A Companion to
George Eliot

Blackwell Companions to Literature and Culture

This series offers comprehensive, newly written surveys of key periods and movements and certain major authors, in English literary culture and history. Extensive volumes provide new perspectives and positions on contexts and on canonical and post-canonical texts, orientating the beginning student in new fields of study and providing the experienced undergraduate and new graduate with current and new directions, as pioneered and developed by leading scholars in the field.

Published Recently

A COMPANION TO
GEORGE ELIOT

EDITED BY
AMANDA ANDERSON
AND HARRY E. SHAW

WILEY Blackwell

This paperback edition first published 2016
© 2013 John Wiley & Sons, Ltd
Edition history: John Wiley & Sons, Ltd (hardback, 2013)

Registered Office
John Wiley & Sons Ltd, The Atrium, Southern Gate, Chichester, West Sussex, PO19 8SQ, UK

Editorial Offices
350 Main Street, Malden, MA 02148-5020, USA
9600 Garsington Road, Oxford, OX4 2DQ, UK
The Atrium, Southern Gate, Chichester, West Sussex, PO19 8SQ, UK

For details of our global editorial offices, for customer services, and for information about how
to apply for permission to reuse the copyright material in this book please see our website at
www.wiley.com/wiley-blackwell.

Library of Congress Cataloging-in-Publication Data

A companion to George Eliot / edited by Amanda Anderson and Harry E. Shaw.
    pages   cm
  Includes bibliographical references and index.
  ISBN 978-0-470-65599-3 (cloth); ISBN 978-1-119-07247-8 (paperback)
  1. Eliot, George, 1819–1880–Criticism and interpretation.   I. Anderson, Amanda, 1960– editor
of compilation.   II. Shaw, Harry E., 1946– editor of compilation.
  PR4688.C57 2013
  823'.8–dc23
                                                    2012046823
A catalogue record for this book is available from the British Library.

Cover image: Samuel Lawrence, Portrait of George Eliot, c. 1857. Reproduced by permission
of the Mistress and Fellows, Girton College, Cambridge

Set in 11/13pt Garamond 3 by SPi Global, Pondicherry, India
Printed and bound in Malaysia by Vivar Printing Sdn Bhd

1   2016

Table of Contents

Notes on Contributors

James Eli Adams is Professor of English and Comparative Literature at Columbia University. He is the author of *Dandies and Desert Saints: Styles of Victorian Masculinity* (1995) and *A History of Victorian Literature* (2009), both of which received a *Choice* award as an outstanding academic title, and the co-editor, with Andrew Miller, of *Sexualities in Victorian Britain* (1996).

Amanda Anderson is Andrew W. Mellon Professor of Humanities and English at Brown University and Director of the School of Criticism and Theory. She is the author of *Tainted Souls and Painted Faces: The Rhetoric of Fallenness in Victorian Culture* (1993), *The Powers of Distance: Cosmopolitanism and the Cultivation of Detachment* (2001), and *The Way We Argue Now: A Study in the Cultures of Theory* (2006).

Isobel Armstrong is Emeritus Professor of English (Geoffrey Tillotson Chair) at Birkbeck, University of London. She has published widely on Victorian literature and culture, particularly poetry, and is currently revising her *Victorian Poetry: Poetry, Poetics and Politics (1993)*. Her *Victorian Glassworlds. Glass Culture and the Imagination* (2008) received the MLA's James Russell Lowell Prize. She has taught at Harvard University and Johns Hopkins University as Visiting Professor.

Alison Booth, Professor of English at the University of Virginia, is the author of *Greatness Engendered: George Eliot and Virginia Woolf* (1992) and *How to Make It as a Woman* (2004), and editor of *Wuthering Heights* (Longmans). Her research exploring the transatlantic reception of authors and biography *of* or *in* groups continues in a digital project, *Collective Biographies of Women* (http://womensbios.lib.virginia.edu), and a book on literary tourism, biography, and museums, "Writers Revisited."

James Buzard is the author of *Disorienting Fiction: The Autoethnographic Work of Nineteenth-Century British Novels* (2005) and *The Beaten Track: European Tourism,*

Literature, and the Ways to "Culture," 1800–1918 (1993), as well as numerous essays on nineteenth- and twentieth-century British literature and culture, the history of travel, and cultural theory. He coedited *Victorian Prism: Refractions of the Crystal Palace* (2007). Buzard is Professor and Head of the Literature Faculty at MIT.

Ian Duncan is Florence Green Bixby Professor of English at the University of California, Berkeley. His books include *Scott's Shadow: The Novel in Romantic Edinburgh* (2007), *Modern Romance and Transformations of the Novel: The Gothic, Scott, Dickens* (1992), *Scotland and the Borders of Romanticism* (coeditor, 2004), and editions of novels by Walter Scott and James Hogg. He is a member of the editorial board of *Representations* and a general editor of Hogg's *Collected Works*.

Simon During is an Australian Professorial Fellow at the University of Queensland. He has previously taught at the University of Melbourne and Johns Hopkins University. His books include *Modern Enchantments: The Cultural Power of Secular Magic* (2001), *Exit Capitalism: Literary Culture, Theory and Post-secular Modernity* (2010), and *Against Democracy: Literary Experience in the Era of Emancipations* (2012).

Monika Fludernik is Professor of English Literature at the University of Freiburg, Germany. Her major fields of interest include narratology, postcolonial studies, law and literature, and eighteenth-century aesthetics. She is the author of *The Fictions of Language and the Languages of Fiction* (1993), *Towards a "Natural" Narratology* (1996), and *An Introduction to Narratology* (2009). She has edited *Hybridity and Postcolonialism* (1998), *Diaspora and Multiculturalism* (2003), *Postclassical Narratology* (with Jan Alber, 2010), and *Beyond Cognitive Metaphor Theory* (2011).

Laura Green is Associate Professor and Chair of the Department of English at Northeastern University, where she has taught since 2001. She is the author of *Educating Women: Cultural Conflict and Victorian Literature* (2001) and of the forthcoming study *Literary Identification from Charlotte Brontë to Tsitsi Dangarembga*.

Rae Greiner received her PhD from the University of California, Berkeley in 2007, and joined Indiana University that year as Assistant Professor of English. She is the co-editor of the journal *Victorian Studies* and has published essays in *Narrative, ELH*, and *Victorian Studies*. Her first monograph, on Adam Smith's theory of sympathy, nineteenth-century realism, and narrative form, is forthcoming from the Johns Hopkins UP.

Daniel Hack is Associate Professor of English at the University of Michigan. Author of *The Material Interests of the Victorian Novel* (2005) and articles in journals including *Critical Inquiry, ELH, Novel: A Forum on Fiction*, and *Victorian Studies*, he is currently writing a book on the uses of Victorian literature in nineteenth-century African American literature and print culture.

Nancy Henry is Professor of English at the University of Tennessee at Knoxville. She is the author of *George Eliot and the British Empire* and *The Cambridge Introduction to*

George Eliot. She is also the co-editor of *Victorian Investments: New Perspectives on Finance and Culture*. Her *Life of George Eliot* was published by Blackwell's Critical Biography Series in 2012.

T. H. Irwin is Professor of Ancient Philosophy in the University of Oxford and a Fellow of Keble College. From 1975 to 2006 he taught at Cornell University. He is the author of *Plato's Gorgias* (1979), *Aristotle's First Principles* (1988), *Classical Thought* (1989), *Plato's Ethics* (1995), *The Development of Ethics* (2007–09), and of *Aristotle's Nicomachean Ethics* (translation and notes; Hackett. 2nd ed., 1999).

David Kurnick teaches English at Rutgers University. He is the author of *Empty Houses: Theatrical Failure and the Novel* (2012), and articles on nineteenth-century literature, queer theory, and the history of the novel.

Carolyn Lesjak is Associate Professor and Graduate Chair of English at Simon Fraser University. She is the author of *Working Fictions: A Genealogy of the Victorian Novel* (2006), as well as numerous articles and contributions to studies of the Victorian novel. Her current book project examines the character and ethics of Victorian object relations. Other projects include work on contemporary Marxist theory and the status of theory and the university within the current neoliberal moment.

Caroline Levine is Professor of English at the University of Wisconsin-Madison. Author of *The Serious Pleasures of Suspense: Victorian Realism and Narrative Doubt* (2003) and *Provoking Democracy* (2007), she is writing a book on form.

Jonathan Loesberg is a Professor of Literature at American University. He is the author of three books, including *A Return to Aesthetics: Autonomy, Indifference, and Postmodernism* (2005), as well as articles on Victorian literature and literary theory. He has recently completed a book on Browning and belief.

Daniel S. Malachuk, Associate Professor of English at Western Illinois University, is the author of *Perfection, the State, and Victorian Liberalism* (2005) and the coeditor with Alan M. Levine of *A Political Companion to Ralph Waldo Emerson* (2011).

Josephine McDonagh is Professor of Nineteenth-Century Literature at King's College London. She is author of *De Quincey's Disciplines* (1994) and *Child Murder and British Culture* (2003), as well as a short volume on *George Eliot* (1997), and coeditor of a number of volumes, most recently *Charles Dickens and the French Revolution* (2009). Her current work is on the nineteenth-century novel and the print cultures of migration.

Stefanie Markovits is Professor of English at Yale University. She is the author of *The Crisis of Action in Nineteenth-Century English Literature* (2006) and *The Crimean War in the British Imagination* (2009).

Jill L. Matus is Professor of English at the University of Toronto, where she also holds the position of Vice-Provost, Students. A Fellow of the Royal Society of Canada, she has published widely on Dickens, Gaskell, George Eliot, and the Brontës and is the author of *Unstable Bodies: Victorian Representations of Sexuality and Maternity* (1995), *Tony Morrison* (1998), *Shock, Memory and the Unconscious in Victorian Fiction* (2009), and editor of *The Cambridge Companion to Elizabeth Gaskell* (2007).

Andrew H. Miller is Professor of English at Indiana University and co-editor of *Victorian Studies*. His publications include the books *The Burdens of Perfection* (2008) and *Novels Behind Glass* (1995). "'Bruising, Laceration, and Lifelong Maiming'; Or, How We Encourage Research" (ELH 2003) concerns Eliot's *Theophrastus Such*. "Lives Unled in Realist Fiction" (*Representations* 2007) and "For All You Know" (in *Stanley Cavell and Literary Studies*, 2012) derive from his current project, *On Not Being Someone Else*.

Hina Nazar is Associate Professor of English at the University of Illinois at Urbana-Champaign. She is the author of *Enlightened Sentiments: Judgment and Autonomy in the Age of Sensibility* (2012) and several articles on Enlightenment literature and moral philosophy, the nineteenth-century novel, and feminist political theory. She is currently at work on a manuscript that explores the interface between contemporary theory and Enlightenment feminism, especially as regards their respective understandings of rationality and education.

Jeff Nunokawa is Professor in the Department of English at Princeton University. He teaches and writes on subjects ranging from the Victorian novel to the history of the essay in English. Currently his most conspicuous scholarly passion consists of writing very brief essays (a paragraph or two in length at most) on an internet platform called Facebook. He has written thousands of them, and a miscellany of them will be published as a book soon.

Adela Pinch is Professor of English at the University of Michigan. She is author of *Strange Fits of Passion: Epistemologies of Emotion, Hume to Austen* (1996) and *Thinking About Other People in Nineteenth-Century British Writing* (2010).

John Plotz is Professor of Victorian Literature at Brandeis University. He is the author of *The Crowd: British Literature and Public Politics* (2000) and *Portable Property: Victorian Culture on the Move* (2008); his current project is "Semi-Detached: The Aesthetics of Partial Absorption."

Bruce Robbins is Old Dominion Foundation Professor in the Humanities at Columbia University. He is the author of *Perpetual War: Cosmopolitanism from the Viewpoint of Violence* (2012), *Upward Mobility and the Common Good* (2007), *Feeling Global: Internationalism in Distress* (1999), *The Servant's Hand: English Fiction from Below* (1986), and *Secular Vocations: Intellectuals, Professionalism, Culture* (1993). He has edited and coedited several books including *Cosmopolitics* (1998) and *Immanuel Wallerstein and the Problem of the World* (2011).

Jan-Melissa Schramm is a Fellow at Trinity Hall and a University Lecturer in the Faculty of English at the University of Cambridge, where she teaches Victorian literature. She is the author of *Testimony and Advocacy in Victorian Law, Literature, and Theology* (2000) and *Atonement and Self-Sacrifice in Nineteenth-Century Narrative* (2012) as well as a number of articles and book chapters on representations of the law in the works of Dickens and Eliot, Victorian satire, and first-person narration. She is also co-editor of *Fictions of Knowledge: Fact, Evidence, Doubt* (2011). She currently holds a Leverhulme Research Fellowship to complete a monograph provisionally entitled "Democracy, Censorship, and Victorian Sacred Drama."

Harry E. Shaw is Professor of English at Cornell University. He is the author of *The Forms of Historical Fiction* (1993), *Narrating Reality: Austen, Scott, Eliot* (1999), and (with Alison Case) *Reading the Nineteenth-Century Novel* (2008).

David Wayne Thomas is Associate Professor of English at the University of Notre Dame and co-editor of the interdisciplinary journal *Nineteenth-Century Contexts*. He has authored a book entitled *Cultivating Victorians: Liberal Culture and the Aesthetic* (2004) and assorted essays treating Victorian literature, literary theory, and the literatures of the British Empire.

Herbert F. Tucker has written extensively on Victorian poetry and poetics, including books on Browning, Tennyson, and nineteenth-century epic. He is associate editor of *New Literary History* and series coeditor in Victorian literature and culture for the press at the University of Virginia, where he holds the John C. Coleman Chair in English.

Lynn Voskuil is the author of *Acting Naturally: Victorian Theatricality and Authenticity* (2004), which includes chapters on the drama criticism of George Henry Lewes and on the forms and function of theatricality in George Eliot's life and fiction. She is currently writing *Horticulture and Imperialism: The Garden Spaces of the British Empire, 1789–1914*, a study that explores Victorian Britain's fascination with exotic plants and horticulture. Voskuil is Associate Professor of English at the University of Houston.

Robyn Warhol, Arts and Humanities Professor of English at Ohio State University, specializes in narrative. She wrote *Having a Good Cry* (2003) and *Gendered Interventions* (1989), and coedited *Feminisms* (1991, 1997) and *Feminisms Redux* (2009).

Alex Woloch is Associate Professor of English at Stanford University. He is the author of *The One vs. the Many: Minor Characters and the Space of the Protagonist in the Novel* (2003) and the co-editor of *Whose Freud?: The Place of Psychoanalysis in Contemporary Culture* (2000).

Michael Wood is Professor of English and Comparative Literature at Princeton University and the author, most recently, of *Yeats and Violence* (2010). Earlier books include *The Magician's Doubts* (1994) and *Literature and the Taste of Knowledge* (2005).

Introduction

Amanda Anderson and Harry E. Shaw

On the eve of her novelistic career, George Eliot wrote an essay for the *Westminster Review*, "The Natural History of German Life" (1856), that ranged widely across discussions of literature, art, science, and social science (or what Eliot classed as "natural history"). In the essay, Eliot famously insists on the importance of fiction in cultivating the sympathies of its readers and in bringing them to a better understanding of those with whom they share their worlds. She argues against idealizing tendencies in the literary and visual arts, especially in portrayals of peasant and rural life, and makes the case for realistic portrayals of ordinary and common people. The German sociologist Wilhelm von Riehl, whose works are under review in the essay, is for Eliot exemplary in his careful, experience-based observations of rural life in his native land. But as important as this essay is for its artistic statement on the cusp of what was to be an impressive literary debut, it is equally important in indicating Eliot's intellectual range and ambition. Indeed, Eliot saw her own literary efforts as actively in dialogue with a broad range of contemporary developments—not only in the social sciences as practiced by people like Riehl, but in philosophy, religion, and science as well. It is for this reason that her work remains responsive to such a broad range of scholarly and critical questions, particularly at a time when scholars in the humanities are exploring interdisciplinary approaches and newly considering the domain of ethics, questions of religion, and a number of issues pertaining to transnational perspectives.

In assembling this Companion, we have therefore tried not only to bring together exciting new work on Eliot by important scholars working in the field, but also to

A Companion to George Eliot, First Edition. Edited by Amanda Anderson and Harry E. Shaw.
© 2013 John Wiley & Sons, Ltd. Published 2016 by John Wiley & Sons, Ltd.

give as full a sense as we can of the ways in which Eliot's work speaks to contemporary intellectual questions. This approach is evident not only in the topical essays gathered under the third and largest section of the Companion, "Eliot in Her Time and Ours: Intellectual and Cultural Contexts," but also in the chapters specifically addressing questions of literary history and form ("Imaginative Form and Literary Context"), individual writings ("Works"), and life and reception ("Life and Reception"). It is often impossible to keep life and art entirely distinct when seeking to make interpretive sense of Eliot's body of work: many of the topical essays thus appeal to the life and especially to the cultural and intellectual milieu Eliot inhabited. As several of our contributors show, Eliot's views on a range of matters, including money, travel, internationalism, and gender, were notably informed by her experience, and many of the essays here help to illuminate this fact, as well as the significant ways in which cultural contexts and norms conditioned her art and thinking. To read these essays is to rediscover the reach of Eliot's artistic, intellectual, and moral achievement, and to recognize her relevance to contemporary concerns in the humanities, including questions of ethics, politics, religion, gender, aesthetics, and the relation between literature and science.

Imaginative Form and Literary Context

When Henry James announced that *Middlemarch* "sets a limit . . . to the development of the old-fashioned English novel," part of his purpose was to pronounce an epitaph that would make room for novels written on different lines from those of Eliot, including his own.[1] The comments made by one great novelist about another have a particular value, even if in the end we cannot agree with them. Today, no writer seems more central to the institution of the British novel than does Eliot. In "The Reception of George Eliot," James Eli Adams explains the progression by which Eliot dropped from the company of major British novelists in the earlier part of the twentieth century, only to be reinstated after World War II. Adams traces in Eliot's own day a growing recognition that she was the premier novelist of her time, but also a growing discomfort about the way in which she increasingly seemed to be using her fiction to convey intellectual and especially ethical doctrine. In the period between Eliot's death and World War II, distrust of the allegedly doctrinal bent of her fiction remained, but a belief in her preeminence did not. This changed in the 1940s. According to Adams, the post-war revival of respect for Eliot rested on two pillars. First, the rich intellectual texture of her novels came to be seen, not as an imposition of alien content on fictional form, but as an integral part of that form. Critics of many persuasions have found Eliot's works useful in exploring society and religion, philosophy and gender. Second, literary critics in the period after World War II learned to read novels in ways that revealed in Eliot an unexpected artistry. This countered the doubts about Eliot's craftsmanship expressed by James, who found in *Middlemarch* excellent parts but an "indifferent whole" (958), a view that recalls the celebrated question he elsewhere asked about novels by Thackeray, Dumas, and Tolstoy: "what do such large loose baggy monsters, with their queer elements of the accidental and arbitrary, artistically *mean*?"[2] In the last half-century, a number of answers to this question have emerged. As we have seen, a standard criticism of Eliot, during her life and beyond, involved Eliot's inclusion of what was seen as "doctrine," and particularly ethical doctrine. Why wouldn't Eliot stick to her story and her characters? Why did the novels have to be so "difficult"? Viewed in the context of form, this became an objection to the way Eliot's narrators "intruded" into her narratives, delivering ideas and sentiments to readers directly, in an attempt to engage the reader in a dialogue about the work instead of using the world of the fiction to enact its meaning. Today, Eliot's narrators are no longer routinely accused of being "intrusive": instead, their contribution to a given novel is more likely to be explored. The essays in this section reflect a broadening of interest in Eliot's narrative craftsmanship: they range from a discussion of Eliot's narrative technique taken as a whole to the examination of her use of a single trope, metaphor.

In "Eliot and Narrative," Monika Fludernik shows how narratology, the formal study of narrative strategies and effects, can powerfully assist us in coming to grips with the form of Eliot's novels. For Fludernik, Eliot's realism depends upon involving the reader. She creates narrators who invite us to share their perceptions and values, their mixture of judgment and sympathy. We become the narrator's accomplices in evaluating the fictional world before us and the characters within it. The narrator sometimes presents external pictures of the characters, forcing us to make sense of hints and clues—one more way of inducing us to share the moral and practical view that characterizes the narrator. A striking example of this technique involves the way in which Hetty Sorrel is presented in *Adam Bede*: as Fludernik shows, her external depiction contrasts strongly with the internal depiction of such characters as Adam. Our involvement in the process of making sense of a character like Hetty is what makes us accept Eliot's narrative world as "real": we come to share the narrator's moral evaluations of characters and incidents, as well as the narrator's depiction of how and why things occur in her world. We take those aspects of the narration to be telling the truth about the fictional world and our world as well—that is, to be "realistic."

In exploring Eliot's artistry, commentators have often attended to her use of metaphor. Fludernik is no exception. She believes that Eliot's metaphors provide yet another way in which we are brought to share a work's complex vision, as we collaborate with the narrator in making sense of the text's metaphors. Michael Wood's "Metaphor and Masque" is wholly devoted to the issue of metaphor in Eliot, which he approaches from a different angle. He is interested less in what happens when we find ourselves as readers sharing the narrator's often ironic metaphors than in how metaphors help Eliot's characters (and us as readers) to understand, and also at times to misunderstand, the world. How do metaphors help Eliot's characters to grasp the reality around them? And how can they (and we) avoid being led by metaphors into misunderstanding? Casaubon in *Middlemarch* entangles himself in error and self-deception when he imagines passion as something that works like a bank account, constantly accruing interest, not as a spring that may in time dry up. How can we avoid such misprision? Wood suggests that Eliot's critics have tended to take one of two views on the place of metaphor in Eliot's fiction, some charting her masterful deployment of metaphorical webs, others concentrating on moments when her control of metaphor seems ready to slip. He believes that neither view should wholly be ignored. Metaphors can illuminate but also distract. Metaphor is useful but potentially dangerous.

In "'It is of Little Use for Me to Tell You': George Eliot's Narrative Refusals," Robyn Warhol provides another narratological view of Eliot's realism, exploring moments that are "unnarratable" either because they are so mundane that they fall beneath the dignity of deserving narration (and are thus "subnarratable") or because they rise so far above the mundane that they become ineffable ("supranarratable"). These varieties of the unnarratable, Warhol argues, allow Eliot to screen out of her fiction narrative clichés, which too often lead in the direction of stereotypical romance, not concrete realism. Eliot's realism also famously demands that we refuse to apply the label of subnarratable to parts of life that not only can be but ought to be narrated: by refusing to deal with such things, romances ignore the conditions of mundane life that permeate the real experience of our fellow human beings. A prime example is again provided by Casaubon in *Middlemarch*. Eliot's narrator insists that we turn our attention to him ("But why always Dorothea?") and also employs disnarration (the narrating of things that do not in fact occur in the text) to present the better self Casaubon might have been were it not for his "egocentric fear" (56). When Eliot's narrator insists that it is easy to depart from reality and difficult to face it, she is urging her readers to focus on the mundane conditions fiction too often neglects. With Warhol's chapter, then, we have moved from James's notion that Eliot's fiction lacks artistic management to the view that even the mundane material Eliot presents is part of her creation of a rich narrative realism.

Does realism require passing beyond the self and its distortions? The accepted view has been that Eliot's realism shows such a dynamic at work among her characters, prompting readers to share it. For Caroline Levine, however, selfishness needs to be directed, not excluded, if realism is to be achieved. In "Surprising Realism" she agrees that we project our imaginings and desires onto the world. She adds, however, that this projection can take radically different forms and sometimes can provide the force we draw on to imagine the situation of others. Levine is particularly interested in Eliot's creation of narrative surprises that move the minds of characters and readers beyond the limits of the self, as happens when, in the closing pages of *Daniel Deronda*, Daniel's explanation of his plan to journey to Israel shocks Gwendolen into the realization of how much larger the world actually is than she had supposed it to be. Though different in focus, Levine's notion of realism seems compatible with those of Fludernik and Warhol. The surprises that propel the reader beyond the self can be seen as leading to the sharing of viewpoints between narrator and reader that Fludernik finds at the heart of realism. And Levine's realist surprises could also lead to the shift in viewpoint about what is narratable that Warhol discusses.

Henry James, it would seem, underestimated the force and subtlety of Eliot's art. In "Two Flowers: George Eliot's Diagrams and the Modern Novel," John Plotz raises doubts about the adequacy of James's pronouncement that *Middlemarch* "sets the limit" to the "old-fashioned English novel." Some have argued that *Daniel Deronda* was a necessary precursor to James's own *Portrait of a Lady*. Plotz goes further, arguing that Eliot's fiction serves, not as the end-point of Victorian social realism, but as a hinge between Victorian and modern fiction. Eliot, like other nineteenth-century realists, uses her characters to provide the multiple perspectives that make a realist hold on reality seem robust and persuasive. She also delves into individual interiority, in a way that anticipates more recent fiction, but when she does so, the force of the external world always lurks in the background, ready to inform our view of the characters and their sense of themselves. Eliot depends on a "semi-detachment" of characters from fictional worlds which allows her to avoid neglecting either self or society.

Works

One remarkable aspect of the post World War II revitalization of interest in Eliot has been its growth to encompass all of her writings. To be sure, her novels have maintained pride of place, but significant discussions have emerged of her essays (along with her essayistic final work, *Impressions of Theophrastus Such*) as well as of her poetry (probably the side of her literary output that has as yet gained the least attention). This Companion offers a variety of approaches to Eliot's works; the essays in this section not only provide new insight into individual works and genres within Eliot's oeuvre, but also together represent an impressive diversity of methodological and thematic interests.

In *Scenes of Clerical Life*, Eliot's earliest work of prose fiction, we see the beginnings of her realism, as she strives to depict mundane reality in a way that will promote our sympathetic understanding. One might suppose that this would mean a rejection of melodrama and romance, but Stefanie Markovits suggests in "*Scenes of Clerical Life* and *Silas Marner*: Moral Fables" that this is not entirely the case. Eliot means to move her readers in *Scenes of Clerical Life*, at times making them part of a "fellowship in suffering" (qtd. on 99), and for this melodrama can prove useful. And in *Silas Marner*, Eliot achieves a remarkable blend of a realistic portraiture of lives on the one hand, and a fairy tale texture on the other. When Eppie appears on the hearth in Silas's cabin and Silas begins to care for her and love her, we find ourselves in the familiar territory of Eliot's country realism. But not entirely. The events (and particularly the way in which Eppie takes the place of Silas's gold) have the ring of a fairy tale as well. These two strands combine in *Silas Marner*, in which "the ideal can serve as that which escapes 'real' embodiment yet still facilitates literature's power to stimulate sympathy, a sympathy not so much of understanding, but one based on our sense of shared incomprehensibility, of shared otherness" (103).

Rae Greiner's "*Adam Bede*: History's Maggots" discovers in *Adam Bede* a similar stress on the incomprehensible, which in this case involves how ideas and the forces of history can be borne into the present by minds and lives that are oblivious of them. In *Adam Bede*, a trope that centrally reflects these unconscious but powerful historical forces is, surprisingly, the maggot, a figure which Greiner traces back to the eighteenth century. A number of the characters in *Adam Bede* are said to be afflicted by maggots. Even Dinah, that most blameless of female characters, has her fervent Methodistical beliefs ascribed to maggots by Mrs. Poyser. But the chief example is Hetty, who evokes in others genuine responses to qualities which they impute to her but which are no part of her own consciousness. Hetty stands as the prime example of a character who acts as the bearer of historical and cultural meaning to which she herself has no access—a surprising development for an author who regularly evokes moments whereby, through the action of a newly roused sympathetic imagination, unconscious views are revealed and if need be corrected.

In Eliot's own day, some readers wished that she had never strayed from the pastoral realism of *Scenes of Clerical Life*, *Adam Bede*, and *Silas Marner*. Even if they accepted the innovations in the novels that followed, they regretted that Eliot had not rested content with the pastoral mode of the earlier works. Modern critics take a different view, with *Middlemarch* as the work that draws most discussion and is considered the summit of her achievement. This Companion is no exception, as our authors turn regularly to *Middlemarch* for examples of the thematic and formal qualities of her fiction.

In "*Middlemarch*: January in Lowick," Andrew H. Miller seeks to illuminate both that novel and Eliot's fiction in general. He suggests that the texture of *Middlemarch* invites us to project ourselves into the fiction and to follow up on its potentialities to the limits, thus experiencing "the promise and peril of entering into states of absorption that offer to make one's actions and world meaningful" (155). As we read, tracing the unfolding of (say) Dorothea's mind, we experience this absorption, which Miller associates with "the difficult discovery or creation of meaningfulness" (163). When absorption is broken off, the threat is that meaningfulness too will be lost. But if we allow ourselves to be too deeply buried, we can also lose track of meaning. Eliot's fiction elicits and weighs our quest for meaning, and Miller reveals how demanding and rewarding responding to her works can be.

How could an author write a novel to follow Middlemarch? Alex Woloch's "*Daniel Deronda*: Late Form, or After *Middlemarch*" describes how Eliot faced this challenge in writing *Daniel Deronda*. He is particularly interested in what happens to *Daniel Deronda*'s system of characters and its exploration of psychology. Gwendolen's egotism lies at the center of much of this, serving as source and figure for the novel's fascination with inner consciousness. We see a kind of division of labor emerge, with Gwendolen attracting to herself moral opprobrium and undergoing hysterical suffering for her selfishness, while the novel's plot acts as a "supreme udder" for Deronda, bringing him things he isn't conscious of desiring. *Daniel Deronda* has often been said to fall into two distinct parts with very different qualities—the love plot involving

Gwendolen, and the "Jewish" plot centered on Deronda himself. (No one would make the same criticism of *Middlemarch*, even though that novel in fact arose from two distinct stories Eliot had been working on.) Woloch is interested, not in championing either "half" of the novel but in understanding, in a systematic way, how its excesses result from internal pressures far stronger than anything we find in *Middlemarch*.

Daniel Deronda is not the only Eliot work with the reputation of being a "problem" novel. For different reasons and to different extents, three other Eliot novels have been considered problem works: *Felix Holt, Romola*, and *The Mill on the Floss*. Complaints about *Felix Holt* have taken a similar form to those about *Daniel Deronda*. *Felix Holt* is said to be divided between a love plot and a political plot, which in turn are split between legalism and abstraction on the one hand, and deep human feeling (and suffering) on the other. The way in which the political interests of the novel are treated has also been considered highly problematic, with the novel's political force losing itself in the sound of wedding bells at novel's end. David Kurnik's "*Felix Holt*: Love in the Time of Politics" recognizes what is at stake here and does not wholly disagree with the novel's detractors. In the end, however, Kurnik is not content simply to explain how its political energy is negated by Felix's abstract beliefs as well as his marriage. He reminds us that there are forces in the novel which elude such negation, and in particular that the suffering and anger of Mrs. Transome escape their local source in her disappointment in love, becoming instead "legible as a diagnosis of the inadequation of the interpersonal and the political" (151).

Romola has posed problems for readers ever since its publication. To many, Eliot's careful and detailed depiction of fifteenth-century Florence has seemed *too* detailed, presenting them with a massive foreign territory lacking a living connection to their present-day interests. In "*Romola*: Historical Narration and the Communicative Dynamics of Modernity," David Wayne Thomas approaches this problem by suggesting that *Romola* is set at the hinge-point between traditional society and modernity. Thomas views modernity through the lens of Jürgen Habermas, who has suggested that for moderns, no longer able to draw their values from tradition, values must be discovered through communicative reason. In Thomas's eyes, *Romola* is designed to test the efficacy of this sort of communication, and other kinds as well. Though at times the novel may suggest that speech cannot register the more profound aspects of our experience, on the whole it views Habermassian communication as our best hope by weighing the strengths and weaknesses of how the novel's characters communicate. In doing so, *Romola* enriches our understanding of our own predicament in the modern world.

We turn now to another novel some readers have found problematic, *The Mill on the Floss*. Eliot interrupted work on that novel shortly after she had begun it, to write "The Lifted Veil," and critics have tended to think that writing the latter somehow made it possible for her to pass beyond the opening of the former. In "*The Mill on the Floss* and 'The Lifted Veil': Prediction, Prevention, Protection," Adela Pinch suggests that we think not of beginnings but instead of endings in addressing both works. What does attending to "the pull of the future in [Eliot's] narrative art" (119) allow us to recognize in *The Mill on the Floss?* For one thing, we become sensitive to patterns in which the novel anticipates its own ending. An example of this is a kind of magical thinking in which caregivers express fears for future events, with the hope that doing so will ward them off: on a number of occasions, for example, Mrs. Tulliver predicts that Maggie will drown—a prophesy which does not succeed in disarming the threat of the future, since drowning still turns out to be Maggie's fate. The grim conclusiveness of the flood that puts a sudden stop to the course of the novel and to Maggie's life has always disturbed readers, seeming to many unexpected (though Eliot had it in mind from the beginning) and impossible to understand. Yet the most important future for any novel, Pinch argues, lies (quite literally) in the hands of its readers. Experiencing the ending of *The Mill on the Floss* can help to prepare us for our own endings and those of the people who matter to us, teaching us to "tolerate the pain of reading tragic endings that seem scripted from the beginning" as well as to live with our responsibility for ourselves and others, accepting "the painful limits of that responsibility."

Critics sometime speak of the poetical resonance of moments evoked by Eliot's novels. Herbert F. Tucker's "Poetry: The Unappreciated Eliot" agrees that there are ties between Eliot's poetry and the novels, but his principal concern is to lead us to take a keener look at the texture and dynamics of Eliot's verse. Her careful craftsmanship is there to be seen for those who take the trouble. Tucker is not suggesting that Eliot is a great poet who has gone unrecognized, but instead a great writer who, in whatever medium she chooses to work, is worth attending to. Tucker's meticulous reading of Eliot's verse reveals a side of her achievement many of us have skipped over.

Eliot's works also include a significant amount of non-fictional prose, in the form of essays she published early in her career as well as the last volume she authored, *Impressions of Theophrastus Such*. These works alone might have provided the foundation for a lesser writer's claim to be remembered, but given the magnitude of Eliot's fictional achievement, it is hardly surprising that both of the critics who write here about them view them in the context of the novels. Jeff Nunokawa's "Essays: Essay v. Novel (Eliot, Aloof)" draws on Eliot's novelistic practice, especially in *Middlemarch*, to remind us of what the essays are not, of how the intelligence behind them fails to mirror the generosity of the narrators of Eliot's fiction. The tone of the essays is characteristically harsh; their voice seems eager to move up and away from their topics, be they "silly" female novelists or fulminating clerics. In the novels, by contrast, the quality of the narrator's presence helps us to view with a sympathetic understanding unappealing characters whom we would otherwise pass over quickly. In illuminating Eliot's final work, James Buzard's "*Impressions of Theophrastus Such*: 'Not a Story'" also discerns problems, but for him these arise from Eliot's own questioning of her fictional methods—a questioning Buzard believes to have made its mark felt in her final novels as well. Eliot becomes uncomfortably aware of the unearned advantage possessed by her narrators, whose omniscience supports sympathy for repellent characters in a way that our limited knowledge can never match. A suspicion of narrative finds its fruition in *Theophrastus Such*, where the first-person narrator is anything but omniscient and the depicted figures are dropped quickly, before they can achieve a status comparable to that of the major characters in the novels, a status that elicits the full sympathy we associate with the narrators of Eliot's fiction.

Life and Reception

The lives of famous authors hold a certain fascination. Eliot's life has always been of interest to her readers, the more so because it ran counter to the conventions of Victorian England. During the early part of her career, when her male nom de plume of George Eliot was the only information about her available, her readers naturally wanted to know more about this male author, indulging in the usual pastimes of conjecture and false attribution. When she subsequently decided to breach her anonymity, the focus shifted to how a woman could have created such fiction. Worries also arose about this particular woman, who had translated texts of "godless" German philosophy and was currently living with a man to whom she was not married. (For all of this, see Adams.) In our own time, concerns arising from Eliot's gender have shifted, but not disappeared. We now find in her a fascinating example of the predicament of female intellectuals during the Victorian period (and our own), while what is taken to be her political conservatism raises the question of whether this powerful woman writer was herself a feminist.

Living with George Henry Lewes placed Eliot in a position of social ostracism. Men would call on her and Lewes; women would not. In time, her celebrity overcame this boundary, but it was real enough when it existed and tended to put Eliot in an awkward position, cut off from the mainstream of society. In "George Eliot Among Her Contemporaries: A Life Apart," Lynn Voskuil shows, however, that a "life apart" was a state she inhabited and to some degree fashioned long before she met Lewes. In her younger years, she broke with her father's religion, causing a rift that never fully healed. Even after she had become recognized as a Victorian sage and her Sunday afternoon salons attracted literati from home and abroad, she continued to set herself apart, particularly from those who viewed her with worshipful eyes. She did this by creating a persona that was at one moment on intimate terms with followers but was at others wrapped in an intimidating mantle of greatness.

Some of those who visited Eliot's Sunday afternoons salon were American, but her influence on the American novel and its influence on her were not limited to personal contacts. In "Feminist George Eliot Comes From the United States," Alison Booth views Eliot in the context of feminism and reform, both in her own day and in ours, chronicling her influence on American women writers including twentieth-century feminist literary critics in the United States. She reveals, on the part of Eliot's American contemporaries, respect and affection mixed with disappointment that Eliot did not embrace feminist ideals more thoroughly and openly. A similar pattern can be discerned with American feminism in our own time: Eliot is admired as an author no one could condescend to, but her gradualist politics are distrusted. Daniel Hack's "Transatlantic Eliot: African American Connections" explores another set of transatlantic bonds, one involving issues of race, in which Eliot drew on Harriet Beecher Stowe's *Dred*, a novel centered on slavery, and a number of Black writers in America drew on Eliot's work. In reviewing *Dred*, Eliot praised that work's depiction of a "conflict of races" and of a people who viewed their scriptures as a living force that could shape present-day action. We can see the same elements in the "Jewish half" of *Daniel Deronda*. Interestingly, when African American writers turned to Eliot, they were most responsive not to *Daniel Deronda* but to Eliot's long poem *The Spanish Gypsy*, with its emphasis on how a heroic champion can help to create a racial tradition. With *Daniel Deronda*, the possession of a rich heritage promises to act as the base from which a currently dispersed people can regain their racial identity; with *The Spanish Gypsy*, such a heritage is what heroic individuals (like the African Americans who drew on that poem) would need to create as part of the task of fostering racial solidarity and rising above race-based deprivation.

Eliot in Her Time and Ours: Intellectual and Cultural Contexts

As we mentioned at the outset of the introduction, Eliot's writings engage a wealth of intellectual, historical, and broadly humanistic concerns. She is interested in science and religion, philosophy and art, ethics and politics, psychology and sociology, finance and law, and the broad cultural and economic developments that attend modernization. As a polymath and a reader of extraordinary range and insight, Eliot brought a great deal of learning to her art, which nonetheless always remained centrally trained on human moral and psychological experience. Indeed, responses to Eliot's preoccupation with the moral life often play an orienting role in commentaries on her art. While she has always had her admirers, there are also those who fault her for didacticism or an unpersuasive idealism. In the past several decades in particular, many critics have sought to show how Eliot's most valued moral practice, sympathetic response to others, is complicated by factors such as egotism, power, or the difficulties attending communication. Much of this work is fundamentally skeptical of Eliotic sympathy and aims to show that despite Eliot's best intentions her novels, in part because of the reach of their psychological and sociological realism, cannot avoid registering skepticism too. Thus while earlier critics found her moralizing to be intrusive and thus aesthetically distasteful, later critics have tended to stress the ideological or mystifying features of Eliot's ethics.

Many of the essays collected here re-situate Eliot's ethics in a way that acknowledges the complexity of her art as well as the philosophical, psychological, and sociological reach of her thinking about the moral life. Without neglecting either the internal tensions of Eliot's thought or the larger cultural forces conditioning her own frameworks, these essays credit Eliot with a more intricate and realistic conception of ethical experience than some of her critics have allowed, often revealing her understanding of the importance of ethics to multiple domains of individual, social, and institutional life. In a ground-clearing philosophical discussion, T. H. Irwin's "Sympathy and the

Basis of Morality" asks whether sympathy, as opposed to general principles, is indeed the basis for morality in Eliot, and if so, precisely what sort of sympathy is advocated or in play. Irwin usefully distinguishes among different types of sympathy (cognitive, affective, and practical), showing that the most important type in Eliot is practical, insofar as it involves moral evaluation of particular situations (realist fiction is of course uniquely suited to this orienting interest in particularity). Irwin suggests, however, that Eliot does not appear to secure practical sympathy as a basis for morality, given characters such as Tito who use affective sympathy manipulatively and who remain firmly within a selfish outlook. By Irwin's account, Eliot herself demonstrates that sympathy may not be enough; we may need general principles and the form of moral judgment associated with them (Caleb Garth's response to Bulstrode is his main example here).

Isobel Armstrong's "George Eliot, Spinoza, and the Emotions" argues for the formative influence of Spinoza's *Ethics* on Eliot's understanding of the passions and the dynamics affecting social emotions more generally. Eliot worked extensively on her translation of the *Ethics* in the mid-1850s, directly prior to her turn to fiction-writing. As Armstrong shows, Spinoza's emphasis on the intense social dynamics of love and hate, compassion and envy, desire and suffering, are revelatory for an understanding of Eliot and help to dislodge the more traditional form of fundamentally rational sympathy that has typically been employed in the analysis of her art. Spinoza's elaboration of the triangulated nature of the passions, the tense mutual imbrications of what we tend to class as positive and negative affects, and the political economies of love and hate (particularly with respect to class and race) provide profound insight into the more challenging and unsettling aspects of Eliot's work. Armstrong's examples include Dorothea's experience of Will's interactions with Rosamond in *Middlemarch* and certain continuities between the two plots in *Daniel Deronda*, both of which exhibit forms of envy, status-anxiety, and anxious projection. Armstrong shows that Eliot's idealism is inseparable from her insight into the ineluctability of powerful passions.

Essays in the volume that situate Eliot in relation to law and to economics further establish the sophistication of Eliot's moral thought, its ongoing engagement with larger social and institutional contexts. Jan-Melissa Schramm's "George Eliot and the Law" demonstrates that Eliot's thinking about the law intersects in productive ways with her abiding interests in justice, fairness, redemption, sacrifice, and mercy. While Eliot possessed considerable knowledge of legal history and doctrine, and respected the law's universalistic aims, her admiration for the law was tempered by an acknowledgment of the limits of legal frameworks. Given the reach and substance of her moral vision, she was especially interested in showing the complexity of motive and action in human drama, something which legal understandings of responsibility and guilt are ill-equipped to capture. Such an insight is certainly present in the presentation of legal assessments of fateful action in both *Adam Bede* and *Felix Holt*. Beyond this, Eliot valued forms of moral response, such as hope and mercy, which exceed strict notions of legal accountability (Schramm notes that such responses are often associated with women and with more private or informal spheres of activity, as in Dorothea's championing of Lydgate after the affair of Raffles's death). With Eliot, fiction becomes a type of advocacy that can extend beyond the field of vision of the law.

In "George Eliot and Finance," Nancy Henry establishes that Eliot's works reflect not only a wide-ranging understanding of financial affairs, but also a particular interest in broad transitions underway in economic life during the nineteenth century. Financial elements and events are central to many of the narratives (wills, debts, inheritances, investments, gambling, speculations), demonstrating Eliot's realistic understanding of the way in which finances shape and affect human relations, both personal and impersonal. Eliot gives special attention to how financial transactions or interests can degrade human relations, from the tendency to put money interests above the affections, to forms of slavery and bondage based on financial dependence. In several instances, valued characters refuse the lure of money (Silas Marner would be the prime example here, but of course Esther Lyon and Dorothea also engage in such refusals). Henry shows the ways in which Eliot balances pragmatic and ethical considerations of money and economic relations, and notes as well that Eliot became increasingly aware of financial dealings as her wealth increased due to her success as an author.

The emphasis on ethics in Eliot has often tended to involve the assumption that larger contexts recede in importance as she hones in on the moral energies of individual lives and interpersonal relations. Many readings of Eliot have charged that politics in her novels are relinquished in favor of ethics; such readings typically class her as a conservative, or at best a conservative liberal. Contributions to this volume usefully reframe these longstanding characterizations of Eliot. In "George Eliot and Politics," Carolyn Lesjak argues that Eliot's emphasis on the interrelated aspects of social life expresses a deeply political conception of the world. For Lesjak, this political view is best understood as a politics of the common(s) and of the commonplace, and it is grounded on a materialist conception of character and of social life. Refusing limited conceptions of Eliot as conservative or liberal, Lesjak points instead toward the radical potential of Eliot's art. Through a close consideration of Eliot's representation of character (and in particular her interest in typicality, commonness, and the unheroic), as well as her interest in forms of indebtedness to others and to the world, Lesjak illuminates Eliot's view of social interdependence.

A similar reconsideration of what have been viewed as politically limiting or conservative features of Eliot's work also animates the contributions by Josephine McDonagh and Daniel Malachuk. In "Imagining Locality and Affiliation: George Eliot's Villages," McDonagh revisits the portrayal of rural and village life in Eliot, arguing against those readings, inaugurated in John W. Cross's *George Eliot's Life as Related in her Letters and Journals*, that see Eliot as nostalgically committed to England's past. McDonagh establishes manifold ways in which Eliot's representation of rural and village life registers historical change and promotes ideals of social cohesion and moral response. Insisting on the influence of two disparate sources on Eliot's thinking about villages—Mary Russell Mitford's serial tales about village life (*Our Village*) and Sir Henry Maine's legal and historical work on the transition from status to contract—McDonagh shows that Eliot's searching understanding of social and moral life is evident in her representational strategies (which typically combine situated and observer perspectives), in her sophisticated treatment of affiliation and inheritance, and in her adaptation of the village concept to the pressures and networks of an increasingly wide and changing world. McDonagh's treatment of Eliot captures at once her strong investment in rootedness and affiliation, especially as they bear upon the moral life, as well as her ongoing encounter, from the early to the late work, with the conditions of modernity.

Daniel Malachuk's "George Eliot's Liberalism" also addresses elements of Eliot's thought that have characteristically been associated with traditionalism or pastoralism. Placing Eliot in relation to republican theory, Malachuk argues that Eliot's sense of the ethico-political life is oriented toward practices and sites that might be comprehended by an enlarged conception of *oikos* (household, family) rather than by the traditional *polis* associated with state-based forms of citizenship. Focusing on the significance Eliot accords to domestic life, marriage, labor, and place, Malachuk reconstructs a powerful conception of civic virtue in Eliot, one that has been lost to view in accounts that impose a narrow conception of liberalism, and of politics generally, on her work. Concentrating on *Felix Holt* and *Middlemarch*, and drawing on disparate influences and thinkers from the liberal tradition, Malachuk helps us to see anew the implications of the narrator's closing assertion that the "effect of [Dorothea's] being on those around her was incalculably diffusive" (qtd. on 381). Similarly, he casts in a new and more politically consequential light Caleb Garth's mode of work, and reconsiders the transformative understanding of marriage that is at play in both novels. The theoretical influences underlying Malachuk's understanding of *oikos* in Eliot range from political philosophy to recent ecocriticism.

Laura Green asks us to reconsider the political implications of Eliot's presentation of women, gender, and sexuality. In "George Eliot: Gender and Sexuality," Green begins by noting the oft-remarked gap between Eliot's own life and her lack of commitment to feminist positions. Green insists that this gap is partially closed by the fact that a conception of women's suffering, linked specifically to crises of desire and vocation, grounds Eliot's realism. While men's vocational struggles are also anatomized in the novels, their experiences lack what Green refers to as "the conclusive significance of women's suffering and loss" (394). Moreover, while many critics have found the lack of fulfillment among Eliot's heroines disappointing, the rendition of the bleak conditions facing aspiring and unconventional women itself bespeaks a feminist consciousness. Beyond this, we can see explorations of sexuality and desire in some of Eliot's work, particularly in relation to the noble heroines. Invoking Katherine Bond Stockton's work on Eliot, Green concludes that Eliot's works invite queer critical analysis, especially given their important departures from traditional heterosexual norms.

In "The Cosmopolitan Eliot," Bruce Robbins establishes the context for a deeper understanding of Eliot's divided attitude toward cosmopolitanism. On the one hand, there is clear evidence that Eliot's scale of aspiration tends not to extend beyond the nation, and that she is committed to the importance of local affiliations and loyalties as the ground upon which moral development rests (for Eliot, indeed, certain forms of cosmopolitanism are simply unlivable, from a moral point of view). On the other hand, Eliot recognizes at key moments the importance of a critical cosmopolitanism able to register the moral problems of imperialism and colonialism. Often such moments of critique are oblique, as in the case of Mr. Brooke's speech on the hustings in *Middlemarch*. We can also find evidence of Eliot's ambivalence in her character system, most notably in *Daniel Deronda*, where the eponymous hero is at once an ideal and a pathology, and Gwendolen Harleth represents cosmopolitanism as malaise. While previous work on Eliot's cosmopolitanism has tended to favor *Daniel Deronda*, Robbins redirects our attention to *Middlemarch*, in which Dorothea's consciousness becomes something of a filter for the pressures of cosmopolitanism, in both its threatening and critical forms (the former is evident in her experiences in Rome, the latter in the novel's opening discussion of the jewels and those who make and sell them). Robbins concludes by suggesting that Eliot's own investments in India opened her thinking to non-stereotypical understandings of foreign labor.

Hina Nazar's "The Continental Eliot" revisits the international dimensions of Eliot's art and thinking from the perspective of intellectual history, exploring the continuities between the continental philosophical tradition, especially in its Hegelian formations, and recent and influential theoretical trends in the humanities which have stressed the situated nature of action and the limited powers of individual agency. Nazar argues that while Eliot is certainly interested in the importance of situated agency and embedded existence, as are the Hegelian critics of Kant, she is also committed to maintaining the importance of individual experience and particularly the capacity of the individual for reflective agency. Nazar sees this emphasis as in large part producing her favoring of fiction as a mode of representation, insofar as it allows for the portrayal of concrete individuals within larger communities and social formations. Indeed, Eliot's novels contain several examples of individuals who move beyond an excessive dependence on others and toward a higher degree of self-scrutiny. For Nazar, Eliot's work serves as an important counterweight to a line of thinking that develops from Hegel up through the critics of Enlightenment including pragmatists, communitarians, and certain post-structuralists. Throughout she shows the centrality of Eliot's critique of religion to her understanding of the importance of autonomy and self-actualization.

While Nazar's essay stresses the critical function of Eliot's relation to religion, Simon During's "George Eliot and Secularism" presents an Eliot who was at once secular and spiritual, dedicated to immanent life or conditions of finitude, but with a profound interest in acknowledging forces that we associate with the religious life. Interestingly, while much of Eliot's thinking led her away from an emphasis on formal religion, her political commitment to community prompted an appreciation of the

Anglican Church, insofar as it provided ethical cohesion in a world eroded by the forces of individualization and modernization. During tracks a very complex social and religious landscape in Eliot, one which includes secular versions of spiritual life as well as guiding forms of non-doctrinal Anglicanism which are socially and ethically useful. During's chapter locates Eliot within an intellectual lineage of spiritual reform reaching back to the Romantics and to Owenism. He sees in Eliot's novelistic project a tension between an aspiration to reach beyond the existing social state (e.g. Deronda's mission) and an affirmation of the importance of Anglicanism as an exemplary site from which to enact situated moral and spiritual engagement with community life (Mr. Irwine, Dr. Kenn, Mr. Farebrother).

Amanda Anderson's "Living Theory: Personality and Doctrine in Eliot," also addresses Eliot's engagement with the critique of religion, but it does so within a consideration of Eliot's ongoing attempt to imagine how one might best live a life consciously informed by doctrine or theory. At the center of Eliot's thinking on these issues, Anderson argues, is a reworking of Feuerbach's emphasis on the importance of personality in mediating belief and an awareness of the sociological and psychological importance of charisma. In *The Essence of Christianity*, which Eliot translated, Feuerbach stresses the psychological dimensions of religious belief, including the need for a personal God (as demonstrated through the Christian Incarnation). Eliot's novels resituate this dynamic within a social context, showing the ways in which individual humans, typically moral exemplars of one sort or another, can come to mediate this need. Anderson argues that as her novel-writing career progresses Eliot becomes increasingly interested in staging dynamic relations between exemplary personalities (heroic protagonists) and charismatic visionaries who still remain within religious frameworks of belief (the key examples here are Romola/Savonarola and Deronda/Mordecai). Eliot's novels ultimately accord value to the interplay of skepticism and aspiration that marks the protagonists' engagements with the visionaries.

One central context for Eliot's long and fundamentally productive argument with religion was of course the emerging influence of science during the nineteenth century. Gillian Beer and George Levine have written important works on the influence of evolutionary theory and scientific thought on Eliot's works.[3] Contributors to this volume have extended this scholarship into areas encompassing sciences of the mind, evolutionary psychology, and the broader history of the human sciences. In "George Eliot and the Sciences of the Mind: The Silence that Lies on the Other Side of Roar," Jill L. Matus explores Eliot's treatment of what her partner, George Henry Lewes, termed the "psychical life." Eliot faced a strong tendency among her contemporaries to reduce mind to the status of an epiphenomenon, a mere by-product of physical events. For Lewes and Eliot, mind had a much broader scope than this, acting as the orchestrator of emotions and sense impressions and the recipient of unconscious mental activity. Thus when Dorothea in chapter 21 of *Middlemarch* is said to have failed to form of her husband's inner life "an idea wrought back to the directness of sense, like the solidity of objects," her failure may be seen as stemming from an insufficiently broad use of the inherent power of the human mind to give ideas such emotional and perceptual force (qtd. on 463). Matus claims that Eliot's fiction comes to concentrate increasingly on individual human minds, with her later novels stressing "the hidden components of consciousness," not the webs of external causation explored so prominently in the earlier ones (464). Yet for all her insistence on the inadequacy of an epiphenomal view of the human mind, that view had its attractions to Eliot, as evident in her treatment of a kind of post-human consciousness in the essay "Shadows of the Coming Race" in *Impressions of Theophrastus Such*.

Ian Duncan's "George Eliot and the Science of the Human" shares with Matus's chapter an attentiveness to Eliot's ability to think beyond the human. Duncan places Eliot within broad developments in science, focusing especially on the growing cultural awareness of the dwarfing of human time in relation to geological time. According to Duncan, it is precisely Eliot's awareness of estranging perspectives on the human that intensifies her humanism; but it is also the case that her works frankly acknowledge the influence of new forms of knowledge on human experience. He traces a range of effects registered through the fiction, beginning with the pressures of organic community on individual growth (in *The Mill on the Floss* and *Middlemarch*) and leading to the post-human futures imagined in her last writings, *Daniel Deronda* and *Impressions of Theophrastus Such*. Duncan reads *Daniel Deronda* as staging a tension between biological and cultural registers, effectively unmooring its characters from the cushioning contexts of provincial life and ultimately evoking larger reaches of an evolutionary time that is at once biological and cultural. Duncan provocatively states that here Eliot is on the verge of writing science fiction.

Jonathan Loesberg's "Eliot, Evolution, and Aesthetics" also explores the interesting relation between the biological and the non-biological registers in *Daniel Deronda*, focusing in particular on the aesthetic. His chapter not only reframes Eliot's relation to Darwinism but also engages new work on evolutionary psychology and aesthetics to tease out a complex negotiation among evolution, art, and moral choice in her late works. For Loesberg, Eliot's consideration of sexual selection in *Daniel Deronda* leads to a greater openness toward an aesthetic mode of self-understanding and value endorsement, a shift enabled by the very emphasis on aesthetic preference (and the break with the strict causality of natural selection) within the theory of sexual selection. Loesberg shows that an emphasis on biological constraint through reproduction (most evident in *Middlemarch*) gives way to a more flexible view of the free play of choice in *Daniel Deronda*, one that resonates with the many ways in which aesthetics exert a powerful force within the field of the novel's action. While Eliot's desire to have art and morality authorize one another is well-known, Loesberg emphasizes the more radical endorsement of the aesthetic that emerges in her last novel.

Across the wide range of topics and texts addressed in this Companion, one gathers a sense of the extraordinary richness of Eliot's oeuvre, and especially of her engagement with some of the most pressing questions of the modern era. That her work continues to repay such sustained engagement, and that the history of criticism on her writings itself tells such a revelatory story for the history of literature and intellectual life more generally, testifies to Eliot's great achievement and her ongoing relevance.

NOTES

1 Henry James, rev. of *Middlemarch*, *Galaxy*, March 1873. Reprinted in *Henry James, Literary Criticism: Essays on Literature, American Writers, English Writers* (New York: Library of America, 1984), 965.

2 Henry James, Preface to *The Tragic Muse*, 1908. Reprinted in *Henry James, Literary Criticism: French Writers, Other European Writers, The Pref-aces to the New York Edition* (New York: Library of America, 1984), 1107.

3 See Gillian Beer, *Darwin's Plots: Evolutionary Narrative in Darwin, George Eliot, and Nineteenth-Century Fiction* (Cambridge: Cambridge UP, 1983, 2000); George Levine, *Realism, Ethics, and Secularism: Essays on Victorian Literature and Science* (Cambridge: Cambridge UP 2008).

Part I

Imaginative Form and Literary Context

1
Eliot and Narrative

Monika Fludernik

With a single drop of ink for a mirror, the Egyptian sorcerer undertakes to reveal to any
chance comer far-reaching visions of the past. This is what I undertake to do for you,
reader. With this drop of ink at the end of my pen, I will show you the roomy workshop
of Mr Jonathan Burge, carpenter and builder in the village of Hayslope, as it appeared
on the eighteenth of June, in the year of our Lord 1799. (*Adam Bede* 5; ch. 1)

Though George Eliot's novelistic oeuvre is generally credited with the authoritative
tone and rational tidiness of the omniscient narrator tradition so prominent in the
realist prose of the nineteenth-century English novel, this cliché only partially succeeds in characterizing her narrative discourse. True, we feel we are in competent
hands when we immerse ourselves in the fictional worlds of Eliot; yet the impression
of authority arises less from a consistent world view that is being propounded than
from our connivance at Eliot's ironies. As in satire, the superiority displayed by the
narrator's delineation of characters' foibles, their self-deceptions and propensity to
slide from ideal conduct, communicates itself to the ideal reader, who comes to share
that ironic aloofness from the lapsarian world and savors the exposure of the protagonists' shortcomings. Since the authorial discourse (to use Stanzel's terminology) is
clearly a knowing one, the reader comes to feel that the narration provides a normative
viewpoint on the fictional world, in which the sarcasm of satiric analysis is humanely
tempered by charitable impulses to explain and excuse the characters' blunders. The
reader is thus led to appreciate the discriminating and sympathetic intelligence of the
narrator.

A Companion to George Eliot, First Edition. Edited by Amanda Anderson and Harry E. Shaw.
© 2013 John Wiley & Sons, Ltd. Published 2016 by John Wiley & Sons, Ltd.

The opening of *Adam Bede* cited above illustrates this intertwining of irony and sympathetic appeal. In this passage the blend of dissonance and consonance (Cohn) arises from a conjunction of two textual strategies that narrative theorists usually believe to be incompatible—(a) metafiction, with a hint at metalepsis, the transgression of ontological boundaries; and (b) the establishment of aesthetic illusion (Wolf) by means of the reader's immersion (Ryan) in the fictional world. In the ironic opening paragraph of *Adam Bede*, the narrator implicitly compares himself with an Egyptian sorcerer, thus seemingly undermining the respectability and credibility of fictional realism. At the same time, s/he works toward immersion by magically projecting the reader into the fictional world, where s/he can "see" what is happening in the carpenter's shop: "It is clear *at a glance* that the next workman is Adam's brother"; "He [Seth] has thrown off his paper cap, and *you see* that his hair is not thick and straight, like Adam's, but thin and wavy, *allowing you to discern* the exact contour . . ." (6; ch. 1; my emphasis).[1] The passage therefore prepares the ground for a metaphorical metalepsis that the narrator's "drop of ink" is able to achieve by means of direct address ("you, reader") and deictic positioning: the shift into the present tense and the references to vision require a transgressive location of the reader within the fictional world.

Eliot displays this technique a second time to even more striking effect in Chapter 5 when we are introduced to Mr. Irwine and the narrator takes the role of our chaperone: "Let me take you into the dining-room, and show you the Rev. Adolphus Irwine, Rector of Broxton. . . . We will enter very softly, and stand still in the open doorway, without awaking the glossy-brown setter who is stretched across the hearth . . ." (54; ch. 5). The narrative positions us behind Mr. Irwine so that "at present we can only see that he has a broad flat back and an abundance of powdered hair" and have to wait until "[h]e will perhaps turn round by-and-by" (55; ch. 5). The narrator even attributes thoughts to the projected reader figure: "You suspect at once"; "which tells you that he is not a young man" (54, 55; ch. 5). All of this is not very radical as metalepsis goes; Charlotte Brontë in *Shirley* has the narrator stand behind the chairs of the three curates and look over their shoulders; her narrator asks the narratee to "[s]tep into this neat garden-house," proposes that "You and I will join the party," and suggests that the time while the curates are at their meal can be used for a little chat: "and while they eat we will talk aside" (6; ch. 1). What is noteworthy in both passages is the conjoining of this strategy of address plus metaleptic metaphor—putting the reader on the scene, so to speak—with an enhancement of sympathetic affect. Reader address and the employment of metalepsis are traditionally believed to produce a breaking of aesthetic illusion; here, in fact, they serve the opposite function of deepening the reader's involvement in the fiction rather than disrupting immersion.[2] The magic trick played by Eliot's narrator persona is of course that of reviving the past by deploying her pen; the presumably heathen visions of the projected Egyptian sorcerer are replaced by the decidedly Christian theater in which Eliot stages her drama of moral failings, tragedy, remorse, and religious atonement and reconciliation. The final realist proof that no malevolent magician has beguiled us with his mischievous tricks comes in another instance of explicit metalepsis in chapter 17, in which the story pauses a little for the narrator to propound her chari-table aesthetics of ugliness and social commitment to the lower classes, noting in an aside that "I gathered [this] from Adam Bede, to whom I talked of these matters in his old age" (*Adam Bede* 179; ch. 17).[3] Despite the ostensible breaking of illusion, the strategy succeeds in authenticating the reality of the fictional world, transforming the invented events of the novel into the supposed factuality of the narrator's personal past. The logical contradiction this entails fails to bother the reader, whose willing suspension of disbelief has made such strides that it reinterprets this logical irritation as a corroboration of the credibility of the narrator persona.

I have taken a route through generalization to foreground the inherent ambivalence of Eliot's writing. In what follows I would like to proceed more systematically by listing prominent features of Eliot's narratorial discourse, mostly focusing on *Adam Bede*. I will first elaborate on the narrator persona's strategies of communication, analysis, and evaluation with an emphasis on metaphor and simile. I will then focus on perspective and focalization. A final section will be devoted to Eliot's irony, par-ticularly in conjunction with metaphor and the use of reflectorization.

Eliot's narrator figures have of course been the object of much literary criticism. A question that has greatly interested narratologists is the presumptive gender of Eliot's narrator personae. As Barbara Hardy (*Particularities* 128–40), Suzanne Graver (278–86), Ansgar Nünning (*Grundzüge* 125–290) and myself ("Subversive Irony"), among others, have pointed out, Eliot's gendering of the narrator figure varies from text to text. Thus, in *Adam Bede,* the narrator takes a consistently male role by means of statements that refer to a man's perspective: ". . . *one* can put up with annoyances in the house, but to have the stable made a scene of vexation and disgust, is a point beyond what *human flesh and blood* can be expected to endure long together . . ." (126; ch. 12; my emphasis). *One* or *humankind* are male, as is the narratee addressed at the end of chapter 50: "That is a simple scene, reader. But it is almost certain that you, too, have been in love—perhaps, even, more than once, though you may not choose to say so to *all your lady friends*" (493; ch. 50; my emphasis).

From *The Mill on the Floss* onwards Eliot starts to vacillate between male and female gendering of the narrator figure in gnomic statements and addresses to a gendered narratee with whom the narrator persona claims communality. Thus, in the following passage from *The Mill on the Floss*, the narrator first identifies with the female experi-ence of bonnets and then takes a typically male perspective:

> English sunshine is dubious; bonnets are never quite secure; and if you sit down on the grass, it may lead to catarrhs. But the rain is to be depended on. You gallop through it in a mackintosh, and presently find yourself in the seat you like best – a little above or a little below the one on which your goddess sits . . . (359–60; bk. 6, ch. 7)

More often, Eliot's narrator persona is androgynous or of neutral gender, as in this comment from *Romola*: "But our deeds are like children that are born to us; they live and act apart from our own will" (219; ch. 16). Although the passage applies to Tito's situation, the insight characterizes a general human conundrum, one that one could also find corroborated in *Adam Bede*.

A second important feature of Eliot's narrator figures is their active philosophizing and moralizing, most commonly in gnomic utterances[4] of considerable length and breadth. Let us consider an example:

> He [Seth] was but three-and-twenty, and had only just learned what it is to love – to love with *that* adoration which a young man gives to a woman whom he feels to be greater and better than himself. Love of this sort is hardly distinguishable from religious feeling. . . . *Our* caresses, *our* tender words, *our* still rapture under the influence of autumn sunsets . . . all bring with them an unfathomable ocean of love and beauty; *our* love at its highest flood rushes beyond its object, and loses itself in the sense of divine mystery. And this blessed gift of venerating love has been given to too many humble craftsmen since the world began, for us to feel any surprise that it should have existed in the soul of a Methodist carpenter half a century ago . . . (*Adam Bede* 37; ch. 3; my emphasis)

Gnomic utterances in Eliot typically start out from a concrete situation or problem in the fictional world—here Seth's unrequited love for Dinah—and return to the particular issue after the narrator's flight of sermonizing. Moreover, such passages frequently deploy the plural pronouns *we* and *our*, establishing with the text-internal narratee but also with the text-external audience a commonality of experience and attitude and thereby soliciting their consent with the expressed views. In the above passage it is love of a deep and venerable kind as a generic human experience that is being described. The point is to allow for an acknowledgment that depth of amatory sentiment is not a privilege of the upper classes but, as a universal human phenomenon, occurs also among "humble craftsmen." The thrust of these observations therefore anticipates the argument of chapter 17, Eliot's plea for the lovability of people "not altogether handsome" (177), and her appeal to her audience to cherish the beauty residing "in the secret of deep human sympathy" (178)—passages in which the narrator moves beyond mere gnomic truths to explicit moral statements in his own voice: "Let us cultivate . . . let us love . . . Paint us an angel . . . but do not impose. . . ."; "It is so needful that we should remember . . ." (all 178), on to statements in the first person: "It is more needful that I should have a fibre of sympathy with that vulgar citizen who weighs out my sugar . . . than with the handsomest rascal in red scarf and green feathers" (179).

Gnomic utterances often presuppose that the characteristic they are about to outline is already well known to the narratee; they are reminding us of a well-known fact rather than pointing out any ingenious insight that the narrator has happened upon. This is frequently made explicit by the anaphoric demonstrative *that*. In the passage cited above, Seth's love for Dinah partakes of "*that* adoration which a young man gives to a woman whom he feels to be greater and better than himself" (37; ch. 3; my emphasis). The *that* underlines our familiarity with the emotion; it calls up our recognition of it, and thereby endorses its appropriateness as a reference for Seth's situation. In *Middlemarch*, Dorothea's way of attiring herself calls up a similar *that*-construction: "Miss Brooke had *that* kind of beauty which seems to be thrown into relief by poor dress" (*Middlemarch* 29; ch. 1; my emphasis).

At times the narrator addresses the reader figure as an arbiter of the point under discussion or even lectures the narratee, as in chapter 17, where the largely gnomic philosophizing develops into a veritable harangue:

> But, my good friend, what will you do then with your fellow-parishioner who opposes your husband in the vestry? – . . . with your neighbour, Mrs Green, who was really kind to you in your last illness, but has said several ill-natured things about you since your convalescence? – nay, with your excellent husband himself, who has other irritating habits besides that of not wiping his shoes? These fellow-mortals, every one, must be accepted as they are: you can neither straighten their noses, nor brighten their wit, nor rectify their dispositions; and it is these people – amongst whom your life is passed – that it is needful you should tolerate, pity, and love: it is these more or less ugly, stupid, inconsistent people, . . . the real breathing men and women, who can be chilled by your indifference or injured by your prejudice; who can be cheered and helped onward by your fellow-feeling, your forbearance, your outspoken, brave justice. (*Adam Bede* 176; ch. 17)

The admonition is directed at a reader figure of flesh and blood, one that knows real people like Mrs. Green and chafes under her husband's untidiness. (Note, incidentally, that the narratee is here decidedly female.) Such reader addresses can be used merely to focus on the representation, as when we read "I beseech you to imagine Mr Irwine . . . in his ample white surplice that became him so well" (*Adam Bede* 197; ch. 18). Here the effect is that of alerting the audience to the picture of peacefulness and benevolence ("the benignant yet keen countenance" and "generous soul") of an Anglican service on Sunday. This is of course an ideological strategy. At other points the narrator engages in a dialogue with the hypostatized narratee:

> Are you inclined to ask whether this can be the same Arthur who, two months ago, had that freshness of feeling, that delicate honour which shrinks from wounding even a sentiment, and does not contemplate any more positive offence as possible for it? . . . The same, I assure you; only under different conditions. Our deeds determine us, as much as we determine our deeds; and until we know what has been or will be the peculiar combination of outward with inward facts, which constitutes a man's critical actions, it will be better not to think ourselves wise about his character. (*Adam Bede* 313; ch. 29)

The passage first involves the narratee in an argument about Arthur, then propounds a gnomic truth ("Our deeds determine us") and by continuing to use the first-person plural pronoun aligns our judgments and our capability of lapsing into wrong with

Arthur's predicament, thus drawing us into a sympathetic and condoning attitude towards Arthur's self-delusions. German literary criticism has coined the handy term *Sympathielenkung* for this technique, literally "directing (the reader's) sympathy (to a character)," to talk about narrative strategies that convey positive or negative attitudes or impressions of a character. Eliot's narratorial discourse clearly moves beyond abstract moralizing and evaluation to deliberate empathetic manipulation and "shaping"[5] of her audience.

There is a comparable moment in *Adam Bede* when Hetty is, for once, seen compassionately. Again, we do not learn what she thinks or feels but confront her as the enigma of suffering hidden behind the screen of touristic pastoralism. The narratee is put into the role of a traveler unaware of the seamy underside of the natural beauties displayed for his gaze. The immersive function of the narratorial communion with the narratee is here fitted with a nasty barb of irony hidden in the fluff of theatrical display:

> What a glad world this looks like, as one drives or rides along the valleys and over the hills! I have often thought so when, in foreign countries, . . . I have come on something by the roadside which has reminded me that I am not in Loamshire: an image of a great agony – the agony of the Cross . . . and surely, if there came a traveller to this world who knew nothing of the story of man's life upon it, this image of agony would seem to him strangely out of place in the midst of this joyous nature. He would not know that hidden behind the apple-blossoms, or among the golden corn, or under the shrouding boughs of the wood, there might be a human heart beating heavily with anguish: perhaps a young blooming girl, not knowing where to turn for refuge from swift-advancing shame . . . (*Adam Bede* 363–64; ch. 35)

The spectacle of bloom and happiness conceals a dark, sad secret. Such secrets often remain hidden to the cursory reader disinclined to delve below the surface or look behind the trees and apple blossoms. The narratee imaginatively adopts the role of a traveler and is exhorted to be aware of latent meanings.

Let me move on to another prominent feature of Eliot's prose, that of her use of metaphor. I would like to distinguish between explicit and implicit metaphor or simile. An explicit metaphor or simile openly declares its metaphoric nature; in the case of a simile by means of a comparative (*like, as*, etc.), in the case of metaphor by the semantic rupture within a sentence from the literal meaning of the surrounding context. Explicit metaphor and simile are phenomena located at the syntactic microlevel of the sentence. Let us look at two examples:

> But it is not ignoble to feel that the fuller life which a sad experience has brought us is worth our own personal share of pain: surely it is not possible to feel otherwise, *any more than it would be possible for a man with cataract to regret the painful process by which his dim blurred sight of men as trees walking had been exchanged for clear outline and effulgent day.* (*Adam Bede* 530; ch. 54; my emphasis)

In this explicit narratorial simile Adam's growing maturity is explained as based on the sorrow he experienced through Hetty's tragedy; his reward of a richer life comes at a cost which is compared to the regaining of sight; the result, however painful the process, overwhelms all memory of previous suffering. In the second example, this time of explicit metaphor, the narrator even adds a metanarrative comment on metaphor:

> Poor Mr Casaubon had imagined that his long studious bachelorhood had stored up for him *a compound interest of enjoyment*, and that *large drafts of his affections* would not fail *to be honoured*; for we all of us, grave or light, *get our thoughts entangled in metaphors*, and act fatally on the strength of them. (*Middlemarch* 111; ch. 10; my emphases)

Here the narrator uses economic metaphors to portray Casaubon's increasing desire for emotional gratification. Casaubon has hoarded up his feelings and invested them in the expectation of deferred marital bliss, a speculation that turns out to be erroneous since the treasure has dried up rather than blossoming into fruit (interest). The narrator's comment on our propensity to act on metaphor is, however, odd since the economic parallel was introduced by the narrator herself and most likely was not a conscious motive in Casaubon's thoughts; Casaubon clearly failed to exercise his emotions in the expectation that they would be available in increased force when at last needed; but did he really conceive of this "hoarding" as a financial transaction, a speculation? It seems more likely that the narrator ironically exposes Casaubon's mode of thinking as *comparable* to the bank model of compound interest, where the money always increases and does not become devalued. The irony consists in the fact that Casaubon's expectations ignore the quality of emotion, that he is unaware that affection is like a spring that may dry up the older one gets.[6] What the narrator really implies is that we often have incorrect notions and that the reason for our misconceptions lies in imposing a structure on reality that is not appropriate to it—a gap in adequation that can be grasped by means of metaphor. Metaphor imposes a frame on a situation that reconfigures the situation from a new perspective; if the metaphor works well, it will allow us to operate more successfully by supplying us with new concepts and outlooks. If it falls flat, as in Casaubon's case, it falsely makes us act on notions that will be disappointed; it deludes us with hopes and lures us to our ruin.

Explicit metaphorizing is one of the prerogatives of Eliot's narrators; unlike Flaubert, Eliot rarely attributes her metaphors to the characters. When Hetty's dread of discovery is figured in a striking simile that anticipates her impending confrontation with the law, the imagery that evokes Hetty's mental condition belongs to the narrator's ironic discourse:

> Hetty looked out from her secret misery towards the possibility of their ["her aunt and uncle"] ever knowing what had happened, *as the sick and weary prisoner might think of the possible pillory*. (*Adam Bede* 336; ch. 31; my emphasis)

The explicit comparison is part of the narrator's rhetoric: suffering is terrible, but it palls before the dread of shameful exposure. Hetty is not the source of this simile.

Let me now turn to *implicit* similes and metaphors. A good example of such implicitness is the gnomic dictum that "people who love downy peaches are apt not to think of the stone, and sometimes jar their teeth terribly against it" (*Adam Bede* 153; ch. 15). This comes at the end of Hetty's depiction as "puss" and a "dear young, round, soft, flexible thing" (152; ch. 15) and Adam's thinking about Hetty "very much in this way" (153; ch. 15). The gnomic statement creates an analogy to the discussed inclination of men to take pretty women as harmless fools and innocent child-like creatures who need to be protected and are apt to be "lovely and loving" (153; ch. 15)—note the alliteration. The analogy of the peach which costs you your tooth applies to the argument that women who look like fruit are apt to be bitten into to the detriment of the male consumer. This analogy is an implicit metaphor. The ostensible message ("Things are not what they seem," "Appearance is not reality") through the verb "love" and the adjective "downy," which echoes women's softness and Hetty's earlier description of having the "beauty . . . of kittens, or very small downy ducks" (83; ch. 7), establishes a primary analogy ("One has to be careful of women's real character just as one has to be careful of stones in peaches") that could be interpreted as metaphorical: women are peaches, and they have stones. Or, analogously: "Hetty is a peach with a stone (for her heart?)." This implicit metaphorical conceptualizing of Hetty is half-corroborated by the opening of the following paragraph: "Arthur Donnithorne, too, had the same sort of notion about Hetty. . . . He felt sure she was a dear, affectionate, good little thing" (153; ch. 15).

The strategy of implicit imagery recurs in Mr. Irwine's cautioning of Arthur:

> You needn't look quite so much at Hetty Sorrel then. *When I've made up my mind that I can't afford to buy a tempting dog, I take no notice of him, because if he took a strong fancy to me, and looked longingly at me, the struggle between arithmetic and inclination might become unpleasantly severe.* (102; ch. 9; my emphasis)

Mr. Irwine is proposing a parable with the moral "Do not get involved where your feelings might get the better of your rational calculations or duties," and this parable is taken from the realm of dog buying. However, implicitly, the analogy suggests that Hetty is the dog, and the cautioning tale in fact anticipates precisely what will happen, though the consequences are much more serious than overdrawing one's account for the acquisition of a puppy. In fact, the whole simile makes much more sense for horse-buying (where the cost might indeed become prohibitive). The dog imagery is extremely appropriate to Adam's view of Hetty as his future wife and to Arthur's patronizing attitude towards Hetty; it captures the men's attitudes towards women: they are fawning spaniels who need to be pampered and they deserve love for the adoration they expend on their masters (husbands); the canine image moreover underlines the domesticity of the vignette in a manner that a horse in the stable could not have done.

From the indirection of such examples of metaphor I would like to turn to another strategy of indirection which is prominent in *Adam Bede*. In the opening chapter of the novel we have Adam stride home to the admiring glance of "an elderly horseman" (12; ch. 1) who is impressed by Bede's stalwart carriage and vigorous walk. In chapter 2, the anonymous horseman pulls up at the Donnithorne Arms, and the "traveller" (17; ch. 2) then proceeds on his journey; it is through his eyes that we view the landscape ("the traveller might exchange a bleak treeless region . . . for one where his road wound under the shelter of woods . . . and where at every turn he came upon some fine old country-seat" [17–18; ch. 2]). Not only what the rider sees but what he might have seen is outlined in detail ("He might have seen other beauties in the landscape if he had turned a little in his saddle and looked eastward" [18–19; ch. 2]). But the main focus of the chapter is his witnessing of the Methodist preaching and thereby the introduction of Dinah Morris to the reader. "The stranger" (22; ch. 2) has extremely favorable impressions of Dinah, thus directing our sympathies towards her and, by his double noting of Adam and Dinah, implying that they are the two main protagonists, whose union will indeed close the novel. The strategy of providing an external viewpoint does not end here.[7] We have noted how Hetty is always presented in terms of how she affects other people watching her: Arthur looking at her in the dairy (83–86; ch. 7), Adam seeing her gather the red currants (219–20; ch. 20), Adam watching for her affections before and after he gives her Arthur's letter (318–23; ch. 30) and when he proposes to her (358–60; ch. 34).

Hetty is rendered almost consistently in external focalization, though often through the internal focalization of other characters' thoughts about her. She is first talked about by Dinah ("that poor wandering lamb, Hetty Sorrel" [34; ch. 3]), then by Lisbeth ("that bit of a wench, as is o' no more use nor the gillyflower on the wall" [45; ch. 4]) before she is noted by the narrator for her vanity (73; ch. 6). Next she is viewed by Aunt Poyser, whose "keen glance" is nevertheless misled in judging Hetty (74; ch. 6). Hetty is described in detail for three pages in chapter 7, all for the benefit of the reader, whose imaginary viewing of her is underlined at every turn (83–85; ch. 7). This series of perspectives continues with the impression that Hetty makes during her trip to Arthur at Windsor, and later at the trial we also get various depictions of her from the witnesses' statements. The problematic positioning of Hetty as the focalized object of other people's vision is therefore a persistent feature of the novel and suggests that she is the object of desire in Lacanian terms as well as, more literally, for the men in the fictional world. Hetty poses an enigma—she seems easily readable through her beauty (the peach), but hides her innermost self by this dazzling and deceptive exterior.

There are of course minor exceptions to this external presentation of Hetty. I will cite one below when I note the novel's extensive use of free indirect discourse. Since we have a very outspoken narrator persona who keeps commenting on the customs and attitudes of the protagonists, psychonarration—the narrator's representation of characters' consciousness—is a recurring strategy that allows for an ironic view of the characters' minds. In fact, as we shall see, the most empathetic passages frequently turn out to be barbed with implicit criticism or judgment.

> Arthur had felt a twinge of conscience during Mr Poyser's speech, but it was too feeble
> to nullify the pleasure he felt in being praised. [psychonarration] *Did he not deserve what
> was said of him, on the whole? If there was something in his conduct that Poyser wouldn't have
> liked if he had known it, why, no man's conduct will bear too close an inspection; and Poyser was
> not likely to know it; and after all, what had he done? Gone a little too far perhaps in flirtation,
> but another man in his place would have acted much worse; and no harm would come – no harm
> <u>should</u> come . . .* [free indirect discourse] (*Adam Bede* 264; ch. 24; my emphasis)

Here Arthur's self-deluding musings are rendered in free indirect discourse; we as
readers do not yet know that he has slept with Hetty, except from the hint at dire
consequences. The passage definitely provides an ironic view of Arthur's mind. By
contrast, when Adam panics that he might have killed Arthur, we have a clearly
consonant, empathetic representation:

> *But why did not Arthur rise? He was perfectly motionless, and the time seemed long to Adam . . .*
> *Good God! had the blow been too much for him?* [free indirect discourse] Adam shuddered
> at the thought of his own strength, as with the oncoming of this dread [psychonarration]
> he knelt down by Arthur's side and lifted his head from among the fern. [narrative]
> There was no sign of life: the eyes and teeth were set. [Adam's impression] The horror
> that rushed over Adam completely mastered him, and forced upon him its own belief.
> He could feel nothing but that death was in Arthur's face, and that he was helpless
> before it. [psychonarration] (*Adam Bede* 301; ch. 28; ellipsis in original)

Here Adam's fear is totally justified and the reader is sympathetically involved with
Adam, whom he or she does not want to see as a murderer. The passage moreover
illustrates Eliot's typical technique of blending psychonarration and free indirect
discourse.

One of the few passages that give us Hetty's thoughts comes in chapter 31, when
she decides she will marry Adam:

> *Why should she not marry Adam? She did not care what she did, so that it made some*
> *change in her life.* [free indirect discourse] She felt confident that he would still want to
> marry her, and any further thought about Adam's happiness in the matter had never yet
> visited her. [psychonarration] (*Adam Bede* 339; ch. 31)

This rendering of Hetty's mind is consonant to the extent that we get an insight into
Hetty's feelings and surmises that are clearly expressive of her wish to improve her
situation. Though her reasons for marriage are wrong, the reader does not yet know
that she is pregnant and cheating on Adam; the end of the previous paragraph in fact
had a gnomic utterance by the narrator which rather suggested she is merely naïve in
wanting to marry without loving her husband: "she was ready for one of those con-
vulsive, motiveless actions by which wretched men and women leap from a temporary
sorrow into a life-long misery" (339; ch. 31). Since the narrator here deceives us into
thinking Hetty is merely unhappy because she no longer has Arthur to dream about,

the irony of her views about marriage is much muted. Eliot's narrative therefore continues to blend irony and sympathy in its preference for external viewpoints and selective representations of consciousness.

In this essay there is no space to elaborate on George Eliot's irony, clearly one of the hallmarks of her prose. What I would like to conclude with is a different narrative strategy that I have discussed in connection with *The Mill on the Floss* and *Romola* (Fludernik, "Subversive Irony"; *Towards a "Natural" Narratology* 182–84), reflectorization.

Reflectorization[8] consists in the miming of a particular story-internal viewpoint by the narrator who adopts the arguments, style, and vocabulary of a person (or, possibly, group of persons) inside the fictional world. This mimicry is mostly ironic: the narrator in the role of the character whose viewpoint he or she has been echoing is unreliable to the extent that we as readers know that these opinions and views are definitely not in line with the overall belief system of the narrator or the text as a whole. Although unreliability is generally considered to be a feature of first-person (homodiegetic) narrative, the posturing of the narrator as in agreement with a character's worldview when we know that this particular standpoint is being criticized seems to allow for the label, particularly since the Boothian disparity between the beliefs of the character and those of the text in its entirety (the "implied author") can be argued to underlie the reader's recognition that there is ironic undermining of the views outlined by the narrator in her/his mimicry. Let us look at an example from *Adam Bede*. The character whose viewpoint is echoed is Arthur Donnithorne:

> he was but twenty-one, you remember; and we don't inquire too closely into character in the case of a handsome generous fellow, who will have property enough to support numerous peccadilloes – who, if he should unfortunately break a man's legs in his rash driving, will be able to pension him handsomely; or if he should happen to spoil a woman's existence for her, will make it up to her with expensive *bon-bons*, packed up and directed by his own hand. It would be ridiculous to be prying and analytic in such cases, as if one were inquiring into the character of a confidential clerk. We use round, general, gentlemanly epithets about a young man of birth and fortune; and ladies, with that fine intuition which is the distinguishing attribute of their sex, see at once that he is 'nice.' The chances are that he will go through life without scandalising any one; a sea-worthy vessel that no one would refuse to insure. (*Adam Bede* 125–26; ch. 12)

The narrator in this passage continues his speculations about Arthur by adopting an attitude about the possible peccadilloes of young gentlemen that emphasizes their harmless and forgivable nature. As the examples indicate, however, these pastimes are far from innocent. The adventures of the "nice" young man are in fact irresponsible aggressions towards his social inferiors, resulting for instance in a broken limb and the man's permanent disability. The "young man of birth and fortune" can afford to pay his way out of his blunders by giving the invalid a pension (which will not enable him to make his life meaningful) and by solacing the grief of the ruined woman with luxurious presents that seem to indicate his esteem for her ("packed up and directed by his own hand") when in fact they debase her as the recipient of superficial concern. This mode of behavior is "ridiculous," yet the narrator uses this lexeme to scoff at those scrutinizing the young man of property's behavior from a too narrow, petty, lower-class perspective (the comparison to the "confidential clerk"). The rest of the paragraph continues in this exculpatory vein, anticipating Arthur's foundering on the rocks of disastrous circumstance, a vessel with a "flaw" in its construction (126). The term *flaw* again plays down the seriousness of the situation, but the consequences of this faulty workmanship in the sinking of the ship ("casualties" including the loss of load and lives of the crew) are tragic indeed. The narrator in this passage takes the role of a person with common-sense attitudes towards young scions of the upper classes. By means of such ironic impersonation he thoroughly discredits the ideology of the gentry, denouncing it from the perspective of the waste caused in humbler lives through the irresponsible and thoughtless sowing of wild oats.

Reflectorization in Eliot is a strategy that serves to enhance the ironies purveyed by the narrator. The technique of reflectorization is often flanked by the delineation of what Alan Palmer has termed "intermental thought," evident for example in the collective thought represented by the "Middlemarch Mind." (See Palmer, "Intermental Thought"; "Large Intermental Units"; *Social Minds* 65–104). Intermentality concerns thoughts and opinions that are shared between people. Most passages of intermental thought are ironic since the village or town are usually mistaken in their views, prejudiced, or otherwise untrustworthy in their outlook. For instance, in *Silas Marner*, the envious and supercilious Miss Gunns are presented as sharing uncharitable views of Miss Nancy Lammeter, views that the narrator is quick to contradict, thus putting down the Gunns' cavillings:

> The Miss Gunns smiled stiffly, and thought what a pity it was that these rich country people, who could afford to buy such good clothes (really Miss Nancy's lace and silk were very costly), should be brought up in utter ignorance and vulgarity. She actually said "mate" for "meat," "appen" for "perhaps," and "oss" for "horse," which, to young ladies living in good Lytherly society, who habitually said "orse," even in domestic privacy, . . . was necessarily shocking. . . . There is hardly a servant-maid in these days who is not better informed than Miss Nancy; yet she had the essential attributes of a lady – high veracity, delicate honour in her dealings, deference to others, and refined personal habits . . . (*Silas Marner* 92–93; ch. 11)

The passage ridicules the snobbism of small-town society and its focus on pronunciation rather than moral character. Another good set of examples of collective thought can be drawn from *Felix Holt* and the depiction of the riot, where diverse groups within the mob are contrasted in their viewpoints.

Let me conclude. When we try to characterize Eliot's narrative, its preponderant features are the presence of a foregrounded, opinionated narrator persona; the high incidence of narratee address and involvement, especially in Eliot's early fiction; a frequent use of explicit and implicit metaphor and simile; a consistent tendency towards irony, reinforced by ironic free indirect discourse, reflectorization, and passages of collective thought; and an inclination to moralize, judge, and philosophize on the human condition, yet in reference to very specific circumstances in the fictional world. Eliot's narrative corresponds to a social reality familiar to its readers, as the prominence of gnomic commentary and the focal use of text-internal observation of characters by others demonstrate. It is precisely this alignment of the represented world with the readers' moral and practical outlook that makes for George Eliot's realism. It is not a realism of descriptive detail *à la* Ian Watt, but a realism of ethical concern and pragmatic life experience. It encompasses, like the holy spirit in Gerard Manley Hopkins's "God's Grandeur," the whole world of great and small, ugly and beautiful, envious and noble, of the egotistic and bilious as well as the modest and passionately spiritual: "Because the Holy Ghost over the bent / World broods with warm breast and with ah! bright wings" (Hopkins 1030).

NOTES

1 Compare also Nünning, *Gründzüge* 161.

2 See Nünning, "Mimesis" and Fludernik, *Introduction* 61 on this counter-intuitive effect of metanarrative, and even metafictional, techniques in realist prose.

3 Compare Nünning's remarks on this in *Grundzüge* 166.

4 The term *gnomic* refers to universally valid dicta.

5 There is no English equivalent of *Sympathielenkung*. (But see Tyson 195–97 on "shaping" our empathy towards Gatsby.)

6 See Hardy (*Novels* 218–20) on the water metaphor in *Middlemarch*.

7 See Shaw (222–25) for further examples of the traveler motif.

8 The term comes from Stanzel (168–84), where it translates the German *Personalisierung*, and echoes what Stanzel calls reflector-mode narrative (*personale Erzählsituation*) in which internal focalization predominates.

REFERENCES

Brontë, Charlotte. *Shirley*. Ed. Jessica Cox. London: Penguin, 2006.

Cohn, Dorrit. *Transparent Minds. Narrative Modes for Presenting Consciousness in Fiction*. Princeton: Princeton UP, 1978.

Eliot, George. *Adam Bede*. Ed. Valentine Cunningham. Oxford: Oxford UP, 1996.

Eliot, George. *Middlemarch*. Ed. W. J. Harvey. London: Penguin, 1986.

Eliot, George. *The Mill on the Floss*. Ed. Gordon S. Haight. Oxford: Clarendon, 1980.

Eliot, George. *Romola*. Ed. Andrew Sanders. London: Penguin, 1986.

Eliot, George. *Silas Marner*. Ed. Terence Cave. Oxford: Oxford UP, 1996.

Fludernik, Monika. *An Introduction to Narratology*. Trans. Patricia Häusler-Greenfield and Monika Fludernik. London: Routledge, 2009.

Fludernik, Monika. "Subversive Irony: Reflectorization, Trustworthy Narration and Dead-pan Narrative in *The Mill on the Floss*." *Yearbook of Research in English and American Literature {REAL}* 8. 1992: 159–84.

Fludernik, Monika. *Towards a "Natural" Narratology*. London: Routledge, 1996.

Graver, Suzanne. *George Eliot and Community: A Study in Social Theory and Fictional Form*. Berkeley: U of California P, 1984.

Hardy, Barbara. *The Novels of George Eliot: A Study in Form*. London: Athlone, 1959.

Hardy, Barbara. *Particularities. Readings in George Eliot.* London: Peter Owen, 1982.

Hopkins, Gerard Manley. "God's Grandeur." 1877. *The Arnold Anthology of British and Irish Literature in English.* Ed. Robert Clark and Thomas Healy. London: Arnold, 1997. 1030.

Nünning, Ansgar. *Grundzüge eines kommunikationstheoretischen Modells der erzählerischen Vermittlung. Die Funktionen der Erzählinstanz in den Romanen George Eliots.* Horizonte, 2. Trier: Wissenschaftlicher Verlag, 1989.

Nünning, Ansgar. "Mimesis des Erzählens: Prolegomena zu einer Wirkungsästhetik, Typologie und Funktionsgeschichte des Akts des Erzählens und der Metanarration." *Erzählen und Erzähltheorie im 20. Jahrhundert: Festschrift für Wilhelm Füger.* Ed. Jörg Helbig. Heidelberg, 2001. 13–47.

Palmer, Alan. "Intermental Thought in the Novel: The Middlemarch Mind." *Style* 39.4 (2005): 427–39.

Palmer, Alan. "Large Intermental Units in *Middlemarch*." *Postclassical Narratology: Approaches and Analyses.* Ed. Jan Alber and Monika Fludernik. Columbus: Ohio State UP, 2010. 83–104.

Palmer, Alan. *Social Minds in the Novel.* Columbus: Ohio State UP, 2010.

Ryan, Marie-Laure. *Narrative as Virtual Reality. Immersion and Interactivity in Literature and the Electronic Media.* Baltimore: Johns Hopkins UP, 2001.

Shaw, Harry E. *Narrating Reality: Austen, Scott, Eliot.* Ithaca: Cornell UP, 1999.

Stanzel, Franz Karl. *A Theory of Narrative.* Cambridge: Cambridge UP, 1984.

Tyson, Lois. *Critical Theory Today: A User-Friendly Guide.* 2nd ed. London: Routledge, 2006.

Watt, Ian. *The Rise of the Novel: Studies in Defoe, Richardson and Fielding.* Berkeley: U of California P, 1957.

Wolf, Werner. *Ästhetische Illusion und Illusionsdurchbrechung in der Erzählkunst. Theorie und Geschichte mit Schwerpunkt auf englischem illusionsstörenden Erzählen.* Tübingen: Niemeyer, 1993.

2

Metaphor and Masque

Michael Wood

". . . not ideas, you know, but a way of putting them" (George Eliot, *Middlemarch*, Chapter 46)

". . . the philosophic door is always open, on her stage" (Henry James, "The Life of George Eliot")

"He did not live in the scenery of such an event" (*Middlemarch* 469; ch. 47). The remark is not a criticism, or an indication of failure; it is a kind of compliment. But it raises, if we pause over it, a whole series of questions—about the connection of scenery to event, about life among scenery, about the risks and comforts of metaphor— and it represents generosity of spirit as an absence of imagination.

The context is Will Ladislaw's consideration of his relation to Dorothea Brooke in a late chapter of *Middlemarch*. The scenery he is not inhabiting surrounds the possible death of Mr. Casaubon and the chance of marrying Dorothea. This is precisely "the ordinary vulgar vision" that Mr. Casaubon suspects Will of entertaining, and even Eliot's narrator finds something odd about Will's innocence in this respect:

> there is no human being who having both passions and thoughts does not think in consequence of his passions—does not find images rising in his mind which soothe the passion with hope or sting it with dread. But this, which happens to us all, happens to some with a wide difference. (468; ch. 47)

A Companion to George Eliot, First Edition. Edited by Amanda Anderson and Harry E. Shaw.
© 2013 John Wiley & Sons, Ltd. Published 2016 by John Wiley & Sons, Ltd.

It happens with such a difference that to some it scarcely happens at all. Will's "dreamy visions of possibility" are not like anyone else's.

> It may seem strange, but it is the fact, that the ordinary vulgar vision of which Mr. Casaubon suspected him—namely, that Dorothea might become a widow, and that the interest he had established in her mind might turn into acceptance of him as a husband—had no tempting, arresting power over him; he did not live in the scenery of such an event, and follow it out, as we all do with that imagined "otherwise" which is our practical heaven. (468–69; ch. 47)

If Will doesn't do what "we all do," he seems to be a contradiction, an impossibility, rather than an exception. The fact can be rescued from its strangeness only by a looser, ampler logic. The easier claim must be that what happens to us all doesn't happen all the time, and isn't the single thing that happens to us. We meet Will at one of those (rare) mental moments without images. This understanding doesn't diminish the surprise, but it does tame the impossibility.

The general proposition—that we think in consequence of our passions, that our minds produce images that soothe or sting those passions—is a familiar part of the moral and psychological fabric of *Middlemarch*. This is why the claim about the scenery is so interesting. It is a claim against the imagination, and it is made in the form of a metaphor, that is, in what Eliot thinks of as the imagination's strongest and most dangerous idiom.

For of course Will is not just not thinking about marrying Dorothea. He *can't* think about it, because in the implied logic of the figure, he would have to be living in a specifiable imaginative space for the idea to enter his mind: in another play, or on another stage, if we take the metaphor to be theatrical; in a different landscape if we take it to be drawn from the natural world. We can note further the suggestion that he must be living in the scenery of some event or events, because we all do; just not this event. Events have their mental scenery. They can occur without it, this happens all the time, that's how we are surprised or devastated. But they can't be imagined without it. The scenery is the imagination of the event, the pictured place where the event waits, and the only place where it can wait, as long as it is an imagined event.

The compliment to Will, then, rests not on a general absence of imagination, or even on an ability just to see things as they are, but on the absence of a local, acquisitive imagining. And yet. Does Eliot, or her narrator, actually, consistently think that all mental events have their scenery, as distinct from their context or their ground or their motivation? Surely the metaphor is doing a very particular kind of work here. Doesn't scenery, whether theatrical or natural, suggest something optional or leisurely, a touch of the artful or the picturesque? Hillis Miller says there is no such thing as a literal meaning—in Eliot, or perhaps in life (66–67). This can't be quite right because, as Nietzsche would say, if there is no literal meaning there is no figurative meaning either. In *George Eliot's Pulse*, Neil Hertz glosses "to take seriously," after de Man, as to take "both literally and figuratively" (85). But it is true that the literal meaning of any metaphor, if not just another metaphor, is another wording, and so can't quite say what the metaphor says. This is one important sense of Donald Davidson's claim that "metaphors mean what the words, in their most literal interpretation, mean, and nothing more" (32). The narrative, substantive content of Eliot's sentence can be expressed—and probably is expressed, when we tell the story of *Middlemarch* to ourselves——in a phrase like "He did not think of such a thing." This must be a large part of what Eliot wants to say, and indeed it is what Lydgate says in non-metaphorical terms when he evokes Will's "romantic disregard" of his "worldly interests" (467; ch. 46). But it isn't what the metaphor actually says. It doesn't even say "His mind formed no picture of such an event," which would still be quite different from living among the event's scenery. Eliot is inviting us not only to understand the sense of the metaphor but to see or feel what it does for her idea, and by implication, to wonder what sort of effect might be achieved by another metaphor— an arena, for example, or a climate—or by a non-metaphorical term like hope or expectation.

Eliot explicitly accepts the traditional definition of metaphor as transferred predication, what Ted Cohen calls seeing one thing as another (8, 9). But her seeing is often so swift and subtle and secure that it can seem to create a new literal realm, a discreet novel within the novel. The old literal meaning doesn't disappear, and still less is it, as Davidson argues for metaphor more generally, devoured entirely by a new literal sense. But as we have just seen it becomes very faint and functional, a narrative marker, a place we prudently remember on the map while we spend our time on other pages of the atlas. Eliot's metaphors impart knowledge, as Nelson Goodman says metaphors do (125), and this is how they mainly work in her prose. But they also represent seductive illusions, and this is how they frequently figure for her characters and in her own theoretical passages on imagery.

We can't be surprised to learn (again) that Eliot worries about the imagination— that she can praise a man for not imagining—even as she sets so much store by the imagination's achievements and possibilities. And to encounter this worry and this investment is, among many other things, to meet up with two distinct and differently valuable critical traditions of thinking about George Eliot and figuration. The first registers and rightly wonders at the reach and power of what Hertz calls Eliot's "metaphorical control," the masterly world of her many and interconnected tropes, explored by Schorer, Hardy, Gezari, and others. This tradition allows for "absolutely no horsing around," Hertz says (20). The other tradition, most marked perhaps in the work of Hertz himself and Mary Jacobus, doesn't exactly horse around either, but it is interested in the proliferating suggestiveness of metaphor rather than stable patterns of imagery, and if it doesn't suggest Eliot's metaphors are out of control, it does place them at the edge of control, ready to slip off into overtime, even into play. Jacobus writes of an "impropriety" in metaphor, an "oxymoronic otherness" (74).

Of course we need both traditions. The second wouldn't exist without the work of the first; and the first is rather prim if we don't complement it with the second. But both traditions, I think, leave unjudged the issue that Hillis Miller settles perhaps too quickly when he says "the only weapon against metaphor is another metaphor" (67), and that Eliot herself never quite closes: namely that of the opposing claims represented by the view that metaphor is unavoidable in affairs of the mind and the view that we might usefully manage without it some of the time or even quite often. At first glance it might seem as if the first position belongs to her mature thinking, and is reinforced on almost every page of *Middlemarch*, while the second position is ironically but firmly declared in a famous passage in *The Mill on the Floss* which contains the lament "that we can so seldom declare what a thing is, except by saying it is something else" (*Mill* 147; bk. 2, ch. 1). My suggestion is that although there are delicate shifts of tone and emphasis and preference over time, and even within individual novels, Eliot never fully accepts or abandons either position, but allows each to become infected, so to speak, by the scenery of the other.

Let's look at the "later" position first, since it seems to be more amply declared. We have already heard a version of it: "there is no human being who having both passions and thoughts does not think in consequence of his passions—does not find images rising in his mind." These are the large cadences of Eliot's best generalizing music, the sentences that so magisterially insist on what "all of us" do, and they recur at crucial moments in *Middlemarch*:[1]

> We are all of us imaginative in some form or other, for images are the brood of desire. . . . (324; ch. 34)

> for we all of us, grave or light, get our thoughts entangled in metaphors and act fatally on the strength of them. (85; ch. 10)

In the first case old Peter Featherstone is imagining the pleasure he will have in annoying his heirs when he is dead, forgetting that his cancelled consciousness is an indispensable part of the deal. In this sense he is caught up in "the fellowship of illusion"; apparently the least fanciful of men, he becomes a victim of a picture, and thus is "imaginative, after his fashion" (324; ch. 34). It seems possible, on the simple evidence of his fantasy—his "chuckling over the vexations he could inflict by the rigid clutch of his dead head" (324; ch. 34)—that Featherstone is enjoying *now* in thought the pleasures he won't have *then* in fact, in which case he would be imaginative after a more creative, less deluded, albeit distinctly malicious fashion. But the narrator firmly excludes this possibility: "he certainly did not make clear to himself that his pleasure in the little drama of which it formed a part was confined to anticipation" (324; ch. 34). Even so, the malice has its energy, and is comically counterpointed after the funeral by Mr. Vincy's attributing the perfectly wrong motive to the dead man:

> "I shouldn't wonder if Featherstone had better feelings than any of us gave him credit for," he observed, in the ear of his wife. "This funeral shows a thought about everybody: it looks well when a man wants to be followed by his friends, and if they are humble, not to be ashamed of them." (334; ch. 35).

The funeral does indeed show a thought about everybody, or at least all the prospective inheritors. And there is a further, melancholy counterpoint in the reminder that the event finds a significant place in Dorothea's mind: "this scene of old Featherstone's funeral . . . aloof as it seemed to be from the tenor of her life, always afterwards came back to her at the touch of certain sensitive points in memory, just as the vision of St. Peter's at Rome was inwoven with moods of despondency" (326; ch. 34).

We can put these reactions—there is a great deal more to be said about this miserable (and entertaining) scene of provincial death—into a sort of parable about the imagination: one person imagines a pleasure he cannot by definition have; another misreads this man's imagination according to his own friendly fashion; and another always remembers the results of the first person's imaginings. We could think the situation as a model of contagion, or proof of the reverse of one of Eliot's most famous sayings. It's true that "there is no private life which has not been determined by a wider public life" (*Felix Holt* 74); but it's also possible that there is scarcely any private event that does not make its way into the lives and minds of others.

But Eliot herself lingers over the relation of the imagination to the imaginer, the pictorial form of what she elsewhere calls a "report of . . . consciousness" (84; ch. 10), and she follows her proposal that "we are all of us imaginative in some form or other" with an unruly suggestion contained in what is effectively a metaphor for metaphor: "images are the brood of desire" (324; ch. 34). They are not just bred or born of desire, they are desire's brood, an implied mob of children or chickens. Because images are figures of desire, and not a reflection of sympathy or knowledge or even need, they are likely to be wrong, and our case will often not be better than Featherstone's as the narrator sees it. But they are not bound to be wrong, only to be freighted with wishing. We are all of us imaginative, but not all in the same way. Imagining is one of the things we do, and we do more of it than we think. But it is not all we do with our minds.

Mr. Casaubon, the instigating instance of the other sentence about what we all do ("get our thoughts entangled in metaphors and act fatally on the strength of them"), is precisely, and not accidentally, the opposite of Will: he is thinking about Dorothea and money, that's the scenery of his event. It's true he's not thinking of her money, or indeed of wanting to marry her, since he's already decided to do that. That is just the problem. He is surprised to discover that although he has "won a lovely and noble-hearted girl" he has not "won delight." He can't make out where his "blankness of sensibility" comes from, and feels himself "in danger of being saddened by the very conviction that his circumstances were unusually happy" (85; ch. 10). The narrator knows what's wrong. Like Featherstone in her view, Casaubon is the victim of a picture, trapped in an image dictated by desire rather than self-knowledge:

> Poor Mr. Casaubon had imagined that his long studious bachelorhood had stored up for him a compound interest of enjoyment, and that large drafts on his affections would not fail to be honoured; for we all of us, grave or light . . . (85; ch. 10)

Actually the trouble is already there in the conventional but still troubling metaphor of "winning" a girl—Mr. Casaubon is no knight and no athlete, and he should pay more attention even to his tired tropes—and I think we are meant to take the wonderful fiscal image as something more than a description of the actual content of Mr. Casaubon's imagination. Novelistically it must be this: he knows he hasn't spent any of the enjoyment to which he was entitled, and now he thinks it's piled up in the bank, and earning a good rate. But morally, the metaphor must rather indicate the style of his mind, the cramped, calculating idea of pleasure of a man who doesn't understand pleasure at all. Indeed the notions of compound interest and the large drafts on his affections may be a touch too witty for him to have entertained them. They seem to be employed on his behalf, and operate like a secondary irony at his expense. If this reading bears any weight, it will suggest that he can't even figure his deceiving imagination in a lively way. All we would know for sure about him is that he is baffled and disappointed, and that he grasps in the third person, as it were, that he should be happy and isn't. It is characteristic of him that he only wants what he thinks he ought to have, that even his sad surprise occurs at a failed remove, mediated by what he thinks others will think. The following sentence is a lesson in self-absorption as self-displacement: "He could not but wish that Dorothea should think him not less happy than the world would expect her successful suitor to be" (86; ch. 10). And in this sense the fine remark about the entanglement of our thoughts in metaphors, opening a host of questions for us, may let him off too easily. Mr. Casaubon can get things wrong and act fatally without any assistance from imaginative error. His literal misprisions will do the trick.

But do the rest of us get our thoughts entangled in metaphors? Do we act fatally on the strength of them? Let's turn to *The Mill on the Floss*. There is no explicit mention of metaphor when we are told that Mr. Stelling had managed to get a few declensions into Tom Tulliver's head by dint of "hard labour," although the idea of labour in this rural setting probably suggests something like digging the earth, and Tom's brain is already pictured as a place, somewhere to get things "into" or not, where things find or fail to find "a lodgment" (146; bk. 2, ch. 1). And there is nothing figurative about Mr. Stelling's basic diagnosis: Tom is stupid, but not naturally stupid; just effectively stupid through obstinacy or indifference to what he is being taught. The narrator confirms this diagnosis is correct, and gives us instances of Tom's intuitive, practical intelligence, and skill in calculating and drawing. "His perceptive powers," the narrator says, "were not at all deficient. I fancy they were quite as strong as those of the Rev. Mr. Stelling" (146; bk. 2, ch. 1).

She means they were stronger, and it's important to bear in mind the humor of this and so many other passages in Eliot, because it alters and multiplies the meanings of the words, so that they are scarcely ever saying only one thing, even when they are talking specifically about calling things by their proper names. Mr. Stelling is mocked for being a pedant, albeit a well-meaning one ("Mr. Stelling was very far from being led astray by enthusiasm, either religious or intellectual . . . he had not wasted his time in the acquirement of anything abnormal" [146; bk. 2, ch. 1]); and Tom is mocked, although rather less at this moment than at others, for being a touch more rustic than he needs to be.

The sequence of thought described to us means that although Mr. Stelling sees Tom as being "in a state bordering on idiocy with regard to the demonstration that two given triangles must be equal," it is the brain of an obstinate rather than a dim-witted child that needs ploughing and harrowing by the "patent implements" of "etymology and demonstrations" (147; bk. 2, ch. 1). The metaphor is not as gratuitous or as cruel as the narrator's discussion is about to make it seem. It's not just any old brain that is like a field; it is a brain that needs preparation for what it is to receive. In any case, "it was [Mr. Stelling's] favourite metaphor, that the classics and geometry constituted that culture of the mind which prepared it for the reception of any subsequent crop" (147; bk. 2, ch. 1). At this point a very fast-moving argument begins.

The narrator says of Mr. Stelling's "theory" that "if we are to have one regimen for all minds, his seems . . . as good as any other" (147; bk. 2, ch. 1)—that is, some minds will respond to being ploughed and others won't, and indeed perhaps more minds will respond to this treatment than will not. But Tom's mind is not one of those, and the narrator exposes the weakness of Mr. Stelling's metaphor through a simile: "I only know it turned out as uncomfortably for Tom Tulliver as if he had been plied with cheese in order to remedy a gastric weakness which prevented him from digesting it" (147; bk. 2, ch. 1). Tom's indifference to demonstrations is implicitly turned into an accidental deficiency, quite outside the domain of the will, but the narrator doesn't pause over this move, which is the effective, sympathetic trigger of the miniature essay on metaphor that follows:

> It is astonishing what a different result one gets by changing the metaphor! Once call the brain an intellectual stomach, and one's ingenious conception of the classics and geometry as ploughs and harrows seems to settle nothing. But then it is open to some one else to follow great authorities, and call the mind a sheet of white paper or a mirror, in which case one's knowledge of the digestive process becomes quite irrelevant. It was doubtless an ingenious idea to call the camel the ship of the desert, but it would hardly lead one far in training that useful beast. O Aristotle! if you had had the advantage of being "the freshest modern" instead of the greatest ancient, would you not have mingled your praise of metaphorical speech, as a sign of high intelligence, with a lamentation that intelligence so rarely shows itself in speech without metaphor – that we can so seldom declare what a thing is, except by saying it is something else? (147; bk. 2, ch. 1)

The double use of "ingenious," the quiet sarcasm in "high intelligence," along with the contrasting assertions of practical sense, suggest a sturdy verbal empiricism, a commitment to calling a brain a brain. But this is part of the rather earnest fun of the passage, its educational mischief, let's say. It can't be its real drift or meaning. Did anyone ever think a metaphor would help with the training of a camel? Was that why it was called the ship of the desert? Would calling it a camel make it any easier to train? A metaphor is not a model, even in this mocking passage, it is a matter of entailment: what follows from one picture will not follow from another, and what is at issue is not the metaphor but its consequences, we might say its scenery.

Indeed the underlying claim here seems to be not that ingenious people have tried and failed to get their language to work but that they haven't cared whether it works or not. The insistence on the practical end of things is not a demand for the abolition of metaphor but a call for the imagination to remember that it inhabits an obstructive physical world. What's wrong with Mr. Stelling's theory is that it is a theory—or rather that it suffers from the failure of attention to concrete realities which has often been seen as one of the vices of theory. The lamentation that Aristotle is invited to compose, then, is not actually a complaint that we should so rarely be able to declare what a thing is except by saying it is something else, but that we far too often don't sufficiently know or care what a thing is, and consequently have no scruple about calling it something else. In this light, Eliot's playful excursion repeats Ruskin's arguments about the pathetic fallacy, and anticipates Susan Sontag's worries about illness as metaphor. What is being defended is not some form of unblinking common sense, but reality itself, composed of the world out there and the minds of other people, and neglected, as it seems, by all those who, like Charles Kingsley in Ruskin's example, would rather personify the sea than look at it ("The foam is not cruel, neither does it crawl"); who think one metaphor is just as good as the next or invariably think their own metaphors are the best, if not the only possible ones; who are too impatient with ordinary or proper names to allow them to do the considerable work they can actually do.

In such a reading, these early remarks both differ and do not differ from the later ones. They are different in their location of the charge of harm. In *The Mill on the Floss* it is the reality of Tom's resistance to learning that is misrecognized, mangled by a general method; and things themselves suffer from being called by names that hide them from the namers. If we translate this preoccupation into the later language, we can say we are all of us imaginative in some form or other, and our preferred form is a refusal of attention to what is before us, an indulgence of the lazy freedom of our minds; that we all of us get our thoughts entangled in metaphors and lose the world itself in the process.

In *Middlemarch* the stress falls on the imagining mind rather than the world, on the internal damage done by the mind's misrepresentations of its interests and preoccupations. The concern about metaphor is not really to be separated from the recurring difficulty certain characters in this novel have in focusing their feelings, either literally or figuratively. We have seen Mr. Casaubon's bafflement by his sadness before his marriage, and during the same time Dorothea is "ashamed of being irritated from some cause she could not define even to herself (88; ch. 10). When she is found crying in Rome she has "no distinctly shapen grievance that she could state even to herself" (192; ch. 20). Such phrases appear repeatedly in descriptions of her moods, and of those of Casaubon and indeed Will. Would she or they be helped by a picture, an image, or to borrow the quoted term, a shape for the irritation or grievance or other condition? They might be, if they didn't get their thoughts entangled in it. Would they be helped by analytic definition of the mental occasion? Again, they might, as long as the definition was not completely wrong, the analyzing mind's delusion. In the second of the quoted instances, we are told what Dorothea is trying and failing to think:

> in the midst of her confused thought and passion, the mental act that was struggling forth into clearness was a self-accusing cry that her feeling of desolation was the fault of her own spiritual poverty. (192; ch. 20)

What's missing is not a picture but an act, and the cry, if it came, would be as literal and analytic as anyone could wish. But would it tell Dorothea the truth of her spiritual condition or merely reflect, accurately but obliquely, the truth of her eagerness to be hard on herself? It seems as if there is nothing that can be said for or against metaphor that can't be said for or against literal speech.

But this isn't the direction of argument Eliot is proposing to us, even though it runs through her novels like an undercurrent. In this larger argument the similarities between the thinking on metaphor in *The Mill on the Floss* and in *Middlemarch* begin to override the differences. To expect an event is to live in its scenery; we are all us imaginative in some form or other; we get our thoughts entangled in metaphors; we can seldom say what a thing is except by saying it is something else. Eliot's ostensive definition of metaphor is logical and psychological rather than grammatical. For her a metaphor becomes a simile, and a lot safer, as soon as its metaphoricity is explicitly announced: as in "throwing herself, metaphorically speaking, at Mr. Casaubon's feet, and kissing his unfashionable shoe-ties as if he were a Protestant Pope (51; ch. 5), or "In this way, metaphorically speaking, a strong lens applied to Mrs. Cadwallader's match-making will show a play of minute causes" (60; ch. 6). An instance from *Daniel Deronda* is even more cautious and explicit: "his heart metaphorically in his mouth" (78; ch. 7). As distinct from literally?

The reverse can happen, a simile can assume the force of a metaphor:

> in certain states of dull forlornness Dorothea all her life continued to see the vastness of St. Peter's, the huge bronze canopy, the excited intention in the attitudes and gar-ments of the prophets and evangelists in the mosaics above, and the red drapery which was being hung for Christmas spreading itself everywhere like a disease of the retina. (194; ch. 20)

The disease takes over our reading as St Peter's takes over Dorothea's memory. The comparison vanishes into the power of the picture: we do not think of red drapery as like a disease, but see only the disease and perhaps even forget just what it was sup-posed to resemble.

A metaphor doesn't have to mislead us or haunt us, but it's not a metaphor in the strong, troubling sense suggested by these novels unless the chance of misleading or haunting is present. The same can be said of images more generally, since they are the brood of desire, but in the key passages we have been looking at Eliot closes in specifically on a particular idea of figuration, on the entangling of thoughts in metaphors, and on the difference made by a change of metaphor, and metaphor's near ubiquity in the mind's reflections on itself and on the world.

We are not condemned to metaphor; we have alternatives; and metaphor is not in itself a mode of error or delusion. But we are metaphor-prone, and metaphor is a liability. We can revise our earlier hesitation—or the hesitation I was attributing to Eliot— between the unavoidability of metaphor and the chance of doing without it even occasionally. The question is more subtle and more pragmatic, and does not involve a balance of opposites. It requires the looser logic we found for our understanding of Will's exemption from what "we all do." We all do it, but not all the time. What we need to think about is when and how. The deep invitation of these novels is to an awareness that is bound to come too late for most of us: the sense of the delusion that flattered us too much for us to detect it, the scenery we lived in because we loved it and not because it was real. Eliot's concern about metaphor is a concern about what Paul de Man calls "the proliferating and disruptive power of figural language" (30), although she would add that such power is not inherently possessed by language but conferred on it, and on pictures, by our desire.

Let's return in conclusion for another look at particular images in *Middlemarch,* all involved with ideas of gesture and deception. When in an early chapter we learn of Will's unfulfilled promise and undecided future, we are told that "the universe had not yet beckoned," and reminded that "we know what a masquerade all development is" (83: ch. 10). The contrast and proof is Casaubon, who has found his vocation and lost his way, unraveled the very idea of development. Some time later we are informed that on her honeymoon Dorothea often chose to drive out of the city of Rome, "away from the masquerade of the ages, in which her own life too seemed to become a masque with enigmatical costumes" (193; ch. 20).

The image of the unbeckoning universe is beautifully false, not because the universe can't literally beckon, in the way the foam can't crawl, but because it *doesn't* beckon, even figuratively. It's not what it does; the very thought of its beckoning is an avoidance of thought. And the image of the theatrical occasion works in two ways. As Davidson says, "there are no instructions for devising metaphors" (31), and these specific metaphors, belonging to the thought-worlds of two individuals, are different in use even when semantically they are much the same. In the first case the masquerade continues the self-deceiving inference of the beckoning, and claims not just that a supposed development like that of Mr. Casaubon is a sham, but that "all development" is. In the second the masque expresses Dorothea's confusion with ornate exactness: the world itself has turned Italianate, mysterious, elegant, and terrifying. She will always live in the scenery of this alien non-event.

NOTE

1   Cf. "We are all of us born in moral stupidity"; "as with all of us, seeking rather for justifica- tion than for self-knowledge." *Middlemarch* 211; ch. 20; 329; ch. 34.

References

Cohen, Ted. *Thinking of Others: On the Talent for Metaphor*. Princeton: Princeton UP, 2008.

Davidson, Donald. "What Metaphors Mean," *Critical Inquiry* 5.1 (1978): 31–47.

de Man, Paul. "The Epistemology of Metaphor," *Critical Inquiry* 5.1 (1978): 13–30.

Eliot, George. *Daniel Deronda*. Ed. Terence Cave. London: Penguin, 1995.

Eliot, George. *Felix Holt*. Ed. Lynda Mugglestone. London: Penguin, 1995.

Eliot, George. *Middlemarch*. Ed. Rosemary Ashton. London: Penguin, 1994.

Eliot, George. *The Mill on the Floss*. Ed. A. S. Byatt. London: Penguin, 1985.

Gezari, Janet. "The Metaphorical Imagination of George Eliot." *ELH* 45.1 (1978): 93–106.

Goodman, Nelson. "Metaphor as Moonlighting." *Critical Inquiry* 6.1 (1979):. 125–30

Hardy, Barbara. *The Novels of George Eliot*. London: Athlone, 1981.

Hertz, Neil. *George Eliot's Pulse*. Stanford: Stanford UP, 2003.

Jacobus, Mary. *Reading Woman*. New York: Columbia UP, 1987.

Miller, J. Hillis. "The Two Rhetorics." *The Mill on the Floss and Silas Marner*. Ed. Nahem Yousef and Andrew Maunder. London: Palgrave, 2002. 57–72.

Schorer, Mark. "Method, Metaphor and Mind." *Middlemarch: Critical Approaches to the Novel*. Ed. Barbara Hardy. London: Athlone, 1967. 12–23.

3

"It Is of Little Use for Me to Tell You": George Eliot's Narrative Refusals

Robyn Warhol

"Nothing 'boring' about the Victorian sensation novel," D. A. Miller has remarked (*"Cage aux folles"* 107). The Victorian enthusiasm over the novel of sensation—the suspenseful and shocking productions of authors like Wilkie Collins or Mary Elizabeth Braddon, or even the Gothic elements in an otherwise realistic text like *Jane Eyre*—has come to be understood as an antidote to the ordinariness of nineteenth-century life in England. With police forces and insurance policies well established, with increasingly comprehensive regulations for controlling everything from labor practices to the water supply, with the ability to traverse the British Isles by regularly scheduled train or to communicate with other citizens through a reliable postal service—in short, with the complete internalization of the mentality of the Panopticon, Victorians led a relatively routinized lifestyle that had been developing in England since the previous century. Just as the early Romantic gothic novel is supposed to have arisen in reaction against the eighteenth-century origins of what was to become Victorian security and monotony, the novel of sensation is now understood as the bourgeois escape from the predictable clockwork of social and economic intercourse in the nineteenth century. Surprise, thrill, revulsion, shock: the literal sensations evoked by sensationalist fiction are supposed to have been the antidote to the common affects evoked by the normal. And because they are extra-ordinary, they are narratable in nineteenth-century British fiction, which is to say they are worthwhile telling and capable of being told.

Even that great chronicler of the normal, George Eliot, experimented with sensation in "The Lifted Veil." But as Miller has also persuasively argued, boredom—

A Companion to George Eliot, First Edition. Edited by Amanda Anderson and Harry E. Shaw.
© 2013 John Wiley & Sons, Ltd. Published 2016 by John Wiley & Sons, Ltd.

the unsensational sensation associated with routine and repetition—had its appeal for Victorian readers, too. Realist novelists plumb the depths of what I call the "sub-narratable," that which is too mundane or too obvious to need saying. For Miller, boredom is a cover story overlaid on paranoia and hysteria. While his account in *The Novel and the Police* of the dynamics of boredom in Trollope's Barsetshire novels seems to me irrefutable within the framework of the psychoanalytic approach he takes, I have been working with the vocabulary of narratology to turn the conversation about boredom and reading in the direction of genre. In previous work I have linked boredom to the genre of serialized fiction, which—in the Victorian era and our own—relies on repetition, flashbacks, and re-iterated backstories to clue in readers who join the series late (*Having a Good Cry* 76–87). The repetition of storyworld details in serialized realist novels only reinforces the boredom inherent in many of those details themselves. The narrators of realist novels from Henry Fielding to George Eliot display a heightened consciousness of the anti-romantic, anti-sensationalist context of the storyworlds they create, defending their narratorial practices against supposed impatience on the part of actual readers who are expecting romance and thrills. Repeatedly, as critics have long acknowledged, narrators in Eliot's novels explicitly refuse to create sensationalist storyworlds. In this essay I will explore another kind of narrative refusal in Eliot's fiction, that is, an expressed unwillingness to relate details that fall outside the category of the narratable in the genre she is developing. Some details, as it turns out, are "subnarratable," too boring or too ordinary even to make their way into the narration of anti-sensationalist anti-romances like *Middlemarch*, even as some other details—the "supranarratable" are too ineffable or too traumatic to be rendered in the narrator's speech.

George Eliot participated self-consciously in the invention of the anti-sensationalist anti-romance, and her narrators' comments about the ordinariness of her characters in her first fictions, *Scenes of Clerical Life* and *Adam Bede*, express the distance the novelist perceived between her own work and the kind of romance she was writing against. The narrator of "Amos Barton" in *Scenes of Clerical Life* offers a riposte to a virtual narratee who questions the likelihood of the refined Countess Czerlaski's "long residence" (58; ch. 7) at the humble Shepperton Vicarage:

> Not having a fertile imagination, as you perceive, and being unable to invent thrilling incidents for your amusement, my only merit must lie in the faithfulness with which I represent to you the humble experience of an ordinary fellow-mortal. I wish to stir your sympathy with commonplace troubles—to win your tears for real sorrow: sorrow such as may live next door to you—such as walks neither in rags nor in velvet, but in very ordinary decent apparel. (59; ch. 7)

What may come off as either false modesty ("not having a fertile imagination") or broad sarcasm ("being unable to invent thrilling incidents for your amusement") on the part of the narrator of "Amos Barton" takes a more sincere turn in *Adam Bede*:

So I am content to tell my simple story, without trying to make things seem better than they were; dreading nothing, indeed, but falsity, which, in spite of one's best efforts, there is reason to dread. Falsehood is so easy, truth so difficult. . . . Examine your words well, and you will find that even when you have no motive to be false, it is a very hard thing to say the exact truth, even about your own immediate feelings—much harder than to say something fine about them which is *not* the exact truth. (194–95; ch. 17)

If the narrators of Eliot's earliest forays into realist fiction earnestly take on the challenge of bridging that gap between what *is* and what *can be told*, Eliot's later works feature narrators who sometimes will refuse to try. The signs of this refusal are unnarration and disnarration, the narratorial markers of the unnarratable that I will discuss at more length below.

In pursuing a mode of narration that would capture something truer than the thrilling amusement offered by romance, Eliot was emulating the narrators of Henry Fielding, who—especially in *The History of Tom Jones, A Foundling*—was explicitly insistent upon differentiating his own narrative practices from those of the writers of romance. Fielding's narrator frequently names himself "a historian" as part of the conceit of the novel's re-presenting something that really happened, rather than trafficking in the fantasies that propel romance. At the beginning of the fifteenth chapter of *Middlemarch*, Eliot's narrator invokes this eighteenth-century predecessor, expressing some anxiety about the degree to which she can imitate the comprehensiveness of his narration. Eliot's chapter begins,

A great historian, as he insisted on calling himself, who had the happiness to be dead a hundred and twenty years ago, and so to take his place among the colossi whose huge legs our living pettiness is observed to walk under, glories in his copious remarks and digressions as the least imitable part of his work, and especially in those initial chapters to the successive books of his history, where he seems to bring his arm-chair to the proscenium and chat with us in all the lusty ease of his fine English. (141; ch. 15)

Granting Fielding the greatness signified by the longevity of his reputation, Eliot's narrator counts herself as part of "our living pettiness," or the apparent triviality of the modern and mundane. The emphasis on the hundred and twenty years since Fielding's death adds another layer of meaning to the idea that a narrator—or the implied author that animates narration—is a "historian," since *Middlemarch* itself is set four decades before its publication.

By citing Fielding's claims that his narrator's extensive commentaries are what she calls "the least imitable part of his work," the narrator of *Middlemarch* expresses both an ambition to aspire to Fielding's mode of narration and a sense of her own novel's difference from Fielding's. As this opening paragraph develops, the narrator reveals that difference to be the respective novelists' sense of what can be included in their narration, which is to say, what is narratable. Fielding, she suggests, had time to disperse his commentary "over that tempting range of relevancies called the universe" (141; ch. 15), because he "lived when the days were longer (for time, like money, is measured by our needs), when summer afternoons were spacious and the clock ticked slowly in the winter evenings" (141; ch. 15). "We belated historians," Eliot's narrator asserts, "must not linger after his example," because it would result in "chat" that would be "thin and eager, as if delivered from a camp-stool in a parrot-house" (141; ch. 15). A parrot house would be a noisy, colorful, smelly, commercially produced and overheated enclosure where a visitor might perch temporarily on a camp-stool carried in for that purpose: the metaphor explains why the kind of "chat" this situation might produce would be "thin and eager," by implying that "belated historians" who dwell in modern chaos have no leisurely opportunity to take the time or to gain as wide a perspective as Fielding could on those spacious summer afternoons and those slow-moving winter evenings of his earlier era. The Victorian relationship to time is different from the Augustans', Eliot's narrator suggests, and if a Victorian narrator were to try to comprehend "the universe" while telling a story, the newly speeded-up and crowded nature of the nineteenth-century universe would render that impossible. Eliot's narrator is as explicit about what she *must* do as about what she can't, in the way of including everything in her narrative commentaries:

> I at least have so much to do in unraveling certain human lots, and seeing how they were woven and interwoven, that all the light I can command must be concentrated on this particular web. (141; ch. 15)

Few readers of *Middlemarch* would be likely to argue that the narrator should say more than she already has. As prolix as she is, however, Eliot's narrator does not say everything she could, as this little disquisition of hers on Fielding suggests.

Unnarration and Disnarration

No novel's narrator, not even the chattiest Victorian or Fielding himself, can say everything pertaining to the storyworld her discourse creates, because some aspects of the storyworld are unnarratable. Every time a narrator elides, represses, suppresses, passes over, leaves out, or ignores some action, utterance, feeling, or impression that implicitly occurs in the storyworld, that gap or lacuna represents an element that is unnarratable for that genre in that era. By adapting a taxonomy of the unnarratable inspired by Gerald Prince's definition of its opposite, the narratable, I have proposed four kinds of unnarratability:

> *subnarratable* (what need not be told because it is too obvious or boring)
> *supranarratable* (what cannot be told because it is ineffable or inexpressible)
> *antinarratable* (what should not be told because of trauma or taboo)
> *paranarratable* (what would not [yet] be told because of literary convention).[1]

Like all realist novels, George Eliot's fictions are subject to the boundaries of what was and was not narratable in her time. Plenty of actions that are supposed to have happened in her storyworlds are antinarratable: Eliot never dramatizes sex scenes, for instance, so that Arthur Donnithorne's seduction of Hetty or Lydgate and Rosamond's wedding night are left entirely to the imagination of those among her readers who want to think about it. Bodily functions are generally absent, as we never see poor alcoholic Janet vomiting after a drinking binge, for example, or Adam Bede going to the loo. For Victorian novelists the antinarratable shades over into the paranarratable, as that which is taboo in nineteenth-century fiction—such as sex or the physical effects of overindulgence in drink—has become commonplace in novels of the twentieth and twenty-first century. The paranarratable is a larger category, in that it also contains plot turns that would not be possible for an Eliot novel to take. For Dorothea to become an unmarried, independent philanthropist at the end of *Middlemarch* is inconceivable, given the Victorian convention of rewarding heroines with attractive husbands in the end. Eliot's narrators, though they leave out the anti- and paranarratable elements of storyworld, do not remark on the omissions. They are simply absent from Eliot's narratives, as are countless other details that might have been mentioned but are neither told nor marked as missing from the text.

Although it would be impossible to conceive of everything that is left out of a Victorian novel, realist narration employs (at least) two devices for marking certain elements that are unnarratable.[2] Like her contemporaries, George Eliot employs both unnarration and disnarration to indicate elements of her storyworlds that her narrator can't or won't narrate, but that the implied author is not willing to leave entirely unremarked. In Eliot's case, these two devices are reserved for marking both the sub- and supranarratable. *Unnarration* refers to those passages in a narrative where the narrator asserts that what happened cannot be recounted, or explicitly indicates that what happened will not be narrated because to do so would be either unnecessary or impossible. "No words can express how she felt when she beheld him once again" would be an example of (suitably archaic) verbal unnarration; a shot of a closed door muffling sounds of violence in the room beyond would be a filmic example.[3] In nineteenth-century realist fiction, unnarration occurs in both a sentimental and a comic mode. Both carry over from the rhetoric of eighteenth-century fiction, where narrators like Fielding's are even more loquacious and more explicit about their narratorial practices than their descendants in the next century. Perhaps the most pointed example of comic unnarration in the eighteenth-century novel would be Lawrence Sterne's notorious inclusion in *Tristram Shandy* of an all-black page, offered as an alternative to the impossible task of articulating the grief occasioned by the death of Yorick. Tristram as narrator relies explicitly on his audience's familiarity with his subject matter: among his many third-person references to his narratee, he habitually makes assertions like, "As the reader (for I hate your ifs) has a thorough knowledge of human nature, I need not say more to satisfy him . . ." (22). If the all-black page is a comically hyperbolic reminder of the incapacity of language to express intense emotion, the offhand bits of unnarration ("I need not say more") are part of the metaleptic machinery driving *Tristram Shandy*'s self-consciousness about the transaction between the fictive text and the real-world reader. Between the unspeakable— the sadness of Yorick's demise—and the expected—what everybody already knows about human nature or indeed, about the way it is typically represented in literary texts—Sterne always plays his unnarrations for laughs, and nineteenth-century narrators often follow suit, though as usual, Eliot's comical employment of this convention is often embroiled with the earnestness of her overall project, as we will see in examples from *Middlemarch* below.

Disnarration refers to those passages in a narrative where the narrator relates something that did not happen, instead of telling what happened. Disnarration can include speculative storytelling ("If George Eliot had lived in Germany, her marriage to George Lewes might have been legally and socially recognized") and another mode of what I will call "counterfictional" narration, where a narrator merely tells what did not happen ("George Eliot did not live in Germany, and her German marriage to Lewes was not recognized").[4] Disnarration of both kinds enacts the refusal to narrate what happened by using negation, subjunctives, or figurative language to articulate something that did not happen, instead. By supplying the details of the disnarrated, this mode of narrative refusal fills in a blank in the story-world but simultaneously erases it, supplying the actual reader with glimpses at possible alternate worlds that could have been better or worse for the characters involved.[5] Unnarration, by contrast, relies on the actual reader to fill in the blanks of what gets marked as un-said.

To provide the critical context for my anatomy of the unnarratable, as well as to place Eliot's narratorial practices in the context of her contemporaries, I will elaborate here on the first two of the four categories of unnarratability—the subnarratable and the supranarratable—before demonstrating how Eliot uses unnarration, disnarration, and figurative language (specifically metonymy) to refuse narrative in *Middlemarch*. These two kinds of unnarratability are the two types that Eliot's narrators typically mark, either by saying they won't tell what happened or by telling something that didn't happen in place of telling what did.

The Subnarratable: What *Needn't* Be Told Because It's Normal

The subnarratable, that which is unworthy of being told, is the equivalent of what Prince calls "the non-narratable," or the "normal" (52). These are events that fall below the "threshold of narratability" because they "go without saying," events too insignificant or banal to warrant representation. As Prince remarks, "If I told a friend what I did yesterday, I would most probably not mention that I tied my shoelaces" (1). For this category, I substitute for Prince's "nonnarratable" my new term, "subnarratable," in order more clearly to distinguish it from the larger term, "unnarratable." In realist fiction, the subnarratable is seldom marked by either disnarration or unnarration; like Prince's "nonnarratable," its presence is typically marked by its absence.

David Herman helpfully observes that

No one building a fictional world can hope to specify every facet of the world, to characterize every element of it exhaustively and from the ground up. Rather, creators of fictional worlds must rely on readers, listeners, or viewers to draw a vast number of inferences about the world under construction—inferences that enable recipients to supply crucial information not explicitly available in the text. (67–68).

Drawing on Marie-Laure Ryan's claim that "we project upon [fictional] worlds everything we know about reality, and . . . make only the adjustments dictated by the text" (qtd. in Herman 68), Herman points out that this is a fundamental principle of constructing storyworlds, and that

> Unless cued to do so by [the text of Kate Chopin's *The Awakening*], I will not assume that during those unsatisfactory conversations Edna has with her husband in the first part of the novel, she is secretly issuing a Klingon battle cry *avant la lettre* or speaking out of her left index finger rather than her mouth. (68)

The conventions of realist narrative operate within the assumptions that Ryan and Herman are here making about storyworld construction. That which is so ordinary it does not require "specification," to use Herman's term, is subnarratable and so does not make its way into the narrative discourse: its very absence from the discourse is what defines it as subnarratable.

When the subnarratable does reach the surface of a text through a narrator's explicit refusal to provide details—as happens in Jane Austen's love scenes, for example—the realist novel can sometimes signal that the novelist is taking a pass on an opportunity for representation that is too banal, too much a cliché to warrant telling (or telling again). In such cases the subnarratable is usually marked by unnarration. Jane Austen, that pioneer of the anti-sensationalist anti-romance, is notorious for her narrator's refusals to fill in the specifics of courtship and marriage, details her twenty-first-century audience would be all too glad to know, judging by the contents of the dozens of adaptations and continuations of her novels that have been published by commercial presses since 2000. Again and again those rewritings of Austen put stilted words in the mouths of Austen's heroines and heroes at the moments which ought to be the climaxes of their marriage plots, but which Austen's narrator pushes aside impatiently as beneath her attention. "I leave it to my reader's sagacity to determine" the specifics of how in *Northanger Abbey* Catherine Moreland and Henry Tilney become a happy couple (215). "I purposely abstain from dates on the occasion [of Fanny Price's engagement to Edmund Bertram after his break with Mary Crawford in *Mansfield Park*], that every one may be at liberty to fix their own, aware that the cure of unconquerable passions, and the transfer of unchanging attachments, must vary much as to time in different people" (436) "What did she say" when Emma answered Knightley's declaration of love? "Just what she ought, of course" (404). With a yawn and a wink, Austen's narrator greets these moments in her heroines' lives as utterly subnarratable. I see this as a crucial part of the novelist's feminist project. Love and weddings are not, after all, what Austen's novels are chiefly about. They are about something else, something of more material significance for the women represented in and by them. The getting-married part of the marriage plot turns out to be normal, ordinary, subnarratable.

Donald E. Hardy notes that narratorial commentary on material that might fall below the threshold of narratability goes back at least as far as Fielding, whose narrator in *Tom Jones* declares,

> When any extraordinary Scene presents itself (as we trust shall often be the Case) we shall spare no Pains nor Paper to open it at large to our Reader; but if whole Years should pass without producing any Thing worthy his Notice, we shall not be afraid of a Chasm in our History, but shall hasten on to Matters of Consequence, and leave such Periods of Time totally unobserved. (74)

Fielding's narrator passes over the subnarratable material with his characteristic bravado and aplomb ("Afraid of a Chasm" in his history? Not he!), but as Michael Rosenblum observes in a discussion of Jonathan Swift's 1727 *Holyhead Journal*, some eighteenth-century literary writing demonstrates a considerable degree of anxiety over what is worth recounting and what is not. Identifying passages in which Swift perseverates over whether or not his narrative warrants telling, Rosenblum states that the two genres having the lowest threshold of narratability are the journal and the letter, whose very purpose is to record circumstantial details which would be of interest only to the addressee, who—in the case of a journal—may be merely the author him or herself. Given eighteenth-century English novels' penchant for presenting themselves to the public as "real" bundles of letters, like Richardson's *Pamela* and *Clarissa,* or "true" first-person journals, like Defoe's *Robinson Crusoe*, and given the literary historical genealogy linking nineteenth-century novels to the epistolary fictions and fictitious autobiographies of the previous century, the minimal degree of consequence required for an action to be narratable in the nineteenth-century novel is understandably low.

For D. A. Miller, though, the level of banality Trollope's novels consistently achieve through their attention to the subnarratable is significant, not because reading Trollope's endless stringing together of unremarkable events is boring (although that is, in itself, interesting to a critic with a psychoanalytic bent), but because that very boredom signifies the repression of the terrible paranoia at the heart of modern consciousness. As Miller says,

> In much the same way that one sinks into the easy chair that is still the most likely place to read Trollope, or sinks into that half-slumber in which his pages there may be safely skimmed, so one falls into *the usual appreciation of his appreciation of the usual* and into the paired assumptions on which it is based: "Life is like this" and "Novels are like this, too." (*The Novel and the Police* 107; emphasis added)

But that easy-chair comfort, that "usual appreciation" of Trollope's "appreciation of the usual," masks the reality of what Miller calls "the terroristic effects of the banality that Trollope, as a matter of principle and program, relentlessly cultivates" (108). Those terroristic effects operate in the service of the consolidation of bourgeois subjectivity, the middle-class state of believing that the way we do things is the way things always have been and always ought to be done (to paraphrase Althusser). Miller points out that not only would individual incidents in Trollope's novels fall under the category of what I am calling the subnarratable, but entire sequences of action in Trollope fail to meet a reasonable threshold of narratability:

> The frequent observation that "nothing happens" in Trollope, absurd if one is counting up narrative incidents, is true enough in the sense that these incidents occur in the absence of that strong teleology which, elsewhere in Victorian fiction, would allow them to gain point (as major climax or minor anticipation, in the beginning, middle, or end). (122)

Attributing this phenomenon to the commercial exigencies of the serial form that is Trollope's bread-and-butter, Miller makes an excellent point. As everybody knows, for a novel to warrant a sequel, it needs to achieve an imperfect closure. If the novel's action is, as Miller describes the plot of *Barchester Towers*, "more a meandering succession of episodes than a dynamic progression en route to Aristotelian catharsis or Freudian working-through" (122), its lack of telos gives the text no major conflict to resolve, no loose ends to tie up. The very subnarratability of Trollope's novels is, then, what gives them their long lease on life as serial installments.

When fictional events are unspeakable, as in instances of the supranarratable or the antinarratable—the narrator's use of unnarration amounts to saying "I can't": "There are no words that can express," "We cannot delineate," and such phrases are moments in which narrators throw up their hands in defeat, performing the ineffability of the characters' emotional experience. The fictional situation is so extraordinary as to be beyond language. But just as frequent among passages of unnarration in nineteenth-century novels are phrases that say, in effect, "I don't need to": when narrators say "It need not be told" or "I need not say more," they acknowledge the complete ordinariness, the predictability of what is happening in the storyworld. Counting on the implied readers' familiarity with textual and actual incidents, the narrators don't bother to go into detail, but they do gesture towards the clichés that they decline to narrate. Scenes covered by this kind of unnarration are marked as boring, banal—they are passed over in accordance with what D. A. Miller has called "an etc. principle."[6]

While the unnarration that says "I don't need to tell you" may occasion frustration on the part of an actual reader who would be interested in the juicy details, the narrator whose unnarration says "I don't want to" is running even more strongly against the grain of readerly desire. Nowhere in nineteenth-century British fiction is this more jarringly displayed than in the famous moment in *Middlemarch* when George Eliot's narrator almost violently shifts her narrative focalization from her heroine's perspective to that of the heroine's husband. Having established a pattern of following a single focal character for three or more chapters before switching to another character's point of view, Eliot's narrator finishes a sequence on Lydgate and the Vincys, then follows Dorothea's impressions through the twenty-eighth chapter of the third volume, "Waiting for Death," and begins the twenty-ninth chapter with the expected continuation, "One morning some weeks after her arrival at Lowick, Dorothea—." Unexpectedly the narrator breaks off with that dash, and embarks on an unnarration of unusual force:

> But why always Dorothea? Was her point of view the only possible one with regard to this marriage? I protest against all our interest, all our effort at understanding being given to the young skins that look blooming in spite of trouble; for these too will get faded, and will know the older and more eating griefs which we are helping to neglect. In spite of the blinking eyes and white moles objectionable to Celia, and the want of muscular curve which was morally painful to Sir James, Mr. Casaubon had an intense consciousness within him, and was spiritually a-hungered like the rest of us. (278; ch. 29)

If the narrator positions this shift as a morally virtuous choice, she also acknowledges her own complicity in the implied reader's desire to keep following Dorothea and her blooming young skin. "I protest against all *our* interest, all *our* effort at understanding being given [italics added]" to the attractive heroine, the narrator claims, simultaneously admitting the fault and objecting to it. Virtuously the narrator continues the chapter by following Mr. Casaubon's "intense consciousness" and anatomizing the spiritual hunger which his white moles and his flaccid muscles distract his in-laws (and the novel's implied reader) from appreciating. The passage stages a conflict between narrative desire—both the narrator's and the implied reader's—and narrative practice. For all her ethical positioning, the narrator is catching herself and her audience in the act of desiring more of Dorothea, and declaring "I don't want to" satisfy that desire.

Of course, the dynamic between the narrator and the implied reader of *Middlemarch* is more complicated than this disingenuous bit of unnarration implies. Despite the narrator's professed intention to devote some interest and some understanding to Mr. Casaubon, the pages that follow "Why always Dorothea?" are typical of the narrator's treatment of Mr. Casaubon throughout the text, in that she employs free indirect discourse both to exhibit and to inculpate Mr. Casaubon's character. The narrator borrows Casaubon's vocabulary and patterns of thinking to exhibit his attitudes towards his young wife: "a man of good position should expect and carefully choose a blooming young lady—the younger the better, because more educable and submissive" (278; ch. 29); "she might really be such a helpmate to him as would enable him to dispense with a hired secretary, an aid which Mr. Casaubon had never yet employed and had a suspicious dread of" (278; ch. 29); "society never made the preposterous demand that a man should think as much about his own qualifications for making a charming girl happy as he thinks of hers for making himself happy" (278; ch. 29). The sympathy for Dorothea that the narrator claims to be trying to re-direct at Dorothea's husband simply won't go there. Even these representations of his inner consciousness function to further enlist the implied reader's sympathy for the charming girl who has mistakenly married him. One page further into this free-indirect-discursive representation of Casaubon's mind, the narrator avers, "For my part I am very sorry for him" (279; ch. 29). Having failed to present Casaubon's character sympathetically by taking his point of view, the narrator shifts into disnarration:

> It is an uneasy lot at best, to be what we call highly taught and yet not to enjoy: to be present at this great spectacle of life and never to be liberated from a small hungry shivering self—never to be fully possessed by the glory we behold, never to have our consciousness rapturously transformed into the vividness of a thought, the ardour of a passion, the energy of an action, but always to be scholarly and uninspired, ambitious and timid, scrupulous and dim-sighted. (279–80; ch. 29)

What this passage says Casaubon actually is—highly taught; a small hungry shivering self; scholarly, uninspired, ambitious, timid, scrupulous, and dim-sighted—is entirely in keeping with the characterization that has been emerging from the narrator's glimpses into his consciousness. Through disnarration, however, the narrator can do what Casaubon cannot, by imagining a better Casaubon who could enjoy his education, be present at the great spectacle of life and liberated from the self, be fully possessed by the glory he beholds, be able to have his consciousness rapturously transformed into the vividness of a thought, the ardor of a passion, the energy of an action. In other words, Casaubon might have been another Dorothea (or another Will Ladislaw, his ultimate foil in the text), were it not for the egocentric fear that cripples him. Here the disnarration, the shadowy representation of what Mr. Casaubon might have been, serves the purpose of the unnarration, the affirmation that Mr. Casaubon's perspective deserves as much attention and understanding as Dorothea's. The fictional reality is that Casaubon is not Dorothea or Will, and while the narrator can declare her sympathy for him as much as she likes, her rhetoric ensures that he can never enlist the same readerly or authorial attention as the young and attractive characters do. "I don't want to" keep talking about Dorothea, the narrator in effect claims through the unnarration at the chapter's beginning, but thwarting the implied reader's desire to stay with the heroine has the opposite effect from the narrator's purported goal. The excursion into Casaubon's consciousness only cements the implied reader's sense of his unworthiness as a husband for Dorothea. This is a paradigmatic example of the ways narrative refusal enacts a perversity that has not often been attributed to the narrators of classic nineteenth-century British novels, particularly not George Eliot.

The Supranarratable: What *Can't* Be Told Because It's Ineffable

The second variety of the unnarratable, "that which is not susceptible to narration," comprises those events that defy narrative, foregrounding the inadequacy of language or of visual image to achieve full representation, even of fictitious events. The supra-narratable is the one of these four types of the unnarratable that most consistently carries a textual marker in the mode of unnarration I have characterized above as "I cannot tell." While subnarratability indicates that something is too ordinary or normal to tell, supranarratability suggests that the ordinariness and normalness of telling makes the narrative act impossible. The supranarratable is the category that often forms the occasion for unnarration in classic realist texts, beginning with Tristram Shandy's recourse to that all-black page as the anti-expression of his grief for "poor Yorick's" death (232) and carrying over in the sentimentalist tradition to narrators' assertions that "I don't think I have any words in which to tell" the specifics of highly-charged emotional scenes, as Louisa May Alcott's narrator puts it in *Little Women* (184).

The narrator of *Adam Bede*, for example, treats Hetty Poyser's beauty as supranarratable. "It is of little use for me to tell you," the narrator claims,

> that Hetty's cheek was like a rose-petal, that dimples played about her pouting lips, that her large dark eyes hid a soft roguishness under their long lashes, and that her curly hair, though all pushed back under her round cap while she was at work, stole back in dark delicate rings on her forehead, and about her white shell-like ears; *it is of little use for me to say* how lovely was the contour of her pink-and-white neckerchief, tucked into her low plum-coloured stuff bodice, or how the linen butter-making apron, with its bib, seemed a thing to be imitated in silk by duchesses, since it fell in such charming lines, or how her brown stockings and thick-soled buckled shoes lost all that clumsiness which they must certainly have had when empty of her foot and ankle;—*of little use*, unless you have seen a woman who affected you as Hetty affected her beholders. (92; ch. 7; emphasis added)

Following the logic of occupatio—the rhetorical figure in which the speaker gives information about something while claiming to be unable or unwilling to speak of it—Eliot's narrator pushes the unnarration of the supranarratable into an extreme zone, where that which can't be expressed comes across in heightened detail. To put it another way, the narrator can give details about the specifics of Hetty's appearance—cheek, pout, eyes, lashes, hair, forehead, ears, clothing, stockings, and shoes—but claims it is of no use unless "you have seen a woman" who had the same effect on her beholders as Hetty. Hetty's body parts can be enumerated, but their impact is ineffable, outside of narratability.

It would be tempting to think of the supranarratable as the opposite of the subnarratable—one being too significant to be representable, the other too insignificant to warrant representation. George Eliot's narrator in *Middlemarch*, however, offers a later Victorian perspective on narratability that blows apart any such neatly binary opposition. Telling of the tears Dorothea sheds after returning from her honeymoon, the narrator claims not to "suppose that when Mrs. Casaubon is discovered in a fit of weeping six weeks after her wedding, the situation will be regarded as tragic." She continues,

Some discouragement, some faintness of heart at the new real future which replaces the imaginary, is not unusual, and we do not expect people to be deeply moved by what is not unusual. That element of tragedy which lies in the very fact of frequency, has not yet wrought itself into the coarse emotion of mankind; and perhaps our frames could hardly bear much of it. If we had a keen vision and feeling of all ordinary human life, it would be like hearing the grass grow and the squirrel's heart beat, and we should die of that roar which lies on the other side of silence. (194; ch. 20)

Dorothea's disillusionment is not unusual enough to move "us," the virtual community constituted of Eliot's narrator, her narratee, and her authorial audience. The heroine's experience is too ordinary to be classified as "tragic." The "very fact of frequency," the inevitability and mundanity of the kind of grief Dorothea is experiencing, don't register as tragic in "the coarse emotion of mankind." Here the narrator comes very close to declaring Dorothea's crying subnarratable, but she takes an unexpected direction in her explanation for mankind's indifference to ordinary feelings. "If we had a keen vision and feeling of all ordinary human life, it would be like hearing the grass grow and the squirrel's heart beat, and we should die of that roar which lies on the other side of silence." If we could clearly see and feel the details of the ordinary, it would kill us; if we could hear the tiny sounds made by every living thing, we would die of the roar. While Eliot's narrator is not exactly saying that the mundane, the usual, and the small are ineffable, she certainly implies that the very imperceptibility of the ordinary makes these seemingly insignificant details impossible to speak about. Here, then, the subnarratable and the supranarratable collapse into each other, as in fact they do in Eliot's own narrative practice. One way to see the narration in *Middlemarch* is as an attempt to record that roar on the other side of silence, or at least to strain to hear what ordinarily makes no sound. Eliot's narrator undertakes to render many of the most unremarkable aspects of her characters' emotional experiences. In spite of the narrator's disclaimer about not being able to hear the grass's growth and the squirrel's heartbeat, everything she says is an attempt at representing subnarratable elements whose very obscurity has rendered them supranarratable.

Eliot is by no means the only Victorian novelist to grapple with the issue of what is and is not representable. In *Resisting Representation*, Elaine Scarry delineates the ways in which Thackeray and Hardy each confront the unrepresentable, in Thackeray's case because the history he seeks to tell is too abstract and in Hardy's because the human body at work, his primary topic, is too concrete. Scarry is especially illuminating in her discussion of Hardy, whose subject, she says, "is not the passage of persons through the world but the passage of embodied persons through the world" (50). I see no reason to dispute Scarry's claim that Hardy "is, on this subject, without peer in the three centuries of the English novel" (50). For Hardy, Scarry argues, "human consciousness is always . . . embodied human consciousness," and work best signifies "his essential subject . . ., the reciprocal alterations between man and world" because work entails "a far deeper embodiment" even than erotics or play, as the human at work "is immersed in his interaction with the world, far too immersed to extricate himself from it (he may die if he stops)" (51, 54, 52). Scarry posits that the body at work "is a subject that in some fundamental ways is very difficult to represent" (60); in this respect it resembles the other topic she has famously studied, the body in pain. The concreteness of work is not its only impediment to representation; another is its endless iteration, which Scarry understands as antithetical to narrative:

> Work is action rather than a discrete action: it has no identifiable beginning or end; if it were an exceptional action, or even "an action," it could—like the acts in epic, heroic, or military literature—be easily accommodated in narrative. It is the essential nature of work to be perpetual, repetitive, habitual. (65)

Just like Dorothea's tears, work is not "unusual" enough to register as a suitable subject for a story, and "the very fact of [work's] frequency" disqualifies it as tragic action. Still, Scarry is able to show how Hardy embeds the tragic action of a novel like *Tess of the D'Urbervilles* in his other strategies for representing work:

> It is not simply the surface of the body but the deep entirety of its interior that is in work put at risk. Tess's encounter with Alec brings about a profound change in her body as it first swells to a large size and then breaks into two: while this particular alteration may belong to the realm of desire rather than work, the encounter is between an employee and her employer . . . and what happens to her is (as is routinely recognized in the twentieth century and as Hardy deeply understood) a hazard of the workplace, an industrial accident. (56)

Scarry contends that Hardy addresses the problem of representing work by textually attaching working characters to the materials of their work through various strategies including metonymy, apposition, and the transformation of verbs into nouns through gerunds. Although each of these features of Hardy's language stands as an attempt to render the concrete activity of work in words, the topic is supranarratable: it eludes narration for all the reasons Scarry enumerates.

George Eliot's quintessential workingman, Adam Bede, has a far less vexed relationship to physical work than poor Tess Durbeyfield. Still, a close look at a scene in the workshop where Adam labors can reveal that Scarry is on to something when she says that the working body is not narratable. Chapter 1 of *Adam Bede*, "The Workshop," offers detailed descriptions of the bodies of Adam ("a large-boned, muscular man, nearly six feet high, with a back so flat and a head so well poised" as to give him a military look) and his brother Seth (whose complexion, eye color, hair color and texture, slightly stooping shoulders, and "coronal arch that predominates very decidedly over the brow" are all itemized) (10; ch. 1; emphasis added). The narrator lingers over parts of Adam's body in particular: "The sleeve rolled up above the elbow showed an arm that was likely to win the prize for feats of strength; yet the long, supple hand, with its broad finger-tips, looked ready for works of skill" (10; ch. 1). By contrast to the description of Hetty at work in the dairy, the rendition of Adam and of Seth does not come couched in disnarration. These male bodies are available for direct narration and inspection, as Hetty's is not. They are also legible, as the reference to Seth's dominant coronal arch—the phrenological location of cautiousness, conscientiousness, and benevolence—indicates (Donovan 107). And yet the movements of their bodies in the act of working are not visible. Through the kind of metonymic connection Scarry predicts, the scene offers the smells (a "scent of pine-wood" mingles with "the scent of the elder-bushes"); sounds ("the sound of plane and hammer," Adam's "strong baritone" singing a hymn, and the way his "sonorous voice subside[s] into a low whistle" when he is concentrating on taking a measurement); and textures (a "rough gray shepherd-dog" lies on "a heap of those soft shavings" that "flew before the steady plane") associated with work, but gives no details—other than Adam's taking that one measurement—of what the workingmen are actually doing (9; ch. 1).

If the unnarratable actions of the carpenters are simply missing from the opening scene in the workshop, in the Poysers' dairy Hetty's work gets summarized, just as Scarry suggests it might, in gerunds that suggest repeated or habitual motions rather than narrating discrete acts:

> And they are the prettiest movements into which a pretty girl is thrown in making up butter—tossing movements that give a charming curve to the arm, and a sideward inclination of the round white neck; little patting and rolling movements with the palm of the hand, and nice adaptations and finishings, which can not at all be effected without a great play of the pouting mouth and the dark eyes. (73; ch. 7)

The narrator might have said, "Hetty tossed"; "she inclined her neck sidewards"; "she patted and rolled"; "she adapted and finished"; or even "she pouted." Instead the description substitutes nominalizations of the action verbs: *tossing, movements, inclination, patting, rolling, adaptation, finishing,* and *pouting.* Eliot's narrator employs other means than disnarration, then, for marking the supranarratable, including the recourse to metonymy and nominalization Scarry observes in Hardy.

The point is not so much that Eliot's narrator might have said more or created and communicated more specific details in her rendition of the storyworlds of *Middlemarch* and *Adam Bede.* Indeed, it's easy to agree with Eliot's narrator that the degree of her concentration on "th[ese] particular web[s]" is enough, and to say of the narrative commentary in these novels (as Samuel Johnson did of *Paradise Lost*), "None ever wished it longer" (*Lives of the Poets* 185). Whether they come in the form of disnarration, unnarration, or figures of speech, narrative refusals serve to express the not-quite not-there of Victorian storyworlds, to draw the authorial audience's attention to the conventional elements of romance, the inexpressible interior and exterior details about characters, and the ordinary actions like work that are not part of the narrative, but are nevertheless present, through these narratorial gestures, in the text. Leave it to George Eliot to disrupt conventional expectations about what need not be said and what cannot be said in the genre she is developing. Her project as a realist novelist is, at least in part, to say it all.

NOTES

1   Prince's *Dictionary of Narratology* defines "the narratable" as "that which is worthy of being told; that which is susceptible of or calls for narration" (56). For more details on my terminology, see "Neonarrative," my contribution to the *Blackwell Companion to Narrative Theory*.

2   The two terms are not intended to include every way that a narrator might mark unnarratability. See my discussion in "Neonarrative."

3   What Donald E. Hardy calls "the announced gap" in narration by Flannery O'Connor is equivalent to my "unnarration."

4   Andrew Miller discusses statements that are counter to "fact" in fiction in terms of "the optative."

5   Dannenberg has elaborated on the structure of "upward" and "downward" counterfactuals and their role in novelistic plotlines.

6   See D. A. Miller, "Narrative and Its Discontents," 43.

REFERENCES

Alcott, Louisa May. *Little Women*. New York: Signet, 2004.

Austen, Jane. *Emma*. Ed. Fiona Stafford. London: Penguin, 2003.

Austen, Jane. *Mansfield Park*. Ed. Kathryn Sutherland. London: Penguin, 1996.

Austen, Jane. *Northanger Abbey*. Ed. Marilyn Butler. London: Penguin, 1995.

Dannenberg, Hilary. *Coincidence and Counterfactuality: Plotting Time and Space in Narrative Fiction*. Lincoln: U of Nebraska P, 2008.

Donovan, Cornelius. *A Handbook of Phrenology*. London: Longmans, 1870.

Eliot, George. *Adam Bede*. Ed. Stephen Gill. London: Penguin, 2008.

Eliot, George. *Middlemarch*. Ed. Rosemary Ashton. London: Penguin, 1994.

Eliot, George. *Scenes of Clerical Life*. Ed. Jennifer Gribble. London: Penguin, 1998.

Fielding, Henry. *The History of Tom Jones, a Foundling*. London: Penguin, 2005.

Hardy, Donald E. "Towards a Stylistic Typology of Narrative Gaps: Knowledge Gapping in Flannery O'Connor's Fiction." *Language and Literature* 14.4 (2005): 363–75.

Herman, David. *Story Logic: Problems and Possibilities of Narrative*. Lincoln: U of Nebraska P, 2002.

Johnson, Samuel. *Lives of the Poets*. London: Bell and Sons, 1890.

Miller, Andrew. *The Burdens of Perfection: On Ethics and Reading in Nineteenth-Century British Literature*. Ithaca: Cornell UP, 2008.

Miller, D. A. "*Cage aux folles*: Sensation and Gender in Wilkie Collins's *The Woman in White*." *Representations* 14 (1986): 107–36.

Miller, D. A. *Narrative and Its Discontents: Problems of Closure in the Traditional Novel*. Princeton: Princeton UP, 1981.

Miller, D. A. *The Novel and the Police*. Berkeley: U of California P, 1988.

Prince, Gerald. *A Dictionary of Narratology*. Lincoln: U of Nebraska P, 1987.

Rosenblum, Michael. "Swift's *Holyhead Journal* and Circumstantial Talk in Early Modern England." *Eighteenth-Century Studies* 30.2 (1996–97): 159–72.

Scarry, Elaine. *Resisting Representation*. Oxford: Oxford, 1994.

Sterne, Laurence. *The Life and Opinions of Tristram Shandy, Gentleman*. London: Penguin, 1967.

Warhol, Robyn. *Having a Good Cry: Effeminate Feelings and Popular Forms*. Columbus: Ohio State UP, 2003.

Warhol, Robyn. "Neonarrative; or, How to Render the Unnarratable in Realist Fiction and Contemporary Film." *A Companion to Narrative Theory*. Oxford: Wiley-Blackwell, 2008. 220–31.

4
Surprising Realism

Caroline Levine

Critics have never agreed on the essential elements of a realist novel. Should realism be defined by its subject matter—the struggle to capture the new living and working conditions that were transforming ordinary life in the nineteenth century, such as poverty, middle-class domesticity, and the shocks of modern technology? Is realism best understood as a struggle for mimetic immediacy, an attempt to make us feel as if we inhabit the same world as the characters? Or is it quite the opposite: are realist novels in fact highly self-conscious about the limits and artifices of representation? Is realism always politically conservative, attempting to persuade readers to accept the realities portrayed as given and unalterable, or does it deliberately draw our attention to the impact of particular historical conditions? Is it a secular philosophical project, linked to empiricism, evolutionary theory, or sociological description, or is it a specifically literary enterprise, rejecting the conventions of allegory, melodrama, and romance, and embracing such formal techniques as visual and psychological detail, free indirect discourse, and omniscience? To be sure, these various approaches are not mutually exclusive, and sometimes they are bound up together: omniscient narration serving the ends of a totalizing ideology, for example, or empiricist philosophy demanding our attention to ordinary experience. But realism remains a mixed and elusive concept, better understood as a series of overlapping currents than as a coherent style or movement.[1]

A Companion to George Eliot, First Edition. Edited by Amanda Anderson and Harry E. Shaw.
© 2013 John Wiley & Sons, Ltd. Published 2016 by John Wiley & Sons, Ltd.

The matter becomes only more troubling when we ask which novels best exemplify the realist project. Victorian writers tend to thwart realist ambitions as often as they fulfill them. Dickens offers exaggerated characters and moralizing endings, but he also deliberately captures the new urban realities of poverty and crime. Trollope reaches for psychological verisimilitude inside comic and contrived plotlines. Gaskell's attention to the gritty experience of industrial labor earns her a place among Victorian realists, but her efforts to resolve the conflicting interests of the different social classes make her novels look more like soothing ideology than complex truth-telling. And Thackeray, who seemed to his contemporaries to have captured bitter truths about the social world, adopts a satirical voice that constantly draws attention to the artifices of narration rather than striving for the immediacy often considered central to the realist project. Starkly different from each other in style and purpose, all of these writers have been at some times included in the realist canon and at other times disqualified from it.[2]

The exception here is George Eliot. No other nineteenth-century British writer seems so indisputably, so thoroughly, so canonically realist. She herself defined realism with explicitness and precision. Indeed, she was probably the very first writer ever to use the term in English.[3] And although she has often been faulted for excessive moralizing and improbable plots, she is rarely excluded from studies of the realist novel, looming large in critical assessments of realism from her own time to ours.

Grasping the specificity of Eliot's realism, then, might get us to something like the heart of Victorian realism. This essay will begin by looking briefly at Eliot's early articulations of realism, published in the 1850s. Here she insists, famously, that the value of realist representation lies in its power to prompt two responses: sympathy and knowledge. Both responses require a certain detachment, the suspension of the desire to project the self onto the other. But sympathy and knowledge both demand attachment too: they depend on the desire to come close to another, to recognize the inevitably social ingredients of selfhood, and to envisage an otherness outside oneself. That is, the task of knowing and feeling for others yields impulses both toward *and* against the self, both desire and denial, both sociability and isolation, both lively fantasies of possibility and the recognition of unyielding otherness. For Eliot, as we will see, it is the imagination that plays back and forth between self and other, always selfish—projecting from the self—and yet acting as precisely the faculty that allows that self to develop a relation to the other. But what is it, exactly, that propels the imagination away from narcissism and toward sympathy and knowledge? I will argue here that Eliot shows herself persistently drawn to moments when imaginative habits are brought to a sudden stop, moments when readers and characters are startled into new perceptions of alterity. From her first writing on realism in the 1850s to *Daniel Deronda*, that is, she puts a remarkable emphasis on surprise. Through revelations and realizations, narratorial interjections and startling plot twists, her realism works when it jolts the imagination into a properly feeling and knowing orientation toward the otherness of the world. This essay will argue that for George Eliot, there is no realism without surprise.

Sympathy and Knowledge

Before I get to the surprises of Eliot's realism, I want to spend a little time with her influential early articulations of the term. In an admiring review of John Ruskin's *Modern Painters*, published in April 1856, Eliot defines "realism" as "the doctrine that all truth and beauty are to be attained by a humble and faithful study of nature, and not by substituting vague forms, bred by imagination on the mists of feeling, in place of definite, substantial reality" (Rev. of *Modern Painters* 180). The realist tries to resist projecting the self on the world—working against the imagination—and struggles instead to know the reality of the world outside of the self, not claiming any immediate or absolute knowledge but nonetheless striving for it through "humble and faithful study." And significantly, realism demands not only knowledge but feeling, too. "It is not enough simply to teach truth . . . we want it to be so taught as to compel men's attention and sympathy" (181).

Just a few months later, Eliot returned to the same theoretical terrain in her famous review of W. H. Riehl's writing on the organic development of the German people, which linked their geography, history, and social structures and beliefs. In "The Natural History of German Life," Eliot made an urgent appeal for a British writer to follow Riehl's lead, writing a book that would convey "a real knowledge of the People" rather than the usual uninformed clichés and prejudices: "the degree in which they are influenced by local conditions, their maxims and habits, the points of view from which they regard their religious teachers, and the degree in which they are influenced by religious doctrines, the interaction of the various classes on each other, and what are the tendencies in their position towards disintegration or towards development" (56). Although Riehl's interest in ethnographic description might seem far afield from Ruskin's concern with painting nature, Eliot casts them as equally good models for fiction-writing. In both cases, she cautions that the realist writer must be willing to work against the projection of the self in order to attend properly to the realities of the world: "The German novelists who undertake to give pictures of peasant-life, fall into the same mistake as our English novelists; they transfer their own feelings to ploughmen and woodcutters, and give them both joys and sorrows of which they know nothing" (62). And again she insists on sympathy as well as knowledge:

> our social novels profess to represent the people as they are, and the unreality of their representations is a grave evil. The greatest benefit we owe to the artist, whether painter, poet, or novelist, is the extension of our sympathies. Appeals founded on generalizations and statistics require a sympathy ready-made, a moral sentiment already in activity; but a picture of human life such as a great artist can give, surprises even the trivial and the selfish into that attention to what is apart from themselves, which may be called the raw material of moral sentiment. (54)

Here, sympathy does not simply emerge alongside knowledge: knowledge can itself provoke and expand sympathy. And crucially, it is a specific kind of knowledge. Misrepresentations are an "evil," while generalizations and statistics require a sympathy already at work. Thus Eliot insists that only a detailed, local, and well-informed "picture of human life" can provoke us into sympathetic responsiveness.

Similar arguments soon followed in the famous chapter 17 of *Adam Bede* (1859), which pauses to reflect on art's purposes. Again Eliot bewails the tendency to impose our own projections on the world: "It is so very rarely that facts hit that nice medium required by our own enlightened opinions and refined taste!" (175). And again she links the sentimentalizing conventions of representation to her readers' harsh judgments of a world that does not live up to art. She calls for an artistic practice that will instead encourage a sympathy for ordinary people:

> These fellow-mortals, every one, must be accepted as they are: you can neither straighten their noses, nor brighten their wit, nor rectify their dispositions; and it is these people— amongst whom your life is passed—that it is needful you should tolerate, pity, and love: it is these more or less ugly, stupid, inconsistent people, whose movements of goodness you should be able to admire—for whom you should cherish all possible hopes, all possible patience. And I would not, even if I had the choice, be the clever novelist who could create a world so much better than this, in which we get up in the morning to do our daily work, that you would be likely to turn a harder, colder eye on the dusty streets and the common green fields—on the real breathing men and women, who can be chilled by your indifference or injured by your prejudice; who can be cheered and helped onward by your fellow-feeling, your forbearance, your outspoken, brave justice. (176)

Only an art that refuses to idealize the world can prompt us into pity, love, and admiration for the "ugly, stupid, inconsistent people" we actually encounter in our daily lives.

Sympathy and knowledge, then, consistently emerge together as the pair of attitudes which realism can foster. But how to describe the specific contours of the relationship between sympathy and knowledge? Critics have largely agreed that both require self-denial, the willingness to set aside selfish desires in order to open oneself up to otherness. Sympathy and knowledge can facilitate one another, then, because both ask us to work beyond egotistical preoccupations and prejudices. Thus George Levine argues that for Eliot, only exceptional outsiders endowed with deep feeling and a readiness to admit unconventional possibilities can begin to grasp reality, the "unapparent relations" that organize the world (343). Suzy Anger argues, similarly, that "holding on to an ego-centered perspective and operating without sympathy," in Eliot, are not only "moral failings" but also "result in misinterpretation" (117). Rachel Ablow casts the relationship between sympathy and knowledge in more ambivalent terms. Eliot, she contends, struggled to resolve the problem of "how to eradicate selfishness while maintaining the self-consciousness necessary for ethical relationships." In order to act ethically, one must feel for others and be aware of oneself, but self-awareness comes perilously close to the selfishness that allows us to see others as mere extensions of ourselves (71). Where many readers have understood sympathetic community to be the goal of Eliot's work (Cottom; Pyle), her insistence on self-negation has also seemed to some critics in our own time punishing and covertly aggressive. A few readers have charged that Eliot's novels consistently register the power and appeal of sadistic desires and isolation, and have argued that the texts themselves point to the fact that sympathetic community is neither desirable nor sustainable (Lane; Miller).

Both those who praise Eliot and those who condemn her for an embrace of self-denying sympathy have tended to rely on starkly opposed categories of experience: social and anti-social, powerful and powerless, selfless and selfish. I want to propose a different hypothesis: that selfishness in Eliot's work is neither an evil to be constantly avoided in all its forms nor a furtively anti-social impulse, but rather an essential element of an always composite selfhood, and a necessary and desirable ground for her realism. Amanda Anderson has argued that Eliot, like other Victorian writers, was in fact deeply interested in investigating multiple and mixed modes of attachment and detachment. Certainly Eliot's fiction presents us with a vast array of possible relations between self and other, both affective and broadly social, including remorse, absorption, desire, compassion, competition, smugness, loneliness, dependence, domination, judgment, rancor, responsibility, curiosity, forgiveness, pride, fear, guilt, self-sufficiency, respect, absent-mindedness, disgust, loyalty, collaboration, critical detachment, historical embeddedness, common sense, and cultural tradition. If we conclude simply that Eliot tried to get beyond selfish desire, we will miss the extraordinary number of ways that the realist novel struggles to think selfishness, rigorously and seriously, as one complex collection of attitudes among others, sometimes overlapping, sometimes interrupting, sometimes overpowering alternatives. When the narrator notes that Maggie Tulliver "threw some exaggeration and wilfulness, some pride and impetuosity, even into her self-renunciation" (386; bk 4, ch. 3), when Fred Vincy agrees to buckle down and work for a living only on condition that he can have some hope of marrying the woman he loves, and when Daniel Deronda marries Mirah even as Gwendolen's needs and desires tug at him, Eliot insists on the mixing of repression, greed, and erotic desire with self-denial, responsibility, and compassion. She repeatedly suggests, too, that selfishness can be oriented toward others. Consider, for example, the desire to please others that pushes Tito Melema into concealment, the appetite for admiration that drives Hetty Sorrel and Rosamond Vincy, and even the appeals to "common sense" that authorize the punishing judgments of gossiping neighbors. But if complex mixtures of egotism and otherness characterize everyone from Hetty and Tito to Dinah and Dorothea, then selfishness might turn out to be more integral to the realist project of sympathy and knowledge than we have been inclined to recognize.

The reason that selfishness is important, I would argue, is that it is bound up with the imagination, and it is the imagination that compels us to sympathy and knowledge. In other words, for Eliot the imagination is both intrinsically selfish and essential to the aims of realism. Forest Pyle explains: "Sympathy is the imaginative impulse that, transcending the egotism and renouncing the desires of self, promises to bridge the epistemological and ethical gap between self and world." But on the other hand, imagination also entails the projection of the self where it does not belong, "the disfiguration of sympathy, the extension of a consciousness deflected and distorted by the 'rebellious murmuring' of subjective desire and thus devoid of sympathy's ethical dimension" (6–7). For Pyle this pull in opposing directions marks the impossibility of Eliot's realism, but the novelist herself seems fairly composed about it, claiming straightforwardly that the selfish imagination is universal. "We are all of us imaginative in some form or other, for images are the brood of desire," the narrator tells us in *Middlemarch* (202; ch. 34); and toward the end of *Daniel Deronda*: "we are all apt to fall into this passionate egoism of imagination" (867; ch. 69).

It would seem that it is neither good nor bad but simply inevitable that the imagination will project the desires and expectations of the self on the world. And it is certainly true that Eliot's characters, virtuous and not, are constantly imposing their own imaginative impulses onto the world, whether they are speculating about realities hidden behind surfaces or wondering about futures yet to unfold: Gwendolen's dread and Maggie's yearning, Dinah's visions and Rosamond's fantasies, Fred's hopefulness and Mordecai's longing, Dorothea's plans and Hetty's dreams, the mutual misunderstanding of Felix Holt and Esther Lyon, the assumptions about beautiful faces that mislead Adam and Romola, the promises that bind Tom Tulliver and Daniel Deronda, and the expectations for marriage that yield tragic outcomes for the Casaubons, the Lydgates, and the Grandcourts.

Realist Surprises

But if the intrinsically selfish imagination is so essential to social relations, then how can it be turned toward sympathy and knowledge? In order to answer this question, I want to turn to a word that has captured very little critical attention in the famous passage from "The Natural History of German Life" we encountered earlier. The word is "surprises." Eliot writes that "a picture of human life such as a great artist can give, surprises even the trivial and the selfish into that attention to what is apart from themselves, which may be called the raw material of moral sentiment." Of course, it makes sense that "the trivial and the selfish" will need to be surprised into attentiveness to something apart from their own interests and pleasures, since they are usually intent, presumably, on doing what they like. The implicit logic of the passage is that such people pick up a novel or look at a painting for pleasure when great art suddenly shakes them into a new consciousness. But this means that art must have some appeal for trivial and selfish people in the first place, if only later to surprise them out of their usual habits. Or to put this another way: realism must feed selfish hungers as well as thwarting them, yielding enjoyment while also jolting readers into a new kind of informed and sympathetic attentiveness. Why else would selfish people begin to read at all? Surprising art, then, must somehow bring off both selfish pleasures and the denial of self that is required for sympathy and knowledge.

Chapter 17 of *Adam Bede*, too, welcomes surprise. It opens with a startled outcry: "'This Rector of Broxton is little better than a pagan!' I hear one of my lady readers exclaim" (175). Eliot's narrator then admits to being glad to have surprised this reader, arguing that it is quite wrong for fiction to allow us to keep going in "undoubting confidence," "without the slightest disturbance of our presuppositions" (176). If in "The Natural History of German Life," Eliot envisioned surprising self-indulgent readers, in *Adam Bede* she enjoys startling self-righteous ones. And apparently these are two sides of the same coin: "I have observed this remarkable coincidence," the narrator tells us, "that the select natures who pant after the ideal . . . are curiously in unison with the narrowest and the pettiest" (183). Both those who seek their own pleasures and those who crave an ideal, morally perfect universe need to be startled by realism.

If surprise plays a crucial role in these early theorizations, Eliot also repeatedly incorporates moments of surprise into the fiction that follows. Let me offer three examples from different moments in Eliot's career. In the first, Arthur Donnithorne gets a jolt from Adam Bede's "hard, peremptory voice" calling him to account for his dalliance with Hetty:

> Arthur paused in surprise. Susceptible persons are more affected by a change in tone than by unexpected words, and Arthur had the susceptibility of a nature at once affectionate and vain. He was still more surprised when he saw that Adam had not moved, but stood with his back to him, as if summoning him to return. What did he mean? He was going to make a serious business of this affair. Confound the fellow! Arthur felt his temper rising. A patronizing disposition always has its meaner side, and in the confusion of his irritation and alarm there entered the feeling that a man to whom he had shown so much favor as to Adam was not in a position to criticise his conduct. And yet he was dominated, as one who feels himself in the wrong always is, by the man whose good opinion he cares for. (297; ch. 27)

Nothing if not mixed—at once affectionate and vain, patronizing and deferential, irritated and dominated, open and stubborn, aware of guilt and eager for respect—Arthur is about to learn that his own pleasures are incompatible with others' good opinions. Both pleasure and the esteem of others are self-centered urges, but the force of Arthur's desire for Adam's esteem—the pull of the other—literally stops him in his tracks. This is neither pure selfishness nor pure self-denial. Eliot calls Arthur "susceptible," a term she will use repeatedly for those characters about to undergo significant surprises. These characters, however self-seeking, are open to the impact of the other.

A moment later, when the susceptible Arthur experiences yet another surprise, we see the dawning of a wholly new set of ethical possibilities:

> The discovery that Adam loved Hetty was a shock which made him for the moment see himself in the light of Adam's indignation, and regard Adam's suffering as not merely a consequence, but an element of his error. The words of hatred and contempt—the first

he had ever heard in his life—seemed like scorching missiles that were making inef-
faceable scars on him. All screening self-excuse, which rarely falls quite away while
others respect us, forsook him for an instant, and he stood face to face with the first
great irrevocable evil he had ever committed. (300; ch. 27)

The effect is momentary, but it lays the groundwork for further moral development.
This moment therefore seems perfectly in keeping with the realism of "The Natural
History of German Life": startled out of narcissistic habits of self-justification, Arthur
finds himself suddenly recognizing Adam's feeling perspective, and through this
sympathetic insight, gaining an excruciatingly vivid new knowledge of himself that
will allow him to change. He is surprised into an attention to that which is apart
from himself, the raw material of moral sentiment.

A remarkably similar scene occurs at the other end of Eliot's career, in *Daniel
Deronda*, when Gwendolen learns of Daniel's decision to leave for the East. Before the
revelation, the narrator tells us that Gwendolen has always imagined Daniel "within
her reach": "her supreme need of him blinding her to the separateness of his life, the
whole scene of which she filled with his relation to her" (867; ch. 69). As the "egoism
of imagination" renders Gwendolen incapable of recognizing Daniel as other, Eliot
recalls the constellation of terms she had put forward decades before in her definition
of realism. The mind produces images out of its own needs and desires, and these
interfere with our attempts to know and sympathize with the alterity of the world.
But only a few pages later, Gwendolen will be shocked into a new kind of consciousness. "A thrill of surprise was visible in her. . . . 'A *Jew*!' Gwendolen exclaimed, in
a low tone of amazement" (872–73; ch. 69). Daniel goes on to explain that he
will dedicate his life to his people, and this stirs her into a wholly new kind of
awareness.

[His words] had inspired her with a dreadful presentiment of mountainous travel for
her mind before it could reach Deronda's. . . . The world seemed to be getting larger
round poor Gwendolen, and she more solitary and helpless in their midst. The thought
that he might come back after going to the East, sank before the bewildering vision of
these wide-stretching purposes in which she felt herself reduced to a mere speck. There
comes a terrible moment to many souls when the great movements of the world, the
larger destinies of mankind, which have lain aloof in newspapers and other neglected
reading, enter like an earthquake into their own lives—when the slow urgency of growing generations turns into the tread of an invading army or the dire clash of civil war,
and grey fathers know nothing to seek for but the corpses of their blooming sons, and
girls forget all vanity to make lint and bandages which may serve for the shattered limbs
of their betrothed husbands. (874–75; ch. 69)

What makes the egotistical Gwendolen particularly susceptible to this new feeling
(as we cannot imagine Grandcourt, for example, would be) is her desire for Daniel's
good opinion, which suggests again that it is a particular kind of selfishness that can
be shocked into sympathy and knowledge. As with Arthur Donnithorne, Gwendolen's

selfishness is already oriented toward others—it is an intrinsically *social* self-regard—
and as with Arthur, her awakening does not prompt her into an impossible ideal of
self-denial. She is still very much at the center of her own consciousness, solitary and
helpless, but now she appears to herself for the first time as from a vast distance, "a
mere speck." Thus Gwendolen remains self-aware at the same time that she undergoes
"a terrible moment" of recognition, as she grasps both the truth and the emotional
agony of a world much larger than herself.

It seems crucial to recognize that it is not only selfish characters in Eliot's fiction
who experience shocking revelations that provoke a new kind of awareness. Take, for
example, the moment when Dorothea first learns the terms of Casaubon's will:

> She might have compared her experience at that moment to the vague, alarmed
> consciousness that her life was taking on a new form, that she was undergoing a meta-
> morphosis in which memory would not adjust itself to the stirring of new organs.
> Everything was changing its aspect: her husband's conduct, her own duteous feeling
> towards him, every struggle between them—and yet more, her whole relation to Will
> Ladislaw. Her world was in a state of convulsive change; the only thing she could say
> distinctly to herself was, that she must wait and think anew. One change terrified her
> as if it had been a sin; it was a violent shock of repulsion from her departed husband,
> who had had hidden thoughts, perhaps perverting everything she said and did. Then
> again she was conscious of another change which also made her tremulous; it was a
> sudden strange yearning of heart towards Will Ladislaw. (304–05; ch. 50)

There is new and transformative knowledge in this surprising revelation, as there was
for Arthur and Gwendolen, but rather than being startled into a sudden recognition
of guilt or insignificance, what Dorothea undergoes for the first time is "a violent
shock of repulsion" from Casaubon. Strangely, that is, her sympathy actually shrinks
in the moment that her understanding grows. This is no moral failure, presumably,
but rather appropriate to the reality, because her capacity for love and pity have always
been too grand for Casaubon, exceeding both his desires and his deserts. Dorothea's
moment of surprise therefore delivers a dose of selfishness with its flash of insight—
a self-protective withdrawal from Casaubon as well as a newly pleasurable kind of
attachment to Will. And I would argue that this lessening of sympathy remains faithful to the terms of realism which Eliot articulated in the 1850s. Dorothea has had
plenty of fellow feeling all along, but too little knowledge. With imagination deluded
until now by "the mists of feeling," even the sympathetic Dorothea must be surprised,
compelled to face the "definite, substantial reality" that Casaubon was vindictive and
suspicious.

This conclusion works against the critical presumption that sympathy is always the
ultimate goal of Eliot's realism. While there is no question that sympathy has crucial
effects in Eliot's fiction, too much sympathy can also obscure alterity: the generous
Dinah misunderstands Hetty even while she lavishes fellow feeling on her, just as
Dorothea feels too close an imaginary communion with Casaubon. "The Lifted Veil,"
Eliot's Gothic novella about a clairvoyant narrator, considers the possibility that there

can be too much knowledge too: access to others' thoughts disgusts and revolts Latimer, who needs less knowledge and more sympathy. If realism calls for *both* feeling and knowledge, then each is only part of the story: sometimes knowledge can go too far, and even sympathy must sometimes be displaced by a sudden knowledge of the otherness of the real.

One element remains constant through these fluctuating ratios of sympathy and knowledge: the need for surprise. *Middlemarch* is chock full of startling revelations that propel characters into reassessments of themselves and their world: Lydgate is surprised out of his preconceptions by Laure, Rosamond, and Dorothea; Dorothea's fellow-feeling startles Rosamond into a new kind of moral action; Bulstrode, Will, and Fred all undergo shocks that compel them to reinterpret their place in the world. And we can find countless examples beyond *Middlemarch*, too. Mr Irwine "saw the whole history now by that terrible illumination which the present sheds back upon the past" (407; ch. 39). *Felix Holt* and *Daniel Deronda* are organized, one might say, around the surprises of discovering one's parentage; Romola must endure the shock of Tito's duplicity; Silas Marner experiences "utter amazement" to find a sleeping child; and *The Mill on the Floss* wakes Maggie repeatedly, excruciatingly, into the recognition that her forgetful distractedness has hurt those whose love she most desperately craves.

Tellingly, Eliot gives us a few characters who think that they are beyond surprise, and these are among her least likable. Grandcourt's soul, Eliot tells us, "was garrisoned against presentiments and fears; he had the courage and confidence that belong to domination" (744; ch. 54). The Alcharisi suggests something similar in her father: "he did not guard against consequences, because he felt sure he could hinder them if he liked" (696; ch. 51). The Rhadamantine Tom Tulliver, who has always enjoyed punishing wrong-doers, experiences no surprise at Maggie's apparent elopement: "Tom, like other immovable things, seemed only the more rigidly fixed under that attempt to shake him" (630; bk. 7, ch. 3). Certain, domineering, and inflexible, these patriarchal despots expect to bring the otherness of the world under their own control and take a sadistic pleasure in quelling the struggling alterity of those they dominate. If they experience surprise, it is only that the women they oppress sometimes manage to break free, but this surprise produces no new insights or new pathways to sympathy, as it might for others. It seems worth noting here that Will Ladislaw and Daniel Deronda occupy the opposite masculine extreme, so susceptible, so open to the possibilities of the future that they long delay settling in any place, or choosing an occupation. As Eliot puts her mind seriously to the problem of gender inequality, she imagines optimal husbands to be so imaginatively open that they are a matter of constant surprise, even to themselves.

It is my contention, then, that Eliot's realism entails something subtly different from self-denial in the service of sympathetic community. It involves surprising people into proper degrees of sympathy in relation to new and revelatory knowledge. In the process, it does not necessarily require a punishing negation of the self but rather an abrupt modification to an existing understanding of the self in relation to a world of

others. Realist surprises are moments of sudden knowledge that compel two kinds of
readjustment: changes in feeling towards others, on the one hand, and a newly pro-
portionate grasp of the relation between the self and the world, on the other.

Realism's Plots

But why, exactly, does surprise function as such a crucial ingredient in Eliot's realism?
The answer, I think, has everything to do with the fact that surprise can happen only
against a backdrop of expectation. There can be no experience of shock unless our
minds swerve from imagined facts or outcomes. Surprise, then, most often takes place
in the context of ongoing imaginative habit: Arthur is shocked out of his sense that
he will always be well-liked; Gwendolen is startled out of habits of self-absorption;
Dorothea is jolted into the recognition that others may be motivated by bitter mis-
trust. As we have seen, both self-regarding and self-denying characters indulge in
imaginative constructions of otherness and project themselves onto the alterity of
the world through the lenses of their own expectation. And because none of us,
however great-souled, can do without the projections of the self that are the work of
the imagination, then selfishness serves as the necessary ground for the operations of
surprise. And one might take this argument a step farther: if otherness emerges only
by way of a recognition that it is something other than the fictions of the imagination,
then it cannot become perceptible *as such* unless the tracks laid by the egotistical
imagination are disturbed by unexpected realities. Alterity cannot appear at all without surprise.

   To be sure, this argument depends in part on certain conventional assumptions
about character that shape the nineteenth-century novel generally. Eliot's characters
become intelligible to us thanks to the repetition of their imaginative habits: how
would we know Hetty without her vanity or Deronda without his responsive generosity? Leo Bersani argues that the realist novel comforts its readers with "an ideology
of the self as a fundamentally intelligible structure unaffected by a history of frag-
mented, discontinuous desires" (56). And yet to assume that realism depends on a
naïve characterological coherence would be to miss what I think is at the heart of
Eliot's realism, which is the potential to change one's mind. Surprises are the moments
in her fiction when character is opened up to transformation. If realism is oriented
toward otherness, seeking to prompt both sympathy (feeling for another) and
knowledge (setting aside projections and conventions to recognize alterity), it must
always be working against the repetitions of the imagination, which is constantly
spinning its own predictable versions of the world. Far from a naïve understanding
of character, this interest in imaginative repetition prefigures theories of mind articulated by later thinkers, from Freud and the pragmatists to contemporary neuroscience.[4] Thus it would be a mistake to claim that Eliot's realism strives for consistency
of character, or for a settled community of values; it strives, rather, for crises of broken
expectation.

What has happened to the reader in all of this? In "The Natural History of German Life" and *Adam Bede,* Eliot focused on surprising her readers rather than her characters, and hers is a realism, famously, that seeks not only to represent the world but to act in that world. Debra Gettelman notes that Eliot in fact routinely surprised her audience. "Reading several of Eliot's novels in serial form, readers often guessed what the next installment would contain and guessed wrong" (25). Certainly Eliot's reviewers often admitted to having been startled. Dinah Mulock, for example, read with "uneasy surprise" that the virtuous Maggie had been carried away with Stephen Guest (Carroll 160). Henry James complained of "dissatisfaction" with Will Ladislaw; he expected that Dorothea and Lydgate would come more closely together, "their momentary contact" suggesting "a wealth of dramatic possibility between them" (*Middlemarch* 580). And Edwin P. Whipple reported on "the almost universal disappointment at the unanticipated conclusion" of *Daniel Deronda* (31). These disappointments may have been quite deliberate. Indeed, the importance of surprising readers may help to explain why Eliot, who wrote so enthusiastically about Dutch painting and German ethnography, chose a narrative form for her own realism. Surprise, after all, is a quintessentially narratable experience, operating along a temporal axis. Eliot's characters are relentlessly forward-looking: they anticipate, fear, calculate, plot, compete, presume, forewarn, speculate, hypothesize, dread, hope, desire, and wonder. And first-time readers, typically drawn along by a keen interest in what is to come, are compelled to follow their temporal lead.[5] Actively guessing, hypothesizing, looking forward, the realist reader, like Eliot's characters, lays down imaginative tracks—expectations, hopes, and assumptions that come from ourselves.

But surprising the reader presents a challenge for the realist project. One of the problems with ordinary life is that it is monotonous, unexciting—plotless. Plot depends on crafty artifices and concealments, which contend against the conventionally realist goal of plausibility. The novelist George Gissing created a fictional writer, Biffen, who asserts that his novel will include nothing but "honest reporting." The result, he acknowledges, "will be something unutterably tedious. . . . If it were anything but tedious, it would be untrue" (1:265). Notably, Eliot repeatedly refuses this kind of tedium, opting for dramatically timed deaths (Maggie and Tom, Casaubon), remarkable coincidences (Raffles happening upon Bulstrode in the same town as Will Ladislaw), happily married endings (Adam and Dinah, Dorothea and Will, Deronda and Mirah), and a startling number of sensational murders and murderous desires (Caterina in "Mr Gilfil's Love Story," Hetty, Baldassarre, Laure, and Gwendolen).

Does thrilling the reader with plot twists and satisfying closures point to a kind of bad faith at the heart of Eliot's realism? Not at all, if surprise acts as the crucial stimulus to both feeling for others and gaining new knowledge. Indeed, seen in this light, sudden coincidences and startling events must be indispensable. I am suggesting, in other words, that plotted surprise is not so much an obstacle to Eliot's realism as it is its constitutive form. Far from striving to follow the routines of day-to-day experience, this is a realism that deliberately incorporates melodramatic and sensational elements. Of course, not all readers would have been shocked by all of Eliot's outcomes, but any surprise can prompt us to recognize that our imaginative habits are limited—that the facts do not always hit that nice medium required by our own enlightened opinions and refined taste, and that the future is not what our imaginations, trapped in settled routines, have prepared us for. Nor is surprise purely a matter of plot: Eliot's famous narratorial interjections—"But why always Dorothea?"—also jar us out of readerly expectations. And Eliot's surprises are characterological too, as she understands the very grounds of selfhood to be built on one's susceptibility to different kinds of surprise. Taken together, plot, narration, and character alike teach us to be ready for the surprises of a world apart from our imaginative projections.

Exciting and sometimes deliberately sensational, this realism does not strive to be punishing. Eliot expected great art to surprise "even selfish and trivial readers" into an "attention to what is apart from themselves," which means, as I suggested earlier, that art must surely indulge their very selfishness, engaging and delighting them before startling them into a new relation to the world. And to excite readers is not to betray the ethical and epistemological aims of realism. After all, selfishness in Eliot is not an obstacle to sympathy and knowledge: it is the imaginative ground that allows these to come into relief.

NOTES

1   For realism's subject-matter, see Auerbach and Menke; for realism as conservative in its attempts at transparency, see Belsey and Bersani; for its self-consciousness about representation and its relation to secular philosophy, see Watt and Levine; for its focus on historical experience, see Lukács and Shaw; for realism's forms, see Agathacleous and Cohn.

2   These disagreements have been going on since the nineteenth century. Eliot herself argued against Dickens as a realist: "We have one great novelist who is gifted with the utmost power of rendering the external traits of our town population; and if he could give us their psychological character—their conceptions of life, and their emotions—with the same truth as their idiom and manners, his books would be the greatest contribution Art has ever made to

the awakening of social sympathies" (*Natural History* 55).

3   The *Oxford English Dictionary* names John Ruskin as the first English writer to use the term realism in 1856, but the term does not appear anywhere in his work in the 1850s. Eliot's 1856 review of Ruskin, however, includes a prominent definition of the term.

4   See Freud on repetition-compulsion (22–24); Dewey on habit (iv); and recent neuroscience, which has embraced the hypothesis of neuroplasticity—the idea that the brain repeats certain connections but can be rewired through the acquisition of new habits.

5   Tina Choi and Harry Shaw have argued that the Victorian novel favored open-ended and contingent plots.

REFERENCES

Ablow, Rachel. *The Marriage of Minds: Reading Sympathy in the Victorian Marriage Plot*. Stanford: Stanford UP, 2007.

Agathocleous, Tanya. *Urban Realism and the Cosmopolitan Imagination in the Nineteenth Century*. Cambridge: Cambridge UP, 2011.

Anderson, Amanda. *The Powers of Distance: Cosmopolitanism and the Cultivation of Detachment.* Princeton: Princeton UP, 2001.

Anger, Suzy. *Victorian Interpretation.* Ithaca: Cornell UP, 2005.

Auerbach, Erich. *Mimesis: The Representation of Reality in Western Literature.* 1953. Princeton: Princeton UP, 2003.

Belsey, Catherine. *Critical Practice.* London: Methuen, 1980.

Bersani, Leo. *A Future for Astyanax: Character and Desire in Literature.* Boston: Little, 1984.

Carroll, David, ed. *George Eliot: The Critical Heritage.* London: Routledge, 2000.

Choi, Tina Young. "Natural History's Hypothetical Moments: Narratives of Contingency in Victorian Culture." *Victorian Studies* 51.2 (2009): 275–97.

Cohn, Dorrit. *Transparent Minds: Narrative Modes for Presenting Consciousness in Fiction.* Princeton: Princeton UP, 1978.

Cottom, Daniel. *Social Figures: George Eliot, Social History and Literary Representation.* Minneapolis: U of Minnesota P, 1987.

Dewey, John. Preface. *Human Nature and Conduct.* By John Dewey. *New York*: Carlton, 1922.

Eliot, George. *Adam Bede.* Ed. Valentine Cunningham. Oxford: Oxford UP, 1996.

Eliot, George. "John Ruskin's *Modern Painters Vol. III.*" Unsigned review. Westminster Review (April 1856). Rpt. in *John Ruskin: The Critical Heritage.* Ed. J. L. Bailey. London: Routledge, 1984. 179–83.

Eliot, George. *Middlemarch.* Ed. Bert G. Hornback. New York: Norton, 2000.

Eliot, George. *The Mill on the Floss.* Ed. A. S. Byatt. London: Penguin, 1985.

Eliot, George. "The Natural History of German Life." *The Westminster Review* (July 1856): 51–79.

Freud, Sigmund. *Beyond the Pleasure Principle.* Trans. C. J. M. Hubback. London: International Psycho-Analytical, 1922.

Gettelman, Debra. "Reading Ahead in George Eliot." *Novel* 39.1 (2005). 25–47.

Gissing, George. *New Grub Street.* 3 vols. London: Smith, Elder, 1891.

Lane, Christopher. *Hatred and Civility: The Anti-Social Life in Victorian England.* New York: Columbia UP, 2004.

Levine, George. *The Realistic Imagination: English Fiction from Frankenstein to Lady Chatterley.* Chicago Georg: U of Chicago P, 1981.

Lukács, Georg. *The Historical Novel.* Trans. Hannah and Stanley Mitchell. Lincoln: U of Nebraska P, 1962.

Menke, Richard. *Telegraphic Realism.* Stanford: Stanford UP, 2008.

Miller, D. A. *Narrative and Its Discontents: Problems of Closure in the Traditional Novel.* Princeton: Princeton UP, 1989.

Pyle, Forest. "A Novel Sympathy: The Imagination of Community in George Eliot." *Novel* 27.1 (1993): 5–23.

Shaw, Harry E. *Narrating Reality: Austen, Scott, Eliot.* Ithaca: Cornell UP, 1999.

Watt, Ian. *The Rise of the Novel.* London: Chatto, 1957.

Whipple, Edwin P. "Daniel Deronda." *North American Review* 124 (1877): 31–52.

5

Two Flowers: George Eliot's Diagrams and the Modern Novel

John Plotz

John Bender and Michael Marrinan have recently proposed that the Enlightenment-era European novel participated in a "culture of diagram" predicated on the epistemological indispensability of establishing multiple viewpoints upon any object of knowledge. This "culture of the diagram," they argue,

> embraces both scientific and aesthetic orientations, notably with shifts in scale, perspective and imaginary points of view that follow from recasting innate and idealized knowledge in terms of the materiality and limits of human perception. (81)

In the scientific realm the crucial technique for this may be the technical diagram, but in the aesthetic realm from the early nineteenth century onwards, free indirect discourse and related formal techniques for presenting subjective standpoints in putatively objective discourse make the novel a crucial site of diagrammatic thinking. I make the case here that in George Eliot's progressively more complex and subtle (in the case of *Impressions of Theophrastus Such*, even baroque) experiments with representing characters' divergent subjective impressions of a shared social realm, we can see those "diagrammatic" techniques put to uses that Bender and Marrinan's model does not quite explain.

Building on the linguistic work of Ann Banfield's *Unspeakable Sentences*, Bender and Marrinan argue for the emerging early nineteenth-century importance of

> those novelistic instances of free indirect discourse where subjective and private internal states are represented impersonally as if present to external perception. Impersonal, third-

A Companion to George Eliot, First Edition. Edited by Amanda Anderson and Harry E. Shaw.
© 2013 John Wiley & Sons, Ltd. Published 2016 by John Wiley & Sons, Ltd.

person grammar produces an effect of mental presence without narrative, analogous to the raw data of physical phenomena produced by recording instruments. (81)

This impersonal subjectivity produces a "now in the past" moment within fictional discourse that Bender and Marrinan see as comparable to the sort of conjectural interpolation of a readerly presence that is evident in the scientific diagrams of Diderot's *Encyclopédie* (1751–72). Consider, for example, how Jane Austen conveys Harriet Smith's excitement at meeting Emma Woodhouse:

> Miss Woodhouse was so great a personage in Highbury, that the prospect of the intro-
> duction had given as much panic as pleasure; but the humble, grateful little girl
> went off with highly gratified feelings, delighted with the affability with which Miss
> Woodhouse had treated her all the evening, and actually shaken hands with her at last!
> (24; ch. 3)

A "culture of diagram" reading would stress the reiterative structure of "grateful" and "gratified feelings" which hints at the gap between the impersonal narrator summing up Emma's reputation at the beginning of the sentence, and the flood of feelings (culminating in the jubilant exclamation point) that occupies the sentence's end. Yet such a diagrammatic reading would also have to find a way to accommodate the persistent line the text draws between reportage and "raw data" even at the moments when subjectivity seems most on display. The exclamation point at once marks Harriet's joy and encourages the reader, relishing Austen's "*frozen* speech" as much as Harriet's warmth, to assume a sardonic distance (Miller 6; emphasis in original).

Brewer and Marrinan want to locate nineteenth-century novels as part of a project—as much epistemological as aesthetic—to make sense of a world where "limits of human perception" can come to be modeled by way of a series of experiments that measure what can be captured and conveyed on white pages intermittently blackened by print. The novel is placed, in their reading, alongside a range of scientific publications, as a particular kind of "working object" in a larger culture of observation and experimentation.

Do George Eliot's novels belong in such scientific company? Readers who recall that Eliot coined the words *high-browed, pre-Raphaelism*, and *self-criticism* have sometimes been tempted to align her scholarly bent with her novels' shortcomings rather than triumphs. Still, alongside her interest in the conduits from scientific investigation to the everyday world, Eliot retained a Dickensian taste for mundane facticity: she is also the writer who ushered into print *wurst, lunch-time, lampshade, thrummed, blondness, kraut*, and (describing a type of music) *pop*. And it may be in the lunch-time, or even the pop Eliot that we find the clearest link to the culture of diagram.

Lukács's defense of the realist novel in contradistinction to the modernist novel offers one influential way to think about Eliot's relationship to the "raw data" account of the novel's capacity to document divergent individuals within a shared social world. For the realist novel, Lukács argues, "man is a social animal" whose "individual existence . . . cannot be separated from the social and historical environment" (19). Within the realist novel

> Solitariness . . . is always merely a fragment, a phase, a climax or anticlimax, in the life of the community as a whole. . . . Solitariness is a specific social fate, not a universal condition humaine. (20)

The understanding of solitude in the realist novel does not in Lukács's account preclude moments of isolation: we might think for example of Louis Trevelyan, the mad protagonist of Trollope's *He Knew He was Right* (1869), whose jealousy pushes him into a doomed misperceptions of a world correctly parsed by everyone else in his social habitus.

By contrast, writes Lukács, man for modernist writers "is by nature solitary, asocial, unable to enter into relationship with other human beings. Man may establish relationships . . . only in a superficial, accidental manner" (20). Once this modernist (i.e. post-realist) writing loses its capacity to align social context with the experiential shape of individual experience (thus generating "concrete potentiality" rather than mere "abstract potentiality") any reliable connective logic vanishes (24). The problem here is that Lukács offers far too simple a model for what happens when fiction turns away from direct representations of the public transactions of a readily decipherable social world: to be impressionistic is not necessarily to be unrepresentative, as Lukács's account asserts.

This chapter argues that Eliot's fictional experiments suggest the need to revisit Lukács's account of the gulf that yawns between socially anchored realism and its subjectivist successors. It also makes the case that we can best locate Eliot by extrapolating the "culture of diagram" into a later nineteenth-century context in which a character's own awareness of what it means to live within a culture of diagram is one of the basic pieces of information that a diagram ought to contain. Examining the work of free indirect discourse in Eliot's novels (*Middlemarch* especially) and the principles of characterization that shape her final book, the generically odd *Impressions of Theophrastus Such*, I argue that Eliot's understanding of the multi-perspectivalism of prose fiction does build upon the "culture of diagram." It does so, however, in large part by forcing a reconsideration of the various axes along which novelistic discourse might seem to offer a privileged vantage.

The result is a novelistic form that fits neither Lukács's notion of a realism that depicts individuals located in their "knowable communities" (to borrow a phrase from Raymond Williams [165]) nor his notion of a modernism that dissevers a character's temporal, spatial, and concrete links in favor of an "abstract potentiality." Rather, diagrammatic logic precisely allows Eliot to make sense of forms of detached knowledge that can arise from known material antecedents. Moreover, looking forward into the early twentieth century, the experiments that Eliot devises in order to explore the extent and the limits of diagrammatic logic become a crucial foundation upon which the modernist novel, particularly in its Jamesian iteration, is built.

Viewpoints

Raymond Williams concludes that Eliot's "critical realism" is ultimately characterized by "withdrawal from any full response to an existing society" (180), but Eliot is in fact grappling with a new set of concerns that begin to arise in the mid-Victorian novel as they had not in predecessors like Scott and Austen—and is doing so despite her own maxim that "It is easier and pleasanter to recognize the old than to account for the new" (*Romola* 5; Proem). Henry James's notion of Eliot as an expert in creating characters who are "solid and vivid in their varying degrees" suggests one way to understand the investigations her novels make possible (James, Rev. of *Middlemarch* 357). James's formulation points to what we might think of as the Eliotic interest in *variable solidity*—characters who are present in all their knotty particularity in one moment, and seem nothing more than a metonym for a general class in the next. One of Eliot's distinctive achievements as a novelist is her capacity to "scale" her characters in this way, to present them as they appear at a given moment to a particular observer. Thus Celia can one day seem to Dorothea nearly an extension of herself. Yet on the next day, informing Dorothea that Sir James is in love with her, she can appear to Dorothea as the repellent personification of the small-minded world: "How can one ever do anything nobly Christian, living among people with such petty thoughts!" (36; ch. 4).

The various ways in which a character can switch roles in the eyes of other characters—or of the reader—are fascinatingly permuted in Eliot. What seems worth stressing about all the ways that Eliot varies the viewpoint, however, is that they depend upon the novel's capacity suddenly to shift not just direction of gaze, but even axis and orientation. Bender and Marrinan point out that the diagrams in the *Encyclopédie* work as effectively as they do because the same page may contain entirely discrepant images: a close-up of a cauldron and a medium view of a kitchen at work, say. There is a version of the same logic at work in Eliot; the moment that a standpoint has been established, it is replaced by a different angle of approach. The novel's art may be to conceal its artifice, but (as Eliot herself suggests in her 1868 "Notes on Form in Art") elaborate infrastructures of tacit knowledge nonetheless underlie what looks like an effortless move in the narratorial standpoint. *Middlemarch* does not read like a technical diagram, nor does it require ponderous critical detachment to parse; but its smoothness should not obscure the considerable conceptual work demanded of the reader in following a chapter from, let us say, its beginnings in a saint's life, through moments of profound individual introspection, before it concludes in a socially awkward confrontation between inimical personalities with awkward secrets to conceal.

This is an effect that narrative film relies on heavily, for example, on the sudden tracking back-and-up that makes so many Hollywood movies feel like the end of Keats's "Eve of St. Agnes," when the perspective suddenly switches to view the entire action of the poem through the wrong end of a microscope: "And they are gone: ay, ages long ago / These lovers fled away into the storm." Eliot, however, approaches the problem of how such shifts can and should occur with a subtlety that noticeably increases throughout her career. Consider the sudden interjection of the narrator into the description of little Maggie Tulliver playing outside Dorlcote Mill in *The Mill on the Floss*:

> It is time the little playfellow went in, I think; and there is a very bright fire to tempt her: the red light shines out under the deepening gray of the sky. It is time, too, for me to leave off resting my arms on the cold stone of this bridge. . . .
>
> Ah! my arms are really benumbed. I have been pressing my elbows on the arms of my chair, and dreaming that I was standing on the bridge in front of Dorlcote Mill, as it looked one February afternoon many years ago. Before I dozed off, I was going to tell you what Mr. and Mrs. Tulliver were talking about, as they sat by the bright fire in the left-hand parlor, on that very afternoon I have been dreaming of. (8; ch. 1; ellipsis in original)

Eliot, having positioned a narrator to provide a framed view of the bygone provincial world, pivots, explicitly overlaying the site of action and the site of experience. The world we dream comes vividly to life, but there are still moments when we will be forced to wake from the dream.

In Eliot's later novels, the diagrammatic logic is so fully woven into the fabric of the work that it requires a closer attention to what's demanded of the reader to make sense of the logic of axial shifting. The result is that certain odd passages—often in free indirect discourse—signal the kind of rapid conceptual shift occasioned by the novel's capacity—taking for granted readers' skill in deciphering such gyrations—to swivel fluently through a scene. Take an early scene from *Middlemarch* in which Will comes to visit Dorothea, a scene that positions the reader in several highly unexpected and original ways in relationship to each character's viewpoint. As the scene begins, Will has successfully plotted a way to see Dorothea alone:

> "Sit down." She seated herself on a dark ottoman with the brown books behind her, looking in her plain dress of some thin woolen-white material, without a single orna-ment on her besides her wedding-ring, as if she were under a vow to be different from all other women; and Will sat down opposite her at two yards' distance, the light falling on his bright curls and delicate but rather petulant profile, with its defiant curves of lip and chin. (354; ch. 37)

The first half of this sentence is presumably from Will's viewpoint: not only because it locates the brown books behind her, thus establishing an angle from which Dorothea is seen, but also because Will (like the narrator, perhaps, but presumably unlike Dorothea herself) is unable to specify what that woolen-white material might be. The second half is just as clearly from Dorothea's viewpoint, delineating Will's profile and conveying to the reader not just Will's good looks, but also Dorothea's attention to them. Even here, though, there is something more than the "raw data" Bender and

Marrinan emphasize. What Dorothea looks like to Will is not defined so much by her dress, whatever the material, but by his finding that she looks "as if she were under a vow to be different from all other women." It's a description that bespeaks his desire to discern facts about her inner life—an inner life understood to be defined by the kind of relationship to her community (as Will imagines it) that such intended difference implies.

Even in this moment of simple perception the reader catches a glimpse of the ways that Will strives to see beyond Dorothea's present appearance to a hypothetical vow. We might say that Eliot does not (as by Bender and Marrinan's logic, she should) reason here like Erving Goffman, whose account of "behavior in public" presumes that a meeting in a given space with given social rules follows the same kinetic logic no matter what persons might be involved in it. Yet the result of that highly personalized account of looking is not immersion in one viewpoint, but an extremely odd pivoting of the viewpoint into something like a common consciousness.

> Each looked at the other as if they had been two flowers which had opened then and there. Dorothea for the moment forgot her husband's mysterious irritation against Will: it seemed fresh water at her thirsty lips to speak without fear to the person whom she had found receptive; for in looking backward through sadness she exaggerated a past solace. (354; ch. 37)

Each looking at the other as a flower is straightforward, but "two flowers" is something else. It is not churlish but crucial to understanding how the diagrammatic logic works to notice that the plural form poses a serious discursive problem. After all, neither Will nor Dorothea can be thinking of two flowers; each has only one flower (one profile, one woolen-white dress) in mind and sight. Only the narrator can bring us each appearing to the other as a flower.

That mutuality is rendered fragile partly by the fact that each must be a flower in the other's eyes, and yet also remain a person seeing the other as a flower. As soon as the effect is defined as shared, moreover, the axis of perception shifts; the floral perception also becomes individuated, and in a way that drives a wedge not only between the two characters but also between the characters and their own past experiences, as they recollect them. Dorothea gazes as she does at Will because he has been "receptive," but the narrator reminds us immediately that in fact she has misremembered, because of her sorrow since; she has "exaggerated a past solace." The exclamation point in Austen functions as a nuanced signal that the narrator has a viewpoint distinct from Harriet Smith's juvenile glee; Eliot, though, is willing to spell out explicitly not only the feeling that Dorothea has, but also its mistaken roots. This is diagrammatic logic with a difference. Eliot is concerned to establish what it means to see things *from somewhere*, but also to underscore the history behind the particular viewpoint from which sense-claims are made.

Middlemarch took on its final form (the merging of two pieces Eliot had been working on separately) when characters antipathetic to one another were forced into contiguity and coexistence—as Welsh points out, the "first chapter drafted with something like the final design in mind" is the election scene where Lydgate casts a vote against Farebrother. The resulting "network of circumstances, opinion and individual motives over time" results in "an intertwining of alien modern beings" such as Bulstrode and Lydgate (Welsh 62). Alongside that forced contiguity of unrelated plots in the same space and time, we also ought to note in Eliot a different kind of pressure, registered in this scene as the discrepancy that arises even between characters' current and past feelings. One result of that discrepancy, which is understood not only as inter- but also intrasubjective, is that memories, even at such moments of intimacy, are inherently unreliable.

> "I have often thought that I should like to talk to you again," she said immediately. "It seems strange to me how many things I said to you."
>
> "I remember them all," said Will, with the unspeakable content in his soul of feeling that he was in the presence of a creature worthy to be perfectly loved. I think his own feelings at that moment were perfect, for we mortals have our divine moments, when love is satisfied in the completeness of the beloved object. (354; ch. 37)

The crucial point about this passage is not so much the presence of the narrator within the scene as the foregrounded awareness of what it means to shift angles. The "two flowers" that Dorothea and Will see in one another are the perfect exemplification of the challenge the novel always takes on: not to provide definitive "raw data" on the subjectivity constituted by an event, but to struggle to make sense of what different things a single event may mean, and then continue to mean, to people who briefly share a space, but who also then have to move onward with their lives.

Such passages signal something highly distinctive and ultimately influential about Eliot's ways of representing her character's thoughts, a shift in available levels and vantage-points, so that the narratorial movement out of the consciousness of Will and Dorothea leads readers to reflect as well on the nature of the consciousness that focalizes their experiences. Not just as a tricksy narrator (who rests his arms on a bridge and an armchair simultaneously) but as the placeholder for some kind of detached viewpoint on one's own life: the "I" who thinks that Will's feelings were perfect is perhaps something like the I who tries to look at one's own life from a partial remove.

Time Slips, Focal Shifts

In what we have seen so far, perspective has changed, but the temporal axis has remained untroubled: Dorothea's memory of her past is wrong, but the narrator is there to set it right. However, one crucial aspect of the diagrammatic logic in Eliot involves the sense that characters are constantly trying to make of their own place along a temporal axis to which they have only highly limited access. Every present, Andrew Miller has argued, tarries with the optative, holding out various possible futures (198). Yet the contingency of such plausible future outcomes does not prevent characters from looking towards their futures in many of the same ways as they look into one another's lives. The subtlety with which Eliot reckons with such forecasting of contingencies signals an innovation: her novels concern themselves not simply with possible outcomes but also with what difference it makes to people to live their lives precisely by concerning themselves with possible outcomes. These are stories, that is, of people who know that their own lives will fall out according to a set of trajectories that may somehow be diagrammed; and the trick will be to find out what diagrams one moves within, and in what relationship to others. When "destiny stands by sarcastic" it is not just the *"dramatis personae"* but also future actions that remain "folded in her hand" (93; ch. 11).

For example, after the melodramatic "discovery" scene in which Dorothea finds Will with Rosamond, he is moved fatalistically to contemplate his future fate. Lydgate and Will both at this moment seem to be slipping into a miserable future caused by provincial exigencies, social tyranny, and the particular brand of *bovarysme* that Rosamond has inflicted on them. Still uncertain of the eventual result of all this the reader, like Will, fears the worst. At this dark moment, Eliot depicts Will providing a narrative template within which all that has happened can be fitted into that plausible worst case outcome.

> It seemed to him as if he were beholding in a magic panorama a future where he himself was sliding into that pleasureless yielding to the small solicitations of circumstance, which is a commoner history of perdition than any single momentous bargain. (772; ch. 79)

Eliot's presumptions here are diagrammatic: the "raw data" of consciousness are made available so that we can form judgments about possible outcomes. However, this is a moment where living inside a culture of diagram provides suitable advantages in understanding what it means for Will to forecast his future based on the glimpses he has. The narrator casts Will's mistake in moral terms: "We are on a perilous margin when we begin to look passively at our future selves" (772; ch. 79). That is, this is Will acting as if he were uncharacteristically will-less. We might push the logic slightly, however, for the point I think is that at a moment like this it is not "raw data" that the reader wants but something a bit more cooked: the truly revealing diagram, looking down the road from this "magic panorama" moment, is not the path to perdition that Will foresees. That road, readers soon discern, belongs rightly to Lydgate.

We might also understand this question of the diagram and its capacity to help Will forecast his future based on present circumstances and what he knows of his capacity not to behave passively in a more self-reflexive way: is the novel too just such a "magic panorama" as Will glimpses? After all, *Middlemarch* too offers us some glimpses of what it must be like to be ourselves, or to be people close to us, at crucial moments in our lives. Viewing the state of these characters, we view ourselves at a partial remove; just as Will steps back here, puts together the pieces, and tries to figure out in what direction his narrative tends, conjecturing a life of Lydgate-like failure. The "magic panorama," though (like Lydgate's objectless dreaming in his study at a similarly dispirited moment), lacks the diagrammatic robustness of the novel itself. By charting the various ways in which characters look towards things that may yet come to pass (and to do so in essence by gazing inward), the novel, unlike the magic panorama, allows readers to catch sight of a series of hypothetical, or virtual, worlds.

The kind of inward-looking social virtuality we have seen here (from the impossible but plausible two flowers to the magic panorama of a nonexistent future) undermines the strong division Lukács draws between the social world of the realist novel and the solitary states of the modernist novel's isolatos. Eliot invokes the counterexample of the magic panorama (like the "images which succeed each other like the magic-lantern pictures of a doze" during Dorothea's moment of sublime disorientation in Rome) in order to clarify by contrast something that the novel actually does make feasible in the way that illusion-inducing devices do not (188; ch. 20). She sees the capacity to hypothesize about future outcomes—to see in one's mind a set of pictures that may or may not apply to oneself—as a mechanism that in fact returns the solitary dreamer to a social world. Even if that dreaming never itself finds a social outlet, the very fact of hypothesizing about how one's path may or may not resemble paths traveled by one's contemporaries is an act of diagrammatic imagination. An attempt, that is, both to make sense of oneself through their fates, and to make sense of their fates through one's own possible futures.

Lukács suggests that the modernist novels err by grounding their account of the human experience in solitude, and neglecting the inevitable sociability of human interaction. Eliot, however, is already grappling with a subjectivity that, while formed out of a social self, always hinges on the capacity of the self to retreat from that social world. Sociability hinges on particular personages who have to be acknowledged in all their distinctiveness—which also means that the work of the novel is to find ways to approach them in their prickly idiosyncrasy, their inherently *unsympathetic* distinctiveness.

> One morning, some weeks after her arrival at Lowick, Dorothea—but why always Dorothea? Was her point of view the only possible one with regard to this marriage? I protest against all our interest, all our effort at understanding being given to the young skins that look blooming in spite of trouble; for these too will get faded, and will know the older and more eating griefs which we are helping to neglect. (271–72: ch. 29)

The function of this memorable rupture is diagrammatic in a straightforward sense, in that it renders visible the tacking required in order to form a sense of the world that will be not only consistent (a single character's views would be that) but also complete and persuasive. Even the notion of the imagination-engendered mirror introduced in Adam Smith's *Theory of Moral Sentiments* (that we know others' feelings by imagining ourselves inside their bodies) would seem a sufficient mechanism to force readers to put themselves in faded as much as in blooming skins. In that sense, this paragraph is structurally comparable to chapter 41 in *Emma*, which without explanation leaves Emma to focalize through Knightley entirely. Such a reading, though, shortchanges the force of the interjection itself: the surprise, the rupture that it adduces, marks the narrator's surprise, even perhaps a slight sense of shame, at her own way of narrating. Without that first, suspenseful half-sentence that found Dorothea about to do something (what is never revealed to the reader) this turn towards Casaubon would be entirely different in more than just tone.

We might summarize all these examples by seeing in them Eliot continuing the diagrammatic logic of the novel as Bender and Marrinan see it emerging in the early nineteenth century—but also pointing out a range of ways in which that logic necessarily falters within a world in which characters themselves are very aware of such diagrammatic potentials. The undiagrammable gaps that Eliot labors to describe are discernible in various directions, even in these brief passages: between characters who only guess at what they see in one another; between the narrator and characters who still conceal even from that narrator some vital aspects of their selves and thoughts; between characters and their own pasts; and perhaps most of all, accumulating out of all such synaptic and semantic gaps, the space that opens between what can be known inside the world of the novel and what readers can know of these characters, from outside their hypostatized world. Rather than making any one of these categories the definitive index of how the Eliotic narrative handles the problem of other minds, however, I would suggest that we think of the whole array of problems Eliot presents as the logical outcome of an admirable but ultimately circumscribed effort to use the diagrammatic logic of prose fiction to form definitive judgments about characters, or about persons. Eliot takes the culture of diagram to the next level, and in so doing she presses its capacities to the breaking point.

Impressions of Theophrastus Such

Thinking about moments of mistaken regard is also a useful way to make sense of Eliot's final book, the 1879 *Impressions of Theophrastus Such*. That work is Eliot's final set of experiments with the ways in which understanding—of self, of others, and of fictional characters available only through a textual world—can fail. Especially in "Looking Inward" and "So Young!" Eliot tests the limits of knowledge about others by exploring sites at which a social environment begins to shape what looks like the closed inner world of character-formation. The book's opening sentence contains its crucial question:

> It is my habit to give an account to myself of the characters I meet with: can I give any true account of my own? (3)

Here the *habit* of giving an account "to myself" of the characters I meet suggests that the question of whether I can give an account of my own (also to myself?) reveals how inwoven the practice of narrative description upon which fiction relies has become. Equally habitual, too, has become the necessary self-revelatory disclaimers that are required to ground the sketches that will follow.

> I am a bachelor, without domestic distractions of any sort, and have all my life been an attentive companion to myself, flattering my nature agreeably on plausible occasions, reviling it rather bitterly when it mortified me, and in general remembering its doings and sufferings with a tenacity which is too apt to raise surprise if not disgust at the careless inaccuracy of my acquaintances, who impute to me opinions I never held, express their desire to convert me to my favorite ideas, forget whether I have been to the East, are capable of being three several times astonished at my never having told them before of my accident in the Alps, causing me the nervous shock which has ever since notably diminished my digestive powers. (3)

This second sentence, with all its odd trailings off and unexpected turns (the "surprise" and disgust" seems at first to refer to his friends' view of Theophrastus, only to be revealed as the reverse) charts the ways in which characters are constituted not just from the inward out, nor solely by their public appearance in the world, but by the internalization of the outward into the inner, so that what others think of us becomes a significant portion of our inner lives.

This is also the problem to which an essay much later in the book, "So Young!," is devoted; it turns on the way that an *enfant terrible* ("Ganymede") has lost touch with what his public actually thinks of him because he remains wedded to a conception of himself as a talent known mainly for his remarkable youth. The central point of "So Young!' is about the quality that Eliot in other contexts refers to as the "inwrought"; that is, the set of exterior sensations that over a time are drawn into one and, for good or ill, come to shape one's experience. As a young man, writes Theophrastus, Ganymede was "only undergoing one form of a common moral disease: being strongly mirrored for himself in the remarks of others, he was getting to see his real characteristics as a dramatic part, a type to which his doings were always in correspondence" (100). The result is that "Ganymede's inwrought sense of his surprising youthfulness had been stronger than the superficial reckoning of his years and the merely optical phenomena of the looking-glass," even when his age and body type have changed so much that "a stranger would now have been apt to remark that Ganymede was unusually plump for a distinguished writer, rather than unusually young" (101).

The writer who continues to be "so young" in his own mind after he has become objectively old and principally plump in the eye of the beholder is an instance of the person for whom what is "wrought back to the directness of sense" is of no benefit in making sense of those around him (*Middlemarch* 205; ch. 21). The "culture of diagram" works well, by Bender and Marrinan's account, if it supplies "raw data" of others' experience to the reader. But what Eliot suggests is that the problem of such data in fact depends on understanding how it has been or will be processed by those whom it had originally struck. By the same token, in Thomas Mann's novels characters sometimes quote as current wisdom the maxims of long dead beloveds; in a long-outdated opinion about democracy in Prussia in *Buddenbrooks* (1901), one can infer everything about the frozen libido of an aged spinster aunt still holding firmly in mind the last intellectual vestiges of a lost first love.

Time Slips the Other Way

Eliot's writing is haunted by and framed by its past. The particular variation that "So Young!" plays on the theme of a socially mediated temporality—that we carry within us as if it were an existential quality the vestiges of what others long ago thought of us—provides a valuable way to go back to Eliot's fiction to make sense of the sorts of self-deceit that such vestiges of the past can engender. "So Young!" explores what it means to be unable to see one's present world (even one's own plump and aging body) because a picture from the past holds one captive. It also helps to clarify what might be understood as the mirror-image of such temporal brainwashing: the life that excludes necessary and formative aspects of the past from conscious knowledge. During his downfall, for example, Bulstrode finds his long-hidden past rising hideously to become a formative aspect of his present ("second") new life in Middlemarch. This is not because anything from that past had been actually unknown to him, but because its becoming known to the town changes what it means to him in the present.

> Into this second life Bulstrode's past had now risen, only the pleasures of it seeming to have lost their quality. Night and day, without interruption save of brief sleep which only wove retrospect and fear into a fantastic present, he felt the scenes of his earlier life coming between him and everything else, as obstinately as when we look through the window from a lighted room, the objects we turn our backs on are still before us, instead of the grass and the trees. The successive events inward and outward were there in one view: though each might be dwelt on in turn, the rest still kept their hold in the consciousness. (615; ch. 61)

Bulstrode's social panic unfolds entirely within his own thoughts. The notion of the "hold" that Bulstrode's past can exercise on him here is one key way to grasp Eliot's account of the way that a set of past events, suitably repeated and internalized, can form a fixed pattern, a stereotype, into which one's current experiences are inextricably cast.

Eliot is writing about the state of being *semi-detached* from one's past, which nonetheless rises before one, ineluctable but somehow only partially tangible, like that "magic panorama" that Will sees as he tries to envision his future (failing, visualizing instead only Lydgate's). The persistence of the past is not a solid but a translucent presence. Like the translucent overlay pages in a childhood book about the body (the blood vessels on one sheet, the nerves on another, eventually the whole body falling into place), these memories, which are swiftly coming to the attention of those around him, exist both within and without Bulstrode.

Again it is worth noting here the space that this semi-detachment makes for Eliot between social realism and modernist isolation as Lukács defines them. This is a solitary occupation, this haunting, and yet it has an inextricably social component: the thoughts of others are a haunting factor even when one finds oneself alone: what rises up alongside the deeds that cannot be recalled, are the thoughts of others about those deeds. Like the chains that mark experience turned into an inescapable legacy in *Great Expectations*, the occurrences in Eliot turn into memories, and from memories, they become facts about the world. Turned into a part of the living past, they move forward with characters, conditioning them and so in turn determining their future actions, which in turn have their own effects, which in turn may or may not become inwrought. The ongoing chain of events, then, is shaped not only by a set of billiard ball collisions between independent actors, but by a ramifying set of previous events turned inward, regaining an outward shape as they are translated into further cascades of actions.

Conclusion

One way of understanding Eliot's relationship to the culture of diagram that preceded her and the modernist novel that followed her is to see the Eliotic conception of semi-detachment as it shaped the work of her successors. Henry James for example discerns in Eliot a way to preserve from the realist novel a commitment to a shared public world, coupled with an attunement to the way that the characters who share that world often, like Bulstrode, are haunted by images that rise before their eyes, temporarily blocking out an otherwise common reality. James's understanding of the novel's capacities precisely arises from his effort to account for that ongoing sensation of partial detachment from and ultimate return to a current reality.

Marcel Proust describes gaining from "Sesames and Lilies" such a pure sensation of Ruskin's mind that an encounter with the actual man would be (as indeed it was when Proust finally glimpsed him at an art gallery) a pale imitation of his legible presence in a book. Henry James understands getting lost inside a book quite differently. Unlike other genres, James asserts in the New York edition preface to *The Ambassadors*, a novel can be both "dramatic" (it can stage scenes plausibly) and "representative" (it can enter into how particular people feel and experience the world). In fact, its capacity to keep the scenic and the mental both afloat within the text is the novel's unique strength: a play gives you only social scenes, a poem only mental states. Novels by contrast at their most "elastic" and "prodigious" are a mixture of the "dramatic" and the "representational." James is asserting here that novels are elastic and prodigious precisely because even as a great scene is happening, even as key "business" gets accomplished, they can move the reader inside the mind of a character who is watching it happen—very often a character who, far from being involved in the scene, experiences it in a profoundly different way from what we might imagine. He accordingly describes the novel's representational successes as being made up of "disguised and repaired losses" and "insidious recoveries" (xxiii; Preface).

James's aesthetic credo here helps clarify the significance of his praise, many decades earlier, for the varying degrees of solidity in Eliot's characters. They vary in their solidity to one another, as much as to the reader, and that variety bespeaks a fundamental fact about the kind of realist yet also modernist novel that James aims to create in Eliot's wake. It is not just readerly attention, but attention in the real world as well, that by James's account is always defined by some mixture of the "dramatic" and the "representational." Thus for Eliot first, and for James following her, the novel is "realist" to the extent that it captures the way each of us makes sense of the world by a complex and only partially traceable mixture of attending and disattending. This rapprochement between mid-Victorian and early modernist aesthetics points to one way Lukács misunderstands the force that the external or objective world may have in a modernist novel. In Proust and Woolf as much as in James, the subjectivity effect within a text never leads to pure temporal flux. The falls into flashback or jumbled *hysteron proteron* begin somewhere, and lead back to questions about the grounds from which such a tumble begins.

In Virginia Woolf too we can see a post-Eliotic register of two warring tendencies tugging at the novel. In Woolf, interestingly, they are also manifested as the war of the present (the now, objective and shareable) and the recollected past, which interjects an inescapable subjectivity into any moment's sensations. Mrs. Dalloway's exasperation with her own memorializing tendency epitomizes the tension perfectly:

> She remembered once throwing a shilling into the Serpentine. But every one remembered; what she loved was this, here, now, in front of her; the fat lady in the cab. (Woolf 12)

The problems of mutual regard I've sketched in *Middlemarch*, and the problems of deformed or temporally disjointed self-regard in *Impressions of Theophrastus Such* strongly suggest that Eliot understands characters in her novels as a series of limited vantage points onto a world that the reader comes to know through a mixture of third-person axioms and first-person observations. Novels that seem to offer the possibility of an impartial and complete third-person vantage point always contain hints of the arms cramped by watching; the flower into which beloved faces are transformed always contains a hint of the peering eyes, the fading skin, beneath.

Mrs. Dalloway's dismay when forced to choose between past and present, like James's sense that occupying oneself with an internal monologue guarantees that one loses what's being said around one, is in some ways as distinctively modernist as is the capacity of Marcel in Proust's novels to flicker from place to place and time to time like a magic lantern show, with recollections and a time-sense dependent on an always internally preserved paratactic logic. However, there is a far greater debt owed by such experiments than is often acknowledged to the palpably experimental semi-detachment Eliot is perpetually refining in her writing: from the numb forearms of

The Mill on the Floss to Theophrastus's admittedly incomplete attempts to understand his own character through an investigation of others, Eliot is working up an aesthetic enterprise predicated not only on the "culture of diagram" that Bender and Marrinan describe, but also on the implications of living in a world where one is forced to consider what it means that others around one are equally making use of such diagrams to comprehend their surroundings. Flowers everywhere.

REFERENCES

Austen, Jane. *Emma*. Ed. Richard Cronin and Dorothy McMillan. Cambridge: Cambridge UP, 2005.

Banfield, Ann. *Unspeakable Sentences: Narration and Representation in the Language of Fiction*. London: Routledge, 1982.

Bender, John and Michael Marrinan. *The Culture of Diagram*. Stanford: Stanford UP, 2010.

Eliot, George. *Impressions of Theophrastus Such*. Ed. Nancy Henry. Iowa City: U of Iowa P, 1994.

Eliot, George. *Middlemarch*. Ed. David Carroll. Oxford: Oxford UP, 1986.

Eliot, George. *The Mill on the Floss*. Ed. Gordon S. Haight. Oxford: Oxford UP, 1980.

Eliot, George. *Romola*. Ed. Dorothea Barrett. London: Penguin, 1996.

James, Henry. Preface. *The Ambassadors. The New York Edition of Henry James*. Vol. 21. New York: Scribner's, 1909. v–xxiii.

James, Henry. Rev. of *Middlemarch*. Unsigned. *Galaxy* 15 (March 1873): 424–28. Rpt. in *George Eliot: The Critical Heritage*. Ed. David Carroll. London: Routledge, 1971: 353–59.

Lukács, Georg. "Ideology of Modernism." *The Meaning of Contemporary Realism*. Trans. John and Necke Mander. London: Merlin, 1963.

Miller, Andrew. *The Burdens of Perfection: On Ethics and Reading in Nineteenth-Century British Literature*. Ithaca: Cornell UP, 2008.

Miller, D. A. *Jane Austen, or the Secret of Style*. Princeton: Princeton UP, 2003.

Welsh, Alexander. "The Later Novels." *The Cambridge Companion to George Eliot*. Ed. George Levine. Cambridge: Cambridge UP, 2001. 57–75.

Williams, Raymond. *The Country and the City*. London: Hogarth, 1985.

Woolf, Virginia. Mrs. *Dalloway*. New York: Harcourt, 1925.

Part II
Works

6

Scenes of Clerical Life and *Silas Marner*: Moral Fables

Stefanie Markovits

Scenes of Clerical Life and *Silas Marner*, the two works that bookend George Eliot's "early" period (Knoepflmacher), have much in common. Both are short in form—the first a collection of three inter-related stories and the second a novella—distinctive for that reason alone given Eliot's general reputation as a writer of massive novels. Both deal thematically with questions of suffering, confession, and redemption, questions that arise in the context of anthropologically-oriented explorations of the state of contemporary religious belief within small provincial or rural communities. Moreover, these tales are not only pastoral (in the generic as well as the spiritual sense of the term) but also set in the past—not the distant past of *Romola* but the more recent past of Marian Evans's Midlands childhood, a past that is viewed as threatened by the forces of modern "improvement" (Eliot, "Amos Barton," *Scenes* 5; ch. 1). And both, as this last fact suggests, are fictions of memory, deeply imbued with personal recollection. As many novice writers have been told, start with what you know, and Eliot's decision to follow this rule was aided by her commitment to documenting the real. Indeed these works participate in (and *Scenes* inaugurates) Eliot's realist agenda, her desire, as she put in most famously in *Adam Bede*, to portray "real breathing men and women" (156; ch. 17) in order to facilitate the sympathetic processes at the heart of her moral project.[1]

Yet for all their realism, both works came to their author in what might be called visionary moments. As Eliot records in "How I Came to Write Fiction,"

A Companion to George Eliot, First Edition. Edited by Amanda Anderson and Harry E. Shaw.
© 2013 John Wiley & Sons, Ltd. Published 2016 by John Wiley & Sons, Ltd.

one morning, as I was thinking what should be the subject of my first story, my thoughts merged themselves into a dreamy doze, and I imagined myself writing a story, of which the title was "The Sad Fortunes of the Reverend Amos Barton." (*Letters* 2:407)

The epiphany was even more startling with *Silas Marner*, interrupting Eliot's research for *Romola*. "I am writing a story which came *across* my other plans by a sudden inspiration," she announced to her publisher, John Blackwood (*Letters* 3:371; original emphasis), later elaborating:

It came to me first all quite suddenly, as a sort of legendary tale, suggested by my recollection of having once, in early childhood, seen a linen weaver with a bag on his back; but, as my mind dwelt on the subject, I became inclined to a more realistic treatment. (*Letters* 3:382)

As this comment hints, these works are representative of Eliot's wider oeuvre not only for their realism—and the forms of morality we associate with that realism—but also for their sometimes uneasy balance between realism and romance, between the everyday and the "legendary." Indeed it is striking that with *Silas Marner*, the story to which F. R. Leavis long ago affixed the tag of "moral fable" (60), realism grows out of the initial romantic vision, and not the other way around. For this reason, these tales help illuminate what Theresa Kelley has called "the peripheral vision of Victorian realist culture—that edge where realist values become blurred and allegory's raids on the verisimilar occur" (218).

But another way the tension between real and ideal can be considered is as a manifestation of that even more fundamental writerly difficulty of how to convert ideas into something substantial enough to be capable of communication. As the author of numerous essays and translations, Eliot's intellectual ability was in no doubt even before she "came to write fiction." Still, her capacity to embody her ideas in stories was untested. Even George Henry Lewes felt uncertainty about her "dramatic power"— a phrase suggesting fear that her plots might not offer sufficient scaffolding to uphold her description but also recalling the embodied presentation of ideas on the stage (*Letters* 2: 407). Such embodiment was essential both to her fictional project and to her moral one; as Adam Smith recognized, sympathy rests on one's ability to imagine oneself bodily into another's subject position. Eliot's narrator offers a related recognition in a much-cited passage from "Janet's Repentance," the third and longest of the *Scenes*:

Ideas are often poor ghosts; our sun-filled eyes cannot discern them; they pass athwart us in thin vapour and cannot make themselves felt. But sometimes they are made flesh; they breathe upon us with warm breath, they touch us with soft responsive hands, they look at us with sad sincere eyes, and speak to us in appealing tones; they are clothed in a living human soul, with all its conflicts, its faith, and its love. Then their presence is a power, then they shake us like a passion, and we are drawn after them with gentle compulsion, as flame is drawn to flame. (263; ch. 19)

Eliot used similar language in a letter to Blackwood voicing her fear that the success of *Adam Bede* might overshadow her earlier work and threaten the publication of a new edition: "I am very anxious that the 'Scenes of Clerical Life' should have every chance of impressing the public with its existence . . . because there are ideas presented in these stories about which I care a good deal, and am not sure that I can ever embody again" (*Letters* 3:240). But while particular embodied ideas might be peculiar to the *Scenes*, the problem of embodiment was not; writing years later to Frederick Harrison, Eliot is still agonizing over "the severe effort of trying to make certain ideas thoroughly incarnate, as if they revealed themselves to me first in the flesh and not in the spirit" (*Letters* 4:300). The question of types of "incarnation" (Carroll 27; Yeazell 109; Nunokawa 284)—and the distinction between fleshly bodies and "ghosts"—keeps arising in relation to both the *Scenes* and *Silas Marner*, showing the kinship at the heart of these two fictional experiments.

Scenes of Clerical Life

Scenes of Clerical Life, first published serially in *Blackwood's Magazine* between January and November of 1857 (a two-volume edition appeared in 1858), declares its interest in embodiment through the metaphor animating its title. While this metaphor might be read dramatically, Ruth Yeazell has suggested why it makes sense to consider it visually; noting the passage above from "Janet's Repentance," she describes how "Eliot worried the question of how ideas may be made flesh, and . . . her self-conscious effort to embody abstractions in concrete particulars prompted her to look for a precedent to the visual art of the seventeenth-century Netherlands" (110). Indeed the *Scenes of Clerical Life* as a whole can seem a kind of "picture-writing of the mind," a phrase Eliot uses in "The Natural History of German Life," an essay written for the *Westminster Review* shortly before her turn to fiction and in which she is working through ideas about realism (*Essays* 267).[2] And while *Scenes of Clerical Life*'s narrator presents himself in the opening pages of "The Sad Fortunes of the Reverend Amos Barton" as a young "member of the congregation" (5; ch. 1)—and sporadically reminds us of his youthful bodily presence within *Scenes of Clerical Life* (see, for example, *Janet's Repentance* 176, ch. 2; 201, ch. 5; 205, ch. 6)—this persona is unstable, frequently being superseded by a wiser, more impartial tone, one closer to that of Eliot's mature narrative voice. Actually, the narrator's recurrent trick of shifting to the present tense in order to describe what he is laying before his reader, helpfully suspending the action to allow our scrutiny (Yeazell 103), can give him the effect of a knowledgeable docent in a gallery, able to point out the significant details of these faded paintings, now some decades old.

Such scrutiny is especially necessary in the first tale because its protagonist, Amos Barton, holds little promise of interest: "he was superlatively middling, the quintessential extract of mediocrity" (40; ch. 5). An ineffectual clergyman burdened financially by an overlarge family and a beautiful but parasitic semi-aristocratic

Countess for a houseguest (her presence precipitates the whisper-slight action of the tale by creating rumors of impropriety that isolate Barton from his community), Amos poses a challenge to the limits of sympathy. As the narrator admits,

> perhaps I am doing a bold thing to bespeak your sympathy on behalf of a man who was so very far from remarkable,—a man whose virtues were not heroic, and who had no undetected crime within his breast; who had not the slightest mystery about him. . . . "An utterly uninteresting character!" I think I hear a lady reader exclaim. . . .
>   But, my dear madam, it is so very large a majority of your countrymen that are of this insignificant stamp. (36; ch. 5)

Already, we see the characteristic mark of Eliot's realism, its moral foundations in the need to enable our sympathies with the average, with "real sorrow: sorrow such as may live next door to you" (50; ch. 7). And if this level of realism is slightly counterbalanced by the idealistic portrayal of Barton's ailing wife, Milly, the "large, kind, gentle Madonna" (15; ch. 2) whose premature death will—in an almost Dickensian fashion—help us to bond in sympathy with her flawed but genuinely grieving husband, such a combination of real and ideal is itself typical of Eliot's later methods (although the reliance on death and the sorrows of the orphaned small children as stimuli to pathos is not).

If the narrator's temporal and descriptive methodology is painterly, the counter-genre to *Scenes of Clerical Life* is the sermon. Eliot's decision to focus her first effort at fiction on the clergy's role during the rise of Evangelicalism is usually read biographically, as a sign that she is working through her early ardent embrace and later abandonment of that movement. But Eliot's interest in the clergy also owes something to their work as men of language, as authors of a peculiarly didactic form of essay. Throughout *Scenes of Clerical Life*, Eliot seems sympathetically alive to the difficult task of didacticism faced by her assorted preachers; early in "Amos Barton," she contrasts her "hero" with the more effectual Mr. Cleves (who, like Mr. Gilfil of her second tale, bears a passing resemblance to *Middlemarch*'s Farebrother), a man possessed of "the wonderful art of preaching sermons which the wheelwright and the blacksmith can understand," because he "knows how to disencumber ideas of their wordy frippery" (47; ch. 6). Amos, though, is proud author of an "extremely argumentative" printed sermon (suggestively, on the subject of "the Incarnation"), which the narrator deems "exceedingly well adapted to trouble and confuse the Sheppertonian mind" of his original audience (30; ch. 3). As Eliot admits,

> Nothing in the world more suited to the simple understanding than instruction through familiar types and symbols! But there is always this danger attending it, that the interest or comprehension of your hearers may stop short precisely at the point where your spiritual interpretation begins. (23; ch. 2)

That is, comprehension may never penetrate the surface flesh to discover the ghostly ideas underneath. But where Barton's art may fail him, his life—at least as embodied

Amos =
Dolly

in Eliot's fiction—succeeds in its educative purpose: "Amos failed to touch the springs of goodness by his sermons, but he touched it effectually by his sorrows" (62–63; ch. 10). As David Carroll notes, "[Amos] becomes, in fact, the incarnation . . . of the beliefs he has been preaching in his ineffectual way to the parish" (46).

Such an interest in the effectiveness of sermons' didactic speech persists in the second and strangest of the stories in *Scenes of Clerical Life*, "Mr. Gilfil's Love Story." We first encounter the Reverend Mr. Gilfil in the "present" of the narrator's childhood, only to be removed, via a telescoping process of explanatory flashbacks, to 1788 and his "antecedent romance" (74; ch. 1), his love for Caterina Sarti, the young Italian-born ward of Sir Christopher Cheverel—and, briefly, even farther back to when Sir Christopher and his wife find and adopt the infant Tina on an Italian journey. The tale begins, however, with a discussion of Gilfil's clerical methods, which include reaching every Sunday into a "large heap of sermons, rather yellow and worn at the edges," from which he extracts a pair at random to present before the parishes within his fold (68; ch. 1). These sermons are themselves well-worn versions of moral fables, offering little more "than an expansion of the concise thesis, that those who do wrong will find it the worse for them, and those who do well will find it the better for them" (72; ch. 1). While much admired by his parishioners, they are so formulaic as to encourage a "flippant town youth" to "declare he could write as good a sermon," which, on a wager, he proceeds to do: "The sermon was written . . . astonishingly like a sermon, having a text, three divisions, and a concluding exhortation beginning 'and now my brethren'" (73; ch. 1). It is as though Eliot were challenging the reader to accuse her own tripartite moral exhortation to her brethren of being similarly formulaic.

Still, sermons and clerical issues play a comparatively minor role in the flashback portions of this second story, the most romantic of the tales (hence the revolutionary setting, which offers little insight into the upheavals agitating "the great nation of France," other than to remark on a parallel in the "terrible struggles" occupying "our Caterina's little breast" [89; ch. 3]). Rather, painting comes front and center. Eliot uses the language of contemporary art to help us picture her scene: the narrator explains that Lady Cheverel "treads the lawn as if she were one of Joshua Reynolds's stately ladies" (78; ch. 2), and we soon learn (as simile is embodied in story) that Sir Christopher has commissioned portraits from the painter himself (84; ch. 2); Cheverel Manor is worthy of "some English Watteau" (78; ch. 2); and crucial scenes take place in galleries lined with "queer old family portraits" (87; ch. 2) or involve Tina's tempestuous smashing of a miniature of her feeble and faithless lover, Captain Wybrow (Sir Christopher's nephew and heir). Actually, the arts in general pervade the story's atmosphere. Tina's charm rests largely on her talents as a singer, and Sir Christopher's passion is architecture: he is in the process of gothicizing Cheverel Manor.

The architectural theme manifests the tale's oddly uneven tone, looking back to the Dickensian gothic of Lady Dedlock's pacing of the ghost's walk at Chesney Wold even as it looks forward sympathetically to the ambitions of Henry James's aesthetes. Plot, too, is macabre—a far cry from the realism of both "Amos Barton" and Mr. Gilfil's tender story of love and loss in the framing portions of his story. Thus Tina removes a dagger from the gallery with which to murder her faithless lover only to discover, upon meeting him, that he has already suffered a heart attack (making her the first of Eliot's quasi-murderers, like Hetty Sorrel, Felix Holt, Laure, Bulstrode, and Gwendolen Harleth). The melodramatic moment elicits a characteristic Eliotian commentary on the complexity of human will. When assured by Gilfil of her innocence, the devastated Tina can only repeat, "I meant to do it." "Our thoughts are often worse than we are, just as they are often better than we are," Gilfil consoles her, "and God"—or, one might add, the novelist—"sees us as we are altogether" (159; ch. 19).

Jane Austen's ghost also hovers over these pages. Eliot was rereading *Mansfield Park*, the most "clerical" of Austen's works, while working on "Mr. Gilfil's Love Story" (Cross 1:306), and Lewes had remarked to Blackwood that Eliot's "represent[ation] of the clergy like every other class" bore a resemblance to Austen's (Cross 1:301). While Tina's status as poor ward in the Cheverel household might remind us of Fanny Price's marginalized position, the more potent link is that between Sir Christopher—perhaps the tale's most interesting tragic center—and Sir Thomas Bertram: both scions of the British aristocracy must learn their fallibility. "It really is a remarkable thing that I never in my life laid a plan and failed to carry it out," Sir Christopher announces ominously (141; ch. 14). Some hours later, after Captain Wybrow's corpse and Tina's flight are discovered, his tone has changed: "God help me! I thought I saw everything, and was stone-blind all the while" (151; ch. 18). Gilfil voices Eliot's moral here, and in *Scenes of Clerical Life* as a whole: "we can hardly learn humility and tenderness enough except by suffering" (150; ch. 18). That this suffering encompasses both the comparative "realism" of Mr. Gilfil's deep but gentle love for Tina and the tempestuous "romance" of her betrayal by Wybrow—indeed that the tale suggests that these two terms and plots are less distinct than they might appear—is key to Eliot's conception of both categories.

Suffering, as much as the titular repentance, also fuels the final story, "Janet's Repentance," which chronicles what happens when "Evangelicalism . . . mak[es] its way" into the small provincial town of Milby (227; ch. 10)—at least Evangelicalism as embodied in the consumptive but potent form of the Reverend Edgar Tryan. Much of the community, like our heroine Janet Dempster and the narrative itself, initially try to repel this advancing spirit with a "No!" as forceful as that expressed by Janet's brutal husband, the lawyer Dempster, in the tale's shocking opening word. As the story unfolds, focus slowly shifts from that broader community to the single, highly idealized figure of Janet Dempster, whose "grandly-cut features," intelligence, and compassion for the poor make her the first of Eliot's magnificent heroines (199; ch. 4). Gradually, we are allowed glimpses back into "the sad growth of home-misery over long years" (208; ch. 7), as we see how Janet's marriage has disintegrated from its initial promise into one of physical abuse (Dempster's of Janet) and alcoholism (of both husband and wife). As in her later fiction, Eliot shows an uncommon preference for tales of marriage over narratives of courtship. It is against this backdrop of marital misery that Eliot can most forcefully display how sympathy with suffering enables change, giving "ideas" the power to be "made flesh" (263; ch. 19).

Once again, sermons play a part in the process of transformation; Janet is initially surprised to discover that Tryan's sermons—which she reads to find fodder for her husband's campaign against the minister—are "not at all what I expected—dull, stupid things—nothing of the roaring fire-and-brimstone sort" (210; ch. 7). But the moment of conversion and repentance (for her crimes to Tryan and her alcoholism) requires a face-to-face encounter with the man, the embodiment of his own ideas, and a recognition of "fellowship in suffering" (237; ch. 12). The encounter, their first verbal one, follows Janet's dark night of the soul, when her husband locks her out after a particularly brutal fight, forcing her to seek refuge with a neighbor. Janet's confession to Tryan is "prompt[ed]" by his own confession of youthful indiscretion; the face-to-face exchange thus enacts the process of sympathy, which, as the narrator explains, "is but a living again through our own past in a new form" (258; ch. 18), the form of someone else's body.[3] Significantly, the narrator had previously explained his perspective on the story using similar terms. Speaking of the "bird's-eye station" from which the "critic" peers down upon Tryan, he distinguishes his own subject-position: "But I am not poised at that lofty height. I am on the level and in the press with him, as he struggles his way along the stony road." "The only true knowledge of our fellow-man," the narrator concludes, "is that which allows us to feel with him" (229; ch. 10). The passage melds the narrator's with his hero's function, even as it suggests why in her later work, Eliot might again aim, albeit with a less embodied narrative voice, to assume the tone of "a member of the congregation." It also helps explain Eliot's turn from criticism to fiction by showing how fiction can offer "a picture of human life" that fosters "the extension of our sympathies," as she put it in "The Natural History of German Life" when explaining why works of art are more effective than "hundreds of sermons" (*Essays* 270).

Still, while this "epoch" (to use Eliot's favorite term for such crises) enables Janet to confess, Eliot does not end her tale here, but rather allows Janet ten more chapters in which to demonstrate the fruits of her repentance, letting her turn her own ideas about right behavior into bodily actions. At first, Janet feels an aimlessness that will prove characteristic of many of Eliot's later heroines: "It is very difficult to know what to do: what ought I to do?" (274; ch. 22). But when her husband falls from his carriage and is mortally injured—precipitating the tale's famous delirium-infused sick-room scene—Janet's own "burden of decision as to her future course" is removed: in the presence of illness, "you may begin to act without settling one preliminary question" (278–79; ch. 24). And when Janet is further freed by Dempster's death (as Dorothea will be freed by Casaubon's), she can set upon her own rescue of the man who has "rescued" her (301; ch. 28) by ensuring that Tryan spend his final, consumption-ridden months in a comfortable home that she has purchased and arranged for him. Tryan's earthly body is laid to rest, but Eliot reminds us that his spirit has found a new fleshly home; while the "simple gravestone in the Milby churchyard" may give his name, "there is another memorial of Edgar Tryan, which bears a fuller record: it is Janet Dempster" (301; ch. 28). Or, rather, "Janet's Repentance."

Silas Marner

"In 'Janet's Repentance,'" Thomas Noble has declared, "the plot itself is a dramatization of the idea" (Eliot *Scenes* xii; Intro.). But *Silas Marner* displays Eliot's purest incarnation of an idea in a plot. As many readers have noticed, the essence of this most schematic of her fictions can be found in Silas's puzzled musings on the tale's pivotal exchange of the weaver's gold for Eppie's golden curls:

> Thought and feeling were so confused within him, that if he had tried to give them utterance, he could only have said that the child was come instead of the gold—that the gold had turned into the child. (120; ch. 14)

The intricate webs of thematic metaphor woven through the later fiction seem here to be condensed in this central plot dynamic, whereby the agency of the child reconnects Silas with his community. A "reversal of the Midas story" (Carroll 153), this plot's simplicity has led readers to liken the novella to a fable or fairytale. But of course, ambiguity remains. Is the transaction one of metamorphosis or incarnation, a lyrical transcendence ("turn[ing] into")? Or is it rather a narrative process of substitution, of going and "com[ing]"? The uncertainty owes something to Eliot's debt to Wordsworth. Perhaps because his *Lyrical Ballads* share in her novella's generic back-and-forth between transcendent (lyrical) and narrative (ballad) impulses, or the "legendary" and the "realistic" (as Eliot labeled the competing modes when describing her tale's germ), Eliot imagined the poet as *Silas Marner's* ideal reader, and she admitted that she had "felt all through as if the story would have lent itself best to metrical rather than prose fiction" (*Letters* 3:38).

This mixed nature also appears in the story's double-plotting (frequently compared to *Daniel Deronda's* combination of the "romantic" Deronda plot with the "realistic" Gwendolen plot), which scholars have been tempted to read as offering modally distinctive accounts of the events in Raveloe. Thus Silas's tale of loss and recovery becomes the stuff of legend, while the parallel tale of Godfrey Cass's escape from an unwanted wife and child and regret for this choice when he and his new wife, Nancy Lammeter, find themselves childless, is considered realistic. Choice proves crucial to distinguishing between the two plotlines and their methods of representation. Godfrey's tendency to "rather trust to casualties than his own resolve" to relieve him from his financial and marital burdens (27; ch. 3) is deemed little better than (and just as false as) his wicked brother Dunstan's faith in his "usual good-luck" (35; ch. 4). Such faith equates with pure egoism or "doing as one likes," as the narrator notes: "Favorable Chance, I fancy, is the god of all men who follow their own devices instead of obeying a law they believe in." So Cass comes to represent Eliot's realistic commitment to what she elsewhere calls the "inexorable law of consequences" (see Shuttleworth 219), or, as she puts it here, "the orderly sequence by which the seed brings forth a crop after its own kind" (71–72; ch. 9). In contrast, Silas's plotline belongs to the realm of fairy or folktale and is in fact ruled by luck. His early expulsion "by lots" from the Calvinist society of Lantern Yard seems to predict how chance governs his entire life, best exemplified by the way his very body is subject to random fits of catalepsy. Eppie's fortunate appearance in place of the deadening gold during one such cataleptic fit thus disrupts any sense of "orderly sequence," sharply bifurcating Silas's life into an unlucky before (his first fifteen years in Raveloe) and a lucky after (the sixteen years with Eppie to which we are privy in the novella's second half), without attributing the split to his own agency. The psychological critic E. S. Dallas picked up on the uncharacteristic nature of this plotline for Eliot: "a hero whose mind is nearly a blank, and whose life is presented as the sport of chance, is at variance with the spirit of her books," which usually operate not by chance but by analyzing the role of "Work and reward, cause and effect" (Dallas 12).

Yet as many have also recognized, these strict oppositions break down under closer analysis. For Joseph Wiesenfarth, the tale's "legend enhance[s] its realism" (228), while Srdjan Smajic has coined the term "supernatural realism" to describe the story's effect, pointing to the novella's much admired chapter 6, which recounts the conversation among the locals of Raveloe at the Rainbow Inn (a name that conjures images of legendary pots of gold) before Silas interrupts it with his announcement of the theft of his hoard. As Smajic points out, while the scene offers the quotidian detail and narrative "filler" we associate with realism, "the realm of the ordinary is here conceived as a portal into the extraordinary and, importantly, back again" (11). Take the long discussion of the ghost haunting Mr. Lammeter's stables, the reality of which is left open to question. As the landlord puts it, "I'm for holding with both sides; for . . . the truth lies between 'em" (52; ch. 6). And at this point the ghostly but real form of Silas himself actually interrupts the discussion. The mingling of realistic and legendary becomes especially apparent by the end of the book, when Marner takes full responsibility for his choice of keeping and raising Eppie. As he puts it to Cass, even if "God gave her to me"—a lucky chance—he did so because Cass had "turned his back on her." Silas uses a politicized moral rhetoric of rights and obligations, the language of the realist novel: "you've no right to her! When a man turns a blessing from his door, it falls to them as takes it in" (164; ch. 19).

Moreover while Silas may be a creature of chance for much of the book, he is also a creature of habit, a category in which Eliot shows intense interest throughout her career and that lies halfway between realistic agency and the more allegorically propelled action of fable and fairytale. Indeed one of the great questions raised by the novella concerns the moral valence of Silas's habitual action in his earlier, hopeless phase. Many readers are repulsed by the vision of Silas weaving away automatically at his loom with "the unquestioning activity of a spinning insect." Yet this habitual activity is also what preserves him through those long wasted years, and Eliot's description of his weaving is far more nuanced than it is sometimes credited with being: "Every man's work, pursued steadily, tends in this way to become an end in itself, and so to bridge over the loveless chasms of his life" (15; ch. 2). That it is better to have love none can doubt, but that it is good to have work as a substitute for love in its absence also seems possible; the weaving emerges as a healthy if similarly habitual counter-activity to the heart-deadening hoarding. In fact, in his routine existence Silas actually resembles Nancy Lammeter, whose rule-bound life might threaten to make her seem like an automaton but whose selflessness and capacity for love save her from our condemnation—contrast Rosamond Vincy, to whom she is in other respects startlingly similar.

Comparable tensions reside in the novella's many prominent objects, which appear like its plot to reify Eliot's usual metaphorical method. Even the hard kernel of action at the center of *Silas Marner* is really an exchange of two things—golden curls and gold—between which Silas must learn the proper distinction. And less plot-bound objects offer related forms of incarnationalism. Consider the "brown earthenware pot" that Silas counts as "his most precious utensil." Even after it is "broken into three pieces," Silas "prop[s]" the "ruin" "in its old place as a memorial" (19–20; ch. 2).[4] Susan Stewart points to the breakage as "the opening of Silas's capacity for . . . true familiarity that is now no longer dependent upon the object, but internalized" (525), but it is just as important that the object is preserved. If "Janet's Repentance" concludes by insisting that Janet has "internalized" a more vibrant form of memorial to Tryan than the stone tablet in the churchyard, *Silas Marner* seems weirdly sympathetic to the need for material containers, even if they are now broken. Later, after Eppie arrives, the pot becomes absorbed into the hearth that it decorates:

> [Silas] loved the old brick hearth as he loved his brown pot—and was it not there when he had found Eppie? The gods of the hearth exist for us still; and let all new faith be tolerant of that fetishism, lest it bruise its own roots. (137; ch. 16)

The habitual affections formed by Silas in his dark years—whether for brown pot, brick hearth, "brownish web" (as the narrator describes his weaving) (20; ch. 2), or even golden coins—may be "fetishism," but they help prepare his heart (in good Positivist fashion) for Eppie's arrival and a new religion of human love.

This salutary side to habits and fetishes, to actions or things that are embodied but from which the ghost of the propelling ideas and motives have vanished, manifests itself in an even more literal fashion in the parable of Dolly Winthrop's lard-cakes.[5] "There's letters pricked on 'em," Dolly tells Silas, pointing out the "I. H. S." which she is surprised to discover the weaver can identify. "I can't read 'em myself," she admits,

> and there's nobody . . . rightly knows what they mean; but they've a good meaning for they're the same as on the pulpit-cloth at church. . . .
>   whativer the letters are, . . . it's a stamp as has been in our house, Ben says, ever since he was a little un. (79; ch. 10)

Just as "the interest or comprehension of" Amos Barton's parishioners "stop[s] short precisely at the point where [their] spiritual interpretation" might begin, Silas and Dolly are both "unable to interpret" the letters (a monogram for Jesus) (80; ch. 10). Yet in their bodily form as lard-cakes, those letters will nevertheless provide nourishment (albeit more to the eager child Aaron than to the rather more ascetic Silas). And as a gift between neighbors, they will nourish the spirit as well as the body. The scene reads less as a parody of the incarnationalism of the rite of communion than a humanist reinterpretation of it.

For all their emphasis on incarnation, *Scenes of Clerical Life* and *Silas Marner* both conclude in spaces that attempt and fail—or, perhaps better, refuse—to embody completely the spirits within. Superimposed, the two volumes' final effects resemble the conclusion of *Wuthering Heights*, where the sight of Catherine and Hareton's well-tended garden is overshadowed by intimations of spectral escapes from Cathy and Heathcliff's grave. Thus if Janet's breast holds the ghostly memory that Tryan's monument can but crudely approximate through its bare-bones inscription, it does so only for the duration of her lifetime. And if the safe realm of Eppie and Silas's happy home is finally "fenced with stones on two sides," it preserves an "open fence" at the front (176; Conclusion), as though to acknowledge not only the impossibility but also the stifling dangers of total containment.

Through these endings, Eliot implicitly addresses the two major concerns that (in addition to the many tropes and themes generally found in the early novels) I began by suggesting as links between *Scenes of Clerical Life* and *Silas Marner*. We see here the confrontation between the real (death, the outside world) and the ideal (Janet's memory, Eppie's Edenic garden) from which Eliot's fiction so frequently arises. But we also see Eliot's acknowledgment that too fleshy an embodiment, too permanent an enclosure, might limit the force of fiction. In fact, the ideal can serve as that which escapes "real" embodiment yet still facilitates literature's power to stimulate sympathy, a sympathy not so much of understanding, but one based on our sense of shared incomprehensibility, of shared otherness. As Eliot recognized, even the most solidly incarnate realism requires a destabilizing remnant of something else—call it lyricism or romance or fable or some "poor ghost" of an idea—to awaken the full potential of the human imagination.

NOTES

1 The works were published in a single volume in 1863, although for the Cabinet edition of 1878, George Eliot decided to issue *Silas Marner* alongside *Brother Jacob* and "The Lifted Veil."

2 Eliot also praises Riehl's work in this essay for offering a "conception of European society as incarnate history" (*Essays* 289).

3 Moments of confession prove climactic for Eliot's later characters, too: consider Hetty Sorrel, Rosamond Vincy, Gwendolen Harleth, and *Silas Marner*'s Godfrey Cass.

4 While Wordsworth's "Michael" supplies *Silas Marner*'s motto, the tale also reads like a comic version of "The Ruined Cottage," the poet's tragic account of a weaver's family's sufferings

at the hands of historical change during the
Napoleonic Wars, and Silas's shattered pot recalls "the useless fragments of a wooden bowl"
discovered by that poem's speaker, which similarly serve as a memorial.

5 "These things are a parable," the narrator of
Middlemarch famously declares when comparing Rosamond's egoism to the effects of a
candle in a pier-glass (248; ch. 27). Here the
"parable" really is a "thing."

REFERENCES

Carroll, David. *George Eliot and the Conflict of Interpretations*. Cambridge: Cambridge UP, 1992.

Cross J. W., *George Eliot's Life, As Related in her
Letters and Journals*. 3 vols. Boston: Dana Estes
& Company, n.d.

[Dallas, E. S.]. Rev. of *Silas Marner*. *The Times*
(London). 29 April 1861. 12.

Eliot, George. *Adam Bede*. Ed. Carol A. Martin.
Oxford: Oxford UP, 2008.

Eliot, George. *Essays of George Eliot*. Ed. Thomas
Pinney. New York: Columbia UP, 1963.

Eliot, George. *The George Eliot Letters*. Ed. Gordon
S. Haight. 9 vols. New Haven: Yale UP,
1954–78.

Eliot, George. *Middlemarch*. Ed. David Carroll.
Oxford: Oxford UP, 1998.

Eliot, George. *Scenes of Clerical Life*. Ed. Thomas A.
Noble. Oxford: Oxford UP, 2000.

Eliot, George. *Silas Marner*. Ed. Terence Cave.
Oxford: Oxford UP, 1996.

Kelley, Theresa. *Reinventing Allegory*. Cambridge:
Cambridge UP, 1997.

Knoepflmacher, U. C. *George Eliot's Early Novels:
The Limits of Realism*. Berkeley: U of California
Press, 1968.

Leavis, F. R. *The Great Tradition*. Garden City, NY:
Doubleday, 1954.

Nunokawa, Jeff. "The Miser's Two Bodies:
Silas Marner and the Sexual Possibilities of
the Commodity." *Victorian Studies* 36.3 (1993):
273–92.

Shuttleworth, Sally. *George Eliot and Nineteenth-
Century Science: The Make-Believe of a Beginning*.
Cambridge: Cambridge UP, 1984.

Smajic, Srdjan. "Supernatural Realism." *Novel* 42.1
(2009): 1–22.

Stewart, Susan. "Genres of Work: The Folktale and
Silas Marner." *New Literary History* 34.3 (2003):
513–33.

Wiesenfarth, Joseph. "Demythologizing *Silas Marner*." *ELH* 37.2 (1970): 226–34.

Yeazell, Ruth. *Art of the Everyday: Dutch Painting
and the Realist Novel*. Princeton: Princeton UP,
2008.

7

Adam Bede: History's Maggots

Rae Greiner

> The *Maggot Bites*, I must begin:
> *Muse!* Pray be civil! enter in!
> Ransack my addled *pate* with Care,
> And *muster* all the *Maggots* there!
>
> (Samuel Wesley, *Maggots*)

Commencing on 18 June 1799, its scenes pungent with wood shavings, Provence roses, and grassy milk, *Adam Bede* opens into the past. Early readers considered it a rural retreat, "a visit to Scotland *minus* the fatigues of the long journey," as Jane Welsh Carlyle wrote, a "crystal-clear, musical, Scotch stream" alongside whose banks one might in fancy lie to escape the "stagnant" landscape of the modern, urban South (17–18). And it looks back to Scotland in another way, reprising Sir Walter Scott's *The Heart of Mid-Lothian*, a tale of sisters, Jeanie and Effie Deans, embroiled in a family drama of illegitimate pregnancy, infanticide, and capital crime. As Scott had done in *Waverley*, Eliot sets her novel sixty years since, the span of a human lifetime. Like Scott, she draws for her material on recent history as well as ancient: the story of convicted child-killer Mary Voce, visited in prison by Elizabeth Evans, Eliot's Methodist aunt; Romantic poems of infanticide and despair, like Wordsworth's "The Thorn"; the pastoral and folkloric traditions; and, of course, the Greeks. Detailing the circumstances of Hetty Sorrel's crime, *Adam Bede* brings tragedy down to earth, and if *The Heart of Mid-Lothian* exaggerated the frequency of child-murder in the era it recounts, the desperate, unwed mother was once again of pressing concern in the wake

A Companion to George Eliot, First Edition. Edited by Amanda Anderson and Harry E. Shaw.
© 2013 John Wiley & Sons, Ltd. Published 2016 by John Wiley & Sons, Ltd.

of the 1834 New Poor Law, which drove her to commit violence against her children and herself.[1] William Burke Ryan's *Infanticide: Its Law, Prevalence, Prevention, and History* (1862) pictured an England littered with infant remains, polluting waters and moldering on land. More figuratively, infanticide in *Adam Bede* thematizes the relation between (female) artist and her literary offspring, along with its (mostly male) lineage. The pressures of generation are everywhere felt in Eliot's first full-length novel: in its complicated lines of inheritance, its concern over what will and ought to survive.

Early reviewers were so taken with *Adam Bede*'s realism as to pass over its shocking homicide, one of several aberrations in a novel otherwise as "matter-of-fact" as bread and sunshine: "the story is not a story," wrote Geraldine Jewsbury in the *Athenaeum*, "but a true account of a place and people who have really lived" (284). Realistically rendering "painstaking honest men" engaged in vital but underappreciated labor, *Adam Bede* portrayed subjects considered far less suitable for art than murder, ordinary people doing unremarkable things (Jewsbury 284.). Thus Eliot's spirited defense of her method in chapter 17, where she insists upon treating seriously the most pedestrian scenes of human life. That effort would remain a moral and aesthetic duty, but *Adam Bede* was faulted from the beginning for breaches against its own aims. "Consequences are unpitying," Mr. Irwine advises Hetty's seducer, Arthur Donnithorne; yet Hetty is issued a last-minute reprieve (156; ch. 16). In Jay Clayton's view, it is left to Thomas Hardy to correct that sentimental error by leading the murderous Tess to the gallows. Eliot "vitiates much of the novel's talk about the inescapable consequences of one's deeds by rescuing Hetty," he writes; "Hardy makes no such mistake" (51). For some, Hetty's rescue, as morally problematic, is akin to the narrator's problematic moralizing, most noticeably in chapter 15's juxtaposition of (bad) Hetty and her (good) cousin Dinah: each is antithetical to realism, betraying the novelist's too-heavy hand in controlling outcomes and directing judgment. Faulting its occasional lapses into the "melo-dramatic and traditional," Jewsbury suggests that the novel's "true genius" lay in what was "most natural," least strange: the less "startling, unequal or spasmodic," the better (284.).

Of course, the ordinary *was* strange. Prior to the mid-Victorian period, most literature had centered on aristocratic figures like Arthur, whose moral levity (along with that of his class) Eliot explicitly critiques. Yet *Adam Bede*'s empirically knowable, concrete reality provides the setting for a meditation on complex historical processes that are surprisingly odd and unpredictable. Historical reality, the novel tells us, can be transmitted through the medium of unknowing minds. Jewsbury captures something of this when she writes that England's "secret" strength lay not in men and women with "lyrically recognized name and fame," but in the "amount of worth that is *un*recognized, that remains dumb and unconscious of itself . . . with a certain honest stupidity that understands nothing but doing its best and doing its work" (284). It is to that class of humankind that Dinah prefers preaching, to those who "seemed to have their eyes no more filled with the sight of the Sabbath morning than if they had been dumb oxen that never looked up to the sky" (83; ch. 8). But unknowing, unfeeling Hetty will matter most to what follows, for her dim comprehension, unredeemed by honest work or emotional intelligence, is at once targeted for vicious attack and presented as a form of unconsciousness through which historical reality reveals itself. That most heartless of girls serves as a vehicle for what is most alive and least mundane in Eliot's world, sympathetic contact with humanity past, present, and future.

Equally surprising, the "maggot"—a minor trope in the novel, indicating a mind gripped by silly ideas—brings Eliot's close association of history and triviality into focus. Together, these figures of the dim and the common form a pattern of meaning and allusion extending through Scott to Samuel Wesley, father to John and Charles, the founders of Methodism, and to Mehetabel (called "Hetty"), a lovesick daughter.[2] For Wesley also authored *Maggots: or, Poems on Several Subjects, Never before Handled* (1685), a hudibrastic collection centered on small, animal subjects: "On the Grunting of a Hog"; "To the Laud of a Shock Bitch"; "On a Supper of Stinking Ducks." Among the least consequential of beings, the maggot is Wesley's muse, engineering both death and creation ("Sometimes *begetting*, sometimes *killing*," as the maggot says) ("Maggot" 69). It is also a powerful agent of history, communicating sentiment between the living and dead. When Wesley's maggot—with its capricious temporal movements, its combining of rude, even disgusting ordinariness with far grander claims about the nature of history—resurfaces in *Adam Bede*, it binds Eliot's primary interests, in the meager and quotidian, and in historical transmission, into a single project. As Harry Shaw has shown, the novel echoes the Apocrypha in recalling those "who have no memorial; who are perished, as though they had never been," but whose "seed shall remain for ever" (qtd. in Shaw 221). As we shall see, maggots preserve hidden things "become as though they had never been born" (qtd. in Shaw 221). As such, they are emblematic of Eliot's realism, which in *Adam Bede* combines local observation with historical processes rather less mundane. Afflicting both Hetty and Dinah, Eliot's maggots hold a singular promise: that perished remains course through us, that the past animates the real even through minds too feeble to know it.

***

Whether she is a "poor wandering lamb," the object of Dinah's compassion, or "the gillyflower on the wall," given to gazing vainly at herself in polished pewter, metal, and wood, Hetty is in many ways lost from the start (31; ch. 3, 41; ch. 4). A kind of infantile deadness defines her, an elemental heartlessness that, next to sociopaths—and kittens—only babies possess. Likening her to newborn animals and stone fruit, the novelist captures her hardness and softness at once. Martin Poyser thinks her "squashy," but to her aunt Hetty is a cherry, pit and all, heart "hard as a pebble" so that "there's nothing seems to give her a turn i' th' inside" (141; ch. 15). Given her beauty, it takes "a very acute personage" to suspect Hetty's hardness; we are "apt not to think of the stone" in the peach, the narrator remarks, and so "jar [our] teeth terribly against it" (139–40; ch. 15). The rock solidity of Hetty's insides, invisible to Adam, is relentlessly pointed out to readers. Cheeks unblushing, Hetty experiences "no thrill" when Adam draws near, feels "nothing when his eyes rested on her"; he doesn't "stir in her the emotions that make the sweet intoxication of young love" (90; ch. 9). Cousin Totty, her pink pockets jingling with Arthur's coin, is to Hetty more nuisance than maternal testing-ground. The novel treats these failures to love as grave moral and emotional shortcomings rather than the ordinary unfeeling of adolescence or unreciprocated desire. That Dinah feels no heat for Seth is chalked up to eccentricity, but Hetty, pink and white, is a hot-house flower, a plant without roots. As Dinah sees it, she has a "blank in [her] nature," an "absence of any warm, self-devoting love" whose most vivid proof is an infant buried alive (143; ch. 15).[3]

Eliot's commitment to a vision of sympathy as combining imagination and emotional amplitude explains why Hetty's mind is as narrow as her heart. Equipped with a bovine intellect, hers is a half life in more ways than one. Hetty hasn't read any novels, perhaps hasn't even seen one; "the words would have been too hard for her" (123; ch. 13). Her waking life scarcely differs from sleep, full as it is of childish imaginings, "fragmentary and confused" (146; ch. 15). Hers is "Hetty's World," an unreal landscape suffused by a "strange, happy languor"; head in the clouds, Hetty's mind is perpetually elsewhere (91; ch. 9). The gardener Craig woos her in a language of strawberries and "hyperbolic peas," for Hetty—animal, vegetable, mineral—seems a brainless being of minimal understanding, shot through with "trivial butterfly sensations," unable to think for herself (88; ch. 9, 227; ch. 22). Others step in to do Hetty's thinking, and, having had "all the business of her life . . . managed for her," she at her most despairing wants exactly that (333; ch. 36). Contemplating suicide, she buoys her spirits by hoping Arthur will "care for her and think for her"; failing this, unconsciousness becomes her "one relief" (329; ch. 35, 347; ch. 37). For some critics, this quality lessens the severity of her crimes, diminishing the distance between Hetty and the infant she kills. Her "amoeba-like unconsciousness of the world outside herself" partly exonerates Hetty, a "mindless victim" incapable of the advanced thought necessary for moral responsibility (Martin 760). A "case of arrested development," "mentally a child," Hetty is "a victim no matter what she may finally do" (Harris 180). Even Hetty cannot say, seems not to know, whether she killed her child. "I didn't kill it—I didn't kill it myself" she cries seconds after admitting, "I did do it . . . I buried it in the wood" (405; ch. 45).

Readers have thought Eliot mean-spirited toward the pretty butter-maker, vindictive in her portrayal of erotic joy, envious of Hetty's plump arms, blooming face. By contrast, Gillian Beer finds in Hetty's voluptuous physicality a condemnation of the fallen woman stereotype. But if she is vibrantly alive, it is mostly in an animal sense, one reason Hetty—tastier than one "Miss Bacon . . . who was called the beauty of Treddleston"—seems perpetually on the verge of slaughter (136; ch. 15). And there is another reason, having to do with the stupid confusion her presence evokes. Even calculating Adam goes soft where Hetty is concerned, "creat[ing] the mind he believed in out of his own" and seeing in Hetty a doting mother and wife (319; ch. 33). He's wrong of course, but he's not the only one. Mindless herself, Hetty projects a baffled mentality into which others are perpetually thrown. Not just men but "all intelligent animals, even . . . women" find themselves unable to turn away from her, a baby, a chit, a naughty little huzzy, a star-browned calf leading you on "a severe steeple-chase," into a mental fog (76–77; ch. 7). She is one of those downy, purring things whose obliviousness fascinates to the point of inciting violence. Eliot worries repeatedly that her words will be "of little use" in capturing the effect Hetty inspires (76; ch. 7). Unless you have "utterly forgotten yourself" in a beauty of that order, you will never understand Hetty's "divine charm" or the desire to stamp it out, an impulse "to crush for inability to comprehend the state of mind into which it throws you" (76–77; ch. 7).

The "state of mind" to which Hetty gives rise, in her fellow characters and in the reader, is central to *Adam Bede*, where, as Murray Krieger has shown, extreme tragic action is averted by way of diminished capacities, at least for some. By "attenuating the process by which [Adam] becomes aware" of the circumstances unfolding around him, Eliot "blunts the consequences of that awareness" (Krieger 211). Adam's slow comprehension of Hetty's betrayal, Arthur's deception, allows him to keep his first, angry impulses in check. Hetty, on the other hand, is just slow. Moreover, her stunted intellect appears to justify her community's response. As Susan Morgan writes, by putting "subhuman" Hetty "beyond the human pale," the people of Hayslope make no serious attempt to understand her actions; they "do not even realize there is any-thing to understand" (272–73). Fiercely resisting mortification as death drops down upon her, Hetty seems to realize what's at stake: "it was almost as if she were dead already, and knew that she was dead, and longed to get back to life again" (347; ch. 37). But it is too late. Frequently called a "thing" by the narrator, Hetty is now nearly a corpse. So, in her way, is Dinah. But where Dinah is "a lovely corpse into which the soul has returned charged with sublimer secrets and a sublimer lover," Hetty is "a beautiful corpse" deprived of "miserable consciousness" (144; ch. 15, 338; ch. 36). When, at the trial, the narrator gazes upon her as on "the corpse we love," her non-equivalence to Adam's long-held idea makes Hetty poignant: "it is the likeness, which makes itself felt the more keenly because something else *was* and *is not*" (387; ch. 43). Adam's view of the "pale hard-looking culprit" proves that others supply Hetty, whose "distractingly pretty looks" have always "meant nothing," with the tender meanings she otherwise lacks (387; ch. 43, 189; ch. 19). He sees "the Hetty who had smiled at him in the garden under the apple-boughs"; the woman in the courtroom is "that Hetty's corpse" (387; ch. 43).

Yet Hetty's hardness seems something more than a personal failing, or a develop-mentally primitive state to be swiftly outgrown, when we recall Dinah's bouts of oblivion, attributed to her having maggots in the brain. Indeed both are accused of harboring maggots—ordinarily a corpse's condition, but here meaning being dead set on outlandish whims, subject to wild, intractable ideas. Suspect thoughts burrow like maggots into the minds of the stricken, threatening to turn them imbecilic. It is difficult to bend maggot-headed people to one's will. According to Martin Poyser, "on'y tradesfolks" are bitten with Methodistical maggots, because exposed (and sus-ceptible) to faddish ideas; "you niver knew a farmer bitten wi' them maggots," he says (173; ch. 18). But secular maggots abound. When Poyser tells his wife of Hetty's notion to become a lady's maid, she responds, "I thought she'd got some maggot in her head" (305; ch. 31). This might be more proof of Hetty's fleeting intelligence, aware only of "the little history of her own pleasures and pains" (331; ch. 36). Yet the queer condition runs in the family, is what most makes Dinah her cousin's kin. "[T]oo much given to sit still and keep to [her]self," the intensely private Dinah is "greatly wrought upon" by thoughts outside her, to which she becomes determinedly fixed (82; ch. 8). Mrs. Poyser's efforts to persuade Dinah to remain at Hall Farm, living "comfortable, like other folks," meet with firm resistance, for Dinah's insides, like Hetty's, are hard to turn: "[i]f anything could turn her, *I* should ha' turned her," Aunt Poyser says (172; ch. 18). But Dinah does only what she sets her mind to do. "When there's a bigger maggot than usial in your head you call it 'direction,'" Aunt Poyser complains, but she might be describing unyielding, unresponsive Hetty instead: "and then nothing can stir you—you look like the statty o' the outside o' Treddles'on church, a-starin' and a-smilin' whether it's fair weather or foul" (73; ch. 6).

It seems, at first glance, there are good maggots and bad. Dinah's mind, radiating "the thought of God," is expansive, generous; sermons pour from her unbidden, "as the tears come," deeply moving in Eliot's cosmology because their meanings are, at base, affective, neither "beginning nor ending . . . in words" (82; ch. 8). Her maggots are of a divine, ego-nibbling variety. When Dinah says "it's my besetment to forget where I am and everything about me, and lose myself in thoughts that I could give no account of," we understand this self-effacement as a state to which Hetty never succumbs (82; ch. 8). One might object that Dinah hasn't any maggots, that what her aunt deems maggoty is evidence of something more like grace. Yet this language strongly echoes Eliot's description of the stupefied effect Hetty's beauty has on us: unless you have "utterly forgotten yourself in straining your eyes after the mounting lark, or in wandering through the still lanes when the fresh-opened blossoms fill them with a sacred, silent beauty," you cannot appreciate the experience involved, the "inability to comprehend the state of mind into which it throws you" (76–77; ch. 7). Dinah's description of being "greatly wrought upon" by forces beyond her power, her speech coming "without any will of [her] own," is very nearly repeated in defending Adam's susceptibility to Hetty's charms (82; ch. 8). "Is it any weakness," the narrator asks, "to be wrought upon by exquisite music?—to feel its wondrous harmonies searching the subtlest windings of your soul, the delicate fibres of life where no memory can penetrate, and binding together your whole being past and present in one unspeakable vibration . . .?" (319; ch. 33). "If not," she continues, "then neither is it a weakness to be so wrought upon by the exquisite curves of a woman's cheek and neck and arms"; for in such beauty we perceive "a far-off mighty love that has come near to us, and made speech for itself there," an "*impersonal* expression" surpassing "the one woman's soul that it clothes" (319; ch.33.). Barbara Hardy writes that Hetty's mind, anchored to experience, has "almost no generalizing power" (36), yet Hetty transmits "impersonal," "unspeakable" expressions unexplained by private subjectivity or experienced life. Conveying "far-off" notions between bodies, baffling

—

rationality, binding past immemorial with present: these are thoughts resembling maggots (82; ch. 8). Worming into others, body and soul, Hetty's is a maggot whose bite is sublime.

That maggot's prehistory is rooted in Methodism and aesthetics. Samuel Wesley considered the maggot his muse. The frontispiece to *Maggots* declares the poems therein the product *of* (not simply *about*) maggots, and written "Because while this foul Maggot bites / [the Author] nere Can rest in quiet" [Fig. 1]. In *The Life of Wesley* (1820), a book Eliot researched for *Adam Bede*, Robert Southey observed that the frontispiece depicts the artist "crowned with a laurel, and with a maggot on his forehead" (2: 269); more suggestively, W. H. Meredith saw in the image "a boy of about fourteen years, but with a face much older," on his brow "a good-sized maggot in the act of biting" (625). "On a Maggot," the title poem, confirms the association: "The *Maggot Bites*, I must begin: / *Muse!* Pray be civil! enter in! / Ransack my addled *pate* with Care, / And *muster* all the *Maggots* there!" (1–4). Yet Wesley's maggots do more than inspire poems. Emissaries of sentiment, they body forth the attitudes and emotions motivating human behavior. With a knack for sexual calamity, the maggot travels at warp speed—"Good *Folks* that Love your Necks, *stand clear!*/ For I must leap *five hundred Year*"—documenting its role in the romantic misadventures of Cleopatra, Dido, and Cupid, himself "a *Maggot* born" (48–49, 77). Literature, the maggot insists, is superior to traditional history in unearthing the sentimental forces driving historical action: "Twas I my self, 'twas I possest, / Scævola's mighty Brain, and Breast; / I was the *Worm in's Crown*, that made, / The *Hec. Porsenna's* camp invade," the maggot brags; or later, of Lucretia, "Pray let not *Livy's Shams* prevail! / I was the *Worm*, in *Pate*, and *Tail*: / That made the *Matron* bravely dye" (25–28, 44–46). These lines advance an (ostensibly silly) idea that philosophers like David Hume and Adam Smith later made legitimate: that history involves the narrative of forces unseen, the "sentiments or designs of men, which pass in their minds" (A. Smith 84).

That Wesley and John Dunton, his publisher and brother-in-law, made a living "composing elegies, epitaphs, and epithalamiums" (Southey 2: 269) helps explain their mutual fascination with "living death" and "waking dream" (Dunton 443). But *Maggots*, read widely, was widely lampooned, most famously by Alexander Pope, whose *The Dunciad* blames maggots for poor rhyme, bad similes, and meandering purpose.[4] By then, as J. Paul Hunter demonstrates, the maggot had become shorthand for expressing a specific aesthetic anxiety, an antagonism toward a "climate of receptivity to innovation for its own sake" (14). A symbol of the "false wit and downright silliness" thought to characterize the vogue for novelty, the maggot emblematized new, bad ideas and the new, bad forms being developed to express them (14). The English novel, among the newest and most maggoty, was one. As early as 1705, Dunton was insistent that writers could be original without falling prey to maggots. Of his "Living Elegy," Dunton writes, "some may think it a little *maggoty*, that I should come again from the Dead to write 'The History of my own Life'"; but, he urges, "cease to wonder at this," for "I have almost finished 'The Funeral of Mankind, or an Essay proving we are all dead and buried, with an Elegy upon the whole Race'" (xv). Such experimentation is ridiculous only to the arch defenders of aesthetic convention, while his "New and Surprising" approach is "far from being *maggoty*; for if a Man must be called a *maggot* for starting Thoughts that are *wholly new*, then farewell invention" (iv).

These objections notwithstanding, Dunton also suggests that the best ideas derive from maggots, outré conceptions resurrected from the grave and gaining credibility later on. "[F]or even Philosophy itself had never been improved, had it not been for new opinions, which afterwards were rectified by abler men, such as Norris and Locke," he writes; "and so the first notions were lost, and nameless, under new superstructures" (iv). Begrudgingly, Dunton had declared, if "my *Ideal Life* must pass for a *maggot*, I must own it my own pure maggot; the natural issue of my brain-pan, bred and born there"; yet he allows for the possibility that one man's maggots are the "lost, and nameless" fodder of future generations' cherished beliefs (xv–xvi). Outlasting the heads and times that house them, maggoty "first notions"—outlandish, discredited—are the invisible bedrock on which subsequent convictions are built (xv).

In looking back to Wesley's *Maggots*, Eliot might have discovered a figure for trivialities whose aesthetic potential and historic significance had been overlooked. As William Empson said, "one of the assumptions of pastoral"—a mode important to *Adam Bede*—is that "you can say everything about complex people by a complete consideration of simple people" (137). Consider Wesley's "On a Cheese: a Pastoral," whose young lovers, Amoretta and Strephon, muse upon "an *Embryo Cheese*" (73) out of which whole worlds are made:

> So the rising Vision shows,
> As when the World from Chaos rose.
> Then 'tis bruis'd, and prest till all
> The pale Tears around it fall.
> Thus when Jove intends to mould
> A Hero out of purer Gold,
> Hee'll shut him up in pain and Care,
> And like Alcides, pinch him there;
> 'Till he by kind Afflictions trod,
> Emerges, more than Half-a-God. (76–85)

Readers of the historian Carlo Ginzburg might hear echoes of the sixteenth-century heretic Menocchio—"miller, carpenter, sawyer, mason, and other things," as he described himself before being burned at the stake—who held the universe a cheese, God a worm living inside it (qtd. in Ginzburg 1). "[I]n my opinion, all was chaos," Menocchio explains, "and out of that bulk a mass formed—just as cheese is made out of milk—and worms appeared in it, and these were the angels," as was God, "he too having been created out of that mass at the same time" (qtd. in Ginzburg 6). The poem's vision of heroism born of affliction has clear resonances with *Adam Bede*, whose hero emerges a bruised but better man. In latter days, folks "who told Hetty Sorrel's story by their firesides" vividly recalled being moved by the "marks of suffering" in

Adam's face; Hetty, meanwhile, looks a "statue of dull despair" (386, 391; ch. 43). Hetty's hardness is given as the reason why her story folds into his in a communal memory dedicated to recalling and retelling Adam's pain. But the living statue is a figure for possession by maggots as well, a reminder that vital historic forces pulse through even the most mindless and hardest of heads. Oblivious herself, Hetty bodies forth history in a Carlylean (and Wesleyan) sense, wherein "the Present holds in it both the whole Past and the whole Future" (T. Carlyle 33). She is that "animating" device enabling the past to commune with the present, without which "we would have neither history nor elegy—only gibberish and unmarked graves" (Rosenberg 13).

Indeed Hetty's beautiful corpse teems with life of which she is unaware. In a remarkable passage, Eliot writes, "Hetty's face had a language that transcended her feelings," adding:

> There are faces which nature charges with a meaning and pathos not belonging to the single human soul that flutters beneath them, but speaking the joys and sorrows of foregone generations—eyes that tell of deep love which doubtless has been and is somewhere, but not paired with those eyes—perhaps paired with pale eyes that can say nothing; just as a national language may be instinct with poetry unfelt by the lips that use it. (258; ch. 26)

Hetty's face, Neil Hertz writes, "incarnates history": it is the "secular or esthetic equivalent of Dinah's trans-personal spirituality, which has its own (*super*natural) history" (105). As Daniel Cottom explains, Eliot "discover[ed] within the unconscious Hetty the discourse of universality upon which all her fiction was based" (166). We might recall the novel's opening image of condensation and long-distance travel: "With a single drop of ink for a mirror, the Egyptian sorcerer undertakes to reveal to any chance comer far-reaching visions of the past," Eliot writes; "This is what I undertake to do for you" with "this drop of ink at the end of my pen" (5; ch. 1). Now consider these lines, from Thoreau's *Walden*: "I sometimes despair of getting anything quite simple and honest done in this world by the help of men," Thoreau complains:

> They would have to be passed through a powerful press first, to squeeze their old notions out of them . . . and then there would be someone in the company with a maggot in his head, hatched from an egg deposited there nobody knows when, for not even fire kills these things, and you would have lost your labor. Nevertheless, we will not forget that some Egyptian wheat was handed down to us by a mummy. (17)

How thoughts enter our heads, move from one mind and generation to the next, is a question tied to the handing down of the seeds of culture, a transmission sometimes done by way of corpses—or by maggots, for not even fire kills these things, which neither time nor death destroys. *Adam Bede's* association of maggots with God and the angels, corpses with historical transmission, and these with both divine Dinah and her fleshly cousin, along with Scott's sisters Deans, purveyors of a fine Dunlop cheese: this concatenation of the rude, slow, earthy, and dumb with sublimity provides an early gloss on Eliot's developing moral-aesthetic sensibility, her insistence that minor things harbor greatness inside them. Thus alongside chapter 17's defense of Adolphus Irwine, Rector of Broxton, and so a turning away from "cloud-borne angels" in favor of "faithful pictures of a monotonous homely existence," are echoes of Samuel Wesley, Rector of Epworth, whose maggots drop in from nobody knows where, piercing the mundane stupidity through which even smart people pass much of ordinary life (161; ch. 17). Cottom writes that in *Adam Bede* (unlike later novels), Eliot adheres to "the methodology of natural history," is "guided not by theory or imagination, but by concrete observation" (xiii, 1). Yet in writing of those "concentrating" moments wherein feelings "scattered through the toilsome years" converge, binding "your whole being past and present," Eliot describes a phenomenon better explained by maggots than empirical science (319; ch. 33). Like drops of Egyptian ink, maggots compress human history into the imaginative forms through which the past, as Edwin Paxton Hood put it, is "perpetually renewed from age to age" (159).

"Worms have played a more important part in the history of the world than most persons would at first suppose" declared Charles Darwin in 1881. "Archaeologists ought to be grateful to worms," for "they protect and preserve for an indefinitely long period every object, not liable to decay, which is dropped on the surface of the land, by burying it beneath their castings" (308, 312). By the end of his career, the entire landscape of human accomplishment had become for Darwin an occasion for thinking about worms, that lowliest of creatures capable of producing "stupendous cumulative effects" (J. Smith 270). Turning the land with what Darwin deems intelligence, worms level the earth, whose whole surface "has passed, and will again pass, every few years through [their] bodies" (313). *Adam Bede* certainly emphasizes the benefits of long labor, including the husbanding of harsh soil, and Darwin's worms seem the zoological equivalent of Eliot's rough humanity, the dumb, unsung heroes of the age. Yet the novel also offers a less gradualist account of human truths unattainable by empiricism or the slow accumulation of metonymic detail. U. C. Knoepflmacher suggests that when, in *Middlemarch*, Eliot "puts on trial Lydgate's empiricist view of reality," the "imitative realism she had practiced in her earlier fiction" also stands accused (47–48). Yet like *Middlemarch*, *Adam Bede* "employs the literature of the sixteenth and seventeenth centuries as a model for its presentation of truth," just as (with "The Lifted Veil") it exonerates certain forms of obliviousness, which, when not sheltering us from the roar on the other side of silence, might provide strange modes of access instead (Knoepflmacher 55). Eliot wrote that the story of Mary Voce "lay in [her] mind for years and years as a dead germ, apparently—till time had made [her] mind a nidus in which it could fructify" as *Adam Bede* (*Letters* 3:175), her agrarian, developmental metaphor harboring the more miraculous suggestion that the mind preserves things, dead and buried, till a time when they can be newly hatched, "nidus" ("nest") the preferred scientific term for describing *not* soil but the animal-vegetable substance encasing maturing insects (including maggots) as they "work their way into life or action a second time," undergo "second birth" (John Hunter, *Essays* 438). Perhaps the

Figure 7.1 Samuel Wesley, *Maggots: or, Poems on Several Subjects*. London 1685, Typ, EC7 W5165 685m, Houghton Library, Harvard University.

greater miracle is that animal-vegetable Hetty now looks to be an emblem of Eliot's mind: incubating maggots, turning the historical imagination into food for worms.

NOTES

1 Gould writes, "[r]eports of 150 dead infants found in the city's streets during 1862 led *The Times* to lament that 'infancy in London has to creep into life in the midst of foes'" (26).

2 Unhappily married after an earlier engagement was broken off, Hetty Wesley penned an epitaph for herself in which she described the "living death" occasioned by her broken heart (qtd. in Southey 2:9).

3 Hetty possibly abandons a living child, hoping, as she says, that "somebody [might] find it" (405; ch. 45).

4 Pope writes: "Maggots half-form'd in rhyme exactly meet, / And learn to crawl upon poetic feet. / Here one poor word an hundred clenches makes, / and ductile dulness new meanders takes; / There motley Images her fancy strike, / Figures ill-pair'd, and Similes unlike" (61–66).

REFERENCES

Beer, Gillian. *George Eliot*. Brighton: Harvester, 1986.

Eliot, George. *Adam Bede*. Ed. Carol A. Martin. Oxford: Oxford UP, 2008.

Eliot, George. *The George Eliot Letters*. Ed. Gordon S. Haight. 9 vols. New Haven: Yale UP, 1954–78.

Carlyle, Jane Welsh. "JWC to George Eliot 20 Feb. 1859." *The Carlyle Letters Online*. Vol. 35. <carlyleletters@dukejournals.org>.

Carlyle, Thomas. *Past and Present*. London: Chapman and Hall, 1843.

Clayton, Jay. "The Alphabet of Suffering: Effie Deans, Tess Durbeyfield, Martha Ray, and Hetty Sorrel." *Influence and Intertextuality in Literary History*. Ed. Jay Clayton and Eric Rothstein. Madison: U of Wisconsin P, 1991. 37–60.

Cottom, Daniel. *Social Figures: George Eliot, Social History, and Literary Representation*. Minneapolis: U of Minnesota P, 1987.

Darwin, Charles. *The Formation of Vegetable Mould through the Action of Worms*. London: John Murray, 1882.

Dunton, John. *The Life and Errors of John Dunton, Citizen of London*. Vol. 1. London: J. Nichols, Son, and Bentley, 1818.

Empson, William. *Some Versions of Pastoral*. 6th ed. New York: New Directions, 1974.

Ginzburg, Carlo. *The Cheese and the Worms: The Cosmos of a Sixteenth-Century Miller*. Trans. John and Anne C. Tedeschi. Baltimore: Johns Hopkins UP, 1992.

Gould, Rosemary. "The History of an Unnatural Act: Infanticide and *Adam Bede*." *Victorian Literature and Culture* 25.2 (1997): 263–77.

Hardy, Barbara. *The Novels of George Eliot: A Study in Form*. London: Athlone, 1959.

Harris, Mason. "Infanticide and Respectability: Hetty Sorrel as Abandoned Child in *Adam Bede*." *English Studies in Canada* 9.2 (1983): 177–96.

Hertz, Neil. *George Eliot's Pulse*. Stanford: Stanford UP, 2003.

Hood, Edwin Paxton. *Thomas Carlyle, Philosophic Thinker, Theologian, Historian, and Poet*. London: James Clarke, 1875.

Hunter, J. Paul. *Before Novels: The Cultural Contexts of Eighteenth-Century English Fiction*. New York: Norton, 1990.

Hunter, John. *Essays and Observations*. Vol. 2. London: John van Voorst, 1861.

Jewsbury, Geraldine. "*Adam Bede*." *The Athenaeum* 1635 (26 Feb. 1859): 284.

Knoepflmacher, U. C. "Fusing Fact and Myth: The New Reality of *Middlemarch*." *This Particular Web: Essays on* Middlemarch. Ed. Ian Adam. Toronto: U of Toronto P, 1975. 43–72.

Krieger, Murray. *The Classic Vision: The Retreat from Extremity in Modern Literature*. Baltimore: Johns Hopkins UP, 1971.

Martin, Bruce K. "Rescue and Marriage in *Adam Bede*." *Studies in English Literature, 1500–1900* 12.4 (1972): 745–63.

Meredith, W. H. "Wesley's Maggots." *The Methodist Review* 15 (1899): 624–28.

Morgan, Susan. "Paradise Reconsidered: Edens without Eve." *Historical Studies and Literary Criticism*. Ed. Jerome J. McGann. Madison: U of Wisconsin P, 1985. 266–82.

Pope, Alexander. *The Works of Alexander Pope*. Vol. I. London: M. Cooper, 1743. English Poetry Online. <http://collections.chadwyck.com>

Rosenberg, John. *Elegy for an Age: The Presence of the Past in Victorian Literature*. London: Anthem, 2005.

Ryan, William Burke. *Infanticide: Its Law, Prevalence, Prevention, and History*. London: Churchill, 1862.

Shaw, Harry E. *Narrating Reality: Scott, Austen, Eliot*. Ithaca: Cornell UP, 1999.

Smith, Adam. *Lectures on Rhetoric and Belles Lettres. Works and Correspondence*. Vol. 4. Ed. J. C. Bryce and A. S. Skinner. Indianapolis: Liberty Fund, 1985.

Smith, Jonathan. *Charles Darwin and Victorian Visual Culture*. Cambridge: Cambridge UP, 2006.

Southey, Robert. *The Life of Wesley and Rise and Progress of Methodism*. 2 vols. New York: Evert Duyckink, 1820.

Thoreau, Henry David. *Walden*. 2nd ed. Ed. William Rossi. New York: Norton, 1992.

Wesley, Samuel. *Maggots; or, Poems on Several Subjects, Never Before Handled*. London: John Dunton, 1685. Early English Books Online.

8

The Mill on the Floss and "The Lifted Veil": Prediction, Prevention, Protection

Adela Pinch

Introduction: Beginnings and Endings

Both begun right around the time of the publication of *Adam Bede* in 1859, Eliot's second novel, *The Mill on the Floss*, and her gothic short story, "The Lifted Veil," are curiously intertwined. The earliest mention of the beginnings of *The Mill on the Floss* appears in Eliot's journal on 12 January 1859. "We went into town today and looked in the Annual Register for cases of *inundation*," she noted, making clear that the plan for the flood at the end of the novel, for which so many readers have found themselves catastrophically unprepared, was present from the beginning (*Journals* 76; emphasis in original). By March or April she had drafted the first several chapters of the novel: it had a beginning, an ending, but no middle.

The mystery concerns what happened next. Eliot put aside her work on *The Mill on the Floss*, and wrote "The Lifted Veil." Her journal entry for 26 April 1859 notes: "Finished a story—'The Lifted Veil'—which I began one morning at Richmond, as a resource when my head was too stupid for more important work" (*Journals* 77). The next day, she resumed her work on *The Mill on the Floss*, completely rewriting the first two chapters, and then researching and drafting the rest at an astonishingly accelerating pace. Eliot wrote the last words on 21 March 1860, sent it off to her publisher, and set off on a much-anticipated trip to Italy with her partner George Henry Lewes the next day.

Given the story of the intertwined writing of *The Mill on the Floss* and "The Lifted Veil," it has been compelling to think of the two as fitting together like pieces of a

A Companion to George Eliot, First Edition. Edited by Amanda Anderson and Harry E. Shaw.
© 2013 John Wiley & Sons, Ltd. Published 2016 by John Wiley & Sons, Ltd.

puzzle: two pieces of unequal size, "The Lifted Veil" as the little, jagged, dark piece. It has been irresistible, that is, to see the writing of that short story as having enabled George Eliot—after an aborted or false beginning to her novel—to have begun *The Mill on the Floss* again, and to bring it to completion. This possibility has seemed as perplexing as it is alluring: how could the gothic horror story about clairvoyance and blood-transfusion have anything to do with the intense, emotional, yet fundamentally realist novel? "The Lifted Veil" has been read variously as "a sort of dumping ground" for dark emotions stemming from events in the author's life in 1859—the pain of her brother's rejection, her sister's death, anxieties about public controversy about her unconventional life and her authorial identity—that needed to be "exorcized" through writing before *The Mill on the Floss* could proceed (Bodenheimer 134). As Eliot's only fiction narrated in the first person, "The Lifted Veil" has been viewed as a place where the author worked out a mode of self-representation before writing the novel that is most clearly drawn on, in transmuted forms, her own life (Swann; Hertz), and anxieties about female authorship (Gilbert and Gubar). Pessimistic about the virtue of sympathy and the knowledge of other minds, "The Lifted Veil" has been seen as a skeptical counter-balance to, or crash test dummy for, some of the key philosophical values embodied in *The Mill on the Floss* and Eliot's later novels (Albrecht; Greiner).

Compelling as such interpretations are, however, it is impossible to know whether there was actually a relationship of cause and effect between the writing of "The Lifted Veil" and the successful completion of *The Mill on the Floss*. However, we can certainly use the intertwined origins of these fictions to intertwine our understandings of them, using one work to illuminate the other. Chronologically, "The Lifted Veil" is embedded inside *The Mill on the Floss*. But in what follows the embedded text will be used to frame a crucial way of reading the larger novel; and in what follows, there will be a shift away from beginnings—and stories of beginnings—to endings, as well as a shift away from the writer's experiences to the reader's. Both the story and the novel are fictions fundamentally and unusually oriented around their endings, and around the ways in which the ends of fictions loom as their characters' futures. "The Lifted Veil"'s opening line is: "The time of my end approaches" (3); Maggie Tulliver in *The Mill on the Floss* asks: "'How long will it be?'" (649; bk. 7, ch. 5). Both written in a year in which George Eliot felt that "the weight of my future life . . . presses upon me almost continually" (*Letters* 3:170), *The Mill on the Floss* and "The Lifted Veil" explore the resources in and of fiction for orienting life and literature toward the future.

The Future in "The Lifted Veil"

Different in genre and mood from anything else Eliot wrote, "The Lifted Veil" is a tale of supernatural powers. The first-person narrator, Latimer, describes—for a reader he imagines in the future after his death—his sensitive, morbid childhood, his early loss of his mother, his strained relations with his wealthy father and his indifferent older brother, his aborted scientific education. A childhood illness in Geneva leaves him with strange mental powers: first visions of the future, and then the ability to read the thoughts of people around him. After his brother's death, Latimer marries the brother's fiancée, the cold, inscrutable Bertha, whom he loves precisely because her thoughts alone are hidden from him, in spite of his clairvoyant knowledge that in the future she will come to hate him. Indeed, after their marriage, the veil hiding her thoughts is lifted. The story culminates in an outlandish episode in which Bertha's dead servant, Mrs. Archer, is fleetingly brought back to life by a blood transfusion, and in her brief return to life reveals Bertha's plan to murder her husband. Like Mary Shelley's *Frankenstein*, Eliot's venture into gothic fiction allowed her not only to experiment with narrative technique, but also to explore contemporary debates in science and pseudo-science: about psychological phenomena, vivisection, and medicine (Flint; Menke).

It is important, however, to discriminate among Latimer's mental powers. His ability to know the minds of others has received the most critical attention, because it seems a power so close to that of the omniscient narrator of the psychological realist novel as Eliot was developing it. But "The Lifted Veil" presents Latimer's mind-reading powers as a subset of a larger, broader power: seeing into the future. His first freaky experiences include a hallucinogenic vision of Prague, which corresponds exactly to his visit to that city several pages later (8–9, 23), and a preview of his first meeting with Bertha, which is also realized one page later (11, 12). His ability to see into minds unfolds from there: "My prevision of incalculable words and action proved it to have a fixed relation to the mental process in other minds," he says (13). The forecasting dimension of Latimer's powers has on the whole received less critical attention than has the mind-reading (exceptions include Swann; Hertz), perhaps because it seems less philosophically rich, more preposterous and crystal-ball-ish than does an engagement with the problem of other minds. However, to recognize the ways in which "The Lifted Veil" subordinates mind-reading to future-casting might shift the ways in which we interpret this gothic tale's potential for helping us understand George Eliot's writing by helping us think about the pull of the future in her narrative art.

In "The Lifted Veil" George Eliot rattles our sense that the primary verb tense of fiction is the past tense, that fiction is about the conferral of the reality-effect of the past tense on things that never happened. The opening paragraphs of "The Lifted Veil" describe what never happened but also what hasn't yet happened. It is an account of what will happen "one month from this day" of the time of narration: "For I foresee when I shall die, and everything that will happen in my last moments" (3). The opening page takes Latimer right to the brink, modulating into the present tense: "Darkness—darkness—no pain—nothing but darkness; but I am passing on and on through darkness; my thought stays in the darkness, but always with a sense of moving onward. . . ." (3; ellipsis in original). At the end of the story, after the retrospective narration that makes up the body of "The Lifted Veil," the narration returns to this moment on the brink of death: "It is the 20th of September 1850. I know these figures I have just written, as if they were a long familiar inscription. I have seen them on this page in my desk unnumbered times, when the scene of my dying struggle has opened upon me . . . " (43; ellipsis in original). What is most striking about comparing the two passages just quoted is their similarities, not their differences. That is, while we may be tempted to read the latter utterance as taking place right in the moment of death itself, the play of verb tenses and markers in both utterances do not make clear that Latimer has "really" arrived in the future at the end. The present tense of "it is the 20th of September" was present in the future-casting version at the beginning as well. The "now" of the end may not be the real future, or the future finally arrived at in the present, but another future-casting vision of this moment, which has been repeated "unnumbered" times. The undecidability of the time in the story at the end, of whether a month has "really" transpired in the story since the opening frame, of course makes us aware that the only real present is the "now" of narrative discourse, and above all the now of reading, "this page" coming to signify not the page Latimer has written, but the page we are reading (Swann 53).

"The Lifted Veil"'s revelation of the centrality of the future to the time frame of fiction may be further underscored by the ways in which Latimer and his creator take pains to naturalize his visions of the future, as if his presentiments of the future are not that different from those of ordinary mortals. First of all, his previsions seem highly selective. Unless we attribute to him unusual levels of deliberate withholding of information, Latimer seems to have had, for example, no idea what was to transpire at Mrs. Archer's deathbed. Such a highly fallible clairvoyant narrator reinforces our sense that it is the author herself who is the only person who can see around a fiction's future corners. Like ordinary mortals, Latimer finds himself looking back and wishing that he "could have had a foreshadowing" of other events, lamenting "that if I had foreseen something more or something different," things would have worked out differently (21). Freaky as his powers are, he appeals to his readers to recognize an affinity between his own glances into the future, and their own: "Yet you must have known something of the presentiments that spring from insight at war with passion; and my visions were only like presentiments intensified to horror" (21). His future-castings, Latimer suggests, are only intensified versions of the ordinary presentiments, forebodings, and fearful obsessions about the future that are part of life, and, according to *The Mill on the Floss* (as we shall see) part of love: " 'love gives insight,' " Philip Wakem tells Maggie, " 'and insight often gives foreboding' " (429; bk. 5, ch. 3).

The notion that forecasting the future is akin to ordinary modes of thinking is an idea that finds support in several important sources in George Eliot's intellectual milieu. Eliot was enormously influenced by her friend and early intellectual mentor Charles Bray's *Philosophy of Necessity* (1841). Bray's "law of consequences"—the principle that all events are necessitated by the conditions that precede them—tethers future outcomes closely to present causes (1:166). In October 1859, Eliot was reading Auguste Comte's *Catechism of Positive Religion,* just translated by her neighbor Richard Congreve (*Journals* 81), in which Comte predicts the logical outcome of the practice of the principles of Positivism in a future in which the religion of Humanity replaces all other religion. In Comte's religion of Humanity, a "Positive conception of the future life" is one in which individuals live on through collective bonds (Comte 104). In the early 1850s Eliot had herself contemplated writing a book to be called *The Idea of a Future Life*, influenced by Feuerbach's *The Essence of Christianity*, which interprets the Christian idea of the future life as simply an imaginative extrapolation of the present: "The future life is this life once lost, but found again, and radiant with all the more brightness for the joy of recovery . . . it is the beauteous present intensified" (Feuerbach 237). Neil Hertz notes that in this conception, the future resembles fiction itself: in turning to the writing of fiction in the later 1850s, he suggests, Eliot had found another way to write books about the idea of a future life (57). In Eliot's intellectual world, in other words, there was a perhaps unusually high interest in, and optimism about, the knowability of the future. Both "The Lifted Veil," and *The Mill on the Floss*, however, derive a great deal of their pathos from the ways in which a commitment to predicting the future renders ever more acute an inability to prevent it.

Predicting the End in *The Mill on the Floss*

To think about *The Mill on the Floss* is to think about its catastrophic ending, in which Maggie and Tom Tulliver are swept to their deaths in a flood of the river Floss that smashes the mill and destroys parts of the town of St. Oggs. It is the single biggest interpretive issue in the novel, and the thing that creates an enormous gulf between an innocent first reading, and a second reading. Any subsequent reading is dominated by the intense gravitational pull of the ending, and a sense of dread and helplessness in the face of coming disaster. It could be objected that *The Mill on the Floss* shares this with any tragic dramatic or narrative work, and indeed theories of tragedy have always loomed large in critical discussions of this novel, from contemporary reviews to more recent assessments of the novel in light of Eliot's own writing on Greek tragedy (Carroll 121–22; Bonaparte). But the dread and helplessness of the repeat reader as she feels herself sucked towards the end of *The Mill on the Floss* is distinctive for at least two reasons. One is the fact that the tragic conclusion involves a sudden and massive natural disaster, which extracts a tragic outcome from any causal chain of human agency among the characters, and pins it to authorial choice. The other reason involves genre. Tom and Maggie Tulliver are protagonists of a *Bildungsroman*, the genre whose plot tracks the growth and development of a literary character from childhood. While *The Mill on the Floss* was certainly not the only tragic *Bildungsroman*, or anti-*Bildungsroman* (Fraiman), the way it demands the witnessing of the proximity of development of children to destruction brings special pain.

These factors may explain why there has been such vigorous debate, since the novel's publication, about whether the tragic ending of *The Mill on the Floss* is justified, or sufficiently prepared for. An early reviewer complained that right up to the end, the novel's "development is languid and struggling," and, using the novel's own persistent water imagery: "the slow, placid, and somewhat turbid stream too suddenly changes to a rushing waterfall; the canal ends in a cascade" (Carroll 139). The Victorian novelist Edward Bulwer-Lytton explicitly contrasted the novel to the standard of classical tragedy: "The Tragic should be prepared for and seem to come step by step as if unavoidable. But that is not the case here" (Carroll 121–22). On the other side are readers who have either seen the tragic ending as completely woven into the fabric of the novel as a whole, or viewed the particularly shocking nature of the ending as entirely necessary. Over the past thirty years, the most eloquent voices expressing the latter view have been feminist critics, who have read the novel's ending as a woman novelist's indictment of the limited plots available in the European literary tradition for female characters such as Maggie (Miller 47); as a symbolic, liberating upwelling of female desire and power (Beer 101–03); or as Eliot's drastic symbolic sacrifice of her character's unconventional life so that she could live, and write, her own (Jacobus 252). The feeling that Eliot engaged in some kind of violent, willful, premeditated sacrifice of her character hangs heavy throughout Eliot criticism, and indeed can be perhaps detected in a remark she made assenting to some of the criticism of her poor pacing in the novel. "My love of the childhood scenes made me linger over them," she wrote, "so that I could not develop as fully as I wished the concluding book in which the tragedy occurs, and which I had looked forward to with *attentive premeditation*" (*Letters* 3:374; emphasis added).

Having begun her work on the novel researching "cases of *inundation*" (*Journals* 76; emphasis in original), Eliot had indeed premeditated the end from the beginning; it was no last-minute sacrifice. But the letter just quoted—with its language of authorial love, development, and "attentive premeditation"—may help us be attentive to the kinds of intimations of the end there are in *The Mill on the Floss*. Far from failing to prepare readers for the ending, there is in fact plenty of forecasting, some of a surprisingly unsophisticated nature. Some of it is voiced by the novel's most unsophisticated character: the unimaginative, bewildered Mrs. Tulliver. "'Maggie, Maggie,'" she nags, "'where's the use o' my telling you to keep away from the water? You'll tumble in and be drownded some day, an' then you'll be sorry you didn't do as your mother told you'" (61; bk. 1, ch. 2). "'They're such children for the water, mine are,'" she says of both Maggie and Tom: "'they'll be brought in dead and drownded some day'" (166; bk. 1, ch. 10). Both Mrs. Tulliver and her sister Mrs. Glegg at different times seriously jump the gun, rushing to the conclusion that Maggie has drowned long before she does (90; bk. 1, ch. 5; 629; bk. 7, ch. 3).

Mrs. Tulliver's utterances function as a species of what scholars of narrative call *prolepsis*: narrative devices by which an author flashes forward to what will be coming down the road (Genette 67–71). Moreover, this species of prolepsis, in which a character within the story itself seems to predict what will happen in it ("homodiegetic prolepsis," Genette 71), can seem ridiculously artificial, even embarrassing in the work of so sophisticated a novelist (D. A. Miller 220). The likelihood that we will view Mrs. Tulliver's utterances as a clumsy narrative device is utterly dependent on our assessment of her character: provincial, limited, unprophetic. We can sharpen our

sense of the unusual awkwardness of Mrs. Tulliver as an instrument of narrative prolepsis by contrasting her utterances to the prophetic utterances of other Eliot characters. In "The Lifted Veil," Latimer's prophetic utterances are integrated into who he
is as a character and as a narrator. Later Eliot characters who seem gifted with foresight,
such as the visionary mystic Mordecai in *Daniel Deronda*, similarly strike us as characters whom the novelist has fully vested with special powers. By contrast, Mrs. Tulliver's homely prophecies can be seen as rudimentary examples of what Roland Barthes
termed "the completeness" ("*la completude*") of even the most sophisticated realist
novels, the way they seem to contain archaic forms of story-telling that put a premium
on everything in the story "matching up," thus creating a kind of surplus of meaning
through which all the parts of the fiction legitimate each other (D. A. Miller 221;
Barthes 112, 85–86).

Mrs. Tulliver's predictions, then, contribute to our sense of *The Mill on the Floss* as
a novel in which literary realism—including the painstaking evocation of the social
contexts that determine the limited world view of a provincial woman such as Mrs.
Tulliver—works in tandem with narrative events, forces, and effects that feel archaic,
elemental. As one earlier reviewer put it, such aspects of *The Mill on the Floss* "seem
to crop out of the rich culture of [Eliot's] mind like the primitive rocks of an earlier
world . . . vestiges of a Titanic time, before the reign of the peaceful gods commenced"
(Carroll 143). We can further specify the role of Mrs. Tulliver's utterances in the fabric
of the novel by focusing on them as instances of a particularly powerful, perhaps
"primitive," but certainly "rich" mental phenomenon. While the sophisticated reader
may instantly decode Mrs. Tulliver's utterances as a narrative device, those utterances
are also instances of psychological phenomena that George Eliot was extremely interested in, not only in *The Mill on the Floss* but also in her later novels: forms of magical
thinking.

In *The Mill on the Floss*, as elsewhere, Eliot is highly attentive to the psychology of
magical thinking: forms of wishful thinking attended by a belief, or at least a hope,
that thinking about something might make it happen—or not happen. In *Daniel
Deronda*, for example, Eliot asks for a toleration of Gwendolen Harleth's belief that
her thinking has killed her husband: her belief, while irrational, is a valuable index
of moral growth. Magical thinking is often wishful thinking about the future, such
as the "mirage" of future glory that Maggie Tulliver paints on "the desert of
the future" (380; bk. 4, ch. 3), Rosamond Vincy's tendency to "rapid forecast" in
Middlemarch, or Hetty Sorrel's dreams of her future as a great lady in *Adam Bede*
(Gettelman 29). In contrast to these more common, self-flattering, and obviously
consoling forms of magical thinking, Mrs. Tulliver's predictions that Maggie will
drown—especially when she utters them, not to Maggie in warning but to herself
"without reflecting that there was no one to hear her"—are instances of apotropaic
magic (166; bk. 1, ch. 10). They are, that is, instances of the way our minds rush
forward to imagine the worst in the hope that the worst, therefore, will be warded
off. Eliot's own term for this kind of thinking is "foreboding," and in *The Mill on the
Floss*, foreboding is not only associated with love ("love gives insight, and insight

often gives foreboding"); but it is also the defining prerogative of adulthood—and in particular, parenthood. In one of the novel's many celebrated utterances about the perspectivelessness of childhood, Eliot notes: "While the possible troubles of Maggie's future were occupying her father's mind, she herself was tasting only the bitterness of the present. Childhood has no forebodings, but then, it is soothed by no memories of outlived sorrow" (145; bk. 1, ch. 9).

Lines such as Mrs. Tulliver's "They'll be brought in dead and drownded some day," in other words, partake of a perverse, through surprisingly common, folk-psychology particular to parenthood: that we can protect our children from the worst by imagining it for them instead. As fatalistic as they sound, such lines may be thought of as a kind of death line that is really a kind of lifeline for both parent and child, a sentence designed to serve as rope with lifesaver tied to the end. We can find mordant, parental magical thinking in the diary that George Eliot's contemporary novelist, and admirer, Elizabeth Gaskell kept of the first years of her first child's life. The diary is full of these kind of death-line/life-line sentences that express simultaneously the need for vigilant attention to signs of danger in the child, the need to prepare herself for the possibility of the child dying, and the wishful thinking that, in attending and writing about this possibility, she could prevent it. "Death," Carolyn Steedman comments, "its nervous anticipation, and the taming of it by evocation were the regular apostrophes of her diary" (Steedman 64). Both Eliot's and Gaskell's emphasis on a kind of parental attentiveness that is inseparable from apotropaic foreboding suggests that such thinking is as integral a part of parental care as feeding and clothing.

To think of Mrs. Tulliver's dire predictions for Maggie and Tom in this context presents us with some interesting interpretive possibilities. It might seem that the two possibilities outlined thus far—seeing her predictions either as a clumsy narrative device to prepare the reader for tragedy, or as instances of a superstitious but common form of parental care—pose a stark choice, like an optical illusion that forces you to see a picture of either a rabbit or a duck. It is a choice between reading at the level of what narratologists call the "discourse"—the choices and activities of the storyteller—or at the level of what they call "the story"—the events and circumstances, including characters, being described (Culler). But the emotions that cling to the level of discourse and the level of story are never quite as distinct as the narratologists make them out to be. As readers, we may register Mrs. Tulliver's utterances as belonging to both registers at once, coloring each other: the narrative device of prolepsis borrows some of the psychological and emotional weight of parental magical thinking.

To make such a link between narrative function and parent-child relations may seem uncomfortably close to suggesting that George Eliot viewed her novels as her children. There is actually some evidence that she did: she referred in a letter to *The Mill on the Floss* as her "youngest child," and George Henry Lewes described her writing of the novel as a form of parental care: rocking the cradle of the "new 'little stranger'" (*Letters* 3:335, 117). Furthermore, reaching the end of *The Mill on the*

Floss was intimately bound up with her anticipation of a new future that involved parenthood (Bodenheimer 192–99). Throughout the time of the writing of *The Mill on the Floss,* Eliot was assuming a new role, via letters, as a virtual stepmother to George Henry Lewes's three sons, all away at boarding school: at this moment they were her "dream children"—as the nineteenth-century essayist Charles Lamb famously described imaginary children—forged in a relationship through writing, hovering between present and future for her. As she raced to finish the novel, Eliot was preparing for a journey which would involve meeting the boys for the first time; one of them was to come live with them. "I hope my heart will be large enough for all the love that is required of me," she confided to a friend (*Letters* 3:232).

Critics, biographers, and ordinary readers wishing to connect *The Mill on the Floss* to Eliot's life have overwhelmingly stressed its relation to her past, and the novel's emphasis in general on history and memory. Set in Lincolnshire in the decades after the Napoleonic Wars, *The Mill on the Floss* both commemorates the slow disappearance of a pre-industrial way of life and evokes Eliot's own childhood. Clearly based on the author's close but painful relationship with her own brother, Isaac Evans, the evocation not only of the relationship between Maggie and Tom Tulliver, but also of the joys and pains of childhood, have been viewed by critics as responses to the Romantic poet William Wordsworth's modes of making poetry out of memory (Homans). But emphasizing the connections between the end of *The Mill on the Floss* and events in the author's future life allows us to think about the ways in which the novel is oriented around the future, rather than the past.

More significant than these associations between writing, parenthood, and the idea of a future life, may be the way the curiously parental nature of prefiguring endings resonates throughout *The Mill on the Floss.* Metaphors evoking parental care and anticipation are structured into the fabric of the novel, attaching to characters in often unexpected ways. For example, near the end of the novel, when Maggie's hopes for a meeting with her cousin Lucy—a meeting she both longs for and dreads—are dashed by the news that Lucy has already left town, Eliot compares Maggie's feelings to the feelings of "those who have known what it is to dread their own selfish desires as the watching mother would dread the sleeping potion that was to still her own pain" (641; bk. 7, ch. 4). In this complex metaphor, care for others is modeled on the excruciating vigilance of the mother who stays up watching over a perhaps sick child, a mother whose worst fear seems to be that she might choose sleep over vigilance: a vigilance about vigilance. That this metaphor is about Maggie Tulliver—so often the object of others' worries—underscores the extent to which *The Mill on the Floss* revolves around anticipating future calamity as a form of care, a desire to protect. And while *The Mill on the Floss* seems to cast vigilant, foreboding thinking as a form of protection and care for others, the question of who is protecting whom is always shifting. For example: as the flood waters of the Floss rise during the final, fatal night, Maggie is awake while others sleep, and becomes extraordinarily active, surprising some of those she seeks to help, including Tom Tulliver's friend Bob Jakins:

The fact that Maggie had been up, had waked him, and taken the lead in activity, gave
Bob a vague impression of her as one who would help to protect, not need to be protected. (650; bk. 7, ch. 5)

Who is the protector, and who is the protected? Who is the imaginer and who is the
imagined? The tragedy of *The Mill on the Floss* is that, while it casts thinking ahead
and narrative prolepsis as forms of love and protection, those actions also make events
happen, and hasten Maggie ineluctably toward her tragic future.

Conclusion: Development, Reading, and the Futures of *The Mill on the Floss*

The Mill on the Floss is unique, even among tragic *Bildungsromane,* in its evocation of
the inherent proximity of development to devolution. Though Eliot read Darwin's
Origin of the Species in 1859 during its composition, the novel unfurls a version of
evolution without evolutionism's typical commitment to progress: "development, for
George Eliot, also entails loss" (Shuttleworth 53). There are precedents for *The Mill
on the Floss*'s embrace of development and decay in other arenas of Victorian science
as well, such as cell theory and physiology, which intuited that, at the level of the
individual organism, the ultimate trend of individual growth was its own individual
extinction. *The Mill on the Floss*, and other theories of development that express development's elegiac side, confront what *Bildung* can look like from the point of view not
of the one developing, but of the looker-on: the hard, unstoppable fact that "a child
grows up, and goes away" (Steedman x).

In *The Mill on the Floss*, one important aspect of *Bildung,* formal education, gets a
pretty mixed report card (Homans; Jacobus), and Maggie's own most significant
experience of book learning is one in which she only learns half the lesson, missing
its "inmost truth" (384; bk. 4, ch. 3). Accidentally coming across the medieval mystic
Thomas à Kempis's book of meditations, *The Imitation of Christ,* Maggie half-learns
its lesson of self-renunciation: she throws herself enthusiastically into what seems to
her a heroic life of self-denial without embracing the hard truth, that "renunciation
remains sorrow" (384; bk. 4, ch. 3). This episode of reading is designed to illustrate
Maggie's passionate nature, and to protest against the limited possibilities for a young
woman coming of age in the world of *The Mill on the Floss,* a world in which self-denial
might appear a rational choice. But in this description of an encounter between
a book and a reader, the deck seems overwhelmingly stacked against the reader: the
book itself appears more uncanny, more genuinely creepy, than anything in the gothic
"The Lifted Veil." The "little, old, clumsy" copy of *Imitation of Christ* that falls into
Maggie's hands seems strangely alive:

It had the corners turned down in many places, and some hand, now for ever quiet, had
made at certain passages strong pen and ink marks, long since browned by time. Maggie
turned from leaf to leaf and read where the quiet hand pointed. . . . She went on from

one brown mark to another, where the quiet hand seemed to point, hardly conscious that she was reading—seeming rather to listen to a low voice. (382, 383; bk. 4, ch. 3)

Pushing out of the past and into what is its future—Maggie's present—this old book seems to compel her, "with all the hurry of an imagination that could never rest in the present," to imagine a strange future for herself (384; bk. 4, ch. 3).

The futures of all books lie in the hands of readers. Maggie—with that "hurry of an imagination that could never rest in the present"—does know that to read a novel is to be engaged in hurrying forward and forecasting the novel's end. This is what she does with Sir Walter Scott's *The Pirate* and with Madame de Staël's *Corinne*: she predicts the endings (401; bk. 5, ch. 1; 432; bk. 5, ch. 4). Maggie cannot tolerate the unhappy futures she forecasts for Scott's and de Staël's heroines: for the former she invents an alternative future; for the latter she refuses to read on. The future is indeed an often intolerable place, for novel characters, and for novel readers. In a short story called "Brother Jacob," George Eliot alludes to the "heroes" of certain novels by the French writer Honoré de Balzac, "whose foresight is so remarkably at home in the future" (56). It is hard to know what Eliot means by this. What would it mean for foresight to be "at home" in the future? Does it just mean foresight that turns out to be right? In "The Lifted Veil," Latimer is someone whose foresight is right, but nothing about him seems at home in the future, or anywhere else. But the people who are at home in a book's future are its readers. *The Mill on the Floss's* future began when it fell into the hands of readers, and continues to do so. For readers of *The Mill on the Floss*, there is no "quiet hand" making little brown marks to point us to the moral, to lift for us the veil that reveals meaning, or to draw a veil for us over the painful parts. But just as we can, if we wish, speculate about the origins of *The Mill on the Floss*, we can speculate on its futures—including its futures that are already past.

The Mill on the Floss's impact on the development of its readers, particularly of generations of nineteenth- and twentieth-century women intellectuals, has been enormous. For example: the French philosopher, novelist, and feminist Simone de Beauvoir was bowled over by Eliot's novel at the age of eleven, and returned to it again and again. In her eighties, she discussed with her biographer what *The Mill on the Floss* had meant to her. Her biographer summarizes:

> It was somehow comforting to read and reread that Maggie Tulliver had no control over the circumstances of her life and her tragic death. It helped Simone de Beauvoir to deal with her own adolescence and to accept how little control she had over it. (Bair 71)

The Mill on the Floss also prompted Simone de Beauvoir to imagine a future as a writer (De Beauvoir 148). Somehow Eliot's novel made it possible for this reader to tolerate the pain of reading tragic endings that seem scripted from the beginning. Perhaps learning this—and learning to tolerate responsibility for oneself and for others, but also to tolerate the painful limits of that responsibility—is the best development anyone can make.

References

Albrecht, Thomas. "Sympathy and Telepathy: The Problem of Ethics in George Eliot's 'The Lifted Veil'." *ELH* 73.2 (2006): 437–63.

Bair, Deirdre. *Simone de Beauvoir: A Biography*. New York: Simon, 1990.

Barthes, Roland. *S/Z*. Trans. Richard Miller. New York: Hill, 1974.

Beer, Gillian. *George Eliot*. Brighton: Harvester, 1986.

Bodenheimer, Rosemarie. *The Real Life of Mary Ann Evans*. Cornell: Cornell UP, 1994.

Bonaparte, Felicia. *Will and Destiny: Morality and Tragedy in George Eliot's Novels*. New York: New York UP, 1975.

Bray, Charles. *The Philosophy of Necessity*. 2 vols. London: Longmans, 1841.

Carroll, David. *George Eliot: The Critical Heritage*. London: Routledge, 1971.

Comte, Auguste. *The Catechism of Positive Religion*. Trans. Richard Congreve. London: John Chapman, 1858.

Culler, Jonathan. "Story and Discourse in the Analysis of Narrative." In Culler, *The Pursuit of Signs: Semiotics, Literature, Deconstruction*. Ithaca: Cornell UP, 1981. 169–87.

De Beauvoir, Simone. *Memoirs of a Dutiful Daughter*. Trans. James Kirkup. Cleveland: World, 1959.

Eliot, George. *The George Eliot Letters*. Ed. Gordon S. Haight. 9 vols. New Haven: Yale UP, 1954–78.

Eliot, George. *The Journals of George Eliot*. Ed. Margaret Harris and Judith Johnston. Cambridge: Cambridge UP, 1998.

Eliot, George. *The Lifted Veil* and *Brother Jacob*. Ed. Helen Small. Oxford: Oxford UP, 1999.

Eliot, George. *The Mill on the Floss*. Ed. A. S. Byatt. London: Penguin, 1979.

Feuerbach, Ludwig. *The Essence of Christianity*. Trans. Marian Evans. London: John Chapman, 1854.

Flint, Kate. "Blood, Bodies, and 'The Lifted Veil'." *Nineteenth-Century Literature* 51.4 (1997): 455–73.

Fraiman, Susan. *Unbecoming Women: British Women Writers and the Novel of Development*. New York: Columbia UP, 1993.

Genette, Gerard. *Narrative Discourse*. Trans. Jane E. Lewin. Oxford: Blackwell, 1980.

Gettelman, Debra. "Reading Ahead in George Eliot." *Novel* 39.1 (2005): 25–47.

Gilbert, Sandra, and Susan Gubar. *The Madwoman in the Attic*. New Haven: Yale UP, 1979.

Greiner, Rae. "Sympathy Time: Adam Smith, George Eliot, and the Realist Novel." *Narrative* 17.3 (2009): 291–311.

Hertz, Neil. *George Eliot's Pulse*. Stanford: Stanford UP, 2003.

Homans, Margaret. *Bearing the Word: Language and Female Experience in Nineteenth-Century Women's Writing*. Chicago: U of Chicago P, 1986.

Jacobus, Mary. "Men of Maxims and *The Mill on the Floss*." In Jacobus, *Reading Woman: Essays in Feminist Criticism*. New York Columbia UP, 1986, 62–79.

Menke, Richard. "Fiction as Vivisection: G. H. Lewes and George Eliot." *ELH* 67.2 (2000): 615–53.

Miller, D. A. *Narrative and Its Discontents: Problems of Closure in the Traditional Novel*. Princeton: Princeton UP, 1981.

Miller, Nancy K. "Emphasis Added: Plots and Plausibilities in Women's Fiction." *PMLA* 96.1 (1981): 36–48.

Shuttleworth, Sally. *George Eliot and Nineteenth-Century Science: The Make-Believe of a Beginning*. Cambridge: Cambridge UP, 1987.

Steedman, Carolyn Kay. *Strange Dislocations: Childhood and the Idea of Human Interiority*. Cambridge: Harvard UP, 1998.

Swann, Charles. "Déjà vu, déjà lu: 'The Lifted Veil' as an Experiment in Art." *Literature and History* 5 (1979): 40–57.

9
Romola: Historical Narration and the Communicative Dynamics of Modernity

David Wayne Thomas

No turn of critical fortunes seems likely to render George Eliot's *Romola* a popular favorite among readers. Eliot herself indicated that the work was, from its conception, not intended to have the same widespread appeal as her previous fictions, with their familiar settings in the English Midlands and their relatively modest claims on her readers' historical sensibilities and concerns (Eliot, *Letters* 4:49). Contemporary reviews, almost without exception, ranged merely from negative to cordial, often indicating that Eliot had in *Romola* shot rather "too high above the heads" of her readers, in Anthony Trollope's words (187). Nonetheless, the novel has long been understood as a rewarding object of study. It is, famously, a product of immense research on Eliot's part, exacting a toll on her that she memorably summarized in a letter: "I began it a young woman,—I ended it an old woman" (Cross 225). The resulting novel has been esteemed for its portrait of republicanism in fifteenth-century northern Italy and even as a guidebook to Renaissance Florence. More meaningful for latter-day literary scholarship, however, is *Romola's* privileged role among Eliot's novelistic meditations on the intersections of individual and political life and on key features of socio-political modernity. Eliot's most popular works have always been those such as *Adam Bede, The Mill on the Floss*, and *Middlemarch*, which give pride of place to the development of moral consciousness at the levels of individuality and immediate communities of feeling. In recent years, however, scholars have brought increasing interest to novels such as *Romola* and *Daniel Deronda* (1876), which more fully incorporate themes of state powers, nationalism, internationalism, and modernity.

A Companion to George Eliot, First Edition. Edited by Amanda Anderson and Harry E. Shaw.
© 2013 John Wiley & Sons, Ltd. Published 2016 by John Wiley & Sons, Ltd.

Key instances of such scholarship include Daniel Malachuk's reading of the novel in connection with Eliot's relations to Victorian liberalism and David Kurnick's view that the eponymous Romola, in her way of mingling energies of ethical investment and detachment, bodies forth certain affective dynamics of modern novel reading. The most substantial precedent to my argument is, however, an account of *Daniel Deronda* undertaken by Amanda Anderson in her book *The Powers of Distance*. For Anderson, *Deronda* explores "intersubjective and collective practices" in such a way as to provide "one of the most rigorous and complicated contributions to the Victorian literature of detachment" (119). Daniel Deronda himself illustrates practices of reflective dialogism, developing his critical understanding through relations of dialogue, real or imagined, with other actors. Anderson also indicates how Eliot puts certain limits on the accomplishments of such reflection: even if Deronda seems typically modern in his cosmopolitan view of Jewish identity, avoiding the programmatic urgency of Mordecai's romantic nationalism, we need also to note Deronda's failure to appreciate the burdens of gender difference borne by his long-estranged mother Leonora Alcharisi, whose access to such a reflective standpoint seems hardly equal to his own. Anderson does not claim that reflective dialogism is some kind of triumphant standpoint. In Eliot's novel, dialogical reflection is a genuine force, both ethically and socio-politically, but it can also have its share in problematic ethical exclusions or blind spots. But this complexity gives us no reason, argues Anderson, to abandon the modern project overall, because reflective dialogism remains a critical mode that can bring such exclusions to light and lead in time to their overcoming.

For purposes of my own reading, Anderson's account of Mordecai is of particular interest. An ardent Zionist and romantic nationalist, Mordecai is broadly analogous to Savonarola in *Romola*, in that Savonarola, too, is defined by his metaphysical and dogmatic allegiances. And just as Daniel is attracted but not fully seduced in the end by Mordecai's appeals, Romola is subdued but only temporarily, and even provisionally, by Savonarola's preachings. Both Deronda and Romola seem in these cases to exhibit something like a modern socio-ethical disposition, one that renders metaphysical and dogmatic allegiances problematic. But even more so than in *Deronda*— more so even than in Eliot's most well-known "social problem" novel, *Felix Holt*— in *Romola* we find Eliot's most developed image of political modernity. The novel shares with *Daniel Deronda* a close-grained attention to the effects on individual temperaments created by the dynamics of modernity while also thematizing politics via Florentine republicanism, which implicates modernity in so far as republicanism fundamentally presupposes a bracketing of the aristocratic, clerical, and monarchical authorities that predominated in feudal times.

My discussion is therefore a kind of bookend to Anderson's reading of *Deronda*, presenting *Romola* as Eliot's attempted reflection on modernity, but I also try to put a more far-reaching emphasis on the thematics of communicative action, to use a phrase widely associated with the work of Jürgen Habermas. For Habermas, the use of language implicates users in an ideal of uncoercive consensus-seeking through deliberation and argument. That viewpoint presupposes an image of human agency guided by rationality. It is a broadly Kantian and so-called antimaterialist viewpoint that literary and social historians have typically regarded with skepticism, as they look instead to more materialist forms of explanation, ranging from general empiricism to Marxism and psychoanalysis. My suggestion is that a Habermasian perspective on the operations of language and communication in *Romola* will help us to comprehend the novel's view of modernity and even to rethink the utility of Habermasian theory for literary-historical reading.

Let me begin with a brief summary of Eliot's *Romola*. The narrative begins in 1492 upon the death of Lorenzo de' Medici, who had been the de facto ruler of Florence during the height of the Italian Renaissance. In the period leading up to Lorenzo's death, resistance to the rule of the Medici family had already been gaining momentum, in part due to the fiery preachings of Fra Girolamo Savonarola, the Prior of San Marco. In addition to their many political entanglements, the Medicis were known for promoting Greco-Roman culture and the arts, concerns that Christian ascetics such as Savonarola would deem problematically worldly and pagan. Our eponymous, fictional heroine is Romola de' Bardi, who serves as an assistant to her father Bardo de' Bardi. A blind scholar, Bardo has cultivated in Romola an intense admiration of Greco-Roman classical culture and imbued her with profound humanist suspicions concerning the claims of Christianity and religion more generally. Into their lives comes the handsome young Greek, Tito Melema, who has arrived mysteriously at Florence with only some jewels to barter and a hope for employment commensurate with his scholarly training. Tito becomes Bardo's new assistant and will marry Romola as well, but his many defects of character gradually become apparent. He secretly supports and occasionally visits Tessa, a local peasant woman whom he impregnates after a faux marriage. We find that his background includes an elderly man named Calvo Baldassarre, who had raised Tito from a very young age, only to have Tito abandon him to languish in slavery. The most hurtful event to Romola comes shortly after the death of her father, when Tito surreptitiously liquidates Bardo's large collection of annotated books and antiquities. It had been Bardo's wish to keep the collection together, the better to establish his legacy as a man of letters. It becomes apparent that Tito is only concerned for himself and the pleasures and honors he can attain in society. At this point, Romola struggles with the realization that she can never fulfill her nature in service as a daughter nor as a wife, and she falls under the influence of Savonarola, who has been drawing crowds with his preachings against the political status quo and the established interests at the Vatican. To turn herself over to Savonarola's guidance is a large step for Romola, who was raised to regard Christianity as a popular fantasy. For some time, she remains enthralled with Savonarola's teachings, but she eventually breaks from him when his activities come finally to seem to her power-seeking and too self-convinced. Tito, in turn, seems on the verge of success in playing his double or even triple games with various political factions, but Baldassarre finally catches him and kills him in revenge. Savonarola himself is imprisoned and executed after Florence's new political and clerical powers come to interpret his preachings as heretical. After Romola leaves Florence with no purpose but dying, she finds herself reborn in tending to a plague-stricken community of Jews. The novel ends with Romola back at Florence, living with Tessa and Tessa's offspring by Tito.

Themes of communication animate all representations of the novel's personages and conflicts, both in historical and fictional contexts. To begin, *Romola*'s images of popular feeling as fickle and volatile would certainly ring familiar for Eliot's Victorian readers in those years leading into the passage of the Second Reform Act in 1867. At the novel's outset, as news spreads of the death of Lorenzo de' Medici, voices rise with vigor but without communicative purpose or destination, "each speaker feeling rather the necessity of utterance than of finding a listener" (18; ch. 1). And much later in the novel, when popular acclaim for the preachings of Savonarola might be thought to redeem in some way the historical pertinence of his massed listeners at a time when corrupt forces were arraying against his teachings, the narrator wryly notes about the populace, "[N]ext to hearing Fra Girolamo himself, the most exciting Lenten occupation was to hear him argued against and vilified" (510; ch. 63). When Eliot highlights questions of communications and rhetoric in her many minor characters and interactions, it is often to comic effect. The loquacious barber Nello explains, "[W]e Florentines have liberal ideas about speech, and consider that an instrument which can flatter and promise so cleverly as the tongue, must have been partly made for those purposes; and that the truth is a riddle for eyes and wit to discover, which it were a mere spoiling of sport for the tongue to betray" (35; ch. 3). When the Medicean conspirators are awaiting trial in prison, the street-purveyor Bratti takes to selling handbills on both sides of the question of whether the conspirators should be punished or not, with one set of handbills headlined "Law," the other, "Justice." Underscoring that the terms "law" and "justice" are here used prejudicially rather than carefully, the narrator observes, "[I]t was an opinion entertained at that time (in the first flush of the triumph of printing) that there was no argument more widely convincing than question-begging phrases in large type"(484–85; ch. 59). An indulgent, perhaps condescending image of popular sensibility emerges also in the defense of public processionals by Bernardo Cennini, a local goldsmith who assisted Lorenzo Ghiberti in the construction of the Gates of Paradise doors in Florence's Battistero di San Giovanni: "the great bond of our Republic is expressing itself in ancient symbols, without which the vulgar would be conscious of nothing but their own petty wants of back and stomach, and never rise to the sense of community in religion and law. There has been no great people without processions, and the man who thinks himself too wise to be moved by them to anything but contempt, is like the puddle that was proud of standing alone while the river rushed by" (91; ch. 8).

While such passages might seem merely decorative and humorous, they also blend seamlessly with the calculated insider maneuverings of the novel's elite political actors, where the ethical and political stakes are more material. Among the novel's significant historical figures is Niccolò Machiavelli, famous as a practitioner of what Habermas would call strategic action as opposed to communicative action—that is, the pursuit of personal ends in relation to another party as opposed to the pursuit of a consensus and understanding with that party. Eliot presents Machiavelli as a savvy observer of his moment's partisan machinations, a young man who has "penetrated all the small secrets of egoism" (393; ch. 45). Eliot also gives us Tornabuoni, among the conspirators who would later be executed for trying to establish Piero de' Medici in power after Lorenzo's death: he tells them that a "wise dissimulation" "is the only course for moderate rational men in times of violent party feeling" (343; ch. 39). Among Eliot's fictional characters, Tito exemplifies the most pernicious form of self-interestedness, in that his thinking fails to rise even to the level of strategic partisanship for locally agreed ends. That is, Machiavelli and his Florentine counterparts can generally be understood, as Eliot's narrator indicates, to share some common concerns by virtue of their traditional attachments and legacies. Like Mafia families or other *sub rosa* collective agents, these figures could assume that certain forms of loyalty remain generally in play. But Tito frequently asks himself what end there could be in life but the pursuit of his own interests and pleasures (115; ch. 11 and 476; ch. 57), and he manages to gain confidence on various political sides precisely because of his alien standing as a Greek (472; ch. 57): his ostensible political partners are not quick enough to realize that Tito does not share a grounding allegiance to any of Florence's inherited social and political arrangements.

Several figures in *Romola* provide more sanguine images of ethical and intersubjective character, but it is notable that they seem perhaps for that very reason to have a more marginal place in the novel's socio-political order. This seems to reflect an intuition on Eliot's part: narrative realism has to acknowledge that practical affairs are in fact dominated, historically, by more cynical energies. (At one point, when Romola asks the double-dealing Tito why he sees fit to make it look as if he is siding with unsavory actors, he answers, "Such relations are inevitable to practical men, my Romola. . . . You fair creatures live in the clouds" [406; ch. 46].) Piero di Cosimo, a Florentine painter, appears here almost in a mischievous way: where most people are taken with Tito's attractiveness, Piero finds his face exceptional for its expression of fear and cowardice, and he calls him to model for a corresponding role in a painting (186; ch. 18 and 257; ch. 28). Romola's step-father Bernardo is another case in point: he exhibits a patient sensibility, strong but accommodating, and it marks him as one of the novel's more perspicacious figures that he also, like Piero, has suspicions about Tito from the outset. He emerges as a judicious figure, however, when he refuses to insist upon his suspicions in the absence of better evidence for them than he has at hand. Romola esteems Bernardo for his capacity to accept Romola's positive attitude toward Tito, evidencing Bernardo's "power of respecting a feeling which he does not share" (179; ch. 17). But it is, at the same time, some indication of his stance's precariousness that Bernardo ultimately falls victim to his own rectitude. Refusing to participate in the hypocrisies and behind-the-scenes alliances that transpire during the crisis of the Republic and define its winners, he is driven to his execution by political expedience.

Unsurprisingly, Eliot's most developed and illuminating images of intersubjective relations arise in her novel's characterizations of its principal figures. At every juncture, Eliot carefully describes the relationships in terms of their communicative dynamics. Although almost everyone finds Tito's external appearance winning, Eliot gives us his disturbing background by letting us overhear his "first colloquy with himself" (98; ch. 9), when it emerges that Tito is ready to rationalize as much as need be his failure to go in search of his adoptive father, Baldassarre, and free him from enforced slavery. This background inevitably gives us pause as readers when we find Romola so ready to resist Bernardo's suggestion that she is won over only by Tito's external appearance. Says Romola, "I love Tito . . . because he is so good. I see it, I feel it, in everything he says and does" (191; ch. 19). But when Romola fancies herself to be experiencing a "mutual consciousness" with Tito (175; ch. 17), the narrator makes plain the distorted nature of her viewpoint, in that Romola really "only read her own pure thoughts" in "the dark depths" of Tito's eyes, rather than seeing there the reality: Tito was actually pleased at Romola's brother Dino dying without revealing Dino's betrayal of Baldassarre (176; ch. 17). The decayed nature of the marital relationship is underscored later when the narrator observes, "Tito and Romola never jarred, never remonstrated with each other. They were too hopelessly alienated in their inner life ever to have that contest which is an effort towards agreement" (399; ch. 46). Even as all the narrative details here paint their relationship in communicative terms, the character of that communication is plainly vexed and misfiring. "In the first ardour of her self-conquest, after she had renounced her resolution of flight [from Florence], Romola had made many timid efforts towards the return of a frank relation between them. But to her such a relation could only come about by open speech about their differences, and the attempt to arrive at a moral understanding." But Tito, notes the narrator, "cared for no explanation between them" (399; ch. 46).

This stalemate breaks up in the critical chapters 46–48, when Romola, from a concern that powerful interests are plotting to murder Savonarola, approaches Tito and asks his help. He assures her that Savonarola will not be allowed to go beyond the city gates and expose himself to such danger. Distrusting Tito, however, Romola elects to bind him further to his word by asking him later to repeat it to her in a public setting. He does so, and she departs, but he is inwardly enraged. Despite what the narrator earlier called Tito's "innate love of reticence" (94; ch. 9), he finally confronts Romola in an effort to steer her away from interference in his political doings: "'Romola,' he began, in the cool liquid tone which made her shiver, 'it is time that we should understand each other'" (412; ch. 48). Of course, Tito means by *understanding* that Romola must agree to submit herself to his will and to keep clear from his practical doings, but Romola's orientation is of another sort. Says she to Tito, "You shut me out from your mind. You affect to think of me as a being too unreasonable to share in the knowledge of your affairs. You will be open with me about nothing" (413; ch. 48).

With this interpersonal impasse laid bare, the novel has little more to do with the relationship, and notwithstanding the deliberateness with which Eliot paints the marriage in terms of its trajectory from mistaken understanding to entrenched antipathy, it might be tempting to say simply that it is one more novelistic bad marriage. But Romola's communicative relations are also dramatized in terms of larger issues of modernity, precisely through the novel's mingling of communicative themat-

ics and historical ambitions. Eliot carefully presents this marital stalemate as a collision between Tito's repressiveness and Romola's cooperative sensibility. This dichotomy
finds expression not only in gender inequality and domestic discord but also in
the political distinction between coercive authority—a hallmark of premodern political order—and the consensual forms of governance that characterize modernity. Eliot
is careful to maintain both the personal and historical facets of this distinction. As
the narrator notes, the "fortunes of Tito and Romola were dependent on certain
grand political and social conditions which made an epoch in the history of Italy"
(205; ch. 21).

In its overlaying of personal and socio-historical energies, *Romola* has a noteworthy
precedent in Walter Scott's *Waverley*, the nineteenth century's preeminent model of
historical novelistic writing and a clear influence on Eliot's narrative. Scott's novel
looks back to the 1740s and the struggle between the Hanoverian dynasty and Stuart
claimants to the throne. *Romola* likewise asks us to keep a bifocal view as readers,
paralleling the narrative's personal energies and its stake in historical processes. But
Eliot goes even further than Scott by refusing to lend much conclusiveness to the
symbolic roles that her key characters are to play. With *Waverley*, Scott plainly wishes
to fashion an elegiac portrait of traditional Scottishness and the Jacobite cause to
which it offered allegiance in opposition to a Hanoverian rule that was understood
to reflect a modern ethos of commerce and realpolitik. Scott's aim is to portray that
image of traditional culture sympathetically while at the same time acknowledging
that modernizing forces must inevitably overwrite traditionalism. In order to read
Romola in such a fashion, we would have to see Savonarola as a counterpart to such
figures as Scott's Highland chieftain Fergus Mac-Ivor. Each figure mingles fervent
support for a traditionalist cause and an appetite for worldly pursuit of that cause.
Each is an insurrectionary figure, eventually executed for his activities by larger forces
in the political establishment. Similarly, we might view Romola as a counterpart to
Fergus's sister, Flora, who shares her brother's political ideals but who programmati-
cally abstains from worldly political actions. Scott's key figures are ultimately elegiac,
however, while Eliot wants something still more subtle and elusive from her central
figures. In Savonarola, we have a figure who points us, not only to energies of fanaticism and power-seeking which must ultimately seem like unstable elements in history,
but also to forms of aspiration and practical idealism which Eliot is at pains to keep
in reserve.

It is tempting to see Romola's relation to Savonarola in the light that we might
see Dorothea Brooke's to Casaubon in *Middlemarch*. In each case an ardent young
woman gives her loyalty to an older male figure of high intellectual standing and
ambition, seeking her fulfillment in service to his vision; in the end, however, she
must strike out on her own after judging that very figure critically for his partialness
of vision and sensibility. In Casaubon's case the turnabout in his standing is plainer,
in that he manifestly fails to rise to his questionable goal of fashioning a Key to all
Mythologies, and what Dorothea once generously understood as his lofty concerns are
exposed in due course for their substantial share of pettiness and anxiety. But Savonarola's failure, situated as it is at a fulcrum point in modern political history, has wider

meanings, partaking in the overdeterminations that inform all historical events. His aspirations and his meaningfulness in Eliot's eyes can therefore never be fully compartmentalized or bracketed away.

A first matter to note about Savonarola is the inspiring effect he has on his contemporaries. He marshals, the narrator says, "a power rarely paralleled, of impressing his beliefs on others, and of swaying very various minds" (207; ch. 21, see also 234; ch. 24). When portraying Savonarola's effects, however, Eliot is at pains to situate his verbal or conceptual powers as secondary aspects of his persuasiveness. Insistently, it is not Savonarola's message that persuades, nor even his rhetorical talents, but instead his "voice" (156–57; ch. 15).[1] Even when Romola is most in the sway of Savonarola, she retains her tendency to recoil from "the wearisome visions and allegories" of Christian preachers, except when those visions are announced from the lips of Savonarola: "she found herself listening patiently to all dogmas and prophecies, when they came in the vehicle of his ardent faith and believing utterance" (388–89; ch. 44). Patently, Romola is not sold on his message but instead on his sensually manifested "presence." Savonarola's message, in other words, does not translate, does not submit to remaining one argument among others.

It is hard to overstate the insistence Eliot brings to the nonconceptual or nonlinguistic nature of Savonarola's power, not only over Romola but more generally. For example, Baldassarre stumbles about Florence with virtually nothing on his mind but vengeance against Tito, but even he will make a point of going to observe Savonarola's appearances (231; ch. 25 and 265; ch. 30). And in this light it seems no coincidence that Baldassarre's character is emotionally driven and emphatically detached from the world of common discourse. He is a ruined scholar who has lost his ability to read and to communicate his feelings. At one point he is called to task for his accusations against Tito, but where an articulate man might have succeeded in convincing onlookers of Tito's perfidy, Baldassarre is left to grope in vain for a way to make his case (352; ch. 39). And it is the exception that proves the rule when Baldassarre is at one point tantalized by a brief, exhilarating recovery of his verbal faculties and scholarly acumen (335; ch. 38). The episode only underscores for us and for him his linguistic and conceptual deficits.

Likewise, Eliot's phrasing consistently connects Savonarola's effects on Romola to various potencies somehow outside language or even opposed to it. Romola is "subdued by the sense of something unspeakably great" when listening to Savonarola, as he waylays her in her attempted flight from Florence. To be sure, when he persuades her to return to her duties in the city, he does use words, but his persuasion appears to rely on other forces. Here is how the novel gives us Romola's submission to his guidance: "Almost unconsciously she sank on her knees. Savonarola stretched out his hands over her; but feeling would no longer pass through the channel of speech, and he was silent" (362; ch. 40).

Eliot here styles speech as limited with respect to feeling, but in due course it will also come to seem that feeling is limited in respect to speech, in so far as Savonarola's authoritativeness as a guide for Romola comes clearly into question. As Eliot's

narrative unfolds, it has to seem that the germinal forces leading to Romola's disenchantment with Savonarola were always waiting in the wings. Several times, the
narrator indicates Romola's partialness of insight into his nature and his effects. Like
a doe-eyed lover, she first sees only the positive in him and not the negative. But later,
as she observes him beginning to show signs of stress and "exasperation" in his public
speeches (441; ch. 52), she begins to attain a less idealizing and blinkered view of
him: "for the moment she felt what was true in the scornful sarcasms she heard continually flung against him, more keenly than she felt what was false" (445; ch. 52).
But the narrative also gives an ephemeral character to Romola's altering viewpoints
on Savonarola, in that she views him critically "for the moment." The fuller unfolding
of this relationship will show us Eliot keeping many aspects of intersubjectivity in
play, ranging from dialogic communication, in which Savonarola will be lacking,
to forces of feeling and perception that cannot be entirely registered explicitly with
language and argument.

But that balanced view emerges only by the novel's end, when Eliot reconstructs
her appreciation for Savonarola's historical meaning. At this earlier juncture, what
undermines Savonarola in Romola's eyes is something more explicitly deliberative:
his unduly categorical conviction that the truth as he sees it will suffice, and that his
truth corresponds to truth for all of Florence in its partisan predicaments. This realization emerges for Romola when she goes to Savonarola to plead for intercession in the
arrest of her confidant Bernardo. Here Savonarola comes to appear to her as an accom-
modator and partisan in his willingness to let Bernardo and other alleged conspirators
die, even though he understands that men like Bernardo are better basically than some
of those on Savonarola's own side, who stand to come off as the victors. Savonarola's
rationale is that worthy men are sometimes casualties in the larger work of God, just
as wicked men can sometimes be a service to that greater good. Romola rejoins, "Do
you, then, know so well what will further the coming of God's kingdom, Father, that
you will dare to despise the plea of mercy—of justice—of faithfulness to your own
teaching . . . ?" "Take care, Father, lest your enemies have some reason when they say,
that in your visions of what will further God's kingdom you see only what will
strengthen your own party." Savonarola bristles at these challenging words: "The cause
of my party *is* the cause of God's Kingdom." Romola's response is likewise firm—"I
do not believe it!"—and Eliot's narrator underscores the depth of this break with
words that indicate once again the novel's continuing concern with language and
communication: "The two faces were lit up, each with an opposite emotion, each with
an opposite certitude. Further words were impossible. Romola hastily covered her
head and went out in silence" (492; ch. 59).

One might certainly understand Savonarola here as vain and arrogant. Indeed,
Romola inwardly abandons her devotion to Savonarola after this encounter for that
reason: "In that declaration of his, that the cause of his party was the cause of God's
kingdom, she heard only the ring of egoism" (510; ch. 63). But the more fully figured
form of her disillusion, in terms of communicative standpoints, is that Savonarola has
shown himself to inhabit a communicative standpoint that Romola can no longer

abide. Or, more exactly, he appears to inhabit one or the other of two unacceptable standpoints. First, in so far as Savonarola's certitude seems grounded in a claim of metaphysical insight, his sensibility must seem to Romola problematically premodern.[2] That is, he has made plain to her his subscription to an ultimately metaphysical and categorical—rather than a practical and deliberative—sense of his own commitments. The alternative possibility is that Savonarola's standpoint expresses his worldly calculation that political action is a game to be played with his interests alone in mind—that is, with supremacy rather than morality or justice in mind. In that light, he comes to look problematically Machiavellian, a practitioner of strategic action rather than of communicative intersubjectivity. That would make him into just one more figure for whom, as Tornabuoni insists at one point, a "wise dissimulation . . . is the only course for moderate rational men in times of violent party feeling" (343; ch. 39). That Romola's underlying orientation is antithetical to that latter view was already suggested earlier in the narrative, when she found herself struggling to think past her increasing suspicions about Tito. Says the narrator, "It belongs to every large nature, when it is not under the immediate power of some strong questioning emotion, to suspect itself, and doubt the truth of its own impressions, conscious of possibilities beyond its own horizon" (244; ch. 27).

And here, with this question of whether and how one might strive to look beyond one's own horizons, is where Romola's orientation, implicitly shared by Eliot herself, comes to overlap with Habermasian perspectives on communicative relations under conditions of modernity. In the recasting of Kantian theory that Habermas undertook in the middle of his career with his two-volume *Theory of Communicative Action*, the need to test and rationalize one's viewpoints appeared as an inherent (if fragile) tendency of communicative relations and language use.[3] To use language, on this showing, is to possess some understanding of intersubjective understanding as such. That is not to say, of course, that one often or even ever inhabits an ideal speech situation, just as, when Kant tells us we know lying always to be immoral, he does mean that we think this is a world in which we don't lie. Instead, the point for Habermas is that language involves its users in presuppositions that situate deliberation and the good-faith seeking of consensus as practical ideals. For Habermas, no modern political community can exhaustively define validity within its own prejudices, because language implicates users in a further ideal of an "unbounded community of interpretation" that can potentially transcend the community's specific context (*Between Facts and Norms* 16).[4] Such a premise has been hard to accept for many literary scholars, ranging from those who feel that his public sphere naïvely or culpably disregards inequities of access and influence by minority or marginalized actors to those who maintain that his later communicative action theory and its "ideal speech situation" simply fails to acknowledge the rhetorical and practical complexities of actual discourse. And indeed, neo-pragmatist critics such as Richard Rorty and Stanley Fish maintain that it is flatly nonsensical to suppose that individuals and communities can stand back from their own assumptions to judge them.

Eliot's concluding characterization of Romola suggests that she shared such theoretical concerns while also trying to respond to them in a way that can help us to
move past them. A first point to note is that the narrator insists carefully on Romola's
final determination in the end to eschew "maxims." The trouble with maxims is their
way of performing as blunt instruments, inadequate to the richness and textures
of subjective embodiment. The novel's earliest engagement with the term gives us
Romola at her own early stage of development, when she is ready to see worthy rectitude in a life of maxims. After she discovers that her long-lost brother Dino has
returned to Florence very ill, as the friar Fra Luca, Romola goes to see him where
he has sequestered himself, secretly, at the Fiesole monastery. She implores Dino to
attempt a reconciliation with their father. In response to Dino's protest that Bardo's
regimen of classical education was an imposition of "worldly ambitions and fleshly
lusts" on him, Romola rejoins that Bardo only "wished you to live as he himself has
done, according to the purest maxims of philosophy." The narrator notes that Romola
"spoke partly by rote, as all ardent and sympathetic young creatures do." But Dino's
resistance is unshaken: "What were the maxims of philosophy to me? They told me
to be strong, when I felt myself weak" (154; ch. 15).

What maxims have to offer, in this light, is a reassuring clarity that is also tinged
with inauthenticity—the element of rote speech in Romola, the threat of imposture
or hypocrisy in Dino. Thus it is a mark of Romola's maturation that she grows beyond
maxims at the end of the novel, when tending to the community of Jews suffering
under pestilence in their isolated settlement. The narrator notes that Romola is
seeing the world from a "new position" since she was revived by a child's cry after
having given herself up to death. Now busy with the Jewish community, "she had
not even reflected, as she used to do in Florence, that she was glad to live because she
could lighten sorrow—she had simply lived, with so energetic an impulse to share
the life around her, to answer the call of need and to do the work which cried aloud
to be done, that the reasons for living, enduring, laboring, never took the form of
argument " (560; ch. 69). Here Eliot brackets—even apparently demotes—the idea
of a life led upon reasoned and fully explicit argument. But it is not exactly the case
that Eliot has steered away from the viewpoint that I have styled above as proto-
Habermasian.

What seems to be enabled by Romola's concluding subjective stance is a moralized
species of humility, an openness to the idea that one's viewpoints might never fully
synchronize with every other rational person's, even as it remains possible for us to
deliberate in good faith with the bearers of those viewpoints. Only when Romola finds
herself in this state does she come around to reconsidering her negative feelings for
Savonarola, who has been tortured and executed as a heretic. She is able to see that
he was the most important force in waking her to a new life. There was, after all,
something that could vindicate Savonarola in Romola's eyes: his *aspiration* to speak
truth. The reflective accomplishment of an orientation is not to be understood principally as a cognitive or epistemological feat but instead as an ongoing premise that

one might maintain with respect to intersubjective potentialities. That premise, in turn, gives us Eliot's distinctively modern vision of conduct, both at the level of personal relations and of socio-political ones.

NOTES

1   For other instances which make a point of Savonarola's voice, see 229 (ch. 24); 246 (ch. 27); 355 (ch. 40); and 361 (ch. 40). Ch. 40 itself is entitled "The Arresting Voice."

2   For a noteworthy discussion of this passage, see Ermarth.

3   Most literary scholarship that attends to Habermas's work emphasizes his image of the eighteenth-century public sphere, as set forth in his first book, the 1962 study *The Structural Transformation of the Public Sphere*. My own appropriation of Habermas draws more substantially on his subsequent work. See Eley for a measured retrospect on English-language scholars and their interest in Habermas's ideas

about the public sphere. For an earlier discussion treating Habermas's later work in the light of literary reading, see Brantlinger.

4   His viewpoint needs to be distinguished from neo-pragmatist standpoints, which typically insist that communities cannot stand back from their own assumptions to judge them. For Habermas, no modern political community can exhaustively define validity within its own prejudices, because language implicates users in a further ideal of an "unbounded community of interpretation" that can potentially transcend the community's specific context (*Between Facts and Norms* 16).

REFERENCES

Anderson, Amanda. *The Powers of Distance: Cosmopolitanism and the Cultivation of Detachment*. Princeton, Princeton UP, 2001.

Brantlinger, Patrick. *Crusoe's Footprints: Cultural Studies in Britain and America*.London: Routledge, 1990.

Cross, J. W. *George Eliot's Life as Related in her Letters and Journals*. Vol. 2. London: Blackwood, 1885.

Eley, Geoff. "Commentary: Politics, Culture, and the Public Sphere." *Positions* 10.1 (2002): 219–36.

Eliot, George. *The George Eliot Letters*. Ed. Gordon S. Haight. 9 vols. New Haven: Yale UP, 1954–78.

Eliot, George. *Romola*. Ed. Dorothea Barrett. London: Penguin, 1996, 2005.

Ermarth, Elizabeth Deeds. "George Eliot's Conception of Sympathy." *Nineteenth-Century Literature* 40.1 (1985), 23–42.

Habermas, Jürgen. *Between Facts and Norms: Contributions to a Discourse Theory of Law and Democracy*. Trans. William Rehg. Cambridge: MIT P, 1996.

Habermas, Jürgen. *Knowledge and Human Interests*. Trans. Jeremy J. Shapiro. Boston: Beacon, 1971.

Habermas, Jürgen. "A Philosophico-Political Profile." *Autonomy and Solidarity: Interviews with Jürgen Habermas*. Rev. ed. Ed. Peter Dews. London: Verso, 1992.

Habermas, Jürgen. *The Structural Transformation of the Public Sphere: An Inquiry into a Category of Bourgeois Society*. Trans. Thomas Burger. Cambridge: MIT P, 1989.

Kurnick, David. "Abstraction and the Subject of Novel Reading: Drifting Through *Romola*." *Novel* 42.3 (2009): 490–96.

Malachuk, Daniel S. "*Romola* and Victorian Liberalism." *Victorian Literature and Culture* 36.1 (2008): 41–57.

Trollope, Anthony. *The Letters of Anthony Trollope*. Ed. N. John Fall. Vol. 1. Stanford, Stanford UP, 1983.

Wihl, Gary. "Republican liberty in George Eliot's *Romola*." *Criticism* 51.2 (2009): 247–62.

10
Felix Holt: Love in the Time of Politics

David Kurnick

What does illicit sex have in common with a well-nigh incomprehensible inheritance dispute? If *Felix Holt, the Radical* is perhaps the most discomfiting of Eliot's major novels, most contemporary readers ascribe this fact to the baldly ideological way in which Eliot handles the political "radicalism" that is its avowed central theme. But this political discomfort is augmented by the plot's awkward embrace of the disparate domains of the erotic and the legalistic. The novel's opening is dominated by Mrs. Transome, the imperious mistress of Transome Court whose long-ago extramarital affair has become a source of constant bitterness and anxiety; its denouement, meanwhile, is precipitated by the revelation of an inheritance plot so complex that Eliot had to consult a lawyer to get it right and the standard modern edition of the novel includes an appendix explaining its tortuous logic.[1] The novel may simply seem stranded between the erotic and the legal, the passionately legible and the forensically recondite—until we recognize that both are emblems of disruption to the community that was such a prized ideal for Eliot. She had long worried over the status of the erotic as the single most narratable threat to the stability of the organic community; her first full-length novel, 1859's *Adam Bede*, seems an almost plotless depiction of a rural community until an extra-marital affair comes close to destroying that world's delicate balance. And if the erotic violates communitarian norms with its violent facticity, the legal threatens the community's health from the other end, that of abstraction: in its rationalized distance from lived experience, the law encapsulates the essence of modernity, a world where face-to-face contacts and the customs that regulate them have been replaced with an abstract set of rules.

A Companion to George Eliot, First Edition. Edited by Amanda Anderson and Harry E. Shaw.

But while the erotic and the legal each in their distinct ways threatens the coherence of the community, the oddest thing about their narrative placement in *Felix Holt* is their firm situation in the past. Eliot is sometimes described as a nostalgic novelist, and her habit of setting her fiction at key moments of the transition to modernity is certainly one key reason for this impression. *Felix Holt* is set during the agitation surrounding the passage of the 1832 Reform Act, the law that began the nineteenth century's gradual march toward universal male suffrage by shifting electoral weight away from depopulated rural boroughs and toward the urban centers that had sprung up during the eighteenth century's industrial takeoff. One might expect Eliot to have arranged her narrative's micro-events to mirror this large-scale sociopolitical shift—to have let the shock of the erotic or the abstraction of the law serve as an allegory for the move into the modern political order. But Mrs. Transome's sexual transgression and the bureaucratic headache of the Transome estate's entailment are both squarely in the past when the novel opens; Loamshire, the allegorically named region in which the novel's action transpires, already seems traversed by the atomizing energies that render inappropriate its pastoral name. The novelistic world that results is the product of a densely multiplanar historical imagination, in which the tectonic shifts that tempt us into drastic before-and-after conceptions of time's movement are undercut by tinier and less easily quantifiable seismic tremors.

Perhaps the clearest expression of Eliot's stringently layered historical understanding is the masterful set-piece that opens the novel. The novel's epigraph is taken from Michael Drayton's seventeenth-century *Poly-Olbion*, a poem describing the topography of England and Wales in patient detail; the section Eliot chooses to head her novel begins with the following words: "Upon the midlands now the industrious muse doth fall, / the shires which we the heart of England well may call" (2). While "industrious" here of course signifies only that Drayton's muse is well-occupied, Eliot's 1866 reader would also have perceived a phonemic nod to the word "industrial"—a term which since the late eighteenth century had been strongly associated not only with modern manufacture but with the swift transformation of the English Midlands where that manufacture was concentrated. With typical economy, Eliot's epigraph thus performs a third-order historical self-reflexivity, first inviting us to apply Drayton's words to the industrialized present; then waiting as we correct ourselves with the realization that they describe the distant past; and finally making us aware that our error was itself of historical interest, a revelation of the historicity of our conceptual and literary language: in the context of the rapidly changing environment in which *Felix Holt* is set, the accidental half-pun of Drayton's fairly bland encomium to the Midlands takes on the tones of prophecy, and of elegy.

This epigraphic play prepares us for the novel's text proper, which begins with the nostalgic observation that "[f]ive-and-thirty years ago the glory had not yet departed from the old coach-roads." Eliot's mid-Victorian readers would have been accustomed to traveling the country by railroad, but the narrator reminds them that within living memory state-of-the-art locomotion was provided by England's coaching-system; the catalogue of this coaching-world's features she goes on to provide—"the great roadside inns," "the smiling glances of pretty barmaids," "the repartees of jocose ostlers" (3; Introduction) encourages us to understand the novel's setting in terms of an overarching then-and-now dichotomy. But no sooner has Eliot enumerated this list than she introduces a third historical moment—that immediately previous world which this coaching-system has just displaced. In the moment in which *Felix Holt* is set, we read, "elderly gentlemen in pony-chaises" can be seen "quartering nervously to make way for the rolling swinging swiftness" of the mail coach, the high-speed conveyance Eliot describes as a "meteoric apparition" in the Midlands countryside (3; Introduction). The sequence comprises a miniature essay on the historiographic imagination, a meditation on the inevitability and the inadequacy of our conceptual Great Divides: the old gentlemen are rattled by the mail-coach's supersession of the "pack-horses" with which they grew up; the railway-savvy reader finds the mail-coach quaint; and yet another moment looms on the horizon, a sci-fi future in which, the narrator conjectures, "posterity may be shot, like a bullet through a tube, by atmospheric pressure from Winchester to Newcastle" (3; Introduction). Faced with this dizzying series of sped-up worlds, the reader is forced to confront nostalgia's essential phenomenological truth and its historiographic distortions.

The complexity of Eliot's vision here—the vertiginously unanchored sense of historical change she offers—can be easy to overlook, partly because of the famous composure of her writing. Raymond Williams, one of Eliot's harshest and most astute critics, misses the passage's ambiguity in a reading that nonetheless valuably makes clear the ideological stakes of Eliot's stylistic control. In *The Country and the City*, Williams argues that the hypothetical coach-journey is an allegory of Eliot's style, which can register the causes of political turmoil—Eliot's coach-rider perceives the poverty of the countryside—but contains it in a detached vision of rural tranquility. The passage, Williams argues, relies on "a willing, lulling illusion of old country life." The effect is to occlude the social strife, contingency, and sheer suffering of the past by means of a bucolic vision of a vanished world: "What is then being brought into view on the box-seat is a political comfort. . . . It is manufacturing and the railways which destroy this old England. The full modern myth comes quite sharply into focus" (179–80). The critique is passionately phrased. But in a curiously unacknowledged way, Williams's central point—that the historical imagination can succumb to prelapsarian visions of a pristine past—might itself derive from the Eliot passage he is discussing.[2]

In deciding, for example, whether the tacit contrastive presence of the railroad in Eliot's opening is a "modern myth" or an analysis of one, it is useful to recall that *Felix Holt*'s opening is developing an allegorical use of transportation modes Eliot had first proposed in her 1856 essay "The Natural History of German Life." Like the novel, the essay uses the railroad as an emblem of historicized perception. "Natural History" is ostensibly an appraisal of W. H. Riehl's proto-sociological portrait of German peasantry, but Eliot makes the review an occasion for a manifesto on novelistic realism. In the essay's opening, Eliot contrasts the images the word *railways* would call up in two hypothetical men: "in the mind of a man who is not highly locomotive," the word will summon visions of his local station or a printed timetable, or fantasies of the rail lines being laid over the globe's farthest reaches; his imagination combines elements of the abstract and the particular but lacks any sense of their concrete inter-relations. "But suppose a man to have had successively the experience of a 'navvy,' an engineer, a traveller, a railway director and shareholder, and a landed proprietor in treaty with a railway company"—for this man the word *railway* will summon "all the essential facts in the existence and relations of the *thing*" (267). That Eliot favors this latter vision as the model for her novelistic practice is clear; and the fact that her list of occupations runs to progressively more abstract relations to the material fact of the railway seems to align her vision with the aestheticizing distance with which Williams charges her. But Eliot suggests that abstraction must be tempered by a more intimate vision when, later in the essay, she commends Riehl for basing his observation on "his wanderings over the hills and plains of Germany"; his method, she approvingly notes, is founded on embodied and "immediate intercourse with the people" (286). The highly locomotive vision needs to be complemented with a more modest, slow-paced—"pedestrian" is the approving term Eliot uses (286)—mode of perception.

The novelistic program that Eliot implicitly calls for here is, if not impossible, at least almost unthinkably challenging. The ideal novelistic vision will cultivate a dauntingly diverse set of relations to the object of representation—to "the *thing*" whose emblem here is the railway: get on the train—but get off the train and walk into the fields; build the railroad—but have the resources to ride it frequently; design it; manage it; own part of it, or own the land on which it has been built. Part of the interest of *Felix Holt* is the way its narrative awkwardness serves to render explicit the deeply ambivalent political and representational demands Eliot attempts to rec-oncile throughout her work. It is fitting, for example, that the novel's introduction concludes with a paragraph (not discussed by Williams) addressing exactly his concern with the ways her novel's pictorialism might occlude the perception of human misery:

> The poets have told us of a dolorous enchanted forest in the under-world. The thorn-bushes there, and the thick-barked stems, have human histories hidden in them; the power of unuttered cries dwells in the passionless-seeming branches, and the red-warm blood is darkly feeding the quivery nerves of a sleepless memory that watches through all dreams. (10–11; Introduction)

These sentences heed the admonition offered in "Natural History" that what might look beautifully composed from afar will yield up its social meaning on closer approach. The introduction closes with the following enigmatic words: "These things are a parable" (11; Introduction)—and the sentence's very mysteriousness highlights Eliot's half-despairing sense of a realistic art's potential impossibility. The gothic image of a blood-infested landscape is a parable—but of what? Behind that question we may hear lurking a larger doubt about the social relevance of creative art more generally. To what concrete reality does aesthetic language pertain?

The most immediate referent the novel offers for these words is Mrs. Transome, whose imposing manner hides a seething pain; the imagistic pattern that attends her throughout the novel picks up the introduction's melodramatic sense of suffering physicality secreted behind a grand exterior: "No one," the narrator tells us, "divined what was hidden under that outward life—a woman's keen sensibility and dread, which lay screened behind all her petty habits and narrow notions, as some quivering thing with eyes and throbbing heart may lie crouching behind withered rubbish" (30–31; ch. 1). As this sentence suggests, the narrator's attitude toward Mrs. Transome verges on the sadistically lurid. When her former lover, the family lawyer Jermyn, speaks to her "in a tone of bland kindness," Eliot writes that "every sentence was as pleasant to her as if it had been cut in her bare arm" (115; ch. 9). The vehemence of this imagery suggests a figurative linkage between Mrs. Transome's plot and the political conflict the book's subtitle would lead us to consider its central narrative concern: in what can seem a symptomatic displacement, the social suffering we know to be behind the political agitation seems to find clearest expression in these gore-filled images of Mrs. Transome's psychological pain. Mrs. Transome's plight is serious enough: she must endure the indifference of her old lover, the tedium of her imbecilic husband, and the disrespect of her son. But it seems insignificant when placed against the socio-economic discontent that fuels the novel's political action—a discontent that finds virtually no narrative elaboration. In this sense, Mrs. Transome's dense condensation of affect (curdled eroticism, resentment, fear, despair, boredom, intellectual contempt) is interesting both for its psychological content and for the very extravagance of its psychologism—a psychologism which seems to signify a foundational disequilibrium between the personal and the political. It is as if Mrs. Transome must feel so many terrible things because she has been consigned the unenviable burden of representing a properly political discontent that has very little to do with her.

But even here, Eliot's interweaving of the allegorical levels of her story makes such distinctions difficult to maintain. The character who most brutally misses Mrs. Transome's suffering is her son Harold, recently returned from fifteen years as a trader in the Ottoman port city Smyrna. Harold's absence has given him a self-satisfied sense of detached insight into the British political system, and on his return he announces his plan to stand for Parliament as a "Radical." Eliot makes clear that Harold's radicalism stems less from a deep commitment to social or economic justice than a general contempt for present-day arrangements. His social vision is tellingly represented by a cartographic sense of Loamshire's geography: "All the country round here lies like a map in my brain," he boasts to his mother (22; ch. 1). His words echo the abstracted perspective Eliot begins by applauding in "The Natural History of German Life," but they come with no second moment of descent to the particular, no willingness to attend to the breathing reality surrounding him. Harold's habit of mental abstraction leads him both to a casual sexism—("he was one of those men," we read, "who are liable to make the greater mistakes about a woman's feelings, because they pique themselves on a power of interpretation derived from much experience" [418; ch. 43]), and, worse, to a kind of moral autism. In the midst of a conversation with

Esther Lyon, the young woman whose hand he seeks in marriage, Harold casually mentions that his first wife "had been a slave—was bought, in fact" (421; ch. 43). The sentence's grammatical abstraction is a chilling indicator of emotional distance; we never learn whether Harold's pluperfect tense and passive voice indicate that he wasn't the buyer, or simply that he's uncomfortable admitting it. Either way, Harold seems not to register that the remark might be the occasion for his listener's moral disquiet. That Harold also fails to notice his mother's mental anguish is, we infer, a result of the same habit of abstraction; and the chain of associations that connects Mrs. Transome to the social suffering secreted in any picturesque landscape therefore makes us sense the essential emptiness of Harold's radicalism. Thus even as Mrs. Transome's pain seems to register a privatization of potentially political meaning, it also serves as a measure of how the personal and the political in Eliot's work become images of one another.

Harold's abstraction is finally disqualified by the novel, but Eliot attempts to embody a viably radical ethico-political vision in her titular hero. Felix is a thoroughly odd character, and much of his unlikeliness stems from the sense that Eliot is using him to encapsulate the strenuous characterological requirements she implicitly lauds in "The Natural History of German Life." Like Eliot's ideal social researcher, Felix has cultivated a wide range of relations to "the thing itself" that is provincial life. The son of a weaver turned apothecary, Felix is a product of a family with a recent toehold in the petite bourgeoisie. But he has rejected this patrimony on discovering that his father's medicines are "as bad as poisons to half the people who swallow them" (61; ch. 5), abandoning his apprenticeship to pursue a course of medical study in Glasgow. (Once again Eliot's contrasting narrative threads create a sense of finely graded moral distinctions: if going away seems necessary to achieve a detached view of English provincial life, going too far away leaves one dangerously disconnected from local reality: Felix's Glasgow is accordingly a more suitable sabbatical location than Harold's culturally and ethnically alien Asia Minor.) But Felix has given up his studies in Scotland, returning to Loamshire to take up training as a watchmaker; he announces proudly that he will "take no employment that obliges me to prop up my chin with a high cravat," and avers that he would have preferred his father had remained a weaver (62; ch. 5). Eliot's purpose in engineering this curious career trajectory seems to be the creation of a hero whose commitment to the material conditions of his class and his location are a matter not of necessity but of conscious reflection; it is as if Felix has needed to temporarily remove himself from his social role so that he can live it as if in the third person, experiencing himself as a kind of representative case.

The details of Felix's past thus appear less psychologically realistic than narratively required: "Glasgow" is the sign of a distance as much characterological as geographic, and "watchmaking" (the details of which we never see Felix engaged in) the sign of a quasi-sociological determination to figure out what makes society tick. Certainly Felix's hostility to personal class advancement has a more than mildly opportunistic air, as when an aspiring politician spends a well-publicized season in a tough job in order to burnish his blue-collar credentials. Indeed, Felix's working-class identity is shown to be in part a matter of calculated effect: when he addresses a restive crowd of working men and urges them to go slow in their demands for the franchise, Eliot writes that "the well-washed face and its educated expression along with a dress more careless than that of most well-to-do workmen on a holiday, made his appearance strangely arresting" (289; ch. 30); the sense of mild theatrics is palpable. And when a friend wonders whether Felix is planning a political career, his response is equivocal: after disdaining the "ringed and scented men of the people," Felix goes on to say, more ambiguously, that he "should like well enough to be another sort of demagogue, if I could" (65; ch. 5). Precisely what will mark his difference from traditional political agitators Felix does not say; but when it becomes clear that he is opposed to the immediate enfranchisement of the working class, we are tempted to conclude that it is this very ineffability that constitutes Felix's politics.

This is the proposal Catherine Gallagher makes in her account of the novel's ideological workings. For Gallagher, Felix's character answers Eliot's desire to conceptualize a "realm of pure value" (233)—a realm distant from the material interests that drive political reality, and one she thought it incumbent on the novelist to represent to the populace. Felix's peculiarity—in particular the sense he radiates of detachment from his own position—is in Gallagher's account the result of Eliot's desire to make him the embodiment of this pure realm. "Felix Holt's face," Eliot writes in a key passage, "had the look of habitual meditative abstraction from objects of mere personal vanity or desire, which is the peculiar stamp of culture" (291; ch. 30). This last word is central in Gallagher's account; it identifies *Felix Holt* as a document of the 1860s' elaboration of the concept of "culture" as a repository of disinterested thought that would also create a brake on mass political agitation.[3] Felix's embodiment of this overtly apolitical space makes him a particularly mysterious character, a politician who never voices a coherent political vision save one of cautious abstention from political action.

Felix's impenetrability is most noticeable when he becomes a player in the novel's central love plot. The ideological standoff between Harold and Felix is intensified when the men become two points in a heavily significant romantic triangle. Esther Lyon is the adopted daughter of the dissenting Reverend Lyon, and for complicated reasons she is the rightful heir to the Transome estate, a fact that compels Harold Transome—who has always assumed he would inherit the Manor—to push his mild interest in her into a marriage suit. But despite having spent her youth yearning for French fashions and genteel society, Esther finds herself drawn to Felix, whose conversation with her mostly consists of hectoring lectures on her intellectual and moral shortcomings. Esther's choice between these two men quickly takes on ethical and aesthetic significance. "In accepting Harold Transome," Eliot writes, Esther comes to feel that she would have to "adjust her wishes to a life of middling delights, overhung with the languorous haziness of motiveless ease, where poetry was only literature, and the fine ideas had to be taken down from the shelves of the library when her husband's back was turned" (426; ch. 44). We might perceive in this dreary prospect an inverted image of Eliot's fantasies for her novel—her desire that it exceed the bounds of run-of-the-mill "literature" to achieve the heights of cultural "poetry." That Esther's choice between suitors is an allegory of Eliot's artistic ambition is clear in the numerous passages in which Esther ponders her enigmatic passion for Felix. "If Felix Holt were to love her," she thinks at one point, "her life would be exalted into something quite new—into a sort of difficult blessedness" (228; ch. 22): the last phrase serves as an excellent description of Eliot's prose, with its sometimes tortuous syntax and its sense of granting laborious access to ever higher realms of insight and compassion. Later, Eliot writes that her heroine feels that "he was an influence above her life, rather than a part of it" (356; ch. 37)—another good description of the intensity of the fictive world, adjacent to but not coextensive with the real one. If Gallagher is right that Felix represents the realm of culture, in falling in love with him Esther appears to fall in love with a fantasy image of a world removed from pettiness, and with the posture of yearning and aspiration this image demands of her. She almost seems to be falling in love with abstraction itself.

And yet it is a testament to the curious honesty of the novel that it remains so alive to the confusions that might attend such an abstracted and idealized character. The climax of the novel is an election riot in which Felix, staunch defender of law and order and a deep skeptic about the value of expanding the suffrage, leads a mob that kills a member of the constabulary. Or does he? Eliot's narrator makes clear that Felix's motivation in assuming the lead of the mob is to avert serious bloodshed, and several characters note that without his intervention the damage to life and property would have been much more grave. But one consequence of Felix's inscrutability is that it is hard to read his intention from his exterior. When Eliot describes Felix's attempt to lead the rioters away from the room where an innkeeper and her servants are cowering, Eliot writes that he "assum[ed] the tone of a mob leader, [crying] out, 'Here, boys, here's better fun this way—come with me!' and drew the men back with him along the passage. . . . He looked, to undiscerning eyes, like a leading spirit of the mob" (315; ch. 33). We have, in a sense, only the narrator's word for it that Felix means well here, and it is a bizarre concomitant of Felix's ineffable nobility that he is able so easily to imitate the opposite quality. Moreover, what makes it easy for Felix to control the mob is also precisely what makes it seem he is leading them: "A man with a definite will and an energetic personality acts as a sort of flag to draw and bind together the foolish units of a mob," Eliot writes (317; ch. 33). The sentence's very equipoise, in failing to specify what might distinguish "binding" a mob from leading one, bears scrupulous witness to how metaphysical is the value with which Felix has been invested by his creator.

Moreover, the trial scene in which Felix is acquitted after Esther's teary testimony is possibly the most critically unloved moment in Eliot's work.[4] Here again, the sense of the novel's bad faith doubles as a kind of honesty, since the very improbability of the character forces on our attention the ideological work he is being made to do. The sense of Felix's singularly problematic status in Eliot's corpus is underlined by the fact that he is the only character she ever resurrected in an extra-novelistic format. Eliot's publisher John Blackwood urged her in 1867 to pen an "Address to Working Men" in Felix's voice for publication in his magazine, the fiercely Tory *Blackwood's*. The idea was for Felix to address the million men newly enfranchised by that year's passage of the Second Reform Act, and in particular for him to explain the duty of self-control required by their new political clout.[5] Eliot's initial response was equivocal: she wrote that "Felix Holt is immensely tempted by your suggestion, but George Eliot is severely admonished by his domestic critic"—that is, her companion G. H. Lewes—"not to scatter his energies" (Cross 25). The play on the gender-drag of her nom de plume is typical of Eliot's correspondence with Blackwood.[6] But this response also makes oblique reference to the multiple and awkward layers of masquerade involved in a middle-class writer taking on the voice of a fictional working-class character in order to address "working men" in the pages of a magazine read by a firmly middle-class audience. In the end, her willingness to wrench her creation from his fictional frame can be seen both as a particularly bald violation of her character's coherence and as a stark admission that there was always something amiss in this character's conception.

Felix argues throughout the "Address" for restraint on the part of his working-class auditors; he warns them in particular that their ignorance of cultural touchstones should make them wary of exercising their political power to make hasty change; he speaks tendentiously of the franchise's "heavy responsibility" and the "terrible risk we run of working mischief" (486). His reasoning in the piece is counterintuitive in the extreme, as when in the course of cautioning against overweening class pride he blames the working class itself for having been ruled by venal overlords: "if we had groaned and hissed in the right place . . . we should have made an audience that would have shamed the other classes out of their share in the national vices" (485). But if the political cynicism of the piece is transparent, it is perhaps even more interesting for the way it seems to violate the precision of Eliot's historical imagination. Between the 1832 Reform Act (in the wake of which the "first," novelistic Felix issues his repeated cries for moderation) and the 1867 Reform Act (after which this second, resurrected Felix makes essentially the same argument), there has intervened a fiercely articulate series of working-class movements—most notably in the Chartists' mass demand for universal suffrage which reached its high point in the 1840s and remained a presence in British politics through the next decade. The second Felix's failure to so much as mention this history, and the ease with which Eliot transports him across this historical and political divide, suggests just how little a creature of his time "he" is. It is the deepest admission of the failure of the novel's historical and political imagination.

If we nonetheless sense that the novel's political and historical truth is not exhausted with Felix, we will have to return to Mrs. Transome, and to the soured desire she represents, for an explanation. Critics who find the book's politics suspect have focused their scorn on Felix and Esther's plot, in particular on the way the potential of political agitation is deflected into a happy marriage at the novel's conclusion. In this, they agree (unlikely though the association seems) with Henry James, who in his review of the novel complained that "we find [Felix] a Radical and we leave him what?—only 'utterly married;'. . . In fact, after the singular eclipse or extinction which [Felix's purported radicalism] appears to undergo on the occasion of his marriage, the reader feels tempted to rejoice that he, personally, has not worked himself nearer to it" (in Carroll 275). But this critical position, in rehearsing the novel's apparent containment of politics by marriage, is better at describing the novel's ideological program than at perceiving those aspects that escape such containment. Feminist criticism—notably that of Gillian Beer and Dorothea Barrett—has been more successful at perceiving what remains ideologically unassimilable in the novel. That excess, as I have suggested, is most visible in the outsize rhetorical and affective presence of Mrs. Transome. Precisely because her anguish is so keyed to her disappointed eroticism and to her exclusion from the masculine domains of the legal and political, Mrs. Transome's bitterness functions as a kind of corrective to the novel's program; if Esther and Felix's romance allegorizes the containment of the political by love, Mrs. Transome's obdurate failure to be consoled by her marriage or by her lover rebukes that containment, and even begins to take on wholly unexpected political shades. As Beer puts it, "the connection between the uselessness of Mrs Transome's growing rage and the deafness of all political parties to what is meant by change, remains the radical insight of the book . . . this book potentiates radical questioning without itself being in command of it" (145, 136).

Indeed, in several of her more apodictic statements Mrs. Transome seems to voice the novel's inadvertent rebuke to its own procedures. When she tells her maid Denner that "a woman's love is always freezing into fear" (374; ch. 39), Mrs. Transome might be not only recalling her experience with Jermyn, but also diagnosing Esther's supposedly more beneficent relationship to Felix. Certainly her words make us remember the terms in which the narrator has described Esther's feelings for Felix—"mortification, anger, the sense of a terrible power over her that Felix seemed to have as his angry words vibrated through her . . . She pinched her own hand hard to overcome her tremor" (124; ch. 10)—and to perceive the mutual antagonism and violence secreted even in the idyllic romance of the novel's marquee couple. And perhaps even more revealing than the content of Mrs. Transome's utterance is its intense epigrammatic energy, its stylistic approximation of Eliot's own prose. To be sure, and as if in response to this threatened convergence, Eliot's narrator almost immediately puts Mrs. Transome in her place, making clear that her verbal compression should not be taken for intellectual depth: "She had no ultimate analysis of things," Eliot writes, almost as if denying Mrs. Transome's application for a position as a social theorist. "She had never seen behind the canvas with which her life was hung" (379; ch. 40).

But in its gratuitousness the denial almost affirms its opposite, and Mrs. Transome's unappeased, perhaps unappeasable frustrations reach beyond their thematic location in the plot to speak to the novel's true radicalism. If the anger, resentment, and disempowerment in this novel are more powerfully expressed in women's relations to men than in workers' relations to factory owners and landholders, this is not merely an ideological displacement. The intensity of Mrs. Transome's anger, the vision of "the dreary waste of years empty of sweet trust and affection" (470; ch. 50) to which the novel abandons her near its close, is finally legible as a diagnosis of the inadequation of the interpersonal and the political. If this novel can appear to be the crudest instantiation of a strategy of liberal avoidance, whereby political trouble is resolved by means of sanitized relations between sympathetic subjects, it more powerfully reads as an exposure of that strategy. "Conversation consists a good deal in the denial of what is true" (279; ch. 29), Eliot's narrator—sounding a bit like Mrs. Transome—at one point affirms, and the novel's pockets of bad feeling speak a crucial truth that its plot attempts to deny: that the political ambitions of modernity are secreted only fitfully in psychological structures.

NOTES

1   On Eliot's consultation with the lawyer Frederic Harrison on the novel's plot details, see Haight 383.

2   For a defense of the historiographic and ideological complexity of *Felix Holt*'s opening segment, see Shaw 224–25.

3   Within a year of the novel's publication, Matthew Arnold would write the articles collected in 1869 as *Culture and Anarchy*. The essays not only popularized Arnold's definition of culture as "the best that has been thought and known in the world" (5), but also explicitly proposed culture as an antidote to mass political agitation.

4   See Shuttleworth 142; Fisher 153; Franklin 101; and Williams's *Culture and Society*, 107.

5   In a revealing comment, Blackwood wrote to a correspondent that the novel's "politics are excellent and will attract all parties" (quoted in Eliot, *Felix Holt* 484)—an assertion that prompts the response that politics that attract all parties probably don't deserve the name.

6   Eliot's coy response is also characteristic of the dramas around authorial agency she repeatedly stages in her fiction. For a searching account of the ways syntax and image register Eliot's ambivalence about the aggression inherent in crafting plots and in animating characters, see Hertz.

REFERENCES

Barrett, Dorothea. *Vocation and Desire: George Eliot's Heroines*. London: Routledge, 1989.

Carroll, David, ed. *George Eliot: The Critical Heritage*. New York: Barnes & Noble, 1971.

Cross, J. W. *George Eliot's Life as Related in her Letters and Journals*. Vol. 3. Edinburgh: Blackwood, 1885.

Eliot, George. "Address to Working Men." *Blackwood's Edinburgh Magazine* Jan. 1868. Rpt. as Appendix B in Eliot, *Felix Holt*.

Eliot, George. *Felix Holt*. 1866. Ed. Lynda Mugglestone. London: Penguin, 1995.

Eliot, George. "The Natural History of German Life." *Essays of George Eliot*. Ed. Thomas Pinney. London: Routledge, 1963.

Fisher, Philip. *Making Up Society: The Novels of George Eliot*. Pittsburgh: U of Pittsburgh P, 1981.

Franklin, J. Jeffrey. *Serious Play: The Cultural Form of the Nineteenth-Century Realist Novel*. Philadelphia: U of Pennsylvania P, 1999.

Gallagher, Catherine. *The Industrial Reformation of English Fiction: Social Discourse and Narrative Form, 1832–1867*. Chicago: U of Chicago P, 1985.

Haight, Gordon S. *George Eliot: A Biography*. 1968. London: Penguin, 1985.

Hertz, Neil. *George Eliot's Pulse*. Stanford: Stanford UP, 2003.

Shaw, Harry E. *Narrating Reality: Austen, Scott, Eliot*. Ithaca: Cornell UP, 1999.

Shuttleworth, Sally. *George Eliot and Nineteenth-Century Science: The Make-Believe of a Beginning*. Cambridge: Cambridge UP, 1984.

Williams, Raymond. *The Country and the City*. Oxford: Oxford UP, 1973.

Williams, Raymond. *Culture and Society: 1780–1950*. New York: Columbia UP, 1958.

11
Middlemarch: January in Lowick

Andrew H. Miller

So, we have entered there where we will never enter, into this scene painted on a canvas. All at once, there we are. We can't exactly say that we have penetrated there, but neither can we say that we are outside. We are there in a manner older and simpler than by any movement, displacement, or penetration. We are there without leaving the threshold, on the threshold, neither inside nor outside—and perhaps we are, ourselves, the threshold, just as our eye conforms to the plane of the canvas and weaves itself into its fabric. (Jean-Luc Nancy, *The Muses*)

Mr. and Mrs. Casaubon, returning from their wedding journey, arrived at Lowick Manor in the middle of January. A light snow was falling as they descended at the door, and in the morning, when Dorothea passed from her dressing room into the blue-green boudoir that we know, she saw the long avenue of limes lifting their trunks from a white earth, and spreading white branches against the dun and motionless sky. (256; ch. 28)

Under a still sky, movement encloses our world: the Casaubons descend with the snow, Dorothea passes from room to room, the lime trees lift their trunks back toward the sky, against which their branches spread. Since we last saw it, the world thus framed has become chilly and pale, but there are dry oakboughs burning in the fire, and they bring a "renewal of life and glow" to the room. In this, we are told, they are like the figure of Dorothea herself:

She was glowing from her morning toilette as only healthful youth can glow: there was gem-like brightness on her coiled hair and in her hazel eyes; there was warm red life in

A Companion to George Eliot, First Edition. Edited by Amanda Anderson and Harry E. Shaw.
© 2013 John Wiley & Sons, Ltd. Published 2016 by John Wiley & Sons, Ltd.

her lips; her throat had a breathing whiteness above the differing white of the fur which itself seemed to wind about her neck and cling down her blue-grey pelisse with a tenderness gathered from her own, a sentient commingled innocence which kept its loveliness against the crystalline purity of the outdoor snow. (256–57; ch. 28)

Dorothea glows in the snowy enclosure, her tenderness glows in the fur, and, we can say, metaphor glows in this metonym.

This device—by which the metonymic unfolding of Eliot's narrative is infused by the metaphors she has previously established—is common enough in the novel which opens, after all, by proposing that we consider our heroine's unfolding life through comparison with that of St. Teresa. Such intensifying infusion will be my initial concern as it radiates out from Eliot's sentences into her enduring preoccupations. Here, it gains force through juxtaposition with another, equally characteristic figure, namely visual juxtaposition itself. Mrs. Casaubon's beauty is thrown into relief by the whiteness of her fur, which in turn stands out against the whiteness of the snow, as the snow itself, cresting the lime-tree branches, stands out against the dun sky. White above a different white against a third and then a fourth: the fineness of the distinctions only thickens Eliot's determination to capture them before they sublime, rather bewilderingly, into a lovely innocence and a contrastive crystalline purity. (Eliot, the model English realist, regularly drives her figures into surreal abstraction.) And both these devices—infusion and visual juxtaposition—are joined here by a third, which I will call intimation. Hair, eyes, lips, throat, neck, pelisse: each of the things described in this sentence is represented by a word, but in sequencing them spatially Eliot intimates something else, the slow cascade of our gaze, represented by no single word but by their syntactic order, so that our sequential assimilation of words corresponds to the fall of our eyes down Dorothea's figure. We too seem to have returned to Lowick and descended into this scene, placed in the negative space etched by Eliot's phrasing. We're present even if unnamed—unless by sentence's end we do find a name for ourselves, or at least a representative, in the fur which trails down Dorothea's features no less than do our clinging eyes.

A space is enclosed, marked off, a canvas framed; and within that enclosed space it can seem that everything named has meanings and everything not named has meanings. The internal relation of these two conditions—the fact of enclosure and the plenitude of meanings—may be read allegorically: consigned to immanence, Eliot produces a novel unprecedented, in the English tradition, in its density of significance. The world is entirely before us. There is nothing else, nowhere else; but in its solitude, this world brims. A couple of paragraphs later, Eliot will speak of a "manifold pregnant existence," a full, enclosed, promising life; but that existence, we're told, is at an unspecified distance, and Dorothea has difficulty maintaining a "sense of connexion" with it (257; ch. 28).

The fantasy of circumscribed but inexhaustible and promising significance close to hand but not in hand is one source of Eliot's allure, inspiring in readers both exhilarated gratitude and an unsettled sense of something perhaps missed. It invites readings that are not close so much as slow: drawn onward as we hold ourselves back, we attempt to absorb all that Eliot may have meant. As we read, time seems *filled*—"as a glass may be filled not just to the level of the rim but slightly above" (Fried *Absorption* 51.) Although *Middlemarch* has long been understood to be the central expression of Eliot's belief in the ethical and aesthetic importance of sympathy, it is also the supreme expression of an even more fundamental insight, one involving the promise and peril of entering into states of absorption that offer to make one's actions and world meaningful. This sustained, demanding engagement with absorption may be among the fundamental reasons so many readers consider *Middlemarch* to be Eliot's greatest novel. But in raising these issues, *Middlemarch* also raises various questions concerning method, and among the first of these is likely to be: how far, in my absorbed solicitation of meaning, should I go? That fur—does it really figure our clinging, descending gaze? Say that it does. Are we then to understand that we should gather from Dorothea her tenderness, and like the fur form with her a comingled innocence, animated and preserved against the cold? It does sound like the sort of attitude Eliot would want to foster. But could she have meant this? Perhaps we've gone too far. Let's continue.

> As she laid the cameo-cases on the table in the bow-window, she unconsciously kept her hands on them, immediately absorbed in looking out on the still, white enclosure which made her visible world. (257; ch. 28)

The glowing that serves as my guiding figure for this passage modulates here into absorption. But Eliot's locution is odd: we're not told that Dorothea is "absorbed in the still, white enclosure"; she is absorbed in *looking* at that enclosure. Eliot thus suggests that Dorothea is uncertainly absorbed both in herself and in something outside of herself, absorbed in her own act of attending to something outside of her. As are we: absorbed in the book in our hands, we are absorbed in a visible world which intimates an invisible one.

Absorption seen in another evidently is itself absorbing: having pictured her heroine absorbed in looking, Eliot escorts us into free indirect discourse. We imagine the contents of Mrs. Casaubon's mind as she imagines the contents of her enclosure, the house of which she is now mistress, while measuring out the coming days, indefinite and directionless:

> The ideas and hopes which were living in her mind when she first saw this room nearly three months before were present now only as memories: she judged them as we judge transient and departed things. All existence seemed to beat with a lower pulse than her own, and her religious faith was a solitary cry, the struggle out of a nightmare in which every object was withering and shrinking away from her. Each remembered thing in the room was disenchanted, was deadened as an unlit transparency . . . (258; ch. 28)

It is a sadly ironic moment: the very act of finding meaning in which we have been engaged, are now engaged, has for Dorothea come to nothing, leaving her with a sense of isolating difference so great as to seem physiological. A picture of skepticism, the room is glowless. And yet the lack of meaning is signified with such fertility: withering, shrinking, disenchanting, deadening, hopes departing. How are we to understand this contrast? Does language stand by sarcastic before the emptiness of the world? Or, are we to think that, if language is so fertile, the world cannot be so empty? Does the fertility of the narrator's expression signal Dorothea's scrabbling desperation? Or—perhaps—it expresses her anger, diffused and deflected, intimated and unexpressed, at those pale-pulsed others who, with baleful touch, turn her walled-in world to lead.

Dorothea finds one immediate response to her skeptical situation in a relationship with a representation of another person, Aunt Julia.[1] Dorothea establishes a connection with a work of art at some distance, a representation of a woman herself pregnant with meaning: Julia is at once Mr. Casaubon's aunt and Will's grandmother, a memory and a hope, as the evening star in the night is nothing other than the morning star of dawn.

> Each remembered thing in the room was disenchanted, was deadened as an unlit transparency, till her wandering gaze came to the group of miniatures, and there at last she saw something which had gathered new breath and meaning: it was the miniature of Mr. Casaubon's aunt Julia, who had made the unfortunate marriage—of Will Ladislaw's grandmother. Dorothea could fancy that it was alive now—the delicate woman's face which yet had a headstrong look, a peculiarity difficult to interpret. Was it only her friends who thought her marriage unfortunate? or did she herself find it out to be a mistake, and taste the salt bitterness of her tears in the merciful silence of the night? (258; ch. 28)

Here as often elsewhere, free indirect discourse allows, exactly, indirection, giving us extraordinary access to intimate elisions, to all the ways the characters do not say—perhaps cannot say—what they may nonetheless know. We do not know what Dorothea knows. Facing her, we share her question: did she find her marriage out to be a *mistake?*

In her invisible, yet more than in her visible world, understanding the meaning of Dorothea's motion is a matter of interpreting metonymically, reading not individual words but their syntax, the unfolding relations within and among sentences. "This motion in narrative," writes Rosemarie Bodenheimer, "in which each sentence rereads and responds to the unstated implications of the one before, is to my mind a most striking (and lifelong) aspect of George Eliot's style. It creates both the dense and muscular demand of her prose, and its peculiar self-enclosure, which makes of the reader not so much a direct addressee as a reminder of other perspectives that the writer is compelled to incorporate, defuse, and transform" (38–39). In passages of free indirect discourse, the resultant effect of syntactic self-enclosure conveys and intensifies the enclosed nature of the character's contemplation. We read from the sequencing of words and sentences to the passage of Dorothea's unstated thought, and our very difficulty in understanding that passage generates an effect of psychological depth sculpted through time:

> What breadth of experience Dorothea seemed to have passed over since she first looked at this miniature! She felt a new companionship with it, as if it had an ear for her and could see how she was looking at it. Here was a woman who had known some difficulty about marriage. Nay the colours deepened, the lips and chin seemed to get larger, the hair and eyes seemed to be sending out light, the face was masculine and beamed on her with that full gaze which tells her on whom it falls that she is too interesting for the slightest movement of her eyelid to pass unnoticed and uninterpreted. The vivid presentation came like a pleasant glow to Dorothea. (258; ch. 28)

Dorothea not only glows but, at last, is glowed upon. She has felt such sentient comingling only rarely, most strikingly with Will. Indeed, his plausibility as a love object rests on his possessing the talent Dorothea imagines here in this portrait of his grandmother, the ability to find interest in the world and, in particular, in Dorothea herself: Will "always seemed to see more in what she said than she herself saw" (339; ch. 37). For Will, the world as it is now, with Dorothea in its foreground, is more full of meaning than initially appears, and it asks to be understood even in its smallest details. (The world is for him primarily aesthetic—more likely to be under-interpreted than over-interpreted.) What Dorothea finds in this work of art is not exactly an interpretation of herself but the promise of her worthiness to be interpreted. She has an immense desire to be found, and her interpretation of Julia's portrait expresses that desire. She thus makes of being intelligible and generously interpreted something erotic. But her discovery of Will's qualities in his grandmother also reveals that she has feelings about Will which she herself does not know. Her absorption thus exposes her to us and we, with a full gaze, see more in her than she sees herself.

"We don't entirely merge with Dorothea," Harry Shaw remarks about another moment in the novel: "we also observe her transmuting the external environment into a subjective symbol" (232). That observing stance, generated by our recognition that Dorothea is interpreting this miniature according to her desires, prepares us for the more starkly distanced position we soon assume:

> The vivid presentation came like a pleasant glow to Dorothea: she felt herself smiling, and turning from the miniature sat down and looked up as if she were again talking to a figure in front of her. But the smile disappeared as she went on meditating, and at last she said aloud—
> "Oh, it was cruel to speak so! How sad—how dreadful." (258–59; ch. 28)

By not naming the figure in front of Dorothea, Eliot conveys the impression that Dorothea is herself avoiding his name and thus avoiding her desire for him. Equally important, the moment of distancing uncertainty this elision causes in us anticipates the effect created by the sudden eruption of quoted speech in the next sentence. Having been absorbed for some pages within Dorothea's associative inner life, we now are given only what we can see and hear from the outside. Her speech comes as a shock in the stillness; our absorption in her is broken. Why should Eliot have broken that absorption and separated us from Dorothea just when she has been absorbed in an act of interpretation? In one's preoccupation with whatever it is that one is interpreting—with an image or with a passage of prose that seems especially rich—one can find oneself alone, one's separateness palpable, abandoned, deep in the labyrinths with a guttering taper. How can you know if you have gone too far? For Eliot it is not—or not only, perhaps not principally—when you learn you have made a *mistake*, but when you look up and discover that you are alone. Dorothea stands and goes to find her husband.

***

I've gone to some lengths to dramatize a reading of this passage in order to bring forward Eliot's fascination not merely with the family of figures that includes glowing, infusion, and absorption but with the vulnerability that such absorption brings with it.[2] In *Middlemarch*, Eliot frames enclosures saturated with significance and represents her characters, Dorothea not alone but above all, attracted to and interpreting that significance; intimating our equivocal presence in those enclosures, she engages us in analogous acts of absorptive interpretation. In this way the novel can glow with meaning and can hold out the promise not only that we will know but will be known. And yet, Eliot also commits her technical dexterity to disrupting that absorption and that promise, often quite violently.

At Lowick, Eliot interrupts absorption by abruptly intruding dramatic speech on pages of modulated narration rendering Dorothea's thoughts. Elsewhere Eliot uses other techniques. Sometimes she sinks us in the events of one plot only to indicate with a glancing, cross-cutting blow that our absorption has made us oblivious of momentous events elsewhere: it's rather pointedly noted that we've been otherwise occupied while Celia has had her baby and Rosamond has lost hers. At other times, we're surprised out of our absorption by recursive movements within a single plot. Fred Vincy rides toward the Garths to tell them that he cannot pay a bill which Mr. Garth has cosigned. As he rides, he dwells listlessly on the scene he will confront at the Garths', absorbed in thoughts of the awkwardness and the inconvenience it will cause not them but himself. He's especially anxious about Mrs. Garth, of whom he is rather in awe. And as we don't know much about her, the narrator gently, insensibly lifts the reins of the story from Fred's hands and helpfully provides several paragraphs of carefully balanced description of her character, stressing her honest industry first as a governess and then as a housewife, now joining the two roles in raising her children; and, as if in illustration of this point, we're ushered to a seat in her kitchen and provided an ostensibly representative scene, rendered dramatically in dialogue, as the industrious, multifariously competent woman teaches her children their grammar lessons while rolling out her pastry dough. Absorbed at length in this vital world of honest daily labor, we're startled when she suddenly exclaims, "Hark, there is a knock at the door!" and in comes Fred with his bad news (231; ch. 24). The lesson that Eliot—multifariously competent herself—has for us requires that we identify not with his self-absorption but with those who suffer from it, and in order to teach us she absorbs us in their kitchen, and punctures that absorption.

A less didactic but more elaborately recursive movement structures the protracted shot-reverse-shot of Dorothea absorbed in looking in the Vatican Museum, a scene which in fact prepares the way for our return to Lowick. Having first seen Dorothea from the perspective of Will and his friend Naumann, we then cycle back through the story of her sublime nuptial misery amid Rome's wreck of gorgeous ideals, all unilluminated by the learning of her husband, and work our way back finally to the Museum, where we find her standing still, staring at a streak of sunlight, in "brooding abstraction" (190; ch. 20). Our chapter-long absorption in the story of her honeymoon thus mimics her absorption at the Vatican, conveying the sense that, in such swollen moments, a whole history can be condensed. But our surprise at discovering ourselves back where we started, rather like the surprise of hearing Fred knock at the Garths' door, disrupts that carefully engineered absorption.

Absorption formally interrupted, then, is a recurring event in reading the novel, varied in means and purpose. So far I have stressed this absorption and its interruption as an experience of characters and readers. But it characterizes the experience of the author, too. And this is perhaps nowhere more evident than in the passage that opens the chapter immediately following that on which I have focused:

"One morning some weeks after her arrival at Lowick, Dorothea . . ." (261; ch. 29). In retrospect, it is the generic quality of this phrase which is most striking. Eliot is going about her business, drawing forward our attention by recalling the opening lines of the previous chapter quoted at the start of this essay: she is at work, routinely absorbed in the task at hand, rendering her heroine's experience in her snowy enclosure, where time passes insensibly, the days differing one from the next only in shading. And, then, famously, the passage of those unremarkable, unremarked-on weeks is juxtaposed with this instant, now, of writing:

> One morning some weeks after her arrival at Lowick, Dorothea—but why always Dorothea? (261; ch. 29)

This movement of thought has been understood to concern point of view, underscoring the importance of sympathetically imagining events from others' perspectives. It is a prelude to the bravura achievement of sympathy with Casaubon, who had been so effectively skewered by the satire of the novel's early pages. And that understanding is reasonable enough—indeed, Eliot tells us to understand it in this way, more or less, in her next sentence. But what is distinctive here is not that we're schooled about perspective—that happens all the time in the novel—but that the narrator is so instructed, that she schools herself. Something has pulled her up short as Dorothea was pulled up short in her boudoir, and that interruption makes us realize that Eliot, too, has been absorbed by a picture of a woman.[3] But what is it that has pulled her

up? In the previous chapter we trailed Dorothea as she passed from the visible representation of Julia to an invisible representation of Will; we then watched as she,
prompted by imagined remarks, abruptly moved to her husband. Now the narrator
follows Dorothea; she moves toward Casaubon, too. And, in both cases, what prompts
this movement appears to be an act of verbal repetition. As Dorothea's dramatic rec-
reation of Will's words jolts her out of her absorption, so here, the simple fact of
writing the word "Dorothea" causes Eliot to surface. She has been absorbed in looking
no less than her heroine, and is wrenched away from that absorption by the iterative
nature of representation. Such surfacing and the absorption it breaks suddenly come
to appear essential features of the act of writing itself.

***

A generation of scholarship on George Eliot devoted itself to the study of representation, language, and interpretation in her novels: criticism by Neil Hertz, J. Hillis
Miller, D. A. Miller and, along different lines David Carroll all contributed to
this theme, concentrating on Eliot's preoccupation with the nature of writing. This
preoccupation, I have been suggesting, informs not only Eliot's explicit references to
linguistic signs and their interpretation, but her representations of absorption—of
characters who are absorbed in their tasks as Eliot herself, at the moment of creating
them, was absorbed in hers. Dorothea's absorption in looking, Fred's absorption in
the scene he pictures for himself, Mrs. Garth's absorption in her daily labors: items
in a long list that also includes Lydgate's youthful absorption in his book on anatomy
as he receives his moment of vocation, Mary's absorbed attentions to the dying Featherstone, and Rosamond's climactic absorption in Will Ladislaw, there in front of
her, glowing in her lifeless home, giving it meaning. All expressions, on this view, of
Eliot's own absorption, pen in hand, in the act of writing—and all exposed to interruption: for every toddling St. Teresa, a rescue of prudent uncles. Eliot is present in
her work not only as an analyst of interpretation, or as subject to linguistic dissemination, but as someone preoccupied with writing as an absorbing but exposed labor. Of
course, other absorbing pursuits are subject to interruption, too: what is Lydgate's
story but a monitory tale of the need to preserve absorption from the interruptions
of money-cares? But, for Eliot, writing holds a special place. Caleb Garth is the most
naturally absorbed character in the novel; he appears fully continuous with his existence. (R. H. Hutton: "The happiest creatures she draws are those who are most able,
like Caleb Garth or Adam Bede, to absorb their whole minds and sink their whole
energies in limited but positive duties of visible utility." [Carroll, *Critical Heritage*
301]). But even Caleb's absorption can be disturbed, we're told, when he is writing,
and his table shaken (374; ch. 40).

While influenced by these literary critics, my present line of thought is more
responsive to the work of the art historian Michael Fried, who conceives of absorption as an aspect of pictorial realism, visible intermittently from Caravaggio through
Chardin and Greuze, appearing again in the nineteenth century with Menzel and

Manet, before reemerging in the recent art photography of Jeff Wall, Thomas Struth, and others. Each of these artists, in varied fashions, responded to visual art's primordial condition of being beheld, its intrinsic sociality, by depicting figures sunk in absorption, unseeing of others. In his work on Courbet, Fried argues that the French painter sophisticated this process by repeatedly transporting himself into his paintings, thus negating his status as their "first beholder" (*Courbet* 98). Doing so allowed Courbet to fancy his canvases forever un-beheld: if he, their "first beholder" did not see them, how could a second or third (*Courbet* 98)? Fried's readings of Courbet's self-portraits, allegories, landscapes, and paintings of women testify to the fertility of this fantasy. Eliot analogously attempts to control relations with her audience and does so by similarly managing writing's primordial condition of being read—*its* sociality. But Eliot, to a greater degree than her French contemporary, recognized the limits of this fantasy—or so I understand from Bodenheimer's study of her letters and novels:

> The appeals to readers and the sudden shifts in perspective that are so central to the effect of George Eliot's prose originate in this always double activity, in which the writer both immerses herself in writing and assumes the position of a suddenly critical reading audience. If that is a defensive posture, it becomes in George Eliot's hands an immensely generative technique. (46)

In *Middlemarch* this generative technique is at work, wherever else, in the running battle between the narrator and those who first appear in the text as "common eyes" (3; ch. 1) and continue to be present through the routine intimations of the passive voice—as when, still in the novel's opening pages, we're told that Dorothea "was usually spoken of" as being remarkably clever (7; ch. 1) and "was regarded as an heiress" (9; ch. 1). Here, and elsewhere, the passive voice exercises Eliot's power, intimating an audience the errors of whom she will silently correct. The stakes of this ongoing, invisible skirmishing with these featureless, faintly characterized beholders eventually emerge in the Finale, when Eliot describes the confused reception that such common eyes give to the books written by Mary and Fred Vincy.[4] Absorbed in her writing, Eliot preempts its reception by serving as its first reader, displacing featureless, oppositional others.

  The understanding of an absorbed Eliot has endured in the book's critical reception. When critics recall the story of her self-identification with Casaubon, or complain about her too vituperative treatment of Rosamond and Celia, or apologize for her laxly admiring attitude toward Will, they suggest that she has been too fully absorbed in her creation.[5] It was this sense of infusing authorial presence that undergirded Henry James's defense of Eliot's dull letters: having "distilled her very substance into the things she gave the world," she had, "therefore, so much the less of it for her casual writing" (Carroll, *Critical Heritage* 492). And when he goes on to speak of "her earnestness, her refined conscience, her exalted state of responsibility" (Carroll, *Critical Heritage* 495), we have one of the most familiar marks of her distilled presence. Eliot is emphatically earnest—which is to say she is not merely unrelievedly serious, but unrelievedly serious *in intention*. Her writing glows with her intentions. "In morality, tracing an intention limits a man's responsibility; in art, it dilates it completely" (Cavell 236); Eliot did not merely accept this dilation of responsibility but embraced it. It exalted her.

And yet, against this picture of *Middlemarch* as infused by Eliot's intentions, consider the opposing view of her as secluded or recessed. Again, James gives the most sophisticated instance, presenting her prose as a series of sequestration effects. Having dwelt on the long years of adulthood in which Eliot wrote no novels and cast no "premonitory rays" of any genius (Carroll, *Critical Heritage* 493), he notes the surprise of her early readers: who was it, they asked, who had been in our midst "taking notes so long and so wisely without giving a sign" (Carroll, *Critical Heritage* 496)? Secluded by her nature—one "deeply reserved" and "not overflowing in idle confidences" (Carroll, *Critical Heritage* 491)—she was further secluded by her irregular union with Lewes, who protectively interposed himself between his wife and the world; she was thus free to produce her creations "in some intellectual back shop or crucible." They "carry to the maximum the indoor quality," are enclosed, walled off (Carroll, *Critical Heritage* 501). Along this line of development, then, the impression is of someone doubly recessed, apart and inscrutable, controlling her relation to the world and her readers, interposing her reflective narrative voice between herself and the world, secluded from others and pressed ironically into seclusion by her very sensitivity, her liability to absorption. "On the whole," she wrote in 1872, "it would be better if my life could be done for me and I could look on" (*Letters* 5:340).

***

Eliot's writing on the aesthetics and ethics of sympathy have been central not only to interpretation of her novels but also to critical reflection on narration more generally; the most prominent and pertinent recent contributors to this long tradition are James Buzard and Amanda Anderson, who have analyzed Eliot's recognition of the dangers, as well as the powers, of extensive sympathizing while tracing its cultural and political consequence. This emphasis on perspective and sympathy accords with a conventional understanding of ethical reflection. We tend, as the philosopher Susan Wolf has most recently remarked, to describe human motivation and to establish normative models of practical reason along two lines: one presents humans as egoists, "moved and guided exclusively by what they take to be in their own self-interest"; the other presents them as capable also of being moved impersonally, by reason or duty (1). These alternatives, I hope, will be familiar to any reader of *Middlemarch*: they define Eliot's overt ethical investments. It is no surprise that, in presenting her picture of conventional moral reflection, Wolf turns to Eliot's friend the philosopher Henry Sidgwick, who, during the years *Middlemarch* was composed, analyzed these alternatives in terms congenial to the novelist, as matters of perspective: he contrasts "the point of view of an individual seeking his own happiness" with "the point of view of the universe" (Sidgwick 186, 417). Eliot's manipulation of perspective aims to exercise the sympathy of characters and readers in order to calibrate properly the relation of egoism to reason or duty in particular situations.

What I have written here clearly bears on (and draws from) this critical tradition. But this picture, natural as it appears, excludes many of the motives and reasons that most centrally shape our lives. As Wolf remarks, we don't always act either out of desire for our own happiness or out of duty; we're also susceptible to other motivations and reasons, most prominently those connected to the need for meaningfulness. "I agonize over the article I am trying to write," she reports, "because I want to get it right—that is, because I want the argument to be sound, the view to be correct, the writing to be clear and graceful. It is not for my sake—at least not only for my sake—that I struggle so with my work. I do not know or care whether it is best for me . . . it is the value of good philosophy that is driving and guiding my behavior" (4–5). Such a behavior is meaningful, and it is that meaningfulness that provides her rationale and motivation. Meaningfulness, she remarks, should be recognized as "a distinct category of value" (53). Focusing on Eliot's manipulations of perspective, our attention centers on the ethical cultivation of sympathy and its obstacles; focusing on her study of absorption, by contrast, draws our attention to something prior to that, the ethical cultivation of meaningfulness and the dangers of its evaporation. Eliot is often concerned with the difficult balance of egoism and duty; she is always concerned with the difficult discovery or creation of meaningfulness, the forming of lives with meaning. This is Dorothea's work, as the snow of Lowick enters her heart.

Of course, as Wolf recognizes, not every activity contributes to meaningfulness. Eliot worries over Dorothea's duty toward her husband before and after his death, and the conflict between her duty toward him and her own happiness is part of the drama. But the peculiar character of that conflict—and much of its emotional power—is given by the cruel thought that his life-work was not worthy of his engagement (and, a separate concern, that he himself was not worthy of Dorothea's). Eliot turns this particular screw because she is committed to cultivating in her readers an emotionally powerful appreciation of meaningfulness and its vulnerability—our engagement with meaningful objects and our desperation when their significance vanishes. This engagement guides Dorothea at Lowick, and has guided me, absorbed in looking at her.

That this fundamental concern with the vulnerability of meaning was an enduring one for Eliot is suggested by a letter she sent to a youthful friend and fellow evangelical some three decades before imagining the enclosure of Lowick. It's a remarkable document, raising in a preliminary way the issues that have preoccupied us across these pages: our intimate displacement within an enclosure dense with meaning uncertainly available; the desire to be intelligible and to be generously understood; and the violent, isolating defeats that our absorbed pursuit of meaning can inflict on those desires. I'll end by reflecting (on) its premonitory rays:

> Mine is too often a world such as Wilkie can so well paint, a *walled-in* world, furnished with all the details which he remembers so accurately, and the least interesting part thereof is often what I suppose must be designated as the intelligent; but I deny that

it has even a comparative claim to the appellation for give me a three-legged stool and it will call up associations moral, political, mathematical if I do but ask it, while some human beings have the odious power of contaminating the very images that are enshrined as our soul's arcana, their baleful touch has the same effect as would a uniformity in the rays of light—it turns all objects to pale lead colour. (*Letters* 1:71)

The young Eliot here escapes the walled-in world that would later threaten her equally young heroine by describing a dramatic confrontation in which the desolation of significance effected by her intimate opposites in meaning-making succumbs to the triumphant flood of adjectival emphasis, the surge of lapidary figures, the rush of allusion in her own writing.

O how lusciously joyous to have the wind of heaven blow on one after being *stived* in a human atmosphere, to feel one's "heart leap up" after the pressure that Shakespeare so admirably describes, "When a man's wit is not seconded by the forward child understanding it strikes a man as dead as a large reckoning in a small room. (*Letters* 1:71)

At this stage it should come as no surprise that the swelling pressures of meaning within an enclosed room can figure writing itself, a place where wit meets, or does not meet, understanding. But, perhaps, we can take one further step. Eliot's final, syntactically difficult allusion is to *As You Like It*, where Touchstone wishes that the woman he loves had the capacity to understand what he has written. Scholars understand that Shakespeare, in writing of death in a small room, was alluding to the murder of Christopher Marlowe, some six or seven years before the play appeared, victim of a deadly misunderstanding over a large bill. Marlowe's violent death; Shakespeare's allusion to it; Eliot's allusion to Shakespeare; and the echo, years later, of that violent allusion in the stived, glowless atmosphere of Lowick: should we understand that the rage over a reckoning has somehow been channeled through this metonymic course to be directed now at the scholar Casaubon, whose solitary tracing of similar allusions is death-dealing? Must Casaubon die so that Dorothea can understand and be understood? Does that sound like the sort of attitude Eliot would want to foster? How far should we go?

NOTES

1 This perfectionist narrative structure, in which a condition of world-withering skepticism is displaced by an encounter with another person, is efficiently described in Hertz's "Two Extravagant Teachings" and in much of Stanley Cavell's writing. Hertz links this issue directly with the question of interpretive limits and explicitly asks how far one can go. The present essay should be understood as a continuation

of thoughts he initiated. That perfectionism was a central feature of Victorian literary and ethical culture is the guiding proposition of my *Burdens of Perfection*.

2 I'm grateful to Evelyn Noell for conversations about this passage and to the other members of the seminar I taught at Indiana University on *Middlemarch* in the Spring of 2011.

3   While analyzing the relation between the "inside" and "outside" of the texts we read, and placing that relation in the context of Victorian "autoethnography," Jim Buzard identifies the narrator's need to "stop herself before going 'too far'" (282) and notes, neatly, the echo of the prudent Mr. Brooke, forever pulling up.

4   Eliot makes related concerns explicit in "Looking Forward," the first essay of *Theophrastus Such*.

5   See, for instance, Hutton's tender defense of Rosamond against Eliot's unfair treatment, and Sidney Colvin's charge that Eliot's representation of Celia wants "impartiality" (Carroll, *Critical Heritage* 337), and Dicey's striking intuition that Eliot was unable fully to transfer Will Ladislaw from her thoughts onto the page (Carroll, *Critical Heritage* 350).

REFERENCES

Anderson, Amanda. *The Powers of Distance: Cosmopolitanism and the Cultivation of Detachment.* Princeton: Princeton UP, 2001.

Bodenheimer, Rosemarie. *The Real Life of Mary Ann Evans: George Eliot, Her Letters and Fiction.* Ithaca: Cornell UP, 1994.

Buzard, James. *Disorienting Fiction: The Autoethnographic Work of Nineteenth-Century British Novels.* Princeton: Princeton UP, 2005.

Carroll, David. *George Eliot: The Critical Heritage.* New York: Barnes & Noble, 1971.

Carroll, David. *George Eliot and the Conflict of Interpretations: A Reading of the Novels.* Cambridge: Cambridge UP, 1992.

Cavell, Stanley. *Must We Mean What We Say?: A Book of Essays.* Cambridge: Cambridge UP, 2002.

Eliot, George. *The George Eliot Letters.* Ed. Gordon S. Haight. 9 vols. New Haven: Yale UP, 1954–78.

Eliot, George. *Middlemarch.* Ed. David Carroll. Oxford: Oxford UP, 1997.

Fried, Michael. *Absorption and Theatricality: Painting and Beholder in the Age of Diderot.* Berkeley: U of California P, 1980.

Fried, Michael. *Courbet's Realism.* Chicago: U of Chicago P, 1990.

Hertz, Neil. "Two Extravagant Teachings." In *The End of the Line: Essays on Psychoanalysis and the Sublime.* New York: Columbia U-P, 1985. 145–57.

Hertz, Neil. *George Eliot's Pulse.* Stanford: Stanford UP, 2003.

Miller, Andrew H. *The Burdens of Perfection: On Ethics and Reading in Nineteenth-century British Literature.* Ithaca: Cornell UP, 2008.

Miller, D. A. *Narrative and its Discontents: Problems of Closure in the Traditional Novel.* Princeton: Princeton UP, 1981.

Miller, J. Hillis. "Narrative and History." *ELH* 41.3 (1974): 455–73.

Miller, J. Hillis. "Optic and Semiotic in *Middlemarch*." *The Worlds of Victorian Fiction.* Ed. Jerome H. Buckley. Cambridge: Harvard UP, 1975. 125–45.

Nancy, Jean-Luc. *The Muses.* Stanford: Stanford UP, 1996.

Shaw, Harry. E. *Narrating Reality: Austen, Scott, Eliot.* Ithaca: Cornell UP, 1999.

Sidgwick, Henry. *The Method of Ethics.* Indianapolis: Hackett, 1981.

Wolf, Susan. R. *Meaning in Life and Why it Matters.* Princeton: Princeton UP, 2011.

12

Daniel Deronda: Late Form, or After *Middlemarch*

Alex Woloch

Is it beautiful or not beautiful to begin a novel with a question? The opening inter-rogative of *Daniel Deronda* is the first of many meta-critical prompts in George Eliot's last novel. It goads the reader not just with a question grounded in the world of the story (how should we understand Gwendolen Harleth's character?) but simultaneously a question about the question (how should we understand a novel that commences in such an odd way?). An incipient sense of self-consciousness is almost unavoid-able: Eliot's opening is conspicuously experimental, unfolding only in contrast to the reader's normative expectations of how a novel starts. Reading can subtly split in this circumstance, catalyzing a double awareness of both story and discourse, mutually implicated with one another but not sealed securely together. The residual force of this sentence—as it calls attention to itself—might then remind us of Mr. Vander-noodt, a minor character in *Daniel Deronda* who, during the tour of the Abbey, "had the mania of always describing one thing when you were looking at another"(358; ch. 35).

Consciousness is, of course, a key term and topic in Eliot's art. Strikingly, the opening of the *second* installment of *Daniel Deronda* depicts precisely such a residual, second-order experience of consciousness within the story itself. It is worth quoting this scene across the threshold of the volume division, from book 1 ("The Spoiled Child") to book 2 ("Meeting Streams"):

> "Miss Harleth, here is a gentleman who is not willing to wait any longer for an intro-duction. He has been getting Mrs. Davilow to send me with him. Will you allow me to introduce Mr Mallinger Grandcourt?"

A Companion to George Eliot, First Edition. Edited by Amanda Anderson and Harry E. Shaw.
© 2013 John Wiley & Sons, Ltd. Published 2016 by John Wiley & Sons, Ltd.

Mr Grandcourt's wish to be introduced had no suddenness for Gwendolen; but when Lord Brackenshaw moved aside a little for the prefigured stranger to come forward and she felt herself face to face with the real man, there was a little shock which flushed her cheeks and vexatiously deepened with her consciousness of it. (90–91; chs. 10 and 11)

The elaboration of Gwendolen's oxymoronic "little shock" describes and generates the effect of intensification that we might see at work in the opening of the novel. Gwendolen's sense of consciousness is alienated from but also implicated in the flush that provokes it. The "deepen[ing]" operates like a pair of mirrors producing a continuous structure of reflection: Gwendolen's "vexatio[n]," at suddenly noticing the flush on her cheeks, only works to produce more of a flush, which in turn could produce more vexation. Flush, vexation, shock, and consciousness blur together and reinforce—or "deepen"—one another. And yet this process takes place in an instant, rendered more conspicuous by the suspension of this moment across the break between books.

***

The reverberating formal deviance of *Daniel Deronda*'s opening is only heightened by its explicit *thematic* proximity to Eliot's own previous novel: "Miss Brooke had that kind of beauty which seems to be thrown into relief by poor dress." Like the novel as a whole, the first line of *Daniel Deronda* is at once deliberately reminiscent of *Middlemarch* (in its immediate aesthetic focus on the female protagonist) and radically dissimilar (withholding a clear sense of who is asking, or who might be the object of, this question). In this way, the opening of *Daniel Deronda*—in addition to foregrounding its own experimental narrative energies—inaugurates the problem of the text's relationship to its immediate precursor, *Middlemarch*. "I have enjoyed *Daniel Deronda because* I have enjoyed *Middlemarch*," says Henry James's Theodora (979) in "the most famous review of the novel" (Gallagher 153). And while readers have long noted the reach of *Daniel Deronda*—singling it out, for example, as a novel that "touches the limits of Victorian fiction" (Hardy 8) or in which "the history of English realism comes to an end" (Tucker 35)—this reach is curiously intertwined with any number of ways that the novel unfolds in close, backward-looking relation to its immediate precursor. Most evidently, the eight-book design, with its insistent chapter epigraphs, locks *Daniel Deronda* into almost awkward structural proximity with *Middlemarch*. It is as though the novel—despite its unorthodox narrative desires—were unfolding in an already occupied, or previously actualized, fictional space. More pervasively, and under the force of this structural repetition, the reader confronts continuities in plot-lines, characters, and the narrator's own position and disposition, that complicate our direct interaction with *Daniel Deronda*.

What can you write after *Middlemarch*? The reach or "grasp" of *Daniel Deronda*—following in the wake of *Middlemarch*'s expansive and synthetic narrative—makes it an exemplary instance of novelistic "late style," at once extending, merely recapitulating, and straining against the novelist's own previous works (and above all its structural twin, *Middlemarch*). If this problem of writing beyond a previous text is, of course, a condition—or opportunity—for many works of art, the serialized, popular realist fiction of the nineteenth century presented a particularly rich matrix for this kind of writerly obstacle and catalyst. Such novels both work to construct an ever more completed, authentic fictional reality and emerge in a literary marketplace that tended to favor prolific and continuous production. To fill out the world—making it credible, compelling, immersive, and saturated with a set of rich fictional personalities—and then to destroy the world, starting again, like an angry god: this often seems like the dual mandate of nineteenth-century fiction (resisted only in the outlying cases of interconnected networks of fiction such as those by Balzac or Trollope). It is a perverse spectacle of aesthetic labor.

This perversity informs what we could call the compositional quandary of *Daniel Deronda*, as it simultaneously seems to build on (or, more negatively: repeat) and to work against the achievement of *Middlemarch*. We can see this quandary echoed within the fictional world itself—for example, in the extreme versions of characters struggling to break from the past (as in Leonora's rebellion against her origins) or to reconnect with it (Mirah's mournful fidelity to her dead mother). Likewise, in Daniel's paradoxical "choice of inheritance," the novel foregrounds an extravagant synthesis that would encompass these two poles. One way to understand these dueling impulses is as they reflect back on, or are drawn out of, Eliot's own writerly situation, post-*Middlemarch*.

Eliot's epic of provincial life doesn't only intensify the general problem (of artistic follow-up) because of its sheer accomplishment, but also, more pointedly and specifically, through its commitment to an "integrated" fictional world. *Middlemarch* famously balances public and private, psychological depth and social expansiveness, perspective and immersion; it seals together the individual and the social and intertwines the vertical movement of the *Bildungsroman* with the horizontal inclusiveness of the social-realist novel. To amplify (and not merely, diminishingly, reproduce) such a framework poses a keen aesthetic dilemma, as the very act of extension can threaten to undermine the harmonious object that it tries to develop. March in any direction and you are no longer in the middle. In this way, *Daniel Deronda*'s experimental thrusts hardly ever entail a simple break from the aesthetics of *Middlemarch*, but more complicated forms of echoing that—just as an echo works both to extend and distort—can seem to subsume and dissolve the former novel simultaneously.

Daniel Deronda is thus renowned both for its aggressive expansion of novelistic scope—most obviously in its insistence on a post-national supra-English perspective, its strategic introduction of "foreign" and "Jewish" identities into the English novel and its countervailing attention to unconscious and semi-conscious states (what Eliot calls "the unmapped country within us" [235; ch. 24])—and for its omissions, lacunas, and generic instabilities.[1] Against a series of terms which readers have reliably applied to *Middlemarch*—expansive, harmonious, balanced, (even "grown-up," in Virginia Woolf's famous comment)—*Daniel Deronda* has long provoked a more unruly set of qualifiers—"elephantine" (Chase 215); the "last, wildest and savviest novel" (Hertz

32); "an outré" and "overwritten novel" (Gallagher 130 and 120), to cite three important examples. (Gallagher's recent discussion offers one particularly elegant model for
a reading that would foreground and work through, rather than shying away from
or ingeniously transcending, the sheer excess or "too much" of *Daniel Deronda*). The
adjectival volatility that the novel has always generated is perhaps the abiding formal
feature of its critical reception. The most well-known instance of this reception occurs
in F. R. Leavis's vociferous argument for the merits of the Gwendolen-centered,
"English" plot of *Daniel Deronda*, which emerges only against his simultaneous repudiation of the Daniel-centered "Jewish" plot. Leavis's opening contention, of the
"remarkable" and "unfortunate" "association of the [novel's] strength with [its] weakness" (93) prompts him to two transgressive critical gestures: imagining a differently
titled novel—*Gwendolen Harleth* (100)—which he would find lurking within Eliot's
actual novel, and calling for an excision of the text (which would substantialize the
fragmentation, or aesthetic splitting, that provokes him): "as for the bad part of *Daniel
Deronda*, there *is* nothing to do but cut it away"(137).

Leavis's essay has generated a lot of critical scorn over the years. But the best criticism of *Daniel Deronda* has often been able dialectically to absorb, rather than simply
negate or transcend, the dissonant note that Leavis (and before him James) sound,
whereas the repudiation of his segregative response can rely, too frequently, on short-
circuiting the question of aesthetics altogether or invoking an idealized category of
unity that discounts the wildness and excess of the novel. In her own most well-known
response to *Daniel Deronda*'s troubled reception, Eliot both wards off and crystallizes
this excess, writing, against those readers who were praising only the Gwendolen
sections, "I meant everything in the book to be related to everything else"(*Letters*
6:290). This comment moves beyond any simple, or settled, architecture of parallelism
to suggest a dizzying, even hallucinogenic network of connections that could, ironically, serve to dislocate and confuse the reader. On the one hand, the cohesion that
Eliot invokes—operating across the many fault-lines in the novel, across its shifts in
generic registers, its varied tempo, its changing vantage-points of distance and immersion, its disarming mixture of precision and coincidence—offers a strangely contained
box within which to press this over-spilling narrative. Such compression might work
to accentuate, rather than smoothing over, the modulations and disparities of the
novel. On the other hand, the proliferating implications of this network—in which
"everything" connects not just to the novel as a whole but to "every" other point in
the narrative—would only serve to refract and multiply (exponentially) the text's
heterogeneities. In Roland Barthes's terms, the *process* of signification would be dramatically foregrounded (even swollen) in such a text but the actual meaning or final
significance always further displaced, like a receding line of horizon. Here we are back
to Mr. Vandernoodt's mania, writ large.

One fairly discrete example of this disruptive effect is the over-and-under principle
through which Eliot weaves many of her seventy chapter epigraphs, so that what
appears in one context as a putatively stabilizing frame for a section of the narrative
gets submerged, at another point, into the narrative proper. Not only are we prompted

to "relate" the varied epigraphs to one another—as these allusions (real or invented) trigger abundant resonances and cross-currents between themselves—we're also often confronted with frames that reappear within the composition itself, or, alternatively, tropes and points of reference within the story that suddenly leap out as epigraphs (and thus mediating devices). For example, near the end of chapter 24 the narrator discusses Gwendolen's "Promethean" despair at her suddenly confined circumstances (235; ch. 24), a reference the reader can't help but relate to the epigraph of chapter 16, which troubles a clear distinction between interior feeling and external action by highlighting "those moments of intense suffering which take the quality of action— like the cry of Prometheus, whose chained anguish seems a greater energy than the sea and sky he invokes and the deity he defies" (139). Examples of such level-jumping, or descent, abound. And while this same kind of inversion (of frame and narrative) occurs in the epigraphs from *Middlemarch*, it is a process that, like so many other things, is intensified in *Daniel Deronda*. This intensification (we can see it, too, in the greater proportion, and unwieldiness, of the invented epigraphs in *Daniel Deronda*) is crucial, as though the latter novel were pausing on signifying processes already at play in *Middlemarch* and, by foregrounding and dilating them, bringing out their latent strangeness and affect. In this way, devices that underwrite narrative authority and stability in *Middlemarch*—these epigraphs themselves, various aspects of Eliot's sympathetic omniscience, the incorporation of complicated analogical reasoning within the unfolding narrative, the system of thematic or characterological parallels and juxtapositions—recur in *Daniel Deronda*, but now, extended and thus rendered more conspicuously as devices, are simultaneously more disorienting.

The *tour-de-force* character of different aspects of *Daniel Deronda* has time and again been noted by readers, and critical attention can easily be transfixed on any number of set-pieces in the novel: episodes, scenes, passages, and even sentences and phrases that stand out as striking, dazzling effects. These effects can function themselves as "little shock[s]," galvanizing—and even glutting or monopolizing—our critical and aesthetic attention but also disrupting the unfolding elaboration of the novel as a whole. ("In perhaps the most astounding moment in *Daniel Deronda*, a book not short of them" James Buzard writes (292–93), in a nice example of the phrasing that this novel has always provoked—and turning his attention, in fact, to what had been a relatively overlooked passage). The effect of such astounding moments, aesthetically speaking, can be like the flooding of a car's accelerator. Certainly a version of this tension is always visible in Eliot and crystallized in the strain of the novelist's omniscient, analytical intelligence in *Middlemarch*, which often seems too conceptually rich, and syntactically compounded, for cohabitation in a novel. These omniscient pulsations—the life-blood of *Middlemarch*—often have a keenly double-edged effect, at once giving the reader maximal leverage on the storied world (the pause allows an unprecedented degree of narrative authority) and functioning as static and interruption (authority only elaborates itself *as* narrative pause, in the technical sense of a radical misalignment of story and discourse). But once more this tension is intensified in *Daniel Deronda*, the dialectic extended and dissolved, the movement between "systole and diastole" (204; ch. 22) made more affectively conspicuous and inextricably linked to the novel's large- and small-scale experiments in plotting, phrasing, representation, and narrative construction.

I've already mentioned the opening question of the novel—a device that increases readerly self-consciousness and establishes, as the first scene unfolds, a deeply experimental approach to consciousness and inter-subjectivity, hinging on the unspoken interactions between Deronda and Gwendolen. Such inter-subjectivity is miniaturized in a much briefer set-piece during the second Thames scene (between Mordecai and Daniel) when Eliot expands a single sentence in order to include the equivalent of a 360° movement that shows Daniel's apprehension of Mordecai's apprehension of himself.[2] I'm less interested here in the quality or ethical implications of this sentence than in its rigorously dramatized ambition, as it strives to effectuate a complete, and in fact bewildering, circuit of recognition, shifting Deronda from subject to object to incipient subject ("beckon[ing] again and again") once more.[3] The sealed quality of this circuit simply literalizes the way in which larger units of narrative in *Daniel Deronda*—building blocks for the inter-connected totality toward which Eliot aspires—so often can stand out or turn in on themselves, creating heightened aesthetic effects that simultaneously put pressure on the dynamic unfolding of the narrative as a whole.

Some but by no means all of the varied "set-pieces" that cry out for attention, beyond the opening lines and opening scene, would include: the single paragraph which dwells on the disturbing *absence* of thought within Grandcourt (268–69; ch. 28); the chapter which inscribes the successful, defiant marriage of Klesmer and Catherine Arrowpoint, as a compressed, oddly isolated, counter-narrative (202–12; ch. 22); the strange description of the "choir long ago turned into stables" (359, ch. 35); the extravagantly peripheral letter from Hans Meyrick (549–53, ch. 52)[4]; or the remarkable "consent" produced in the proposal scene between Grandcourt and Gwendolen, which carries each character's intensified effort to entwine agency with passivity to a limit-point ("'Do you command me to go?' . . . 'No' . . . 'You accept my devotion?' . . . 'Yes,' came as gravely from Gwendolen's lips as if she had been answering to her name in a court of justice" [257; ch.27]). This scene is already understood *as* remarkable—or an "astounding moment"—by the novel itself, which quickly comments on its own narrative accomplishment: "Was there ever before such a way of accepting the bliss-giving 'Yes'?" (257). ("Was ever woman in this humor wooed? / Was ever woman in this humor won?," soliloquizes Richard III in lines perhaps echoed here by *Daniel Deronda*, and touching, again, on Shakespeare's own virtuosic construction of this character and scene.)

This virtuosic explicitness in *Daniel Deronda* has many other manifestations. Barbara Hardy comments on the way that *Daniel Deronda* (unlike *Middlemarch*) shows its own construction—"a novel which reveals (or betrays) the large effort of imagination which has gone into it" (9)—and we can see this also in ways large and small, from the curious use of parentheticals to describe Grandcourt's silences (92–93; ch. 11)[5] to the disruptive entry of a crucial, and intensely realized, character in so tight—and so *late*—a space within the narrative (Leonora)[6]—followed by the entry of a still *later* character (Lapidoth), whom Neil Hertz aptly describes as "the last significant figure in George Eliot's fiction . . . [he] figures in only four chapters of this long novel, but he figures memorably, as a *tour de force* of caricatural realism and as the focus for some of the book's most *astonishing* language" (122, emphases added). The provocative inscription (and ejection) of both of these "late" characters exemplifies the way that Eliot ramifies the consequences of signification itself, as the aesthetic intensity of these portraits, functioning both magnetically and disruptively for the reader, bleeds into the social and characterological configuration of these fictional persons within the narrative as a whole. Put differently, the potential affective stakes of the "set-piece," as an aesthetic device—isolated, charismatic, disorienting, and, finally, vulnerable (within the construction of the text as a whole)—is here fully realized in terms of the referenced world itself, pulled back into the story, given social and characterological ballast. It is impossible to separate figure from ground, the referential configuration of these disappearing characters and their coordinated place within the narrative as a whole.

***

But this has, of course, long been the case in *Daniel Deronda*, well before we reach this point in the narrative. The fissure between Gwendolen and Daniel, as dueling or potential protagonists within the narrative, brings us back to *Daniel Deronda*'s strained refraction of the integrated world of *Middlemarch*, both in the extremes that each of these two central characters—and these two projects of characterization—represent for Eliot and in their configuration *as* mutually co-implicated, and thus incomplete, centers within the narrative as a whole. I've suggested how the famous opening of the novel—as it generates an incipient awareness of the discourse itself—finds a referentially-grounded echo in the opening of book 2, with the "little shock" that is associated with Gwendolen's disjunctive, reverberating sense of consciousness. One of the last examples of such mild shock is the jarring appearance of the name "Gwendolen Grandcourt," written by the co-protagonist herself, on the novel's final page. The surprising introduction of this appellation, for the first and only time, has two inter-related effects: it insists on demonstrating a continued psychological fissure within the diminished heroine, now built definitively into the unfortunate name that she carries (and writes), and it conveys the sense of new information, and new questions, still unfolding in the discourse, even here at the very end. In this way, once again, a disjunction of consciousness, or identity, bleeds into the unsettled elaboration of the discourse itself, and critics have likewise pointed out the disorienting effect of marking Gwendolen's final narrative manifestation in the conspicuously mediated form of this brief letter. (As Adela Pinch describes this "disappearance into writing": "Gwendolen has been transfigured into italicized writing, a brittle form that seems far removed from her spectacularly physical presence throughout the novel" [153–54]).

Gwendolen's uneasy, reverberating consciousness is, I've been suggesting, foregrounded from the beginning as both a manifestation of, and a referentially-grounded channel for, the text's narrative and aesthetic intensities. We could argue, in fact, that it is only this engagement with Gwendolen's consciousness that motivates and justifies the aesthetic logic of *Daniel Deronda*'s many "astounding moments." The *excess* in Gwendolen's experience of selfhood—precisely that "Promethean" feeling of "anguish [which] seems a greater energy than the sea and sky he invokes and the deity he defies"—has such a curious place within the logic of this novel (and in the history of the novel as genre): at once the quality which the narrative decries—dismisses and diminishes—and an energizing source for the novel's own wrought intensity. Recent commentary on *Daniel Deronda* has focused on the resonant convergences between the ethical and aesthetic practice of the Eliotic narrator—her sympathy, her detachment, her omniscience, her mobility—and the embodied, emplaced character of Deronda himself. The figure of Deronda, in these accounts, can be understood as either a concrete, even pragmatic actualization of these narrative desires (threading, for example, between detachment and immersion) or an uncanny, unsettling disruption of them.[7] But if Gwendolen's egotism might seem a far cry from the telos of Eliot's sympathy, we could also understand it as just that: not the mechanism, certainly, for sympathy but its end-point and justification. "Mr Casaubon had an intense consciousness within him"(253; ch. 29), the narrator writes in her paradigmatic brief for the putatively distributed sympathies of *Middlemarch*, and it is this set of terms—not simply consciousness, but an "intense" consciousness, and further, the odd, reverberating sense *of* a consciousness "within" oneself—that structures the movement at the beginning of book 2 in *Daniel Deronda*. Although it is explicitly repudiated, the intensified "egotism" of Gwendolen is here the very currency of novelistic representation: both in an ethical sense (as it exemplifies the self-grounded, non-instrumental depth of *every* person, which the novel as genre aspires to recognize) and in an aesthetic sense (as, without such propulsive interiority, the core technologies of novelistic psychologization would simply wither away).

Daniel Deronda's presentation of Gwendolen thrives on these tensions. Gwendolen's selfishness pulls the novel into a tight, claustrophobic circumference, markedly at odds with—or one of the dissociated extremes of—*Middlemarch*'s synthetic amplitude. In this sense, she is an anti-hero *par excellence*, not merely as a central character depicted primarily in terms of her flaws rather than virtues, but as her centrality, embedded in the essential formal and generic logic of the text, produces and amplifies these very flaws. This definition of the anti-hero understands the most accomplished of such figures as a problem of *form* (how they are emplaced, as "heroes" or potential heroes, within a narrative system) rather than content (how we confront their charismatic vices), and thus as a site that can provoke structural, rather than merely ethical, judgment and disorientation. In the simplest sense, we could say that this novel's conspicuously experimental bearing hinges on this odd, intimate interaction of a fully sympathetic narrative with such a complete agent of egotism. (What would finally be either the purpose or the process of sympathy without this horizon of absolutely insistent consciousness?) *Middlemarch* obviously valorizes Dorothea Brooke more, but *Daniel Deronda* gets closer to Gwendolen. What might be aversion in *Middlemarch* can become "repulsion" in *Daniel Deronda*. As Pinch says, Gwendolen has a "spectacularly physical presence." And because the distance between the narrator and the character is greater, the reverberations of Gwendolen's own sense of self are more noticeable within the narrative and free-indirect discourse in *Daniel Deronda*, as it absorbs the impress of Gwendolen's acutely-experienced consciousness, more volatile. The text has numerous points where the distinction between analytic description and emotive reenactment blurs. When the narrator states that "this man's speech was like a sharp knife drawn across her skin" (512; 48), or "[s]he was perfectly silent, holding up the folds of her robe like a statue" (113; ch. 13), it is difficult to say if the novel is analyzing, borrowing, reinforcing, contextualizing (and thus critiquing) or taking advantage of (and thus implicitly valorizing) Gwendolen's perspective. (In the second example, is Gwendolen like a statue or acting like a statue?) And while the novel enacts—first tonally and then structurally—a critique and correction of the "poor spoiled child" it would be difficult to isolate not just the "presence," but the sheer generativity of Gwendolen's egotistical perspective, which, to use one of Eliot's own favored metaphors, seeps into the narrative's own astounding construction like "sap into leafage" (102; ch. 11).

My argument for the strange alliance of the novel's intensities and Gwendolen's own would underlie a fairly disturbing account of the narrative organization of *Daniel Deronda*. Jane Austen's *Emma* is, in my view, perhaps the most rigorous and structurally-realized exploration of the intricate, mutually constitutive relationship between a central character's "egotism" and the very narrative elaboration of centrality. The only Austen text, of course, with such an eponymous character, *Emma* is a case-study in the dissonant energies that are released—or escape—in the necessarily imperfect sealing of character to title, a process which is almost *guaranteed* to unduly amplify the egotism, or imperious ballast, of the central figure. (In this sense, I am suggesting that "love of self" is not the flaw of this novel's protagonist, but the flaw of the novelistic protagonist as such, insofar as the novel tends so reliably to build centrality through the representation of interiority). The displacement effectuated in *Daniel Deronda* is of a different sort: it is as though the narrative had split the characterological traits of Emma (that "disposition to think a little too well of herself " [7; ch. 1]) and the structural prominence that attaches to and generates these traits. The text thus presents us with a curious chiasmus between Gwendolen and Deronda—the agent of egotism is gradually excluded from the narrative-system (or, more precisely, the text inscribes such exclusion *through* this agent) while the agent of sympathy is harnessed into a secured position and identity (or again, becomes the figure through which we can see this process of securing take place). Egotism—a more valuable novelistic capacity, I am arguing, than we might at first imagine—is the site of a structural abnegation; disinterestedness bestowed with an Emma-like ability of generating resilient reward. In Bernard Paris's elegant formulation of this, "[t]he universe of the novel is ordered in such a way as to honor Deronda's defenses" (182): in other words, the narrative structure itself responds to Daniel—amplifying his wishes, turning desires into discoveries—as Gwendolen might vainly, erroneously, imagine the "universe" will respond to her. This reading would emphasize the ways in which Gwendolen's fundamental character doesn't radically change (she can be wonderfully selfish even in the narrow zeal of her remorse, or what the narrator calls "the lava-lit track of her troubled conscience" [661; ch. 66]) and how the structure of the narrative—despite the character's attraction to disinterestedness—comes to serve, and thus make visible, Deronda's interests. The most well-known example of such a fit—between the protagonist's perspective and the narrative's structure—is, of course, the way that Deronda's origins seem as much to emanate from as to form his desires; in this category, as well, would be the gradual process by which Daniel transfers Mirah from being an object of moral to romantic gratification. The reach and ambition of the narrative—the sense in which Eliot is straining toward new novelistic pathways—makes these constrained dialectics of discovery, where we can only find what we have been looking for, that much more troubling. There is a profound relationship here between what the novel enacts and the character denies: Daniel's thought processes often hinge on double negatives—his "suppressed consciousness that a not unlike possibility of collision might lie hidden in his own lot" (322; ch. 33), "a feeling quite distinct from compassionate affection" (398; ch. 37), "a repugnance to affirm or deny" (567; ch. 53) his love of Mirah. In all these instances Daniel can't quite bring himself to identify with what he wants or desires (in the same way the novel often shows Daniel in the act of hiding himself by observing others).

Gwendolen's diminishment within the novel is not just marked in relation to the rise of the "Jewish plot" but also by the brutality of her marriage. The key turning point occurs at the end of chapter 31 and the break from Gwendolen that ensues. We see Gwendolen put on the diamonds; then, "after [a] long while," we see instead Grandcourt *seeing* her, "pallid, shrieking as it seemed with terror, the jewels scattered around her on the floor. Was it a fit of madness?" (303; ch. 31). This displacement is echoed by the novelistic structure: we read of Gwendolen next in the fifth book ("Mordecai") when Daniel meets her for the third time and now, as opposed to their reunion in book 4, we re-encounter her from Daniel's perspective (348; ch. 35), and wearing the diamonds. This gap—between Gwendolen "shrieking as it seemed with terror" and later wearing these same jewels—is by far the biggest lacuna up to this point in her story, and it is etched into the narrative structure as a whole: if Gwendolen is absented, in this way (and in this state), across the mid-point of the novel, the rest of book 5 focuses on Daniel and, crucially, *extends* this focus seamlessly across the division between books 5 and 6. The shift away from Gwendolen thus stretches from that single moment at the end of chapter 31 into the structure of the novel: the orientation of the narrative is now firmly determined.

I'm most interested in the initial sentence of chapter 32, however, precisely as it functions as the *opposite* of a set-piece, an unwieldy sentence whose awkwardness, I would argue, helps to mark, as well as enact, the displacement that is occurring:

Deronda, on his return to town, could assure Sir Hugo of his having lodged in Grandcourt's mind a distinct understanding that he could get fifty thousand pounds by giving
up a prospect which was probably distant, and not absolutely certain; but he had no
further sign of Grandcourt's disposition in the matter than that he was evidently inclined
to keep up friendly communications. (304)

Is it beautiful or not beautiful? The syntactically-clotted sentence ("of his having
lodged," "than that he was evidently inclined") momentarily makes the mechanisms
of sequencing and emplotment conspicuous, as though, under the force of that shift
away from Gwendolen, we were witnessing this construction from an estranged angle.
And largely through the redundant, slightly confusing use of the third-person pronoun,
the sentence seems to draw Grandcourt, Deronda, and Sir Hugo together, as though
Gwendolen's suffering were set against this entire range of male figures.

The "bad" sentence gains meaning through its very hollowness, both as it contrasts
with the text's many "astounding moment[s]" and as it occupies, in fact, a structurally
significant position, at the hinge of that turning from Gwendolen to Daniel. The
ironies here suggest the intricate ways in which the narrative structure both reinforces
and complicates that key ethical paradigm developed from within the story: Daniel's
remonstrance to avoid activities, like gambling, in which "our gain is another's loss"
(284; ch. 29). It is one of the fascinating ironies of the novel that the source for Daniel's sensitivity to such a form of injury—he imagines that Sir Hugo is his father and
has disavowed his mother—turns out to be illusory; and arguably, by confirming
Leonora as merely "an instrument" (567; ch. 53) of transmission between himself and
his grandfather, Daniel enacts the very imagined displacement that has focused his
ethical indignation. (In another example of such *withdrawn* injury, Lydia Glasher,
established as the other major victim of such dispossession, ends up the rightful owner
of Grandcourt's main estate; even as, in the gradual transmutation of his relationship
with Mirah, Daniel realizes that he might have "introduce[d] himself where he had
just excluded his friend" [401; ch. 37]).

These complications redound back on the opening scene: what Daniel calls
"the little affair of the necklace" (280; ch. 29) but which Gwendolen insists on
prioritizing. "And Gwendolen? She was thinking of Deronda much more than he
was thinking of her"(467; ch. 44). Such asymmetry would seem to undermine
Daniel's ethical reading of gambling, as the relative significance or insignificance of
the "affair of the necklace" would itself be merely another index of Gwendolen's own
displacement, by Daniel, as narrative center. But the narrative structure also, ironically, confirms Gwendolen's perspective, since this affair is *the* great set-piece of
Daniel Deronda, locked into prominence by the astounding temporal organization
of the novel, which snakes back twice toward its own beginning, each time newly
revealed as a middle. In this way the famous commitment of *Daniel Deronda* to
"set[ting] off *in media res*" (3; ch. 1) is also a way to hold the reader within the self-
enclosed grip of the narrative structure, where the tensions between gain and loss,
exclusion and inclusion, and the daring confusion of egotism and sympathy continue
to reverberate.

NOTES

1   "I wonder what he accomplished in the East?" begins the conversation in James (974); for an astute recent analysis of "Eliot's curious withdrawal in the face of Jewishness" (90) see Plotz. See also Rosenthal's ingenious reading of how *Daniel Deronda* breaks from the integrative aesthetics of Eliot's earlier fiction, to prioritize "rigid laws that operate at the large scale" and "unconditioned autonomy at the individual scale" (778).

2   "[Daniel's] eyes caught a well-remembered face looking toward him. . . . It was the face of Mordecai, who also, in his watch toward the west, had caught sight of the advancing boat, and had kept it fast within his gaze, at first simply because it was advancing, then with a recovery of impressions that made him quiver as with a presentiment, till at last the nearing figure lifted up its face toward him—the face of his visions—and then immediately, with white uplifted hand, beckoned again and again" (422; ch. 40).

3   We could contrast this with a passage from the next book that emphasizes the absolute *non*-recognition between Lush and Gwendolen, as Gwendolen, trying to turn away from the demi-villain, notices that Lush is *not* looking at her and infers that he must have seen her earlier, when she was not looking at him (476; ch. 45).

4   The appropriate pivot in Chase's influential deconstructive reading.

5   This forms a crux, for example, in Tucker's ambitious argument (77–81) and also in Shaw (247–48).

6   Another long-standing crux and a fulcrum of interpretation, see, for example, Anderson and most recently Kurnick.

7   For a key example of the former see Anderson, 119–46; for the latter, Hertz, 122–37 and Gallagher 144–51.

REFERENCES

Anderson, Amanda. *The Powers of Distance: Cosmopolitanism and the Cultivation of Detachment*. Princeton: Princeton UP, 2001.

Austen, Jane. *Emma*. London: Penguin, 2003.

Buzard, James. *Disorienting Fiction: The Autoethnographic Work of Nineteenth-Century British Novels*. Princeton: Princeton UP, 2005.

Chase, Cynthia. "The Decomposition of the Elephants: Double Reading *Daniel Deronda*." *PMLA* 93.2 (March 1978): 215–27.

Eliot, George. *Daniel Deronda*. Oxford: Oxford UP, 2009.

Eliot, George. *Middlemarch*. New York: Bantam, 1985.

Eliot, George. *The George Eliot Letters*. Ed. Gordon S. Haight. 9 vols. New Haven: Yale UP, 1954–78.

Gallagher, Catherine. *The Body Economic: Life, Death, and Sensation in Political Economy and the Victorian Novel*. Princeton: Princeton UP, 2006.

Hardy, Barbara. Introduction. *Daniel Deronda*. By George Eliot. Ed. Barbara Hardy. London: Penguin, 1967. 7–30.

Hertz, Neil. *George Eliot's Pulse*. Stanford: Stanford UP, 2003.

James, Henry. "*Daniel Deronda*: A Conversation" in *Literary Criticism: Essays on Literature, American Writers, English Writers*. New York: The Library of America, 1984. 974–94.

Kurnick, David. *Empty Houses: Theatrical Failure and the Novel*. Princeton: Princeton UP, 2011.

Leavis, F. R. *The Great Tradition*. London: Penguin, 1962.

Paris, Bernard J. *Rereading George Eliot: Changing Responses to Her Experiments in Life*. Albany: State U of New York P, 2003.

Pinch, Adela. *Thinking About Other People in Nineteenth-Century British Writing*. Cambridge: Cambridge UP, 2010.

Plotz, John. *Portable Property: Victorian Culture on the Move*. Princeton: Princeton UP, 2008.

Rosenthal, Jesse. "The Large Novel and The Law of Large Numbers; Or, Why George Eliot Hates Gambling." *ELH* 77.3 (2010), 777–811.

Shaw, Harry E. *Narrating Reality: Austen, Scott, Eliot*. Ithaca: Cornell UP, 1999.

Tucker, Irene. *A Probable State: The Novel, the Contract and the Jews*. Chicago: U of Chicago P, 2000.

13
Poetry:
The Unappreciated Eliot

Herbert F. Tucker

Opportune Anomaly

Nobody appreciates George Eliot's poetry. It's a shame, but it's a fact. It's also one of those embarrassing bumps in the road of literary history that can precipitate fresh recognitions. Making good on this potential will not come easy just now. Anyone who sets out to champion the substantial body of verse that Eliot produced, nearly all of it during the decade between 1865 and 1875 when her reputation as a novelist advanced from strength to strength, risks stepping forward as a crank: a whistle-blower in the decorous house of fiction, if not a saboteur in the prosperous industry of Eliot scholarship. For several generations now it has been possible to publish acclaimed books on the novels that drop no hint about the poetry; it has become normal practice to allude in passing to "Armgart," say, or *The Spanish Gypsy* as a handy biographical voucher, or a resonator furnishing harmonic background for a thesis in gender or race. At most the critic cuts and pastes, without further comment, a bit from "O May I Join the Choir Invisible" or "A College Breakfast-Party," to sweeten an argument that has been cinched already by scrutiny of the fiction—a gesture unruffled by Eliot's own practice of auto-epigraphy (see Price) and undeterred by the irony cast on such practice by chapter 1 of *Middlemarch*.

It's one thing when a failure to appreciate Eliot's poetry stems from authentically experienced distaste, as surely it does for some among us now, and as demonstrably it did among outspoken critics in her day. I am about to commend to notice the grounds such critics gave for disliking poems that they had in good faith read. But

A Companion to George Eliot, First Edition. Edited by Amanda Anderson and Harry E. Shaw.
© 2013 John Wiley & Sons, Ltd. Published 2016 by John Wiley & Sons, Ltd.

first let me highlight what makes such articulate evaluation commendable: the rarity with which critical evaluation as such plays even a cameo role in the way we read Eliot now. Nowadays our failure to appreciate her poetry is precisely that: a failure to go so far as *appreciate* it, assess its worth, take its measure by taking our own stand for or against it and so declaring ourselves in the process. What may it mean that Eliot the poet goes unappreciated even in this root sense? Candor obliges me to raise a possibility which optimism hastens to downplay: namely, that the academic cultivation of niche expertise has reached a point where specialists in fiction are, *ipso facto* and in their own professional judgment, disqualified to hold opinions about poetry. Readers caught in that snare will presumably skip this chapter anyway, which can by definition address nothing they acknowledge a stake in. And yet our quaint-sounding topic of poetry-appreciation opens to view an issue in which they, like the rest of us, are crucially involved if seldom aware: the academic decline of evaluative reading, whether in its own right or as a critical heuristic.

This is an enormous issue, of which Eliot's case offers pointed illustration. When did eminent criticism last trouble itself centrally with how good Eliot's writing was, good at what, and with what arc of rise or fall? If it seems beside the point to put such questions to "Janet's Repentance" or *Romola*, much less *The Mill on the Floss*, then so much the worse for the quality of our engagement with those works. Take the excellence of *Adam Bede* for granted long enough, and your grasp of that excellence as a vital property of the book, locally actualized page by page, will slacken. Admittedly it's impossible to imagine these days, except as a stunt or joke, a direct inquiry into the literary worth of *Middlemarch*. It and *Daniel Deronda* are by now too big to fail. With the author's unappreciated poetry, however, it is another story: the fact that nobody adores or analyzes it opens a rare opportunity, within the negligently received canon of a writer indubitably canonical, to appreciate Eliot's writing as if for the first time, and with consequences for the larger oeuvre that look, from here, intriguingly hard to predict.

As if for the first time, because precedents do exist for frontal evaluation of the poems. The most of it, and the best, occurs in review essays that appeared shortly after publication of *The Spanish Gypsy* (1868) and then *The Legend of Jubal and Other Poems* (1874, expanded 1878). These volumes engrossed the attention of superior writers who knew they were reviewing a superior writer, and in whose reports the mingling of diplomatic reception with puzzled disappointment not only betrays the practical limitations of critical vocabulary from the nineteenth century but also underscores, in dispiriting retrospect, the worse curbs under which criticism has labored with Eliot's poetry across the twentieth. What is most bracing about the responses registered by Henry James, William Dean Howells, and John Morley among other contemporaries is not their careful praise but the frankness with which they censure Eliot's shortcomings, as gauged, on one hand, against cherished ideas about modern poetry and, on the other, against her own manifest achievement in the art of modern prose. On the whole these critics balk at the verse, which may abound in "grace and delicacy of phrase" (Morley 283) but also betrays prosodic missteps in its "hard, sharp, and galvanic" meter (Skelton 477, also Howells 381; Minto 514). Formal deficiencies on this order are outward signs of an inward flaw that is reckoned more damaging still. Because the poetry has been too long and too cerebrally incubated to wear "the shape spontaneously assumed by the writer's thought" (Morley 281), because it proffers so odd "a mixture of spontaneity of thought and excessive reflectiveness of expression" (James 485), it forfeits that "spiritual translucence" (Howells 381) and "high subtle transcendental mood of feeling" (Skelton 474) which mainstream Victorian poetics steadily looked forward—and up—to. Rose Elizabeth Cleveland's 1885 book on the poems, long the only study of its kind, took this transcendentalism to an orthodox extreme: the poetry fails because the agnostic poet lacks the true faith. Even for secular-minded reviewers of *The Spanish Gypsy*, a ponderous intellection cumbers Eliot's verse as it doesn't her prose, which, in a set passage from the Proem to *Romola* that more than one reviewer cited for contrast, outsoars the verse "in imaginative breadth and force" and is "in the highest sense poetic" (Morley 281; Howells 383).

Clumsy or acute, here at least are critical judgments one can work with, for example by comparing in some detail the panoramic openings of *Romola* and of *The Spanish Gypsy*, book 1 or 3. Much less useful is the choir impalpable of latter-day response, in faint perfunctory rehearsal of ideas that for Eliot's first responders had been incisively fresh. Patronizing the poetry as "innocuous" (Hanson 268) or "pedestrian" (Lisle 263) and praising its "gracefully controlled" style for "deftness and economy" (Pinion 132, 156) are two sides of the same dispensation from scrutiny. There is a little more traction, but not much, in a recent summary judgment that Eliot's "inversions, archaisms, and monotonous smooth regularity are compounded by sentimental and lofty tones" (Hardy xxiv). Although Barbara Hardy doesn't pause a beat here over the syntactic, lexical, and prosodic features she patronizes from afar, we might find the "compound" strong stuff if we were to do so—might find it moving rather than sentimental, elevating rather than lofty—but then the whole point of this sentence, coming from a doyenne among critics of Eliot's fiction, is to excuse the student in advance from undertaking anything of the kind.

Eliot's "verse does not sing" (Ashton 64); it is too "epigrammatical, metaphorical" for that. (And never mind squaring these descriptors with that sentimental loftiness we just heard about.) Of course it doesn't sing, to ears that are busy not listening. Of course poems that are read as if their form in verse were an accident best ignored will look funny; and, since the literary mind's ear may doze but never really slumbers, they will sound funny too. "That the poems are so pedestrian, in fact, may tempt us to overlook their real importance," an importance which, for the exceptionally forthright critic here quoted, inheres uniquely in the themes they treat (Lisle 263). We need frame no case for George Eliot as an unsung lyric genius—and no such case will be forthcoming in this chapter—in order to agree that reading her or any poet's verse as wrong-footed prose (i.e. for its thematic content alone), means decreeing a pseudo equivalence between verse and prose that tilts the balance in prose's favor and handicaps verse just where it is strongest. A nuanced appraisal of Eliot's varying power in both literary media entails respecting the difference between them, which is to say, at a minimum, respecting verse's charter to embody thought and enact emotion within the language that makes it up. Only thus may we hope to understand why this author committed some of the best years of her life to poetry and why, within the terms of that choice, she made the prosodic and generic choices she did. It's not over till the great lady sings; and she won't sing until we break prose's conspiracy of silence and listen.

Soundings

Turning to Eliot's first public trial of the resources of verse, *The Spanish Gypsy*, consider for starters the street-performer Pepíta,

> Who stands in front with little tapping feet,
> And baby-dimpled hands that hide enclosed
> Those sleeping crickets, the dark castanets.

(1.58)

The first two lines tap a kitschy vein that no Victorian poet did without. But then the phonemes of "enclosed" scatter across the next line a life of their own: "crickets" makes a nice if obvious onomatopoeia, and nicer still is the resumption of its click in the clack of "dark castanets," redoubling the double *k* from "crickets" within a fourth-foot spondee long enough to open up the space between adjective and noun for a syncopated flamenco staccato. Or revisit the same Plaça Santiago when, tragedy swelling toward its catastrophe, the massed Zíncali gypsies swear fealty to Fedalma as her assassinated father breathes his last:

> The shout unanimous, the concurrent rush
> Of many voices, quiring shook the air
> With multitudinous wave: now rose, now fell,
> Then rose again, the echoes following slow,
> As if the scattered brethren of the tribe
> Had caught afar and joined the ready vow.

(4.350)

A novelist may set out to describe waves of echoing sound; a poet gets to graph them on the oscilloscope of the blank-verse line. This may be seen, better yet heard, by tracking the long *o* from line 3 down to line 6, in its gradually blunted recurrence from the exactly echoed "rose" into "slow," across the reverberant cross-current of unstressed *o* syllables from "echoes" and "following," until the distant return of "vow" two lines later makes no more than an eye-rhyme with "slow," even as it faintly revoices the diphthong from the initiating "shout" back in line 1. The effect is as grandiloquent here as our first passage was racy, and in each case with good reason. Turn the page of Eliot's book for a third example conjoining tragic pathos with

subtlety of touch, as the now apostate renegade Don Silva walks out of his beloved's
life forever, cursed with the safe-conduct of a Cain:

> Slowly he walked, reluctant to be safe
> And bear dishonoured life which none assailed;
> Walked hesitatingly, all his frame instinct
> With high-born spirit.

(4.353)

The reader who fails to hesitate over "hesitatingly" has not been paying attention to
the iambic pentameter. Steadied on either side with metered stateliness, the rhythm
all but crumbles in line 3 into a trochee, an iamb, and then a caesura-spavined anapest
enacting the footing of a broken hidalgo whose constitutional inability *not* to walk
tall forms half the tragedy of Eliot's relentless plot.

Each of the above passages enacts a performativity in which Eliot's adroit versification abounds, through the wielding of meter as through the deployment of "vowels
turned / Caressingly between the consonants, / Persuasive, willing" (1.19). Eliot seems
less to plume herself up in such passages than delightedly to honor the capacities of
a medium that she not only has studied to master (see the prosodic analyses in her
notebooks [Pratt and Neufeldt]) but moreover finds to be a regular source of unexpected prompts to fresh expression. Verse maximizes the writerly inspiration that form
incites: "thought-teaching form" is how *The Spanish Gypsy* puts it (1.53)—not, as
theme-driven criticism supposes, "thought, teaching form." That technique is ingredient in creativity, that inspiration flows both ways between the artist's intention and
instrument, constitutes the credo of Eliot's surrogate craftsman of "perfect violins, the
needed paths / For inspiration and high mastery" ("Stradivarius" 24–25). There is a
remarkable passage in "The Legend of Jubal"—title piece of Eliot's two poetic collections and arguably her signature essay in practical poetics (but see Solie 117–18)—
in which, as the idea of music dawns on its antediluvian inventor, the word "form"
resounds over and over. The din of laboring humanity graduates from noise to music
only when it is "Wrought into solid form" (321). While "Jubal must dare as great
beginners dare, / Strike form's first way in matter rude and bare" (340–41), music
repays the investment "With form-begotten sound" (335). The fecundating agency
of form within the musical arts (including song or poetry) recapitulates for Jubal what
his blacksmith brother Tubal-Cain has earlier learned in forging the technical crafts:

> Each day he wrought and better than he planned,
> Shape breeding shape beneath his restless hand.
> (The soul without still helps the soul within,
> And its deft magic ends what we begin.)

(204–07)

A poetic celebration of origins, "The Legend of Jubal" keeps inaugurations and aims
in mutual play through the verbal starts and stops of rhyming couplets like the

parenthesis here, where the end-rhyme "begin" illustrates in miniature the thought-teaching power of a form-begotten sound, its formally punning paradox a brief token of poetry's inner need for that seeming outsider, the verbal framework. Thus the narrative couplets of "How Lisa Loved the King" establish medieval Spanish chivalry as instinct "With beauteous response, like minstrelsy / Afresh fulfilling fresh expectancy" (24–25), a simile that earns its keep when the expectation-fulfilling rhyme realizes in form the idealism it speaks of.

Blank verse works from a subtler palette, but the metered line in itself also suffices for play on beginning and ending, as appears near the close of "A Minor Prophet": "Full souls are double mirrors, making still / An endless vista of fair things before / Repeating things behind" (295–97). A rearview mirror is not a pierglass; still, these lines if read off as prose resemble a *Middlemarch* style just enough to throw into relief the breaking and mending of sense that verse enjambment effects as prose cannot. Underscoring the temporality of articulation, the unfolding of Eliot's lineated sense throws into relief the difference between repetition and identity, a difference that gives meaning to time, holding open the space of even minor prophecy, and with it the poem's hedged but genuine utopianism. A few lines later in "A Minor Prophet" this difference emerges in the blank verse's sudden flirtation with rhyme: idealism burgeons

> At labours of the master-artist's hand
> Which, trembling, touches to a finer end,
> Trembling before an image seen within.
>
> (304–06)

"Hand" and "end" don't rhyme, quite, but the placement of "end" at line's end suggests that they might mate in an imperfect world, even as the image they convey brings home the blessed discrepancy between what "Jubal" called the "soul within" and "soul without," between an inspiring "image seen within" and the executive explorativeness of the master-artist's refining hand.

The music and the motion for which we have thus far sampled Eliot's versification display a self-awareness that can boost consciousness of verbal phenomena across the board. Whatever we make, in *The Spanish Gypsy*, of the turmoil Don Silva suffers between love and duty, cosmopolitan reason and peninsular breeding, Gothic and Catholic makeup, we should note that Eliot set her anatomy of early-modern man to a lexical accompaniment that staged the ethnical-ethical contest in an arena of etymology. Watch the Saxon and Latin elements circle each other:

> Silva was both the lion and the man;
> First hesitating shrank, then fiercely sprang,
> Or having sprung, turned pallid at his deed
> And loosed the prize, paying his blood for nought. . . .
> Deliberating ever, till the sting
> Of a recurrent ardour made him rush

Right against reasons that himself had drilled
And marshalled painfully. A spirit framed
Too proudly special for obedience,
Too subtly pondering for mastery:
Born of a goddess with a mortal sire,
Heir of flesh-fettered, weak divinity,
Doom-gifted with long resonant consciousness
And perilous heightening of the sentient soul.

                                                                (1.73)

Too systematically allotted, perhaps, and too coldly fused, to be mistaken for Shake-speare's or Milton's, this interleaving diction nevertheless evinces a way with words that is Shakespearean and Miltonic. It is, for that matter, Johnsonian; linguistic curiosity sharpened by such an anatomy of character in verse might nourish study of Eliot's prose as well, and might elicit fresh analyses that put formal and cultural reading in each other's neighborhood, and debt.

Lexical analysis ratcheted up one order of magnitude becomes discourse analytics, of a Bakhtinian sort that despite its current vogue is too little practiced on an author whose stylistic accomplishment goes without saying. The overtness with which Eliot the poet switches among various registers of style may have things to teach us—questions to prompt us to ask again—about heteroglossia in her prose. Here follows a passage, from *The Spanish Gypsy*, framing a scene where Silva and some street performers in his employ visit the astrologer Sephardo:

A room high up in Abderahman's tower,
A window open to the still warm eve,
And the bright disc of royal Jupiter.
Lamps burning low make little atmospheres
Of light amid the dimness; here and there
Show books and phials, stones and instruments.
In carved dark-oaken chair, unpillowed, sleeps
Right in the rays of Jupiter a small man,
In skull-cap bordered close with crisp gray curls,
And loose black gown showing a neck and breast
Protected by a dim-green amulet;
Pale-faced, with finest nostril wont to breathe
Ethereal passion in a world of thought;
Eyebrows jet-black and firm, yet delicate;
Beard scant and grizzled; mouth shut firm, with curves
So subtly turned to meanings exquisite,
You seem to read them as you read a word
Full-vowelled, long-descended, pregnant—rich
With legacies from long, laborious lives.
Close by him, like a genius of sleep,
Purrs the gray cat, bridling, with snowy breast.

A loud knock. "Forward!" in clear vocal ring.
Enter the Duke, Pablo, and Annibal.
Exit the cat, retreating toward the dark.

(2.189)

I quote in full to show how often, and how easily, the multi-tasking style shifts back and forth among inventory and overview, listing and interpreting, immediate scenery and "pregnant" traditionary background, literal and figurative registers; and then how quickly, in the last three lines, the description these devices evoke folds up and slips into the pocket of plot. To make the eloquent abstraction of "Ethereal passion in a world of thought" consort with a flatfooted "Exit the cat" is a sort of trick in which Eliot's narrative prose excels, usually without awakening more than a passing recognition that she has woven "poetic" and "prosaic" elements together. Such commingling of styles emerges more diagrammatically, and so more strikingly, when it takes place on verse's premises; and a study of the novels that bore the poems in mind should be impelled thereby to a nearer look and a finer appreciative vocabulary. "Right in the rays of Jupiter a small man": how uncanny the co-presence of the homely close-up with the interplanetary long shot; how oddly right that "Right."

Pulse Taking

None of the foregoing poetry-appreciation refutes the objections we heard earlier from Eliot's first critics, who were happy to temper critique by conceding that this or that passage shed transient luster on what remained a generally disappointing performance. Challenging these objections on their own ground requires correlating the general with the particular, and reasoning downwards from the leading themes of Eliot's poetry to their specific prosodic instantiation. These themes prove to be remarkably consistent, across the poetry and also with animating concerns of the fiction, under the sign of synecdoche, or the problem of the one and the many. Aspects of the problem just detained us in "The Astrologer's Study," where the reciprocal bearing of singularity and generality emerged in the enumeration of details soliciting interpretation ("to read them as you read a word"), and also in the strong association between a thing's meaning and its history. Writ large, this association is ubiquitous in the fiction, where the gravitas the past imposes on the present, and the bearing of broad systems on local nodes, are the silver and golden keys to Eliot's representational realism. Likewise her moral vision, in verse as in prose media, turns on the synecdochic relation between individual ego and social collectivity (see Krasner). At each point along the continuum from lyric to epic, subjectivity in Eliot's poems is destined to possess what the allegorically schematic dialogue "Self and Life" calls the knowledge, won through "anguish," of "fellowship more vast" (72). It is the surest commonplace in Eliot criticism that the novels bestow such knowledge on their protagonists through the access of sympathy, by an accretive process whose ultimate warrant lies in the reader's experience of sympathy with the sympathies those protagonists learn to feel. Among the poems only *The Spanish Gypsy* and "Armgart" are long enough to attempt this gradual moral adjustment of ego to other, and it is hard to resist the consensus that the dramatic hybrid form of these two works enjoys only indifferent success. Armgart and Fedalma seem brought to their knees—or hoisted to their pedestal—by the force of sheer authorial conviction, rather too thinly clad as an abrupt twist in the story.

These results suggest we look elsewhere in the poetry for an equivalent to the narrative sympathy that sustains moral realism within the novels. We find it, I think, in a different experience of sympathy: the musically rhythmic sway that was Eliot's pulse in verse (see Weliver; Picker; Solie). In *The Spanish Gypsy* the "large music rolling o'er the world" at times whelms what Zarca fanatically dismisses as "the round of personal loves," "A miserable, petty, low-roofed life" (3.270), and at other times it uplifts life's pettinesses into significant participation in the course of history, felt "Swift as the wings of sound yet seeming slow / Through multitudinous pulsing of stored sense / And spiritual space" (3.237: an elusive image, which swims into ken when we ponder how "stored sense" bides its time in the printed lines of a poetry book). Eliot's epic carriage declares itself again in a late passage on "the dire hours / Burthened with destiny," which

>   sweep along
> In their aërial ocean measureless
> Myriads of little joys, that ripen sweet
> And soothe the sorrowful spirit of the world.
>
>   (5.363)

The enjambed modifier "measureless" spans the synecdochic gap between whole and part. Syntactically the word hovers between the high "ocean" of heaven's immensity and the sheer proliferant "Myriads" of realia in the world; yet on either construction there is a soothing countercharm to enormity in the wavelike measure of verse, intimating an order that inheres in the ripening course of time. Multitudinousness has a pulse to it; take that pulse, and you apprehend the world's body.

Hence flows the affection with which Eliot's muse stoops to the quotidian region of "dull brown fact" (1.49), "the streets, the shops, the men at work, / The women, little children—everything, / Just as it is when nobody looks on" (1.95). The prosaic poetic of such writing is in one sense familiar from Eliot's defense of Dutch realism in *Adam Bede*. Things change, though, when it is in verse that "The crones plait reeds, or shred the vivid herbs / Into the caldron" (3.239): objects seem denser, actions more deliberately outlined. Occasionally with Eliot, as with her admired Wordsworth, a piece of prose seems to have wandered into verse by accident:

> Within the prettiest hollow of these hills,
> Just as you enter it, upon the slope

> Stands a low cottage neighbored cheerily
> By running water, which, at farthest end
> Of the same hollow, turns a heavy mill,
> And feeds the pasture for the miller's cows.
>
> ("Agatha" 53–58)

Yet even here, where the poet aims at a modesty befitting her idyllic endorsement of a vital, frugal plainness, the enjambment that lineation creates in verse however prosy begins, almost in spite of itself, to trace the contoured Alpine landscape and embody its sloping flow. To think of a certain mill on the Floss—from the novel that has most signally elicited literary criticism tending, for worse (Freeman) and for better (Stewart), toward poetically-normed response—or to think of Dorothea Ladislaw's "incalculably diffusive" lot at the finale of *Middlemarch*—is to appreciate Eliot's wager that the acoustic sympathy verse bears would temper the loss of the part in the whole, would measure (if not, exactly, calculate) the diffusion of the individual into the collective. Hence her own cheerful audition for "the choir invisible / Whose music" gives promise "of a good diffused, / And in diffusion ever more intense" ("O May I Join the Choir Invisible" 40–43). Hence the enshrinement of her Moses, not in a tomb but "as Law," to the accompaniment of what sounds very much like the Lord's own poetry: "mysterious speech, / Invisible Will wrought clear in sculptured sound" ("The Death of Moses" 118–22). And hence, alas, the reckless and reader-vexing insistence of *The Spanish Gypsy* on individual submission to world-historical imperatives of blood and tribe that are borne to the reader, as to Fedalma dancing in the public square, on the vibrancy of solo aria and not much else: a wing, we might say, and a prayer.

Indeed, the dismay that readers from the first have expressed at Fedalma's rendezvous with destiny may arise in response to a certain ambivalence in Eliot about poetic form. She revered it, and at the same time she mistrusted it. She worked it with so self-conscious an insistence because she wasn't quite sure that it worked. The air of calculation that her critics complain about arises from a virtually Stradivarian approach to the instrumentality of the verse medium, which she seems typically to *use*, like a power tool marvelously effective in the execution of a preconcerted design. (If only in this sense, the canard that Eliot wrote *The Spanish Gypsy* out fully in prose before translating it to verse—hardly credible in itself—has a certain *prima facie* plausibility. Beyond question it was at this same time she confessed to "the severe effort of trying to make certain ideas thoroughly incarnate, as if they had revealed themselves to me first in the flesh and not in the spirit" [*Letters* 5:300]). Eliot tasked poetry to do so much because she believed it could do anything, which is why in the poems she carried favorite theorems to extremes that in her prose were more prudently buffered and hedged (Armstrong 371; Reynolds 305). Yet at the same time, and by the same token, she seldom writes as if she has abandoned her agenda and taken the leap of poetic thinking for its own sake. It is therefore the more remarkable when, once in a great while, the musical flood of significant sympathy drains off, and she is stranded in spare random thoughtfulness, like her Fedalma here:

> the glow dies out, the trumpet strain
> That vibrated as strength through all my limbs
> Is heard no longer; over the wide scene
> There's nought but chill gray silence, or the hum
> And fitful discord of a vulgar world.
>
> (3.279)

This passage anticipates the fine metaphysical zeroing-out in which the entire epic concludes, as Don Silva, yearning toward the horizon after Fedalma's unreturning ship, "knew not if he gazed / On aught but blackness overhung by stars" (1.375). Yet Fedalma's earlier passage is if anything more blank than this tragic fall of the curtain: the mind in its very disempowerment is delivered over to a poverty in which one wishes George Eliot the poet had known how to dwell.

This wish is met, and thereby whetted, by the survival of an exceptional verse sketch from Eliot's notebook that went unpublished for a century. "In a London Drawing-Room," anticipating the verse of another poet named Eliot yet unborn, stands comparison with the poetry of urban anomie at which Tennyson and Baudelaire had tried their hand not long before Eliot composed it—jotted it, rather, in a mode of unbespoken bricolage whose vitality differs signally from most of what she saw fit to print:

> The sky is cloudy, yellowed by the smoke.
> For view there are the houses opposite
> Cutting the sky with one long line of wall
> Like solid fog: far as the eye can stretch
> Monotony of surface and of form
> Without a break to hang a guess upon.
>
> (1–6)

The poem begun in these lines goes on for a dozen more, concluding with a speculative simile that compares the urban prospect to "one huge prison-house and court / Where men are punished at the slightest cost" (17–18). A conclusion well enough in its way; but in bending the poem into conformity with her habitual interpretive processing Eliot's conclusion sets off by contrast the rawer-minded impressionability of her speculative opening gambit. The scholar who first published "In a London Drawing-Room" in 1959 aptly judged that it turns, almost uniquely within Eliot's work, "upon the nature of the world perceived" and not "upon the *way* in which consciousness perceives" (Paris 549; see also Stephen 171). For once, the images do the thinking rather than illustrate a thought. This preconceptual quality of suspended "guess" apparently caught the poet's appreciative eye as it still does ours, for she made of it a chapter epigraph in *Felix Holt*. A separate study of the verse epigraphs Eliot placed in her novels might well show that fragmentary shapes liberated her, as poems fully rendered for publication didn't, to engage in this species of impromptu "thought-teaching form." John Morley and Henry James were on to something: Eliot's poetry would probably have amounted to more had she taken such liberties more boldly.

Amateur Standing

Eliot's care to see into print only poems that were finished, nay accomplished, may be linked to a last noteworthy feature of her career in verse: its deliberate dilettantism. She made it a point to come before the public in the character of a minor poet, which in her special case meant a major novelist keeping her hand fresh in a sister art (see Tucker). The case this chapter has framed for the excellence of her handiwork, while it seems to contradict this appreciation, actually sustains it deep down. So does the remarkable fact that the portfolio of Eliot's published poems is so diversified in genre, whether we look to verse structures or larger poetic kinds. "The Legend of Jubal" and "How Lisa Loved the King," extended heroic-couplet narratives set in ancient days, display the closest resemblance anywhere in the corpus, yet in their narratorial manner and typical handling of the coupleted unit they are as distinctly different as the ages of the Patriarchs and of Chivalry that they respectively treat. Among the subgenres in blank verse "Agatha" is a pastoral idyll of Tennysonian stripe, "Armgart" a closet drama, "A Minor Prophet" a double-focused elliptical monologue à la Browning, "Stradivarius" an anecdotal fable with one foot in history, "A College Breakfast-Party" an academic eclogue, "The Death of Moses" an epyllion that feels lifted from the last book of some Miltonic *Mosiad*, and "O May I Join the Choir Invisible" a humanist hymn (see Vogeler). "Brother and Sister" with its eleven Shakespearean sonnets earns a decent corner in the Victorian tradition of themed lyric sequences. The other poems in rhyme include a Shelleyan allegory ("Self and Life"), one love song with a refrain and one without ("Two Lovers," "Sweet Evenings Come and Go, Love"), and a parable on the fortunes of poetry ("Arion"), written in the form of Marvell's Horatian ode. We glanced above at discursive heteroglossia within the strenuous *Spanish Gypsy*; that poem's bid for epic standing is formally pronounced in the encyclopedic diversity of its generic constituents: verse but occasionally prose, narrative but more often dramatic dialogue, and into the bargain a respectable chapbook's worth of highly various lyrical songs.

The sheer versatility within this poetic output is so remarkable that we should reckon it an important part of the performance. Eliot appears on purpose to have avoided repeating herself. The overall effect is that of a virtuoso recital, undertaken as if to show, with each genre and mode on exhibit, how very well she could carry it off and then, dusting off her hands, to go on and excel at something else. A passing exchange from "Armgart" offers a virtual gloss on this phenomenon:

> I have known
> A man so versatile, he tried all arts,
> But when in each by turns he had achieved

> Just so much mastery as made men say,
> "He could be king here if he would," he threw
> The lauded skill aside.

(242–47)

This cool dabbler, the worldly Graf Dornberg goes on to relate, held that it was the fate of "excellence" to wind up "Huddled in the mart of mediocrities" (255–59). That Armgart unequivocally pooh-poohs this idea does not mean Eliot did. At all events it is quite suggestive that she should have both thought it up and then subjected it to scorn, on the part moreover of a diva heroine whose tragedy will be entailed by precisely what it cautions against, putting all your eggs in one basket.

As the exchange from "Armgart" shows she suspected, Eliot's versatility while praiseworthy invited a negative appreciation as well. There is a sense, especially within the Romantic climate that governed most Victorian poetry, in which excellence as such is not the mark of genius but its muzzle, the snaffle in Pegasus' teeth. In this sense we may regard Eliot's versatility as betokening the declining of an option, the renunciation of a pioneer's major stake in any one mode of poetic art, a shying away from the glory that was to be won, if at all, at a higher risk of inspired failure than she stood ready to assume. Reluctant to embrace poetry as an exploratory medium, she remained content to practice it illustriously, which is to say, by and large, as an illustrative medium instead. A number of interlocking reasons no doubt underwrote this reluctance (see Wade): an abashed veneration, in which most of her contemporaries participated, for the greatness of poetry; a compensatory corollary suspicion, likewise widely shared, that poetry's grandeur was not compatible with modern life; the belittling gravamen of Victorian gender politics as it bore on an art historically dominated by men (see LaPorte; Hadjiafxendi); even the cruel ageism that made poetry a young writer's game, a slippery slope for the middle-aged adventurer. These obstacles notwithstanding, suffice it to observe at last that, within the select circle of modern authors who have cultivated both novels and poems with signal distinction—Goethe, Scott, Hugo, Hardy, Lawrence, Updike—she remains, pending a candidate or two alive at this writing, and with all respect to that scintillating flash in the pan Emily Brontë, a woman without peer.

REFERENCES

Armstrong, Isobel. *Victorian Poetry: Poetry, Poetics and Politics*. London: Routledge, 1993.

Ashton, Rosemary. *George Eliot*. Oxford: Oxford UP, 1983.

Cleveland, Rose Elizabeth. *George Eliot's Poetry and Other Studies*. New York: Funk & Wagnall, 1885.

Eliot, George. *The Complete Shorter Poems of George Eliot*. Ed. Antonie Gerard van den Broek. 2 vols. London: Pickering, 2005.

Eliot, George. *The George Eliot Letters*. Ed. Gordon S. Haight. 9 vols. New Haven: Yale UP, 1954–78.

Eliot, George. *George Eliot's "Middlemarch" Notebooks: A Transcription*. Ed. John Clark Pratt and Victor A. Neufeldt. Berkeley: U of California P, 1979.

Eliot, George. *The Works of George Eliot: The Spanish Gypsy*. Edinburgh: Blackwood, 1878.

Freeman, John. "George Eliot's Great Poetry." *Cambridge Quarterly* 5.1 (1970): 25–40.

Hadjiafxendi, Kyriaki. "Voicing the Past: Aural Sensibility, The Weaver-Poet, and George Eliot's 'Erinna.'" *Studies in the Literary Imagination* 43.1 (2010): 95–118.

Hanson, Lawrence and Elisabeth. *Marian Evans and George Eliot: A Biography*. Oxford: Oxford UP, 1952.

Hardy, Barbara. *George Eliot: A Critic's Biography*. London: Continuum, 2006.

Howells, W. D. "George Eliot's *Spanish Gypsy*." *Atlantic Monthly* 22 (1868): 380–84.

James, Henry. "George Eliot's *The Legend of Jubal*." *North American Review* 119 (1874): 484–89.

Krasner, James. "'Where No Man Praised': The Retreat from Fame in George Eliot's *The Spanish Gypsy*." *Victorian Poetry* 32.1 (1994): 55–74.

LaPorte, Charles. "George Eliot, The Poetess as Prophet." *Victorian Literature and Culture* 31.1 (2003): 161–77.

Lisle, Bonnie J. "Art and Egoism in George Eliot's Poetry." *Victorian Poetry* 22.3 (1984) 263–78.

[Minto, W.] Untitled Review. *The Examiner* 16 (1874): 513–14.

[Morley, J.] *"The Spanish Gypsy*." *Macmillan's Magazine* 18 (1868): 281–87.

Paris, Bernard J. "George Eliot's Unpublished Poetry." *Studies in Philology* 56.3 (1959): 539–58.

Picker, John. *Victorian Soundscapes*. Oxford: Oxford UP, 2003.

Pinion, F. B. *A George Eliot Miscellany: A Supplement to Her Novels*. London: Macmillan, 1982.

Price, Leah. *The Anthology and the Rise of the Novel*. Cambridge: Cambridge UP, 2000.

Reynolds, Margaret. "Poetry of George Eliot." *The Oxford Reader's Companion to George Eliot*. Ed. John Rignall. Oxford: Oxford UP, 2000. 304–08.

Skelton, J. Untitled review. *Fraser's Magazine* 78 (1868): 468–79.

Solie, Ruth A. "'Music their Larger Soul': George Eliot's 'The Legend of Jubal' and Victorian Musicality." *The Figure of Music in Nineteenth-Century British Poetry*. Ed. Phyllis Weliver. Farnham: Ashgate, 2005. 107–31.

Stephen, Leslie. *George Eliot*. 1902. London: Macmillan, 1913.

Stewart, Garrett. *Novel Violence: A Narratography of Victorian Fiction*. Chicago: U of Chicago P, 2009.

Tucker, Herbert F. "Quantity and Quality: The Strange Case of George Eliot, Minor Poet." *Journal of George Eliot-George Henry Lewes Studies* 60–61 (2011): 17–30.

Vogeler, Martha. "The Choir Invisible: The Poetics of Humanist Piety." *George Eliot: A Centenary Tribute*. Ed. Gordon S. Haight and Rosemary T. VanArsdel. London: Macmillan, 1982. 64–81.

Wade, Rosalind. "George Eliot and Her Poetry," *Contemporary Review* 204 (1963): 38–42.

Weliver, Phyllis. *Women Musicians in Victorian Fiction, 1860–1900*. Farnham: Ashgate, 2000.

14
Essays: Essay v. Novel
(Eliot, Aloof)

Jeff Nunokawa

We will begin in the middle of a forest, very far from the resounding voice we hear so much in the essays; in the middle of a forest where we hear the sound of a man, not accustomed to doing so, in the midst of changing his mind: stopping in the woods for a second time; stopping in his tracks for the first; opening his mind and his heart, after having closed them for what surely seemed, to all concerned, forever; stopping in the darkest of all unloving places, the place past all forgiveness; stopping to turn and see in a different and unexpected light, an old friend who has done him and all he cares for, a world of harm; stopping so, a man named Adam struggles to become a new man:

> There was silence for several minutes, for the struggle in Adam's mind was not easily decided. Facile natures, whose emotions have little permanence, can hardly understand how much inward resistance he overcame before he rose from his seat and turned towards Arthur. Arthur heard the movement, and turning round, met the sad but softened look with which Adam said,
>
> "It's true what you say, sir: I'm hard—it's in my nature. I was too hard with my father, for doing wrong. I've been a bit hard to everybody but. . . . I've known what it is in my life to repent and feel it's too late: I felt I'd been too harsh to my father when he was gone from me—I feel it now, when I think of him. I've no right to be hard towards them as have done wrong and repent." (470; ch. 48)

Those who have encountered Adam Bede, or any nature so fixed, will know to heed the baptismal ordeal he must suffer to be softened so: an ordeal as awesome as the act

A Companion to George Eliot, First Edition. Edited by Amanda Anderson and Harry E. Shaw.

of repentance that it witnesses and gives its best to emulate. For a man with a mind so made up, to reverse, upon review, its final verdict—"I've no right to be hard towards them as have done wrong and repent"—spells out, as surely as any sign from anywhere here, or on high, ever could, a second birth. Such upsettings of settled thought—always decisive, whether quaking or quiet—are as regular as the turning of the tide or the changing of the clocks in the world Eliot measured and surely helped to make.

Thus the flood that ends *The Mill on the Floss*: the flood that washes away an adamant brother's bill of divorcement, sundering him for what he had thought forever from a rampant and too loving sister—his settled reasons for the separation, lost now in the amazement of her amazing effort to rescue him:

> It was not till Tom had pushed off and they were on the wide water—he face to face with Maggie—that the full meaning of what had happened rushed upon his mind. It came with so overpowering a force—it was such a new revelation to his spirit, of the depths in life that had lain beyond his vision, which he had fancied so keen and clear— that he was unable to ask a question. . . . Thought was busy though the lips were silent: and though he could ask no question, he guessed a story of almost miraculous, divinely protected effort. But at last a mist gathered over the blue-gray eyes, and the lips found a word they could utter: the old childish—"Magsie!" (455; bk. 7, ch. 5)

In the light of the "revelation to his spirit" brought on by the liquefaction of all the lines separating the damned from the saved, a hard brother, hardened by a hard life, becomes tender enough to wonder again, wonder beyond all the bounds of what he can see or count—he guessed a story of almost miraculous, divinely protected effort; tender enough to recall by its name his first affection for the errant sister he had long ago given up for lost. Here is a sea-changing apocalypse, which after all the waters have drawn back, shows the grounds for companionship that surpasses all alienation: "The tomb bore the names of Tom and Maggie Tulliver, and below the names it was written—'In their death they were not divided'" (457; bk. 7, ch. 6).

The crisis of consciousness which rocks beyond recognition a man's whole measure of another, and his whole means of measuring him, and, vaster, his means of measuring anyone or anything at all—"it was such a new revelation to his spirit, of the depths in life that had lain beyond his vision, which he had fancied so keen and clear"—is the crisis that constitutes the very grounds of continued companionship with that other, by the lights of the world that Eliot helped so much to make a world for us.

As experts in the Constitution of Eliot will surmise, the foundational grounds I have in mind are discovered in a strange letter lodged at the heart of *Middlemarch*:

> One little act of hers may perhaps be smiled at as superstitious. The 'Synoptical Tabulation for the use of Mrs. Casaubon', she carefully enclosed and sealed, writing within the envelope, 'I could not use it. Do you not see now that I could not submit my soul to yours, by working hopelessly at what I have no belief in?—Dorothea.' Then she deposited the paper in her own desk. (539; ch. 54)

Anyone who knows Eliot will feel something dearer and deeper than indulgent amusement when they hear tell of this latter-day Theresa, beseeching an ear which gave little sign of hearing what she had to say when he was alive, hoping it might somehow hear her now—though now there can be no reasonable doubt but that "the silence in her husband's ear was never more to be broken" (482; ch. 48). Those of us who love and honor Eliot are more than merely amused or mildly touched by this quaint and curious effort to speak to the dead: those of us who love and honor Eliot cannot help but feel that we are in the presence here of our author's Apocalyptic Book— written in a strange, cipher code which by virtue of its outlandish faith, reaches us, even now: those of us who love and honor Eliot cannot help but read in the widow's note to her dead husband the central tenet of its real author's real religion: the higher criticism we hear in a narrative voice whose every sentence sounds out the belief that both the minds she speaks of, and the minds she speaks to, no matter how removed, might at any moment be loosened from the fixed belief that it possesses the "Key to all Mythologies" (*Middlemarch* 280; ch. 29); or even the small-case key to a single other mind.

Any mind might be loosened, I suppose—even, one made up, seemingly for all time:

> As long as the English language is spoken, the word-music of Tennyson must charm the ear; and when English has become a dead language, his wonderful concentration of thought into luminous speech, the exquisite pictures in which he has blended all the hues of reflection, feeling and fancy, will cause him to be read as we read Homer, Pindar and Horace. Thought and feeling, like carbon, will always be finding new forms for themselves, but once condense them into the diamonds of poetry, and the form, as well as the element, will be lasting. (*Essays*, "Tennyson's Maud" 190–91)

The "wonderful concentration of thought into luminous speech, the exquisite pictures in which he has blended all the hues of reflection, feeling and fancy"—will draw the eye that has dwelt on *Middlemarch* to those gems whose gleams of light, near the first words of the book, flow through even the tautly woven protections of a puritan mind, with all the power of the last:

> "How very beautiful these gems are!" said Dorothea, under a new current of feeling, as sudden as the gleam. "It is strange how deeply colors seem to penetrate one, like scent. I suppose that is the reason why gems are used as spiritual emblems in the Revelation of St. John." (13; ch. 1)

A hard, well-cut gem encasing the flashes of a last and lasting light: I do not suppose there could be a better emblem for the object that Eliot as Critic values most of all—the finished work of art; the fully made man; the final act of justice.

And anything short of such completion must be regarded by her lights as mortally defective; as mortally defective as a man who, no matter how successful in the eyes of the world, does not finish what he started—"His skill was relied on by many paying patients, but he always regarded himself as a failure: he had not done what he once meant to do" (*Middlemarch* 835; Finale); as morally defective as the rude mechanics who leave off their tasks at the first sound of the closing bell, and thus subject themselves to Adam's terrible swift tongue:

> [O]bserving the cessation of the tools, [Adam] looked up, and said, in a tone of indignation,
> "Look there, now! I can't abide to see men throw away their tools i' that way, the minute the clock begins to strike, as if they took no pleasure i' their work, and was afraid o' doing a stroke too much." (12–13; ch. 1)

No surprise, I suppose, that what most appeals to the judge whose chambers we most often enter in Eliot's essays are works which are, one way or another, *complete*, since such work matches the proclivity for comprehensiveness that marks a magisterial temperament uninterested in entertaining a verdict that might require re-visiting. Canonizing or condemning; delivering its subject to the permanent collection, or discarding it from the pantheon—in any case, once the opinion is handed down, there is no calling back.

***

And here now, I will brave the objections of Adam Bede and his guild, to suspend my own argument, for a moment, well before it is done: I would be unable to complete my case were I not to stop long enough to mention to you that I prosecute it under duress: I wouldn't be able to finish this brief essay were I not to stop long enough to admit to you that, with some exceptions (they are few; we will visit one of them later), I find it nearly unbearable to read or write about Eliot's own. You will see, I hope, why I cannot make myself very interested in the persona who prevails there—someone who takes scant interest in me, or much more to the point, in *anyone*—at least for a length longer than the time that it takes for her to render her verdict on them. Anyone who cares for the narrative voice at home in Eliot's novels (the voice that makes us feel at home, there, ourselves), cannot help but feel at least a little betrayed and surely more than a little put off by the legalistic sterility that has taken its place, divested of the fictional narrator's grace-noting signature style, a whole worldview that we have been instructed to designate by Eliot herself, *primus inter pares*, by the single word of "sympathy."

Absent now the passionate regard, all concerned with lingering for however long it takes to measure the size, the shape and growth of the heart and mind of someone else; in its place, the quickest of glances at the someone else who dwells behind the scene of an action, an archive, a monograph, a monument in stone or sermon— a judicious, even judicial disinterestedness that potentiates the smooth protocol of irreversible verdict and unquestionable authority that reigns in the essays. The powers of judgment by which one of the great assessors in the history of English literature weighs with imperturbable self-assurance, the exact worth of the arts and acts of men and women, taken as individuals or as a whole: these are present and accounted for, in the essays. In fact the essays rather concentrate and render conspicuous this power of judgment: what is compressed and rendered glaring in the brevity of an essay is spread across the fiction, as the broad atmospheric moral authority that presides more obliquely (though no less surely) over the entire horizon of the novels.

What is missing is the other side, the inside story: the one arranged by a sensibility determined not merely to condemn or condone the ordinary and extraordinary business of even the most unusual or ordinary, lovely or unlovely, people or peoples, but to compassionate them as constant companions, as well. The speaker in the essays is as deliberately edifying as the narrative voice whose storied sympathy presides over the novels, but as quickly detached from the characters it judges as the voice from the novels remains enduringly close to them. Except in the form of abstract, *ex cathedra* instructions whose form contradicts and thus rather undoes the familiar call (never more familiar than it is in Eliot) to love your actual and not merely your putative neighbor, there is little sign of that narrator—so loved for her loving—who cares to know the inmost workings of the hearts and minds of everyone in town—able to do so, in no small part, because she cares so much to do so—even, indeed especially, after the first or last call of public judgment has been made about their outward actions and aspects. It's as if her schooling in moral and aesthetic law has trained the voice of the essayist to sound out only the dry, or at most wry sentence of the verdict—the voice of justice without much mercy—too busy evaluating her subjects (a doggedly inhumane ecclesiastical pronouncer; those silly women novelists with their insupportably stilted style) to feel much for them—to feel much for them, once she is done passing judgment on them (*Essays*, "Evangelical Teaching," "Silly Novels").

Those familiar with the world the novels bequeath to us, always thickly populated, indeed quite constituted by the actions and reactions of people upon one another, will find the grounds of the essay a far flatter and dryer earth, one riveted by judgments that, once delivered, are done with their subject once and for all. Like the backside of a censorious brother, or an indelible last Will and Testament, or the stiff sound of a primary school teacher's report—"Another indication of Young's deficiency in moral, i.e., in sympathetic emotion, is his unintermitting habit of pedagogic moralizing" (*Essays*, "Wordliness and Other-Worldliness: The Poet Young" 379)—the sense (no *sensibility*) that presides over the essays appears deaf to all appeals.

All (almost all, anyway), of its sentences seem to come from on high and return there, as quickly as possible—verbalizing some view, whose native grounds, if not exactly nowhere, are at least someplace very distant from the particular cases that the narrator of the novels appears always to dwell amidst—particular cases that Eliot the essayist, like a traveling magistrate, will visit, and then leave behind, as quickly as possible and once and for all—"The sum of our comparison is this" (*Essays*, "Wordliness and Other-Worldliness: The Poet Young" 385): the "this" summarized, our essayist is done with her subject, which falls away from the sphere of her interest with the alacrity of last month's Topic A.

Eliot makes as little room for the possibility of surprise (a change of mind; a reversed train of thought; a seeing things new) in the essays as she makes much for it in the novels—whether in the forest where Adam meets Arthur for the last, but really the first time, or in the town whose main topic is always one or another way of "Showing That Old Acquaintances Are Capable of Surprising Us" (*Mill* 435; bk. 7 ch. 3)—like the surprise that Mrs. Glegg winds up defending Maggie Tulliver, cast out by those who had heretofore more or less consented to live with her, for a crime of passion (dire, though not dark; a crime of passion which was something at least a lot like love). Thus a heart-strong and headstrong girl finds comfort in the house of her most rebarbative relative, who had always before been first to condemn her for considerably fewer cardinal sins.

No such relenting in the essay. The results can sometimes be hilarious, but they are hardly ever humane. Thus, to revisit Eliot's most enduring opinion—"Silly Novels by Lady Novelists": having satisfied itself that those she prosecutes deserve no pity, the essay is more than pleased to give them none:

> We had imagined that destitute women turned novelists, as they turned governesses, because they had no other "lady-like" means of getting their bread. On this supposition, vacillating syntax and improbable incident had a certain pathos for us, like extremely supererogatory pincushions and ill-devised nightcaps that are offered for sale by a blind man. (303)

Like the provincial princess who reigns at the beginning of Eliot's last novel, the author of "Silly Novels by Lady Novelists" appears to take a puerile sadist's intent, intense delight in the easy target—a small sized aquarium to which she is happy to apply a Gatling Gun.

Sheltered from dire material want, any other human susceptibility of her Lady Novelist (the ordinary desire, for example, to seem wiser or more worldly, not to mention richer or prettier or shapelier, than she is), Eliot appears happy to forget as she sets about demolishing, by means of a satiric voice so unsympathetic that it would seem, at first sound, to fall almost entirely outside the range of voices we would recognize from the novels, the legibly ludicrous affectations that grow out of these homey, homely aspirations—"a quite playful familiarity with the Latin classics—with the 'dear old Virgil,' 'the graceful Horace, the humane Cicero, and the pleasant Livy'" (305).

Now and then we meet a variation on the satiric voice that speaks here in the novels—listen to Gwendolen (not to mention the narrator whose consciousness when she covers that princess in exile, covers herself in the same mean-girl sarcasm); Gwendolen, who has herself the makings of the dilettante lady writer, and who makes her first enemy of a confirmed one—"squat" Mrs. Arrowpoint, whose tome on Tasso—"Home-made books must be so nice"—we have no reason to believe anyone especially

wished longer, or to be more exact, taller—except for the author herself: "My Tasso
. . . I could have made it twice the size" (46; ch. 5). Like Gwendolen whom she
resembles more than she would ever admit in open court—Gwendolen who is hardly
inclined to tarry long enough to consider the sight of the smarting Mrs. Arrowpoint,
after she has delivered her arrow to the heart of the homey novelist—the essayist is
hardly inclined to look back to consider the carnage she has left behind.

As vast as the distance between London and Palestine, is the difference between
such satire and the sympathy by which Eliot petitioned to vacate any version of
the nullification order that philosophers for a long time now have called the problem
of other minds—or should I say, in the case of Eliot, the problem of other hearts?
Both, of course: the epistemological ethos Eliot enshrines in her fiction established
its precedence by the merging of pity and perception, eliding the difference between
the receptive powers of the heart and the mind, as surely as other forms of faith
routinely sanctify and receive their power of sanctification by means of the marriage
of the figurative and literal. No more than the body and the spirit can be separated,
can sympathy from the science that Eliot did as much as anyone to advance. Like
an anatomy lesson that blossoms, under your nose, into a blazon of affection for all
the catalogued parts, the labor of careful description becomes itself the way you
care for what is being described. Sometimes this care is as sweet as your feelings for
that kid whose heart, however errant and erroneous, is always in the right place; that
kid whose transgressions you are perfectly willing to forgive in advance; a feeling of
charity which gives us standing to engage with the inner hearing of his hot-blooded
speciousness:

> Fred had been rewarding resolution by a little laxity of late . . . the last fortnight Mary
> had been staying at Lowick Parsonage with the ladies there . . . and Fred, not seeing
> anything more agreeable to do, had turned into the Green Dragon, partly to play at
> billiards, partly to taste the old flavour of discourse about horses, sport, and things in
> general, considered from a point of view which was not strenuously correct. He had not
> been out hunting once this season, had had no horse of his own to ride, and had gone
> from place to place chiefly with Mr Garth in his gig, or on the sober cob which Mr
> Garth could lend him. It was a little too bad, Fred began to think, that he should be
> kept in the traces with more severity than if he had been a clergyman. . . . And now,
> Mary being out of the way for a little while, Fred, like any other strong dog who cannot
> slip his collar, had pulled up the staple of his chain and made a small escape, not of
> course meaning to go fast or far. There could be no reason why he should not play at
> billiards, but he was determined not to bet. As to money just now, Fred had in his mind
> the heroic project of saving almost all of the eighty pounds that Mr Garth offered him.
> . . . Nevertheless, it must be acknowledged that on this evening, which was the fifth of
> his recent visits to the billiard-room, Fred had, not in his pocket, but in his mind, the
> ten pounds which he meant to reserve for himself from his half-year's salary (having
> before him the pleasure of carrying thirty to Mrs. Garth when Mary was likely to be
> come home again)—he had those ten pounds in his mind as a fund from which he might

risk something, if there were a chance of a good bet. Why? Well, when sovereigns were flying about, why shouldn't he catch a few? He would never go far along that road again; but a man likes to assure himself, and men of pleasure generally, what he could do in the way of mischief if he chose, and that if he abstains from making himself ill, or beggaring himself, or talking with the utmost looseness which the narrow limits of human capacity will allow, it is not because he is a spooney. Fred did not enter into formal reasons, which are a very artificial, inexact way of representing the tingling returns of old habit, and the caprices of young blood: but there was lurking in him a prophetic sense that evening, that when he began to play he should also begin to bet—that he should enjoy some punch-drinking, and in general prepare himself for feeling "rather seedy" in the morning. It is in such indefinable movements that action often begins. (*Middlemarch* 670–72; ch. 66)

Who could tell at what point exactly the analysis of motivations become affection for the motivated? No way of knowing when knowing turns into caring here, anymore than either Mary or Fred could tell you when the charms of their childhood companionship turned into the current of a life-long one. Who in their right mind and heart would even care to try?

Of course, it's easy enough to admit some fondness for Fred Vincy, and especially after this full press courting of the dimensions of his subjectivity (an operation that, pulling out the stops, crosses the line that separates the narrator's psyche from that of her characters; the extra inning set piece our narrative playbook calls free indirect discourse and which Eliot made into a whole new game). Aside from Mrs. Garth, who being at the short end of all the wishful thinking admitted here, will be forgiven her immunity to his charms, can help but love Fred Vincy, at least a little, after this full accounting of all that wishful thinking? But the blending of perception and pity that Eliot spent her talent cultivating, communicating, and commending, that blending blesses even the most repellent characters, simply by the virtue of its sustained attention to the affective accidents and silent motives that move them to a destruction more or less richly deserved. We gladly join the narrator in the fellowship of this sustained attention (itself the very form of care), even when we know in advance what our finding will be.

To understand is to forgive—at least a little. Eliot does not mean for Harriet Bulstrode to be alone in the room, as she undergoes the ordeal of stripping her mind of all the glitter of small-town illusion to render herself fit to accompany her husband after the public exposure of his hypocrisy and perfidy have condemned them both to a social death in life (exile, disgrace): Eliot has arranged for all of us to be present there, as well. For Eliot, at least the Eliot we care best to know, there can be no understanding of what men and women do apart from the subjective poise, poisonings, and passions that went into their production. Even—in fact, especially—those most culpable or comic have the motives that make them so fully aired, extenuating circumstances that will render our judgment of them at least a little more mild than it would be otherwise. No work or deed, no matter how covered in foolishness or wickedness; no matter how trivial or cardinal; can be understood unless it is recognized as part of a ratio whose other term is the trembling human being who performs them, the human face (at least a little divine, always, all too human—"Doubtless some ancient Greek has observed that behind the big mask and the speaking-trumpet, there must always be our poor little eyes peeping as usual and our timorous lips more or less under anxious control" [*Middlemarch* 280; ch. 29]); the human face we recognize, and remain with, at last—even Bulstrode, of all people, that saintly kill joy whose demolition only a Saint would fail to observe without at least a little pleasure has his day in the Court of Compassion.

Count the careful pages that Eliot dedicates to explaining the turns of consciousness and willed and semi-willed unconsciousness which lead Bulstrode step-by-step down the road to perdition. The psychological conditions that enable what a man wills to write, say, or do goes a long way to defining it, according to the point of view of the narrator who presides in Eliot's novels—not a subjective theory of value, exactly; more like a subjectivity theory of value. In any case, the meaning of what a man wills to write, say, or do cannot be told apart from the circumstances that brought on that will, and thus cannot be told apart from the very long time together we must spend with that character in order to tell those circumstances. Thus, in the sphere of human action, no fact, even the most condemnable or commendable is bare, not even the most bare faced thievery:

> That was the bare fact which Bulstrode was now forced to see in the rigid outline with which acts present themselves to onlookers. But for himself at that distant time, and even now in burning memory, the fact was broken into little sequences, each justified as it came by reasonings which seemed to prove it righteous. Bulstrode's course up to that time had, he thought, been sanctioned by remarkable providences, appearing to point the way for him to be the agent in making the best use of a large property and withdrawing it from perversion. Death and other striking dispositions, such as feminine trustfulness, had come; and Bulstrode would have adopted Cromwell's words—"Do you call these bare events? The Lord pity you!" (618–19; ch. 61)

By the lights of Eliot's restorative history, pity is wanted more *from* those who discern events only after they have been dislocated from the subjective grounds where they grew than it is *for* them. And to fully consider those extenuating and extending circumstances, you have to care enough about them, to spend considerable time with them, both before and after any official or officious verdict—far more time than a busy judge pressed to finish opinions by deadlines and word counts can spare.

On the other hand, there are those (we love them best) who have a lifetime for such companionship:

> He dared not look up at her. He sat with his eyes bent down, and as she went towards him she thought he looked smaller—he seemed so withered and shrunken . . . she said,

solemnly but kindly—'Look up, Nicholas.' He raised his eyes with a little start and looked at her half amazed. . . . (*Middlemarch* 750; ch. 74)

The Puritan banker, from the depths of his bared, minimal, self has reason to be amazed. What he beholds is the woman who cares for him transfigured into a knowing being who has been vested with the power of objective observation. "He seemed so withered and shrunken": the tender intuition of intimacy ("her woman's solicitude shaped itself into a darting thought that he might be going to have an illness" [613; ch. 61]) is certified (again through the grammatical offices of free indirect discourse) as a truth, universally acknowledged.

But as much as we know about them, as much as Eliot devotes all of her epic powers of empathic conveyance to the benefit of our understanding, no less striking, and, I will argue, far more telling, is what remains *beyond* our comprehension; what *baffles* our comprehension. Listen again to the coda of Eliot's bravura transcription of Fred Vincy's wishfulness, as he tarries on the verge of self-destruction: "Fred did not enter into formal reasons, which are a very artificial, inexact way of representing the tingling returns of old habit, and the caprices of young blood." Wonderstruck by the fidelity of the recording Eliot has given us of what goes on in a young man's mind, even the quickest of us may be forgiven for passing over all that is confessed here, which is, for the record, nothing short of the admission that even the subtlest sympathetic ear is powerless before the bar that separates it from the other side of silence, the existential sequestration that keeps apart any representation of motives, from what actually moves. Exquisite symphonic arrangement! But in the end, a miss as good as a mile—as little able to fathom the depths of heart and mind it labors so carefully to comprehend as one of those silly novels whose falsification of true feelings Eliot delights in demolishing.

As Eliot would map its motions, our heart is moved as much—more—by the knowledge that its knowledge of the one we love fails, as by the knowledge that our knowledge of the one we love succeeds: that when all our reasoning is said and done, all our representations rested, all our passionate pointing, spent—oh, there's still so much we'll never know! As Fred prepares to feel rather seedy in the morning, is there more going on within and beyond his consciousness than his advocate so brilliantly surmises? Is there less? And do we not love him not less but more, because we cannot put the question to rest? And Harriet Bulstrode, for all that she suddenly knows about her husband, her continued espousal of him is premised at least as much on what she doesn't know, as what she does:

> He raised his eyes with a little start and looked at her half amazed for a moment: her pale face, her changed, mourning dress, the trembling about her mouth, all said, "I know"; and her hands and eyes rested gently on him. He burst out crying and they cried together, she sitting at his side. They could not yet speak to each other of the shame which she was bearing with him, or of the acts which had brought it down on them. His confession was silent, and her promise of faithfulness was silent. Open-minded as

she was, she nevertheless shrank from the words which would have expressed their mutual consciousness, as she would have shrunk from flakes of fire. She could not say, "How much is only slander and false suspicion?" and he did not say, "I am innocent." (750–51; ch. 74)

The full-souled willingness of this half-knowing woman to follow the man she married into the wilderness ("her hair down. . . . like an early Methodist" [750; ch. 74]), is raised to its sublime finish at the end of the novel: "the effect of her being on those around her was incalculably diffusive" (838; Finale).

If you love the world you share with those who have come before you, those who, right now, inhabit this world with you, and those who will pass into it after you have passed out of it, surely a part of that love is for that part of this world which must remain removed from all sureness. We hold this truth to be self-evident: who you are derives in part from what they were; and, in turn, part of those who come with you, and after you, derives, in part, from you.

What parts? That is less evident, and that uncertainty, I submit to you, is as much a reason for our love of the world as any certainty. We declare and manifest our engagement with this world, our world, at least as much because we know we cannot know, as because we sometimes think we can.

And here, at last, we turn back to a place in the essays where we find Eliot staying a little longer than absolutely necessary; seeming a little sorry to leave us. Here, near the end of "The Natural History of German Life": "We must unwillingly leave our readers" (*Essays* 298). Never mind, for now, what follows these lines. Consider only the feeling of regret, new to our ears, so accustomed to the magistrate who passes her sentence and then moves quickly on.

For once, Eliot the essayist seems as sorry to leave us, as someone who loves us is happy, after a time apart, to see us. As happy to see us as the stranger, the sermonizer at the end of *Adam Bede*: the stranger who lingers on horseback at the outskirts of a meeting of early Methodists at the start of a novel, before he makes away (he is a magistrate, and doubtless much business calls him elsewhere); the stranger, so pleased, after a separation that stretches across the whole length of the novel, to meet again the girl whose preaching, early on, had struck him with wonder, and seemed to suspend his powers of judgment—"the voices of the Methodists reached him, rising and falling in that strange blending of exultation and sadness which belongs to the cadence of a hymn" (34; ch. 2); the stranger, that magistrate, who, in the end, opens the prison door to allow the preacher girl to visit the condemned—"'Come then,' said the elderly gentleman, ringing and gaining admission; 'I know you have a key to unlock hearts'" (447; ch. 45).

"We must unwillingly leave our readers." Here, at last, in the midst of an essay, someone as unwilling to leave us as she might be someone or something she loves, and we can be forgiven for thinking that we are in the fleeting presence here of something like love; something like the affection silently dwelling in the picture of the world which she leaves us as she leaves us so unwillingly—the essay's final scene:

"the sun is only just touching the mountain-tops, and all along the valley men are stumbling in the twilight" (*Essays* 299). Loving this twilight picture, at least as much for its lack of light as its promise of a new sun: could this be a little like loving the reader she is sorry to leave as much for what she doesn't know about him, as for what she does?

References

Eliot, George. *Adam Bede*. Ed. Stephen Gill. London: Penguin, 1985.

Eliot, George. *Daniel Deronda*. Ed. Terence Cave. London: Penguin, 1995.

Eliot, George. *Essays of George Eliot*. Ed. Thomas Pinney. New York: Columbia UP, 1963.

Eliot, George. *Middlemarch*. Ed. Rosemary Ashton. London: Penguin, 2003.

Eliot, George. *The Mill on the Floss*. Ed. Gordon S. Haight. Boston: Houghton, 1961.

15
Impressions of Theophrastus Such:
"Not a Story"

James Buzard

When may we look forward to seeing or hearing of another fascinating book from Mrs Lewes? (William Blackwood to G. H. Lewes, 16 May 1878, qtd. in Ashton 360)

I was thinking principally of Vorticella, who flourished in my youth . . . as the authoress of a book entitled "The Channel Islands, with Notes and an Appendix." I would by no means make it a reproach to her that she wrote no more than one book; on the contrary, her stopping there seems to me a laudable example. What one would have wished, after experience, was that she had refrained from producing even that single volume. . . . (*Impressions* 121)

Of all George Eliot's works, her last, *Impressions of Theophrastus Such* (1879), is the one most readers have wished Eliot—"Mrs Lewes," above—had "refrained from producing." From the book's first respondents—her devoted, dying partner George Henry Lewes and her supportive publishers, the Blackwoods—down to more recent ones, reactions to the volume have ranged from the tactful less-said-the-better attitude to the openly hostile. Evidently William Blackwood, writing to Lewes for news, was hoping for a new novel, a successor to the colossal *Middlemarch* and *Daniel Deronda*; Eliot had told him nothing of her plan for a collection of ruminative essays, mainly about the foibles of various character types, presented as the work of a crotchety fellow with a peculiar name. To be sure, the book sold well, but almost anything by Eliot would have done so, on the strength of the reputation she had built over two decades as one of Britain's premier novelists. How many buyers actually made it through

A Companion to George Eliot, First Edition. Edited by Amanda Anderson and Harry E. Shaw.
© 2013 John Wiley & Sons, Ltd. Published 2016 by John Wiley & Sons, Ltd.

Impressions we cannot know. As Nancy Henry points out in the introduction to her edition of the work, the early critics "were generally unimpressed with either the intellect or the humour displayed by the great national novelist in her first book of essays" (Henry xiii). Reviews took umbrage at the aggressive intellectualism, the overwrought prose style, the "hyper-self-consciousness of [the] narrative as a whole" (Bodenheimer 158). As Henry notes, "even the *Times*, which called the book 'emphatically a work of genius', doubted it could ever be popular 'in the ordinary acceptation of the word' . . ." (xiv).

More recent critics and biographers have continued to give *Impressions* short shrift. The pioneering modern biography by Gordon Haight makes no comment on the quality of the book and confines itself to the briefest of summaries of its contents (521–22). The volume on Eliot in the *Critical Heritage* series does not include a single review of *Impressions*: it does print a portion of W. H. Mallock's 1879 piece on the volume, but only that portion dealing with Eliot's earlier career (see Carroll 448–60). Others have been more explicit in expressing their displeasure at this unlovely work having the audacity to crown Eliot's career. Biographer Frederick Karl declared *Impressions* "the least satisfactory of Eliot's publications, perhaps because it fell between the memoir she disdained to write and the desire, near the end of her life, to write more freely about more personal things" (570). To Rosemary Ashton, the character studies in *Impressions* "often leave a dull and bitter taste, being mere sketches of human limitations such as a Casaubon, a Tito, or a Bulstrode would have been if they had not been imaginatively embedded in a fully realized community and engaged in the shifting and dramatic interaction of a plot." She adds, "it is in the nature of the minor genre to which *Theophrastus Such* belongs to lack plot, development, drama, light and shade, movement and feeling"—in other words, all those attributes that make Eliot's novels such superior instances of *their* genre (Ashton 360).

Ashton's judgments might seem to commit the common error of faulting a work for not being a different kind of work. The last letter Lewes ever wrote, a note accompanying the manuscript of *Impressions* to John Blackwood, emphasized that the book "is *not* a story" (Haight 515). Only one of the eighteen essays in the volume—the fable-like "How We Encourage Research"—carries out anything like a continuous narrative, and the meagerness of the fictional world it spins out over a dozen pages can indeed make one pine for the light and shade, movement and feeling of Eliot's novel plots. But perhaps Ashton, in laying stress upon all those qualities not to be found in this book, comes close to grasping its relation to the novels: for, from a certain perspective, *Impressions* comes to appear not just "not a story," but a refusal to traffic in storytelling. Returning to nonfiction prose late in her career, Eliot stepped away from narrative and into a form contrapuntal to the novels whose connection to Eliot's fictional practice might be found in its seeming exaggeration of a resistance to narrative not unknown to the great novels themselves. To acquire this perspective, we will have to revisit the issue of Eliot's relationship to the natural-scientific ideas of Lewes, specifically those bearing on the biological concept of life and the relationship between the organism and the surrounding medium in which it has its being.

We will need to consider the implications of such ideas for the writing of fiction. And finally we will have to take stock of the only other work of first-person narration in Eliot's oeuvre ("The Lifted Veil"), to see what arises from the exercise of connecting it to *Impressions*. But first we should have a look around the volume itself, and situate it in relationship to that "minor genre" Ashton referred to above.

The ancient Greek Theophrastus (c. 370–288 BC) was a pupil of Aristotle and successor to him as head of the Peripatetic School of Athens. Among his many writings was a book called *The Characters*, consisting of sketches of thirty negative personality types. Rooted in the ethical teachings of his master, Theophrastus's analysis focused on the way behavior, hardened by repetition into habit, yielded identifiable, predictable character—this word deriving from the Greek verb *charassein*, to stamp with an impression, as in coining. "States of character," Aristotle had declared in his *Nicomachean Ethics*, "arise out of like activities": taking the impress from our own behavior, "we become just by doing just acts, temperate by doing temperate acts, brave by doing brave acts" (29). The implications of such a viewpoint were not limited to the sphere of personal morality but extended into politics as well, "for legislators make the citizens good by forming habits in them, and this is the wish of every legislator, and those who do not effect it miss their mark, and it is in this that a good constitution differs from a bad one" (Aristotle 29). Thus a work like *The Characters* aimed not simply at exposing personal failings but at identifying ways in which the political community as a whole was failing at the education of its citizens and those citizens failing in turn to make a healthy community. This distinction would hold for Eliot's *Impressions*, as well: essay 16, "Moral Swindlers," for example, protests a perceived Victorian tendency to reduce the moral sphere to merely personal interactions, in violation of Aristotle's insistence that ethics be considered as an element in "the constitution and prosperity of States" (130).

Theophrastus's *Characters* also became a catalyst for the Greek theatrical style known as New Comedy, associated primarily with the dramatist Menander. Its traces could be felt as well in the Roman comic theater of Plautus and, more directly, in such imitative texts as Diogenes Laertius's *Ethical Characters* (c. 230 BC).

With the reclamation of the classical heritage in the Early Modern period, the character study enjoyed a resurgence that lasted well into the eighteenth century. The reader of Eliot experiences a particular fillip upon learning that one Isaac Casaubon published a Greek text and Latin translation of the *Characters* in 1592, bringing the ancient Theophrastus generations of new readers, imitators, and adapters. "In England," writes the critic G. Robert Stange, "the Theophrastan pattern was very quickly domesticated, reaching what is perhaps a culmination in the *Microcosmographie* of John Earle (1628)" (314). The most famous of modern Theophrastans was the Frenchman Jean de la Bruyère, who published his *Les Caractères, ou les Moeurs de ce siècle* in 1688, and whose "influence [in Eliot's book] is so pervasive as to make him the guiding spirit of *Impressions of Theophrastus Such*" (324). "[E]ssentially a set of essays on the manners and morals of his time, illustrated by brief sketches of characters who represent the tendencies he is discussing," la Bruyère's book provided Eliot with a more flexible template than she could have found in her Greek original, and it shared with hers a notable emphasis on the literary life (324). But even more recent models were ready to hand for the form and style of *Impressions*. Stange points out that an acquaintance of Eliot's, R. C. Jebb, had "revived English interest in Theophrastus's *Characters* with his excellent new translation [of 1870], annotated and with a lively introduction" (323). Eliot could thus "assume that many of her readers had some knowledge of the form and that her title, *Impressions of Theophrastus Such*, would be understood to suggest both her debt to the Theophrastan tradition and, in its creation of a fictitious author, her departure from it" (323–24). As for the character of that fictitious author, Stange finds "a parallel in [Charles] Lamb's Elia, the maimed eccentric who suffers inwardly but loves his fellow men and teaches his readers to love them too" (326). Ultimately the "long tradition of moralist as victim of society" goes back to Aesop, "the lame slave whose wisdom we find the more acceptable because it issues from an author so seemingly harmless" (326). Yet Stange also detects a "debonair sophistication" in Eliot's Theophrastus that "reminds one . . . of another nineteenth-century essayistic persona who has been too little regarded: Vivian, the figure George Henry Lewes created for his columns of dramatic criticism in the *Leader*" (326–27).

The title of George Eliot's final book could not be more open in acknowledging its generic affiliations, and the Aristotelian roots of Theophrastan tradition show in the text from time to time. In one essay we read, "One cannot give a recipe for wise judgment: it resembles appropriate muscular action, which is attained by the myriad lessons in nicety of balance and of aim that only practice can give" (105). Elsewhere, however, we find Eliot's persona confessing that had he been in the Athens of his ancient namesake, "I might have objected to Aristotle as too much of a systematiser, and have preferred the freedom of a little self-contradiction as offering more chances of truth" (16); and it would be a mistake to look for any very organized plan beneath the surface differences from essay to essay. À la Bruyère, not all the pieces in the collection fit squarely within the conventions of the Theophrastan character book. Essay 10, "Debasing the Moral Currency," develops no central character and consists simply of generalized complaints about aspects of Eliot's contemporary culture. Number 17, "Shadows of the Coming Race," stages a debate rather than highlighting a distinct personality type. Number 18, "The Modern Hep! Hep! Hep!," by far the longest in the volume, foregrounds neither a character nor the distinctive narrator in the course of presenting its argument about the virtues of national identification, even for the diasporic Jews. Following on from her last novel, *Daniel Deronda*, Eliot concludes her final book with a defense of modern Zionism on the grounds that

An individual man, to be harmoniously great, must belong to a nation . . . if not in actual existence yet existing in the past, in memory, as departed, invisible, beloved ideal, once a reality, and perhaps to be restored. A common humanity is not yet enough to feed the rich blood of various activity which makes a complete man. The time is not come for cosmopolitanism to be highly virtuous, any more than for communism to suffice for social energy. (147)

As her career drew to a close, the cosmopolitan intellectual Mary Ann Evans repudiated cosmopolitanism, through her mediating personae George Eliot and Theophrastus Such, as incapable—at least so far—of centering us morally and intellectually.

And then there are the first two essays in the volume, which may cause us to reflect on the title's final word, "Such." Henry questions whether we are to take "Such" as the narrator's surname, even though it is "placed so as to imply a patronym" (xvi). She points out that, in the Greek Theophrastus's work, each sketch began with the formula *toiontos tis, hoios*, which means "such a type who" tends to act in a certain way. Henry advises that we treat the title of the work as announcing the book's aim of giving us "impressions of Theophrastus, such a type who . . ."—with the specification of his tendencies and character to be provided by the essays that exhibit his sensibility. And the first two essays in the book do what the ancient Theophrastus never attempted: they focus on the character of the figure who will characterize others in the subsequent essays. Whereas the Greek original never brings the analyst into view, Eliot's essay 1, "Looking Inward," presents the narrator as an aging bachelor whose interaction with others has taken him on a journey from the "stupidity of a murmuring self-occupation" (10), through a phase of extreme detachment, to an asserted re-identification with his subjects. He will criticize their shortcomings but will not exempt himself from his charges against them. Anticipating the empathetic form of understanding (*Verstehen*) that Wilhelm Dilthey would soon establish as central to the human, as opposed to natural, sciences, Theophrastus declares, "No man can know his brother simply as a spectator" (4; see Palmer 98–123). "Thus if I laugh at you, O fellow-men! If I trace with curious interest your labyrinthine self-delusions, note the inconsistencies in your zealous adhesions, and smile at your helpless endeavours in a rashly chosen part, it is not that I feel myself aloof from you: the more intimately I seem to discern your weaknesses, the stronger to me is the proof that I share them. How otherwise could I get the discernment?" (4). Essay 2, "Looking Backward," situates the narrator historically and culturally, presenting him as the product of a rural childhood bearing similarities to Eliot's own and grounding his worldview in his father's post-Napoleonic English conservatism. Theophrastus's assertion that his "eyes have kept their early affectionate joy in our native landscape, which is one deep root of our national life and language" (22) continues a running theme of Eliot's novels, one that had been manifested most recently in *Daniel Deronda*, with its narrator's contention that "[a] human life . . . should be well rooted in some spot of a native land, where it may get the love of tender kinship for the face of the earth . . ." (*Deronda* 22; ch. 3). While these pieces provide us with the most direct access to the character of our narrator, they problematize the very notion of direct knowledge or self-knowledge where character is concerned—since, as Aristotle held, the formation of our characters cannot be divorced from our broader political or cultural context, and since, as Eliot's narrator insists, we need each other as a means of knowing ourselves, and ourselves as means of knowing each other. "I am obliged to recognize," Theophrastus comments in the opening essay, "that while there are secrets in me unguessed by others, these others have certain items of knowledge about the extent of my powers and the figure

I make with them, which in turn are secrets unguessed by me" (4). No wonder, then, if Eliot "disdained" to write a memoir. What Theophrastus calls the "natural history of my inward self" proceeds not simply by introspection, but by a method of comparison that involves continual tacking back and forth across the boundaries of the self. "It is my way," he states, "when I observe any instance of folly, any queer habit, any absurd illusion, straightway to look for something of the same type in myself, feeling sure that amid all differences there will be a certain correspondence . . ." (104; see Graver 66–68).

No novelist rivals Eliot for keen perception of the human liability to self-delusion, to confuse how things are with how we would like to believe them, to act as if we were the center of things and other people merely actors in our drama rather than possessors of their own centers of consciousness and interested points of view. In the words of her Theophrastus, "There is no knowing all the disguises of the lying serpent," our self-misleading consciousness (108). Her decision to begin *Impressions* by diverging so strikingly from its Greek model, with two essays on the particular and partial perspective of her narrator, may amount to a comment of sorts not only on the Aristotelian tradition of her original but also on her own customary practice as a novelist. For one thing, her update on the character book rejects the notion that the philosopher can treat his own viewpoint as unproblematic or impartial. Eliot's foregrounding of her Theophrastus may also indicate a decision to step away from the kind of narrator she had commonly employed throughout her novels: that supreme work of fiction by way of which so many works of fiction come to us, the third-person narrator who stands outside the action narrated and commands the power to enter into the separate consciousnesses of numerous characters, swooping into and out of their minds to reveal their unspoken thoughts and interpretations of the world they inhabit. In all but one of her fictions Eliot made masterful use of this narrator to reveal both the "secrets in [the self] unguessed by others" and the truths of self unguessed by that very self. It was with the aid of this all-too-familiar and yet magically weird storytelling device that Eliot had written novel after novel advancing and exemplifying her claim that "[t]he greatest benefit we owe to the artist, whether painter, poet, or novelist, is the extension of our sympathies" (*Selected Critical Writings* 263). "Art," she went on, in her 1856 review "The Natural History of German Life," is a mode of amplifying experience and extending our contact with our fellow-men beyond the bounds of our personal lot" (*Selected Critical Writings* 263–64). Eliot's art accomplished this not only by introducing us to kinds of people we tend not to run across, people of remote historical periods or alien cultures or classes, but by taking us inside the perspectives of others, perspectives that, like our own, are definitively limited, liable to distortion according to self-interest, but capable of expansion by means of productive decentering. In *Impressions of Theophrastus Such*, Eliot distanced herself from the most fundamental element of her sympathy-extending fiction, almost as if she had come to regard it as an act of bad faith, a fantasy, in her narrator's terms, of "non-human independence" or even one "form of the disloyal attempt to be independent of the common lot . . ." (12). As Rosemarie Bodenheimer puts it, "[i]f a writer's writings are, as [Eliot] insisted, her 'chief actions,' her final action was an explicit abandonment of the all-wise narrative voice that had promised so much to many of her readers" (265).

Eliot's doing this seems to have involved the imaginative exercise of reaching back to the time before she had become a writer of fiction. *Impressions* was written during the last summer she was to spend with her partner Lewes, whose declining health may have led Eliot to reassess their life and work together over the previous twenty-four years. It was Lewes who had encouraged her to begin writing fiction in the first place, in September 1856 (see *Selected Critical Writings* 322); before then she had been a translator and author of (by convention) non-attributed magazine pieces. Taking an outlandish male pseudonym for her final book may have constituted a self-reflexive gesture toward the moment she first took "George Eliot" as the pseudonym for her novels, the cover under which she, who had begun living with the married Lewes and so cut herself off from family and polite society, might be permitted to address the public. Certain traits of her Theophrastus appear to derive from the experience and character of Herbert Spencer, with whom she had been intimate before meeting Lewes. In these and other ways, *Impressions* "is full of allusions to the period in her life before she was established" (Henry ix). The Theophrastus of "Looking Inward" presents himself as the author of a single published book, "a failure," a "humorous romance, unique in its kind, [which] I am told is much tasted in a Cherokee translation . . ." (6–7). His literary fate could be an exaggerated version of what Eliot's own might have been had her fiction not won the admiration of British readers. Gratuitous success among a people immeasurably remote from his experience just accentuates Theophrastus's failure to reach his own people: he has become the proverbial prophet without honor in his own country.

In fact, it is possible to read the first essay in *Impressions* as describing a process in which Theophrastus, a distinct individual and so, like all of us, starting out in "self-occupation," seems to travel near to the antipodes of that position, approaching the condition of a third-person narrator with regard to the world he inhabits. Having overcome that initial "self-partiality," he has acquired "a habit of mind which keeps watch against [it]," and he has gone farther still (10). Noticing that others confide in him freely, he also perceives "that he is evidently held capable of listening to all kinds of personal outpouring without the least disposition to become communicative in the same way" (11). Becoming habituated to this one-sided flow of personal information, he finds,

> [w]hile my desire to explain myself in private ears has been quelled, the habit of getting interested in the experience of others has been continually gathering strength, and I am really at the point of finding that this world would be worth living in without any lot of one's own. Is it not possible for me to enjoy the scenery of the earth without saying to myself, I have a cabbage-garden in it? (11)

Such a stance is reminiscent of the one Daniel Deronda found himself in before he discovered his racial identity as a Jew and, with it, a cause to devote himself to. The young Daniel exhibited a "many-sided sympathy"—comparable perhaps to Theo-phrastus's "habit of getting interested in the experience of others"—which "had so wrought itself to the habit of seeing things as they probably appeared to others, that a strong partisanship, unless it were against an immediate oppression, had become an insincerity for him" (*Deronda* 364; ch. 32). Before acquiring the consider-able cabbage-garden of Judaism and Zionism, Daniel exemplified the condition of a radically centrifugal sympathy, his "half-speculative, half-involuntary identification of himself with the objects he was looking at" leading him to wonder "how far it might be possible to shift his centre till his own personality would be no less outside him than the landscape" (*Deronda* 189; ch. 17). It is as if Daniel had learned the lessons of Eliot's earlier fiction all too well, evacuating all sense of self in his lavish imagina-tive investment in the lots of others.

No sooner does Theophrastus describe this spectatorship to the brink of which his sympathetic listening has brought him than he pulls himself abruptly back from it. Construing oneself as the third-person narrator of one's world is no less problematic than is the narcissism of construing oneself its protagonist. "But this sounds like the lunacy of fancying oneself everybody else and the disloyal attempt to be independent of the common lot, and to live without a sharing of pain" (12). The pain to be shared includes the sometimes caustic judgments Theophrastus metes out in his subsequent essays, for, as he says, "[t]hough not averse to finding fault with myself, and conscious of deserving lashes, I like to keep the scourge in my own discriminating hand" (6). This sado-masochistic image captures the intensity with which Eliot and Theophras-tus recoil from the earlier novelistic argument that art must always be spreading our sympathy: follow that argument to its extreme, and we find, not the productive decentering of our native self-partiality, but the ethical nullity of the pre-Zionist Deronda, for whom "plenteous, flexible sympathy had ended by falling into one current with that reflective analysis which tends to neutralize sympathy" (*Deronda* 364; ch. 32). As Theophrastus puts it in essay 13, "How We Come to Give Ourselves False Testimonials, and Believe in Them," "a too intense consciousness of one's kinship with all frailties and vices undermines the active heroism which battles against wrong" (105). Even the balm of sympathy must be checked in its outflow, the traffic at the border of self and others rigorously patrolled, lest we lose our ability to operate effec-tively in the world.

The recommendation of Eliot's later works is that selfishness must be countered by nationalism but that nationalism must provide the outer limit of our identification with others. As essay 18, "The Modern Hep! Hep! Hep!," formulates it, "Affection, intelligence, duty, radiate from a centre, and nature has decided that for us English folk that centre can be neither China nor Peru" (147). Or, more crudely: "I am not bound to feel for a Chinaman as I feel for my fellow-countryman" (147). And so we find across the essays of *Impressions* a recurrent emphasis on English men and women's failures to sustain the community they owe each other, their petty conflicts and self-aggrandizings, their mental laziness, their fatal tendency to forget the fragility of the national culture they hold as entailed inheritance. The diasporic Jews are admirable for heroically sustaining their national spirit throughout centuries of the severest trials, and in stark contrast to "our willing ignorance of the treasures that lie in our national heritage, while we are agape after what is foreign . . ." (159). "We have been severely enough taught," says Theophrastus, "(if we were willing to learn) that our civilization . . . is helplessly in peril without the spiritual police of sentiments or ideal feelings" (86)—without, in other words, the "living force of sentiment in common which makes a national consciousness" (147).

The somewhat fanciful notion of a distinct individual or fictional character under-going a transformation into something resembling the detached third-person narrator of an Eliot novel found expression twenty years before *Impressions* in the only other work Eliot narrated in the first person, the macabre story "The Lifted Veil." As with *Impressions*, the tale was written at a time of particular challenges for Eliot, who in 1859 "was suffering from the consequences of her anonymity being breached" and had thus become keenly "sensitive to the difficulties of her position as a writer, dif-ficulties intensified both by her sex and her anomalous social position as the unmarried partner of Lewes" (Shuttleworth xv). Not only can the Latimer who tells this tale foresee what's going to happen, as both third- and retrospective first-person narrators can do; in what seems a nightmarish caricature of an Eliot novel's sympathy-spreading narrator, he is privy to the thoughts of others. As Sally Shuttleworth has demonstrated, Eliot had derived from Lewes's work in the natural sciences a perspective from which each living organism is conceived not as a discrete monad but as constantly engaged in "interaction with a surrounding environment" (Shuttleworth xxi). In *Comte's Phi-losophy of the Sciences* (1853), Lewes had written that "so far from organic bodies being independent of external circumstances they become more and more dependent on them as their organization becomes higher, so that *organism* and *medium* are the two correlatives of life" (qtd. in Shuttleworth xxi). Eliot would adopt a similar view of the relationship between fictional characters and the social, historical, and topographical elements of their environment. In a letter about her novel *Romola*, she declared, "It is the habit of my imagination to strive after as full a vision of the medium in which a character moves as of the character itself" (qtd. in Shuttleworth xxi). In "The Lifted Veil" we confront the unsettling spectacle of a protagonist "entirely open to his sur-rounding medium," unable to "police his boundaries" (Shuttleworth xxii). And in *Impressions of Theophrastus Such*, written when Eliot was forced to contemplate the prospect of living without the barricade Lewes had long provided for her, we meet with another variation on this porous border between individual being and environs. For all that he pulls himself back from the edge of extreme detachment, the narrator who foregrounds himself so markedly in the opening essays tends to flicker in and out of view as we proceed through the collection as a whole. We are apt to forget his mediating presence at times, to think we are reading the voice of Eliot herself (which indeed we may be), so thoroughly does this initially discrete first-person narrator appear to vanish into his words describing the talk, the texts, the thoughts, and the behavior of others, past, present, and, in dystopic imagination, future. An occasional reminder of his presence can seem but the dying ember of his separateness, so much insisted on at the book's beginning. At times he may feel comparable to figures who manage to be voices without quite becoming characters in modernist literature: figures like T. S. Eliot's Gerontion, or his Sibyl and Tiresias in *The Waste Land*, or the thing-like narrator of Beckett's *The Unnameable*. All these witnessing figures occupy an unstable position somewhere between human and inhuman, character and non-character. But overall, the effect we are likely to feel is that of the boundaries painstakingly erected between Theophrastus and his medium, Theophrastus and his creator, tending to disappear.

It is in this tendency to undo what *Impressions* first sets out to do that we find a counterpoint to a tendency in the novels. I have written elsewhere about the possibility that, at some point in her novelistic career, Eliot may have come to be aware of and somewhat skeptical about her own powers as a storyteller to enter into the mental life of even the least prepossessing of figures and to elicit our interest and sympathy on the figure's behalf. Even though she does not actually do so, the sense that she might if she wished may have made Eliot realize that she too had to pull up short before falling into an abyss she had dug herself. She may have felt the need to impede the further progress of that process her novels so regularly set in motion: the mobilization of our sympathy not just for the easy-to-sympathize with or the figure of heroic dimensions, but with characters who are "superlatively middling, the quintessential extract of mediocrity" ("Amos Barton," *Scenes* 85; ch. 5). Eliot's fiction always gravitates toward characters who are definitively situated in their time and place: it works on behalf of characters, such as Maggie Tulliver in *The Mill on the Floss*, not elevated above the webs of custom that make up collective life but borne along—to switch to another of Eliot's favorite metaphors—upon the pitiless current of a delimiting social medium. But for narrative to happen, the boundary between major characters for whom we are to cultivate our sympathy and minor ones who *constitute* a portion of that medium in which the major ones live must be held in place; otherwise we confront the possibility of a novel in which *every* character might turn into a major one. To give free rein to her matchless powers of circumstantial analysis and sympathetic understanding would obliterate the distinction between character and medium—a prospect nothing less than calamitous for the future of the novel, grinding forward movement to a halt with its open-ended pluralizing of perspectives (see Buzard 282–83). So it is that, at some point in the career of the novelist who had praised the reviled casuists for their sensitivity "to the special circumstances that mark the individual lot" and used her narrative art to inculcate "a wide fellow-feeling with all that is human," an infusion of anti-narrative energy came to seem necessary, to restrain the excess to which her narratives seemed liable (*Mill* 628; bk. 7, ch. 2).

It seems to me that, when she stepped away from novel writing in her last book, *Impressions of Theophrastus Such*, Eliot moved to the opposite situation. Stange points out that "[i]t is the Theophrastan practice to isolate character, presenting each figure as a separate study, but George Eliot enmeshes her characters in a discursive text and often involves them in a narrative situation" (324). This act of enmeshing and situating, like the effort to delineate Theophrastus as a distinctive character in the first two essays, sets in motion narrative expectations which it is the task of the essays in *Impressions* systematically to frustrate, for in this anti-novel, no character, not even the narrator, is permitted to be major for long. If the novels might drive themselves toward extinction by (even in prospect) refusing to demote any character to minorness, *Impressions* lifts a series of weirdly named minor figures, starting with Theophrastus himself, briefly out of that medium they comprise, dropping them back into the stream as soon as their identifying features have been noted. Minutius Felix, Glycera, Merman, Grampus, Lentulus, Hinze, Touchwood, Spike, Mordax, Pummel, Mixtus, Scintilla, Euphorion, Ganymede, Pepin, Vorticella—names like these, allegorical, mythological, natural-scientific, absurd, rise and fall before our eyes essay after essay, each exemplifying some fault of modern English culture, each studied like a specimen, none permitted to acquire the slightest narrative traction. The closest we get to a narrative generating sympathy for anyone's point of view is in "How We Encourage Research," but there we watch the hapless Merman strive to make a place for himself in the intellectual community, only to be punished and excluded by its gatekeepers, after which they appropriate his ideas. As in this case, several other essays take up failings particular to the literary or intellectual life, such as essay 14, "The Too Ready Writer" (on Pepin, who publishes too much and cultivates an unearned knowingness), essay 15, "Diseases of Small Authorship" (on Vorticella, who preens herself on her single book), or essay 8, "The Watch-Dog of Knowledge" (on Mordax, who refuses to learn anything from others). In essay 4, "A Man Surprised at his Originality," Lentulus belittles the accomplishments of poets and philosophers without ever producing works of his own. "He admitted," we read, "that he did contemplate writing down his thoughts, but his difficulty was their abundance. Apparently he was like the woodcutter entering the thick forest and saying, 'Where shall I begin?'" (45). This figure exemplifies the egoism of refusing to let his ideas be checked by those of others: "the total privacy in which he enjoyed his consciousness of inspiration was the very condition of its undisturbed placid nourishment and gigantic growth" (46–47). Preserving his so-called ideas from traffic with the world, Lentulus dies without publishing a word and earns the mordant comment, "Blessed be the man who, having nothing to say, abstains from giving us wordy evidence of the fact . . ." (48). Hinze, in essay 5, "A Too-Deferential Man," commits the opposite offense of overvaluing the opinions of his contemporaries. His is "an attitudinizing deference which does not fatigue itself with the formation of real judgments" (55). Elsewhere we read (in essay 12, "'So Young'") of Ganymede, a man trapped in a self-conception he has clearly outlived, and (in essay 9, "A Half-Breed") of Mixtus, another man pining for the early aspirations his own life choices have systematically betrayed.

As these examples suggest, it is possible to discern patterns among the separate essays, but the book as a whole offers no systematic cataloguing of character flaws, and in some cases those receiving analysis seem of little moment. *Impressions* is a scatter-shot performance, occasionally incisive as only Eliot can be but frequently dragged down by a labored prose style that seems almost a self-parody of her usual elegant complexity. The characters pass before us and away again, largely unreflective on their own behavior or circumstances or history, like the "emmet-like" minor characters of *The Mill on the Floss*, doomed to be "swept into the same oblivion with the generations of ants and beavers" (*Mill* 362; bk.4, ch.1). Indeed, the penultimate essay, number 17, "Shadows of the Coming Race," dwells with gallows humor on the prospect of humanity's superseding by machines, which will possess "the immense advantage of banishing from the earth's atmosphere screaming consciousnesses which, in our comparatively clumsy race, make an intolerable noise and fuss to each other about every petty ant-like performance . . ." (139). Considering the cast of characters presented in *Impressions*, and the way they are presented, it can become difficult to sustain the notion that Theophrastus is being ironic when he writes of humankind's "futile cargo of consciousness screeching irrelevantly, like a fowl tied head downmost to the saddle of a swift horseman" (141). It sounds rather as if Theophrastus, and perhaps Eliot too, were wishing that horseman rode faster still, en route to the obsolescence of self-important humanity. The generosity with which Theophrastus began the volume, proclaiming to his readers and subjects, "Dear blunderers, I am one of you" (4), has given way to a dyspepsia and misanthropy as extreme as the book's commitment to forestalling any kind of narrative interest or character development. These traits help account for the fact that, like its characters, this last book of Eliot's passed before its public and passed away again. It has not even succeeded among the Cherokees.

REFERENCES

Aristotle. *The Nicomachean Ethics*. Trans. David Ross. Oxford: Oxford UP, 1988.

Ashton, Rosemary. *George Eliot: A Life*. London: Penguin, 1997.

Bodenheimer, Rosemarie. *The Real Life of Mary Ann Evans: George Eliot, Her Letters and Fiction*. Ithaca: Cornell UP, 1994.

Buzard, James. *Disorienting Fiction: The Autoethnographic Work of Nineteenth-Century British Novels*. Princeton: Princeton UP, 2005.

Carroll, David, ed. *George Eliot: The Critical Heritage*. New York: Barnes & Noble, 1971.

Eliot, George. *Daniel Deronda*. Ed. Terence Cave. London: Penguin, 1995.

Eliot, George. *Impressions of Theophrastus Such*. Ed. Nancy Henry. Iowa City: U of Iowa P, 1994.

Eliot, George. *The Mill on the Floss*. Ed. A. S. Byatt. London: Penguin, 1979.

Eliot, George. *Scenes of Clerical Life*. Ed. Jennifer Gribble. London: Penguin, 1973.

Eliot, George. *Selected Critical Writings*. Ed. Rosemary Ashton. Oxford: Oxford UP, 1992.

Graver, Suzanne. *George Eliot and Community: A Study in Social Theory and Fictional Form*. Berkeley: U of California P, 1984.

Haight, Gordon S. *George Eliot: A Biography*. London: Penguin, 1992.

Henry, Nancy. "Introduction" to Eliot, *Impressions of Theophrastus Such*. vii–xxxvii

Karl, Frederick R. *George Eliot: Voice of a Century*. New York: Norton, 1995.

Palmer, Richard E. *Hermeneutics: Interpretation Theory in Schleiermacher, Dilthey, Heidegger, and Gadamer*. Evanston: Northwestern UP, 1969.

Shuttleworth, Sally. Introduction. *The Lifted Veil and Brother Jacob*. By George Eliot. London: Penguin, 2001. xi–l.

Stange, G. Robert. "The Voices of the Essayist." *Nineteenth-Century Fiction* 35.3 (1980): 312–30.

Theophrastus. *The Characters of Theophrastus*. Trans. Eustace Budgell. 3rd ed. London: Printed for Jacob Tonson, 1718.

Part III
Life and Reception

16
The Reception of George Eliot

James Eli Adams

Was she beautiful or not beautiful? and what was the secret of form or expression which gave the dynamic quality to her gaze? Was the good or evil genius dominant in those beams? Probably the latter; else why was the effect of unrest rather than of undisturbed charm? (Eliot 7)

The character of Gwendolen Harleth, whose unsettling charm is evoked in these opening lines of *Daniel Deronda*, may seem worlds removed from that of her creator. But from the first appearance of "George Eliot," that author also was an object of fascination. Initially the allure was that of a guessing-game: who was the unknown writer behind such distinctive and extraordinarily popular fiction? When the author's identity was revealed—George Eliot was not a rural clergyman, but a woman, and not just any woman, but the translator of "godless" continental thought, who was living with a married man not her husband—the interest became more troubled. How could the charming scenes of *Adam Bede* have proceeded from such a mind? Most reviewers acknowledged the charm, but they began to worry over the moral design informing it: might there indeed be some evil genius at work in a celebration of traditional rural society that proceeded from an "atheistic" writer? Even if the increasingly insistent "analysis" and narratorial commentary did not adulterate the moral force of the novels, did they not interfere with the more fundamental pleasures of character and plot? And then the intractable discords of gender: how could such erudition and insight and imagination belong to a woman?

A Companion to George Eliot, First Edition. Edited by Amanda Anderson and Harry E. Shaw.

In all these tensions, one feels an unexpected resonance in the final sentence of that opening paragraph of *Daniel Deronda*: "Why was the wish to look again felt as a coercion and not as a longing in which the whole being consents?" On the one hand, after the deaths of Dickens and Thackeray, Eliot held an unquestioned eminence as the greatest living English novelist, one who had elevated the very stature of the genre. But as her novels moved away from "entertainment" they also prompted a reception at once more deeply personalized and more intellectually strenuous than those of her predecessors, more like that of a sage or prophet or "sibyl." The contours of her sensibility were inseparable from provocations to rethink the character of both fictional form and modern thought, and increasing numbers of readers found the added effort merely provoking. Following her death, that intellectual burden precipitated a rapid eclipse of her reputation, as it was aligned with a rigid didacticism (personified with various degrees of misogyny), against which critics celebrated the emergence of modernist technique freed of moral constraints. Since World War II, however, the distinctive ambitions of her art have restored it to a place of crucial importance in the history of the English novel and the intellectual life of the nineteenth century.

In the beginning was the style. There was nothing like it, "little or no family resemblance with that of any living author" (Carroll 67), and critics marveled at its distinctive power. In 1862, with the appearance of Eliot's fourth book, *Silas Marner*, one reviewer concluded "that any author should be able to produce a series of works so good in so very peculiar a style, is as remarkable as anything that has occurred in the history of English literature in this century" (Carroll 170). Most critics, perhaps taking their cue from the first title, *Scenes of Clerical Life*, found a helpful vocabulary in visual art: "a new novelist, who to rare culture adds rare faculty, who can paint homely every-day life with great humor and pathos, and is content to rely on the truth of his pictures for effect" (Carroll 67). More specifically, they gestured toward the paradigm of Dutch genre painting, which had wide currency as an emblem of novelistic description well before Eliot invoked it in chapter 17 of *Adam Bede*. The correspondence was manifold: her works offered humble, rural, domestic subject matter, finely-detailed and faithful to the reality they depict, but also informed by "humour and pathos" (a conjunction echoed in numerous reviews), a "sobriety" and absence of exaggeration that lent dignity to the "homely" or "mean" life represented. The effect, reviewers agreed, was that of direct transcription, whether from memory or immediate experience ("somehow we never find ourselves attributing invention to the author" [Carroll 89]). That emphasis would return to haunt reception of Eliot's later novels, but it also captures a revealing tension: reviewers applaud the accuracy with which the author depicts a way of life that (they confess) is unknown to them. This subtle dissonance suggests that Eliot's images gratified a powerful, nostalgic fantasy of rural life, which satisfied by its very remoteness from the modern city, particularly as an image of social order and harmony alien to experience in the metropolis. Hence the peculiar emphasis of E. S. Dallas's rapturous review of *Adam Bede* in *The Times* ("its author takes his rank at once among the masters of the art"):

unlike novelists preoccupied with "the difference between man and man," here is one who recognizes "that we are all alike—that the human heart is one" (Carroll 77). This Wordsworthian refrain pointedly echoes the burden of Gaskell's industrial novels (*North and South* had appeared in 1855), which are more overtly preoccupied with class tensions, to which they apply the universal balm, "we have all of us one human heart." From the outset of her career, sympathy in Eliot's fiction similarly seemed a vehicle of both personal insight and social cohesion.

"There is not much of a story," even Dallas had to concede, and criticism of Eliot's plots became a refrain throughout her career. But the intrusion of melodrama in Hetty's last-minute pardon could not obscure "the great charm" centered in the characters, above all Mrs. Poyser: many critics likened her to Dickens's Sam Weller, and she likewise served as a high-water mark for readers disappointed by the later career. As they savored the atmosphere and idioms of farming life, few reviewers noted a moral design beyond the dignity accorded the characters and their humble piety. Anne Mozley, however, pointedly observed "that the most absorbing and original novel we have had for many a year is also the most sternly moral" (Carroll 95). Emphasis on what Eliot "teaches"—in *Adam Bede*, "that the past cannot be blotted out, that evil cannot be undone" (Carroll 89)—would become the dominant note of critical assessment across the spectrum of appreciation.

Appreciation of *The Mill on the Floss* was decidedly more guarded. The revelation of the novelist's identity, along with the prominence given to Maggie's character, triggered a flood of comparisons to Austen and Brontë, most often to Eliot's advantage. She combined Austen's "minuteness and archness of style," one remarked, with Currer Bell's "delight in depicting strong and wayward feelings" (Carroll 115). But the handling of Maggie's passion unsettled many, and conjured "the worst luxuriance of that petty realism" still associated primarily with French writers (Carroll 150). Most reviewers recognized ambitions beyond mere titillation: "it is one of the grandest and most subduing, as it is one of the boldest pictures ever attempted, of the way in which the soul makes trials for itself" (Carroll 125). But the same reviewer underscored the novelist's "deep responsibility" in the handling of passion, and complained that nothing was served "by bringing into clear and powerful light its perverted and unwholesome growths" (Carroll 130). The flash point was Maggie's capitulation to Stephen Guest, which nearly all readers greeted with incredulity and outrage, as implausible and degrading to both heroine and reader. Some of this was familiar squeamishness: "the whole delineation of passionate love, as painted by modern female novelists, is open to very serious question. There are emotions over which we ought to throw a veil . . ." (Carroll 119). But a sense of decorum merged with complaints of narrative distortion that have persisted throughout criticism of the novel. Stephen seemed hopelessly unworthy of Maggie's attention, and Maggie's responsiveness thus compounded a perceived disjunction between the final volume and the first two—one of the rare criticisms that Eliot herself conceded (Carroll 121). A more encompassing reservation, which gained force over the course of Eliot's career, worried over the lack of consolation in the fictional design: "for whose profit or entertainment does she work out effects so darkly displeasing with a brush so mercilessly fine?" (Carroll 148). Dinah Mulock, anticipating a central uneasiness over *Middlemarch*, complained of "the same dreary creed of overpowering circumstance": "a creed more fatal to every noble effort, and brave self-restraint—above all to that humble faith in the superior Will which alone should govern ours—can hardly be conceived" (Carroll 159). "What does it all come to," wrote another, "except that human life is inexplicable, and that women who find this find the feeling painful?" (Carroll 117). Eliot's moral ambitions thus prompted debate as to whether "spiritual doubts and conflicts" were an appropriate subject for the novelist. Representing them, some thought, trivialized their force, but more sympathetic readers thought that such engagement elevated the novel as a literary form: "The author is attempting not merely to amuse us as a novelist," wrote Dallas, "but, as a preacher, to make us think and feel. The riddle of life as it is here expounded is more like a Greek tragedy than a modern novel" (Carroll 135).

In all of the debate over Maggie's conduct in *The Mill on the Floss*, one point of nearly unanimous praise remained the pictorial technique, centered in "the profoundly-studied and perfectly executed picture of the whole group of Dodsons and Tullivers" (Carroll 142). Even a hostile reviewer conceded that they possessed "a charm unsurpassed" for "those who like Dutch painting" (Carroll 147). This quality was even more prominent in *Silas Marner*, which returned to the more humble milieu of *Adam Bede*, to the great relief of most critics: "There is nothing like the inanity of Stephen Guest or the spiritual conflicts of Maggie. . . . We are left unembarrassed to enjoy those pictures of humble life which have constituted the great merit of George Eliot's works" (Carroll 174). For the *Westminster* reviewer, it was "undoubtedly the finest" of her works: "Nothing can be more profound than this picture of the manner in which all human beings are influenced by their environment, the consequences of this most wonderful fitness between the characters and the scene of their life" (Carroll 187). Here is an echo of the sociological emphasis Eliot had found in Riehl's *Natural History of German Life*, as well as a hint of *The Origin of Species*, published just two years before.

For readers who savored in Eliot's novels this sense of ethnographic fidelity to a distinctly English rural milieu, *Romola* came as a shock, and for most a disappointment. A genius that drew so powerfully on personal experience was sure to be confounded, they concluded, in an effort to evoke fifteenth-century Florence. Although a number of readers praised the characterization of Tito and Savonarola, it quickly became a cliché that the novelist had been lost in the antiquarian (Carroll 208). "There is a theatrical element in the studied accuracy of dress, scenery, and detail" (Carroll 197); her portrait "has resulted only in an accumulation of details" (Carroll 215). In Leslie Stephen's damning posthumous verdict, it was all "a magnificent piece of cram" (Carroll 479). But Eliot's impulse to work against the grain of her own gifts called attention to an engagement with contemporary thought in the mirror of history, which made it a favorite of critics such as Pater, who shared her interests in the Renaissance as a reference point for modern cultural reflection. R. H. Hutton praised her insight into "the conflict between liberal culture and the more passionate form of the Christian religion in that strange era, which has so many points of resemblance with the present" (Carroll 200). But this very project also called attention to the peculiar strains to which Eliot's speculative ambition subjected narrative form—a tension that would become increasingly prominent in reception of her work. Even the *Westminster* reviewer, who pronounced it "the author's greatest work," noted that the novelist's bias toward "moral conceptions rather than towards sensuous, much less passionate ones" led her to present actions "rather as problems than as facts." Hence even the most compelling scenes "were so philosophically treated, and so full of the subtlest analysis of the varying motives which struggle for the mastery in the actors, that we are in constant danger of being more attracted by the treatment of the moral question than interested by its bearing on the fate of those whom it affects" (Carroll 213, 216).

This verdict left the elitist consolation of imagining *Romola* as caviar to the multitude: "How then shall a book which touches on the finest chords of the human heart with a delicacy that proclaims the last results of modern culture be heard among the coarse appeals to curiosity or passion which occupy the public ear?" (Carroll 216). But such disdain for the broader reading public—soon to be echoed in controversy over Swinburne's *Poems and Ballads*—also provoked more concerted analysis of "the last results of modern culture" from those less sympathetic to its aims. An important 1863 assessment of Eliot's career by Richard Simpson, a liberal Catholic writing in the *Home and Foreign Review*, professed appreciation for her novels but underscored the "atheistic theology" informing them, which he attributed to the influence of Goethe mediated by G. H. Lewes. The absence of religious faith was incarnated in the moral doctrine of "Renunciation": "we must content ourselves with the knowable and the attainable; we must renounce ideal and absolute happiness. . . . The surest way to reap all the enjoyment of life is to take a kind of sentimental pleasure in sorrow and suffering, as giving a mysterious grandeur to the soul" (Carroll 247). That this skepticism had eluded so many readers was testimony to Eliot's skills as a novelist.

Reviews of *Felix Holt* gave new prominence to this secular morality—often in conjunction with protests against received wisdom that Eliot's distinction was largely "the excellence of a painter like Teniers . . . as if [*Adam Bede*] contained no more than a photographic reproduction of the life of midland dairies" (Carroll 253). The hero embodied, as John Morley put it, "what may without offense be called modern paganism," which "makes way where a cut-and-dried theology was worthless" (Carroll 257). R. H. Hutton called Felix "a quite new . . . type" of "merely secular and industrial nobleness," naturally recalling Adam Bede. But like most critics he found Felix unappealing—"a harsh mutilated sort of figure" (Carroll 259)—which was a major flaw in what was, like all Eliot's works, "essentially a novel of character." Although many praised the portraits of Mrs. Transome and Harold, the lack of a strong protagonist joined with the notoriously intricate inheritance plot to reinforce old complaints about unsteady narrative structure. In what other writer, asked the young Henry James, "could we forgive so rusty a plot . . . such a disparity of outline and detail . . . so much drawing and so little composition?" (Carroll 273–74)

The relatively modest sales of *Felix Holt*, coupled with the newly ambitious scope of *Middlemarch*, encouraged Eliot to undertake an unusual scheme for publishing the new work: it would appear in four volumes rather than three, but would first be issued serially in eight lengthy parts, initially bi-monthly. The shifting responses of critics as the novel unfolded became an intellectual drama in its own right, as immersion in the novel's characters animated passionate, sometimes plaintive responses to the perceived bleakness of the novel's ultimate conclusions. R. H. Hutton's installments in *The Spectator* are particularly telling. Like many readers he was puzzled by the "prelude" but enjoyed the early characterization, and found the second book "very tranquil reading," but by book 4 any sense of the merely obligatory has dropped away: "We all grumble at *Middlemarch* . . . but we all read it, and find that there is nothing to compare with it appearing at the present moment . . . and not a few of us calculate whether we shall get the August number before we go for our autumn holiday." By book 6, "Middlemarch bids more than fair to be one of the great books of the world," and his summary account reaffirms that verdict: "say what we may, it is a great book" (Carroll 287, 290, 302, 314).

That conclusion had been hard-won, and Hutton's reservations were widely shared. They centered on what most felt was a newly-insistent polemical burden—although its precise contours were elusive. Many complained that the narrator's ironic "chorus," which had distinguished Eliot's moral commentary throughout her fiction, had become newly insistent and unsympathetic, even "acrid," particularly in depicting the conventional femininity of Rosamond and Celia. As the conservative *Saturday Review* complained, "All the weak and mean and knavish people are blond . . . and blue eyes are uniformly disingenuous" (Carroll 319). The Prelude encouraged many to see in this emphasis an engagement with "the 'Woman's' question," as Hutton put it (the scare quotes hinting his uncertainty as to the agenda), but the ultimate fates of the main characters seemed at odds with this design. More generally, the acerbic characterization seemed but one aspect of "a running fire of criticism," which ostentatiously displayed "the authoress's excessive, almost morbid intellectual ability," as Hutton complained (Carroll 294); nearly every reviewer noticed the prominence of scientific discourse ("too often an echo of Messrs. Darwin and Huxley," Henry James pronounced [Carroll 359]). Some of this vocabulary flowed from the particulars of Lydgate's medical career, but it was of a piece with a more fundamental skepticism, which had become an acknowledged ground of her work, but had never seemed so disturbing. It was best evoked by Sidney Colvin, who described Eliot's achievement as a presentation of "the old world" in terms of the new. The old was that of her early experience of provincial life; the new contained "the elements of her reflection" on that experience:

> the many-sided culture which looks back upon pleasure with analytic detachment; the philosophy which declares the human family deluded in its higher dreams, dependent upon itself, and bound thereby to a closer if sadder brotherhood; the habit in regarding and meditating physical laws, and the facts of sense and life, which leads up to that philosophy and belongs to it; the mingled depth of bitterness and tenderness in the human temper of which the philosophy becomes the spring. (Carroll 332).

The burdens of "spiritual doubts and conflicts" sounded in reviews of *The Mill on the Floss* thus take on new urgency, and with them the crucial issue of what sorts of consolation we are to expect of fiction. Even Colvin, applauding the venturesome intellect, found the ending of the story so "uncomfortable" that it seemed an artistic failure. Unlike French writers, Eliot is engaged "with the properly moral elements of human life and struggling," but while she "rouses, attaches, and elevates" as they do not, her works leave us wondering if "a harmonious and satisfying literary art is impossible under these conditions." "Is it that a literature, which confronts all the problems of life and the world, and recognizes all the springs of action . . . is it that such a literature must be like life itself, to leave us sad and hungry?" (Carroll 338). As Hutton put it, "In reading the highest scenes of *Middlemarch* we have a feeling as if the focus of all light and beauty were cold" (Carroll 314). The plaintive note strikingly anticipates the reception of Hardy's later works.

Such disappointment revivified the familiar tension between the "matter" and "manner" of the telling, often in pleas for a representation free of "theory" or "analysis," an art which readers continued to find epitomized in *Adam Bede*. Thus the *Saturday Review* applauded "the ideal storyteller whose primary impulse is a story to tell, and human nature to portray—not human nature as supporting a theory, but human nature as he sees it" (Carroll 315). A. V. Dicey in *The Nation* felt "inclined more than half to curse the day when George Eliot began to reflect rather than to copy," but took comfort that when she "forgets theories and has no time to make reflections, the whole power of simple, direct description is still as strong as ever" (Carroll 351–52). Unsurprisingly, this emphasis crowded aside attention to the larger design of the book, the intricate dynamics of the "web" that figured so prominently in the revaluation of Eliot's achievement a century later. But that neglect also underscored the feature that redeemed the book for most readers: the power and range of Eliot's characterization. (Ladislaw was the one character repeatedly signaled out as a failure.) "The book is like a portrait gallery," the *Saturday Review* marveled, "all are photographed from the life" (Carroll 319). Trollope, Hutton remarked, "scours a still greater surface of life with at least equal fidelity," but cannot approach the depth of Eliot's: "[h]is characters are carved out of the materials of ordinary society; George Eliot's include many which make ordinary society seem a sort of satire on the life behind it" (Carroll 302). "Her novel is a picture," Henry James pronounced, "vast, swarming, deep-colored, crowded with episodes." As usual, he complained of the larger design—it was "a treasure-house of details . . . but an indifferent whole"—and echoed the consensus that it was "too clever by half." But he also suggested the inadequacy of those criteria: "It is not compact, doubtless; but when was a panorama compact?" (Carroll 353, 354). And he concluded, "In spite of all these faults . . . it remains a very splendid performance. It sets a limit, we think, to the development of the old-fashioned English novel" (Carroll 359). Eliot clearly had become central to James's vision of a new kind of English novel.

Few novels could have rivaled the gripping reception of *Middlemarch*, but *Daniel Deronda* attracted unusual hostility on two broad fronts. The first was the familiar set of complaints attached to the predominance of "theory" and "analysis" in Eliot's technique. George Saintsbury's *Academy* review summed them up: "a tendency to talk about personages instead of allowing them to develop themselves, a somewhat lavish profusion of sententious utterance, a preference for technical terms in lieu of the common dialect . . . and a proneness to rank debateable positions and one-sided points of view among the truths to which it is safe to demand universal assent" (Carroll 371). In the reception of Deronda these familiar criticisms were compounded by uneasiness with the world of Jewish life and faith that Deronda ultimately embraces as his own, but which the majority of readers found vague, alien, or downright offensive. It was not merely that Deronda, "the blameless young man of faultless feature," seemed unreal, an embodiment of "certain views and theories" rather than of richly observed character (Carroll 379), but that the doctrine of Mordecai was to most (Christian) readers utterly arcane, not "connected with anything broadly human," as Saintsbury put it (Carroll 375). The *Saturday Review*'s parochialism was unusually blunt: "What can be the design of this ostentatious separation from the universal instinct of Christendom . . .?" (The reviewer began to answer his own question by noting that "fidelity to race stands with this author as the first of duties and virtues" [Carroll 377, 379].) Even the sympathetic R. H. Hutton, who found the portrait of Deronda "a noble one," complained that "so much pain has been expended on *studying* rather than *painting* him" that he remains elusive, and his ultimate departure for the East leaves one "feeling uncomfortably that he is gone on a wild-goose chase,—to preach ideas which have only been hinted, and which must rest on a creed that has hardly been hinted at" (Carroll 368, 370).

This criticism would reverberate for nearly a century, thrown into relief by effusive praise for "the English half" of the novel, centering on "signal triumphs of portraiture" in Gwendolen and Grandcourt. Henry James, who had been "ravished" by the opening book of the novel (which appeared in eight monthly parts), ultimately found the character of Deronda "a brilliant failure," but proclaimed Gwendolen "a masterpiece," and critics have noted its impact on his own *Portrait of a Lady* (1881) (Carroll 424, 422). James's ambivalence in the face of Eliot's achievement—it was "the weakest of her books" and yet "the book is full of the world" (Carroll 421, 433)—had become so acute that he framed his ultimate review as a fictional dialogue, "Daniel Deronda: A Conversation," in which his own critical surrogate, Constantius, steers a course between adoration and disdain. As with *Middlemarch*, the larger design of the book was obscured by attention to individual portraits and the texture of the unfamiliar subject matter, but several critics suggested that Eliot had indeed pressed beyond "the old-fashioned English novel" into the land of romance. This view was argued most forcefully by R. E. Francillon in the *Gentleman's Magazine*, who stressed a difference in kind from her earlier novels, "in conception, scope, circumstance, and form." The realism of the early novels, which "will soon require an archeological museum for their illustration," had been discarded for a timeless realm of psychic struggle, preoccupied with "the mesmeric effect of personality" (Carroll 396, 394, 388). On this view, Deronda has less in common with Lydgate than with Spenser's Red Cross Knight.

Soon after Eliot's death the swelling debate over the prominence of "theory" and "analysis" in her work solidified into the view that her "teaching" was too often a rigid and inartistic didacticism. The shift is registered in many reviews of John Cross's *Life* (1885): "It was the fatal and feminine idea of a mission which pursued her, and which made her look at adverse critics not as at possibly mistaken tasters of a work of art, but as good or bad men who sympathized or did not sympathize with her gospel" (Carroll 488). A sneering misogyny became even more prominent in W. E. Henley's 1890 attack, which offers unattributed "epigrams" mocking Eliot—"Pallas with prejudices and a corset"—and her works: "it is doubtful whether they are novels disguised as treatises, or treatises disguised as novels" (Haight 1965: 162). But the much more sympathetic Henry James passed a similar verdict to more damning effect. In his review of the *Life*, he argued that Eliot viewed the novel as "not primarily a picture of life, capable of deriving a high value from its form, but a moralized fable, the last word of a philosophy endeavouring to teach by example." The priority attached to moral reflection, he continued, entails "that she proceeds from the abstract to the concrete; that her figures and situations are evolved, as the phrase is, from her moral consciousness, and are only indirectly the product of observations. They are deeply studied and elaborately justified, but they are not *seen* in the irresponsible plastic way" (Carroll 497–98).

This is at once the culmination of Victorian response to George Eliot and a harbinger of modernist aesthetics. James's view stands on its head the early reception of Eliot, but it also caps a growing consensus that "reflection," as James put it, had crowded aside "perception." At the same time, his appeal to "the irresponsible plastic way" grounds the novelist's craft in "free aesthetic life," a vision and sensibility untrammeled by moral burdens (Carroll 497). Some version of this axiom informs the consistent depreciation of Eliot across the first half of the twentieth century, in which a recoil from Victorian didacticism is infused with a vigorous misogyny. Oliver Elton in 1920 allows that Eliot is "an artist," but argues that "while exhaustively describing life, she is apt to miss the spirit of life itself"; still, "it is best to remember that George Eliot is a woman, and that her sensibility is true to the better habit of her sex, even if it will not do for our rougher one"—although "we" may still imbibe her "medicine" in small doses (Haight 1965: 198). Lord David Cecil, *Early Victorian Novelists* (1934), wishes to argue that she is "a great writer," that *Middlemarch* bears comparison with *War and Peace*, and that her achievement stands at "the gateway between the old novel and the new," but he cannot resist conjuring up the author's homely image: "That osseous lengthy countenance, those dank, lank beads of hair, that anxious serious conscientious gaze, seem to sum up and concentrate in a single figure all the dowdiness, ponderousness, and earnestness which we find most alien in the Victorian age" (Perkin 103). (Such portraits, almost burlesques of Pater's Mona Lisa, are staples of Eliot's reception up through World War II.) Albert Baugh's *Literary History of*

England (1948) relegates Eliot to a chapter entitled "Other Novelists of the Mid-Century," in which Samuel Chew affirms, "No other Victorian novelist of major rank is so little read today. The effort to lift her fiction to a higher plane . . . though it brought her immense temporary prestige, has ultimately been responsible for this decline" (Baugh 1378).

There were a few pointed rejoinders to such characterizations, most notably Virginia Woolf's centenary tribute in the *TLS* in 1919 (to which we'll return). But the major revaluation set in only after World War II, along two critical frontiers. In Britain, F. R. Leavis in *The Great Tradition* (1948) took up the long-standing moral debate by promoting Eliot to the pantheon of "the few really great" novelists, who "not only change the possibilities of the art" but are "significant in terms of the human aware-ness they promote; awareness of the possibilities of life" (Leavis 2). Leavis, repudiating a critical emphasis he traces back to Flaubert, frames his argument as a running attack on the pursuit of "form" at the expense of "life." Quarreling specifically with James's phrase, "not *seen* in the irresponsible plastic way," Leavis argues that novelistic form is a matter of "responsibility toward a great human interest . . . a responsibility involv-ing, of its very nature, imaginative sympathy, moral discrimination and judgment of relative human value" (Leavis 29). This emphasis in many ways returns us to the debates of the 1870s, as does Leavis's mode of argument, which is essentially an astute character criticism dependent on lengthy excerpts from the novels, particularly *Daniel Deronda* (where Leavis echoes Victorian depreciation of the Jewish "half"). But the assessment claimed wide attention, in part through Leavis's characteristic truculence (Lord David Cecil is a particular *bête noire*) but more substantially through his atten-tion to James's deep affinities with Eliot, which culminates in the claim that *Portrait of a Lady* would never have been written had James not read *Gwendolen Harleth* ("as I shall call the good part of *Daniel Deronda*").

Across the Atlantic, the relationship of "life" and "form" tended to be reversed. Under the ascendancy of the so-called "New Criticism," which celebrated literary form as an autotelic organic unity, American reconsideration of Eliot began with a strenuous *separation* of the novel from "life." In a groundbreaking 1949 essay, "Fiction and the Matrix of Analogy," Mark Schorer argued that the novel, though it might seem con-taminated by its proximity to ordinary life, could indeed repay the close formal analy-sis typically reserved for lyric poetry. The novel "bears an apparently more immediate relation to life than it does to art, thus easily opening itself to first questions about conduct," Schorer notes, but "a novel, like a poem, is not life, it is an image of life: and the critical problem is first of all to analyze the image." Schorer accordingly analyzes the role of metaphor as an organizing structure in *Middlemarch*, concluding that it is "a superbly constructed work," but that what makes it so "is thematic rather than dramatic unity" (Schorer 539, 558).

The renewed appreciation of Eliot's novels, focused in a growing consensus that *Middlemarch* was one of the greatest novels in the language, figured centrally in the profound reorientation of literary criticism after World War II, when late-Victorian "appreciation" (still the genre of Cecil and arguably even Leavis) increasingly gave way to academic "interpretation" and "close reading," as the expansion of higher education accommodated more scholars and more scholarly journals, which triggered a corresponding boom of publication that increasingly confounds summary. In this environment, the complex play of image and figure in Eliot's fiction offered rich occasion for New Critical close reading. At the same time, as the shock waves of modernist narrative receded and the "Victorian" reclaimed interest as something more than a polemical foil, critics offered newly exacting accounts of the rhetorical strategies in her works. The merging of moral interest and formal design was the focus of John Holloway's *The Victorian Sage* (1953), which aligns Eliot with Carlyle and Arnold, among others, in studying the play of figuration and character as an instantiation of each sage's distinctive ethos. The most important early book-length studies still bear a marked revisionary design. Barbara Hardy's *The Novels of George Eliot: A Study in Form* (1958) signals its aim in the subtitle, claiming for Eliot a formal complexity rivaling that of James or Proust or Joyce. W. J. Harvey, *The Art of George Eliot* (1962) gives greater attention to the moral designs of Eliot's fiction, but connects these to a wide-ranging analysis of narrative structure and stylistic technique directed against broadly Jamesian strictures and condescension.

Jerome Beaty's book-length study of the development of *Middlemarch* (1960) confirmed the status of the novel, which over the next two decades became a critical touchstone, and a particularly telling index of changing intellectual climate. The novel has been especially central to ongoing debates about the nature of realism, which were revivified with the rise of deconstructive reading. It is the focal point of two early essays in that vein by J. Hillis Miller, "Narrative and History" (1974) and "Optic and Semiotic in *Middlemarch*" (1975) and receives searching scrutiny in D. A. Miller's importantly different analysis of realism, *Narrative and Its Discontents* (1981), as well as in two important early responses to deconstruction, George Levine's *The Realistic Imagination* (1981) and David Lodge's "*Middlemarch* and the Idea of the Classic Realist Text" (1981), and more recently Harry Shaw's *Narrating Reality: Austen, Scott, Eliot* (1999). "*Middlemarch*, Chapter 85: Three Commentaries," by Barbara Hardy, J. Hillis Miller, and Richard Poirier (1980) helpfully gathers divergent approaches.

These varied formal engagements flourished in conjunction with renewed interest in the large intellectual contexts and aspirations of Eliot's fiction—a recovery greatly assisted by Gordon Haight's monumental edition of her correspondence (1954–78). The "theories" that had so troubled earlier readers came to seem crucial to understanding not only the fiction but nineteenth-century thought generally. Basil Willey's *Nineteenth-Century Studies* (1949), an influential mapping of "the history of moral and religious ideas in the century," gave prominent place to Eliot's relation to German thought, which is further developed in Rosemary Ashton, *The German Idea* (1980). The religious context figures centrally in U. C. Knoepflmacher, *Religious Humanism and the Victorian Novel* (1965). Her engagement with broadly positivist social theory is treated in Suzanne Graver, *George Eliot and Community* (1984) and a host of other studies have been devoted to more specific social dynamics. Alexander Welsh, *George Eliot and Blackmail* (1986), notably reads Eliot's career in light of the burgeoning "information culture" of the nineteenth century, within which anxiety over the potential alienation of personal identity is registered in preoccupation with hidden pasts. Marxist accounts of Eliot have tended to focus on *Felix Holt*, as does the most sustained New Historicist treatment, the chapter on *Felix Holt* in Catherine Gallagher's *The Industrial Reformation of English Fiction* (1986). Tellingly, Eliot's novels have attracted relatively little work in a Foucauldian vein, perhaps because the celebrations of duty and renunciation so insistently hedge the fantasies of freedom and knowledge on which such readings hinge.

Eliot's engagement with science, so prominent in early reviews, curiously received little attention until the 1980s, when it was taken up in a host of studies, most importantly Sally Shuttleworth's *George Eliot and Nineteenth-Century Science: The Make-Believe of a Beginning* (1984) and Gillian Beer's highly influential *Darwin's Plots: Evolutionary Narrative in Darwin, George Eliot, and Nineteenth-Century Fiction* (1983). Both of these works discover in Eliot's engagement with natural science not merely a vocabulary but far-reaching implications for narrative structure. More recently, Nicholas Dames (*The Physiology of the Novel*) and other scholars have extended this line of analysis to cognitive science, studying Eliot's understanding of an emergent scientific psychology and physiology, including the work of her partner G. H. Lewes.

A less systematic but arguably more profound dimension of Eliot's career is the force of gender, which shaped the reception of her fiction from the outset. Initially, the discovery of her identity underwrote extensive attention to the author's personal life, comparisons with Austen and the Brontës, as well as the stereotyping of various aspects of her achievement in the familiar binaries; occasionally it also prompted a category crisis ("*Adam Bede* was thought too good to be a woman's story" [Carroll 115]). But as early as 1863 Richard Simpson attributed a more complex role to gender by arguing that "the supremacy of passion" in her works was the byproduct less of personal experience or fantasy than of the social position of "the authoress"; the celebrity of authorship places her in "the male position," and thus "the male ideal become hers,—the ideal of power,—which, interpreted by the feminine heart and intellect, means the supremacy of passion in the affairs of the world" (Carroll 241). Crude as this may be, it anticipates much later feminist engagement with the works as in various ways symptomatic of the social obstacles confronting an intellectual woman. Virginia Woolf's 1919 appreciation famously praises *Middlemarch* as "the magnificent book which with all its imperfections is one of the few English novels written for grown-up people" (Woolf 172), but the distinctive emphasis of the essay is less Eliot's literary craft than Woolf's acute sympathy with Eliot's own struggles, which she finds reflected (often in disabling fashion) in Eliot's heroines: "their story is the incomplete version of the story of George Eliot herself" (Woolf 176).

With the rise of feminist criticism in the 1970s, Eliot's heroines seemed newly vexing. Ellen Moers in *Literary Women* (1976) flatly claimed that Eliot "was no feminist," because her novels are devoted not to the lot of woman generally but to a fantasy of personal "distinction," which is based not in the heroine's deeds "but in her capacity to attract attention and arouse admiration" (Moers 194). Later works, most notably

Alison Booth's *Greatness Engendered* (1992), offered more sympathetic assessment in Eliot of what Moers found only in *Daniel Deronda*, "a realistic and tolerant appraisal of the difficulties of a woman's life" (Moers 196). But Eliot's celebration of kinship, duty, and renunciation frustrated critics looking for models of feminine autonomy and self-assertion—which were more readily available in the works of Charlotte Brontë. As Gilbert and Gubar point out in *The Madwoman in the Attic* (1978)—whose very title enshrines Brontë as the central reference point in "a distinctively female literary tradition"—"every negative stereotype protested by Charlotte Brontë is transformed into a virtue by George Eliot" (Gilbert and Gubar 498). At the same time, their study epitomizes the impact of feminism in revaluing a feature of Eliot's writings that had been deprecated by earlier critics (even Woolf): what Leavis called "a need or hunger . . . that shows itself to be insidious company for her intelligence" (Leavis 39). The power of feminine desire is no longer an embarrassment, but a central appeal of the novels, as when Gilbert and Gubar savor the irony by which Maggie Tulliver is "most monstrous when she tries to turn herself into an angel of renunciation," in an exemplary eruption of "authorial vengeance" against feminine submission and the patriarchal norms it incarnates (Gilbert and Gubar 491).

These pioneering studies encouraged a newly exacting attention to structures of affect, desire, and repression in Eliot's writings, which were further stimulated by psychoanalytically-inflected French feminism, Michel Foucault's rethinking of sexuality, and the emergence of queer theory. Although *The Mill on the Floss* has been especially prominent in such accounts, John Kucich offered a more through-going rethinking of "inwardness" in Eliot's fiction in *Repression in Victorian Fiction* (1987). Neil Hertz, *George Eliot's Pulse* (2002), employs a broadly deconstructive approach to elicit a constriction of experience in stigmatized characters who function as surrogates of the author. Rosemarie Bodenheimer, *The Real Life of Mary Ann Evans* (1994), offers the most subtle exploration of the novels in a biographical context.

Critical developments over the past twenty years have given special prominence to *Daniel Deronda*. "The Jewish half" so long deprecated by critics seems newly resonant for its representation of personal identity and political life in a global context, shaped by race, religion, culture, and nationality—a set of concerns stimulated by postcolonial criticism in the early 1980s and given new urgency by international conflicts over the past decade. Nancy Henry, *George Eliot and the British Empire* (2002) offers the fullest study of this larger context. The insistent association of femininity with performance has prompted a rich convergence of interests central to feminism and queer theory, frequently centering on the figure of Alcharisi, as Deronda's mother was known in her stage career. As the novel gestures toward a model of cosmopolitanism, and scrutinizes the moral work of "culture" seemingly embodied in Deronda himself, it also has figured prominently in reassessments of Victorian liberalism, most notably in Amanda Anderson's *The Powers of Distance* (2001). But perhaps all of us who are devoted to literature catch a glimpse of ourselves in Eliot's hero; her works seem an inexhaustible inheritance, in which we, like Deronda, have found a vocation.

References

Anderson, Amanda. *The Powers of Distance: Cosmopolitanism and the Cultivation of Detachment.* Princeton: Princeton UP, 2001.

Baugh, Albert C., ed. *A Literary History of England.* New York: Appleton-Century-Croft, 1948.

Beaty, Jerome. *Middlemarch from Notebook to Novel: A Study of George Eliot's Creative Method.* Urbana: U of Illinois P, 1960.

Beer, Gillian. *Darwin's Plots: Evolutionary Narrative in Darwin, George Eliot, and Nineteenth-Century Fiction.* 3rd ed. Cambridge: Cambridge UP, 2009.

Bodenheimer, Rosemarie. *The Real Life of Mary Ann Evans: George Eliot, Her Letters and Fiction.* Ithaca: Cornell UP, 1994.

Booth, Allison. *Greatness Engendered: George Eliot and Virginia Woolf.* Ithaca: Cornell UP, 1992.

Carroll, David, ed. *George Eliot: The Critical Heritage.* London: Routledge, 1971.

Dames, Nicholas. *The Physiology of the Novel: Reading, Neural Science, and the Form of Victorian Fiction.* Oxford: Oxford UP, 2007.

Eliot, George. *Daniel Deronda.* Ed. Terence Cave. London: Penguin, 1995.

Gallagher, Catherine. *The Industrial Reformation of English Fiction: Social Discourse and Narrative Form, 1832–1867.* Chicago: U of Chicago P, 1985.

Gilbert, Sandra and Susan Gubar. *The Madwoman in the Attic.* New Haven: Yale UP, 1979.

Graver, Suzanne. *George Eliot and Community: A Study in Social Theory and Fictional Form.* Berkeley: U of California P, 1984.

Harvey, W. J. *The Art of George Eliot.* Oxford: Oxford UP, 1969.

Haight, Gordon S., ed. *A Century of George Eliot Criticism.* Boston: Houghton, 1965.

Hardy, Barbara. *The Novels of George Eliot: A Study in Form.* London: Athlone, 1959.

Hardy, Barbara, J. Hillis Miller, and Richard Poirier. "*Middlemarch*, Chapter 85: Three Commentaries." *Nineteenth-Century Fiction* 35.3 (1980–81): 432–53.

Harvey, W. J. *The Art of George Eliot.* London: Chatto, 1962.

Henry, Nancy. *George Eliot and the British Empire.* Cambridge: Cambridge UP, 2002.

Hertz, Neil. *George Eliot's Pulse.* Stanford: Stanford UP, 2003.

Holloway, John. *The Victorian Sage.* New York: Norton, 1965.

Knoepflmacher, U. C. *Religious Humanism and the Victorian Novel: George Eliot, Walter Pater, and Samuel Butler.* Princeton: Princeton UP, 1965.

Kucich, John. *Repression and Victorian Fiction.* Berkeley: U of California P, 1987.

Leavis, F. R. *The Great Tradition.* New York: Stewart, 1948.

Lodge, David. "*Middlemarch* and the Classic Realist Text." *The Nineteenth-Century English Novel: Critical Essays and Documents.* Ed. Arnold Kettle. 2nd ed. London: Heineman, 1981. 218–31.

Miller, D. A. *Narrative and Its Discontents.* Princeton: Princeton UP, 1981.

Miller, J. Hillis. "Narrative and History." *ELH* 41.3 (1974): 455–73.

Miller, J. Hillis. "Optic and Semiotic in *Middlemarch*." *The Worlds of Victorian Fiction.* Ed. Jerome H. Buckley. Cambridge: Harvard UP, 1975. 125–45.

Moers, Ellen. *Literary Women.* Garden City, NY: Doubleday, 1976.

Perkin, J. Russell. *A Reception-History of George Eliot's Fiction.* Ann Arbor: UMI Research, 1990.

Schorer, Mark. "Fiction and the Matrix of Analogy." *The Kenyon Review* 11.4 (1949): 539–60.

Shaw, Harry. *Narrating Reality: Austen, Scott, Eliot.* Ithaca: Cornell UP, 1999.

Shuttleworth, Sally. *George Eliot and Nineteenth-Century Science: The Make-Believe of a Beginning.* Cambridge: Cambridge UP, 1984.

Welsh, Alexander. *George Eliot and Blackmail.* Cambridge: Harvard UP, 1985.

Willey, Basil. *Nineteenth-Century Studies.* New York: Columbia UP, 1949.

Woolf, Virginia. *The Common Reader.* New York: Harcourt, 1953.

17
George Eliot Among Her Contemporaries: A Life Apart

Lynn Voskuil

And now, O most unreasonable Sarah [*sic*] mine, you ask me to tell you all about myself, when you send me not a word of *yourself*. Do I not live with myself and tire of myself until I have no need of metaphysics to make me believe that there is nothing certain but that *self* exists? And you after all your philosophical lectures to me, would keep me on a spot where I have already pirouetted until I am giddy, until I am one of the most egotistical speakers and writers in this world of egotists. (George Eliot to Sara Hennell, 30 August 1842 [*Letters* 1:144–45; emphasis in original])

To characterize George Eliot "among her contemporaries" is a dauntingly ambitious task for an expansive book (as her many biographers have demonstrated), not to mention a brief essay like this one, because the scope of Eliot's intellectual and literary circles was enormous. Very few Victorians were more widely read than Eliot or more intimately acquainted with the intelligentsia of nineteenth-century England. She *knew* her literary and intellectual contemporaries—their ideas and philosophies, their sensibilities and affections—more widely and trenchantly even than did her partner George Henry Lewes, that extensively networked man-about-town. And as her remarkable letters demonstrate, she was a convivial person who sought an active social life and delighted in her friends. Yet she did indeed live her life "apart" from her contemporaries in consequential ways, her scandalous but carefully considered elopement with the married Lewes only the most obvious in a series of episodes that continue to defy precise categorization in Victorian terms. Indeed, the conditions of her relationship with Lewes capture the paradox of Eliot's very conspicuous seclusion: while Eliot cherished and protected what she called the "dual solitude" of her life with

Lewes, their romantic and professional partnership was also one of the most watched and discussed relationships in Victorian England (*Letters* 3:460). The daily solitude of Eliot's life was, of course, enforced to a great degree (at least in the 1850s, before her authorial fame) by a cruelly gendered double standard that permitted Lewes to conduct a social life with his Victorian contemporaries after their transgression became known, but denied Eliot the same pleasures. Well before she had even met Lewes, however, Eliot perceived herself to live "apart" from others, conceptualizing a complex notion of the "ego" (and herself as an "egotist") that animated interactions with her contemporaries and emerged as a knotty issue in her fiction. Throughout her life, Eliot formed friendships and professional relationships, developed crushes and romantic attachments, and most significantly wrote her novels conditioned by a sense of isolation that was at once emotional, intellectual, cultural, and aesthetic.

The epigraph to this essay evokes the paradox of Eliot's life apart and suggests a structure for my exploration here. It is an excerpt from an early letter to Sara Hennell, written in the heady, liberating days when Eliot was actively abandoning restrictive Evangelical beliefs and reveling in her new friendships with Sara and with Charles and Cara Bray, all free-thinking, liberal people of the sort she had not known in her childhood neighborhood at Griff. A relief after the earnest propriety of Eliot's letters to Maria Lewis, her delight in Sara is palpable: she leaps, in the larger letter, from image to image that bespeak the joy of her new friendship, and in this portion toward the end she gleefully "pirouettes" with the sheer pleasure of it. Significantly, though, her pirouette—a dance routine that is fixed and solitary—casts her in the role of "egotist," a lone performer who whirls dizzily without a partner. Just as she would later do in her "dual solitude" with Lewes, Eliot visualizes herself here as alone yet displayed, certain only of her own egotistical stance in this "world of egotists." This enigma, Eliot's posture of standing apart in a full and active world, is consistent throughout her life but takes particularly poignant forms early and late, during her turn away from orthodox religious belief in her early twenties (about the time she wrote the letter to Sara) and again during her fifties, when she was enjoying a fully achieved literary fame and conducting salons on Sundays in her own drawing-room. Exploring these two moments will show how Eliot's full participation in Victorian social and intellectual life relied paradoxically on her careful cultivation of a life apart.

Fellowship and Isolation

The contours of Eliot's journey away from Evangelicalism are well known and variably narrated by recent Eliot biographers and scholars like Gordon Haight, Ruby Redinger, and Rosemarie Bodenheimer (*Real Life*). The most abrupt and decisive moment of departure occurred on Sunday, 2 January 1842, when the 22-year-old Mary Ann Evans refused to go to church with her father, a rebellious position that troubled Robert Evans deeply and prompted him to decline the sacrament when he attended services without her (*Letters* 1:124). Eliot's defiance was all the more pronounced because Lewis, her early teacher and Evangelical mentor, was visiting the Evans's home for the holiday and tried to persuade her friend, over the ensuing few weeks, to recant her position. Eliot, as we know, stood firm in her intellectual and theological conviction during what she called the "Holy War" (*Letters* 1:133), crafting a letter to her father in February 1842 that stated her own position with integrity but also with heartfelt regard for his (*Letters* 1:128–30). While Eliot never fully reconciled with her father, they eventually worked out a truce that made it possible for her to live with him—and even, on occasion, to accompany him to church—and she nursed him lovingly in his final months.

The move that seemed impetuous and ill-conceived to Eliot's family and conservative friends had in fact been evolving for a long time. And in its development, we can see early images of Eliot's life among, and apart from, her contemporaries. In social and intellectual terms, Eliot had formed a close, tight community by the time she was in her late teens. The earliest of Eliot's extant letters—to Lewis—dates from early 1836, when she was sixteen and writing frequently to the pietistic Lewis as well as to Martha Jackson, her friend from a later school in Coventry. While she had formed close emotional connections with Lewis and Jackson, a crucial aspect of her relationship with them was intellectual (as was the case with all her close friends, throughout her life); indeed, we should think of Eliot's contemporaries not only as the friends and family she knew personally but also as the many people whose books she read and whose ideas she carefully weighed and considered—and discussed frequently with her intimate companions. As an Evangelical teenager, Eliot devoured heavy theological tomes—"I am generally in the same predicament with books as a glutton with his feast" (*Letters* 1:11), she confessed to Lewis—and parsed them in her correspondence. In one letter to Lewis in 1838, for example, she moves from "Mr. Craig's lectures on Jacob" to "Archbishop Leighton's Commentary on St. Peter," "Mr. Williams's account of his missionary enterprises in the South Seas" and finally the "Life of Wilberforce" (*Letters* 1:11–12). Discussing books and ideas, in both person and print, was far more than an intellectual exercise to Eliot, however, for she clearly identified closely with the authors she read and the characters they sketched. She imagined Wilberforce, for instance, as both a mentor and a fellow sinner. "There is a similarity, if I may compare myself with such a man," she wrote to Lewis, "between his temptations or rather besetments and my own that makes his experience very interesting to me. O that I might be made as useful in my lowly and obscure station as he was in the exalted one assigned to him" (*Letters* 1:12). In the process of discussing such books, Eliot deepened the emotional connections of her personal friendships but also began to envision a circle of companions that was far broader than the people she knew in her small Coventry neighborhood.

At the same time, even in these early years, Eliot subjected her friends and intellectual companions to piercing analytical scrutiny. If Eliot's prodigious habits of mind naturally distinguished her from many of her contemporaries in Victorian England, she was just beginning to discover the power of her intellect in the late 1830s and to understand the social ties it could both nurture and rupture. Even so, she never feared to follow her intellect wherever it would lead her. In 1840, for instance, Eliot wrote to Lewis about two books by William Gresley, a popularizer of Tractarian thought who targeted a wide audience. "I want to know your opinion of them," Eliot said to Lewis before she offered her own straightforward critique. "Mine is this: that they are sure to have a powerful influence on the minds of small readers and shallow thinkers, as, from the simplicity and clearness with which the author, by his beau idéal characters, enunciates his sentiments they furnish a magazine of easily wielded weapons for *morning calling* and *evening party* controversialists . . ." (*Letters* 1:45; emphasis in original). In 1839, Eliot read Leveson Vernon Harcourt's *The Doctrine of the Deluge; Vindicating the Scriptural Account from Doubts which have been Recently Cast Upon It by Geological Speculations* (1838), a book calculated to shore up Evangelical belief against the evidence of "'science falsely so called,'" as Harcourt put it (vi). Eliot was not impressed with his argument, as she indicated in another letter to Lewis, spinning out a sardonic trope that anticipates the famous "disease of the retina" used much later in *Middlemarch* (182; ch. 20). "After tracing the image of the Ark and Mt. Ararat through the faded tapestries that line the temple of mythological history, until one is ready to fancy one sees the first in a linen chest and the last in Vandyke's frills, just as objects in [*sic*] which we have long gazed remain on the retina when we would fain be rid of them," she wrote to Lewis, "the author deduces from the doctrine of the deluge that of baptismal regeneration and I humbly opine supports or rather shakes a weak position by weak arguments" (*Letters* 1:34). If the execution is clumsy, Eliot—just twenty years old when she wrote this—nonetheless trenchantly dismisses an argument defending the principle of Scriptural inerrancy, a belief fundamental to Evangelicalism and the communities formed by a shared Evangelical faith.

In these very early letters, even in the stilted respectability of the letters to Lewis, we can thus already see the first stirrings of the authoritative intellect that would later find voice in Eliot's mature fiction. And in her raw exegetical talent—the precocious pleasure she took in interpreting Scripture and theological arguments—we can recognize the outlines not only of the translator but also of the narrator who would later place such a premium on hermeneutical perspective and point-of-view. The audacity and wit with which she offered many of her pronouncements suggest a bookish but not pedantic adolescent who was quickly maturing into an undaunted intellectual. The apparent confidence with which the twenty-year-old Eliot voiced her theological and intellectual opinions, however, belies another, more emotionally fragile persona that is likewise visible in her youthful letters, one that found expression in Eliot's frequent lamentations about her irrepressible ego and her "besetting sin. . . . Ambition" (*Letters* 1:19). "I am as usual becoming egotistical . . ." she wrote to Lewis (*Letters* 1:6), in one of many references to what she thought of as her overweening self-centeredness. In Eliot's teenage years, of course, the frequent self-denunciations and efforts to repress her ambition can be attributed in part to her cultivation of an Evangelical piety and a spiritual persona acceptable to her mentor. The habitual condemnations of her own ego, in other words, may be read as an effort not only to be a good Christian but also to strengthen the bonds that tied her to Lewis. But the concept of ego—specifically her "own egotism, mopping and mowing and gibbering," as she wrote later to her friend John Sibree (*Letters* 1:251)—remained a potent and emotionally challenging concept throughout her lifetime, one that she returned to repeatedly in both her letters and her fiction.

By introducing the notion of "another persona," I do not mean to encourage a quasi-Freudian interpretation of Eliot's psyche for our purposes here. Nor do I share Redinger's view of a "double consciousness" that separated Eliot's critical and creative faculties, as if her psyche could be precisely divided in two and those faculties neatly parceled out (334–35). Instead, I see a complex personality that paradoxically integrated intellectual audacity with crippling self-doubt. In her early years, Eliot's concept of ego was as much spiritual as psychological, and it later played a crucial interpretive role in her fiction (as in the famous pier-glass metaphor from *Middlemarch* [248; ch. 27]). Although she did endure painful bouts of self-consciousness and self-critique throughout her life, moreover, her self-perception of an outsized ego cannot be attributed wholly to a proclivity for self-effacement, even of the Evangelical sort. Eliot was, after all, a "massive, powerful personality," as John Cross put it after her death (3:311); and even in her twenties, she recognized the formative role played by her well-stocked intellect and her assertive passions in relationships with other people. Most crucial for our purposes here, Eliot's concept of the ego illuminates how she thought of herself in relation to others, mediating her relationships with various people throughout her life and conditioning her sense of isolation from her contemporaries.

An extended metaphor from an early letter illustrates these tendencies with special poignancy. The letter is dated 20 July 1840, after Eliot's denunciations of Harcourt's "doctrine of the deluge" and Gresley's shallow exposition of Tractarian ideas, a time when her letters offered variable hints that Evangelical thought was beginning to lose its force. Writing to Lewis once again, Eliot bemoans the "bodily debility" (another constant throughout her life) that "has of late made me a slave to a train of morbid fancies" and laments her inability to cultivate a strong faith that would enable her to "scarcely miss inferior comforts" like physical health (*Letters* 1:57, 59). Addressing this issue further, Eliot gradually unfolds an image that is at once startling, frightening, and moving. "We are like poor creatures of whom I have read," she continues,

> who, for some cause or other, having been thrust out of a ship by their companions, try to grasp first one part of the vessel then another for support, until by the successive lashes that are given to make them loose their hold, they have no fingers left by which to venture another hopeless experiment on pitiless hearts. So we, having *voluntarily* caused ourselves to be cast out as evil by the world, are continually indicating a vacillation in our choice by trying to lean on some part of it within reach, and it is mercy that orders the lashing of our disobedient fingers, even though for a time we be faint and bleeding from the correction. (1:59; emphasis in original)

This image is ambiguously referenced and framed. In the context of the letter and its immediate topics, the simile appears to parallel "we"—Christians who fail to rest in

God—with shipwrecked people who are grasping for a place in the lifeboat. In the parsed image, "it is mercy" to be lashed in this scenario, even to the point of faintness and bleeding, because the lifeboat represents the creature comforts of this world; better to be cast away into turbulent waters because they stand for the act of letting oneself sink into the "fountain" of God's promises, another watery image invoked a few sentences earlier (*Letters* 1:59). Resting in God is thus equated with submersion in rough waters, a tersely frightening reversal of the comparison we might expect—the comparison of God's love with a providential raft—and suggestive of the imagery coloring the particular strain of Evangelicalism that Eliot inhabited.

Beyond the topical context of the letter, though, this image emerges just as Eliot was beginning to seriously question, and sharply critique, the Evangelical faith that gave form and content to her communal life. Without that faith—and without the dogma that grounded it so firmly—Eliot would have envisioned herself, just as most Evangelical Christians would, as cut off from a community of believers, the only community she had known and the one that she thought had nourished her best. The larger emotional context of this ambiguous image, then, may well have been one of self-doubt and spiritual anxiety in a more expansive sense than is suggested by the immediate topic of the letter, a condition whose implications would have been shattering to someone so eager for intimacy and emotional commitment. At the same time, the simple act of letting go, of sinking into a sea of secularism, would also have seemed attractive, especially if the alternative meant hanging on to a faith that entailed repeated appeals to people who would persistently repudiate her evolving beliefs. Either way—as an image of either sinful resistance to God or resignation to secularism—Eliot figures herself here as cruelly cut off from her fellows, as someone who cannot find relief and comfort either within a group or apart from it.

As Eliot continued to withdraw from her Evangelical friends, she found other ways to conceptualize community. By 1842, she was avidly reading and absorbing the second edition of Charles Hennell's *An Inquiry Concerning the Origins of Christianity* (1838; second edition 1841), the book in which she found "what were to be," as Barry Qualls describes them, "the fundamental beliefs of her 'religious' life" (121). Hennell was the brother of Sara, Eliot's correspondent in our epigraph, and also of Cara Bray, and the emotional intimacy Eliot found within this new circle of friends was only solidified by the compatibility of their progressive ideas with her changing beliefs. These new beliefs included the argument that Christianity was the most morally admirable natural religion, an argument that fulfilled Eliot's need to venerate the faith of her childhood without requiring her to tolerate the Evangelical dogma she had gradually discarded. Hennell also figured Jesus Christ not as a divine miracle-worker but as a singular, gifted man who experienced "feelings and powers common . . . to all men" (296); with his very human characteristics, this Jesus was someone Eliot could identify with rather than merely venerate or fear, just as she had done with the figure of Wilberforce several years earlier. Later, when Eliot translated first David Friedrich Strauss's *Das Leben Jesu* (*The Life of Jesus*, Eliot's translation 1846) and then Ludwig Feuerbach's *Das Wesen des Christenthums* (*The Essence of Christianity*, Eliot's translation 1854), she discovered similar ideas expressed with greater sophistication, ideas that also offered new conceptions of community. From Feuerbach in particular, she derived an emphasis on forms of feeling and sympathy that had the potential for sociability. "Feeling is sympathy; feeling arises only in the love of man to man," Eliot translated. "Sensations man has in isolation; feelings only in community" (283). Such ideas, of course, are familiar to all readers of Eliot's fiction. When she first experienced a new depth of sympathetic community in the 1840s, however—in her personal friendships with the Brays and Hennells themselves and in the books that also began to widen her intellectual community—the effect was transformative. It is no wonder that she pirouetted across the pages of her letter to Sara.

These new circles of friends and ideas gave Eliot a new sense of herself in the world, a vision of intellectual and emotional companionship that her childhood relationships could not provide. The Brays and Hennells, moreover, also gave Eliot her first and probably most important entrée into the world of the nineteenth-century British intelligentsia. Through them, for example, she met John Chapman, the London publisher who released Eliot's translation of Strauss and later hired her to become the editor of the *Westminster Review*, the radical journal he had purchased in 1851. As editor of this significant organ of mid-century radical thought, Eliot met and worked with many leading Victorian intellectuals, including Herbert Spencer, James Anthony Froude, Harriet Martineau, William Makepeace Thackeray, Bessie Parkes and Barbara Leigh Smith, the physician Sir David Brewster, the scientists Thomas Henry Huxley and Richard Owen, the Italian revolutionary Giuseppe Mazzini, and perhaps even Karl Marx, who visited the *Westminster* office at least once (Haight 99). And through Spencer, Eliot met Lewes, who was to play such a crucial personal and professional role in her adult life. As editor, she read and commented on articles authored by a number of these people, became friends with many of them and the probable lover of a few—and never stopped reading and discussing current ideas and philosophies. If the Hennells and Brays were the focus of Eliot's emotional and intellectual life in her twenties, when she was nursing her father in Coventry, her circle expanded rapidly and widely in her thirties, when she moved to London and became the administrative and editorial center of the radical community.

By 1852, then, when Eliot assumed her position at the *Westminster Review*, she had forged the intellectual and communal ties that might have enabled her to move beyond the feelings of isolation and egotism marking her youth. She had become, after all, one of the best-connected intellectuals in mid-nineteenth-century London, a position unusual for anyone but especially for a Victorian woman. The paradox of Eliot's "life apart," however, was to persist throughout her life, for she was never able to fully conquer her self-perception as an isolated egotist, no matter how assiduously she cultivated sympathetic connections in both her fiction and her life. This sense re-emerges in other, important images, most notably in the conclusion to *The Mill on the Floss*, where the vision of turbulence and watery submission from her twenties is reinvoked with startling force. Familiar to all readers of this novel that follows the struggles of a young girl trying to subdue her assertive, ambitious personality, the final scene portrays rising flood waters eventually claiming Maggie and Tom Tul-liver in what Eliot the novelist may have envisioned as a similarly merciful submission to a boundless turbulence that links Maggie forever to her brother. By the time *The Mill on the Floss* was published in 1860, Eliot had been with Lewes for six years and had become the lionized author of the widely acclaimed and beloved *Adam Bede*. But her feelings of exile remained strong and were perhaps even intensified in later years by her careful cultivation of the role of "George Eliot," a role she played to a large and worshipful audience.

Being "George Eliot"

Even before Eliot and Lewes returned from Germany as an unlegalized couple in 1855, they were already the scandalous object of speculation and gossip in London. What Eliot had portrayed as their "little island of repose" in Weimar was now an enforced isolation, at least for her (*Letters* 2:173). For the first five weeks following their return, in fact, Eliot didn't see Lewes at all, and the few friends who knew the full story feared that Lewes had abandoned her to endure the cruel fate of the Victorian fallen woman (Haight 176). Lewes did not abandon her, of course, and they soon moved to new lodgings in Richmond, just a few steps from Kew Gardens. For the next several years, however, Eliot did exist largely within a small community that was willing to defy Victorian condemnation of her transgression. As mentioned above, while social con-ventions permitted Lewes to pursue a large and varied social life, Eliot's movements were much more restricted—a condition that many respectable people condoned. Eliot herself did not always regret the isolation, in part because it gave her time to read widely and begin to work on her fiction without a hovering audience of expectant friends and acquaintances; she also said she craved the "dual solitude" with Lewes (*Letters* 3:460). This state of enforced isolation, moreover, occasioned the gatherings that eventually grew into the Sunday salons at the Priory, the London house Lewes and Eliot bought in 1863. While most Victorian women avoided social contact with Eliot in the 1850s and much of the 1860s—except those who were "either so éman-cipée as not to mind what the world says about them," as one visitor noted, "or have no social position to maintain" (qtd. in Haight 409)—men were not similarly pro-scribed from interaction with her; Lewes and Eliot's male friends were thus frequent visitors on Sunday afternoons when it was known that they would both be "at home." Gradually, as Eliot's literary fame grew, the censures waned. By 1870, when she was beginning to work on *Middlemarch*, she was much more widely accepted in polite society, and Sunday afternoons at the Priory had become an established social institu-tion for the London intelligentsia, attracting visitors as varied as Charles Darwin, Robert Browning, Ralph Waldo Emerson, and Ivan Turgenev. Once again, Eliot was at the center of Victorian intellectual life, just as she had been almost twenty years earlier as the editor of the *Westminster Review*.

The 1870s was a decade of mature achievement for Eliot, with the publication of both *Middlemarch* in 1871–72 and *Daniel Deronda* in 1876. It was also the decade when the "George Eliot cult" (Bodenheimer, *Real Life* 242) reached its most fevered pitch. The combination of Eliot's fiction and her outsized personality drew worshipful readers toward her almost inexorably, with many sending gifts and effusive, even eroticized, letters. As Bodenheimer has suggested, it's not clear that Eliot fully recognized the process of her transformation into a "cultural icon," and "acting the sage in public pronouncement" was a role she had assiduously tried to avoid (*Real Life* 233, 240). Even so, the letters she and Lewes exchanged with many of her fans do suggest that the two of them worked together to cultivate the role of "George Eliot," albeit at home, before a domestic audience, and perhaps with little deliberate calculation. And in these later performances of literary celebrity, we see once again the paradoxical cultivation of Eliot's "life apart" from her Victorian contemporaries. At this point, however, it was the very condition of her fame that isolated her, in particular the way that she and Lewes managed her public image and authorial role.

The circumstances of Eliot's life by this time, of course, were dramatically different from those of her adolescence and young adulthood. As a successful novelist, for one thing, she no longer needed to worry about income, as she had been compelled to do after her father's death, when she accepted the editorial position in London. As a revered writer, for another, she was surrounded constantly by a community of like-minded people and could select her companions without the anxiety that attended her withdrawal from the Evangelical community in the 1840s. In some cases, though, Eliot and Lewes cultivated relationships with the most abjectly worshipful fans and mediated those relationships by positioning Eliot on an authorial stage, a position that effectively isolated her once again. The theatrical qualities of her position were not lost on her viewers. Eliza Lynn Linton, for example, observed that she never forgot "her self-created Self." "Her gestures were as measured as her words . . ." Linton wrote. "She was so consciously 'George Eliot'—so interpenetrated head and heel, inside and out, with the sense of her importance as the great novelist and profound thinker of her generation, as to make her society a little overwhelming . . ." (99). While Linton was not one of Eliot's worshippers, this assessment captures the distancing effects of her authorial performance. Even her most adoring fans, moreover, commented on her intimidating theatrical qualities, as in Roland Stuart's description of his first meeting with Eliot. "Her voice can only be compared to that of Sarah Bernhardt—in her melting moods," he wrote; "its tones were so low and soft, and at the same time so musical, that once heard it could never be forgotton" (22). As the son of Elma Stuart, one of Eliot's most faithful followers (and one of her most prolific gift-givers), Roland echoed his mother's effusive admiration—but nonetheless noticed Eliot's theatrical qualities, comparing her to one of the most imposing stage actresses of the nineteenth century.

Remarks like these recall Eliot's vision of herself as the solitary dancer in her early letter to Sara Hennell, even as they evoke the theatrical features of certain characters from her novels. Linton's comments, for example, recall Eliot's representation of "sincere acting" in *Daniel Deronda* (539; ch. 51)—a concept I discuss elsewhere (130–39)—reminding us that performers like Alcharisi and Gwendolen Harleth frequently struggle with isolation and egotism in her fiction even as they are surrounded by fans and spectators. For our purposes here, however, the late Victorian cult of personality is more directly relevant as a cultural context for understanding Eliot's authorial act in her final decade. The idea of unique, larger-than-life personalities was gaining wide currency in the late nineteenth century as a way to frame and view not only stage actors but also celebrities more generally. On the one hand, a "personality," even a famous one, was often perceived to be intimately present and accessible; on the other, such a personality was also thought to be intimidating and commanding. In this vein, while the late Victorian actor Henry Irving was considered to be supremely authentic and personal, even on stage and in character, he was also regarded as "magnetic" and "forceful" (Voskuil 195). "You *have* to look and listen to [him] whether you want to or no," wrote one observer of Irving both on and off stage (Craig 84; emphasis in original). In the same decades, Eliot was described in similar terms. Roland Stuart, for example, goes on to characterize his boyhood meeting with Eliot in the 1870s as self-revelatory and transformative. "Above all else," he recalled,

> it was her eyes which impressed you—and she possessed that magnetic power of looking down into your soul and of drawing you out and making you speak of yourself—at the same time giving you the impression that she was deeply interested in your doings and all that concerned you. I was a mere schoolboy at the time, but I can remember my intense pride in our friendship, and the feeling that one could open one's heart to her and tell her *everything*, being sure of being understood. (22; emphasis in original)

Striking in this passage is his perception of a personality that is at once intimate and coercive. Although Eliot becomes his close friend, she also sets all the terms of their relationship: utterly exposed, he empties himself before her commanding gaze. More than merely theatrical, as in Linton's portrayal, Eliot is here depicted as magnetically irresistible.

For the Stuarts, mother and son, such magnetism was unproblematic and praiseworthy. For other admirers, though, Eliot's imperious form of intimacy was often difficult to negotiate, especially for other women, who seemed to be subjected to this dynamic more frequently than men (though Cross and perhaps Lewes himself may be exceptions). Chief—and most explored—among these relationships is Eliot's conflicted, eroticized friendship with Edith Simcox, the feminist activist who was helplessly smitten with Eliot and recorded her unrequited passion in the secret diary she entitled *Autobiography of a Shirtmaker*. The political and erotic aspects of Eliot's relationship with Simcox have been amply and excellently considered by Bodenheimer ("Autobiography"), Gillian Beer, Ellen Rosenman, and Martha Vicinus, needing no further analysis here. More pertinent to my current purpose is the emotional dynamic that characterized Eliot's friendships with Simcox and other acolytes, friendships that

Rosenman has aptly described as "approach-avoidance relationships" (314) and that recapture some of Eliot's adolescent efforts to tame her personality. By the 1870s, the references to egotism and her "besetting sin. . . . Ambition" (*Letters* 1:19) had largely disappeared from Eliot's letters; and the Evangelical dogma that informed some of those early references had long since been abandoned. But her concern with egotism and self-importance remained strong, re-emerging in her fiction as an idealized form of self-renunciation in characters like Maggie Tulliver and Gwendolen Harleth. Even more pertinently, some of Eliot's own youthful agonies of self-doubt and isolation reappeared in her worshipful fans, enforced by Lewes and Eliot's shared cultivation of "George Eliot," the great author and personality.

Simcox embodies these qualities most poignantly and revealingly. Like Roland and Elma Stuart, she was irresistibly drawn to Eliot, often waiting in anguish for a reply to her notes or a summons to the Priory. Many of their interactions are familiar from Eliot's earlier friendships—at least if Simcox's detailed transcriptions of their conversations are to be trusted as accurate. In one exchange, for example, they discuss Cardinal Thomas Wolsey, Cardinal Armand Jean du Plessis de Richelieu, William Ewart Gladstone's speeches, Benjamin Disraeli's novels and foreign policy, and a recent article in the *Cornhill* on Alfred Tennyson (*Autobiography* 109). Just as she had done with Maria Lewis over forty years earlier, Eliot once again exercises her prodigiously informed intellect as an important aspect of her intimate relationships. Intermixed with these moments of discussion, moreover, are excruciating accounts of Simcox's efforts to "be good" and suppress her "selfish greediness" (*Autobiography* 47, 141), accounts that also echo Eliot's own adolescent letters in their very anguish. For Simcox, being "good" largely meant emulating Eliot's idea of self-renunciation, whether that was embodied by Eliot herself or by her fictional characters. In the diary, she identifies with both Gwendolen Harleth and Maggie Tulliver (102, 141), two of the most chastened figures in Eliot's *oeuvre*, and tries hard to practice the "arts of self-discipline" (*Autobiography* 110). Although Simcox often resisted the models that she found in Eliot's person and fiction—the diary is rife with "arguments she mounted against the George Eliot she had constructed as an inner interlocutor," as Bodenheimer puts it ("Autobiography" 401)—her agonized musings manifest a striking similarity between what she calls her "habit of self-suppression" (154) and Eliot's own youthful efforts to subdue her "ego."

Clearly, Simcox often experienced, and possibly sought, long periods of debilitating isolation in her relationship with Eliot, cultivating her own "life apart" from conventional society. But what of Eliot herself? How did she experience this relationship? No definite answer to that question can be provided because none of Eliot's letters to Simcox has survived (Haight 495–96). Some inferences may be drawn, however, both from Simcox's text and from letters Eliot and Lewes wrote to other effusive fans. While the Eliot of Simcox's *Autobiography* is undoubtedly Simcox's own creation, it is also clear that Eliot, with Lewes's help, both courted and snubbed Simcox, sometimes accepting and even encouraging her emotional advances and at other times coldly rejecting them with that "approach-avoidance" dynamic that Rosenman has identified

(314). The correspondence with Elma Stuart bears similar marks of warmth and subtle withdrawal, though with far less erotic intensity than we see in Simcox's diary. As Vicinus has suggested, Eliot often forced "her young admirers to be self-controlled in the face of her own capriciousness" (125). The interactions thus established—and we should recall that Lewes and Eliot often encouraged these acolytes—would necessarily have isolated Eliot as well, reinvoking her longstanding sense of isolation by mediating these relationships with her own performative, magnetic personality, the "self-created Self" that Linton saw (99). By emphasizing the theatrical qualities of the "George Eliot" persona, I do not mean to suggest that Eliot could have enjoyed an unmediated, authentic relationship with Stuart, Simcox, or anyone else, had she simply been "herself"; like all of us, then and now, Eliot and her companions inhabited the social and cultural roles available to them, even as they challenged some of the conventions of those roles. I do mean to suggest, however, that by fashioning and managing "George Eliot" as they did, Eliot and Lewes not only revived Eliot's youthful self-renunciation in her followers but also continued to cultivate communities within which she could live an emotional and psychological "life apart." Ironically, in many ways, this persona undermined the sympathetic connections she had sought so hard to establish in her life and her fiction.

When Lewes died on 30 November 1878, Eliot endured one last excruciating period of self-seclusion and despair. "She cannot bear it," Simcox wept to her diary: "there have been unendurable sorrows, but I do not see how any can equal hers" (52). For once, Eliot and Simcox were emotionally synchronized. Overcome with grief, Eliot did not leave her room for more than a week, or leave the house until early February, more than two months after Lewes's death. Eliot's own journal for 1879 testifies to her almost mute desolation, beginning with the laconic entry on 1 January: "Here I and Sorrow sit," a quotation from Shakespeare's *King John* (III.1.73; qtd. in Eliot, *Journals* 154). Other, later entries bespeak her ongoing, isolated anguish: 6 January: "Feeling ill—weary and heavy laden" (157); 10 February: "Suffering and deeply depressed" (162); 26 March: "Weather still cruel, and my soul in deep gloom" (167); 3 October: "Tears, tears" (183). Finally, on 29 November 1879, the eve of the first anniversary of Lewes's death, Eliot writes this entry: "Reckoning by the days of the week, it was this day last year my loneliness began. I spent the day in the room where I passed through the first three months—I read his letters, and packed them together, to be buried with me. Perhaps that will happen before next November" (187). Seeking ongoing communion with the companion who had helped her craft a "life apart," she spent much of 1879 preparing Lewes's unfinished *Problems of Life and Mind* for publication and, on the anniversary of his death, reliving her seclusion.

In 1880, Eliot's final year of life, she became Mrs. John Cross, a union that confounded her wide circle of Victorian contemporaries and continues to bewilder readers, critics, and biographers today. Rather than advance any focused reading of Eliot's final act, I prefer to see this unorthodox version of a conventional marriage as yet one more episode in her "life apart," a life I have tried to analyze briefly as a series of paradoxically conspicuous seclusions that are echoed in her novels. John Kucich, going some-what against the conventional critical grain, sees in Eliot's fiction a similar isolation, one that belies her famous pursuit of fellow feeling and sympathetic community. "As much as she seems concerned with human fellowship," Kucich writes, "at the same time—less consciously, perhaps—Eliot sought to meliorate isolation by deepening it, in a way that might make the self into a world sufficient to itself" (119). This per-suasive reading of Eliot's fiction is paralleled by the paradoxical events of her life, most notably by the emotional satisfaction she found in both community and self-renunciation. In the young Eliot who pirouetted for Sara and in the much older Eliot who performed authorship for her acolytes, we see the same personality: a self that found itself only in a life apart.

REFERENCES

Beer, Gillian. "Knowing a Life: Edith Simcox—Sat est vixisse?" *Knowing the Past: Victorian Literature and Culture*. Ed. Suzy Anger. Ithaca: Cornell UP, 2001. 252–66.

Bodenheimer, Rosemarie. "Autobiography in Fragments: The Elusive Life of Edith Simcox." *Victorian Studies* 44.3 (2002): 399–422.

Bodenheimer, Rosemarie. *The Real Life of Mary Ann Evans: George Eliot, Her Letters and Her Fiction*. Ithaca: Cornell UP, 1994.

Craig, Arthur Gordon. *Henry Irving*. London: Blom, 1930.

Cross, J. W. *George Eliot's Life as Related in her Letters and Journals*. 3 vols. New York: Harper, n.d.

Eliot, George. *Daniel Deronda*. Ed. Graham Handley. Oxford: Oxford UP, 1998.

Eliot, George. *The George Eliot Letters*. Ed. Gordon S. Haight. 9 vols. New Haven: Yale UP, 1954–78.

Eliot, George. *The Journals of George Eliot*. Ed. Margaret Harris and Judith Johnston. Cambridge: Cambridge UP, 1998.

Eliot, George. *Letters from George Eliot to Elma Stuart, 1872–1880*. Ed. Roland Stuart. London: Simpkin, 1909. *Hathitrust.org*. Web. 17 Nov. 2011.

Eliot, George. *Middlemarch*. Ed. David Carroll. Oxford: Oxford UP, 1996.

Eliot, George. *The Mill on the Floss*. Ed. Gordon S. Haight. Oxford: Oxford UP, 1980.

Feuerbach, Ludwig. *The Essence of Christianity*. Trans. George Eliot. New York: Cossimo, 2008.

Gresley, W[illiam]. *Clement Walton; or the English Citizen*. London: James Burns, 1840. *Google Books*. Web 27. October 11.

Gresley, W[illiam]. *Portrait of an English Church-man*. London: J. G. and F. Rivington, 1838. *Google Books*. Web. 27 October 2011.

Haight, Gordon S. *George Eliot: A Biography*. Oxford: Oxford UP, 1968.

Harcourt, L. Vernon. *The Doctrine of the Deluge; Vindicating the Scriptural Account from the Doubts which have Recently Been Cast Upon It by Geological Speculations*. Vol. 2. London: Longman, 1838. *Google Books*. Web. 25 Oct. 2011.

Hennell, Charles Christian. *An Inquiry Concerning the Origin of Christianity*. London: Smallfield, 1838. *Google Books*. Web. 10 Oct. 2011.

Kucich, John. *Repression in Victorian Fiction: Charlotte Brontë, George Eliot, and Charles Dickens*. Berkeley: U of California P, 1987.

Linton, Elizabeth Lynn. *My Literary Life*. London, 1899. *Google Books*. Web. 25 Nov. 2011.

Qualls, Barry. "George Eliot and Religion." *The Cambridge Companion to George Eliot*. Ed. George Levine. Cambridge: Cambridge UP, 2001. 119–37.

Redinger, Ruby V. *George Eliot: The Emergent Self*. New York: Knopf, 1975.

Rosenman, Ellen Bayuk. "Mother Love: Edith Simcox, Maternity, and Lesbian Erotics." *Other Mothers: Beyond the Maternal Ideal*. Ed. Ellen Bayuk Rosenman and Claudia C. Klaver. Columbus: Ohio State UP, 2008. 313–34.

Simcox, Edith. *Autobiography of a Shirtmaker*. Ed. Constance M. Fulmer and Margaret E. Barfield. New York: Garland, 1998.

Strauss, David Friedrich. *The Life of Jesus, Critically Examined*. 4th ed. Trans. Marian Evans. New York: Calvin Blanchard, 1855.

Stuart, Roland, ed. *Letters from George Eliot to Elma Stuart, 1872–1880*. London: Simpkin, 1909. *Hathitrust.org*. Web. 17 Nov. 2011.

Vicinus, Martha. *Intimate Friends: Women Who Loved Women, 1778–1928*. Chicago: U of Chicago P, 2004.

Voskuil, Lynn M. *Acting Naturally: Victorian Theatricality and Authenticity*. Charlottesville: U of Virginia P, 2004.

18

Feminist George Eliot Comes from the United States

Alison Booth

No one ever has doubted that George Eliot was English. Unlike many of the writers in the English canon, she was actually born and raised in an accessible county in England (Warwickshire, also known as Shakespeare Country) rather than Scotland, Ireland, Wales, or Yorkshire. She never traveled to the United States, unlike Charles Dickens, Harriet Martineau, and many other celebrated Victorian writers—though in the end she married an American man twenty years her junior. Her contacts with American writers, including Harriet Beecher Stowe and Elizabeth Stuart Phelps, were usually through the medium of letters only. Yet there are many reasons to take a transatlantic perspective on Eliot as a woman writer. A special relationship in litera-ture as well as in reform movements had been growing between Britain and the United States in her lifetime, when works made their way into print abroad more easily than individuals made the journey (Giles; McGill). However secure Eliot may be in the category of *English* literary history, then, it is worth questioning that demarcation. There was an international engagement with a "reform aesthetic" in her day (Cotugno), and today the boundaries of national literatures seem more permeable than ever.

The matters of nationality are scarcely more defined than the questions of gender. Marian Evans Lewes Cross was undoubtedly an English *woman*, but everyone knows her by her male pseudonym. Eliot's early publications anonymously or pseu-donymously masked her female identity, and her later narrators seem to transcend individuality and gender. Yet it was as a woman who exceeded her sex that she was

A Companion to George Eliot, First Edition. Edited by Amanda Anderson and Harry E. Shaw.
© 2013 John Wiley & Sons, Ltd. Published 2016 by John Wiley & Sons, Ltd.

revered, according to the trope of manly genius united with feminine heart and body (Gilbert and Gubar 479–83). The first full-length biography of Eliot, by Mathilde Blind, was part of the Famous Women series (published in 1883 in London and Boston). Two decades later, Leslie Stephen published a biography of Eliot in the English Men of Letters series (London and New York, 1902). While her categorization by gender might seem debatable (famous woman, man of letters), audiences recognized her as a model of women's achievement regardless of nationality. Yet she ducks when asked to stand for a feminist cause. A mentor or friend to a range of women, she has long been reproached for failing to promote women's rights. An English woman writer, not quite a feminist, whose life broke the domestic mold yet who gave her heroines little outlet for their talents, who never traveled to the United States— why claim that a feminist George Eliot came from the United States?

In one sense this is literally the case. When academic feminist criticism established a foothold in the United States about a century after Eliot's death, she inevitably dominated rediscovered traditions of women's writing. Less obviously, she provides a model for biographical and contextual approaches to *reception* history or responses over time to a writer's personality and oeuvre. Eliot and her contemporaries favored biographical criticism, and my focus on Eliot's correspondence with several women writers follows this approach. At the same time, much as Victorians believed in a "spirit of the age" or cultural environment, recent studies place Eliot within historical contexts such as racial theories or imperialism (Carroll; Stern; Henry). I zoom in on the contexts of transatlantic feminist reception. Perhaps it comes down to taking a good look at Eliot's impact on American women writers and feminist criticism in the United States.

To pursue the transatlantic and feminist reception history of Eliot in this chapter, I set aside movements for suffrage or education or abolition; instead, I feature Eliot's feminist reception in the twentieth century followed by Eliot's correspondence with American women writers. The "George Eliot Question" is best addressed out of chronological order in spite of the importance of nineteenth-century movements and contemporary events. After considering feminist reception of Eliot since about 1975, I glance at evidence for her transatlantic relations, literary and social, during the novelist's lifetime and after. I will note both how Eliot was packaged for American readers and how she affiliated with Anglo-American middle-class women committed to reform causes and an artistic vocation. Eliot's relations with Stowe were interwoven with mutual friends including Phelps and Annie Fields, though she met only the last. In exchanges among these women writers, I find intersecting patterns from the mundane to the subliminal: from dangerous attachments to brothers to dutiful alliances with scholars or optimal companionate union; illness or hardship under the compulsory work of writing; the writer's search for a suitable home for receptions, family life, or solitude. Eliot's transatlantic correspondence and her North American reception also touch on overarching themes of aesthetics and social justice and progress that preoccupy the history of criticism on her works.

The George Eliot Question and Feminist Criticism
of Women Writers

The international women's movements around the 1970s found a stronghold in higher education in the United States, initially in departments of literature. Eliot featured prominently, like a monument in a public square, in the literary landscape at the time. Although like many Victorians Eliot had fallen rather out of fashion for the first decades of the twentieth century, critics concerned with writing by women (and there were some before 1975) saw Eliot as a trump card along with Jane Austen, the Brontës, and Emily Dickinson. The lives of writers in groups had long been studied, now and then admitting the anomaly such as Mary Wollstonecraft Godwin Shelley among the Romantics. In such biographical cultural history, Eliot had fared quite well, for instance as translator of Ludwig Feuerbach, successor to John Stuart Mill at the *Westminster Review*, or friend of Herbert Spencer. Gordon S. Haight, Thomas Pinney, and other academics in North America laid the groundwork of biographical scholarship on Eliot in the 1960s, though there had been key British readings of her novels in the spirit of F. R. Leavis's *The Great Tradition* of 1948. Generally at mid-century, however, the standard method disregarded biography and context; a great work of art was said to transcend its origins and milieu. In other words, it was accepted practice to pick and choose the world's great works while ignoring the different conditions in which they were produced or the shifting standards of assessment. If the argument were whether women could attain greatness, there were few models as compelling, in any language, as Eliot. Perhaps this was a misconceived argument—as indeed Eliot's works often imply. (Think of the ironic wish, in the Prelude to *Middlemarch*, for a strict "level of feminine incompetence"[*Middlemarch* 3; Prelude].) The current criteria sought works of art that demonstrated the capabilities of a genre, a common psychological condition, the ironies of language, or the frustrations of the individual in society. Eliot's works scored high on these criteria, though methods would have to change if many other women writers were to be recovered. Inevitably, American feminist studies of women writers by Ellen Moers, Elaine Showalter, and Sandra Gilbert and Susan Gubar as well as Rachel M. Brownstein, Nancy K. Miller, and others featured Eliot, beginning within established critical methods.

Consider an early classic of American feminist criticism, Ellen Moers's *Literary Women* (with the polemical subtitle, *The Great Writers*), published in 1977. I would not call this book transatlantic; it compares representatives of many languages and largely disregards borders, dates, or periodization (though it is somewhat concerned with biography). Moers, as if echoing the Prelude of *Middlemarch*, repeatedly cautions, "there is no single female tradition in literature," "no single female style" (62–63). Indeed, Moers returns to Eliot throughout her book without making her the supreme model for all women writers. Sandwiched between Moers's denials of unified gender difference, Moers quotes Eliot's "pseudo-scientific" "theory about female creativity" in "Woman in France: Madame de Sablé" (Moers 63; *Essays* 53). The abhorrent Victorian belief in national-racial types and in-born gender leads to Eliot's theory: given "the physiological characteristics of the Gallic race," Frenchwomen may be clever but they are quick and shallow. The Teutonic type, "the larger brain and slower temperament of the English and Germans," may make Teutonic women "dreamy and passive" (*Essays* 55). The original article does raise a still relevant kind of question about different contexts; reviewing biographies of seventeenth-century Frenchwomen, it asks "What were the causes of . . . earlier development and more abundant manifestation of womanly intellect in France?" (*Essays* 55). (We might ask, why did feminism succeed in academia sooner in the United States than in Britain, France, or Germany?) Moers reads "self-revelation" in the racial contrast: Marian Evans in 1854, not yet "George Eliot," thought her own Teutonic-style "absorption of ideas" prevented inspired creativity (63).

If we rename these psychological types fox vs. hedgehog, I would call Moers a ("Gallic") fox, darting among women writers across periods and borders. Two pages before this characterization of Eliot, Moers features Emily Dickinson, who "read and reread every Anglo-American woman writer of her time: Helen Hunt Jackson and Lydia Maria Child and Harriet Beecher Stowe and Lady Georgiana Fullerton and Dinah Maria Craik and Elizabeth Stuart Phelps and Rebecca Harding Davis and Francesca Alexander and Mathilde Mackarness and everything that George Eliot and Mrs. Browning and all the Brontës wrote" (61). Such a reading list now seems well ahead of its time, with obscure writers who never won the formalist merit badges of the 1970s. A far more inclusive "checklist of women writers" grew and grew at the back of Moers's book, with an extensive entry on Eliot and connections drawn among Eliot and Stowe and Margaret Fuller and Phelps and many other American and European women writers.[1]

Looking back, we should thank the borderless critical methods of the day for opening up interpretation of many women writers together. But feminist criticism also required consideration of biography, since the fact of being female shaped the career and reception, and biography places the writer in her lifetime and nationality. Gilbert and Gubar's *The Madwoman in the Attic* (1979) adds even more confident biographical diagnosis than we see in Moers's version of Eliot. In some ways, *Madwoman* hearkens back to Eliot's essays "Woman in France" and "Margaret Fuller and Mary Wollstonecraft." Gilbert and Gubar begin the second of their two intricate chapters on Eliot with her comments in letters on the example of Margaret Fuller's life (*Letters* 2:15). By the end of the chapter's second paragraph, the comparison between Eliot's and Fuller's lives leads to Dickinson's comment on Mrs. Lewes: "She is the Lane to the Indes, Columbus was looking for" (Gilbert and Gubar 480). Soon, the critics are drawn to Eliot's strong reading of Stowe in key essays that appeared just as the Englishwoman was about to attempt her first fiction: "Why can we not have pictures of religious life among the industrial classes in England, as interesting as Mrs. Stowe's pictures of religious life among the negroes?" Eliot asks in "Silly Novels by Lady Novelists" (*Essays* 319; Gilbert and Gubar 482). Stowe, Louisa May

Alcott, and Elizabeth Gaskell cluster around Eliot in this passage in *Madwoman* to illustrate "the tension for these women between masculine and feminine roles" (482–83). As many have noted, Eliot admired Stowe's reforming fiction, but she also advocated realism on both aesthetic and moral grounds. In "[Three Novels]," Eliot praises Stowe's *Dred* (1856) (Stowe has "surpassed" Scott in scenes of religious life), but objects to the flat or black-and-white characterization: all her "negroes" are "superior to the mass of whites"; "if the negroes are really so very good, slavery has answered as moral discipline" (*Essays* 327). For Gilbert and Gubar, women writers provide each other with ominous models of how to repress murderous rage without being silenced altogether—the chapter is entitled "George Eliot as the Angel of Destruction."

Eliot loomed large in a wide range of foundational feminist literary criticism in the United States. Such criticism persists in probing Eliot's resistance to women's liberation (Rosenberg). We might say, if her heroines are so capable of selfless sacrifice, then gender inequality has answered as moral discipline (Booth; Claybaugh 130). The stifling of female ambition in Eliot's works is the central theme again in Showalter's "The Greening of Sister George," an influential contribution to reception history. Showalter revealed that British women felt daunted by Eliot's example, whereas American "counterparts" could approach her more informally and "less as Eliot's disciples" (Claybaugh 133). According to Showalter, Eliot's reputation revived earlier in the United States than in Britain, through women writers such as Gertrude Stein, Edith Wharton, and Willa Cather as well as Gail Godwin and Joyce Carol Oates (298 n. 16). More recently, Monika Mueller interlinks Eliot and various American writers with regard to representation of race, gender, and cultural development (13–20); Mueller calls attention to Eliot disciple Cynthia Ozick (193–233), who objected to the premise of a female tradition.

Like Ozick, Eliot resists a feminist agenda, though she associated with various reformers and made limited contributions to causes such as *The English Women's Journal* or Girton College for women (Booth 37–45). Kate Flint elegantly synthesizes the feminist critique of Eliot's "reluctance, or inability, to deliver up unequivocally feminist messages" (161). Flint points to biographer Mathilde Blind's rather awestruck resistance to Eliot's doctrine of "resignation" subordinating "personal happiness to the social good" (Blind 10, 224; Flint 160–61). In part because Eliot was "mistrustful of creating idealistic exceptions" (Flint 161), and because of her conservative view of laws of social development, her works do not pave the road to liberation in feminist terms. It can be "misguided" as well as "disappointing" to expect this (Flint 163).

Many have cited Florence Nightingale's review of *Middlemarch* in 1873 (Showalter 305–06 n. 37), in which she objected to limiting Dorothea to remodeling a few cottages on a country estate, when in reality women like Octavia Hill (whose sister had married Lewes's son) had taken on urban housing reform on a large scale (Claybaugh 129–30). In a transatlantic frame of reception history, such objections stand out clearly. Usually in the same breath that recalls Nightingale's review, critical essays on Eliot cite the letter from an American, Harriet Pierce, responding to *The Spanish Gypsy*: why should "noble women always fail," against the wishes and indeed the reality of the times? (Flint 161; Claybaugh 129). Whereas many interpreted Eliot's courage to live with a married man as an act of feminist heroism, they found that the eminent novelist repeatedly closed down the heroine's career. Perhaps realism called for such confinement, but Eliot's disregard of exceptional women seems to prescribe a feminine moral mission associated with conservative views on women's "possible maternity" (*Letters* 4:467–68; Flint 162–63). Motifs of feminine altruistic or selfless power run through both American and British literature in this era, including Fuller's *Woman in the Nineteenth Century*, which Eliot favorably reviewed (Adams 160–63), and the influential novel-poem about a woman poet, *Aurora Leigh* by Elizabeth Barrett Browning. Arguably, Eliot adapts the same tradition of sentimentalism-as-reform-advocacy that inspired Stowe's portrayal of saintly slaves, and a decidedly transatlantic strain of belief in archetypes of feminine sacred power, not only through Anna Jameson's *Sacred and Legendary Art* but also through Fuller. Eliot heroines certainly fill the role of a virgin saint or the Madonna (a nickname that Lewes encouraged for his partner). Eliot's objections to idealized versions of the victims of prejudice and her secular rationalism did not lead her to avoid the symbolism of religion and persistent myths of gender difference that grant a spiritual and aesthetic power to women. Phelps's reply to *Middlemarch*, *The Story of Avis*, could be seen as carrying forward Fuller's, Barrett Browning's, and Eliot's spiritual aesthetics of gender in a realist portrayal of the life of a woman artist in New England.

Transatlantic Literary Relations and Reform

Eliot's responses to the Woman Question were framed within the transatlantic context. Studies of Eliot's American connections have often confined themselves to passing observations about Nathaniel Hawthorne or Stowe (Mueller 51–53)—the influence of *The Scarlet Letter* on *Adam Bede*, of *Dred* on *Daniel Deronda*. Not that an English author was likely to be deemed derivative of American literature; as in Canada's relative stature to the United States today, the asymmetrical exchange between "American" and "English" literature and writers mattered a great deal more to the aspiring party than to the dominant tradition. And yet publishing conditions as well as debates and campaigns for reform were transatlantic, and Eliot's works had continuing popularity in the United States, as in adaptations of her novels in silent film (Griffith, "American Screen"). Gordon Haight noted that the *Westminster Review* regularly reviewed "'Contemporary Literature' of England, America, Germany, and France" as the owner John Chapman wished to promote "his transatlantic market" (97). In the United States, *The Mill on the Floss* was reviewed in *Godey's Lady's Book*, a dominant women's magazine; *Romola* was a bestseller (Griffith, "Romola"); *Daniel Deronda* was serialized in *Harper's*. Just as there were spin-off revisions of *Uncle Tom's Cabin*, Eliot's work could prompt rebuttals. Many readers resisted the ending of *Daniel Deronda*—Daniel's narrative reverses the plot of Jewish conversion to Christianity, and Gwendolen's plot leaves her a widow without Daniel. To compensate, the American Anna

Clay Beecher produced an anti-Semitic sequel, *Gwendolen: or Reclaimed* (Flint 173). John Picker, speculating that the unknown Beecher might be a distant relative of Stowe, shows that this novel was published anonymously in 1868 to look like a volume in the Harper Library Edition of Eliot's novels (Picker 380).

There are still potential surprises in the dissemination of Eliot in the United States. To a lesser extent than Dickens, Eliot was commodified in many forms. There is the well-known episode of the Scotsman Alexander Main, a Victorian version of a blogging fan, who assembled *Wise, Witty, and Tender Sayings of George Eliot*, an anthology of excerpts published in 1872 by her own publisher, Blackwood, in Edinburgh and London but not, apparently, in the United States (it went through some ten editions by 1896), though many libraries in the United States own a copy. But American publishers repackaged the great novels as well, notably as children's books with colorful covers, large type, and charming illustrations. Both Julia Magruder's *Child-Sketches from George Eliot* (1895) (with a chapter on Marian Evans's childhood) and Kate Sweetser's *Boys and Girls from George Eliot* (1906) (part of her series of children "from" Dickens, Thackeray, or History) blend passages from the novels with connecting summary, offering "pretty" and "true pictures" (Sweetser, Preface). Such anthologies perhaps give more encouraging examples than complete stories of adulthood in the light of common day. Eliot's own life became a model narrative in more than thirty collective biographies of women published in the United States between about 1876 and 1934 (Booth, CBW). For instance, the American James Parton (whose wife was the popular writer Fanny Fern) edited *Eminent Women: A Series of Sketches of Women Who Have Won Distinction by Their Genius and Achievements as Authors, Artists, Actors, Rulers, or within the Precincts of the Home* (New York and Philadelphia, 1880). In spite of Eliot's marital and religious irregularity, she is right up there with Queen Victoria and Martha Washington, Barrett Browning as well as Stowe and Louisa May Alcott, in this distinguished set.

Along with transatlantic circulation in print came visiting and correspondence; such encounters document the intersections of social reform, publishing practices, and reception. In 1848, Marian Evans conversed with Ralph Waldo Emerson and impressed him with her "calm, serious soul," when he visited the Brays, her friends in Coventry (Blind 74; Haight 65–66). Guests at Chapman's house, 142 Strand, when Eliot resided there included Horace Greeley and William Cullen Bryant, and the Swedish author Frederika Bremer stayed there for a month after her American tour (Haight 99–100). Bremer was much celebrated and befriended in international reform circles; her translator Mary Howitt also enjoyed a North American as well as British audience. Since the first World's Anti-Slavery Convention in London, the abolitionist and women's-rights causes circulated internationally (Anderson). Yet after the Civil War, American literati made their pilgrimage to Eliot's Sundays at the Priory, in London, expecting to join a visible, well-documented choir of literary reception rather than politics.

Henry James is often mentioned as a successor to Eliot, as when he shares a chapter with Eliot in Amanda Claybaugh's transatlantic study of the reforming "purpose" that was demanded of prestigious nineteenth-century fiction. James had reviewed Eliot's novels, had visited her home, and in due course reviewed John Cross's *George Eliot's Life, as Related in her Letters and Journals* in 1885, deploring the "grayness of tone" that comes through the letters. Rosemarie Bodenheimer's study of Eliot's life in letters begins with a sketch of Henry and his sister Alice James's similar revulsion from Eliot's epistolary personality. Alice James, in a passage frequently quoted in feminist studies, excoriated the "ponderous dreariness" of Cross's collection, which produced a nightmarish impression of "mildew, or some morbid growth" (Bodenheimer 1–2). Eliot's descriptions of physical sufferings are insufferable to Alice James; where is the sharp intelligence and humor of the novels? Bodenheimer perceives a complex performance in the letters; the descriptions of illness are symptomatic of Eliot's over-compensation for success: "how necessary it was to her to be seen as a sufferer rather than as one of the ambitious, authoritative narrators of her books" (164). Certainly, Eliot accompanies expressions of affinity with women writers with testimony to her depression, pains, and doubt, replying, for example, to the American journalist Harriet Pierce with an insistence that creation left her in a "postpartum" exhaustion (Bodenheimer 162–63). In her transatlantic correspondence, Eliot was not only nego-tiating limits on the woman who has it all but clarifying her positions on religion, family and parenthood, colonial exploitation and race, the critical reception of high and popular art, illness and fears of mortality. It was a heavy freight for bun-dles of handwritten pages to transport overseas and into future biographies and collections.

As North American Anglophilia became more respectable, Americans could cherish Eliot's vivid depictions of scenes of childhood in the rural homeland, even as she might be admired for her cosmopolitan learning. The admixture of realism and social reform with Madonna-like sacrifice also could be linked to a shared Anglo-American fascina-tion with Italy. For Eliot as for Fuller and such American artists as Harriet Hosmer, Italy was the land of aesthetic depths and opportunities. Eliot nevertheless remained outside the Italian expatriate communities that in due course included Henry James. Eliot's research in Italy led to a historical novel, *Romola*, with close affinity to elements of Hawthorne's *The Marble Faun* (Mueller) and Stowe's *Agnes of Sorrento*. The closest intersection of Stowe's and Eliot's careers came in 1861, when Stowe's *Agnes of Sorrento* was serialized in the prestigious London journal, *Cornhill*. Eliot was concerned that her novel *Romola*, also set in early modern Italy, was to appear in the same venue (Haight 355–56; Sheets).

Harriet Beecher Stowe, James T. and Annie Fields, and the Brother Question

Eliot noted *Uncle Tom's Cabin* in her essays and was aware of Stowe's tour in England in 1853. Stirring up abolitionist support, Stowe had transmitted "The Affectionate and Christian Address of Many Thousands of Women of Great Britain and Ireland, to Their Sisters, the Women of the United States of America" (1853), with some 500,000 signatures (Claybaugh 83) by women of all ranks. In 1863, in the midst of ongoing British support for the slave-holding South, Stowe published *A Reply . . . In Behalf of Many Thousands of American Women*, acknowledging the "international expression of a moral idea," the idea of a shared Anglo-American, womanly "common cause" to abolish slavery as a violation of the family and of Christian divine law (3–7). James T. Fields had published a version of Stowe's counter-appeal and in turn published the British activist Frances Power Cobbe's "Rejoinder" in the *Atlantic Monthly* in 1863; George Eliot praised Cobbe's reply in a letter to her close friend Sara Hennell on 9 March 1863 (Cross 2: 253; Mitchell 131–32). It was in May 1869 that Stowe first wrote to Eliot to praise her work (Haight 412–13). Stowe's letter is a kind of Georgic written from Mandarin, her estate in Florida—Eliot's reply repeats her phrase, "we live in an orange grove." On 8 May 1869, Eliot attributes a delayed response to her just returning from Italy, and immediately wishes Stowe to envision the "paralyzing" "mental sickness" that results from the creative labor that Stowe's sympathy helps to justify (*Letters* 5:29). Eliot recalls that her "first glimpse of [Stowe] as a woman came through a letter" (5:29) shared by Mrs. Follen during the first furor over *Uncle Tom's Cabin* (5:30). Eliot continues, "I have rarely had your image in my mind without the accompanying image (more or less erroneous)" of an "ardent Scholar" husband, Calvin Ellis Stowe, one "richer in Hebrew and Greek than in pounds or shillings" (5:30). As we shall see, the Stowes in turn got a fixed idea that Lewes was the original of Casaubon in *Middlemarch*; it is as if Marian and Harriet shared the experience of partnership with the life-deadening scholar. (In 1869 Eliot's letter portrays Lewes's research as a progressive, flexible inquiry, not a Key to All Mythologies in the later phrase [5:30].) Stowe has expressed concern that her *Oldtown Folks* will not appeal to English readers; Eliot counters that "any sort of exquisiteness" in a "widely circulated book" is likely to have beneficial influence only through "a few appreciative natures"; "how slowly the centuries work toward the moral good of men" (5:31). This not very reassuring anticipation of Stowe's reception in England leads Eliot to the topic of her religious beliefs, "wide subjects" likely to be misconstrued in the "narrow and fragmentary" medium of a letter, but Stowe is to be trusted: "for you have had longer experience than I as a writer, and fuller experience as a woman, since you have borne children and known the mother's history from the beginning" (5:31). While Eliot's correspondence stresses her caring for her husband's adult sons, she avers that Stowe's "abundant family" must make a "paradise" (*Letters* 5:31; Bodenheimer 163–64).

On matters including aesthetics and religion the two women novelists differed significantly—in particular on the issue of accurate portrayal of the victims of oppression (Claybaugh 130–34)—but they recognized a shared purpose in such novels as *Dred* and *Daniel Deronda* (Cotugno 123–28). Eliot had reviewed *Dred* (1856), a novel that anticipates Eliot's clever, vain, materialistic heroines in *Felix Holt* or *Daniel Deronda* and her treatment of prejudice, race, rebellion, self-sacrifice. Thematically, *Daniel Deronda* displaces slavery and enfranchisement from contemporary frames (it is set during the Civil War) to a world-historical narrative associated with Exodus.

Many have linked the concluding emigration to the Holy Land with the recolonization that concludes *Uncle Tom's Cabin*. In *Dred*, Stowe no longer is a proponent of Liberian resettlement and has added some complexity to her racialist theories. Fittingly, it was Stowe to whom Eliot wrote the much-quoted justification of "the Jewish element in 'Deronda' . . . to rouse the imagination of men and women to a vision of human claims in those races of their fellow-men who most differ from them in customs and beliefs" (*Letters* 6:301; Haight 487).

Stowe took part only vicariously in American visits to Eliot. James T. Fields, editor of the *Atlantic Monthly* from 1861–71 and partner in the prestigious importer of English literature, Ticknor & Fields, ensured reciprocal readership of English and American authors. Having helped to receive Dickens on his American tours and to launch Hawthorne's career, Fields regularly paid his summer's rounds of calls in England. Fields published Stowe's works from 1860–71; at the urging of his wife Annie Fields, he published Phelps's debut best-seller *The Gates Ajar* in 1868, and in the same year Ticknor & Fields published *The Spanish Gypsy* (it sold 8,000 copies [Haight 406]). In May 1869 Fields visited the Priory "to propose a uniform American edition of the works of George Eliot" and arrange to publish "Agatha" in the *Atlantic Monthly* for £300 (Haight 411). Annie Fields joined him in a visit the following week, bringing James Russell Lowell's daughter (411). The transatlantic bond was firmly established. James T. Fields's literary memoirs, a sequence of parlor conversations in his own home, reminisces about his visits in the homes of English authors—and of Hawthorne: "Our Whispering Gallery" appeared anonymously in *The Atlantic Monthly* in 1871 and was then issued as a book, *Yesterdays with Authors*. Fields's sessions of literary gossip were announced, appropriately, alongside the United States serialization of *Middlemarch* in *Harper's Weekly* from 16 December 1871 to 15 February 1873.[2] Eliot is missing from Fields's gallery, no doubt because he possessed no portrait or memorabilia, little more than a business relationship. An English woman writer might become a friend of an American publisher—Mary Russell Mitford appears at length in Fields's book—but perhaps an irreproachable private life was a prerequisite for a literary friendship of that sort. The case was somewhat different for Fields's wife, Annie, who lived into the next century and belonged to an advanced and prominent circle of women in the arts. (After her husband's death, Sarah Orne Jewett became Annie Fields's companion, and Harriet Prescott Spofford featured both writers in a eulogistic biographical collection, *A Little Book of Friends* [1916].)

Annie Fields, a poet and keeper of a literary salon in Boston, published her own version of "yesterdays with authors," *Authors and Friends* (primarily of American authors such as Henry Wadsworth Longfellow, but including the Tennysons), first serialized in the *Century* in 1893, and published as a book in 1897. In the chapter "Days with Mrs. Stowe," Fields portrays herself as an intermediary between two women writers in different ways enduring magnificent servitude. Before turning to Eliot, Fields quotes letters from Stowe in Florida, lamenting the house in Hartford that won't sell: "there's no earthly sense in having anything,—lordy massy, no!" and again to Mrs. Fields, "I am a slave, and bound thrall to *work*" (Fields 208–09). Without remark on the abolitionist's questionable language and condition as plantation owner post-Emancipation, Fields continues:

> In the summer of 1869 there was a pleasant home at St. John's Wood, in London, which possessed peculiar attractions . . . other drawing-rooms were gayer, but this was the home of George Eliot, and on Sunday afternoons the resort of those who desired the best that London had to give. Here it was that George Eliot told us of her admiration and deep regard, her affection, for Mrs. Stowe. Her reverence and love were expressed with such tremulous sincerity that the speaker won our hearts. . . . Many letters had already passed . . . and she confided to us her amusement at a fancy Mrs. Stowe had taken that Casaubon, in "Middlemarch," was drawn from the character of Mr. Lewes . . . it was impossible to dispossess her mind of the illusion . . . the source of much harmless household amusement at St. John's Wood. I find in Mrs. Stowe's letters some pleasant allusions to this correspondence. . . . "We were all full of George Eliot when your note came, as I had received a beautiful letter from her. . . . She is a noble, true woman; and if anybody doesn't see it, so much the worse for *them*." (209–10)

Stowe promised, once, to bring Eliot's letters to Boston to share with Fields. Fields allows time to blur in this recollection, as Casaubon had yet to appear in print in the summer of 1869.

In the literary memoir of 1893, Fields continues as go-between. Stowe's letter to Eliot dated "Orange Blossom Time, Mandarin, March 18, 1876," according to Fields, is "one of the most beautiful and interesting pieces of writing she ever achieved" (211); *Authors and Friends* transcribes excerpts. Stowe evokes a happy family circle wintering as if in Sicily. She thanks Eliot for a letter of sympathy "about my brother's trial; it was womanly, tender, and sweet. . . . After all, my love of you is greater than my admiration, for I think it more and better to be really a woman worth loving than to have read Greek and German and written books" (Fields 212). The letter shifts to express intimacy with her brother Henry Ward Beecher, the celebrity abolitionist preacher, recently defendant in a sensational trial for adultery: "This has drawn on my life,—my heart's blood. He is myself; . . . he has been from childhood of an ideal purity. . . . Well, dear, pardon me for this outpour. I loved you,—I love you,—and therefore wanted you to know just what I felt" (214–15). Fields, as redactor of Stowe's letter, disregards the scandal that had rocked reform circles (Victoria Woodhull, suffragist and medium, had declared that Beecher practiced free love). Nor does she underline the brother-sister attachment, though surely that heightens the interest of the letter. Now we hear the letter's resonance for the recipient, author of the "Brother and Sister" sonnets (dated 31 July 1869, published 1874 [Haight 472]) as well as *The Mill on the Floss*, and Stowe could have had the English author's fraternal attachment in mind. Instead Fields highlights intimacy between women. Stowe's "interest in any woman who was supporting herself, and especially any one who found a daily taskmaster in the pen, and . . . one possessed of great moral aspiration half paralyzed in its action because she found herself in an anomalous . . . position, made such a woman like a magnet to Mrs. Stowe" (Fields 215).

This episode irresistibly recalls another time when Stowe was magnetically drawn to a controversial defense. In general Eliot's and Stowe's correspondence skirts controversy to find comfort in shared careers and family cares. But Stowe hit a nerve when she exposed Lord Byron's incest with his half-sister, first in an article "The True Story of Lady Byron's Life" (*Atlantic Monthly* and *Macmillan's* 1869) followed by the book *Lady Byron Vindicated* (1870). Eliot wished Stowe had remained silent on the Byron question much as she herself abstained from comment on the Woman Question.[3] Stowe sent Eliot the article (*Letters* 5:53–54), and Eliot in turn wrote with concern to her friends: "I cannot help being sorry that it seemed necessary to publish what is only worthy to die and rot. After all Byron remains deeply pitiable" (*Letters* 5:54); Stowe's publication does a "heavy social injury of familiarizing young minds with the desecration of family ties" (5:56). To Stowe, she wrote that she would "have preferred that the 'Byron question' . . . not be brought before the public" (5:71). T. Austin Graham associates Stowe's vindication with Mary Wollstonecraft's, with Mill's *The Subjection of Women*, and the concept of women's enslavement to men (175). A lifelong devotee of the poet Byron, Stowe presents Byronic characters in *Dred*, including the heroine's dissolute brother with the poet's family name, Gordon (Graham). I would add the even more Byronic intimacy between Nina Gordon and her enslaved half-brother Harry, manager of her estate; the opening scene, as Harry watches Nina display new clothes and boast of her three fiancés, leads the reader to see him as another would-be lover. Nina, like Gwendolen, is a captive in a market in which men hold legitimate as well as illegitimate ownership. The women novelists with deep attachments to brothers diverge on the Byron question, as Eliot censures Stowe's defense of Lady Byron.

Elizabeth Stuart Phelps and the Woman Question

Discussions of Eliot's transatlantic connections usually link Stowe with another epistolary friend, Elizabeth Stuart Phelps, a neighbor of Stowe's in Andover.[4] Phelps and Eliot exchanged fifteen letters, between Phelps's first, on 26 February, 1873 and Eliot's last reply four months before she died in 1880—more than any "other American woman correspondent, excluding Harriet Beecher Stowe" (Griffith, "Epistolary" 94–95). Their exchange measures national differences: Phelps claims the right of an intrusive American to expect political forcefulness, Eliot affirms that Americans should go further in the "experiment" of women's education: "America is the seed-ground and nursery of new ideas," she wrote to Phelps (Blind 246). A later letter to Phelps attests to Eliot's "gratitude to another of kindred feeling who has long entered into the meaning of 'America' for my thought" (*Letters* 7:134; Griffith, "Epistolary" 99). Phelps began by affirming *Middlemarch*: "You have written the novel of the century—but that is one matter; you have almost analyzed a woman—and that is quite another. . . . I believe it remains for you to finish what you have begun." As Eliot herself knew, people would say Dorothea ought never to have married, but

Phelps demurs, "Rather should she never accept wifehood as a métier" (95). She urges Eliot to write a novel of "the Coming Woman"; "I would fain add to your laurels those of being the apostle of the 'Woman Question'" (96).

Whereas Eliot admires Stowe's balance of art and life yet objects to her ideal characterization, Phelps commends Eliot's career but objects to her failure to plot a woman's mission in art. Phelps subsequently wrote to Eliot for biographical information for lectures at "the College of Boston University, the new and so far successful co-educational experiment; . . . I was so fortunate or unfortunate as to be the first woman chosen in our day . . . to lecture before a college" (Griffith, "Epistolary" 96–97; Bodenheimer 235). The series focused on Eliot—probably her first appearance in academic feminist studies—and was avidly received by Eliot's devotees; Phelps repeated the lectures elsewhere (Coultrap-McQuin 174–75). Responding to *Daniel Deronda*, Phelps pleads, "Give us our more Christian book I pray you for the sake of Christ and for the sake of womanhood" (Griffith, "Epistolary" 97). In 1875, she mentions a visit to "Mrs. Stowe's pretty Florida home . . . I like to hear one great woman speak of another as she spoke of you" (Griffith, "Epistolary" 96). Answering the Woman Question in their own lives proved costly; for Eliot and Phelps, creative effort meant illness. "Something is the matter with my hand; I am hardly strong enough to write today," writes Phelps (Griffith, "Epistolary" 97). The postscript invites Eliot to visit her "old maid's Paradise" at the seashore, not far from "my friend Mrs. James T. Fields of Boston, whom I think you have met" (98). Again, the struggle of *The Story of Avis* (1877) is dramatized in a letter that Phelps scrawls with a hand "crippled by six-months' wrestling with my novel" (Griffith, "Epistolary" 98). The influence of Eliot and other women writers is inscribed in *The Story of Avis*, with its epigraphs (one from "Armgart") and its allusions to Barrett Browning's *Aurora Leigh* (Carrion 122–23). Since her best-selling *The Gates Ajar* (1868), Phelps had reached a "mass audience" with stories of "feminist heroines" (Griffith, "Epistolary" 94), and something of what Eliot would have called the "oracular" school. But the portrait of the visual artist as a young woman in *Avis* resonates with passages in *The Mill on the Floss* and *Middlemarch* that read like ecphrastic animations of pre-Raphaelite paintings while they indict the objectification of woman as work of art. It is intriguing that Phelps, aspiring to the model of Eliot's novels and career, published an article in the *Independent* in praise of marriage between older women and younger men (Carrion 120).

Few women writers throughout history have received the attention and preservation devoted to George Eliot and hence to her connections to Stowe and Phelps. A biographical approach reveals a transatlantic coterie of women writers, Eliot's influence in American literature, and dissemination of the English woman novelist as host, correspondent, author of exemplary works, and biographical model. The affinities and differences in these epistolary friendships bring out attachments to brothers; evoke sympathy for the pangs of suffering genius; provoke pity for bondage to a Dryasdust husband; or commend self-determination through artistic vocation and successful partnership, even with a much a younger man. In correspondence Eliot's practical engagement with the success and the potential of contemporary women stands out more sharply than in her fiction and poetry, which draw on an international sentimental mythos of feminine self-sacrifice. Later generations of feminists continued to expect, with Phelps, that Eliot be the apostle of the Woman Question. How little it may seem to limit Eliot's cosmopolitan, enduring works that she was born a girl in provincial England, and yet how much can be gained from retracing such biographical and contextual delineations—even as our expanding literary history stretches the boundaries of gender and nationality. Today, a feminist account of George Eliot builds upon the history of her North American reception.

Notes

1   Blind begins her biography with a challenge to "Woman in France," presenting Eliot and other English women writers as proof of genius to rival the French (1–10). In *Literary Women*, some fifty pages of alphabetical entries summarize oeuvres and relations of women writers, a kind of database before computers: e.g. "'Silly Novels by Lady Novelists' . . . on Stowe . . .; 'Belles Lettres' . . . on *Dred* . . .; . . . on *Aurora Leigh*"; "The GE Letters . . . to Stowe on *Deronda* . . .; quoting Margaret Fuller" (Moers 287–88). Phelps appears in the Addendum without annotation (321).

2   Advertisements for *Middlemarch* and other works by English and American authors in

Harper's periodicals, and for Field's *Yesterdays with Authors* published by Osgood, appear in adjacent columns in *The Literary World* 1 January 1872 (a Boston monthly).

3   Eliot's phrase "Byron question" echoes "the Woman Question," used or addressed in letters dated 21 and 23 August, 21 September, 4 October 1869.

4   Phelps's autobiography, *Chapters from a Life* (1896), has chapters on Stowe, Longfellow, Child, and others. She dedicated a poem to George Eliot (Carrion 120–21).

References

Adams, Kimberly V. *Our Lady of Victorian Feminism: The Madonna in the Work of Anna Jameson, Margaret Fuller, and George Eliot*. Athens: Ohio UP, 2001.

Anderson, Bonnie S. *Joyous Greetings: The First International Women's Movement, 1830––1860*. Oxford: Oxford UP, 2001.

Blind, Mathilde. *George Eliot*. Boston: Roberts Brothers, 1883.

Bodenheimer, Rosemarie. *The Real Life of Mary Ann Evans: George Eliot, Her Letters and Fiction*. Ithaca: Cornell UP, 1996.

Booth, Alison. CBW. *Collective Biographies of Women*. U of Virginia Library. 2011. Web. 21 September 2011. <http://womensbios.lib.virginia.edu>.

Booth, Alison. *Greatness Engendered: George Eliot and Virginia Woolf*. Ithaca: Cornell UP, 1992.

Carrion, Maria Dolores Narbona. "Nineteenth-Century American Women Writers' European Connections: The Case of Elizabeth Stuart Phelps." *New Perspectives in Transatlantic Studies*. Lanham, MD: UP of America, 2002. 117–29.

Carroll, A. *Dark Smiles: Race and Desire in George Eliot*. Athens: Ohio UP, 2003.

Claybaugh, Amanda. *The Novel of Purpose: Literature and Social Reform in the Anglo-American World*. Ithaca: Cornell UP, 2006.

Cognard-Black, Jennifer. *Narrative in the Professional Age: Transatlantic Readings of Harriet Beecher Stowe, George Eliot, and Elizabeth Stuart Phelps*. London: Routledge, 2004.

Cotugno, Clare. "Stowe, Eliot, and the Reform Aesthetic." *Transatlantic Stowe: Harriet Beecher Stowe and European Culture*. Ed. Denise Kohn, Sarah Meer, and Emily Bishop Todd. Iowa City: U of Iowa P, 2006. 111–30.

Coultrap-McQuin, Susan. *Doing Literary Business: American Women Writers in the Nineteenth Century*. Chapel Hill: U of North Carolina P, 1990.

Cross, John W. *George Eliot's Life*. 3 vols. New York: Harper, 1885.

Eliot, George. *Essays*. Ed. Thomas Pinney. New York: Columbia UP, 1963.

Eliot, George. *The George Eliot Letters*. Ed. Gordon S. Haight. 9 vols. New Haven: Yale UP, 1954–78.

Eliot, George. *Middlemarch*. Ed. Bert. G. Hornback. New York: Norton, 2000.

Fields, Annie. *Authors and Friends*. Boston: Little, 1897. Web. 7 Sept. 2011.

Fields, James T. *Yesterdays with Authors*. 1871. Boston: Houghton, 1900.

Flint, Kate. "George Eliot and Gender." *The Cambridge Companion to George Eliot*. Ed. George Levine. Cambridge: Cambridge UP, 2001. 159–80.

Gilbert, Sandra M., and Susan Gubar. *The Madwoman in the Attic: The Woman Writer and the Nineteenth-Century Literary Imagination*. 2nd ed. New Haven: Yale UP, 2000.

Giles, Paul. *Transatlantic Insurrections: British Culture and the Formation of American Literature, 1730–1860*. Philadelphia: U of Pennsylvania P, 2001.

Graham, T. Austin. "The Slaveries of Sex, Race, and Mind: Harriet Beecher Stowe's Lady Byron Vindicated." *New Literary History* 41.1 (2010): 173–90.

Griffith, George V., ed. "An Epistolary Friendship: The Letters of Elizabeth Stuart Phelps to George Eliot." *Legacy* 18.1 (2001): 94–100.

Griffith, George V. "George Eliot on the American Screen." *Nineteenth-Century Women at the Movies: Adapting Classic Women's Fiction to Film*. Ed. Barbara Tepa Lupack. Bowling Green, OH: Bowling Green State U Popular P, 1999. 299–318.

Griffith, George V. "Romola on the American Stage." *The George Eliot Fellowship Review* 20 (1989): 23–27.

Haight, Gordon S. *George Eliot: A Biography*. Oxford: Oxford UP, 1968.

Henry, Nancy. *George Eliot and the British Empire*. Cambridge: Cambridge UP, 2002.

Magruder, Julia. *Child-Sketches from George Eliot*. Boston: Lothrop, 1895.

Main, Alexander. *Wise, Witty, and Tender Sayings of George Eliot*. Edinburgh: Blackwood, 1872.

McGill, Meredith L. *American Literature and the Culture of Reprinting, 1834–1853*. Philadelphia: U of Pennsylvania P, 2007.

Mitchell, Sally. *Frances Power Cobbe: Victorian Feminist, Journalist, Reformer*. Charlottesville: U of Virginia P, 2004.

Moers, Ellen. *Literary Women: The Great Writers*. Oxford: Oxford UP, 1977.

Mueller, Monika. *George Eliot U.S.* Madison, NJ: Fairleigh Dickinson UP, 2005.

Parton, James. *Eminent Women: A Series of Sketches of Women Who Have Won Distinction by Their Genius and Achievements as Authors, Artists, Actors, Rulers, or within the Precincts of the Home*. New York: Alden; International; Philadelphia, Hubbard, 1880.

Picker, John M. "George Eliot and the Sequel Question." *New Literary History* 37.2 (2006): 361–88.

Rosenberg, Tracy S. "The Awkward Blot: George Eliot's Reception and the Ideal Woman Writer." *Nineteenth-Century Gender Studies* 3.1 (2007): n. pag. Web. 14 June 2011.

Sheets, Robin. "History and Romance: Harriet Beecher Stowe's *Agnes of Sorrento* and George Eliot's *Romola*." *Clio* 26.3 (1997): 323–46.

Showalter, Elaine. "The Greening of Sister George." *Nineteenth-Century Fiction* 35.3 (1980): 292–311.

Spofford, Harriet Elizabeth Prescott. *A Little Book of Friends*. Boston: Little, 1916.

Stephen, Sir Leslie. *George Eliot*. English Men of Letters Series. London: Macmillan, 1902.

Stern, Kimberly J. "A Common Fund: George Eliot and the Gender Politics of Criticism." *Prose Studies* 30.1 (2008): 45–62.

Stowe, Harriet Beecher. *A Reply to "The Affectionate and Christian Address of Many Thousands of Women of Great Britain and Ireland, to Their Sisters, the Women of the United States of America"*. London: Low, 1863.

Sweetser, Kate Dickinson. *Boys and Girls from George Eliot*. New York: Harper, 1906.

19

Transatlantic Eliot: African American Connections

Daniel Hack

George Eliot makes a brief appearance in the philosopher Kwame Anthony Appiah's 2007 essay "Ethics in a World of Strangers: W. E. B. Du Bois and the Spirit of Cosmopolitanism." Arguing that the great African American intellectual and activist cultivated a stance of "partial cosmopolitanism" (32), Appiah turns to *Daniel Deronda* to explain what he means by this term. According to Appiah, Du Bois resembles the protagonist of Eliot's last novel in his ability to treat "local allegiances" as neither absolute nor irrelevant, and to "combine . . . recognition of the need for partiality and the value of difference with the recognition of the value of encounter across identities" (33). Using Eliot's phrasing, Appiah claims that Du Bois, like Deronda, manages to affirm "the noble partiality which is man's best strength" without rejecting a broader loyalty to humanity, and to recognize the benefits of having "as wide an instruction and sympathy as possible" while also embracing "the closer fellowship that makes sympathy practical" (33).

Eliot's appearance in Appiah's essay is confined to this one paragraph, and Appiah makes no claim that Eliot's work played any role in Du Bois's thinking; indeed, the same paragraph appears again, virtually verbatim, in the preface to Appiah's subsequent book on cosmopolitanism, only this time shorn of any mention of Du Bois. Appiah is plainly more interested in using Eliot to articulate his own ideal of "partial cosmopolitanism" than in exploring or even claiming any connection between the author of *Daniel Deronda* and the author of *The Souls of Black Folk*. And indeed, evidence of such a link is scant: for example, Du Bois includes "George Eliot's novels"

A Companion to George Eliot, First Edition. Edited by Amanda Anderson and Harry E. Shaw.
© 2013 John Wiley & Sons, Ltd. Published 2016 by John Wiley & Sons, Ltd.

in a long list of readings he recommends in a lecture on education, but he does not single them out for discussion ("Education" 13); and while two of the key terms of *The Souls of Black Folk*, "the veil" and "double consciousness," both appear in Eliot's novella "The Lifted Veil," they bear very different meanings in the two works.

Nonetheless, as this chapter will show, there is in fact a significant history of, in Appiah's phrase, "encounter across identities" between African American writers and Eliot. Moreover, these encounters tend to engage the very issues of racial identity and cosmopolitan encounter Appiah himself invokes Eliot to address. In contrast to Appiah, however, other African American writers, however cosmopolitan in their own tastes and range of reference, tend to invoke Eliot in the course of affirming a commitment to racial identity which often comes at the expense of more universal commitments—and they often cite Eliot herself in support of such affirmations.

Eliot and "the Negro Novel"

The interest of African American writers in Eliot to be traced below would not seem to reflect or respond to a corresponding interest on her part: there is no evidence that Eliot ever read anything written by an African American or even met an African American (although she did see the celebrated African American actor Ira Aldridge perform scenes from Shakespeare, pronouncing him "pitiably bad" [*Letters* 2:301]). Eliot never invented a character of black African descent and her writings include few references to blacks. However, this lacuna should not be mistaken for a lack of interest in "race" as a concept and category; on the contrary, world history itself for Eliot consists largely in the development, clash, and mixing of races. Moreover, Eliot's treatment of race depends in part on writings *about* (if not *by*) African Americans, in particular what Eliot called "the Negro novel" ("Stowe's *Dred*" 380). To some extent, then, efforts to relocate or reimagine Eliot's writings in an African American context mirror Eliot's own transatlantic translation.

Eliot uses the phrase "Negro novel" in her review of Harriet Beecher Stowe's 1856 novel *Dred: A Tale of the Great Dismal Swamp*, crediting Stowe with having "invented" this type of novel in her earlier *Uncle Tom's Cabin* (1852). Eliot praises Stowe for her originality, on the one hand—"Inventions in literature are not as plentiful as inventions in the paletot and waterproof department" ("Stowe's *Dred*" 380)—and for her conformity to a valued model, on the other: like Walter Scott's *Ivanhoe*, Eliot writes, *Dred* takes as its topic "that *conflict of races* which [French historian] Augustin Thierry has pointed out as the great source of romantic interest"; also like Scott's work, "Stowe's novels have not only that grand element—conflict of races; they have another element equally grand . . . the exhibition of a people to whom what we may call Hebraic Christianity is still a reality . . . and by whom the theocratic conceptions of the Old Testament are literally applied to their daily life" ("Stowe's *Dred*" 380; emphasis in original). While noting some "artistic defects," Eliot concludes by emphasizing that *Dred* is "a great novel" ("Stowe's *Dred*" 381).

Eliot began her own career as a fiction writer within days of writing this review in September 1856. Yet rather than writing about "conflict of races" or attempting to capture "a national life in all its phases," she began by writing about a small, homogeneous community; and rather than depicting a people to whom Hebraic Christianity is still a reality and who exhibit "wild enthusiasm" and a "steady martyr-spirit," she wrote of characters incapable of ascending from the material to the spiritual plane and asked her readers to see "the poetry and the pathos, the tragedy and the comedy, lying in the experience of a human soul that looks out through dull grey eyes, and that speaks in a voice of quite ordinary tones" (*Scenes* 44). In short, Eliot's first work of fiction, the novella "The Sad Fortunes of the Reverend Amos Barton," is something of an anti-*Dred*.

Over the course of Eliot's career as a writer of fiction and poetry, however, the elements of Stowe's work she praised gain prominence in her own writing. This development may have been encouraged by the correspondence between the two writers, which began with an admiring letter from Stowe to Eliot in 1869 and continued intermittently until Eliot's death. Stowe's presence looms largest in Eliot's last novel, which is also the novel Appiah seizes upon: *Daniel Deronda*, which Laura Doyle, in one of the very few discussions of Eliot in relation to African American literature, has dubbed a "race epic" (333). In this novel, as several scholars have observed, not only does Eliot incorporate the two "grand element[s]" she identifies in Stowe's (and Scott's) fiction, but she also borrows and adapts formal elements of Stowe's novels, including character types, plot developments, and *Daniel Deronda*'s very narrative structure (Cotugno, Marotta, Mueller). Both of Stowe's "Negro novels" leave their mark on *Daniel Deronda*, but it is *Dred* in particular that *Daniel Deronda* echoes.

Dred's title character is a prophet-figure who leads a hidden community of fugitive slaves and uses Biblical, apocalyptic rhetoric to preach violent resistance to the slave order. However, Dred is not introduced in the novel that bears his name until more than a third of the way through. Stowe begins instead with the story of Nina Gordon, the beautiful, somewhat silly but good-hearted young mistress of a Southern plantation. The plantation is run for Nina by her slave Harry, who is loyal, well-educated, extremely competent, and—as he knows but she does not—Nina's half-brother, the son of her father and a slave. Harry will be torn between his loyalty to Nina, in particular his desire to protect her property from the interference of her ne'er-do-well brother, Tom, and his desire for freedom and resentment at the manifest injustice of his status as compared to his half-brother's. Nina herself is involved in a courtship plot with Edward Clayton, a handsome, earnest gentleman who aspires to do good in the world but is stymied by his belief that all careers involve unacceptable moral compromises. Under Clayton's influence, Nina becomes more serious, but various plot developments prevent them from marrying. Eventually, Nina dies, and both Harry and Clayton end up in Dred's camp in the swamp. By the novel's end, Dred too has died, and Clayton has founded an interracial settlement in Canada, with Harry as one of its leaders.

Daniel Deronda recalls *Dred* in several ways, beginning with its titular gambit (if not its title itself): although Deronda, unlike Dred, appears in the first chapter of the novel that bears his name, he then disappears from the novel until midway through the second of its eight books. It is difficult to think of a third novel that ignores its title character for so long early on, making it unclear why the novel bears that character's name. Eliot seems here to be adopting Stowe's tactic of disorienting her readers to prepare them for their eventual reorientation, as typically marginalized characters and groups take center stage. In both novels, this reorientation is accompanied by a generic shift as well: each begins with a realist courtship plot featuring a young upper-class woman—who, in both works, is labeled a "spoiled child" (Stowe 20, *Deronda* 5; bk. I)—before introducing racial plots which disrupt the novel's conventional plotting and protocols. These plots feature prophet figures—Dred and Mordecai—whose claims to have "visions" and "second sight" (Stowe 274, *Deronda* 497; ch. 40, 471; ch. 38) are treated gingerly by the respective narrators, but are supported by the narratives themselves.

When Daniel Deronda finally does take center stage in the novel that bears his name, he incorporates elements of both Edward Clayton and Harry: he shares Clayton's earnestness and potentially paralyzing idealism, and like Clayton plays the role of improving mentor and (differently) thwarted romantic-interest to the beautiful "spoiled child"; like Harry, he will feel caught between this woman's reliance on him, on the one hand, and the urgings of a charismatic visionary that he become a leader of his race, on the other. Just as Dred identifies Harry as his people's Moses, so too does Mordecai explicitly identify Daniel as a latterday Moses, and in making this identification both Dred and Mordecai emphasize their hoped-for disciple's beneficial education in the dominant culture: "'Brethren,' said Dred, laying his hand upon Harry, 'the Lord caused Moses to become the son of Pharaoh's daughter, that he might become learned in the wisdom of the Egyptians, to lead forth his people from the house of bondage'" (454); "'it is a precious thought to me that he has a preparation which I lacked, and is an accomplished Egyptian'" (657; ch. 52).

The use of Moses and the Israelites as figures for enslaved African Americans was of course quite common in the nineteenth century; what we see in *Daniel Deronda*, though, is the use of a story about enslaved African Americans as a template to tell a story about contemporary Jews. Eliot departs from her model in many ways, but some of these departures are themselves quite telling. In the present context, the most significant difference between the two novels lies in the competing resolutions the authors devise to the "conflict of races" they depict. Whereas Harry never has to choose between his competing loyalties—he joins Dred's band of fugitives only after Nina dies, and ultimately prospers in the interracial community founded by her lover—*Daniel Deronda* offers no comparable vision of interracial coexistence. Instead, the novel insists on the starkness of Deronda's choice between Jewish and English identities, as he and his Jewish bride Mirah head off to Palestine, leaving behind England and the devastated Gwendolen. If *Dred*, then, ends by celebrating cross-racial alliances

and integration, *Daniel Deronda* affirms the model of racial relations Deronda, following the Jewish grandfather of whom he learns late in the novel, calls "separateness
with communication" (725; ch. 60), and Eliot renders the separation much more vivid
than the communication.

Eliot's departure from *Dred* produces the tension between Daniel Deronda's rhetoric
and *Daniel Deronda*'s denouement that makes the novel a problematic choice for
Appiah to enlist on behalf of partial cosmopolitanism (but see Anderson for a defense
of the novel's cosmopolitanism). Ironically, though, it is precisely Eliot's departures
from "the Negro novel" in *Daniel Deronda* and elsewhere that will resonate most
with African American writers in the late-nineteenth and early-twentieth centuries.
That is, although invocations and adaptations of Eliot's work typically eschew the
ultimate form this commitment takes in *Daniel Deronda*—the establishment of a
separate homeland—they tend to cluster nonetheless around aspects of Eliot's oeuvre
that emphasize racial identity, solidarity, and exclusivity, including a plot Eliot pio-
neers that is not present in Stowe.

African American Deployments of Eliot

The heyday of Eliot's presence in African American literature and print culture comes
in the late nineteenth and early twentieth century. Not surprisingly, this presence
takes a range of forms, from brief quotations to extended allusions and borrowed plot
devices, and both the intensity and explicitness of engagement vary. However, patterns
and key texts do emerge. In particular, while African American writers may invoke
Eliot to demonstrate their own sophistication or cosmopolitanism, they do not tend
to invoke her in support of cosmopolitanism per se. On the contrary, as suggested
above, they often call on her in the course of, or in support of, their own affirmation
of a specifically racial identity and project.

The most prominent citations of Eliot in African American letters appear in *A Voice
from the South*, by Anna Julia Cooper. Published in 1892, *A Voice from the South* collected recent speeches and essays by Cooper, a well-known writer, lecturer, and teacher.
Cooper's focus throughout her book is on race relations, with an emphasis on the
treatment and prospects of African American women. Cooper makes her own subject-
position clear at the outset, as the title page reads "By A Black Woman of the South"
(with Cooper's name appearing as the copyright holder), and the book's introduction
asserts this subject's uniqueness and inimitability: "as our Caucasian barristers are not
to blame if they cannot *quite* put themselves in the dark man's place, neither should
the dark man be wholly expected fully and adequately to reproduce the exact Voice
of the Black Woman" (52; emphasis in original). This stance notwithstanding, Cooper
chooses to preface both of her book's two sections with epigraphs from Eliot. The
epigraph for Part I, which focuses on the role of women, is drawn from one of Eliot's
more obscure works, "How Lisa Loved the King," a long poem (approx. 700 lines)
based on an episode in Boccaccio; Cooper strings together two five-line passages that

celebrate the loving attention "Royal-hearted Women" pay to "needy, suffering lives in lowliest place" (50). The epigraph for the wider-ranging Part II (which also carries an epigraph from Robert Browning) is a passage from *Felix Holt* demanding "a free-man's share" in political life—"to think and speak and act about what concerns us all" (120).

The citation of canonical Western authors by African American writers at this time served clear political as well as literary and rhetorical purposes, as it made a claim for knowledge of and participation in the dominant cultural tradition; around a decade later in *The Souls of Black Folk* Du Bois would provide the most celebrated expression of this idea by declaring "I sit with Shakespeare and he winces not . . ." (74). Nonetheless, there is an apparent tension between Cooper's emphasis on speaking in her own voice as a black woman and the prominent place she accords the white Eliot. Yet the use of Eliot can be seen as less an act of deference or subordination than one of affiliation and even appropriation. Or, more precisely, affiliation with regard to the first epigraph, and appropriation with regard to the second, for while the first epigraph is relatively straightforward in its deployment, the second one is trickier: unlike the first Eliot epigraph, as well as the Browning one, which are attributed to their authors with no identification of the works from which they are drawn, this epigraph is attributed to "Felix Holt," with no mention of the author. This shift suggests that Cooper is quoting not just the novel *Felix Holt* but the character Felix Holt—but she is not: the lines are in fact spoken by an unnamed "speaker" whose demand for immediate universal suffrage is contested by Felix himself and implicitly rejected by Eliot.

Cooper's sly use of Eliot tells us more about Eliot's prestige in the late-nineteenth-century United States, on the one hand, and the uses of the Western canon in general for African American writers, on the other, than about any special resonance Eliot's work in particular might have had for African Americans. The desire to cite Eliot in support of one's cause leads at times to even greater acts of decontextualization and distortion, as in a 1903 editorial in the *Colored American Magazine* titled "Steadfast-ness." This piece begins with lines from Eliot's 1868 poem *The Spanish Gypsy*:

> Nay, never falter, no great deed is done
> By falterers who ask for certainty.
> No good is certain but the steadfast mind,
> The undivided will to seek the good;
> 'Tis that compels the elements, and wrings
> A human music from the indifferent air.
> The greatest gift a hero leaves his race
> Is to have been a hero.

"What an inspiration for each one of us in these beautiful lines of George Eliot's," exclaims the editor. Very quickly, though, the editorial tacitly rewrites Eliot to promote a religious message not discernible in the lines quoted: "Certainly a steadfast mind and a trusting heart will enable us all to more nearly do our whole duty as God

shall show it to us. . . ." Indeed, Eliot's passage seems a singularly poor choice of a
text from which to draw the lesson that "much of the present discontent between
mankind everywhere," including "the vexed 'Race Problem,'" could be easily settled
"If the Church of Christ today would but follow the single teachings of their great
leader, look upon God as their Father, and mankind as their brethren" (240): the lines
quoted form part of the successful effort by Zarca, the king of the gypsies, to convince
his long-lost daughter, Fedalma, to abandon the life she has lived in Spain and join
him in establishing a separate homeland for their people. Not only does the poem not
support the editorial, then, but instead it contradicts it.

Such citational ignorance or indifference is common, perhaps even the norm, in the
print culture of the time (if not all times). With reference specifically to Eliot, Leah
Price has shown that numerous brief excerpts from Eliot's writings were already circulating in Anglo-American culture by the 1870s (with equivocal support from Eliot
herself), detached from their original text and valued for their purported wisdom and/
or cultural capital. "What do we live for if it is not to make life less difficult to each
other.—George Eliot" reads a bit of filler lodged between advertisements for Dr.
Kline's Great Nerve Restorer and Cascaret's Candy Cathartic in an 1898 issue of the
Afro-American newspaper (the sentence is from *Middlemarch*). Yet it would be a mistake
to read all citations of Eliot in African American literature and print culture as reflecting a lack of interest in or knowledge of the cited work as a whole, let alone uncon-
cerned with the specificity of the passage quoted. Surprisingly, given its minor place
in current Eliot scholarship, the poem from which the *Colored American* wrings its
wonted music constitutes the major counterexample: of all Eliot's works, *The Spanish
Gypsy* looms largest in African American literature and print culture for roughly the
half-century following its initial publication, and—the *Colored American* editorial
notwithstanding—it is deployed in ways that bespeak not just its general presence in
the wider culture but also its specific resonance for African Americans. What's more,
in the majority of cases invocations of the poem serve not (only) to demonstrate the
author's own cultural literacy but rather, or primarily, to advance a race-based agenda.
If for Appiah, then, *Daniel Deronda* is the exemplary work of partial cosmopolitanism,
for these African American writers, *The Spanish Gypsy* stands as the exemplary work
of cosmopolitan partiality.

The first African American writer to bring *The Spanish Gypsy* to bear on the concerns
of African Americans was in all likelihood Frances Ellen Watkins Harper. Best known
today for her novel *Iola Leroy*, to which we will return, Harper's long career as a poet,
novelist, lecturer, and activist began before the Civil War and lasted into the twentieth
century. Harper discusses and quotes extensively (some fifty lines) from *The Spanish
Gypsy* in "A Factor in Human Progress," an 1885 essay arguing for the importance
of "the training of the morals" in addition to "the education of the intellect" (276).
After asserting that an individual's "education is unfinished" if "he prefer[s] integrity
to gold, principle to ease, true manhood to self-indulgence" (276), Harper turns to
the scene in *The Spanish Gypsy* in which the Gypsy chieftain Zarca reveals to Fedalma—
before whom "the vista of the future is opening with all the light and joy of young

wedded love in a ducal palace" (276)—that she is his daughter and calls upon her to join her ancestral people. Harper quotes Fedalma's stunned reaction, as she grapples with the notion that she belongs to

> a race
> More outcast and despised than Moor or Jew. . . .
> A race that lives on prey, as foxes do
> With stealthy, petty rapine; so despised,
> It is not persecuted, only spurned,
> Crushed under foot . . .

followed by Zarca's surprising response:

> You paint us well.
> So abject are the men whose blood we share;
> Untutored, unbefriended, unendowed;
> No favorites of heaven or of men,
> Therefore I cling to them!
>
> (qtd. in Harper 277)

As David Kurnick has observed, this exchange strikingly presents the gypsies' abjection and even dehumanization as reason to identify or affiliate with them (503); in contrast to *Daniel Deronda*, as he also notes, Eliot has no interest "in making the case for gypsy peoplehood by appealing to a proud cultural tradition" (504). These aspects of the poem appeal to Harper and writers who follow her, who will emphasize both their race's downtrodden, stigmatized condition and what they see as its lack of history. (Indeed, this latter emphasis seems at least as important as the greater citability of verse in accounting for the more visible presence of *The Spanish Gypsy* than *Daniel Deronda*.) However, while Kurnick further argues that "Eliot's concern in *The Spanish Gypsy* is precisely to work out a model of an affiliative politics that would not be guaranteed by religious, national, or cultural prestige" (504), African American writers tend instead to emphasize those moments in the poem that look ahead to the future achievement of such prestige as a source of solidarity. Thus, Harper quotes the remainder of Zarca's long speech, including his declaration that

> Because our race have no great memories
> I will so live they shall remember me
> For deeds of such divine beneficence
> As rivers have, that teach men what is good
> By blessing them.
>
> (qtd. in Harper 277)

"Where in the wide realms of poet[r]y and song," Harper exclaims, "will we find nobler sentiments expressed with more tenderness, strength and beauty?," and she celebrates the effects of "the recital, or the example of deeds of high and holy worth" on a "people," no matter how "low down [they] may be in the scale of character and condition" (278; correction in original).

Following Harper's lead, later writers also approvingly quote passages from *The Spanish Gypsy* that call for the uplifting of a downtrodden, stigmatized race. For example, Emmett J. Scott, the Executive Secretary of the Tuskegee Institute, turns to Eliot's poem in the first chapter of *Tuskegee and Its People: Their Ideals and Achievements* (1905). Arguing that "the school teaches no more important lesson than that of cultivating a sense of pride and respect for colored men and women who deserve it because of their character, education, and achievements," Scott "borrow[s] a line from George Eliot" to drive home the importance of "pride of race"; indeed, he borrows ten lines—those quoted above, beginning with "Because our race has no great memories," followed without a break, as if part of the same sentence, by lines Zarca speaks later in the same scene:

> And make their name, now but a badge of scorn,
> A glorious banner floating in their midst,
> Stirring the air they breathe with impulses
> Of generous pride, exalting fellowship
> Until it soars to magnanimity.

(qtd. in Scott 23–24)

For Scott, the appeal of Eliot's lines stems from their eloquent and authoritative affirmation of the crucial role "race pride" plays in "race development" for a stigmatized race—but also, more specifically, for a race that cannot turn to its past to cultivate that pride or counter that stigma. We see this even more clearly in "Club Movement among Negro Women," a 1902 essay by Fannie Barrier Williams, a leader of that movement. Although the essay appears in a volume expansively titled *Progress of a Race; or, The Remarkable Advancement of the American Negro from the Bondage of Slavery, Ignorance and Poverty to the Freedom of Citizenship, Intelligence, Affluence, Honor and Trust,* Williams's emphasis falls squarely on the barrenness of the past: "In America," she declares, "the Negro has no history, no traditions, no race ideals, no inherited resources, either mental, social or ethical, and no established race character" (230). According to Williams, then, the task of "colored women" is to help "make history for a race that has no history," to furnish "material for the first chapter which shall some day recite the discouragements endured, the oppositions conquered, and the triumph of their faith in themselves" (231). This ambition, Williams declares, resembles that of "old Zarca in George Eliot's 'Spanish Gypsy,'" and she too quotes the passage about transforming "a badge of scorn" into "a glorious banner." "No race can long remain mean and cheap," she comments, "with aspirations such as these" (231).

The rhetoric of Williams's passage as a whole suggests a familiarity with *The Spanish Gypsy* that extends beyond the passage she cites. But her discussion also provides a striking foil to Eliot's "Notes on the Spanish Gypsy and Tragedy in General," an obscure essay which Williams is less likely to have known: in this short piece, first published posthumously in John Cross's 1885 life of Eliot, Eliot characterizes Zarca's tragedy as "the struggle for a great end, rendered vain by the surrounding conditions of life," and her thoughts then move to consideration, as brief as it is rare in her writings, of blacks—and more specifically, black women:

> A woman, say, finds herself on the earth with an inherited organisation: she may be lame, she may inherit a disease, or what is tantamount to a disease: she may be a negress, or have other marks of race repulsive in the community where she is born, &c., &c. . . . It is almost a mockery to say to such human beings, "Seek your own happiness." The utmost approach to wellbeing that can be made in such a case is through large resignation and acceptance of the inevitable, with as much effort to overcome any disadvantage as good sense will show to be attended with a likelihood of success. (Eliot, *Spanish Gypsy* 276).

The modest course of action Eliot prescribes for her "negress" contrasts strikingly with the Zarca-like ambitions Williams ascribes to her "Negro women." It is not at all clear, though, that the former's resignation would be more in keeping with the spirit of *The Spanish Gypsy* itself than would the latter's activism, since Zarca's failure to achieve his grandest aspirations does not discredit the aspirations themselves or the spirit that motivates them.

Yet despite Williams's alignment of Negro clubwomen's ambitions on behalf of their race with Zarca's, the Zincali leader's grandest and most specific aspiration has no place in her scheme. This is particularly striking because Zarca's aspiration points to the most obvious point of convergence between Eliot's gypsies and African Americans: Zarca's goal—which he announces in the very next line of the speech Williams and Scott both quote—is to "guide [their] brethren forth to their new land" where they will "make a nation," and this "promised land" is in Africa, where the Zincali originate (*Spanish Gypsy* 106, 115, 114). That is, although the Zincali are not "Negro," they are African. The drift of Eliot's thought to the "negress" in her "Notes" on the poem may well have been spurred by this common geography. The converse, however, does not seem to have been the case: at least, African American writers who cite *The Spanish Gypsy* never explicitly address the African origins or destiny of the Zincali, nor do they quote the passages mentioning Africa. Williams may compare her clubwomen's ambitions to Zarca's, yet the idea of emigration to Africa goes against the grain of her project—and goes unmentioned.

The general African American lack of engagement with the emigration plot of *The Spanish Gypsy* is particularly striking given the fact that emigration to Africa was a live issue at the time. The silence concerning Zarca's plan seems less a matter of ignorance of or indifference to the particularities of Eliot's plot than its active suppression by writers drawn instead both to the rhetoric of specific passages and to other aspects of the story Eliot tells. In a rule-proving exception, one newspaper editorial from 1902 does compare the leading advocate of emigration, Bishop Henry Turner, to Zarca—only to reject their shared position ("Bishop Turner"). But if we turn to contemporaneous African American fiction, we see that a number of works adopt or adapt the basic plot of *The Spanish Gypsy*—or rather, the basic plot shared by both Eliot's race epics, *The Spanish Gypsy* and *Daniel Deronda*—while stopping short of their shared conclusion or solution of emigration (which is shared as well by *Uncle Tom's Cabin*, though not *Dred*). In this plot, as experienced by both Fedalma and Deronda, individuals 1) grow up as members of their society's dominant race or nationality, 2) discover as young adults that their parentage assigns them instead to a stigmatized minority, 3) are in a position to continue "passing" with the identity they grew up with, but 4) choose instead to embrace their newly discovered lineage, despite the stigma attached to it. For all the secrets of lineage revealed in Victorian novels, this particular plot of unwitting passing and discovered identity is extremely rare: while Eliot saw fit to use it twice, there are virtually no other well-known examples in all British literature. By contrast, a number of nineteenth- and early twentieth-century American writers—most of them African American—constructed this same scenario, and did so almost invariably in stories about African American identity.

Although its greater prevalence in the United States suggests that this plot was more at home there, Eliot does not seem to have borrowed it from an American source. By contrast, several African American writers do seem to have had Eliot's versions of it in mind when they constructed their own. Evidence of Eliot's influence takes various forms, and in isolation some traces of her work might seem rather attenuated. However, the larger pattern carries a cumulative impact, and in a remarkable coincidence—too remarkable, that is, to be viewed as a coincidence—two of the authors who write narratives with this plot are also among those who quote *The Spanish Gypsy* in their nonfiction prose.

One of these authors is Frances Harper, who again plays a key role. As we saw, Harper quotes and discusses *The Spanish Gypsy* extensively in an 1885 article. Harper published four novels, two of which feature the plot of unwitting passing. The first of these, *Minnie's Sacrifice*, appeared serially in the Philadelphia-based *Christian Recorder* (published by the African Methodist Episcopal Church) in 1869—just one year after *The Spanish Gypsy's* publication. *Minnie's Sacrifice* tells the story of two mixed-race individuals, Minnie and Louis, both of whom are raised believing they are white. Minnie learns of her African American lineage from her mother and Louis from his grandmother (both of whom are black), and both eventually embrace this lineage and identity, with their feelings of personal loyalty supplemented by gratitude for specific acts of rescue. After Minnie and Louis marry, they commit themselves to working for the good of "the colored race" (85–86), a goal to which Louis reaffirms his commitment at novel's end, after Minnie is murdered by white supremacists. Reinforcing the novel's message of racial loyalty, a concluding author's note incorporates the logic and even the language of *The Spanish Gypsy*: just as, in one of the passages Harper later quotes, Zarca responds to Fedalma's repeated characterization of the Zincali as "despised" by declaring "So abject are the men whose blood we share/. . . . / Therefore I cling to them!," Harper announces here that "The lesson of Minnie's sacrifice is this, that it is braver to suffer with one's own branch of the human race,—to feel, that the weaker and the more despised they are, the closer we will cling to them, for the sake of helping them . . ." (90).

Like *Minnie's Sacrifice*, Harper's last and best-known novel, *Iola Leroy, or Shadows Uplifted* (1892), tells the story of two individuals who learn of their African American ancestry as young adults, and who refuse opportunities to pass as white. As in the earlier novel, these refusals (by Iola Leroy and her brother Harry) are motivated first by love of family and later by a desire to help uplift the race. Harper does introduce one character, Dr. Latimer (no relation, it seems, to the narrator of Eliot's "The Lifted Veil," also named Latimer), who gives voice to a more cosmopolitan, universalist stance—"instead of narrowing our sympathies to mere racial questions," he declares, "let us broaden them to humanity's wider issues" (260). However, Latimer also argues that "out of the race must come its own thinkers and writers" because "No man can feel the iron which enters another man's soul" (263). Iola herself calls Latimer's own refusal to pass "the grandest hour of his life" (265) and the source of her admiration for him, an admiration which culminates in their novel-concluding marriage.

Like Frances Harper, Fannie Barrier Williams not only cites *The Spanish Gypsy* but also writes a version of it—in Williams's case, in one of her very few forays into fiction. "After Many Days" tells the now-familiar story of a privileged young woman who is raised as white but learns that her mother was African American, indeed a slave (the story is set in the 1880s), and who comes to take pride in this lineage and openly avow it. In a departure from both *The Spanish Gypsy* and Harper's novels, however, the story ends on a note of interracial harmony—literally so, as Gladys Winne and her white fiancé come together while the voice of a white singer "mingl[es] in singular harmony with the plaintive melody as sung by a group of dusky singers" (238). Strikingly, though, the story says nothing about the couple's future, a silence which reads less as a betrothal-plot convention than an implicit acknowledgment of the difficulty of imagining this future.

Williams's "After Many Days" was one of several short stories featuring the plot of unwitting passing to appear in the first decade of the twentieth century in *The Colored American*—ironically, the same newspaper we saw quoting *The Spanish Gypsy* with seeming indifference to its actual content. Marie Louise Burgess-Ware's "Bernice, the Octoroon," which ran nine months after Williams's, adds further, telling twists to its version of the story, and points us toward a conclusion. Like Eliot's Fedalma, when Burgess-Ware's Bernice learns of her ancestry she refuses to continue living as a member of the dominant race, proclaiming that "if one drop of that despised blood flows in my veins, loyal to that race I will be" (257). Also like Fedalma, Bernice takes this step even though she believes it will separate her from her beloved, who is white. However, Burgess-Ware's denouement revises Eliot's: in the poem Fedalma's beloved Silva tries and fails to renounce his Spanish identity and become a gypsy so that he can still be with Fedalma, whereas in the story, Bernice's fiancé eventually learns that he too is a mulatto. Eliot's Silva ends up killing Fedalma's father and himself dying; in Burgess-Ware's story, by contrast, Bernice and Garrett end up happily married and active on behalf of "the race with which they are identified" (275). This revision moves "Bernice, the Octoroon" closer to *Daniel Deronda* while maintaining the anticosmopolitan commitment to racial exclusivity common to both of Eliot's texts as well as much of the tradition tracked here.

By the time of Burgess-Ware's story, enough stories of unwitting passing and affirmed identity had been published that the lineage of any particular text was as mixed as that of the characters who inhabit them. The careful formulation "the race with which they are identified," for example, echoes a passage in *Iola Leroy* where Iola looks ahead to "a brighter future for the race with which she was identified" (219–20). Thus, some of the ways in which Bernice resembles Fedalma are also ways in which she resembles her immediate precursor Gladys as well as Harper's earlier unwitting passers, and in some ways Bernice's story differs greatly from Fedalma's. Yet George Eliot's place in this body of work had not become "incalculably diffusive" by 1903, as Eliot describes Dorothea Brooke's "effect . . . on those around her," in the famous last sentence of *Middlemarch* (838; Finale). Instead, there are signs that Eliot's association with the plot focused on here persisted. Thus, Marie Louise Burgess-Ware herself calls attention to the link between "Bernice, the Octoroon" and *The Spanish Gypsy* by giving Bernice the same last name as Fedalma's beloved: Silva. The use of this name also adumbrates the story's departure from the poem, as the assignment of the fiancé's last name to the heroine foreshadows their eventual union, a union denied Fedalma and Silva. A finely calibrated allusion such as Burgess-Ware's helps ensure that Eliot's presence in African American literature and print culture, unlike Dorothea's influence on those around her, remains visible, even calculable.

References

Afro-American (Baltimore) 16 Apr. 1898: 3. *Proquest Historical Newspapers*. Web.

Anderson, Amanda. *The Powers of Distance: Cosmopolitanism and the Cultivation of Detachment*. Princeton: Princeton UP, 2001.

Appiah, Kwame Anthony, et al. *Justice, Governance, Cosmopolitanism, and the Politics of Difference: Reconfigurations in a Transnational World*. Berlin: Humboldt U, 2007.

"Bishop Turner." Editorial. *The Freeman* (Indianapolis) 3 May 1902: 4. *America's Historical Newspapers*. Web. 9 June 2011.

Burgess-Ware, Marie Louise. "Bernice, the Octoroon." 1903. *Short Fiction by Black Women, 1900–1920*. Ed. Elizabeth Ammons. Oxford: Oxford UP, 1991. 250–75.

Cooper, Anna Julia. *A Voice from the South*. 1892. Rpt. in *The Voice of Anna Julia Cooper*. Ed. Charles Lemert and Esme Bhan. Lanham: Rowman, 1998.

Cotugno, Clare. "Stowe, Eliot, and the Reform Aesthetic." *Transatlantic Stowe: Harriet Beecher Stowe and European Culture*. Ed. Denise Kohn, Sarah Meer, and Emily B. Todd. Iowa City: U of Iowa P, 2006. 111–30.

Doyle, Laura. *Freedom's Empire: Race and the Rise of the Novel in Atlantic Modernity, 1640–1940*. Durham: Duke UP, 2008.

Du Bois, W. E. B. "Does Education Pay?" *Writings by W. E. B. Du Bois in Periodicals Edited by Others, 1891–1909*. Ed. Herbert Aptheker. Vol. 1. Millwood, NY: Kraus-Thomson, 1982. 1–18.

Du Bois, W. E. B. *The Souls of Black Folk*. 1903. Ed. Henry Louis Gates, Jr., and Terry Hume Oliver. New York: Norton, 1999.

Eliot, George. *Daniel Deronda*. Ed. Terence Cave. London: Penguin, 1995

Eliot, George. *The George Eliot Letters*. Ed. Gordon S. Haight. 9 vols. New Haven: Yale UP, 1954–78.

Eliot, George. "Harriet Beecher Stowe's *Dred*, Charles Reade's *It is Never Too Late to Mend* and Frederika Bremer's *Hertha*." *Selected Essays, Poems, and Other Writings*. Ed. A. S. Byatt and Nicholas Warren. London: Penguin, 1990.

Eliot, George. *Middlemarch*. Ed. Rosemary Ashton. London: Penguin, 1994.

Eliot, George. *Scenes of Clerical Life*. Ed. Jennifer Gribble. London: Penguin, 1998.

Eliot, George. *The Spanish Gypsy*. Ed. Antonie Gerard van den Broek. London: Pickering, 2008.

Harper, Frances Ellen Watkins. *A Brighter Coming Day: A Frances Ellen Watkins Harper Reader*. Ed. Frances Smith Foster. New York: Feminist, 1990.

Harper, Frances Ellen Watkins. *Iola Leroy, or Shadows Uplifted*. 1892. Ed. Frances Smith Foster. Oxford: Oxford UP, 1988.

Harper, Frances Ellen Watkins. *Minnie's Sacrifice, Sowing and Reaping, Trial and Triumph: Three Rediscovered Novels*. Ed. Frances Smith Foster. Boston: Beacon, 1994.

Kurnick, David. "Unspeakable George Eliot." *Victorian Literature and Culture* 38.2 (2010): 489–509.

Marotta, Kenny Ralph. *The Literary Relationship of George Eliot and Harriet Beecher Stowe*. Diss. Johns Hopkins U 1974. Ann Arbor: UMI, 1974.

Mueller, Monika. *George Eliot U.S.: Transatlantic Literary and Cultural Perspectives*. Madison, NJ: Fairleigh Dickinson UP, 2005.

Price, Leah. *The Anthology and the Rise of the Novel, from Richardson to George Eliot*. Cambridge: Cambridge UP, 2000.

Scott, Emmett J. "Present Achievements and Governing Ideals." *Tuskegee and Its People: Their Ideals and Achievements*. Ed. Booker T. Washington. New York: Appleton, 1905. 19–34. *Alexander Street Press*. Web. 20 May 2001.

"Steadfastness." Editorial. *Colored American Magazine* (Boston) January 1903: 240. *Hathi Trust Digital Library*. Web. 14 June 2011.

Stowe, Harriet Beecher. *Dred: A Tale of the Great Dismal Swamp*. 1856. Ed. Robert S. Levine. Chapel Hill: U of North Carolina P, 2000.

Williams, Fannie Barrier. "After Many Days: A Christmas Story." 1902. *Short Fiction by Black Women, 1900–1920*. Ed. Elizabeth Ammons. Oxford: Oxford UP, 1991. 218–38.

Williams, Fannie Barrier. "Club Movement among Negro Women." *Progress of a Race, or, The Remarkable Advancement of the American Negro*. J. W. Gibson and W. H. Crogman. Atlanta: Nichols, 1902. *Hathi Digital Trust Library*. Web. 17 May 2011.

Part IV
Eliot in Her Time and Ours: Intellectual and Cultural Contexts

20

Sympathy and the Basis of Morality

T. H. Irwin

The Neglect of Sympathy

According to George Eliot, "the greatest benefit we owe to the artist, whether painter, poet, or novelist, is the extension of our sympathies" (*Essays* 270–71). While we might agree that artists can produce this effect on us, we might ask why it is a benefit, and why it is the greatest benefit. Her answers to these questions reveal her views on the place of sympathy in morality.

The extension of sympathy is the particular role of the artist as opposed to the theorist. Eliot describes herself as an "aesthetic" teacher, who rouses "the nobler emotions which make mankind desire the social right" (*Letters* 7:44).[1] She is not a "doctrinal" teacher who argues theoretically about moral questions. She aims to help readers to appreciate "those vital elements which bind men together and give a higher worthiness to their existence," and to free them from "transient forms on which an outworn teaching tends to make them dependent" (*Letters* 4:472).

This particular gift of the artist is important because it disposes us to favor the moral outlook ("the social right"), and to understand it better than we would understand it if we thought it depended on "transient forms" and "outworn teaching." In her view, morality does not need any theological foundation and is better off without it. Her Christian opponents, the preacher John Cumming and the poet Edward Young, falsely suppose (in her polemical representation of them) that morality needs the support of the Christian dogma of post-mortem rewards and punishments for good and bad behavior. They assume, and they take Christianity to assume, that morally

A Companion to George Eliot, First Edition. Edited by Amanda Anderson and Harry E. Shaw.
© 2013 John Wiley & Sons, Ltd. Published 2016 by John Wiley & Sons, Ltd.

right action rests on the desire for one's own happiness and aversion from one's own misery.

The basic error in these Christian views is their failure to recognize that sympathy is the basis of morality and religion.[2] Sympathy is important partly because morality requires concern for the good of others for its own sake, not simply as a means to one's own good. The theological approach presents only a "squinting virtue"; it squints because it overlooks the immediate and appropriate motive for virtuous action, and always looks for the less obvious egoistic motive.[3] Sympathy, on the contrary, is non-egoistic.[4]

But not all non-egoistic motives are appropriate for morality. Eliot also attacks the view that the glory of God should be the only motive for morally correct behavior. Though this motive is non-egoistic, it still diverts us from sympathy, the true source of morality, toward a source of immorality.[5] Sympathy, therefore, is essential to morality not only because it is non-egoistic, but also because it is directly appropriate.[6] Eliot's objections to a theological alternative to sympathy apply equally to any utilitarian or deontological foundation that tries to replace the sympathetic basis of the different duties and virtues.

This polemic recalls the contrast that Henry Fielding draws between the amiable Tom Jones and the unattractive theological voluntarist Thwackum and the rationalist Square. Fielding's contrast sets Francis Hutcheson's belief in a moral sense against these other views of the basis of morality. Eliot, however, agrees (directly or indirectly) with Adam Smith's rejection of a simple appeal to a moral sense, and shares his ambition of explaining morality by appealing to psychologically simpler elements. Like Smith, she appeals to sympathy.[7]

Types of Sympathy

To see why Eliot thinks sympathy is important, and to see what is important about it, we may usefully raise some simple questions about the elements of sympathy. We might think of it in three ways:[8]

1. We may say that A has some sympathetic understanding of B (or "empathy" for B) if A grasps how B feels in B's situation. A lacks this understanding if A can only represent how A would feel if A were in B's situation with A's mental life. If A thinks of B wearing a gray suit with brown shoes, A may reflect that A would not be embarrassed in such a situation, and so A may infer that B need not take any trouble to wear black shoes. If A understood that B is embarrassed to be seen in brown shoes and a gray suit, A might realize that (e.g.) B has a good reason to buy a pair of black shoes to wear with a gray suit. Let us call this cognitive sympathy.

2. A may make B's supposed affective state vivid to A. A may notice B approaching a precipice, believe that B is afraid, and begin to feel some of the fear that he attributes to B. Let us say that A has affective sympathy for B. This affective sympathy

is not sufficient for cognitive sympathy; if A's belief about B's fear at the edge of the precipice is false, A's sympathetic fear does not result in cognitive sympathy for B. Nor is affective sympathy necessary for cognitive sympathy. Even if A cannot feel any of the embarrassment that B would feel in wearing a gray suit with brown shoes, A may recognize B's embarrassment.

3. A may be sympathetic to B in so far as A recognizes what is bad about B's situation, and weighs B's interests appropriately in deciding how B is to be treated. If A is a judge and B expects a sympathetic hearing from A, B expects that A will take the appropriate account of (e.g.) B's justified grievances. Let us say that A displays practical sympathy to B. This practical sympathy is logically independent of both cognitive and affective sympathy. A need not have any view about how B feels, and need not have any feelings based on true or false beliefs about how B feels. A gives B a sympathetic hearing in so far as A responds appropriately to the injustice that B has suffered.

These three types of sympathy are differently related to morality. The first two are defined independently of morality; their descriptions do not presuppose that the relevant cognitive and affective conditions are connected to morality or to moral judgment. Practical sympathy, however, is described as recognizing what is bad, and as responding appropriately. An agent cannot display these attitudes without some grasp of morality, and we cannot attribute these attitudes to someone without making moral judgments on our own account.

But though these types of sympathy are different, it is neither accidental nor wholly misleading that we speak of sympathy in all three cases.[9] For sometimes one of them leads naturally to the others. When A hears what has happened to B, A may correctly recognize through imagination the pain B feels, and the imagination may be vivid enough to make A feel the same sort of pain, which may lead A to try to get rid of B's pain. This natural sequence of types of sympathy may induce us to suppose that the sequence is necessary, and in particular that practical sympathy must be based on cognitive and affective sympathy, and that cognitive and affective sympathy must lead to practical sympathy. Since practical sympathy requires a correct moral outlook, we may readily infer that cognitive and affective sympathy ensure a correct moral outlook.

Morality Founded on Emotion, not Principle

Why, then, is sympathy the foundation for morality? We have seen that a non-instrumental attitude to morality need not rely on sympathy. A deontological attitude chooses right action because it is right, and not only for some ulterior result. According to Kant, sympathy is an inappropriate foundation for the right moral motive. Among English moralists, Richard Price and Joseph Butler anticipate Kant on this point. They both take the conscientious attitude to be distinct from sympathy, and they both take it to include an essentially rational element. What, then, is Eliot's objection to a rationalist account of the foundation of morality?

In her view, emotions are essential to moral virtues because they express our reactions to particular situations, and only secondarily apply to generalizations.[10] Just people, for instance, respond to particular acts of injustice with the appropriate indignation, and their recognition of a general requirement to be just is secondary.[11] General principles are summaries and reminders; they affect us in so far as they recall the particular situations that arouse our emotions. Their secondary moral significance is derived from the primary moral significance of the responses to particular situations that they recall.[12] This outlook is both particularist (in so far as it takes responses to particular situations to be primary) and sentimentalist (in so far as it takes emotion and sentiment to be primary).

For this reason, Eliot accepts a sentimentalist account of the formation of practical sympathy. My previous description of practical sympathy made it logically independent of cognitive and affective sympathy, but if Eliot is right, it is not psychologically independent of them. On the contrary, the appropriate emotions are the only route to the correct judgments and responses that constitute practical sympathy. She therefore takes cognitive and affective sympathy to be the foundation of practical sympathy.[13]

Sympathy: Indicative or Constitutive?

Eliot implicitly claims, therefore, that our best guide to the morally right is the response of the sympathetic observer. But this implicit position needs further interpretation.

According to an indicative (or detective) interpretation, the responses of the sympathetic observer are better at the detection of what is morally right than any other method would be. The fact that a particular chicken is male or female is independent of the judgment of the chicken-sexer; but we may have no better access to this fact in the new-born chicken than the judgment of a chicken-sexer, who may not rely on any general rules. To defend this indicative view, we need some reason to believe that moral facts about right and wrong exist objectively, independently of our responses to actions and people. Some have rejected this objectivist view of moral facts, on skeptical grounds; they maintain we have no good grounds for believing in any such facts.

Skepticism about objective moral facts may incline us toward a constitutive, rather than an indicative, interpretation of the role of the sympathetic observer. According to this interpretation, the responses of the sympathetic observer do not detect, but constitute moral rightness. If someone has been appointed president of a university to fill a recognized vacancy and according to the recognized procedures, there is no further question "But is she really the president?" The following of the appropriate procedure is all that there is to becoming president. Similarly, the responses of the sympathetic observer are all there is to rightness, and no further question arises about whether these responses in this situation really give us the right conclusion.

This constitutive view combines skepticism about objective moral facts with an anti-skeptical view about moral judgments. We do not seem to be ignorant about right and wrong; on the contrary, our strong moral reactions to different types of situations seem to be a reliable source of moral convictions. But if this is so, and they are not reliable about objective moral facts, moral convictions are not about objective moral facts, and moral rightness and wrongness do not consist in any objective facts. Moral judgments are judgments not about objective facts to which we lack cognitive access, but about our reactions to different situations.

This version of a constitutive view is too simple to be plausible. For my moral judgments are not merely reports of how I react. I can be correct or incorrect, and I expect other people to agree with me. Moreover, my reactions are often self-interested, biased, and thoughtless, whereas we do not expect correct moral judgments to have these features. We can understand moral judgments if we suppose that they attempt to describe the response of the impartial sympathetic observer, and that they are correct when they describe this response correctly.

This is a mere sketch of the constitutive account of sympathy (or the moral sense) and moral facts, as Hutcheson, David Hume, and Smith develop it. But even the sketch suggests that one might prefer it to an indicative view, because it avoids some disputable claims about objective moral reality. But it commits itself to different disputable claims. If we know how a sympathetic observer reacts, we can still ask how these reactions are related to morality. We need some argument to show that there is nothing more to morality than the reactions of a sympathetic observer.

Some of Eliot's remarks on morality and sympathy might be taken to favor a constitutive view. She rejects a narrow conception of morality that confines it to the performance of a short list of duties in a strictly private sphere and refuses to extend the domain of morality to larger questions that affect the well-being of society. In answer to that narrow conception, she argues that we should define morality (and even "morality") as the product of knowledge and sympathy, which we might understand as the product of cognitive and affective sympathy.[14] But it would probably be unwise to suppose that she clearly distinguishes and affirms the constitutive conception. It is useful to keep both conceptions in mind while we consider her remarks on sympathy. She may implicitly assume one or the other conception, or she may rely on each conception in different places; and one or the other may fit her claims on behalf of sympathy.

Sympathy and Accuracy

According to Eliot, novels may free us from the "vulgarity of exclusiveness," which makes us indifferent to the welfare of people who are too remote from us, or too different from us, to be direct objects of our sympathy (*Essays* 270). If we cannot imagine what it is like to live someone else's life and to feel what they feel, we are likely to be relatively indifferent to their well-being. But the artist can change this indifference. If we learn that so many million people are starving, the appeal to our conscience, as Eliot says, presupposes "a sympathy ready-made, a moral sentiment already in activity" (*Essays* 270). If we do not already care about what happens to other people, mere information about what is happening to them will not move us. But the artist can do something to change people who lack ready-made sympathy and active moral sentiment. By making us aware in imagination of what it is like to be one of these people, through a detailed description of their environment and their mental life, the artist "surprises even the trivial and the selfish into that attention to what is apart from themselves, which may be called the raw material of moral sentiment" (*Essays* 270). The description catches our attention, which would not otherwise be aroused by the bare mention of people who are remote from our immediate interest. Our attention results in cognitive and affective sympathy, which are not the same as moral sentiment, but nonetheless change our moral outlook.

Eliot sets out these aims in "The Natural History of German Life," her review of two books by Wilhelm von Riehl. Riehl's works are valuable because they accurately present Germans as they are. A novelist reasonably aims to arouse "the nobler emotions which make mankind desire the social right," but unreal stereotypes of (for instance) ignorant but virtuous rustics in "social novels" impede the desire for the social right.[15] If, for instance, *Adam Bede* presented a society of cheerful, contented, virtuous rustics, we might think that rural society is quite all right as it is. If it presented them as living a bestial existence with only the most primitive mental life, we might think that no elements of the social right can be found there. Charles Dickens is open to criticism for his idealizations. His physical descriptions are accurate, but his descriptions of the mental lives of his subjects are false. These false elements may mislead us about the social right.[16]

This criticism of Dickens is open to doubt. If practical results (the arousal of a desire for the social right) are the standard for evaluating a description, we might still wonder why some false descriptions might not lead us to draw the right practical conclusions. Eliot does not show that no false descriptions could have this effect. In her defense we might observe that the appropriate desire for the social right demands extended sympathy that is directed toward the people who need it. Since the people who need it are mostly quite unlike Fagin or Little Dorrit, reactions to Dickensian characters may not fit ordinary people who need extended sympathy. Sympathy is not a mere quantity of other-directed energy that might fuel sympathy for anyone we choose, in the way that the same petrol may be used to fuel any car we choose for any journey we choose. Since it involves a series of judgments about particular cases, it will be more useful if the particular fictional cases are fairly similar to the particular actual cases that will need our sympathy, and if the similarities are fairly easy to discern. Dickensian extremes (in Eliot's view) are not suitable for this purpose.

The demand for accurate description of characters and situations, therefore, results from Eliot's particularism. Perhaps we could learn appropriate general principles from extreme or unrealistic situations; indeed, these might be especially useful for this purpose. But if moral judgment requires particular judgments and recognition of similarity without reference to general principles, something closer to "natural history" is better for the formation of the right sort of moral judgment.

Though Eliot does not explicitly distinguish these three types of sympathy, the differences between them may help to explain some of what she says. When she claims that the novelist may surprise us into extended attention, she has something short of practical sympathy in mind. And if she identifies extended attention with extended sympathy, or takes the latter to follow necessarily from the former, she recognizes a type of sympathy that is distinct from practical sympathy. Whereas one might plausibly treat cognitive and affective sympathy as raw material for moral sentiment, practical sympathy is not raw material, but a part of moral sentiment. The benefit we owe to the novelist is extended cognitive and affective sympathy, not practical sympathy or moral sentiment. She does not say what else we need if we are to pass from extended cognitive and affective sympathy to moral sentiment itself.

The Escape from Moral Stupidity

But though she does not answer this question, she has more to say, or to convey, about the role of extended cognitive and affective sympathy in the formation of moral sentiment. Her novels would fulfill the role she describes in "The Natural History of German Life" if they simply presented a suitable variety of characters whose different mental lives were described fully enough to catch our attention. By reflecting on the different characters of Mrs. Poyser, Hetty, Rosamond, Gwendolen, Daniel Deronda, Casaubon, Savonarola, and so on, we might find our attention caught, and we might understand these different types of people better. But this is not all we get from the novels. We also watch different characters undergo the process that Eliot wants her readers to undergo.[17] We should, therefore, be able to form a clearer idea of the extension of sympathy by watching how it happens in the novels. Perhaps we can see how it is connected to moral sentiment.

In *Middlemarch* Dorothea's attention is extended by her understanding of Casaubon's distinct mental life.[18] Her recognition of a distinct consciousness that might not correspond exactly to one's own initial expectations of another person is connected with emancipation from egoism.[19] While Dorothea was already aware of the general truth that other people had distinct mental lives that were not designed to fit into her plans, this had been the awareness of reflection rather than feeling. But now she grasps it as feeling, rather than mere reflection, from seeing it in a particular case. She has been surprised into attention to a consciousness distinct from, and not subservient to, her own. She has acquired affective sympathy, which increases her cognitive sympathy, and allows her to apply it to this particular case.

Dorothea's experience releases her from "moral stupidity," a combination of selfishness with a view of the world as designed to suit one's own aims. We emerge from moral stupidity when we learn that the world is not arranged for our benefit. We also seem to emerge from selfishness and self-absorption; Dorothea begins to show more practical sympathy for Casaubon as he actually is, rather than as he would be if he fitted into her plans for herself. Towards the end of the novel, Rosamond emerges from moral stupidity with more difficulty. She responds to Dorothea's and Lydgate's affective and practical sympathy, and learns to care about them in their own right.[20]

On this basis we might argue that Eliot has described the natural growth of the emotions that ensure practical sympathy, and that therefore she has described the growth of the correct moral outlook that gives other people their appropriate weight in one's own choices. Indeed, we might use this account of moral development to support a constitutive, and not a merely indicative, view of the role of sympathy in morality. If Eliot's particularism is correct, and if the emotions of the impartially sympathetic person are our means of access to the morally right and wrong choices in particular cases, perhaps it is simply an illusion to suppose that we can measure the responses of the impartially sympathetic person against some independent standard of right and wrong. In other words, we may be tempted to allow our moral psychology and epistemology to determine the metaphysics of morality. While I do not mean to suggest that Eliot asks these questions, she may reasonably be taken to suggest answers to them. Moreover, if she has these answers in mind, her claims about the benefit we owe to the novelist are not at all exaggerated.

But is it plausible to claim that the necessary or usual result of the extension of attention and affective sympathy is practical sympathy? If I emerge from moral stupidity by learning that the world is not already adapted to my selfish ends, I might infer that I will have to adapt it by my own effort. This inference need not make me any less selfish. Greater cognitive sympathy with other people may help me to manipulate them more skillfully for my own purposes. My affective sympathy with others may secure their trust, and so make them easier to manipulate. This form of selfishness does not seem to involve the wishful thinking that Eliot describes as moral stupidity. But if it is possible, the extension of sympathy does not seem to ensure emancipation from the selfish outlook.

Tito Melema in *Romola* seems to illustrate this possibility. Tito manipulates different sorts of people—Baldassarre, Bardo, Romola, Savonarola, Tessa, Florentine and French politicians. He is able to manipulate them because they trust him. They trust him because he seems frank, open, and agreeable, but also because he knows what to say to them and what aspects of them he needs to appeal to in order to gain their friendship and confidence. He would not know what to say if he did not know what they are like, and how they are different from him. It would be difficult to represent Tito as immersed in "moral stupidity" on the ground that he sees the world as an udder to feed his supreme self. If he had held this view of the world, he would not have been as bad as he is. Perhaps Hetty in *Adam Bede* is the sort of person who never gets beyond the naïve condition that Eliot calls moral stupidity. But Tito is not like her. He seems to have extended his sympathy but used his extended sympathy for the wrong purposes.

One might reject this conclusion about Tito, on the ground that he has acquired only cognitive sympathy, but not affective sympathy. If he had really been able to represent other people's feelings, so that he felt how they felt, he would have cared more than he actually cares about their sufferings. Though he knew what Baldassarre was like and how he felt, he did not really share his suffering, but simply took further precautions against him.

It is true that Tito is not described as affectively sympathetic to the people whom he understands well enough to gain their confidence. Perhaps Eliot would say this in answer to the suggestion that he is sympathetic but selfish. But would this be a good answer? Affective sympathy does not necessarily seem to produce practical sympathy. We might be able to imagine the sufferings of others so vividly that we share them; we might even find it painful to share them; but this pain might not deter us from trying to benefit ourselves at their expense.

Does this conception of affective sympathy miss Eliot's point about the effects of genuine sympathy? Baldassarre, we might argue, found it not only painful, but intolerable, to be betrayed by Tito. If, therefore, Tito had felt what Baldassarre felt, he would also have felt it to be intolerable. Since he does not feel this, he lacks real affective sympathy with Baldassarre.

This argument, however, proves too much, because it implies that we lack affective sympathy for someone else unless we endorse their evaluation of the pain they suffer. Perhaps a child cannot bear to be denied something that is bad for him; but we do not lack affective sympathy simply because we deny it to him. If affective sympathy required us to endorse the other person's evaluation, it would lead to immoral conclusions. Hence Tito's failure to endorse Baldassarre's evaluation does not show that he lacks morally appropriate affective sympathy.

We may certainly agree that Tito has not emerged from moral stupidity, if emergence from it requires the formation of practical sympathy. But agreement on this point is no help to Eliot. Practical sympathy already presupposes morality; to say that he lacks practical sympathy just tells us what we already know, that he lacks morality. We still do not know what aspect of the sympathetic basis of morality he lacks.

Tito, therefore, seems to provide a good example of someone who attends to the distinct mental life of other people, and therefore has emerged from moral stupidity, but has still not acquired practical sympathy.[21] Eliot gives us a good reason to conclude—whatever she concludes—that the process she describes in Dorothea and in Rosamond may result either in more effective and more sensitive practical sympathy or in greater skill in selfish manipulation.

The Relation of Sympathy to Morality

This conclusion raises an objection to a constitutive view of the relation of sympathy to morality. If sympathy consists only in cognitive and affective sympathy, the outlook of the sympathetic observer is not the moral outlook. In Tito Melema cognitive and affective sympathy do not ensure practical concern for the good of others, and, since we take the moral outlook to include such a concern, sympathy is insufficient for the moral outlook. To defend the constitutive view, we would have to show that it is a mistake to require the moral outlook to include concern for the good of others. But that requirement is not only reasonable in itself, but also central in Eliot's conception of morality.

But if she is to defend the indicative view, she needs to presuppose some conception of morality that does not simply define it as the outlook of the sympathetic observer, but requires effective concern for the good of others besides oneself. And for reasons we have seen, she cannot plausibly maintain that sympathy detects what is morally right, so understood. Hence she seems to give no good reason to accept the indicative view either.

These remarks about the relation of sympathy to morality may not contradict anything that Eliot says. She claims only that the novelist can catch and extend our attention, and thereby extend our sympathy. She takes extended attention to be only the raw material of moral sentiment. It may be unfair to criticize her for exaggeration of the moral importance of sympathy, if we stick to what we can find in the novels.

The criticism, however, does not seem wholly unfair. The passages we have quoted from the essays do not suggest the subordinate role for sympathy that we have described. If she had recognized that sympathy is a subordinate element in the moral outlook, she might reasonably have been expected to say more than she says about the other components of a sound moral outlook. She might, for instance, have drawn a less sharp contrast between the "men of maxims" and the sympathetic observer of particular situations. She contrasts the sympathetic observer with the people who rely exclusively on general rules, and she remarks that we go wrong if we rely on general rules without sympathetic observation of particulars. She does not, however, remark that the converse is also true.

This observation needs to be qualified. Eliot describes Daniel Deronda as a victim of enlarged sympathy that threatens to result in practical paralysis. But he does not escape this paralysis by coming to accept moral principles that are external to sympathy. He seeks and finds "the influence that would justify partiality" in his discovery of his Jewish origins.[22] This particular social connection concentrates his sympathies in a particular direction and prevents their paralyzing dispersal. This is not the limitation of sympathy by maxims.

A more pertinent example is the treatment of Caleb Garth in *Middlemarch*. He is Bulstrode's agent, and has the opportunity to help Mary and Fred by securing the tenancy of Stone Court for Fred from Bulstrode. But, having learned from Raffles about Bulstrode's past, he decides to resign as Bulstrode's agent and to do nothing about Stone Court.[23] He does not lack sympathy for Mary and Fred or for Bulstrode, but it does not change his mind about what he has to do. Bulstrode's reply offers three or four "pleas that might be adapted to his hearer's mind"—conscience and God (perhaps identified), sympathy, and self-interest.[24] But they do not move Caleb.[25] He rejects a purely theocentric view of conscience. He admits the legitimacy of an appeal to sympathy, but denies that it requires him to agree with Bulstrode. He refuses to be connected with someone who has done what Bulstrode has done.[26]

Caleb's reply might be found unsatisfactory. His later statement of his resolution is no clearer:[27] If he simply meant that he would find it painful to work with Bulstrode, he might appear selfish. Should he not prefer the happiness of others—Fred, Mary, all the people who would benefit from his connection with Bulstrode—to his own happiness? We would misunderstand the point, however, if we took him in this way. He would be unhappy because he is convinced it would be wrong to profit from wrongdoing, even if it benefited himself and others.

Though Caleb refuses to work for Bulstrode, he also promises not to betray him. He states a general rule that includes an appropriate qualification, and assures Bulstrode that he will keep this qualified rule.[28] This chapter begins by quoting the rule from Sirach: "If thou hast heard a word, let it die with thee." (Sirach 19:10). Though Eliot does not say so, Caleb's qualification of the rule also comes from Sirach: "With friend or foe do not report it, and unless it would be a sin for you, do not disclose it" (19:8).

Caleb appears to oppose the view of Dr. Kenn in *The Mill on the Floss*. Whereas Dr. Kenn rejects the view of the men of maxims and is guided by his sympathies in the particular case, Caleb is a man of maxims, even of Biblical maxims, which he follows without reference to his sympathies. This opposition, however, is only superficial. Since Caleb denies that his moral outlook depends on a reference to God, and he expresses his pity for Bulstrode and his affection for Mary and Fred, he recognizes the legitimate pleas of sympathy and particular circumstances. But he decides that they do not justify him in profiting from wrongdoing. His judgment on this point is sounder than that of the thoughtful and educated Lydgate.

We might infer from this case that morality cannot be reduced to sympathy, but, on the contrary, sympathy needs to be guided by morality. If Caleb had been moved by sympathy, and had not recognized that the course of action suggested by sympathy would be wrong, apparently he would have acted wrongly by accepting any connection with Bulstrode. But is this conclusion too dogmatic? Perhaps Eliot simply points out the complexity and difficulty of Caleb's position, and does not unequivocally endorse the decision he makes.

But even if we concede this point, we do not reduce the distance between sympathy and morality. If the sympathetic outlook were the moral outlook, we would have no reason to doubt that the decision prompted by fully-informed sympathy is morally right. In fact, however, Caleb's reflection and decision raise morally relevant questions that an appeal to sympathy does not answer. We draw mistaken moral conclusions from her novels if we concentrate on the extension of sympathy. For in some especially difficult moral situations sympathy leads us astray unless it is guided by virtue and sound moral judgment.

If this is a reasonable estimate, Eliot's view about the greatest benefit we owe to the novelist is mistaken, or at least incomplete. She regards her novels as means to the extension of our sympathy. But they also show why sympathy is an unsuitable foundation for morality.

How, then, should we estimate her claim to be an "aesthetic" teacher, who rouses "the nobler emotions which make mankind desire the social right"? Reflection on her novels may reasonably be expected to arouse these emotions in readers who approach them with moderately sound moral beliefs. But the sound beliefs have to come from elsewhere. Cumming and Young would have good reason to welcome this conclusion. She accuses them of obstructing true moral development by ignoring "the direct promptings of the sympathetic feelings."[29] But they might fairly observe, on the basis of her novels rather than her polemical essays, that the direct promptings of the sympathetic feelings may also obstruct true moral development if they are not guided by true moral principles.

NOTES

1 This and the following extracts from the letters are quoted and discussed by Harvey, 38–52.

2 Eliot outgrew her early admiration for Young because she realized that he was deficient in the appropriate sort of sympathy. "[With some exceptions] . . . there is hardly a trace of human sympathy, of self-forgetfulness in the joy or sorrow of a fellow-being, throughout this long poem . . ." (*Essays* 371–72). Where Young fails, Cowper succeeds, despite his harsh and gloomy Calvinistic outlook. "Yet, see how a lovely, sympathetic nature manifests itself in spite of creed and circumstance! . . . that close and vivid presentation of particular sorrows and privations, of particular deeds and misdeeds, which is the direct road to the emotions" (*Essays* 381–72).

3 "And his ethics correspond [sic] to his religion. He . . . never changes his level so as to see beyond the horizon of mere selfishness. . . . Virtue, with Young, must always squint— must never look straight toward the immediate object of its emotion and effort" (*Essays* 378).

4 Eliot speaks of "a delicate sense of our neighbour's rights, an active participation in the joys and sorrows of our fellow-men, a magnanimous acceptance of privation or suffering for ourselves when it is the condition of good to others, in a word, the extension and inten-

sification of our sympathetic nature . . ." (*Essays* 375).

5 "But next to the hatred of the enemies of God . . . , there perhaps has been no perversion more obstructive of true moral development than this substitution of a reference to the glory of God for the direct promptings of the sympathetic feelings . . . only in proportion as it is compassion that speaks through the eyes when we soothe, and moves the arm when we succour, is a deed strictly benevolent" (*Essays* 187).

6 "I am just and honest . . . because, having felt the pain of injustice and dishonesty toward myself, I have a fellow-feeling with other men, who would suffer the same pain if I were unjust or dishonest toward them. . . . I have a tender love for my wife, and children, and friends, and through that love I sympathize with like affections in other men. It is a pang to me to witness the sufferings of a fellow-being . . ." (*Essays* 373–34).

7 Readers who want fuller discussion of moral philosophers I mention might consult Whewell (especially relevant since he is a contemporary of Eliot), Schneewind, Gill, Irwin (vol. 2). Dixon (ch. 3) discusses Eliot's views on altruism and sympathy.

8 This division is derived from, though not identical to, distinctions marked by Adam Smith.

9   Anger (80) first mentions sympathy as a capacity to imagine another's state of mind, but also describes it as being identical to, or closely connected to, altruism.

10 "Now, emotion links itself with particulars, and only in a faint and secondary manner with abstractions. . . . Generalities are the refuge at once of deficient intellectual activity and deficient feeling" (*Essays* 371).

11 "Another indication of Young's deficiency in moral, i.e., in sympathetic emotion, is his unintermitting habit of pedagogic moralizing . . . in proportion as morality is emotional, i.e., has affinity with Art, it will exhibit itself in direct sympathetic feeling and action, and not as the recognition of a rule. Love does not say, 'I ought to love'—it loves. Pity does not say, 'It is right to be pitiful'—it pities. Justice does not say, 'I am bound to be just'—it feels justly. It is only where moral emotion is comparatively weak that the contemplation of a rule or theory habitually mingles with its action . . . the minds which are pre-eminently didactic—which insist on a 'lesson,' and despise everything that will not convey a moral, are deficient in sympathetic emotion" (*Essays* 379).

12 "The casuists have become a byword of reproach; but their perverted spirit of minute discrimination was the shadow of a truth to which eyes and hearts are too often fatally sealed,—the truth, that moral judgments must remain false and hollow, unless they are checked and enlightened by a perpetual reference to the special circumstances that mark the individual lot. All people of broad, strong sense have an instinctive repugnance to the men of maxims; because such people early discern that the mysterious complexity of our life is not to be embraced by maxims, and that to lace ourselves up in formulas of that sort is to repress all the divine promptings and inspirations that spring from growing insight and sympathy" (*The Mill on the Floss* 437–38; bk. 7, ch. 2). Surprisingly, Fleishman (55–56) takes Eliot's particularism to be similar to Mill's utilitarianism. Some pros and cons of particularism are discussed in Hooker and Little.

13 When Eliot edited G. H. Lewes's work for posthumous publication, she inserted several references to sympathy (see Dixon 110; Collins 484–92). Her attitude to Lewes's views on altruism and its origins is discussed by Shuttleworth (170).

14 "Let our habitual talk give morals their full meaning as that conduct which, in every human relation, would follow from the fullest knowledge and the fullest sympathy—a meaning perpetually corrected and modified by a more thorough appreciation of dependence in things, and a finer sensibility to both physical and spiritual fact. . . ." (*Theophrastus Such* 241; "Moral Swindlers"). This is appositely quoted in a good short account of Eliot's ethics by Holloway (125–26).

15 "But our social novels profess to represent the people as they are, and the unreality of their representations is a grave evil. The greatest benefit we owe to the artist, whether painter, poet, or novelist, is the extension of our sympathies. Appeals founded on generalizations and statistics require a sympathy ready-made, a moral sentiment already in activity; but a picture of human life such as a great artist can give, surprises even the trivial and the selfish into that attention to what is apart from themselves, which may be called the raw material of moral sentiment" (*Essays* 270).

16 Dixon (110) notices Eliot's use of the Comtean term "altruism" (not a favourite term of hers) in her description of Dickens's picture of the working classes.

17 This process is studied at length by Paris, with references to different characters in the novels (chs. 3, 7–9).

18 "Today she had begun to see that she had been under a wild illusion in expecting a response to her feeling from Mr Casaubon, and she had felt the waking of a presentiment that there might be a sad consciousness in his life which made as great a need on his side as on her own" (205; ch. 21).

19 "We are all of us born in moral stupidity, taking the world as an udder to feed our supreme selves: Dorothea had early begun to emerge from that stupidity, but yet it had been easier to her to imagine how she would devote herself to Mr Casaubon, . . . than to conceive with that distinctness which is no longer reflection but feeling . . . that he had an equivalent centre of self, whence the lights

and shadows must always fall with a certain difference" (*Middlemarch* 205; ch. 21).

20 Some readers may believe that this is an exaggeration of Rosamond's progress in sympathy.

21 Ermarth describes contrasting degrees of sympathy in Tito and Romola (27–31). It is not clear how far Ermarth's conception of sympathy (27) corresponds to Eliot's conception.

22 "But how and whence was the needed event to come?—the influence that would justify partiality, and make him what he longed to be, yet was unable to make himself—an organic part of social life . . ." (336; ch. 32). The effects of sympathy on Deronda are discussed by Jaffe (ch. 5).

23 "Caleb felt a deep pity for him [Bulstrode], but he could have used no pretexts to account for his resolve, even if they would have been of any use" (683; ch. 69).

24 "'You are a conscientious man, Mr Garth—a man, I trust, who feels himself accountable to God. You would not wish to injure me by being too ready to believe a slander', said Bulstrode, casting about for pleas that might

be adapted to his hearer's mind. 'That is a poor reason for giving up a connection which I think I may say will be mutually beneficial'" (683; ch. 69).

25 [Caleb] "But my brethren who went up with me made the heart of the people melt; yet I wholly followed the Lord my God" (Joshua 14:8).

26 "'I would injure no man if I could help it', said Caleb; "'even if I thought God winked at it. I hope I should have a feeling for my fellow-creature. But, sir—I am obliged to believe that this Raffles has told me the truth. And I can't be happy in working with you, or profiting by you. It hurts my mind'" (683; ch. 69).

27 "'But I have that feeling inside me, that I can't go on working with you. That's all, Mr Bulstrode'" (684; ch. 69).

28 "'As to speaking, I hold it a crime to expose a man's sin unless I'm clear it must be done to save the innocent. That is my way of thinking, Mr Bulstrode, and what I say, I've no need to swear'" (*Middlemarch* 684; ch. 69).

29 *Essays* 187; see Note 7 above.

REFERENCES

Anger, Suzy. "George Eliot and Philosophy." *The Cambridge Companion to Eliot*. Ed. George Levine. Cambridge: Cambridge UP, 2001. 76–97.

Collins, K. K. "G. H. Lewes Revised: George Eliot and the Moral Sense." *Victorian Studies* 21.4 (1978): 463–92.

Dixon, Thomas. *The Invention of Altruism: Making Moral Meanings in Victorian Britain*. Oxford: Oxford UP, 2008.

Eliot, George. *Daniel Deronda*. Ed. Graham Handley. Oxford: Clarendon, 1984.

Eliot, George. *Essays of George Eliot*. Ed. Thomas Pinney. London: Routledge, 1963.

Eliot, George. *Impressions of Theophrastus Such*. London: Virtue, n.d.

Eliot, George. *Middlemarch*. Ed. David Carroll. Oxford: Clarendon, 1986.

Eliot, George. *The George Eliot Letters*. Ed. Gordon S. Haight. 9 vols. New Haven: Yale UP, 1954–78.

Eliot, George. *The Mill on the Floss*. Ed. Gordon S. Haight. Oxford: Clarendon, 1980.

Ermarth, Elizabeth Deeds. "George Eliot's Conception of Sympathy." *Nineteenth-Century Fiction* 40.1 (1985): 23–42.

Fleishman, Avrom. *George Eliot's Intellectual Life*. Cambridge: Cambridge UP, 2010.

Gill, Michael B. *The British Moralists on Human Nature and the Birth of Secular Ethics*. Cambridge: Cambridge UP, 2006.

Harvey, W. J. *The Art of George Eliot*. London: Chatto, 1961.

Holloway, John. *The Victorian Sage*. London: Macmillan, 1953.

Hooker, Brad and Margaret Little, eds. *Moral Particularism*. Oxford: Oxford UP, 2000.

Irwin, T. H. *The Development of Ethics.* 3 vols. Oxford: Oxford UP, 2007–09.

Jaffe, Audrey. *Scenes of Sympathy: Identity and Representation in Victorian Fiction.* Ithaca: Cornell UP, 2000.

Paris, Bernard J. *Experiments in Life: George Eliot's Quest for Values.* Detroit: Wayne State UP, 1965.

Schneewind, Jerome B. *The Invention of Autonomy: A History of Modern Moral Philosophy.* Cambridge: Cambridge UP, 1997.

Shuttleworth, Sally. *George Eliot and Nineteenth-Century Science: The Make-Believe of a Beginning.* Cambridge: Cambridge UP, 1984.

Whewell, William. *Lectures on the History of Moral Philosophy in England.* London: Parker, 1852.

21

George Eliot, Spinoza, and the Emotions

Isobel Armstrong

Introduction: The Importance of Spinoza

"Mind—I really want this," George Eliot wrote to Sara Hennell on 28 February 1847. What she wanted so emphatically was the edition of Spinoza's works that she had been forced to return, with some irritation, to Dr. R. H. Brabant, the man who had introduced her to German criticism. She asked Sara to obtain from the publisher, John Chapman, whom she had recently met, "the same edition if possible" (*Letters* 1:232). (The payment of the two-shilling carriage cost caused problems right until September.) She seems to have been contemplating a translation of Spinoza's work as early as 1849, though she disavowed this possibility in a letter to Charles Bray, arguing that a translation in itself would not help unless the complexity of his thought could be understood (*Letters* 1:321). Whether she read G. H. Lewes's article on Spinoza in the *Westminster Review* in 1843, "Spinoza's Life and Works," later to be incorporated in his *Biographical History of Philosophy* (1857), it is hard to say. She was not to meet him until 1851. Certainly, the first major piece of work she undertook after she and Lewes decided to live together in 1854 was a translation of the *Ethics*, begun in Berlin three months after their union was consolidated. "Wednesday [November] 8. Began translating Spinoza's Ethics," her journal records (*Journals* 33). It was an enthusiasm both of them had, for Lewes was working on his life of Goethe, with whose respect for Spinoza she was familiar. "Read, at dinner, his [Goethe's] wonderful observations on Spinoza. Particularly struck with the beautiful modesty of the passage in which he says he cannot presume to say that he thoroughly understands Spinoza' (*Journals*

A Companion to George Eliot, First Edition. Edited by Amanda Anderson and Harry E. Shaw.

40). Her translation was never published in her lifetime. It lay dormant until 1981, when it was edited by Thomas Deegan.

The *Ethics* was a formative text. It does not merely supplement what we know of Eliot's response to the affects through the classical idea of sympathy, but provides a new perspective on her writing. Spinoza helps us thematize elements of her work, but the account of the affects derived from him is important not simply at the thematic level but as a structural and organizing principle of the novels. From 1847 to 1856 when the translation was completed, nearly ten years, Spinoza was on her mind. In the almost two years it took to complete the translation, she was saturated in Spinoza's thought. Her journal records a virtually daily discipline of translation. The terse "Worked at Spinoza" or merely "Spinoza," is recurrent throughout the weeks in Germany and dominated her time (*Journals* 33–47). Through colds, through headaches—"Head not clear, so I did not get through much of Spinoza this morning" (38)—through the impossibly cold winter in Berlin, she continued her work unremittingly. Lewes subsequently withdrew the translation from Bohn in an argument about terms (the bad-tempered correspondence is conveniently collected in an appendix to Dorothy Atkins's *George Eliot and Spinoza*), and Eliot's reaction to this is not recorded. But it is astonishing that neither of them subsequently pursued a publisher for this publication-ready manuscript. Even though, as later work indicates, Lewes's attachment to Spinoza was lifelong (Lewes, *Problems* 333–52).

The effect of this break is the tacit assumption among critics and biographers that Spinoza dies out of Eliot's life after 1856. The exception is Dorothy Atkins's work, mentioned above. His formative influence can be seen right up to *Daniel Deronda*, indeed, particularly in this work. She connected Jewishness with Spinoza, not only because Spinoza was a Jew, though an excommunicated one, but because while she was translating the *Ethics* Jewishness was a theme in her German life. Lewes acted Shylock in company with the actor, Dessoir, who visited them, and at another party:

> I was amused to see that the young women's feeling towards the Jews was not much above that of Gratiano and co. Frau Gruppe when running through the wonderful speech "Hath not a Jew eyes" etc turned round to us and said "They don't feel – they don't care how they are used." (*Journals* 39)

Thus race and the politics of community were bound up with Spinoza from the beginning. Proposition 46 of the *Ethics* is apposite: if someone imagines himself threatened by a person "under the universal name of class or nation," he will "hate, not only that person, but everyone of the same class or nation" (Eliot [trans.], *Ethics* 178).

Traditions of Affect

Eliot read Charles Darwin's *The Expression of the Emotions in Man and Animals* (1872) eagerly, and Angelique Richardson has brilliantly demonstrated the significance of this modern text for her. I concentrate on older traditions governing the affects and the expression of emotion available to Eliot. One, the distortion and anamorphosis of the "Grotesque" associated with Dickens, was explicitly repudiated by G. H. Lewes, and by Eliot as merely "the external traits of our town population" (*Selected Essays* 111). We meet the term "sympathy," another tradition, frequently in Eliot's work. Here it is, famously, in a prose essay, "The Natural History of German Life," and a novel, *The Mill on the Floss*:

> The greatest benefit we owe to the artist, whether painter, poet, or novelist, is the extension of our sympathies. (*Selected Essays* 110)

> . . . the mysterious complexity of life is not to be embraced by maxims . . . to lace ourselves up in formulas is to repress all the divine promptings and inspirations that spring from growing insight and sympathy. (518; bk. 7, ch. 2)

This use of the term "sympathy" as the willing projection of imagination into the condition of another derives, of course, from Enlightenment aesthetics and in particular from Adam Smith's adumbration of sympathy as the basis of the social affects in his *Theory of the Moral Sentiments*. We have no immediate experience of what other men feel except by imagining through our own senses what that might be and putting ourselves in the place of the other. Smith gives the famous example of "our brother" on the rack (2). To "change places in fancy" through "fellow-feeling" with the sufferer activates our own senses and feelings so that we summon them up and "copy" them to arrive at an imaginative identification with his torture, becoming "in some measure the same person with him" (3).

Eliot widened and deepened the idea of sympathy. Smith set many limits on the range of imaginative sympathy: though he admitted that sympathy was precipitated by corporeal impulses—anticipating a blow to another "we naturally shrink and draw back our own leg" (4)—he deemed it "indecent" (52) to express the passions springing from the body, sexual feeling, pain, or hunger. Physical pain could not be the source of tragedy—"What a tragedy would that be, of which the distress consisted in a colic" (60). He ruled out the seemingly anti-social identifications, such as empathy with love (which publicly expressed incited ridicule), or anger. Propriety, reserve, and distance govern sympathy, and above all the sense that the imagination is over against and outside the body. Despite his instance of the person on the rack, for the would-be sympathizer the imagination of familiar and fortunate conditions more readily appeal to the imagination.

Eliot spoke, on the contrary, about the extension of the sympathies, and saw feeling as a deeply corporeal experience. Rather than the total identification of empathy, a critical sympathy that explored difference was her aim, as Elizabeth Deeds Ermarth has argued. One can see this in the deliberate movement from centers of consciousness in *Middlemarch* and in the "intensive patterning" (Hardy 10) of rotating stories in the novel, which brings parallel narratives into contrast with one another. The projection of feeling brings understanding in its train. The experience of the expressive emotions draws us nearer to communal life, as in *The Spanish Gypsy*, when Fedalma gives way to impulse and dances, discovering that the release of feeling in the physical power of dance gives her an intense emotional identification with the watching crowd. Sympathy dissolves her sense of self.

> Oh! I seemed new-waked
> To life in unison with a multitude—
> Feeling my soul upbourne by all their souls,
> Floating with their gladness! Soon I lost
> All sense of separateness: Fedalma died
> As a star dies, and melts into the light.
> I was not, but joy was, and love and triumph.
>
> (1:93)

Eliot invoked the principle of sympathy at crucial moments of authorial comment. "I share with you this sense of oppressive narrowness; but it is necessary that we should feel it, if we care to understand how it acted on the lives of Tom and Maggie," she wrote, in *The Mill on the Floss*. It was a narrowness felt by the characters themselves as a young generation, but "to which they have been nevertheless tied by the strongest fibres of their hearts" (284; bk. 4, ch.1). The cardiac metaphor of fiber beautifully suggests the organic filaments of vein, artery, and corpuscle—the tie to the environment is corporeal and comes from within—at the same time as it indicates the external presence of net and bond. The tactics of this appeal for an assent to complexity are subtle. The writer performs the act of imagination herself as she identifies with the supposed thoughts of a cosmopolitan reader—"I share with you"—asks for a reciprocal act of understanding, and then proceeds to generalize the experience of "young natures in many generations" in an assent-building move. If this agreement is granted, the metaphor of simultaneous bondage and organic, corporeal fusion with an environment that culminates the appeal consolidates both the contradiction of the Tulliver experience and the reader's consent to it through the imaginative projection of sympathy.

For all its skill, however, this rhetoric of sympathy, combining rational generalization, performative imaginative projection, and metaphor, establishes a certain distance both from the Tullivers' emotional experience and from the act of projection itself. Its appeal for affective inwardness describes the act of sympathy as a *possible* lived experience rather than evoking it. The request for sympathy "produces" sympathy as a form of meta-commentary. It's a description at one remove. Sympathy's lack of closeness to the ontological experience of emotion could make Eliot the object of a critique, such as Nietzsche's, that abjured her conscientious "bluestocking" morality (80).

And yet there is plenty of expressive emotion in Eliot's novels. With a well-bred recoil, Virginia Woolf complained of Eliot's emotionalism—"the brewing and gathering and thickening of the cloud which will burst upon our heads at the moment of crisis in a shower of disillusionment and verbosity." Eliot herself, in her "Notes on

Form in Art," affirmed that poetry, by which she included all literary production, consisted of "relations and groups of relations" that "are more or less not only determined by emotion but intended to express it" (*Selected Essays* 233). "*Poetry* begins when passion weds thought by finding expression in an image; but *Poetic Form* begins with a choice of elements, however meagre as the accordant expression of emotional states" (*Selected Essays* 235).

"Sympathy" is less likely to explain these "emotional states," I believe, than an understanding of Eliot's response to Spinoza. This helps to restore the "salt and spice" that William Hale White (also Spinoza's translator) missed in accounts of Eliot. I turn now to what Eliot's translation of the *Ethics* would have shown her. The final section considers form and emotional states in *Daniel Deronda*, with a brief preface on *Middlemarch*.

Spinoza on Love and Hate

The only book-length study of Spinoza's thought and its relation to George Eliot, Atkins's admirable *George Eliot and Spinoza*, makes it clear that Eliot was attracted to his thought by a number of general principles. Spinoza's refusal of an anthropomorphic God, who would be, as Lewes reminded his readers in 1857, a God of "blind cupidity and insatiable avarice" (*Biographical History* 407), was one of these. The paradoxical thinking that led to such statements as "we desire nothing because we judge it to be good, but on the contrary, we call it good because we desire it" (Curley 175), conduces to the "spice" that Hale White recognized in Eliot. Atkins believes that the overcoming of bondage to the passions through rational understanding was of prime importance to Eliot, as to Spinoza. Her analysis of *Adam Bede* shows how Adam overcomes this bondage. She sees the novels as structurally organized round antithetical characters who transcend bondage or succumb to it. "Often characters are paired thematically—Hetty Sorrel with Dinah Morris, and Gwendolen Harleth with Daniel Deronda—to show parallel struggles for freedom from bondage" (10). Her reading of Spinoza is characterological and individual whereas Eliot also saw his significance for social and even socio-economic experience. In the interest of establishing general moral patterns, Atkins ignores the detailed inventory of emotional states that appears in Part Three of the *Ethics*. Understandably, since at first sight Part Three, adopting the model of geometrical proof, documents varieties of emotional and passional experience that seem "self-evident axioms" (20). But it is clear that Eliot understood the significance of this section of the *Ethics*, which she completed translating in London on 11 April 1855. Earlier, writing to Bray in 1849, she had referred to this seeming obviousness. It is as if we are listening to "a conversation of a person of great capacity who has led a solitary life, and who says from his own soul what all the world is saying by rote" (*Letters* 1:321).

As examples of this seeming self-evidence we might quote Propositions 22 and 25.

> *If we imagine someone to affect with joy a thing we love, we shall be affected with love towards him. If, on the other hand, we imagine him to affect the same thing with sadness, we shall also be affected with hate towards him.* (Curley 166)
> Eliot: If we imagine a person as causing pleasure to the being we love, we shall love this person. If, on the contrary, we imagine him as causing pain to the beloved being, we hate him. (*Ethics* 109)

> *We strive to affirm, concerning ourselves and what we love, whatever we imagine to affect with joy ourselves and what we love. On the other hand, we strive to deny whatever we imagine affects with sadness ourselves or what we love.* (Curley 167)
> Eliot: We strive to affirm of ourselves or of the being we love what we imagine affecting us or the beloved being with pleasure: on the contrary we strive to deny that which we imagine affecting us or the being we love with pain. (*Ethics* 111)

Eliot grasped that these statements belong to an account of a network of inter-related and interactive emotional conditions that spread from the self and other to the other's other and beyond. In Part Three of the *Ethics*, "On the Origin and Nature of the Emotions," she found a reading of the emotions—a raw, voracious, ruthless, importunate, and incremental energy—that is quite unlike the rational moral affective structures at work in Adam Smith's theory. Spinoza's striving, desire-centered being is alien to Smith's account of the self's knowing projection of the imagination into the condition of the other in recognition of fellow feeling. "*Each thing, as far as it can by its own power, strives to persevere in its being,*" and this striving is "*nothing but the actual essence of the thing*" (Curley 159). "Every thing, as far as in it lies, strives to persevere in its existence," Eliot's translation runs (*Ethics* 100). Instead of the displacement of the self in the act of sympathy we have the peremptory desire of the being who swings between love and hate and whose measure of experience is not the other but "someone like us" (Curley 168). Where Smith is essentially Cartesian, assuming that the mind has power over the body as it strives to change places in fancy with another being, Spinoza denied this distinction and to him its specious freedom. It is a fallacy that "*the mind can have absolute dominion over its affects*" (Curley 153). Though at the mercy of hunger, for instance, "the infant believes he freely wants the milk" (157). "So the infant believes that it freely seeks the breast," Eliot writes more graphically (97). Yet the advantage of this very bondage is that the affects do not fall out of consciousness as extraneous, invasive elements, hostile to rationality. They are what makes consciousness work. For Spinoza body and mind, extension and thought, are two aspects of the same reality working in parallel. They are of one another, not over and against each other. Affects are generated in and through the body, and it is through the corporeal experience of the body that *images* are aroused (Curley 168). Imaging and the imagination are at the core of all affective experience. (And perhaps we might even say, all experience.) Spinoza sometimes writes as if these *are* the affects: "the images of things are the very affections of the human body" (171).

If we imagine; he who imagines; whatever we imagine. These are constant and invariable formulations used in almost all the Propositions concerning affect and whenever Spinoza wants to describe the arousal effected by emotion in the body. The subject does not *immediately* think or feel, it imagines. The arousal of imagination is continuous with the body, and reacts with it. It is a bodily form of knowledge, the consequence, though Spinoza does not say so, of the passing into consciousness of sense stimuli. To imagine an affect is to have it and to have it is to imagine it. Thus the imagination is the source of the greatest ecstasy—"the image in the lover of the loved thing's joy" (166); "Joy posits the existence of the joyous thing" (167)—and the greatest anguish, as the being is torn apart by hatred and envy.

The imagination is not an extension of self. It is immediate, coercive, fiercely corporeal, and involuntary. It lives in the eternal present, and is therefore outside time (168). Like so many Spinozan structures, this freedom from temporality has positive and negative possibilities. At once in thrall to the present, the mind is yet freed into infinity: when it loves its love is infinite, as God's is, and as it is an attribute of God. When it hates, exactly the same conditions operate, and the infinite present captures hate. Projection implies space and time. Rather than constituting projection the imagination is importunately mimetic. It appropriates the affects of the other and desires the other to love and hate the same things as it loves and hates (Proposition 31). And yet precisely because it *is* an image and not a wholly physiological impulse an affect image is a primitive form of knowing, the first epistemological moment, and initiates that process by which we know what we feel and feel what we know. The mind, intellect, mediates images, and, as we shall see, this gap between image and idea is what can enable the overcoming of bondage to the passions. But this mediation is equally capable of incrementally intensifying the violence of the affects by the sheer reflexive insight a being may gain into its imagination through the imagination.

In the *Ethics* Spinoza sets up both a logic and a phenomenology of the affects. His propositions are set up as geometrical axioms because, like geometry, the affects are part of nature, or what he would call "Substance," and cannot fall outside it. All the emotions and passions he documents are derived from just three elements—striving, or desire, pleasure, and pain. Desire is the dynamic that activates pleasure and pain. It is the agent of change. Pleasure, joy, bliss, or blessedness is an active emotion, transforming the body's energy involuntarily. Spinoza reserves the term "emotion" for these. Pain, sadness, or suffering, lack, and fear, are passive feelings, essentially depleting and negative, likewise draining the body of energy. Spinoza reserves the term "passion" for these feelings, which act upon the body. The privation that pain sets in motion means that the self's constitutional lack disables it from finding ideas adequate to an understanding of it—we might say it is impossible to theorize its lack. Impossible because the subject tries to deny and repress lack. The energy of joy is conducive to theorization. We recognize this tri-partite constellation of feeling later in the work of Freud. But there is no unconscious in Spinoza's logic. Pleasure and pain have their counterparts in love and hatred. Love and hatred are inherently social: they are necessitated by other people. "Hence there is nothing more useful to man than man" (Eliot [trans.], *Ethics* 169). The sociality of the affects, however, work in equal and opposite ways, they can be creative and destructive. And this leads to a complex insight: as well as reaching deep into communal life, both emotions and passions depend on a logic of self-augmentation and incremental aggregation. They are self-compounding as they encounter the pathways or alternatively the blocks to energy. Hatred is libidinal. It is always in surplus.

Spinoza's bias is toward an analysis of hate because the destructiveness of hate is so powerful—"But here we attend only to hate," he says at almost midpoint in Part Three (Curley 167). The formulations of hatred are particularly brutal as in Propositions 23, 24, 32 and 39:

> *He who imagines what he hates to be affected with sadness will rejoice.* (166)
> *If we imagine someone to affect with joy a thing we hate, we shall be affected with hatred to him also.* (167)
> *If we imagine that someone enjoys something that only one can possess, we shall strive to bring it about that he does not possess it.* (171)
> *He who hates someone will strive to do evil to him.* (174)

"[M]en are naturally inclined to hate and envy" (182) through the logic of desire and striving itself. If one's essence is to strive, the mind cannot but imagine also the state of lack: depleted by this knowledge men are "glad of their equals' weakness and saddened by their equals' virtue" (182). In place of these almost Blake-like axioms of hell, Spinoza held that the neediness of hate can be destroyed by love (Proposition 43). This is partly because the active striving for bliss is stronger than the drive of passion, with its diminished power of action (bliss isn't generated by blocks and denials), and partly because of the inherent power of mind to move from the states of sense perception bound up with the image, to an understanding of the limits of reason and to the positing of a directly felt experience—"Joy posits the existence of the joyous thing" (67). When we move to *Daniel Deronda*, much that is said of pride and contempt, and the critique of compassion as a form of envy, will be relevant. Spinoza in fact warned that the codifications he offered were actually forms of the same feelings in different social situations, and that names for emotions do not actually correlate with them (Proposition 52). What seems to have fascinated Eliot was the intricacy of Spinoza's emotional and social logic. An example of this intricacy is the analysis of jealousy.

> *If someone imagines that a thing he loves is united with another by as close, or by a closer, bond of friendship than that with which he himself, alone, possessed the thing, he will be affected with hate towards the thing he loves, and will envy the other.* (Proposition 35, 172)

This seems an obvious enough point to make, but the subtlety is in the working out of this postulate. In Proposition 34, Spinoza has already demonstrated the generative power of loving through the exultation that *being* loved by the other—another social act—confers on us. This exultation incrementally increases the more we see that we are the cause of this love. Desire for joy releases further rejoicing and desire for joy, of and in the other and of and in ourselves. Feeling comes in aid of feeling, as Wordsworth would have said. Spinoza sets no limit, no terminal point, on this inherently social rejoicing and striving. Love is infinite, but so is jealousy. It is also inherently social. The rejoicing of love brings its penalty, as the lover needs to imagine the loved one bound to him as closely as possible. Desire is compounded if the lover knows that another desires the loved one, but it is both compounded and checked by a double image: of the loved one, and of the being who has displaced him. A double hatred emerges, of the formerly loved one, and of the loved one's lover. Spinoza describes this as a triple anguish or "sadness" (as lack and depletion are often termed)—love and hate and envy compounding one another in proportion to the intensity of the original love. The loved one begins to be the object of hate "because he [the lover] imagines that what he loves affects with joy what he hates (173)." The final anguish is in the contradictions of feeling: "he is forced to join the image of the thing he loves to the image of him he hates" (173).

It is not for nothing that Spinoza ground lenses. The dioptric effects of the image and its exponential intensification to infinity, and the capacity of the lens to bend light and reverse the image must have entered his reckoning. In the case of jealousy Spinoza explicitly directs us to sexual love, with its carnal obsession with the other's body. But his reference to Ovid, and his recognition of the intensity of all love and hate, gave him an understanding of the complexity of feeling that we only find much later in psychoanalysis, and perhaps not even then. It is this tangle of complexity (the web of feeling) that Eliot found so arresting, I suggest. And the deep connections of feeling and the body were another source of her interest.

Middlemarch and *Daniel Deronda*

In *Middlemarch* the detachment of authorial comment and the gravitas with which it is associated often gives way to outbursts: "We are all of us born in moral stupidity, taking the world as an udder to feed our supreme selves" (211; ch. 21) That early translation of the *Ethics*, "So the infant believes that it freely seeks the breast," is behind this account of the supreme self's hubris. Eliot comes near to paraphrasing here in this same outburst Spinoza's belief that an ontological understanding of the passions depends on a precision of vision that goes beyond reason into pure clarity of insight: "that distinctness that is no longer reflection but feeling—an idea wrought back to the directness of sense, like the solidity of objects" (211; ch. 21).

But the narrative goes beyond allusion. In the moment of Dorothea's experience of betrayal by Will, Eliot uses Spinoza to structure her character's emotion with the immediacy of a writer who has internalized and lived philosophical meaning rather than abstracting it. It is the force of images that tear Dorothea's heart and create "waves of suffering," just as these waves of suffering produce images themselves, living in her mind with coercive intensity. "There were two images—two living forms that tore her heart in two." The iteration of "two . . . two . . . two" persistently doubles her anguish in the exponential way we have seen Spinoza describe, just as the rhetorical questions—"Why . . . Why . . . Why . . . ?" (786; ch. 80) express the pain of destructive feeling that destroys, and yet augments itself with incremental energy. The two images of Will are simultaneously corporeal and mental. One, "with the nearness of an answering smile," is the Will who offered her redemption from Casaubon's coldness. Like tears, a smile is of the body, responsive to the other. Here it must be a "parting vision": it is through vision that "she discovered her passion to herself in the unshrinking utterance of despair." The second image of Will is of the betrayer: following her like the shadow of her own body, a "detected illusion" that was nevertheless "persistently with her, moving wherever she moved" (786; ch. 80), Eliot evokes an optical obsession with images. The logic or trajectory of jealousy, with its contradiction between two images that we have seen Spinoza trace, is at work here in the "fire" of Dorothea's anger, compounding "scorn," "indignation," "jealous offended pride," "spurning reproach." Rosamund is the unnamed third here. Boldly, Eliot attributes sexual jealousy to a woman, going beyond Spinoza's more conventional association of masculinity and jealousy, but the same conditions occur: "he is forced to join the image of the thing he loves to the image of him he hates" (Curley 173).

The Spinozan elements of *Daniel Deronda* are different. Whereas in *Middlemarch* the poetics of Dorothea's jealousy might be described in Eliot's definition of poetry—"*Poetry* begins when passion weds thought by finding expression in an image"—the formal organization of *Daniel Deronda* relates to her claims about emotion and form—"but *Poetic Form* begins with a choice of elements, however meager, as the accordant expression of emotional states" (*Selected Essays* 235). Formal relations in a work of art are founded on or consonant with an emotional pattern that orders and is ordered by feeling. What might be seen as formal antitheses in the novel—the "realist" text and the mythopoeic text, the country house realist novel of class and power built round Gwendolen and the allegory of Jewish nationhood built round Mordecai, the opposition between the Gwendolen-Grandcourt formation and Deronda, who is to "migrate" to the Jewish allegory—are not antitheses but complementary forms of each other. They all have at their core the depleting "sadness" or "pain," as Spinoza is translated, of contempt, on which class has become predicated in a self-reinforcing manner, confirming an economic system. Correspondingly contempt distorts and paralyses the body by repressing the flow of feeling, which returns as violence. These are the "relations" that are, as Eliot put it, "determined" by emotion and that also "express" it.

To begin with a small but audacious act of Lydia Glasher's. Despite her bitter dispute with Grandcourt about the return of his diamonds, "She ventured to lay her hand on his shoulder. . . . "Light a cigar," she said, soothingly, taking the case from his breast-pocket and opening it" (316; ch. 30). It is a "caressing" sign of "mutual fear," Eliot writes, but it is also a gesture of bodily familiarity that speaks of years of past sexual intimacy. It is unthinkable to imagine Gwendolen ever undertaking such an action. Indeed, in one of those inconspicuous but telling moments of detail, the cigar-smoking Grandcourt later meets his wife's carriage approaching their Grosvenor Square house, and instantly assumes formal, conventional relations: "He threw it away and handed her out" (537; ch. 48).

It is through the body that the shaping emotions of the novel are made known. As Spinoza repeatedly remarks, pain, sadness, with its many manifestations of hate, envy, and contempt, checks the energies of the body and restrains the power of action. As Eliot put it, pain "restrains the effort by which man perseveres in his existence" (Deegan 120). "I hate to see a woman come into a room looking frozen," Grandcourt says, after forcing Gwendolen to wear the diamonds (387; ch. 35). By this time Gwendolen *is* frozen, with fear of her husband—"He delights in making the dogs and horses quail" (386; ch.35)—but she has always been "frozen." Her decision, at the start of the novel, to adopt the role of Hermione, frozen into a statue, as a tableau, is both apposite and profoundly ironic. She has edited out the wonder of Leontes' discovery—"She's warm" (*Winter's Tale* 5.3.109). When she does come alive it is by being galvanized by panic and hysteria as the wall panel falls open, revealing "the dead face and the fleeing figure" (51; ch. 6) that is to haunt her consciousness with nameless dread—"She looked like a statue into which a soul of Fear had entered": "how dare you open things that are meant to be shut up" (20; ch. 3). Panic, fear, and nameless dread are her element. The words "dread" and "fear" are key terms for her. Gwendolen's frigidity, her "susceptibility to terror" (53; ch. 6), her attacks of agoraphobia, her fear of being alone at night, a fear that makes her sleep in her mother's room, must be attributed to a dread of "things that are meant to be shut up." One of these is her own paralyzed sexuality, an unresolved rivalry for her mother's affection that refuses the possibility of libido—"Why did you marry again, mamma? It would have been nicer if you had not" (17; ch. 3). Another is her insecure class status, exacerbated by the peripatetic continental wanderings prior to the settlement at Offendene. Rivalry and contempt for other women, whether it is Catherine Arrowpoint or Juliet Fenn, a defensive sense of her entitlement and an insistence on her standing as a lady, are strategies of denial. The ego wards off what will damage it, Spinoza remarks. In many ways Grandcourt and Gwendolen are ideal foils for one another. Grandcourt's contempt, his "negative mind" (532; ch. 48), is actually dependent on people to despise: his total indifference to admiration, "just as much as desire, required its related object—namely, a world of admiring or envying spectators: for if you are fond of looking stonily at smiling persons, the persons must be there and they must smile—a rudimentary truth which is surely forgotten by those who complain of mankind as generally contemptible, since any other aspect of the race will generally disappoint the voracity of their contempt" (531; ch. 48).

It is customary to set Daniel, with his ethical sensitivity and compassion, in moral opposition to Gwendolen (and to Grandcourt), as she does herself. Yet it is worth remembering that Spinoza held that compassion and envy are dialectically related forms of one another. "We see, then, that from the same property of human nature from which it follows that men are compassionate, it follows that the same men are envious and ambitious" (Curley 171). We see another's joy in possession as an "obstacle to our joy." Knowing the depletions of envy we understand the depletions of the person who lacks something, a knowledge that is also a lack, an "obstacle to our joy." We "pity the unfortunate and envy the fortunate" (171) on the same terms. In the same way, "dread," "disdain," and "mockery" are perverted and negative forms of "wonder" (181–82). Daniel also has his share of "dread" and fear, and for the same reasons as Gwendolen—he has a terror of being declassed. As a child he almost hysterically claims the status of gentleman when asked if he would like to be a singer, and as a young man he wants above all to be an "Englishman" (164; ch. 16). "It was the habit of his mind to connect dread with unknown parentage" (183; ch. 19). Mother loss haunts them both: "The desire to know his own mother . . . was constantly haunted with dread" (182; ch. 19). Daniel's "self-repressed exterior" (180; ch. 19), his inability to choose a profession, his fluctuating capacity to be at once "fervidly democratic" (327; ch. 32) and an apologist for the class system, his bodily investment in sympathy, in which "his own personality would be no less outside him than the landscape" (169; ch. 17), an investment that made sympathy a self-blocking mechanism that neutralized sympathy itself (327; ch. 32), may seem the antithesis of Gwendolen's frozen paralysis. Yet it is another form of it, a check on the vital energies and powers of action equally powerful. The closed panel for Gwendolen and the locked chest that holds the secret of Daniel's birth, hold terrors for them. Both play fast and loose with their father's jewelry, Gwendolen tries to sell her necklace, and Daniel pretends to pawn his father's ring. Jewels, that sign which connects sexuality (for Freud jewels and genitalia are interchangeable in dreams) and genealogy, join Grandcourt's poisoned diamonds as the site of perverted transmission.

Eliot's achievement in *Daniel Deronda* is not to have confined contempt and repressed sexual feeling to the psychology of individuals but to have portrayed it as the structure of feeling in a whole society. She is clear that class boundaries are the product of historical and economic forces. Grandcourt's fortune is founded on the Midland miners who work underground in Lydia Glasher's neighborhood (just as Gwendolen's is lost in mining shares). However, boundaries are also sustained by the casual contempt of class feeling, in Grandcourt's and Mrs. Davilow's dismissal of the supposedly illegitimate Deronda (both use the same phrase) as of no "consequence" (294, 299; ch. 29), or Lady Pentreath's belief in "blood": "there's no blood on any side. . . . And we all know how the mother's money came" (367; ch. 35), she remarks of the Arrowpoints. Contempt and hatred are in alliance, Spinoza said. Violence is endemic to the society Eliot portrays. It is apposite that at one of Gwendolen's earliest social engagements with Grandcourt the discussion should turn to the atrocities of Governor Eyre in Jamaica (296; ch. 29). (Later in an aside Eliot remarks that a Grandcourt colonial policy would deem it "safer to exterminate than to cajole" [539; ch. 48].) At the Grandcourt wedding, a girl is disillusioned by her mother: "Oh child, men's men. . . . I've heard my mother say Squire Pelton used to take his dogs and a long whip into his wife's room, and flog 'em there to frighten her" (317; ch. 31). Concealed violence and its concealed erotic suggestiveness may account for the way superfluous children abound in the novel, as if reproduction takes a statistical revenge on the bourgeois family's erotic life: there are Mrs Davilow's four superfluous daughters, and Gwendolen, the many Mallinger daughters, the many Gascoigne sons, Mrs. Glasher's four illegitimate children in comparison to her single deceased legitimate son, and Princess Halm-Eberstein, with the five children that followed Daniel's birth.

The extreme "voracity of contempt" in English society is the systemic anti-Semitism reserved for the Jews. The mimetic contagion of affect ensures its continuance. The Arrowpoint parents' paranoia about Klesmer's "foreign look" (221; ch. 22), the Meyrick hope that they might "neutralise the Jewess" in Mirah, the MP, Bult's assumption that Klesmer "was not a serious human being" (215; ch. 22), the Princess's self-hate, Daniel's early prejudice as he fails to recognize the dignity of the Cohen family, this structure of feeling is recognized by Mordecai when he speaks of a history of "contempt" of Jews (478; ch. 42). His own employer, the bookseller, Ram, has internalized this contempt. We remember Proposition 46 of the *Ethics*: if he imagines himself damaged by someone "under the universal name of class or nation," a man will "hate . . . everyone of the same class or nation" (Eliot [trans.], *Ethics* 178). Here the damage is fantasmatic, the hate real. In the "Hand and Banner" tavern, debaters question whether hatred on both sides can ever be overcome.

From networks of contempt to hope, from dread to wonder, from skepticism to veneration, from the paralyzed body to the transcendence of the body, from blocked powers of action to liberated powers of action, from the choked class structure of contemporary England to a visionary republic to center the Jewish diaspora. The movement to the obsessed Mordecai brings with it a change of register and poetic eloquence that have persuaded readers to think of the visionary "half" of the novel as that which appears to be a corrective or counteracting force to the "realist" text. Chapter 38 initiates this change. Mordecai's prophetic status as one who "wrought so constantly in images" (429; ch. 38), his visionary yearning to "glorify the possibilities of the Jew" (428; ch. 38), the appearance of Deronda under a golden sky to confirm his longing, this turn to second sight, and Eliot's deep respect for the emaciated man who is explicitly compared with the ascetic Spinoza (427; ch. 38), who is twice mentioned in her *Daniel Deronda* notebooks (356, 421), have also persuaded readers to assume that this must be Eliot's as well as Deronda's "alternative" to the exhausted culture of modernity portrayed in the "realist" side of the novel.

But what if this "half" of the novel could be seen not as a counteracting force to its realist side, but the counterpart of it? Not an antidote but its fevered idealist double? Obsession is as saddening and depleting as cynicism. The wasted body is the shadow of the paralyzed body, just as the fervent intensity of hope is the shadow of Mordecai's culture's extravagant refusal of it. One might claim that his culture "produces" Mordecai. There is an uncanny parallel between Mordecai and Gwendolen. "I saw my wish outside me" (632; ch. 56), she says, of the drowning Grandcourt, her obsessive images of his death horribly realized. Mordecai's visionary excitement could turn "his wishes into overmastering impressions, and made him read outward facts as fulfillment" (465; ch. 41): for such a mind "imagined deeds" have the force of reality. "The event they hunger for or dread rises into vision" (427; ch. 38). In the same way there is an uncanny parallel between the nation state of modern European nationalism and Mordecai's ideal and idealist state: growth is impossible unless "our race takes on again the character of nationality" (484; ch. 42). "Each nation has its own work. . . . But . . . Israel is the heart of mankind" (481; ch. 42).

To see Mordecai as part of the problem explored by the novel rather than its solution does not in the least diminish its power. The "relations" that are "determined" by emotion and that also "express" it are just as searching and profound. And, moreover, they weld the seemingly torn halves of the novel together irremediably. There's an element of criticism of Spinoza here, despite his powerful presence. His model of emotion that posits opposing feelings as the creation of the same structure can lock the self into deterministic paradigms from which there is no escape—dread and wonder, contempt and veneration, compassion and envy. Eliot took from him an intransigent understanding of the intensity of the passions and the logic of their formative violence. But she also stood outside him. Perhaps his disturbing insight into what Lewes described as "the deepest and darkest passions" (*Goethe* 1:11) was a check on publishing that translation?

REFERENCES

Atkins, Dorothy. *George Eliot and Spinoza*. Salzburg: U of Salzburg, 1978.

Curley, Edwin, ed. and trans. *A Spinoza Reader. The Ethics and Other Works*. Princeton: Princeton UP, 1994.

Eliot, George. *Daniel Deronda*. Ed. Edmund White and Hugh Osborne. New York: Random House, 2002.

Eliot, George. trans. *Ethics*. By Benedict de Spinoza. Ed. Thomas Deegan. Salzburg: U of Salzburg, 1981.

Eliot, George. *George Eliot's Daniel Deronda Notebooks*. Ed. Jane Irwin. Cambridge: Cambridge UP, 1996.

Eliot, George. *The Journals of George Eliot*. Ed. Margaret Harris and Judith Johnston. Cambridge: Cambridge UP, 2000.

Eliot, George. *The George Eliot Letters*. Ed. Gordon S. Haight. 9 vols. New Haven: Yale UP, 1954–78.

Eliot, George. *Middlemarch*. Ed. Rosemary Ashton. London: Penguin, 2003.

Eliot, George. *The Mill on the Floss*. Ed. A. S. Byatt. London: Penguin, 2003.

Eliot, George. *Selected Essays, Poems and Other Writings*. Ed. A. S. Byatt and Nicholas Warren. London: Penguin, 1990.

Eliot, George. *The Spanish Gypsy*. 3rd ed. London: William Blackwood, 1868.

Ermarth, Elizabeth Deeds. "George Eliot's Conception of Sympathy." *Nineteenth-Century Fiction* 40.1 (1985): 23–42.

Hardy, Barbara. *The Novels of George Eliot*. London: Athlone, 1963.

Lewes, George Henry. *Biographical History of Philosophy*. 2 vols. London: John W. Parkes, 1857.

Lewes, George Henry. *The Life and Works of Goethe*. 2 vols. London: David Nutt, 1855.

Lewes, George Henry. *Problems of Life and Mind Second Series*. London: Trubner, 1877.

Lewes, George Henry. "Spinoza's Life and Works." *The Westminster Review* 39 (1843): 372–407.

Nietzsche, Friedrich. *Twilight of the Idols*. Trans. Michael Tanner and R. J. Hollingdale. London: Penguin, 2003.

Richardson, Angelique. "George Eliot, G. H. Lewes, and Darwin: Animals, Emotions and

Morals." *After Darwin: Animals, Emotions, and the Mind*. Ed. Angelique Richardson. Amsterdam: Rodopi, 2013. 130–63.

Shakespeare, William. *The Winter's Tale, The Complete Works*. Ed. Stanley Wells and Gary Taylor. Oxford: Clarendon, 1988.

Smith, Adam. *The Theory of Moral Sentiments*. 11th ed. 2 vols. Edinburgh: Bell & Bradfute Lackington, Allen & Co., 1808.

Woolf, Virginia. *Times Literary Supplement* 20 Nov. 1919.

White, William Hale. *Athenaeum* 28 Nov. 1885.

22

George Eliot and the Law

Jan-Melissa Schramm

In January 1866, whilst immersed in the composition of *Felix Holt*, George Eliot entered into an extensive correspondence with the renowned positivist lawyer Frederic Harrison, of Lincoln's Inn (*Letters* 4:214–65). The purpose of their exchanges was initially to ensure the accuracy of the narrative sequence by which the novel's heroine, Esther Lyon, might plausibly be identified as the heiress to the Bycliffe estate, but as time passed, Harrison's sympathetic reception of her ideas encouraged Eliot to articulate a more general aesthetic manifesto. Prompted by Harrison to consider the ways in which literature might legitimately claim to educate its audience, Eliot observed:

> I think aesthetic teaching is the highest of all teaching because it deals with life in its highest complexity. But if it ceases to be purely aesthetic – if it lapses anywhere from the picture to the diagram – it becomes the most offensive of all teaching. Avowed Utopias are not offensive, because they are understood to have a scientific and expository character: they do not pretend to work on the emotions, or couldn't do it if they did pretend.

Her own methodology, she tells Harrison, has involved "the severe effort of trying to make certain ideas thoroughly incarnate, as if they had revealed themselves to me first in the flesh and not in the spirit" (*Letters* 4:264–65). This is a rich but provocative description which seeks to hold in tension a number of potentially contradictory ingredients: that moral instruction in art should be "incarnational"—embodying the value of "that life [. . . of] conscious voluntary sacrifice" which remains man's highest ideal (*Romola* 50; Proem)—tethers Eliot's prose to Christian theology even as she seeks

A Companion to George Eliot, First Edition. Edited by Amanda Anderson and Harry E. Shaw.
© 2013 John Wiley & Sons, Ltd. Published 2016 by John Wiley & Sons, Ltd.

to discard its reliance on miracles. But it also raises questions of form. For whilst Eliot's narrator in *The Mill on the Floss* declares her distrust of the abstract judgments of "men of maxims" and her preference for a generous sympathy with the messy complexity of lived experience (628; bk. 7, ch. 2), her own novels are punctuated by epigraphs and lapidary generalizations which suggest instead the value of the proverbial distillation of wisdom (Price 119–28). That these crucial strands of Eliot's thought are investigated in dialogue with a lawyer is, I would argue, no coincidence: throughout her life, Eliot's engagement with the law was profound and searching—her letters, notebooks, and novels reveal that she returned time and time again to questions of justice (both individual and institutional) and their complex relationship to broader ideas of ethics, social and political equality, and the impartial interpretation of legal and scientific evidence (Schramm, *Testimony* 130–34; Welsh, *Strong Representations* 62–76). For Eliot, these questions of justice and fairness were inseparable from the form in which they were represented—she knew only too well that different discursive forms produced different types of knowledge—and her deep understanding of the law ensured that her fiction was ideally placed to interrogate this interrelationship of rhetoric and responsibility.

Eliot's knowledge of the law was acquired from a number of sources. She shared the taste of her mid-Victorian generation for the vivid legal scandals described in the daily newspapers: when the claim of the famous impostor, Arthur Orton, to the vast Tichborne estate was heard in 1872, she was one of the many members of the public who crowded into the galleries of the Court of Common Pleas to hear the celebrated oratory of John Coleridge and the wise observations of Chief Justice Alexander Cockburn on the bench. Eliot's response to the case, however, was multi-faceted: whilst she enjoyed the challenges it posed for a reading of character, she also used the occasion to think about the ways in which conflicting testimonies should be interpreted and to consider the socio-political implications of the extension of the franchise (*Letters* 5:243, 257). Eliot's fluency in the lexicon of Victorian jurisprudential thought arose in part from her extensive acquaintance with some of the leading legal minds of her day—alongside Harrison, we find amongst her social circle the family solicitor Henry Sheard,[1] the influential criminal jurist James Fitzjames Stephen, and the famous Professor of Jurisprudence Sir Henry Sumner Maine. But her program of reading was even more extensive in its reach: her early editorial work for the *Westminster Review* reveals her understanding of penal legislation in relation to phrenology,[2] and, later, the notebooks she compiled for use in the composition of her novels display her interest in such topics as the work of the Wesleyans in prisons and madhouses (Weisenfarth 24–25), the legal implications of religious tolerance (Weisenfarth 53–54), continental conceptions of evidence (Baker 1:193–207), and testamentary succession and the position of women (Pratt and Neufeldt 202–07, 259–64). This material was extracted from sources like the sixth edition of William Best's *Principles of the Law of Evidence* (1875), Charles Clode's *Military Forces of the Crown* (1869), Maine's *Ancient Law* (1861), and the works of John Austin and Jeremy Bentham.

Eliot's grasp of the law was remarkable in its own right, but perhaps her greatest gift was an ability to place "black-letter law" in conversation with the wider epistemological debates of her times—debates, for example, about the status of religious evidence in an era of increasing secularization, the reliability of the Scriptures, the factual status of miracles, and the explanatory power of scientific paradigms. (That some of her most searching analysis of the interpretation of evidence is undertaken in *Romola*, a historical novel set in fifteenth-century Florence, is particularly good evidence of this.) Eliot asked what guaranteed the effective operation of moral discernment and legal judgment if the status of Biblical truth as supernatural revelation was open to question. The mid-Victorian decades saw significant legal reform, of criminal trial procedure, and of the relationship between the common law (administered in the common law courts like the High Court and the King's Bench) and equity (a supplementary system inherited from medieval conceptions of the "conscience of the King," administered in the by now notoriously inflexible Court of Chancery). As Simon Petch has shown, like her contemporaries F. D. Maurice and Alfred Lord Tennyson, Eliot "responded to the mid-Victorian reorganization of [the] country's traditions and institutions by examining the national conscience" (133–34). According to Petch, this generation of literary authors "put their various configurations of law and conscience in relationship to a sense of justice which is unconstrained by the machinery of the law" (136). Ultimately, they contributed to a larger conversation at mid-century about the origins of our moral sense: "do right and wrong in law arise from the nature of things, or are they created by human institution?" (130).

In this essay, I would like to situate Eliot's compelling representation of fictional trials—both criminal and civil—alongside these larger questions of moral obligation, duty, and individual or national "conscience." Of all the mid-Victorian novelists, she possessed arguably the keenest sense of the ways in which law was a product of its socio-cultural context even as it attempted to distance itself from the strategies of persuasion that it shared with rhetoric and fictional story-telling: whilst Eliot was aware of the value of impartiality and objectivity—and of the quest for precision which marked the law's aspiration to the status of a "science"—she was only too aware of its imbrication in the subjective realm of affect, sympathy, or prejudice. The corpus of her writing reveals her sense that the tragic burden of judgment—the need to end a case and reach a decision—leads to the exclusion of certain types of evidence and the marginalization of certain voices. Her understanding that the law is complex in its application is manifest in the frequency with which she stages a competition between what we might call first- and third-person perspectives of human experience (which generates a provocative—if painful—tension between eye-witness testimony and a professional knowledge of character based on inference alone). And even as she sought to ground her own narrative realism in the rules of evidence which governed the provision of accurate evidence in a court of law, she revealed time and time again her willingness to reach beyond law's formalism—to offer her readers a more abundant economy of hope and mercy.

Eliot and the Criminal Law

Eliot claimed for her realism a probabilistic and evidentiary verisimilitude that owed much to legal praxis: her narrator in *Adam Bede*, for example, famously asserted that the story was told "as precisely . . . as if I were in the witness-box, narrating my experience on oath" (193; ch. 17), and almost all her novels reflect upon the role of the state in the regulation of human behavior. Eliot's earliest fictional work, *Scenes of Clerical Life*, contains a number of ethico-legal themes and tropes which address questions of fairness, justice, redemption, and sacrifice, and *Adam Bede* (her first full-length novel) scrutinizes the impact of legal proceedings on a community. In *Adam Bede*, the immature and selfish Hetty Sorrel is seduced by the young squire Arthur Donnithorne and subsequently accused of murdering her illegitimate child; in the representation of this terrible trial, Eliot reveals her deep understanding of the laws which govern the assessment of evidence and the complex inter-relationship of law and morality more generally. Adam's interactions with Arthur are characterized by missed opportunities for confession and repentance (illustrating, along the way, Eliot's awareness that the criminal law is only one aspect of the process by which neighbors must deal with the social discord caused by violent transgression). Adam yearns for "justice . . . [he] wants [Arthur] to feel what [Hetty] feels" (459; ch. 41)—and the wise clergyman Mr. Irwine momentarily fears that the two men will return to the primitive and destructive form of trial by battle which they had contemplated earlier in the novel. Mr. Irwine counsels restraint: professional trial procedures have replaced older forms of revenge for a reason. *Lex talionis* (the Old Testament law of "an eye for an eye") should be repudiated and a careful discrimination of varying degrees of culpable intention undertaken in its stead. This will depend upon careful scrutiny of the evidence, and Eliot is attentive to the ways in which this evidence is presented to the court—from the medical evidence (which is "heavy on [Hetty]" [466; ch. 42]) to the persuasive power of legal oratory. Given her extensive reading, it is unsurprising that Eliot is also aware of the technicalities of criminal trial procedure of the period: Hetty is represented by counsel but, as the case takes place prior to the enactment of the Prisoner's Counsel Act in 1836 (which extended full representation to those accused of felonies such as murder [Langbein 252–343]), he cannot address the jury on her behalf; he can only, in Bartle Massey's phrase, "make . . . a deal to do with cross-examining the witnesses and quarrelling with the other lawyers" (465; ch. 42). Without the benefit of full legal representation, Mr. Irwine is left to speak to Hetty's "unblemished" character:

> This testimony could have no influence on the verdict, but it was given as part of that plea for mercy which her own counsel would have made if he had been allowed to speak for her – a favour not granted to criminals in those stern times. (473; ch. 43)

In *Felix Holt*, also set prior to 1836, Eliot returns to the role of lay speech in a criminal courtroom as she probes Felix's motives for seeking to give his own description of the riot which has led to his trial for manslaughter: in Felix's case, Eliot seeks to assert the integrity of male working-class speech:

> Even if the pleading of counsel had been permitted (and at that time it was not) on behalf of a prisoner on trial for felony, Felix would have declined it: he would in any case have spoken in his own defence. He had a perfectly simple account to give, and needed not to avail himself of any legal adroitness. (467; ch. 37)

Eliot valorizes his plain Protestant sincerity: "The sublime delight of truthful speech to one who has the great gift of uttering it, will make itself felt even through the pangs of sorrow" (564; ch. 46)—ornamental legal rhetoric, on the other hand, may serve to obfuscate the truth, particularly if it goes so far as to establish a "sham defence" which bears little relation to the genuine facts of the case. Eliot shows herself perfectly well informed about the license of counsel controversy which accompanied the enactment of the Prisoners' Counsel Act (suggesting that barristers would offer relativistic rhetoric for hire), and she clearly sees fiction as a type of advocacy which is thus placed in a combative relationship with its legal equivalent. The move from an amateurish to an adversarial model of the criminal trial had been controversial, and like her peers, Charles Dickens, Elizabeth Gaskell, William Thackeray, and Anthony Trollope, Eliot critiques professional legal speech for its lack of commitment to the discovery of impartial "truth" (Schramm, *Testimony* 101–44).

But Eliot was not interested in the rules of legal procedure solely for their own sake (although, as her correspondence with Harrison suggests, she was committed to historical accuracy as a narrative virtue). Instead, she was profoundly attentive to the contrasting epistemological value of different types of speech, and throughout her career she returns to this question of how first-person speech will differ in its probative weight from the third-person, external account of an individual's character offered by a bystander, or a legal professional, or a doctor. In *Adam Bede*, for example, the tale as told by the prosecution will vary greatly from that confessed by Hetty herself: how is the attentive juror (a metonym for the responsive reader) to accommodate the two? For this reason, Eliot stage-manages the participants' performance at the trial to maximize its confrontational ethical value: initially, it is Adam who is martyred by suffering when the eye-witness testimony of Hetty's alleged guilt is revealed to him, and Eliot delays our access to Hetty's own voice to ensure that the testimony she finally offers is elicited by religious exhortation rather than legal interrogation. Whilst Hetty awaits execution, it is Dinah, the Methodist lay-preacher, who urges, "Hetty, we are before God. He is waiting for you to tell the truth" (489; ch. 45). Eliot avoids easy religious consolation—"It was the human contact [Hetty] clung to, but she was not the less sinking into the dark gulf" (487; ch. 45)—yet Hetty responds to Dinah's request. But what she speaks of is not murder but neglect: "I did do it, Dinah . . . I buried it in the woods . . . and I went back because it cried"—but at the same time, "I didn't kill it—I didn't kill it myself" (491; ch. 45). Hetty had been condemned throughout the narrative for her hardness of heart, her absence of maternal tenderness, yet Eliot here is suggesting the difficulty of apportioning guilt even in seemingly self-evident cases. This is not a miscarriage of justice (Hetty is not wrongfully suspected, like Maggie in *The Mill on the Floss* or Lydgate in *Middlemarch*)—but nor is Hetty a callous killer: like Bulstrode in *Middlemarch* and (to a lesser extent) like Gwendolen in *Daniel Deronda*, in her self-absorbed egotism she had yearned for ease—for the removal of that which caused her pain and suffering. It is fitting that Eliot allows Hetty to be rescued from the scaffold as a consequence of a petition for mercy, although her fate remains harsh: transported to Australia, she dies on her way back to England—arguably something of a scapegoat for the lesson that Arthur must learn: "There's a sort of wrong that can never be made up for" (590; Epilogue).

The extent of a defendant's guilt for something which he or she may have wished for, but played an ambiguous role in bringing about, is something Eliot returns to time and time again in her fiction: to resort to deliberate violence is to be obviously culpable, but what is Hetty's guilt for abandoning a child when she seems incapable of effective moral discernment? What is the extent of Arthur's guilt for taking advantage of her youth and vanity? In *Felix Holt*, what is Felix's culpability for the manslaughter of a policeman when the death was the unintended consequence of an attempt to lead a rioting mob away from dwelling-houses? In *Middlemarch*, what is Bulstrode's guilt for allowing an alcoholic to be treated in accordance with the "standard" medical practice of the day? Is this complicated by the fact that Lydgate had alerted him to the potentially fatal risks of this "standard practice"? And in *Daniel Deronda*, does Gwendolen have an obligation to attempt to rescue her brutal, drowning husband (Rodensky 132–70)? Eliot asks if our duties extend to rendering the best medical treatment to those who blackmail us, or throwing a rope to a husband who will otherwise die. A comparison with the work of Eliot's contemporary, Dickens, is salient here. Whilst Dickens tends to insist on an almost Evangelical economy of character (in which goodness should be unstained and exemplary and in which evil is palpable and manifest), Eliot is far more interested in ambiguous cases of culpability (such as acts of omission, with unforeseen consequences, or incidents in which criminal intention may be complicated or confused). In place of Orlick and Rigaud, Eliot offers us Felix and Bulstrode. And whilst Dickens tended to observe human behavior from the outside, depicting criminal action but eschewing a psychologically-focused approach to its narration (John 5), Eliot was fascinated by the ethical value of intention (Rodensky 88–132): whilst she recognized that our bad deeds have a life of their own, to be assessed independently of any moral vacillation that preceded their commission, she also acknowledged what Mr. Lyon in *Felix Holt* calls that "invisible activity of the soul whereby the deeds which are the same in the outward appearance and effect, yet differ as the knife-stroke of the surgeon, even though it kill, differs from the knife-stroke of the wanton mutilator" (*Felix Holt* 548; ch. 44). The result is the Victorian period's most compelling portrait of the complexities of human intention and agency.

For all of the ways in which Eliot's narratives differ from those of Dickens, they nevertheless share real structural affinities in their treatment of transgressive behavior. In the case of both writers, when their protagonists are accused of serious crime, such accusations are habitually shown to be wrongful and their innocence is established at the point of narrative closure; female protagonists must habitually display high standards of virtue; and potential miscarriages of justice (like Hetty's condemnation to death, and Felix's conviction) are corrected by novel's end. In terms of their larger economies of value, then, both Dickens and Eliot express a hope that legal justice and poetic justice may coincide: they celebrate innocence, self-sacrifice, and mercy (Schramm, *Atonement* 25–32, 227–30). But Eliot in particular is aware of some of the ways in which these moral qualities are potentially incommensurable. To prize innocence above all else is to leave little room for the wisdom acquired through painful and occasionally grubby experience: to prize justice (the treatment of like cases as alike) is to leave little room for the operation of mercy (which insists on the extension of leniency in deserving cases). Whilst Eliot is clearly interested in what J. S. Mill famously identified as the most important feature of justice in the public imagination—that an individual be accorded their "just deserts" (Mill 257)—Eliot still suggests that this standard should be exceeded by the individual in private life: that both forgiveness and goodness should be cultivated in self-abnegating abundance.

Eliot was also aware of the complex relationship between cause and effect, particularly insofar as it impacted upon conceptions of crime and punishment. Can we learn from our mistakes if we pay no price for them? For the Evangelical thinkers who had influenced Eliot in her youth, an innocent substitute (Christ) had already paid the penalty of sin in man's place so that individual offenders may consequently avail themselves of God's mercy—this enabled God's law to be upheld even as pity is extended to those who truly repent: a complex equation which allegedly demonstrated God's equitable judgment. In this way, the theology of the atonement reconciled the apparently incommensurable values of justice and mercy. But when she lost her Christian faith, Eliot came to share the widespread fear that repentance enabled men to escape too easily the consequences of their actions, which potentially provided errant individuals with their most effective moral education (Schramm, *Atonement* 217–22). Mid-Victorian authors repeatedly returned to this seminal question: should mercy and pity prevail over the demands of justice, or should man be "reformed" by the harsh and irrevocable consequences of what Eliot in *Romola* represents as "the deeds [that] are like children . . . born to us" and "which live and act apart from our own will"? (219; ch. 16).

Eliot's answer to this most difficult of questions encompassed both Christian hope (whilst she lost faith in the miraculous dimension of the Biblical narratives, she nevertheless continued to hold tightly to their ethical teaching) and a truly tragic awareness that forgiveness was not always sufficiently capacious to heal the wounds of the past. There is plenty of textual evidence to support the argument that Eliot prioritized mercy above stricter legal notions of our "just deserts": in *The Mill on the Floss*, for example, as the notoriously litigious Mr. Tulliver dies, he asks "'Does God forgive raskills? . . . if He does, He won't be hard wi' me" (464; bk. 5, ch. 7), whilst Maggie dies clinging to the "Unseen Pity that would be with her to the end" (649; bk. 7, ch. 5). But Arthur's lesson in *Adam Bede*—that restitution can never be made for some deeds—has already been alluded to, and throughout her career Eliot articulated the fear that poor moral choices mark families for generations with "some hard entail of suffering" that cannot easily be erased (*Felix Holt* 83; Introduction).

Eliot clearly felt that she had two models available to her as she sought to represent a community's response to the disruptive effects of transgression: the classical model, which tended towards severity, and the Christian, which offered some grounds for a belief in the possibilities of personal and communal healing. In cases where Eliot chooses to prioritize forgiveness above the narrowness of justice strictly conceived, it is women who tend to embody these merciful qualities (Watt 179-83). Dinah preaches God's mercy to Hetty in the condemned cell in *Adam Bede*: Maggie's instinctively sympathetic nature enables her to "feel for" individuals in place of the pharisaism which drives both her father and her brother in *The Mill on the Floss*. But it is in *Felix Holt* and in *Middlemarch* that Eliot undertakes her most sustained analysis of the relationship between gender and merciful judgment.

In March 1859, whilst travelling on the continent, Eliot and G. H. Lewes read aloud to one another Elizabeth Gaskell's *Mary Barton* (Haight 258), in which the eponymous protagonist saves the man she loves from the gallows by the discovery of alibi evidence and the provision of loving testimony at his trial. As Hilary Schor has noted, Felix's trial for manslaughter in *Felix Holt* owes much to Gaskell's precedent (187–88), but whilst Gaskell opted for a melodramatic acquittal of the innocent working-class exemplar, Eliot's more sophisticated treatment of evidence and the role of feelings in the judicial process inevitably complicated the narrative sequence. Esther had initially hoped that her favorable testimony would lead to Felix's immediate release:

> If it was the jury who were to be acted on, she argued to herself, there might have been an impression made on their feeling which would determine their verdict. Was it not constantly said and seen that juries pronounced Guilty or Not Guilty from sympathy for or against the accused? She was too inexperienced to check her own argument by thoroughly representing to herself the course of things: how the counsel for the prosecution would reply, and how the judge would sum up, with the object of cooling down sympathy into deliberation. (570–71; ch. 46)

That Esther's evidence does not produce an instantaneous acquittal is part of Eliot's exploration of this complex relationship between feeling and fact, intuition and knowledge, sympathy and judgment. Whilst her fiction is committed to the promotion of sympathetic feeling, she nevertheless acknowledges the value of "cool . . . deliberation" and impartiality (even as she notes that knowledge is so difficult to separate from prejudice, "for the very truth hath a colour from the disposition of the utterer" [549; ch. 44]):

Esther's deed had its effect beyond the momentary one, but the effect was not visible in the rigid necessities of legal procedure. The counsel's duty of restoring all unfavourable facts to due prominence in the minds of the jurors, had its effect altogether reinforced by the summing-up of the judge. Even the bare discernment of facts, much more their arrangement with a view to inferences, must carry a bias: human impartiality, whether judicial or not, can hardly escape being more or less loaded. It was not that the judge had severe intentions; it was only that he saw with severity. The conduct of Felix was not such as inclined him to indulgent consideration, and, in his directions to the jury, that mental attitude necessarily told on the light in which he placed the homicide. Even to many in the court who were not constrained by judicial duty, it seemed that though this high regard felt for the prisoner by his friends, and especially by a generous-hearted woman, was very pretty, such conduct as his was not the less dangerous and foolish, and assaulting and killing a constable was not the less an offence to be regarded without leniency. (573–74; ch. 46)

Yet Esther's testimony—that Felix "is very noble . . . and he could never have had any intention that was not brave and good" (573; ch. 46)—produces a "stirring of heart in certain just-spirited men and good fathers among them, which had been raised to a high pitch of emotion by [her] maidenly fervour":

during the trial Sir Maximus was wrought into a state of sympathetic ardour that needed no fanning. . . . 'That girl made me cry . . . she's a modest, brave, beautiful woman. I'd ride a steeplechase, old as I am, to gratify her feelings. Hang it! the fellow's a good fellow if she thinks so.' . . . The rector had not exactly the same kind of ardour, nor was he open to precisely that process of proof which appeared to have convinced Sir Maximus; but he had been so far influenced as to be inclined to unite on the side of mercy. (575–76; ch. 47)

Eliot restricts the operation of "feeling" to its proper place in the adjudicative process: it should not color the interpretation of factual material at the trial stage, but a "memorial to the Home Secretary" wins Felix early release from his sentence of four-years' imprisonment—as Harold Transome tells Esther, "I think your speaking for him helped a great deal. You made all the men wish what you had wished" (589; ch. 50). Eliot positions Esther even more firmly as the figure of mercy or equity in the novel when she extends to the suffering Mrs. Transome the pity which her son Harold denies her: "I would bear a great deal of unhappiness to save her from having any more" (596; ch. 50).

If Esther's role in *Felix Holt* is supplementary to legal process (just as the operation of equity was designed to supplement the operation of the common law), then another legal model serves as the organizing principle of the closing chapters of *Middlemarch*. Earlier in her life, Eliot had been greatly impressed by the work of her friend Anna Jameson, and Jameson's study *Shakespeare's Heroines* (1832) offered a particularly compelling portrait of Portia, the advocate of mercy in *The Merchant of Venice*. When Lydgate is wrongfully suspected of complicity in the (possible) murder of Raffles by

Bulstrode, Dorothea undertakes to act as his counsel in conversation with their mutual neighbors. But unlike a professional representative, her advocacy arises from a conviction of his innocence: "You don't believe that Mr Lydgate is guilty of anything base? I will not believe it. Let us find out the truth and clear him!" (730; ch. 72). Eliot eschews the route of public interrogation—that would involve the disgrace of "setting the magistrate and coroner to work"—and affords Dorothea the opportunity to rehabilitate Lydgate's character: Dorothea "disliked this cautious weighing of consequences, instead of an ardent faith in efforts of justice and mercy, which would conquer by their emotional force" (733; ch. 72). As Mr. Farebrother the clergyman notes, "It is true that a woman may venture on some efforts of sympathy which would hardly succeed if we men undertook them" (735; ch. 72). Whilst Lydgate is paralyzed by both the pragmatic difficulty of proclaiming his innocence ("[t]he circumstances would always be stronger than his assertion" [738; ch. 73]) and the extent of his economic dependence upon Bulstrode (which he acknowledges may have compromised his independence upon the discovery of Raffles's corpse), Dorothea remains confident that "the truth would clear [him]" (762; ch. 76). Lydgate finds it "a comfort . . . to speak where belief has gone beforehand" (762; ch. 76) and Dorothea serves as his conduit in transmitting his exculpatory account of events to the community and most significantly, to his unsympathetic wife, Rosamond. It is clear that Eliot sees Dorothea's feelings here as generous and benevolent—like Dickens, she suggests that women preside over a particularly charitable jurisdiction of judgment—yet at the same time, Eliot saw no need for women to play a more prominent role in public affairs: Dorothea's efficacy as an advocate is predicated upon its restriction to the private realm. In fact, whilst Eliot signed Barbara Bodichon's petition for an extension of the property rights of married women (presented to Parliament in 1856 [*Letters* 2:225–26]), she did not otherwise actively campaign for women's rights or a wider participation of women in the public sphere (Haight 396), and we are left with the paradox that she attributed great power for good to women in her novels (and recognized their capacity for merciful intervention in human relations) yet simultaneously retreated from a more formal call for gender equality. Her heroines perform the crucial ethical work of pity and forgiveness in her narratives, yet they remain curiously supplementary to the male world of justice and political power (also see Krueger 12–18).

Eliot and the Civil Law

Whilst Eliot's primary interest lay in the complexities of human intention, and thus in the criminal law which purported to regulate transgressive behavior, a number of her novels also depend for their resolution upon civil litigation (that is, cases relating to contractual disputes and issues of inheritance). In 1859, Eliot consulted the family solicitor, Henry Sheard, about the lawsuit which ruins the Tullivers in *The Mill on the Floss*, and her correspondence with John Blackwood reveals that Sheard read portions of the text to ensure that her representation of Pivart's case against Tulliver was accurate and that the timetable for the sale of the Tulliver's property under the decree of Chancery was plausible (*Letters* 3:246, 262–67). By far the most complex civil case to feature in Eliot's fiction, however, was the transmission of the Bycliffe estate in *Felix Holt*: in addition to the law of entail discussed in depth in the correspondence with Harrison (*Letters* 4:214–65), the plot of *Felix Holt* also featured acts of blackmail (Welsh, *Blackmail* 11–25) and the recognition of long-lost heirs (Cave 212–15). *Felix Holt* foregrounds two episodes of recognition, in which the community attempts to assimilate two stories of severance and voluntary exile—the return of the prodigal son Harold Transome, after fifteen years away in the East, and the exchange of identities through which Maurice Christian Bycliffe becomes Henry Scaddon. Both cases involve the protagonists in the discovery of their parentage: Harold must come to terms with the fact that he is the illegitimate product of his mother's affair with the hated family lawyer, Matthew Jermyn, whilst Esther discovers, through a story evidenced by the traditional tokens of recognition (lockets and a curl of hair), that she is the heir to the Bycliffe estate. Both are compelled to acknowledge the mandates of bio-logical inheritance, in a wider metaphorical exploration of the "statutes" which bind us. In her epigraph drawn from *Agamemnon*, Eliot chooses to illuminate the intracta-bility of consequences—"'Tis law as steadfast as the throne of Zeus / Our days are heritors of days gone by" (582; ch. 48).

As with the technicalities of criminal trial procedure, Eliot does not portray the particulars of civil disputes solely for their own sake. Cases of contested inheritance carry a particularly rich metaphorical resonance for Eliot. On the one hand, as George Semmel contends, Eliot's autobiography—notably the breach with her father occa-sioned by her severance with Evangelicalism—invested her writing with a particular commitment to the myth of virtuous dispossession: her fiction repeatedly reaffirms the choice of moral sentiments and substance above birth and blood when marital ties and heirships are at stake (Semmel 45). Esther in *Felix Holt* and Gwendolen in *Daniel Deronda* both manifest their increasing moral maturity by the alignment of their sympathies with the dispossessed inheritors (the Transomes, in *Felix Holt*, and sup-posedly the eponymous protagonist in *Daniel Deronda*, although subsequent events disprove Gwendolen's initial suspicion that Daniel is the illegitimate son of Sir Hugo Malinger). On the other hand, the significance of the concept of inheritance is con-stitutional, and Eliot displays a particularly conservative and Burkean treatment of the theme in her fiction. Following the publication of *Felix Holt*, her publisher Black-wood had written to Eliot, asking if Felix could be persuaded to address the people: "When the new Reform Bill comes into operation the working man will be on his trial and if he misconducts himself it will go hard with the country" (*Letters* 4:398)— Blackwood felt Eliot was ideally positioned to offer a call to restraint. She agreed and an "Address to Working Men, by Felix Holt" appeared in *Blackwood's Magazine* in January 1868. In this printed "oration," Felix purports to speak both to and for the English working class but the sentiments he expresses are far from radical. According to Felix, the motif by which future social amelioration can best be apprehended is that of inheritance. He argues that the endowed classes, in the inheritance from the past, hold the precious material without which no worthy, noble future can be moulded. Many of the highest uses of life are in their keeping; and if privilege has often been abused, it also has been the nurse of excellence.

To jeopardize the security of the upper classes is thus to endanger the intellectual wealth which they hold in trust: to resort to violence would be to "injure your own inheritance and the inheritance of your children" ("Address," *Felix Holt* 624–26). To appreciate the mutual nature of this shared inheritance is to work for the reconciliation of the classes, not to advocate open antagonism or armed conflict: "the highest interest of mankind must at last be a common and not a divided interest" ("Address," *Felix Holt* 613–14).

In *Felix Holt* and *Middlemarch*, Eliot extends her analysis of human behavior to include the impact of political representation on questions of justice: completed on either side of the enactment of the Second Reform Bill and set at the time of the First Reform Act (1832), these novels are both preoccupied with the ways in which authentic representation—of oneself, of another, of "the people" in a reforming House of Commons—may be undertaken. A legal system depends for its efficacy and its fairness upon a stable constitution. As Cathrine Frank, Catherine Gallagher and Semmel have noted, the analysis of the election at Treby Magna in *Felix Holt* allows Eliot to place this interrelationship under particularly topical scrutiny: in the assessment of responses to political electioneering, she parodies individual self-interest as the test of political commitment, but she nevertheless fails to embrace a fully representative model of reform. In a letter to Blackwood on 20 February 1874, Eliot famously professed herself "no believer in Salvation by Ballot" (*Letters* 6:21–22): in Gallagher's analysis, Eliot believes that the working man *should* be represented—but in fiction rather than in Parliament, for "literary practice [was the] primary mechanism for social reform [and a]s such, it becomes an alternative, at least for the foreseeable future, to political representation" (224). But the trial of Felix Holt further complicates this model as it promotes the Rousseauian belief that a man is the best representative of his own interests—that any representation by proxy, whether professional or political, is inherently liable to distortion. However, even as it critiques these legal and political systems, fiction is tainted by the self-reflexivity of the debates, for it too is dependent upon the vicarious or "virtual" representation of one person's interests by another.

For Eliot, as for other mid-Victorian novelists, much emphasis is placed on cultivating the altruism and generosity which would enable neighbors and strangers alike to avoid litigation. The Biblical hope that Christian brothers should not resort to adversarial combat in courts of law is one shared by the world of Eliot's novels, and she works hard to advocate non-legal forms of dispute resolution. The types of mutual accommodation which may be achieved in Eliot's marriages serve as a template for wider social reconciliation, and again, the public significance of seemingly very private actions is made particularly manifest in *Felix Holt*. Esther is offered two alternative paths by which the competing litigious claims to the Transome estate may be resolved, thereby placing, in the terms of Andrew Miller's analysis, second-person relations under tremendous social and political strain (Miller 25). Were she to marry Harold, "all scandal, all hatching of law-mischief, may be avoided, and the thing may be brought to an amicable conclusion" (457; ch. 36) by the union of the "rational claim" (Harold's, based on long, undisturbed possession) and the "legal claim" (Esther's, after the seemingly "arbitrary" death of Tommy Trounsem [454; ch. 36]). On the other hand, Esther could seek ownership of the estate in her own right, "sanctif[ied]" by "an undefined sense of Nemesis" following her father's death in wrongful imprisonment (475; ch. 38). Yet ultimately her sympathetic identification with the dispossessed is too great for her to assert such a claim, and Esther chooses instead the path of renunciation, preferring a "lot" which embraces both love and voluntary poverty. Whilst Eliot's realism is dependent upon a legal attentiveness to particulars, an imitation of the laws of evidence and a jurisprudential wisdom in the assessment of motive and intention, she nevertheless counsels her reader to follow Esther's example and leave the law behind. And for Eliot, fiction provides us with a moral education far in excess of anything which "black-letter" law can offer.

NOTES

1 Sheard was instructed to draw up Eliot's and G. H. Lewes's wills in November 1859 (*Letters* 3:205, 212) and in the same month he was consulted about T. C. Newby's efforts to publish a sequel to *Adam Bede* (*Letters* 3:208–9, 212–3).

2 For example, in 1854 she edited George Coombe's lengthy article entitled "Criminal Legislation and Penal Reform": see *Letters* 8:75–111.

REFERENCES

Baker, William, ed. *Some George Eliot Notebooks*. 4 vols. Salzburg: U of Salzburg P, 1976–85.

Cave, Terence. *Recognitions: A Study in Poetics*. Oxford: Clarendon, 1988. Rpt. 2002.

Eliot, George. *Adam Bede*. Ed. Margaret Reynolds. London: Penguin, 1994.

Eliot, George. *Daniel Deronda*. Ed. Barbara Hardy. London: Penguin, 1986.

Eliot, George. *Felix Holt*. Ed. Peter Coveney. London: Penguin, 1987

Eliot, George. *The George Eliot Letters*. Ed. Gordon S. Haight. 9 vols. New Haven: Yale UP, 1954–78.

Eliot, George. *Middlemarch*. Ed. Rosemary Ashton. London: Penguin, 1994.

Eliot, George. *The Mill on the Floss*. London: Penguin, 1985.

Eliot, George. *Romola*. Ed. Andrew Sanders. London: Penguin, 1980.

Eliot, George. *Scenes of Clerical Life*. Ed. David Lodge. London: Penguin, 1985.

Frank, Cathrine O. *Law, Literature and the Transmission of Culture in England, 1837–1925*. Farnham: Ashgate, 2010.

Gallagher, Catherine. *The Industrial Reformation of English Fiction: Social Discourse and Narrative Form 1832–67*. Chicago: U of Chicago P, 1985.

Haight, Gordon S. *George Eliot: A Biography*. Oxford: Clarendon, 1968.

John, Juliet. *Dickens's Villains: Character, Melodrama, Popular Culture*. Oxford: Oxford UP, 2003.

Krueger, Christine. *Reading for the Law: British Literary History and Gender Advocacy*. Charlottesville: U of Virginia P, 2010.

Langbein, John. *The Origins of Adversary Criminal Trial*. Oxford: Oxford UP, 2003.

Mill, John Stuart. "Utilitarianism." 1861. *Essays on Ethics, Religion, and Society*. Ed. J. M. Robson. Toronto: Toronto UP, 1967.

Miller, Andrew H. *The Burdens of Perfection: On Ethics and Reading in Nineteenth-Century British Literature*. Ithaca: Cornell UP, 2008.

Petch, Simon. "Law, Equity, and Conscience in Victorian England." *Victorian Literature and Culture* 25.1.(1997): 123–39.

Pratt, John Clark, and Victor Neufeldt, eds. *George Eliot's "Middlemarch" Notebooks*. Berkeley: U of California P, 1979.

Price, Leah. *The Anthology and the Rise of the Novel*. Cambridge: Cambridge UP, 2000.

Rodensky, Lisa. *The Crime in Mind: Criminal Responsibility and the Victorian Novel*. Oxford: Oxford UP, 2003.

Schor, Hilary. "Show-Trials: Character, Conviction, and the Law in Victorian Fiction." *Cardozo Studies in Law and Literature* 11.2 (1999): 179–95.

Semmel, Bernard. *George Eliot and the Politics of National Inheritance*. Oxford: Oxford UP, 1994.

Schramm, Jan-Melissa. *Testimony and Advocacy in Victorian Law, Literature, and Theology*. Cambridge: Cambridge UP, 2000.

Schramm, Jan-Melissa. *Atonement and Self-Sacrifice in Nineteenth-Century Narrative*. Cambridge: Cambridge UP, 2012.

Watt, Gary. *Equity Stirring: The Story of Justice Beyond the Law*. Oxford: Hart, 2009.

Weisenfarth, Joseph, ed. *A Writer's Notebook 1854–1879*. Charlottesville: U of Virginia P, 1981.

Welsh, Alexander. *George Eliot and Blackmail*. Cambridge: Harvard UP, 1985.

Welsh, Alexander. *Strong Representations: Narrative and Circumstantial Evidence in England*. Baltimore: Johns Hopkins UP, 1992.

23
George Eliot and Finance

Nancy Henry

"She used to adore her husband, and now she adores her money . . . "[1]

George Eliot never constructed a financial plot as dramatic as those found in W. M. Thackeray's *The Newcomes* or Anthony Trollope's *The Way We Live Now*, but she used financial networks to establish connections among individual characters, communities, and nations. Unlike some of her contemporaries, she was not nostalgic for a pre-capitalist past. As a successful author, she took advantage of the most sophisticated investment opportunities that Victorian Britain had to offer, and in each of her novels, she drew on historically specific financial details to enhance the social medium in which her characters develop. She did not romanticize human relationships as existing apart from economic interests; rather, in her fiction, she confronted the reality that all social relationships, including those within families, are also economic relationships, whether in pre-capitalist societies or within the various stages of modern capitalism represented in her novels.

Eliot's writing presents a spectrum of financial dealings from the collection of rents to pawnbroking, domestic and foreign banking, mortgages, and speculative ventures in horses, manufactured goods, real estate, and mines. Characters in financial professions include the bankers Harold Transome (*Felix Holt*) and Mr. Bulstrode (*Middlemarch*), pawnbrokers Mr. Dunkirk (*Middlemarch*), Mr. Cohen and Mr. Weiner (*Daniel Deronda*), as well as the speculators Mr. Lassman (*Daniel Deronda*) and Sir Gavial Mantrap (*Impressions of Theophrastus Such*). In her work as a whole, Eliot examines the ways in which human relationships might be reduced to the most elemental monetary

A Companion to George Eliot, First Edition. Edited by Amanda Anderson and Harry E. Shaw.
© 2013 John Wiley & Sons, Ltd. Published 2016 by John Wiley & Sons, Ltd.

exchanges, whether in literal slavery or in the marriage market. At the same time, each of her works represents a local economy connected to national, foreign, and colonial markets.

Characteristically, Eliot does not view the simpler financial relationships of the past as superior to the more complicated ones of the present. Rather, her fiction represents economies in transition. For example, in *The Mill on the Floss* (set roughly in the 1830s), Tom Tulliver speculates in the foreign trade of manufactured goods and also rises within a company that is implementing the very steam-powered mills that will supplant his father's traditional water-turned mill. Kinship networks persist in these transactions, but their influence is weakening as commercial and financial exchanges follow developing technology in manufacturing and transportation to become ever more complex and impersonal. Yet complexity and impersonality are not in themselves bad: the fact that Mr. Tulliver knows the lawyer Wakem—the "devil" responsible for his financial ruin—does not make his suffering any less than that of Gwendolen Harleth in *Daniel Deronda* (set 1864–66), whose family loses a fortune originally made on a plantation in the West Indies (where they have never been) in the failure of a banking house due to speculations by a man they have never met.

Over the course of her career, Eliot's attitudes toward wealth shifted as her knowledge of the developing financial system in Victorian Britain and its empire increased. This change follows from her altered social and economic position as she evolved from a self-supporting editor and journalist living modestly in lodgings to one of England's most highly-paid authors with a diversified, income-generating stock portfolio managed by the banker, John Walter Cross, whom she would eventually marry. She negotiated the most profitable contracts for her work while resisting the temptation to place financial remuneration over artistic integrity. Eliot's mixed emotions about being wealthy are evident in the plots of her later work, in which characters including Eppie in *Silas Marner*, Esther in *Felix Holt*, Dorothea in *Middlemarch*, and Gwendolen in *Daniel Deronda*, renounce the prospect of wealth in favor of higher personal values of love and duty. Her conflicted feelings about wealth may have influenced the form of her art, as her determination not to write for money (i.e., to write what would be popular and sell) was transmuted into her experimentation with genres, including both short verse and longer poems, which were not likely to be profitable. Ironically, these experimental departures from the realist English novel were made possible only by the freedom from financial concerns that her popularity afforded.

Beginnings

Eliot's fiction traces the development of an increasingly complex global financial system up to her own time with a constant awareness that financial relations have always characterized both the public and private spheres. *Romola* looks back to the international influence of fourteenth-century "Sicilian creditors" (44; ch. 5) and the centrality of the "Monti or public funds" to fifteenth-century Florence (184; ch.

19). In the British, Napoleonic War economy of *Adam Bede*, Mrs. Poyser supplements her tenant farmer husband's income by running a dairy, and Adam contemplates the purchase of a carpentry business before he becomes, like Eliot's father, the estate manager for the local squire. *Silas Marner* represents the last of a "race" of cottage weavers who exchanged their goods directly for gold coins. *The Mill on the Floss* parallels the fall of the miller Mr. Tulliver with the rise of the capitalist Guest family. *Felix Holt* and *Middlemarch*, both set at the time of the First Reform Act (1832), represent unevenly developed financial systems in which feudal tenant/landlord relationships co-exist with a global economy of trade and banking. In *Felix Holt*, Jermyn speculates in the development of a spa resort with investments from Sir Maximus Debarry (40; ch. 3), and the Englishman Harold Transome works as a merchant banker in Smyrna. In *Middlemarch*, Mr. Vincy gains social stature by running a successful silk-dyeing business and Bulstrode's provincial bank is so profitable that he is able to purchase the property of Stone Court to elevate his social status. Finally, Eliot turned to more modern financial systems in the two works set closest to the time of their composition in the 1870s, *Daniel Deronda* and *Impressions of Theophrastus Such*, both of which represent speculators in mines (Mr. Lassman and Sir Gavial Mantrap).

In her poem "The Legend of Jubal," Eliot freed herself from the burden of her usual historical accuracy and offered a myth of her own creation about the invention of money itself. Her narrator designates this invention as a sign of the fall from an original state of nature into a state of civilization and culture, an overall theme of the poem, which has at its center the invention (or discovery) of music. Tubal Cain, her archetypal blacksmith, represents industrious physical labor in contrast to his more poetic brother Jubal, who is inspired to create music in part by listening to the sound of Tubal's hammer. In her poem, it is Tubal Cain who fashions the first coins:

> Thus to mixed ends wrought Tubal; and they say,
> Some things he made have lasted to this day;
> As, thirty silver pieces that were found
> By Noah's children buried in the ground.
> He made them from mere hunger of device,
> Those small white discs; but they became the price
> The traitor Judas sold his Master for;
> And men still handling them in peace and war
> Catch foul disease, that comes from appetite,
> And lurks and clings as withering, damning blight.
>
> (*Shorter Poetry* 1:48; lines 225–33)

Here she ranges from her elaboration of the stories told in Genesis about the descendants of Cain and Noah to the betrayal of Jesus in the New Testament (Matthew 26:15) to a vague present when men still handle the modern equivalent of silver coins first forged by Tubal. Her language emphasizes that Judas's betrayal was a sale of one human being by another. Money stands beside art (music) at the origin of culture, and implies that the two aspects of civilization, money and art, would remain forever antithetical yet inseparable. In the mythic register of the poem, she is able to characterize greed for money as a "foul disease," while in her other fictional representations of historically specific contexts, she explores the more subtle psychological forms that greed would take.

All of Eliot's fiction addresses the complex relationship between blood and money, including the archaic remnants of a feudal system of primogeniture and entail, which co-exist with sophisticated modern instruments, such as wills, investments, and trusts. She establishes these fundamental elements of blood and money in the first scene of her first published story. "The Sad Fortunes of the Reverend Amos Barton" opens at the fireside of Mrs. Patten, "a childless old lady, who had got rich chiefly by the negative process of spending nothing" (*Scenes* 8; ch.1):

> Mrs Patten's passive accumulation of wealth, through all sorts of "bad times," on the farm of which she had been the sole tenant since her husband's death, her epigrammatic neighbour, Mrs. Hackit, sarcastically accounted for by supposing that "sixpences grew on the bents of Cross Farm;" while Mr Hackit, expressing his views more literally, reminded his wife that "money breeds money." (*Scenes* 8; ch. 1)

Mrs. Patten's gossipy neighbors resort to the metaphors of growing and breeding to express the reality that, in the early decades of the nineteenth century, money saved, even if only deposited in the provincial bank, generates interest. The scene anticipates and stresses the importance that financial themes would have in all of her later work and includes the familial politics of inheritance. Like old Mr. Featherstone in *Middlemarch*, Mrs. Patten intends to disappoint relatives who are hopeful of receiving a legacy after her death. The all-knowing narrator tells us:

> She used to adore her husband, and now she adores her money, cherishing a quiet blood-relation's hatred for her niece, Janet Gibbs, who, she knows, expects a large legacy, and whom she is determined to disappoint. Her money shall all go in a lump to a distant relation of her husband's. (*Scenes* 9; ch.1)

In one half-sentence, the narrator sums up the life of Mrs. Patten: "She used to adore her husband, and now she adores her money." This trajectory of a life is reversed in the plot of *Silas Marner*, in which the miser who adores his money comes to adore his adopted daughter. The corruption that accompanies the adoration of money is further suggested by the childless widow's unnatural but all too common hatred of her blood relation, and in this way Eliot also emphasizes that blood and money are the fundamental elements upon which financial systems are built.

In the second story included in *Scenes of Clerical Life*, "Mr. Gilfil's Love Story," set at the end of the eighteenth century, another widowed tenant, Mrs. Hartopp, debates with her landlord, Sir Christopher, about her competency to manage the farm from which he intends to evict her. After arguing that she has "sold the hay, an' corn, an' all the live things, an' paid the debts, an' put the money out to use . . . ," she argues further that she knows "a deal o' farmin'," and "there was my husband's great-aunt managed a farm for twenty year, an' left legacies to all her nephys and nieces" (*Scenes* 82; ch. 2). The scene represents more than an encounter between members of the most widely divergent of social classes, the aristocratic Sir Christopher and his peasant tenant; it shows that, even in this late eighteenth-century context, the paying of debts, the investment of money (putting it "out to use"), and the significance of wills were essential aspects of life for both tenants and landlords. The central fact of "Mr. Gilfil's Love Story" is the childless Sir Christopher's legal obligation to leave his estate to his unworthy nephew.

These encounters with provincial women in Eliot's fiction, albeit in generations prior to Eliot's own, reveal her personal experience with the management of money in all classes of English society. Sir Christopher and his wife are based on the Newdigates, the aristocratic family whose estate was managed by her father Robert Evans. Throughout his life (1773–1849) and until his son Isaac took over the management of the Newdigate estate, Robert Evans was in the service of this family, which was engaged in complex legal suits over the ownership of the property. The contesting of the Newdigate will, which caused Robert Evans much aggravation as the mediator between landlords and tenants, influenced Eliot's representation of legal disputes.

Blood and Money

Legal suits are central to what is considered Eliot's most autobiographical novel, *The Mill on the Floss*, in which she fictionalized the family of her mother, Christiana Pearson Evans, in the four Dodson sisters and their spouses. The Dodson sisters are comic figures in *The Mill on the Floss*, but their comic role comes in the service of a commentary on money in relation to families. Their provincial middle-class tribalism dictates duty to "kin" understood largely in terms of money. Her narrator contextualizes the saving and cautiously investing ways of these dominant women who place the utmost importance on the correctness of their wills and the distribution of their wealth according to strict rules of respectability. The hierarchy of kin to be left legacies by the Dodson sisters is particularly important since two of the married sisters (Mrs. Glegg and Mrs. Pullet), like Mrs. Patten, are wealthy but childless. Mrs. Glegg would not think of disinheriting her sister's children because of a quarrel with their father: "in the matter of wills, personal qualities were subordinate to the great fundamental fact of blood; and to . . . not make your legacies bear a direct ratio to degrees of kinship was a prospective disgrace that would have embittered her life" (134; bk. 1, ch. 13).

Mrs. Glegg particularly upholds the strict family traditions of the Dodson sisters. She and her husband are united in being of a "a money-getting, money-keeping turn" (126; bk. 1, ch. 12). The narrator notes that their values reflect an earlier era:

> The inalienable habit of saving, as an end in itself, belonged to the industrious men of business of a former generation, who made their fortunes slowly, almost as the tracking

of the fox belongs to the harrier—it constituted them a "race," which is nearly lost in these days of rapid money-getting, when lavishness comes close on the back of want. (127; bk. 1, ch. 12)

Comically and critically as she portrays the Gleggs, Eliot obviously felt some respect for their conservative attitude toward money in contrast to the ethos of the more precarious mid-century credit economy which prevailed at the time she was writing the novel.[2] And yet it is through Mrs. Glegg that Eliot presents the temptation to venture capital as irresistible to money-loving spirits.

When Mrs. Glegg thinks of "calling in" the money she has lent to her brother-in-law Mr. Tulliver after a family dispute, Mr. Glegg warns her:

"But if you'd like to call it in, don't do it in a hurry now, and breed more enmity in the family—but wait till there's a pretty mortgage to be had without any trouble. You'd have to set a lawyer to work now to find an investment and make no end o' expense." (129–30; bk. 1, ch. 12)

Appealing to their shared conservative natures, Mr. Glegg cautions against calling money in until it can be put out without added expense in a "pretty mortgage," a term reflecting what might be called an aesthetics of investing well appreciated by the money-getting couple.

The Glegg marriage is unusual at a time when marriage meant that a wife's money belonged to her husband because, as Mr. Glegg remarks, his wife has been "allowed to keep her own money same as if it was settled on her" (130; bk. 1, ch. 12). Their finances are separate and Mrs. Glegg can do as she likes with the money inherited from her father. Further emphasizing the economic basis of the marriage, the narrator tells us that Mr. Glegg is "extremely reticent about his will" and Mrs. Glegg has determined in advance that if he does not provide for her sufficiently, she would "cry no more than if he had been a second husband" (131; bk. 1, ch. 12). Her sympathy will be in proportion to the settlement upon her.

This establishment of the Gleggs' finances becomes important later in the novel when Tom Tulliver and his friend Bob Jakin scheme to send out "a bit of cargo to foreign ports" (291; bk. 5, ch. 2). Tom and Bob naturally think of approaching Mrs. Glegg with this opportunity to multiply her money by investing in their scheme. Upon learning that the speculators hope for a return of ten or twelve percent, Mrs. Glegg demands to know why she had not been told about such modern ventures: "then why wasn't I let to know o' such things before, Mr. Glegg?" (297; bk. 5, ch. 2). With Bob promising her "six or seven per zent" after Tom has taken his share, the men prevail upon her to part with her money, and she gives Tom the capital to make the speculation.

Tom is "so well pleased with the prospect of a speculation that might change the slow process of addition into multiplication," that he resolves to undertake it despite the reluctance of his father who had "speculated in the purchase of some corn, and had lost by it" (291; bk. 5, ch. 2). His father has been so reduced by his debt that he now equates the loss of money with loss of his very life and begs Tom not to risk it. The narrator explains that Tom does not tell his father about the ultimately successful venture by way of an observation about blood relations, a theme that recurs in her early work: "it was that disinclination to confidence which is seen between near kindred—that family repulsion which spoils the most sacred relations of our lives" (302; bk. 5, ch. 2). At once generalized and personal, the gratuitous line suggests that in addition to primitive notions of duty, what binds us to family members—by blood and by marriage—is our monetary relationship with them. It is both a realistic analysis of the economics within families and an indictment of blood ties and of marriage. Just as Maggie conceals her relationship with Philip Wakem (an enemy because his father financially ruined her father) and Mr. Glegg keeps his will a secret from his wife, so Tom keeps his speculations a secret from his father until they have earned him enough to redeem the mill.[3]

George Eliot's Wealth

At the time Eliot wrote *The Mill on the Floss*, her communication with her brother Isaac was limited to the receipt of annuity checks (a legacy from their father), which he sent her via a solicitor. The reason for the break with Isaac was her union with G. H. Lewes, with whom she was living. Lewes was tied to his wife Agnes by his legal obligation to support her and her children. Eliot's domestic situation now included a close sibling bond and a legal marriage that were both reduced to cash payments. Furthermore, she earned enough money from *The Mill on the Floss* to begin investing in stocks, and in 1860 she purchased two thousand pounds' worth of shares in the Great Indian Peninsula Railway, which paid five percent, more than the Consols or Funds but was still a security rather than a speculation (Henry 78). It is in this context that, while she was affirming her decision to live with Lewes and act as stepmother to his three sons, and while she was pursuing new means of increasing her own wealth, she wrote *Silas Marner*, a novel that morally affirms the value of love for human beings over the love of money.

Eliot's knowledge about economics and finance prior to beginning her career as an investor was derived from a combination of personal experience and reading. Her friendship with the Coventry ribbon manufacturer Charles Bray and her observations of John Chapman's financial mismanagement of the *Westminster Review* exposed her to the challenges of running a business. Her readings in political economy as editor of the *Westminster Review* in the 1850s, especially the liberal *laissez faire* theories of John Stuart Mill, were influential to her thinking throughout her career.[4] She was also familiar with the broad critiques of capitalism by Thomas Carlyle and John Ruskin. In 1840, she read Carlyle's *Chartism* (*Letters* 1:71) in which he famously laments that "Cash Payment has become the sole nexus of man to men!" (61). Writing in the tradition of Carlyle, Ruskin complained about the absence of "social affection" in theories of political economy. When Eliot read his *Political Economy of Art*, she condemned his "stupendous specimens of arrogant absurdity on some economical points" (*Letters* 2:422).[5] While Carlyle and Ruskin romanticized a medieval past of feudal relationships based on honor and loyalty, Eliot took a more realistic historical perspective. *Silas Marner*, however, offers a fable in which the sudden loss of accumulated wealth creates the conditions for a pure and redeeming love.

In this cultural as well as biographical context, *Silas Marner* may be read as an apology for the wealth that Eliot was now earning and as an ultimately unconvincing reassurance that human love can exist outside of self-interest and monetary entanglements. She was inspired to write the uncharacteristic short novel following *The Mill on the Floss* and while she was contemplating *Romola*. Early in the novel, Silas Marner responds to a betrayal by his best friend and his fiancée, and his rejection by the religious community of which he is a member, by becoming a recluse and miser, and the rest of the story recounts his reintegration into the community of Raveloe through his love for his adopted daughter Eppie, who comes to him after his fetishized gold coins have been stolen. Only in the state of poverty created by the theft of the coins can Silas realize the value of love untainted by monetary interests.[6]

Of Human Bondage

While Eliot may have thought Ruskin's economic critiques were absurd, she was interested in the fundamentally economic nature of social bonds. She viewed the exchange of human beings for money as taking various, historically specific forms. In *Adam Bede*, for example, Adam frees his brother Seth from having to serve in the militia by paying for a substitute (210; ch. 19). In *Daniel Deronda*, Mirah's father attempts to sell her in marriage to a Count, while Gwendolen's family pressures her to sell herself for money in marriage to Grandcourt.

Slavery does not feature prominently in Eliot's fiction, though its shadow is seen in *Daniel Deronda*, which is set during the American Civil War, and in which Mrs. Davilow's income is generated by money inherited from her father, who owned a plantation in Barbados. Gwendolen does not consider the origins of the money, but its derivation is implicitly tainted with the past of slave labor. The frequently-quoted conversation in *Daniel Deronda* about the problem of the blacks in the post-slavery sugar economy of Jamaica in the 1860s (ch. 29) recalls Eliot's story "Brother Jacob" in which David Faux imagines that when he goes to the West Indies after stealing his mother's guineas, he would marry a gullible princess. When that misguided venture fails, he opens a confectioner's shop (under the name of Edward Freely), an enterprise dependent on imported sugar.

In 1856, Eliot reviewed Harriet Beecher Stowe's anti-slavery novel *Dred, A Tale of the Great Dismal Swamp* for the *Westminster Review*. Avoiding the politics of the novel, which are more radical than those of *Uncle Tom's Cabin*, she focuses on questions of realism and refers to the demoralization of oppressed peoples as a matter of realist aesthetics. Later, after the end of the American Civil War and abolition of American slavery, Eliot engaged in a correspondence with Stowe and clearly saw a parallel in the moral undertaking of the latter's anti-slavery novels and her own positive representation of the Jews in *Daniel Deronda* (*Letters* 6:301).

While the contemporary reality of slavery remains a background presence in her other fiction, Eliot treats slavery directly in *Romola*. In events that occur prior to the action of the novel, Tito and his adoptive father Baldassarre are traveling to the Greek island of Delos in separate galleys when Baldassarre's ship is intercepted by Turkish pirates. Tito learns from the crew of the companion galley that a man was seen falling overboard, but others on the ship were taken as prisoners and most likely later subjected to hard labor as slaves (94–95; ch. 9). Tito's own galley subsequently suffers shipwreck. Having survived, Tito finds his way to Rome and then Florence, where he sells the jewels in his possession (which belong to his father). With 500 gold florins in his possession, he must decide whether to seek out his father and pay a ransom to liberate him from slavery, or use the money to advance his own career. Rationalizing that Baldassarre might have been the man who fell overboard (and secretly hoping that this is the case), he chooses to use the money himself. This failure to honor a human bond (albeit not a blood one) and repay the debt he owes Baldassarre for rescuing him from the streets as a child, echoes thematically throughout the novel. The narrator remarks that even an unlovable man such as Baldassarre deserves the "love that is rooted in memories and distils perpetually the sweet balms of fidelity and forbearing tenderness" (96; ch. 9). This was the love Eliot had represented in *Silas Marner*, but in *Romola*, she confronts its starkest form of betrayal. Tito might have redeemed his father, but he chooses to put his money "out to usury" and collect the interest instead (94; ch. 9).

In introducing Romola di Bardi and her father Bardo, Eliot's narrator details the history of the family in specifically financial terms. In the fourteenth century, the Bardis were a banking family "standing in the very front of European commerce—the Christian Rothschilds of that time—undertaking to furnish specie for the wars of our Edward the Third" (43; ch. 5). When their "august debtor left them with an august deficit," it caused "a ruinous shock to the credit of the Bardi" and "a commercial calamity along all the coasts of the Mediterranean" (44; ch. 5). The narrator continues with the modern parallels that suggest Eliot's moral opinion about bankruptcy in Victorian Britain, observing of the Bardi that "like more modern bankrupts, they did not, for all that, hide their heads in humiliation; on the contrary, they seemed to have held them higher than ever" (44; ch. 5).[7]

But in the Bardi family's reduced state at the end of the fifteenth-century, Bardo is a "moneyless, blind old scholar" (45; ch. 5) who knows nothing about his own finances and debt. He cares only that his library be preserved, leaving his daughter Romola and her godfather, Bernardo del Nero, to worry about how the library might remain intact, rather than being sold to pay off his debts:

> Bardo assented with a wave of the hand when Bernardo told him that he thought it would be well now to begin to sell property and clear off debts—being accustomed to

think of debts and property as a sort of thick wood that his imagination never penetrated, still less got beyond. (184; ch. 19)

Treacherously, Tito enters the scene as Romola's intended husband, and appears to interest himself in the project of saving Bardo's library: "And Tito set about winning Messer Bernardo's respect by inquiring, with his ready faculty, into Florentine money matters, the secrets of the *Monti* or public funds, the values of real property, and the profits of banking" (184; ch. 19). But rather than use this knowledge to honor Bardo's wishes after his death, Tito sells the library for a profit without telling his wife. Her shocked response—"You have sold them?"—signals the second of Tito's betrayals of his human bonds for cash (272; ch. 32).

In her next novel, *Felix Holt* (set 1832–33), Eliot integrates slavery into a nineteenth-century English setting when Harold Transome purchases and marries a Greek slave while he is working as a merchant and banker in Smyrna, concealing the marriage from his family in England.[8] It is an indication of Harold's character that he went to Constantinople under the patronage of a relative and was intended to enter a life of public service as a diplomat. But in a rather preposterous offstage plot twist, he saves the life of an Armenian banker and takes the opportunity of the banker's gratitude to enter the world of international commerce and finance, giving up that life when he comes into his property back in England (23; ch. 1).

In addition to an inheritance plot complicated by adultery, illegitimacy, and adoption, *Felix Holt* also recounts the attempt by lawyer Jermyn (Harold's biological father) to turn Treby Magna into a fashionable spa resort. The speculation, which occurs prior to the main action of the novel in a depressed, post-Napoleonic War economy, fails at least partially because the area has been marred by the "coal-mines and the canal" (40; ch. 3). The empty building intended for the Spa eventually becomes a "tape manufactory" (41; ch. 3). Jermyn's failed venture connects him to his illegitimate son Harold, whose character is implicitly condemned by his preference for a career of banking and by his marriage (if it was a marriage) to the unnamed, now-deceased Greek slave by whom he has a son. The references in the novel to financial speculations at home and abroad, and to the persistence of slavery with which English subjects were complicit, show that even Eliot's novels of English rural life represent England's connections to global markets for money, commodities, and persons. Invoking various forms of slavery in *Romola*, "Brother Jacob," *Felix Holt*, and *Daniel Deronda*, she emphasized the tendency throughout history to reduce human beings to a monetary price. This literal selling of people is a basis from which, through comparison and contrast, she explores the other ways in which—even in the most advanced societies—personal and financial interests were inseparable.

Human Transactions

In *Middlemarch* the web of social and familial relationships that entangles the multiple plots is also distinctly financial. Featherstone's and Casaubon's wills, Lydgate's debt, and Bulstrode's past and present business practices situate finance at the center of her "study of provincial life." Mr. Vincy's apparently profitable silk trade, for example, is carried on only with money from his brother-in-law Bulstrode's bank (98; ch. 12). Bulstrode's power depends upon the fact that he knew "the financial secrets of most traders in the town and could touch the springs of their credit" (145; ch. 16). Mr. Vincy's son Fred expects to inherit his uncle Featherstone's estate, but old Featherstone accuses him of a conflict of interests: "You like Bulstrode and speckilation better than Featherstone and land" (103; ch. 12). Placing Fred in the hopeless position of proving that he has not speculated on his expectations, Featherstone demands a testimonial from Bulstrode that Fred has not speculated before he will provide his eager nephew with a cash advance.

In contrast to other characters' preoccupation with various forms of speculation and investment, Caleb Garth represents the work ethic that was idealized earlier in *Adam Bede*. Caleb defines "business" as honest labor. Like Eliot's mythical figure Jubal: "The echoes of the great hammer where roof or keel were a-making, the signal-shouts of the workmen, the roar of the furnace, the thunder and plash of the engine, were a sublime music to him" (235; ch. 24). All such honest labor "acted on him as poetry without the aid of poets, had made a philosophy for him without the aid of philosophers, a religion without the aid of theology" (236; ch. 24). Labor, in short, is sublime to Caleb: "But he could not manage finance," a fact that causes practical problems for him and his family (236; ch. 24). While involvement in banking and business professions in and of itself could not constitute a condemnation of character for Eliot, it seems that the removal of finance from the more direct forms of productive labor offered opportunities for corruption that her fiction exposes and criticizes.

The banker Bulstrode's history is particularly relevant to the consideration of finance in Eliot's novels because of the way it touches upon the inextricability of familial and monetary matters. Bulstrode was once a fervent member of a "Calvinistic dissenting church at Highbury" in London who was inclined to the ministry and to missionary work (578; ch. 61). Employed in a London pawnbroking business with shady dealings, he chooses to ignore the establishment's trade in illegal goods. When his employer Mr. Dunkirk dies, Bulstrode marries the much older widow and heiress. He pays Raffles to cover up the whereabouts of Mrs. Dunkirk's estranged daughter and grandson, thereby ensuring that he will inherit her fortune when she dies. Finding his way to Middlemarch, he marries a local woman, Mr. Vincy's sister Harriet, and also establishes a bank and a charitable hospital. In this way, he seeks to erase his past sins, becoming all the more pious in an inward state of guilt, which he is forced to confront when Raffles returns to blackmail him with the information that the disinherited grandson, Will Ladislaw, is now living in Middlemarch. The narrator asks: "The profits made out of lost souls—where can the line be drawn at which they begin in human transactions?" (579; ch. 61).[9]

Joshua Rigg, Featherstone's illegitimate son, arrives in Middlemarch to receive the inheritance expected by the disappointed Vincy and Featherstone relatives. He had been "educated only by the opportunities of a clerk and accountant in the smaller commercial houses of a seaport" (387; ch. 41). While there, he "looked through the windows of the money-changers as other boys look through the windows of the pastry-cooks" (488; ch. 53). Here Eliot recalls David Faux in "Brother Jacob," who had chosen the profession of confectioner after looking in at just such pastry-cook windows. For Rigg: "The one joy after which his soul thirsted was to have a money-changer's shop on a much-frequented quay . . . to look sublimely cool as he handled the breeding coins of all nations, while helpless Cupidity looked at him enviously from the other side of an iron lattice (488; ch. 53). Rigg's preference for money-changing over land owning signals his status as a low character. Ironically, Bulstrode, who began his career as a pawnbroker, purchases the property that Rigg inherited from Featherstone.

While we do not know whether Bulstrode's original employer, the pawnbroker Dunkirk, was Jewish, we know that pawnbroking, like more advanced forms of finance, was a profession associated with Jews, and that in the town of Middlemarch, Dunkirk's grandson Ladislaw is rumored to be the "grandson of a thieving Jew pawnbroker" (727; ch. 77). Eliot was well aware of these associations of Jews and finance, and she both drew on the connections and criticized the stereotypes throughout her late work. For example, she refers to the Bardi as "Christian Rothschilds" in *Romola*, and in *Middlemarch*, she leaves Ladislaw's Jewishness in doubt. In her last two works, however, she confronted directly the long history of Judaism and capitalism.[10]

An Aged Commercial Soul

In *Impressions of Theophrastus Such*, Sir Gavial Mantrap is a speculator who loses, leading Theophrastus to invoke "the widows, spinsters, and hard-working fathers whom his unscrupulous haste to make himself rich has cheated of all their savings" (129; ch.16). In *Daniel Deronda*, Mrs. Davilow informs her daughter Gwendolen that "Grapnell and Co. have failed for a million and we are totally ruined," referring vaguely to "Mr. Lassman's wicked recklessness, which they say was the cause of the failure" (10; ch. 2).[11] With the crash of Grapnell and Co., Mrs. Davilow has become a victimized widow cheated of her savings and struggling to "pay the liabilities" on her lost investments (10; ch. 2). Upon learning this news, Gwendolen, who is gambling in the German spa resort of Leubronn, visits a pawnbroker, Mr. Wiener, to exchange a necklace for cash. Receiving less then she expected, she thinks: "these Jew pawnbrokers were so unscrupulous in taking advantage of Christians unfortunate at play!" (14; ch. 2). The offstage failure of the discount house and the pawned necklace begin the novel by highlighting images of unmarried women who view themselves as victims of the dishonest financial transactions of Jewish men.

Failing and being ruined are the standard metaphors for financial loss, and just as Eliot morally opposed the gambling in which Gwendolen engages in Leubronn, so she objected to the too easy forgiveness of debt, as implied in passing references from the comparison of the Bardi to modern bankrupts in *Romola*, to "the petty sums which any bankrupt of high standing would be sorry to retire upon" in *Middlemarch* (320; ch 35) and the observation in *Daniel Deronda*: "Fanaticism was not so common as bankruptcy" (435; ch. 41). Theophrastus remarks ironically of Sir Gavial that he was "actually reduced to live in comparative obscurity on his wife's settlement of one or two hundred thousand in the consols" (129; ch. 16). Gwendolen's family is not destitute, but it is the loss of her family's money, the shame of becoming a governess or living in "Sawyer's Cottage," that drives her to marry the wealthy aristocrat Grandcourt.[12]

This upper-class form of prostitution represents a parallel experience to the more sordid life of Mirah Lapidoth, whose father would have sold her in marriage had she not run away. Similarly, the high finances that ruin a family of investing heiresses are merely a more expensive and socially respectable form of gambling than that practiced by Mirah's father, the Jewish gambling addict Lapidoth. This juxtaposition between high and low forms of financial transactions structures the plots of *Daniel Deronda*. It is seen in the two Ezra Cohens. The one (Mordecai) is sublimely spiritual. Like Bardo di Bardi, he has evolved from his commercial ancestors into a moneyless scholar. Ezra Cohen the pawnbroker, however, has a "taste for money-getting [that] seemed to be favoured with the success which has been the most exasperating difference in the greed of Jews during all the ages of their dispersion" (441; ch. 42). The Jews are no greedier than their Christian counterparts, but their "difference" is their success at getting money. The narrator remarks of Cohen's young son Jacob: "His small voice was hoarse in its glibness, as if it belonged to an aged commercial soul, fatigued with bargaining through many generations" (329; ch. 33). Lapidoth's gambling "mania" is a perversion of his passions. The unhappy Polish immigrant can find no home in the world and views even his children as potential sources of money to feed his habit.

Daniel Deronda develops the figure of the Jewish pawnbroker, which had been introduced in *Middlemarch*, though with an intentional ambiguity. Will Ladislaw's grandfather is only rumored to be a "Jew pawnbroker," while Mr. Wiener and Mr. Cohen are specifically Jewish. The notion that such figures were modern embodiments of the Jewish condition of dispersion and of an "aged commercial soul" is a reflection on the complex relationship between the Jews and capitalism that Eliot addresses directly in the last chapter of *Impressions of Theophrastus Such*, "The Modern Hep! Hep! Hep!" Surveying Jewish history, her narrator Theophrastus observes of the Jews that "their cupidity and avarice were found at once particularly hateful and particularly useful" (151; ch. 18). He berates his contemporary members of the Liberal party for "insisting that the Jews are made viciously cosmopolitan by holding the world's money-bag, that for them all national interests are resolved into the algebra of loans" (155; ch. 18). He rehearses an argument made against Benjamin Disraeli, for example, that the Jewish "monetary hold on governments is tending to perpetuate in leading Jews a spirit of universal alienism (euphemistically called cosmopolitanism)" (157; ch. 18). "The Modern Hep! Hep! Hep!" explains the historical conditions that have led the Jews into financial professions from pawnbroking to international finance.

From the economic nature of familial bonds to England's involvement in global financial networks dating from the fourteenth century, money, economics, and finance are central to Eliot's writing. She examines the starkest reduction of familial relations to cash payment when Tito fails to pay his father's ransom and Harold Transome purchases a slave wife. At the other extreme, her work is set within international, financial networks, emphasizing that England's economy has been global at least since the Bardi-funded English wars in the fourteenth century, and suggesting that in the nineteenth century, the global economy is completely established, with provincial men speculating on foreign cargoes and working as bankers in Smyrna. Furthermore, in her last book, she criticizes the contemporary view that cosmopolitanism means placing financial networks before national loyalties and that it is a reason for condemning Jews from small pawnbrokers to the Rothschilds.

At the end of her career and life, Eliot's familial and financial relationships were more closely intertwined than ever. She was connected to domestic, international, and colonial financial networks through the investments she made with the profits from her writing. When Lewes died in 1878, his widowed daughter-in-law and two grandchildren moved from South Africa to London, perhaps expecting to live with George Eliot. She chose instead to support them financially. In 1880, she married Cross, the banker who had managed her finances for over a decade. In this sense, the importance of financial contexts to her exploration of character and personal relationships throughout her fiction did not reflect cynicism or a nostalgia for pre-capitalist times, but rather reflected the reality of social relations as she lived and experienced them.

NOTES

1   "The Sad Fortunes of the Reverend Amos Barton," *Scenes of Clerical Life* (9; ch. 1).

2   See Coleman.

3   On disclosure and secrecy in the *The Mill on the Floss*, see Poovey, "Writing about Finance in Victorian England."

4   See Coleman (ch. 2). See also Blake.

5   His essays condemning political economy (collected as *Unto This Last* in 1862) originally appeared in the *Cornhill Magazine* shortly before Eliot began her serialization of *Romola* in that journal. "Unto this Last" is a Biblical quotation from Matthew 20:1–16 in which Matthew is quoting Zechariah 11:13. The passages refer to the thirty pieces of silver that Eliot would invoke in "The Legend of Jubal."

6   On *Silas Marner*, see Nunokawa.

7   On the Bardi's business transactions, see Hunt.

8   On the contexts and implications of Harold's Greek slave, see Carroll.

9   Bulstrode's history is echoed in that of Mixtus in *Impressions of Theophrastus Such*, who was once a dissenting "visitor and exhorter of the poor in the alleys of a great provincial town" and a disciple of an "eloquent congregational preacher" (75; ch. 9). Mixtus ends, however, as a wealthy businessman, and "in his active superintendence of commercial undertakings he has contracted more and more of the bitterness which capitalists and employers often feel to be a reasonable mood towards obstructive proletaries" and is "indistinguishable from the ordinary run of moneyed and money-getting men" (80; ch. 9).

10   On Will's Jewishness, see Kaufman. On the Jews and capitalism, see Muller.

11   The crash of Grapnell and Co. is generally assumed to be based on the failure of Overend and Gurney in 1864. See Elliott.

12   On bankruptcy in Victorian fiction, see Weiss.

REFERENCES

Blake, Kathleen. *The Pleasures of Benthamism: Victorian Culture, Utility, Political Economy*. Oxford: Oxford UP, 2009.

Carlyle, Thomas. *Chartism*. 1839. 2nd ed. London: Chapman & Hall, 1842.

Carroll, Alicia. *Dark Smiles: Race and Desire in George Eliot*. Athens: Ohio UP, 2003.

Coleman, Dermot. "Being Good With Money: Economic Bearings in George Eliot's Ethical and Social Thought." Diss. U of Exeter, 2011.

Eliot, George. *Adam Bede*. Ed. Valentine Cunningham. Oxford: Oxford UP, 1996.

Eliot, George. *Brother Jacob. Silas Marner, The Lifted Veil and Brother Jacob*. Ed. Peter Mudford. London: Everyman, 1996. 305–end.

Eliot, George. *The Complete Shorter Poetry of George Eliot*. Eds. A. G. Van den Broek and William Baker. 2 vols. London: Pickering, 2005.

Eliot, George. *Daniel Deronda*. Ed. Graham Handley. Oxford: Oxford UP, 2009.

Eliot, George. *Felix Holt*. Ed. Fred C. Thomson. Oxford: Oxford UP, 1988.

Eliot, George. *The George Eliot Letters*. 9 vols. Ed. Gordon S. Haight. New Haven: Yale UP, 1954–78.

Eliot, George. *Impressions of Theophrastus Such*. Ed. Nancy Henry. Iowa City: U of Iowa P, 1994.

Eliot, George. *Middlemarch*. Ed. David Carroll. Oxford: Oxford UP, 1997.

Eliot, George. *The Mill on the Floss: Complete Text with Introduction, Historical Contexts, Critical Essays*. Ed. Nancy Henry. Boston: Houghton, 2004.

Eliot, George. *Romola*. Ed. Andrew Brown. Oxford: Oxford UP, 1994.

Eliot, George. *Scenes of Clerical Life*. Ed. Thomas A. Noble. Oxford: Oxford UP, 1988.

Eliot, George. *Silas Marner. Silas Marner, Lifted Veil and Brother Jacob*. Ed. Peter Mudford. London: Everyman, 1996.

Elliott, Geoffrey. *The Mystery of Overend and Gurney: A Financial Scandal in Victorian London*. London: Methuen, 2006.

Hunt, Edwin S. "A New Look at the Dealings of the Bardi and Peruzzi with Edward III." *Journal of Economic History* 50.1 (1990): 149–62. *JSTOR*. Web. 15 Oct. 2011.

Kaufman, Heidi. *English Origins, Jewish Discourse, and the Nineteenth-Century British Novel: Reflections on a Nested Nation*. University Park: Pennsylvania State UP, 2009.

Muller, Jerry Z. *Capitalism and the Jews*. Princeton: Princeton UP, 2010.

Nunokawa, Jeff. *The Afterlife of Property: Domestic Security and the Victorian Novel*. Princeton: Princeton UP, 1994.

Poovey, Mary. *Genres of the Credit Economy: Mediating Value in Eighteenth- and Nineteenth-Century Britain*. Chicago: U of Chicago P, 2008.

Poovey, Mary. "Writing about Finance in Victorian England: Disclosure and Secrecy in the Culture of Investment." *Victorian Investments: New Perspectives on Finance and Culture*. Eds. Nancy Henry and Cannon Schmitt. Bloomington: Indiana UP, 2009.

Weiss, Barbara. *The Hell of the English: Bankruptcy and the Victorian Novel*. Lewisburg: Bucknell UP, 1986.

24

George Eliot and Politics

Carolyn Lesjak

Everything is "Poltics"

In one of the many plays on language that occur in Charles Dickens's *The Pickwick Papers*, Mr. Pickwick, in his interview with the Count, notes that "The word politics, Sir . . . comprises, in itself, a difficult study of no inconsiderable magnitude." The Count, happy with this description, and "drawing out the tablets again" to record it, replies "'ver good—fine words to begin a chapter. Chapter forty-seven. Poltics. The word poltic surprises by himself—' And down went Mr Pickwick's remark, in Count Smorltork's tablets, with such variations and additions as the Count's exuberant fancy suggested, or his imperfect knowledge of the language, occasioned" (207; ch. 15).

"Ver good—fine words to begin a chapter" on politics indeed. Mr. Pickwick's definition of politics and the Count's humorous mistranslation of his words perfectly capture how much politics is a matter of translation and how expansive *and* wayward its definitions can be. The exchange is both a classic Dickensian moment and, in a more serious vein, identifies the not "inconsiderable magnitude" of politics, and enacts its slipperiness as a term, the way it can move from comprising to surprising, from an object of study to a subject that takes on a life of its own—about which it becomes hard to say what *isn't* politics. In fact, Georg Lukács links a recognition like Mr. Pickwick's to the whole project of realism itself:

> An unbiased investigation of life . . . leads easily enough . . . to the discovery which had long been made by the great realists of the beginning and middle of the nineteenth

A Companion to George Eliot, First Edition. Edited by Amanda Anderson and Harry E. Shaw.
© 2013 John Wiley & Sons, Ltd. Published 2016 by John Wiley & Sons, Ltd.

century and which Gottfried Keller expressed thus: "Everything is politics." The great Swiss writer did not intend this to mean that everything was immediately tied up with politics; on the contrary, in his view – as in Balzac's and Tolstoy's – every action, thought, and emotion of human beings is inseparably bound up with the life and struggles of the community, i.e., with politics; whether the humans themselves are conscious of this, unconscious of it or even trying to escape from it, objectively their actions, thoughts and emotions nevertheless spring from and run into politics. (9)

Lukács extends his claim by underlining that "the true great realists not only realized and depicted this situation—they did more than that, they set it up as a demand to be made on men [*sic*]," demonstrating that the separation of "the complete human personality into a public and a private sector" was "a fiction of capitalist society" (9) and hence in need of debunking.

It might seem strange to begin a discussion about George Eliot's politics with Dickens and Lukács. After all, Eliot's voice could not be more different from Dickens's: Terry Eagleton, for example, notes that "whereas Dickens's prose is declamatory and impressionistic, Eliot's sentences unroll like undulating hills, full of wry asides and scrupulously qualifying sub-clauses." Moreover, there is a politics to these stylistic qualities: "You can tell that George Eliot is a liberal," says Eagleton, "by the shape of her sentences" (163). Likewise, Lukács's Marxist politics seem a far cry from Eliot's judicious, ameliorative politics, not to mention the added fact that Eliot, even more so than Dickens, is noticeably absent from Lukács's account of nineteenth-century realism. Despite these differences, however, Eliot, like Dickens and Lukács, shares a commitment to the belief that everything truly is politics, which, in turn, necessitates experimentation with form and character in order to find the means by which to demonstrate the deep relatedness of all aspects of social life.

For Eliot, I argue, this belief finds expression in her commitment to the common(s) and the commonplace, a commitment grounded in a materialist view of character that both draws on older eighteenth-century practices of character-building and refashions them in response to the pressures of a globalizing mid-nineteenth-century world and the new kinds of social bonds it brings into being. In its emphasis on the collective nature of "character," in both senses of the word, moreover, her politics of the common is irreducibly ethical and political and forestalls the critical tendency to see them as competing emphases. By foregrounding the materiality of Eliot's realism and by extension her politics, I hope to counter the *de rigueur* association of her writing with a predictable liberalism and to suggest some of the ways in which she may be more relevant to twenty-first century readers than she has appeared to be.

In Defense of the Common

George Eliot famously pauses in the middle of *Adam Bede* to clarify her role as a novelist and ours as readers. She distinguishes her realism from older, conventional narratives, composed by "clever [novelists]," at once refusing to produce the idealizing representations she imagines her reader demanding and establishing the terms of her own narrative, which rely on the commonplace rather than the clever and require her to "creep servilely after nature and fact" (221; ch. 17). Throughout the chapter, Eliot makes her case for focusing on the "great multitude" as opposed to the "rarity," the "old women scraping carrots with their work-worn hands" (224) as opposed to the "cloud-borne angels . . . and heroic warriors." The homely, the commonplace, "the middle," the vulgar, the coarse: these are the stuff of realism and those "select natures" that fail to see this are akin to the "narrowest and pettiest" (229) of people.

But equally the homely, the middling, and the common are the actual people inhabiting Eliot's realist text. There is a slippage, that is to say, between the stuff of realism and its characters that makes characters akin to "nature and fact," to the "common things" Eliot's narrator is after. No less material than the world of which they are a part, they put up material resistance to being read, by the narrator or the novels' readers, in merely self-serving ways. In perhaps the most oft-quoted line in the chapter, the narrator writes that she "[aspires] to give no more than a faithful account of men and things as they have mirrored themselves in my mind" (221). Not only are men and things equated here, but the language that Eliot uses to describe their effect on the narrator is not as straightforward as it might initially seem. Rather than referring to the way in which these things are "mirrored in [her] mind," which would grant to the mind a preeminence, they have "mirrored *themselves* in [her] mind, suggesting that they too embody a form of material agency.

The intimate reciprocity between characters and things at the center of Eliot's realism has a number of eighteenth-century antecedents from Cowper and Words-worth to *Chrysal, or the Adventures of a Guinea* and other modes of "characteristic writing." I, however, want simply to note how indebted Eliot's notion of commonness is to this range of writing practices and how, in her hands, they combine to produce the specifically "materialist standards" (Knoepflmacher's term) of her realism. In her early essay, "Worldliness and Other-Worldliness: The Poet Young," for example, Eliot contrasts Edward Young's apophthegmatic other-worldly appeals to Cowper's grounded "worldliness," in which "no object is too small to prompt his song"; and "his song is never trivial, for he is alive to small objects, not because his mind is narrow, but because his glance is clear and his heart is large" (*Selected Essays* 209). The common, as Eliot interprets Cowper, is both near at hand, found as it is in small, common objects, and expansive and worldly in its capacity to prompt fellow feeling. Fellow feeling, for Eliot, is equally prompted, however, by another vision of commonness found in characteristic writing: the idea of character types. Type in this tradition had to do with literal typefaces and the impressions characters make as well as the literal impressions necessary to inscribe characters on a page. This model of type recognizes the profound materiality of character in a most literal sense and, as I will show, counters or at least fractures the equation of nineteenth-century British realism solely with the ideology of liberalism and the consolidation of a capitalist world economy, captured most succinctly in Eagleton's claim that "liberalism and the realist novel are spiritual twins" (164). Eliot not only directly references this tradition—the very chapter in *Middlemarch* that begins with Eliot comparing her craft to Henry Fielding's also names *Chrysal* among Lydgate's juvenile reading—but also incorporates and amends it within her most iconic novels, novels that have been lauded, historically and, as I am suggesting, erroneously, for representing an idealist concept of interiority as the essence of personality—a concept linked to the individualist politics of liberalism. Lauren Goodlad assumes this conception of character in her study of the liberal Victorian state: "Throughout the century Britons tenaciously imagined themselves through character, an antimaterialist concept of the individual" (*Victorian Literature* xii).

But time and time again Eliot's fiction belies this definition of character. Repeatedly and emphatically, Eliot highlights the material, collective nature of character and the material, collective politics such a vision of character entails. At the most obvious level, character types and commonness work by dint of their reproducibility: it is only by capturing what is typical or common, what is shared by others, that a type makes sense. When first introduced, the narrator says of Arthur Donnithorne, for example, "If you want to know more particularly how he looked, call to your remembrance some tawny-whiskered, brown-locked, clear-complexioned young Englishman whom you have met with in a foreign town, and been proud of as a fellow-countryman" (105; ch. 5). Likewise, Amos Barton in "The Sad Fortunes of the Reverend Amos Barton," is a man "very far from remarkable,—a man whose virtues were not heroic, and had no undetected crime within his breast . . . but was palpably and unmistakably commonplace" (*Scenes* 38; ch. 5). A man of "insignificant stamp (*Scenes* 38; ch. 5)," he shares his being with 92 out of a 100 similarly "commonplace people" about whom the narrator asks, "Nay, is there not a pathos in their very insignificance—in our comparison of their dim and narrow existence with the glorious possibilities of that human nature which they share?" (*Scenes* 39; ch. 5). And of course *Middlemarch* announces its concern with commonness and the "middling" in its title, a concern that pervades the novel and which Eliot explicitly theorizes in the preface and conclusion as well as throughout the novel. As with Amos Barton, the novel employs the language of unheroic or "unhistoric acts," which in turn echoes Eliot's description of *The Mill on the Floss* as a tragedy of "millers and other insignificant people" (207; bk.3, ch. 1). "But we insignificant people with our daily words and acts," the narrator assures *Middlemarch*'s readers, "are preparing the lives of many Dorotheas, some of which may present a far sadder sacrifice than that of the Dorothea whose story we know" (838; Finale). Even as Eliot, then, acknowledges earlier in the novel how difficult it is to avoid singling out individual characters from the store of common characters when she asks, "but why always Dorothea?" (278; ch. 29), she ends the novel by recognizing multiple Dorotheas, some of whom may have it far worse than "our" Dorothea: "ours" in the sense that, as social beings, we—countless, nameless others—necessarily help "prepare the lives" of others; and "ours" insofar as we share a common indebtedness to one another, regardless of how presently unequal actual social arrangements might be. In the contemporary language of the commons (to which I will return below),

Michael Hardt and Antonio Negri express this indebtedness thus: "Being, after all, is just another way of saying what is ineluctably common, what refuses to be privatized or enclosed and remains constantly open to all. (There is no such thing as a private ontology.)" (181).

Eliot's ethical commitment to the "superlatively middling" (*Scenes* 42; ch. 5) is nothing if not fraught however, as the tension within this phrase might suggest. First, there is the problem of narrative voice or idiom: the sense, as Raymond Williams has argued, that Eliot's defensiveness about her own common characters and her consequent need to justify the narrative attention she gives them mark the limits of her own class position. Anxious in the company of her imagined middle-class readers, she becomes "self-conscious . . . placating and appealing to what seems a dominant image of a particular kind of reader" (172), thereby falling into a new form of patronage. Second, throughout Eliot's oeuvre, she grapples with the issue of whether "seeing truly and feeling justly was enough to guarantee the moral effect of her stories without the help of an element of idealisation (196)" as David Lodge paraphrases U. C. Knoepflmacher. And finally, there is the sense of discomfort, in general, regarding what it means, exactly, to envision a politics premised on the "superlatively middling"—especially when this description, used to characterize Amos Barton, is followed by a further description of him as "the quintessential extract of mediocrity" (42). It is precisely in the visceral unease elicited by the celebration of mediocrity, though, that the forward-looking aspects of commonness as a radical politics are to be found.

Adam Bede provides perhaps the best early example of the coordinates of Eliot's politics of the common in its explicit linking of its common characters to the historical commons. To begin, in chapter 17 Eliot cautions that common characters, like the world, are "not just what we [as readers] like," not there to be touched up and not "entirely of [the narrator's] own choosing" (221). In short, "men and things" may teach us—readers and realist writers alike—about a kind of "material recalcitrance," which, in a different context, Jonathan Goldberg characterizes as a recognition of the ways in which "reality presses on us, resists our attempts to reduce or refuse it, chastens grandiosity or fantasies of omnipotence" (375). Indeed, we might see in Eliot's version of this material recalcitrance echoes of Marx's famous passage from *The Eighteenth Brumaire* that "men make their own history, but not of their own free will; not under circumstances they have themselves chosen but under the given and inherited circumstances with which they are directly confronted." As Richard Dienst carefully parses the phrase "given and inherited," "What might sound like Marx's redundant stuttering seems on reflection to be especially well phrased. Given *and* inherited, what's taken and what's received, what remains *and* what is passed along: the phrase opens up several distinct settings in which historical circumstances confront us and are confronted, where the dispositions of agency and determination still remain to be seen" (159).

Now George Eliot is no Karl Marx, but her representations of the common types peopling *Adam Bede*—the artisan, the Methodist preacher, the dairymaid, the farmer's wife—nonetheless produce a vision of "the commons" that presupposes a radical transformation of day-to-day material reality almost unthinkable within the economic structure of the time. Take Mrs. Poyser, who, along with her husband, Martin Poyser, are farming tenants on the old Squire's estate. Like characters of her ilk in other Eliot novels, she is routinely gathered into the plural, as in "the Poysers," finding her non-descript place alongside others such as the Dodsons and the Gleggs in *The Mill on the Floss*. Yet confronted with the old Squire's proposition to expand her dairy operation by taking on more dairy-land from a neighboring farm in exchange for ceding some of their plowing land to a new tenant—which we can see as a microcosm for the historical process of enclosure—Mrs. Poyser, as the title of this episode's chapter indicates, "has her say out." Specifically, she systematically rebuts the Squire's claims regarding the common ground upon which such an exchange would be made. Throughout his appeal, the Squire couches the exchange in terms of a "mutual advantage"(390; ch. 32) and assumes, moreover, that the Poysers will agree with him. Mrs. Poyser, however, immediately identifies how unequal such an exchange must be: she bluntly states that she won't take on any more dairy work simply to line the Squire's pockets, presents a sustained analysis of the dangers of specialization, and identifies the division between classes inscribed in the Squire's offer. "I know there's them as is born t' own the land, and them as is born to sweat on 't," Mrs. Poyser declares, "and I know it's christened folks's duty to submit to their betters as fur as flesh and blood 'ull bear it; but I'll not make a martyr o' myself . . . for no landlord in England, not if he was King George himself" (392; ch. 32). Mrs. Poyser explicitly links the deference required by social relations to the economic structure undergirding them, namely private property. Lest we assume that this constitutes an idiosyncratic outburst on Mrs. Poyser's part, she and the narrator make clear she speaks for the parish; a chorus consisting of two servant girls, a waggoner, and "sour old John," not to mention a bull-dog, a terrier, a sheep-dog, and a hissing gander, confirms Mrs. Poyser's claim. Humorous as this particular collective might be, the resistance to the given it dramatizes has potentially dire consequences, for in the course of the conversation the Squire has threatened to cancel the Poysers' lease if they refuse to go along with his plan. The presumption and heat of class privilege quickly replace the liberal, polite language of mutual advantage.

Although the Poysers are ultimately spared the loss of their land and livelihood, the violence the Squire threatens—essentially that of enclosure—nonetheless is made good, in displaced form, in Hetty Sorrel's fate. Wooed and impregnated by the old Squire's son, Arthur, Hetty, the dairymaid on the Poysers farm, ultimately ends up killing her baby and being sentenced to death—a sentence transmuted by Arthur's last-minute appeal into transport to Australia (where, it should be noted, eighty percent of the prisoners were sent for crimes against property). Significantly, Arthur's overriding ambition is to become a "model landlord," which he interprets as furthering the project of enclosure while simultaneously earning the respect and admiration of his laborers. In an overdetermined conversation with Mr. Irwine, in the chapter that immediately precedes Eliot's mission statement about realism, Arthur boasts that he can tame the ire roused by another tenant's enclosure of common land simply by being nice; as he assures Irwine, "I don't believe there's anything you can't prevail on people to do with kindness" (215; ch. 16). Needless to say, there is a terrible irony in Arthur's claim, given Hetty's tragic end. Utterly transformed and aged by his dalliance with Hetty, Arthur leaves his father's estate and only returns to his home—and to the narrative—in the epilogue, set eight years after the end of the story. He confesses to Adam Bede that he "[makes] no schemes now" (582; Epilogue) and, echoing what Adam had told him years ago, concludes that "There's a sort of wrong that can never be made up for" (584).

This "mixed, entangled affair" (221)—a phrase Eliot uses in Chapter 17 to describe the project of realism—begins to conjure the multiple materially and figuratively related notions of indebtedness composing *Adam Bede*'s narrative. Common types like Mrs. Poyser and Arthur are indebted to the other nameless characters making them legible types in the first place. And when character is envisioned as an exchange between common things, whether in the form of characters in relation to each other or to the world, the supremacy of the internal over the external, of mind over matter or nature or fact or other minds, is undercut—a formulation that will find expression in *Middlemarch*, when Eliot's narrator links the most immaterial of perceptions—feeling—to the concreteness of things, writing about Dorothea that "it had been easier to imagine how she would devote herself to Mr. Casaubon, and become wise and strong in his strength and wisdom, than to conceive with that distinctness which is no longer reflection but feeling—an idea wrought back to the directness of sense, like the solidity of objects—that he had an equivalent centre of self, whence the lights and shadows must always fall with a certain difference" (211; ch. 21). Such an equation gives to feeling a materiality that feeling itself would seem to belie, and connects this "thingness" or solidity to nothing less than psychological interiority, on the face of it one of the least "solid" attributes of selfhood.

By giving characters the solidity of objects, material types thus potentially enact a profound leveling of the social, phrased here as the granting of an "equivalent centre of self." Crucially, though, as the narrative of enclosure at the center of *Adam Bede* demonstrates, our indebtedness to others is subtended by property relations such that any vision of equivalence remains at worst, ideological, and, at best, utopian within capitalism. *Adam Bede* shows us both in the twinned narratives of the verbal exchange between the Poysers and the old Squire and the sexual one between the "model landlord" and the dairymaid. Key here, as well, is Raymond Williams's insistence that "as the economy develops, enclosure can never really be isolated from the mainstream of land improvements, of changes in methods of production, of price-movements, and of those more general changes in property relationships which were all flowing in the same direction: an extension of cultivated land but also a concentration of ownership into the hands of a minority" (97). Mrs. Poyser, in essence, rejects the "economics of specialization and scale" (99), in turn resisting the constellation of economic and social changes wrought by agrarian capitalism.

But the novel isn't only backward looking or nostalgic, as its setting in 1799, sixty years before it was written, might suggest. Such a reading ignores the importance of form with respect to types, the fact that Eliot's view of the past encompasses not only "emerging or fading types" (Bowlby xvi) but future types not yet realized in Eliot's own time. Type in the material sense figures a form of commonness that is always also a story about forms of indebtedness, about the fact that our debts to other selves and to the world go hand-in-hand. In *Adam Bede*, as well as elsewhere, Eliot sees these debts as at once metaphorical and literal (just like "character"), at once about inter-subjective relations and economic structures. In this light, Dorothea's claim at the end of the *Middlemarch* that she will "learn what everything costs" (812; ch. 83) looks less like a capitulation to the given than an acknowledgment that all relations are inescapably economic in nature—and that the "cost" of these debts has yet to be learned. Equally, it does not partake of the movement with which Andrew Miller characterizes Eliot's method: "Like the auction and the pawnshop, *Middlemarch* moves away from a narrowly materialist understanding of goods; instead of translating goods into their exchange value, however, she rewrites them as aesthetic objects" (216). In an early letter written to the Brays and Hennells in which she responds to the 15 May 1848 revolution in France and the proposed impeachment of one of its leaders, Louis Blanc, she envisions in the future "a day . . . when there will be a temple of white marble where sweet incense and anthems shall rise to the memory of every man and every woman who has had a deep '*ahnung*,' a presentiment, a yearning, or a clear vision of the time when this miserable reign of Mammon shall end" (*Letters* 1:267). Not just the enthusiasms of a young "Mary Ann" Evans, the mature George Eliot of *Middlemarch* also underscores the utterly structural nature of "Mammon" in the current day. Filling in Lydgate's history, the narrator writes, "He was but seven-and-twenty, an age at which many men are not quite common—at which they are hopeful of achievement, resolute in avoidance, thinking that Mammon shall never put a bit in their mouths and get astride their backs, but rather that Mammon, if they have anything to do with him, shall draw their chariot" (142; ch. 15). If in her letter the realization of a genuine commonwealth takes shape as a utopian impulse, a looking back from a better future in which the present has been overcome, in *Middlemarch*, Lydgate's future makes clear that nineteenth-century Britons are still fully within the "miserable reign of Mammon."

The way out, however, is never envisioned through the recovery of a lost common; instead, much as Hardt and Negri and David Harvey emphasize with respect to the commons today, it is at once an aim and something "perpetually being produced" (Harvey 259) given the ineluctably collective nature of social life. In "Janet's Repentance," the last story of *Scenes of Clerical Life*, set in the 1830s, the common as a literal piece of communally-owned land already no longer exists. The description of Paddiford Common, where Methodist Rev. Mr. Tryan lives and preaches, pointedly draws attention to the changed nature of the common by this time: "As long as Mr. Tryan's hearers were confined to Paddiford Common—which, by the by, was hardly recognisable as a common at all, but was a dismal district where you heard the rattle of the handloom, and breathed the smoke of coal-pits—the 'canting parson' could be treated as a joke" (197; ch. 2). Similarly, in the much earlier 1799 setting of *Adam Bede*, another Methodist preacher, Dinah Morris, chooses to live in an equally "dismal district." In both cases, Dissent and the development of manufacturing districts characterize a newly conceived common and make it a potent site of the present economic transformations accompanying the industrial revolution. The commons, in this context, figures something potentially new in the making, what Williams calls "active community"; as he argues, "In many parts of rural Britain, a new kind of community developed as an aspect of struggle, against the dominant landowners or, as in the labourers' revolts in the time of the Swing machine-smashing and rick-burning or in the labourers' unions from Tolpuddle to Joseph Arch, against the whole class-system of rural capitalism. . . . In many thousands of cases, there is more community in the modern village, as a result of this process of new legal and democratic rights, than at any point in the recorded or imagined past" (104).

Whether seen as process or future achievement, a politics of the commons, as Eliot envisions it, is humbling; it involves a decentering and literal objectification of self (think of Eliot's poetically declarative statement in *Middlemarch* that "I know no speck so troublesome as self" [419; ch. 42]), a recognition of how much we owe to others, of how much we are never simply ourselves. In this way, it shares certain qualities with Barbara Hardy's analysis of the chorus in Eliot. In her reading of *Scenes of Clerical Life*, for example, she notes the multiple roles the chorus has: it is not only background and agent ("from *Amos Barton* to *Middlemarch* the collective personality of the community acts as a causal agent, making and breaking relations"), but also has a formal function, moving the narrative between individual and collective views, "from the shot in the dark to the truth; from the isolated creature to the diffused and comfortable warmth of the crowd; from tension to casual humour." In its unsettling of the individual the chorus shows that "one man's tragedy is everyone else's comedy"; but, "there is usually also the moment when one man's tragedy becomes everyone's tragedy" (21–22). But unlike the chorus, the commons brings into view the fact that any worthy notion of sociality must be grounded materially, not only in the common (as in the crowd, the commonplace) but in the common good. A politics of the commons, as Lydgate's fate confirms, does not permit the material realities of the world to be neglected. Recall his intellectual and class "prejudice," when he first arrives in Middlemarch, that he need not "think of furniture at present" (150; ch. 15) and the fact that his disregard for its cost—literally and figuratively—is central to his fall. It is also a politics in which a more routine politics cannot be evaded, in which everything is politics. Recall Lydgate's gradual absorption into Middlemarch's local politics via the hospital debate and how his vote in the end cannot be separated from his self-interest despite his avowed intention to remain apart from "small social conditions"; "For the first time," the narrator explains, "Lydgate was feeling the hampering thread-like pressure of small social conditions, and their frustrating complexity. . . . However it was, he did not distinctly say to himself on which side he would vote; and all the while he was inwardly resenting the subjection which had been forced upon him" (180; ch. 18). In the end Lydgate naturally succumbs to Bulstrode's pressure and votes for Mr. Tyke rather than Mr. Farebrother (his name says it all). His initial indecisiveness, however, is symptomatic of the complex set of considerations that inform any notion of the common good and the multiple forms of indebtedness that comprise it: its constitution, in short, is an open question, which Dienst, in the context of our current debt crisis, phrases thus: "It is only in the experience of the insistence of indebtedness that one can keep faith with the need to be rid of it, and the desire to construct different bonds in common" (136).

The Commons and the World

In response to reviews of *Daniel Deronda*, Eliot took umbrage at her readers' inclination to "cut the book into scraps and talk of nothing in it but Gwendolen," claiming that she "meant everything in the book to be related to everything else there" (*Letters* 6:290). By the latter half of the nineteenth century, the idea that everything was related to everything else had taken on an increasingly global scope. As Christopher Hitchens notes in his defense of *Daniel Deronda*, the "writing of the novel took place against a background of expansion and innovation—especially the opening that resulted from the digging of the Suez Canal. That is why its action can for the first time comprehend a world outside England" (10). Likewise, Goodlad identifies these "globalizing dynamics" with the existence of "actually existing cosmopolitanisms" in the nineteenth century. Against Fredric Jameson's claim that the representational and political problems attendant on a global economy are not really felt until the advent of modernism, Goodlad proposes that the period during which Eliot and other realists were writing was "noteworthy for its reinvention of empire at a time when Britain was also reinventing itself as a mass democracy" ("Cosmopolitanism's Actually Existing Beyond" 405). In other words, the spatial disjunction Jameson identifies with modernism—between lived (metropolitan) experience and (imperial) structure—impacted realist practices. As a result, nineteenth-century realism needs to be understood in terms of a "Victorian geopolitical aesthetic." In the brief remaining space, I want to suggest that Eliot's politics of the commons is inherently cosmopolitan in its "insistence on indebtedness." At the same time, however, the very dislocations accompanying an expanding, international economy often led Eliot away from the radical premises and promises of the commons toward more partial, nationally- or class-based solutions, even as her own novels narrate the historical passing of those solutions.

On her list of what's not in *Middlemarch*, Gillian Beer includes, as the most obvious absence, *Middlemarch*. As she explains, "the main thing not to be found in Middlemarch, the town, is *Middlemarch*, the book. . . . The disparities between topic and writing are striking. The town of Middlemarch is provincial; the writing of *Middlemarch* is urban, cosmopolitan even. The concerns of the people are local, of the writing polymathic" (17). This tension, Beer argues, is "supple," prompting questions about the distance between *Middlemarch*'s time of writing and its first readers and the conditions depicted in Middlemarch—"How much have things changed? How capable are they of change?"—as well as "wry comparisons" between events in the novel and current events, from bank crises to reform bills to the position of women (17–18). Beer's point is well taken, but increasingly, and even in *Middlemarch*, "outsider" characters themselves either provide or yearn for an expansive, cosmopolitan view of the world—while also desiring the rootedness of provincial life. This outsider viewpoint is frequently associated with Jews, gypsies, and other Bohemian types, such as Will Ladislaw in *Middlemarch*, the artist Klesmer in *Daniel Deronda*, and Daniel Deronda himself. Tellingly, for our purposes, gypsies are also linked directly to a literal common, Dunlow Common, in *The Mill on the Floss*. When Maggie Tulliver determines to run away after pushing Lucy Deane into the mud, she reasons that "she had been so often told she was like a gypsy and 'half wild' that when she was miserable it seemed to her the only way of escaping opprobrium and being entirely in harmony with circumstances, would be to live in a little brown tent on the commons . . . she would run straight away till she came to Dunlow Common, where there would certainly be gypsies, and cruel Tom, and the rest of her relations who found fault with her, should never see her any more" (112; bk.1, ch. 11). Although Maggie's scheme is related with irony, in part because Maggie immediately reads her relationship to the gypsies in hierarchical terms—"the gypsies, she considered, would gladly receive her and pay her much respect on account of her superior knowledge" (112)—they are nonetheless figured as radically Other, living on the fringes of St. Oggs (Maggie is disappointed to find them "in a lane, after all, and not on a common . . . for a mysterious illimitable common where there were sand-pits to hide in, and one was out of everybody's reach, had always made part of Maggie's picture of gypsy life" [115; bk.1, ch. 11]).

Later incarnations of gypsy-like figures retain this radical otherness in a serious vein; they explicitly function as an "outer conscience" (Gwendolen's description of Deronda [833; ch. 64]), which unsettles the domestic, English center of Eliot's earlier texts. Types like Arthur, described above as someone "whom you have met with in a foreign town, and been proud of as a fellow-countryman" (*Adam Bede* 105) are, within the expanded world of *Daniel Deronda*, nothing to be proud of. They, like Gwendolen and her gambling, are made pejoratively common by Deronda's gaze. The effect is very much like that on Dorothea, when Ladislaw informs her of how outmoded Casaubon's research is. Coming from elsewhere, lacking clear lines of pedigree and inheritance, without property, wandering figures like Ladislaw, Klesmer, and Deronda also build on the spatial aspect of otherness that is part of Maggie's image of "gypsydom" and that, in *Mill*, prefigures Maggie's later trip down the river and "out of everybody's reach" for a time. But this, exactly, is the rub. The challenge the politics of a commons raises for Eliot and her twenty-first-century readers is how to imagine and represent our common, quotidian, and embodied life in relation to a seemingly abstract, often invisible, structure of wider relations, without succumbing to the fantasy of detachment, of being "out of everybody's reach" and hence free from social attachments, which has been connected, historically, to the ideal of cosmopolitanism. The concept of "actually existing cosmopolitanism," utilized by Goodlad and explored by Bruce Robbins et al. in *Cosmopolitics*, aims to uncouple this association by "scaling down," "pluralizing and particularizing" the term cosmopolitanism. "We are connected," Robbins writes, "to all sorts of places, causally if not always consciously, including many that we have never traveled to, that we have perhaps only seen on television—including the place where the television itself was manufactured. It is frightening to think how little progress has been made in turning invisibly determining and often exploitative connections into conscious and self-critical ones, how far we remain from mastering the sorts of allegiance, ethics, and action that might go with our complex and multiple belonging" (3). Or, as Goodlad phrases this project in the Victorian context, a practice is needed that "would enunciate the geohistorical as well as expressive dimensions of Victorian globality, exploring the sinuous interchange between embedding structures and embodied ethics" (400).

Eliot's language of the commons thickens these contemporary discussions of "cosmopolitanisms" in its twinned emphases on the materiality of character and the materiality of the world. The common and the commons, in this view, are inseparable from one another, the idea of an ethics separable from politics unthinkable. Again, this is not to say that the specific plans Eliot comes up with—Deronda's nationalistic vow at the end of *Daniel Deronda*, for example—are to be embraced. Nor is it to ignore the fears of certain commoners, such as the industrial working class, which limit Eliot's conception especially of the intellectual commons. In the "Address to Working Men" appended to *Felix Holt*, Eliot, in the voice of Holt, invokes an intellectual commons as "that treasure of knowledge, science, poetry, refinement of thought, feeling, and manners, great memories and the interpretation of great records, which is carried on from the minds of one generation to another." But, prefatory to this description, she writes,

> just as there are many things which we know better and feel much more strongly than the richer, softer-handed classes can know or feel them; so there are many things – many precious benefits – which we, by the very fact of our privations, or lack of leisure and instruction, are not so likely to be aware of and take into our account. Those precious benefits form a chief part of what I may call the common estate of society: a wealth over and above buildings, machinery, produce, shipping, and so on, though closely connected with these; a wealth of a more delicate kind, that we may more unconsciously bring into danger, doing harm and not knowing that we do it. (621; Appendix A)

The danger of destroying these "precious benefits" justifies the novel's conservative, gradualist politics, but also jars just enough to require an explanation. "Now the security of this treasure," she adds, "demands, not only the preservation of order, but a certain patience on our part with many institutions and facts of various kinds, especially touching the accumulation of wealth, which from the light we stand in, we are more likely to discern the evil than the good of" (621). The move away from an inclusive notion of the "common estate of society" is followed directly by a reminder of the importance of "the accumulation of wealth" to any notion of the commonwealth.

In this regard, it is instructive to see the novel often paired with *Felix Holt*, namely *Romola*, as affording Eliot a defamiliarizing lens (fifteenth-century Florentine politics) through which to read the dynamics of a political and cultural revolution, which in the case of *Felix Holt* is too close for comfort (the period of the First Reform Act in 1832 refracted through the time just prior to the passing of the Second Reform Act in 1867). After all, *Romola*, unlike *Felix Holt*, offers a true radical in the figure of Savonarola, and a vision of an alternative politics in Machiavelli. Gary Wihl argues, in fact, that critics have missed a crucial aspect of *Romola*'s politics by focusing almost exclusively on Eliot's reading of J. S. Mill and Matthew Arnold while writing it and thereby neglecting her intellectual interest in Machiavelli. Calling *Romola* "a truly Machiavellian novel" (250), Wihl aims to "put the novel in dialogue with two strands of political thought: cultural liberalism, which promotes a politics of disinterestedness down through the legacy of Matthew Arnold, and republican humanism, which rejects abstract rights and principles of equality in favor of moral action within the public sphere" (259). Perhaps not coincidentally, within the modern political thought that comes to link the conception of republic to property (above all, in Hobbes), Hardt and Negri identify in Machiavelli an alternative path, "which poses the poor as not only the remainder left by the violent appropriation conducted by nascent powers of capital, not only prisoners of the new conditions of production and reproduction, but also a force of resistance that recognizes itself as exploited within a regime that still bears the marks of the common: a common social life, common social wealth" (52). For our purposes, it is significant that *Romola* enacts a historical and ongoing struggle between fundamentally opposed worldviews and class positions (the Florentine poor and the pro-Medicean forces) *and*, at least for a time, advocates for the poor in the language of a common life: "the inspiring consciousness breathed into [Romola] by Savonarola's influence that her lot was vitally united with the general lot had exalted even the minor details of obligation into religion. She was marching with a great army; she was feeling the stress of a common life" (552; ch. 56). Moreover, these common bonds supplant familial ones and prompt Romola's realization vis-à-vis her marriage that "the law was sacred. Yes, but rebellion might be sacred too. . . . It flashed upon her mind that the problem before her was essentially the same as that which had lain before Savonarola—the problem where the sacredness of obedience ended, and where the sacredness of rebellion began" (553). This is a rare position for Eliot to lend voice to, and one quite different from *Felix Holt*'s cautionary tale regarding the preservation of Britain's cultural inheritance. It is also a position that Eliot's critics found surprising, in part because it seemed to downgrade the role of "those precious benefits" necessitating order in *Felix Holt*; as Wihl notes, "many readers of the novel, from Browning onward, have wondered why Eliot practically avoided discussion of the rich artistic legacy of Florence in the novel" (249).

Far from an idiosyncratic aberration, however, the struggle in *Romola* between the common lot and the privileged Medicean elite dramatizes the stakes involved in a politics of the commons, a politics that necessarily threatens class privilege and its particular forms of inheritance, cultural and otherwise. To be sure, Eliot rarely takes us to the brink of revolution, as she does in *Romola*. But that does not mean that it isn't the logical outcome of her politics given its sustained commitment to the common(s) and its increasing awareness of the global aspects of the commonwealth. We might think of this commonness in terms of what Jameson refers to as "a kind of universal plebeianization on the social and political level: and this word is meant in some strong and positive Brechtian sense as an abandonment of privilege and a new and universal equality" (12). In short, in this utopian future, an actually existing "middlingness" or commonness—the key terms of Eliot's realist politics—would be the desired end.

REFERENCES

Beer, Gillian. "What's Not in *Middlemarch*." *Middlemarch in the Twenty-First Century*. Ed. Karen Chase. Oxford: Oxford UP, 2006. 15–35.

Bowlby, Rachel. Foreword. *Adventures in Realism*. Ed. Matthew Beaumont. Oxford: Wiley-Blackwell, 2007. xi–xviii.

Dickens, Charles. *The Pickwick Papers*. London: Penguin, 2000.

Dienst, Richard. *The Bonds of Debt*. New York: Verso, 2011.

Eagleton, Terry. *The English Novel: An Introduction*. Oxford: Blackwell, 2005.

Eliot, George. *Adam Bede*. Ed. Stephen Gill. London: Penguin, 1987.

Eliot, George. *Daniel Deronda*. Ed. Barbara Hardy. London: Penguin, 1986.

Eliot, George. *Felix Holt*. Ed. Peter Coveney. London: Penguin, 1984.

Eliot, George. *The George Eliot Letters*. Ed. Gordon S. Haight. 9 vols. New Haven: Yale UP, 1954–78.

Eliot, George. *Middlemarch*. Ed. Rosemary Ashton. London: Penguin, 1994.

Eliot, George. *The Mill on the Floss*. Ed. A.S. Byatt. London: Penguin, 2003.

Eliot, George. *Romola*. Ed. Andrew Sanders. London: Penguin, 1980.

Eliot, George. *Scenes of Clerical Life. Novels of George Eliot*, Vol. IV. Edinburgh: Blackwood , n.d.

Eliot, George. *Selected Essays, Poems and Other Writings*. Ed. A. S. Byatt and Nicholas Warren. London: Penguin, 1990.

Goldberg, Jonathan. "On the Eve of the Future." *PMLA* 125.2 (2010): 374–77.

Goodlad, Lauren M. E. "Cosmopolitanism's Actually Existing Beyond: Toward a Victorian Geopolitical Aesthetic." *Victorian Literature and Culture* 38.2 (2010): 399–411.

Goodlad, Lauren M. E. *Victorian Literature and the Victorian State: Character and Governance in a Liberal Society*. Baltimore: John Hopkins UP, 2003.

Hardt, Michael and Antonio Negri. *Commonwealth*. Cambridge: Harvard UP, 2009.

Hardy, Barbara. *The Novels of George Eliot: A Study in Form*. London: Athlone, 1963.

Harvey, David. "*Commonwealth*: An Exchange." *Artforum International* 48.3 (2009): 210–262.

Hitchens, Christopher. "In Defense of *Daniel Deronda*." *Threepenny Review* 39 (1989): 9–12.

Jameson, Fredric. "A New Reading of *Capital*." *Mediations* 25.1 (2010): 5–14.

Knoepflmacher, U. C. *George Eliot's Early Novels: The Limits of Realism*. Berkeley: U of California P, 1968.

Lodge, David. "The Making of 'George Eliot': *Scenes of Clerical Life*." In Lodge, *The Year of Henry James; or, Timing is All: The Story of a Novel*. London: Harvill, 2006.

Lukács, Georg. *Studies in European Realism*. 1848. Trans. Edith Bone. New York: Grosset, 1964.

Miller, Andrew H. *Novels Behind Glass: Commodity Culture and Victorian Narrative*. Cambridge: Cambridge UP, 1995.

Robbins, Bruce. "Actually Existing Cosmopolitanism." *Cosmopolitics: Thinking and Feeling Beyond the Nation*. Eds. Pheng Cheah and Bruce Robbins. Minneapolis: U of Minnesota P, 1998. 1–19.

Wihl, Gary. "Republican Liberty in George Eliot's *Romola*." *Criticism* 51.2 (2009): 247–62.

Williams, Raymond. *The Country and the City*. Oxford: Oxford UP, 1973.

25

Imagining Locality
and Affiliation:
George Eliot's Villages

Josephine McDonagh

In an early chapter of *Daniel Deronda*, the narrator pauses, in typical George Eliot style, to present to her readers a piece of proverbial wisdom (Price 145). Turning Wordsworthian sentiment into a universal, usable truth, she extols the virtues of a settled childhood:

> A human life, I think, should be well rooted in some spot of a native land, where it may get the love of tender kinship for the face of earth, for the labours men go forth to, for the sounds and accents that haunt it, for whatever will give that early home a familiar unmistakable difference amid the future widening of knowledge; a spot where the definiteness of early memories may be inwrought with affection, and kindly acquaintance with all neighbours, even to the dogs and donkeys, may spread not by sentimental effort and reflection, but as a sweet habit of the blood. (*Daniel Deronda* 50; ch. 3)

This entwining of landscape and memory is a familiar motif in all Eliot's works, yet it is all the more potent for being expressed here in the novel most explicitly concerned with the restless movement of people. Paradoxically, *Daniel Deronda* yearns for but never actually achieves for any of its characters this "spot of a native land."

Questions of locality and affiliation are central to all Eliot's novels. So too, in a more muted way, are states of dislocation. This is hardly surprising given that all were written against a backdrop of radical social and demographic change. Eliot's own moves from country to city were part of the national traffic of population from villages to towns and cities (Feldman). Moreover, in the period of Eliot's lifetime, an

A Companion to George Eliot, First Edition. Edited by Amanda Anderson and Harry E. Shaw.
© 2013 John Wiley & Sons, Ltd. Published 2016 by John Wiley & Sons, Ltd.

unprecedented number of people, including her stepsons, undertook further journeys across oceans and national borders to settler colonies on the other side of the world, often never to return (Belich; Henry 42–76). Eliot herself directly profited from the new readerships that this wave of emigration provoked (Cross 1:5). As recent scholarship has noted, in this global context, sense of place and community became more highly-charged terms than they once appeared to be (McDonagh, "Space"; Plotz 1–23; Baucom 3–40). Discussion of Eliot's more complicated relationships to places has tended to focus on her late works, *Daniel Deronda* and the *Impressions of Theophrastus Such*, in which she adopts the readily recognizable position of the cosmopolitan (Anderson 119–46). Even in the early works, however, Eliot's sense of place is produced from a distance, and in complex relations to past and future maps.

How did Eliot imagine locality and affiliation? Often in the form of a village.[1] Villages abound in her fiction, but their role is never simple. They are both residual social forms, and organisms through which to imagine the future; and they range across the globe, from her native Warwickshire to faraway India. Here I follow the idea of the village as it operates within her works, as, variously: the location of recollections of her childhood, and a symbol for national life (part 1); the basis of a form of representation embedded in her own practices of realism (part 2); and a model for both a cosmopolitan modernity, and a primitive past (part 3).

Villages Remembered and Imagined

At the time when she died in 1880, Eliot had already established a reputation as a nostalgic chronicler of provincial England. Her death inspired a flurry of biographical writings that embedded this view in critical opinion yet more deeply. Most significant among these was her widower, John W. Cross's *George Eliot's Life as Related in her Letters and Journals* (1885), which published extracts of her personal letters and diaries, many for the first time. Weaving these together with passages of her novels, Cross produced a seamless narrative of a life's work dedicated to the retrieval, and preservation, of a lost England, known in her infancy and lovingly retold in her fictional works. His work had a circular logic to it. What better way to evoke the landscape of Eliot's childhood than with examples taken from her novels? And what better way to establish the reality of those novels than by presenting them as memories, emanating from the soil of her experience? Cross turned the novels into something approaching autobiographies, documentary records of the authentic historical past.

There is certainly enough material in Eliot's own private writings to endorse this view. Her journals convey the belief that she wrote from memory and from the advantage of local knowledge. The "germ" of *Adam Bede*, she recorded in her journal, was a true story told to her by her Methodist aunt—"an anecdote from her own experience" (*Letters* 2:502); while *Scenes of Clerical Life* was planned as "a series of stories, containing sketches drawn from my own observation of the clergy" (*Letters* 2:407–08). Some early readers were so thoroughly convinced by this relationship to lived experience that, rightly or wrongly, they recognized their relatives within her stories (Haight 245). The anonymity of Eliot, combined with the familiarity of the people and places she described, led others to claim authorship of the early works, in particular one Joseph Liggins, "the son of a baker" from a village close to Eliot's family home, who had been sent down from Cambridge, and was now living on the Isle of Man (Haight 244). While Liggins's campaign to claim authorship led Eliot to reveal her identity, at least to her publisher and close friends, it also served to reinforce the sense that her fiction was a picture of a real experience of English society in the remembered past, a record of life as it had been, and to which it might one day be restored (Bodenheimer 130–34).

Biographical readings of Eliot's fiction have tended to follow Eliot's own prompts, and their reinforcement in Cross's account of her life. Most of her fictional works, apart from the historical novel *Romola,* are located in the English Midlands within the living memory of her family. In their first critical assessments, the early works, especially *Scenes of Clerical Life, Adam Bede*, and *The Mill on the Floss*, held a privileged status for depicting the scenes of the author's biographical origins, and drawing on early memories of family members and neighbors (Wah 372). "We have it on very good authority," wrote Mathilde Blind in 1882, "that Mrs Hackit, in 'Amos Barton,' is a faithful likeness of George Eliot's mother," and so on (Blind 10–11). So too their settings: Eliot based the village of Shepperton, in *Scenes of Clerical Life* and *Adam Bede*, on Chilvers Coton, near Nuneaton, the village in which she was born; and the architectural details described at length in the opening paragraph of "Amos Barton" were those of the parish church.

Throughout her works, the social formation of the village is evident as both a residual presence and a social ideal. George Willis Cooke set the tone for the appreciation of Eliot as a writer of village life in his *George Eliot: A Critical Study* (1883), one of the early biographical studies. For him, she was the novelist of "the pleasant country, the common people, the quiet villages" (2), despite the fact that the more mature works, especially *Middlemarch* and *Daniel Deronda*, were concerned with larger conurbations, stately homes, and cosmopolitan resorts. Even in the late works, however, the village setting is retained: in *Middlemarch,* for instance, much of the activity takes place in the outlying village of Lowick, often represented as a place of bucolic leisure, in which, for instance, the Reverend Farebrother installs "a pair of beautiful goats to be pets of the village in general, and to walk at large as sacred animals" (772; ch. 80). In all her works, the village provides a compelling model of social cohesion. Dorothea's grand vision of social good is achieved in the context of village life. Following her night of emotional distress that leads to the novel's dénouement, she looks out of the window and sees

a man with a bundle on his back, and a woman carrying her baby; in the field she could see figures moving – perhaps the shepherd with his dog. Far off in the bending sky was the pearly light; and she felt the largeness of the world and the manifold wakings of men to labour and endurance. (776; ch. 80)

This silent image of social cooperation that is the culmination of the novel is a scene of rural labor—a man and a woman setting about their day's business, a shepherd and a dog, and, by implication, a host of agricultural laborers rising to work—set against the backdrop of a shining pastoral landscape, a view from the village of its surrounding world.[2] She retains the village as a social ideal in *Daniel Deronda* too, where at the end of the novel, Diplow, the "idyllic" village (870; ch. 69), presents a model of social inclusiveness that suggests a vision of the "national centre, such as the English have, though they are scattered over the face of the globe" (875; ch. 69), for which Daniel strives on behalf of the Jewish people.

The village thus provides a living environment for the moral dramas that play out in Eliot's fiction. The villages which Eliot describes are places with stable and traditional communities, into which strangers can be co-opted. Silas Marner, for instance, having been expelled from his native industrial town, moves to Raveloe, a village where he lays down roots with a newly acquired family. The village absorbs Silas through its customary culture, despite his incomer status. The final images of the story affirm his acceptance in both the local community and the natural environment: Eppie's wedding, for example, happens at the "one time of the year which was held in Raveloe to be especially suitable for a wedding," when "the great lilacs and laburnums in the old-fashioned gardens showed their golden and purple wealth about the lichen-tinted walls," "a time when a light bridal dress could be worn with comfort and seen to advantage" (241; Conclusion). In the village, nature and society are parsed together in the natural rhythms of the seasons.

Rather than an autobiographical record, therefore, the village settings are part of the symbolic world that Eliot depicts, and onto which she projects strong moral values. In all Eliot's novels, characters' affiliation to their locality is a fundamental strand in their ethical make up. We are moved to admire the characters who enjoy deep relationships with places more than those who lack a stable home. Dinah Morris, the heroine of *Adam Bede*, says that she has been "planted" in Snowfield, and Mrs. Poyser warns that "there is no more moving [her] than the rooted tree" (518; ch.49; McDonagh, "*Adam Bede* and Emigration" 38). In Dinah's case, the language of rooting is striking because, paradoxically, at the beginning of the novel she is an itinerant preacher. By the end, having been uprooted from Snowfield, she is replanted in Hayslope. The stability that she achieves over the course of the novel provides a steady measure against which to judge Hetty's deviant self, as she trails across the country in search of Arthur, and finally is transported to Australia as a convict for the likely murder of her child. Similarly, we are asked to "pity" the morally dubious Gwendolen Harleth of *Daniel Deronda* for the fact "that Offendene was not the home of [her] childhood, or endeared to her by family memories" (50; ch.3). While Hetty's "crimes" made her homeless, by contrast, it is Gwendolen's homelessness that appears to have caused her moral shortcomings. Later she will be "removed to" and "settled in" Offendene, but the legalistic vocabulary of forced evictions ("removal" and "settlement" are the terms used in connection with the eviction of claimants on the poor law [McDonagh, "On Settling"]), and her evident discomfort, or "pang," at the end of the novel, ensure that we are convinced that her final home has become neither "native" nor "settled."

The language of "roots" is abundantly evident in all Eliot's works, and it projects a rural, and by association, village ambience onto psychological and moral analyses. In the town, by contrast, people are deemed unable to plant roots, and the environment unnatural or artificial. Even though the major characters in her novels are rarely farmers or agricultural laborers—she chooses instead artisans, such as carpenters (Adam Bede), weavers (Silas Marner), or watchmakers (Felix Holt)—the novels highlight the work of planting, husbanding, and cultivating, through a heavily metaphorical vocabulary that sees such work as the bedrock of English society. In *Adam Bede* the narrator tells us that

> you and I are indebted to the hard hands of such men [rural labourers] – hands that have long ago mingled with the soil they tilled so faithfully, thriftily making the best they could of the earth's fruits, and receiving the smallest share as their own wages. (562; ch 53)

It is not just that they are traditional workers who continue the labor or their forefathers; through their work they literally make the landscape which readers imagine that they inhabit. Although "soil" is more often noted as the dirt on people's feet than in a field, (McDonagh, "*Adam Bede* and Emigration" 38) nevertheless the image of "hard hands" "mingling with the soil" is a powerful emblem of English traditional society that pervades all Eliot's works, and which puts this form of village labor at the moral, economic, and aesthetic heart of national life.

The village is part of nature, just as the wedding, in *Silas Marner*, is part of time. Eliot embeds her moral and social views in the very fabric of the world she describes. The vocabulary of roots belongs to the domain of plants, of botany and agriculture, rural landscapes, and the village as the social form of country life. In mid-nineteenth-century everyday life too, as Eliot was well aware, "roots" provided an idiom for the discussion of emigration, in that emigrants "planted" new settlements. This usage resonates in the novels too, especially in her late novel, *Daniel Deronda*. In this, the botanical language of roots and plants combines with a biological language of blood and racial inheritance. In the passage cited at the head of this chapter, a "spot of a native land" provides an arena for both customary practices ("the labour men go forth to"), and a set of familiar sights and sounds, which together provide the foundations for a benign affective attitude ("kindly acquaintance with all neighbours, even to dogs and donkeys") that will "spread" "as a sweet habit of the blood."

The layers of association here, from land to culture to body to blood, indicate the intricacy with which Eliot considers the landscape, not as a neutral backdrop to social life, but as referencing an accretion of different arguments about human culture and its social forms. It reminds us that the "reality" of the novels was not found but constructed, and that when she wrote and published her novels she was responding to contemporary debates about affiliation and belonging. This requires us substantially to refine the view expressed by Cross and the other biographers of the mid-1880s who established the tradition of memorializing her as the nostalgic guardian of old England.

Village Realism

Ideas about rural living were at the heart of Eliot's ideas about realism and the possibilities of fictional representation. As she developed and refined her practices as a writer of fiction she returned frequently to the idea of a village. In July 1856, during the period in which she carried out her initial experiments with fictional forms, and before the launch of her career as a novelist, she published an essay in the *Westminster Review* entitled "The Natural History of German Life," on the work of the German sociologist, Wilhelm Heinrich von Riehl. Eliot appears to have derived many of her ideas from Riehl's work, including the notion that realistic representation should be based on close observation and experience rather than suppositions drawn from theoretical principles, and also the idea that its subject should be ordinary or "common" people depicted in their natural habitats, rather than idealized or "preternaturally virtuous" characters in exotic or romantic settings (Graver 28–36). She also took from him a decidedly anti-town sensibility.

Eliot developed these ideas in her fictional works, but the essay on Riehl is important because it produces a very clear spatial economy, which is evident not only in the implicit claim that the rural peasant class, rather than urban people, are the privileged subjects of realistic depiction. It is also apparent in the proposition that the viewer should stand close to his subjects, practically engaged with them, rather than on high and at a distance. There is a localism in Riehl's method that Eliot admires and seeks to emulate. In the bravura passage at the opening to the essay, she contrasts the ideas that the word "railway" might summon up first in those who have "concrete acquaintance with railways," and second in those of "wide views and narrow experience" (*Selected Essays* 107–08). In Eliot's hierarchy of thought, the former is better than the latter. For the latter, their lack of particular engagement would lead them to talk, impractically in Eliot's view, "of a vast network of railways stretching over the globe, of future 'lines' in Madagascar, and elegant refreshment rooms in the Sandwich Islands . . . " (*Selected Essays* 107). She meant the incongruity of "elegant refreshment rooms" in the South Pacific to amuse readers, for whom the exotic location would summon savage natives rather than railway commuters; although of course, the lingering suggestions that railway travelers might be savages too, and that savages might eat sandwiches, improves the joke considerably. Throughout the essay, Eliot aligns the global, the abstract, and the theoretical with urban "democratic and socialistic" movements that had driven the revolutions of 1848 ("they have made this special study of a single fragment of society the basis of a theory which quietly substitutes for the small group of Parisian proletaires or English factory-workers, the society of all Europe—nay, of the whole world" [*Selected Essays* 129]). In contrast, she associates "concrete" experience with local knowledge, and rural environments with what she calls "incarnate history," and a convincing and truthful representation of reality.

The country village emerges here as the *locus classicus* of realistic representation, and the peasant, its inhabitant, is its agent. The peasant embodies the very region in which he lives. Writes Eliot,

> among the peasantry it is the race, the district, the province, that has its style; namely, its dialect, its phraseology, its proverbs and its songs, which belong alike to the entire body of the people. This provincial style of the peasant is . . . , like his *physique*, a remnant of history to which he clings with the utmost tenacity. (114; emphasis in original)

Here is a complete union of people and places, present and past, impossible in fast moving and unstable urban settings, which, following Riehl, she evokes as hotbeds of revolutionary ideas. Hence the deficiencies of Charles Dickens and Eugène Sue, whose urban novels she considers to be superficial, unable to grasp the psychological makeup of the town-type. Eliot's armory of organic metaphors is mobilized in her account of Riehl: "The nature of European men," by which she means the rural peasantry, "has its roots intertwined with the past"; in England, on the other hand, "we have to recall it by an effort of memory and reflection" (*Selected Essays* 128–29). In "memory and reflection" we hear an echo of Wordsworth, and an English poetic endeavor to restore living links with the past. Riehl adds both weight and urgency to this English literary project, revealing the social and political effects that "intertwining" English "roots" in the lost landscapes might achieve.

It is no coincidence that Eliot should have written these words while she was simultaneously engaged in early experiments in fiction writing. The essay on Riehl (July 1856) sits between her review of Ruskin's *Modern Painters* (April 1856) which praises Ruskin for teaching "the doctrine that all truth and beauty are to be attained by a humble and faithful study of nature" (*Selected Essays* 368), and her excoriating critique of novels by women writers, "Silly Novels by Lady Novelists" (October 1856), "drivelling narrative, which, like a bad drawing, represents nothing, and barely indicates what is meant to be represented" (*Selected Essays* 158). All three essays were published in the *Westminster Review*, and take up questions regarding realism and the limits of representation. At the very same time she embarked on her own attempts at fiction writing. In her journal entry, "How I Came to Write Fiction," dated 6 December 1857, she describes the long gestation period, during which she experimented with fictional modes. Her first attempt, "an introductory chapter describing a Staffordshire village," was "pure description," but gradually she developed in addition "dramatic power," wit, and finally "pathos" (*Scenes* 351, 352, 353; Appendix). Significantly, during this experimental phase, her story moves from "a Staffordshire village" to the village of her childhood home in Warwickshire, and settings shift from an unremarked present to a carefully documented recent past. Following Riehl her fiction aims accurately to represent the daily lives of village people, through concrete detail of their material lives, and like Riehl, she proposes to understand the people, through their relationships to their material environments.

From the very opening of "Amos Barton," Eliot's narratives are saturated with concrete detail, the thick detail that Riehl advocates. This serves initially to locate the narratives in time. For example, the architectural features of Shepperton Church, described in the first chapter of the story, demonstrate the building's new look, achieved over the last twenty-five years. While "its substantial stone tower," and "clock" remain constant, "in everything else," she writes, "what changes!": the church's "slated roof," "old steeple," "windows . . . tall and symmetrical," "outer doors . . . resplendent with oak-graining," and "inner doors reverentially noiseless with a garment of red baize" (*Scenes* 7; ch. 1). The renovation of the church is a motif throughout the story, and underlines the fact that "Amos Barton," in common with all the stories in *Scenes of Clerical Life*, is set precisely in the recent past. Concrete detail is thus crucial to the work of "memory and reflection." Yet if the fiction aims to rejoin present and past, it gives no coherent account of whether, and how, the two have been severed. Despite a list of reforms that have occurred between then and the "now" of the narrative—"the New Police [1829], the Tithe Commutation Act [1836], [and] the penny-post [1840]" (7; ch. 1)—the difference between past and present is presented less as a definitive break, but instead rather more vaguely as that between a "picture" ("dear, old, brown, crumbling, picturesque"), and the abstract representations of architectural planners ("diagrams, plans, elevations, and sections"); or between "a drama" and the "mechanical affair of official routine" (7–8; ch. 1). Within these representational regimes, details signify differently as, on the one hand, sensory elements within an embodied past, and on the other hand, disembodied signs within a bureaucratized and desensitized present. In Eliot's fiction, the two regimes of detail run concurrently and both contribute to her own realist style: details in her narratives are both part of the depiction of an embodied past, and also of an abstracting and "mechanical" present; and they simultaneously produce an immediate sense of sensory presence, and the remote point of view of a distant narrative voice. The latter is not exactly the "diagrams, plans, elevations and sections" that she refers to in "Amos Barton," although a tendency to abstract is shared by both. In Eliot's narrative, the descriptive regimes of past and present, and, by extension, of country and town, are woven together into the fabric of her narrative style.

A vivid example of this double technique in "Amos Barton" is the description of a scene in the dining room in Milby Vicarage, in the neighboring town, where the gathered clerics discuss the presumed goings-on in Shepperton. Through the complex use of concrete detail, the passage draws in its readers, by subjecting them to a shared sensory experience; yet it also adopts a scientific narrative stance which describes the same experience in a distanced and abstract way:

> Pleasant . . . to enter a comfortable dining-room, where the closely-drawn red curtains
> glow with the double light of fire and candle, where glass and silver are glittering on
> the pure damask, and a soup-tureen gives a hint of the fragrance that will presently rush

out to inundate your hungry senses and prepare them, by the delicate visitation of atoms, for the keen gusto of ampler contact! (53; ch. 6)

The material details here serve to produce these affects: the type and quantity of detail generates a sensory overload (the light is "double," the fragrance "rush[es]," the senses are "inundate[d]") which overwhelms characters and readers alike; yet the very same details provide the material for the objective or scientific mode of the narrator, achieved in part through a Latinate ("visitation") and scientific ("atoms") vocabulary. As readers we oscillate between identification with the characters, and being analysts of them. But the description also serves to imply that human characters are always subject to the affects of the sensory world around them; the material world is animated, and humans, in contrast, made passive. At this particular juncture, the description carries a subtle irony, as it provides the backdrop to the clerics' discussion of Amos Barton's dubious appetites: witnessed in his multitudinous children and his suspicious friendship with the beautiful Countess who has taken up residence in his house. The joke they labor over is whether he dines "at six" with the Countess, thus neglecting his wife, or that he dines "with six," that is with his six children (56–57; ch. 6). Either way, he is too lusty for a country cleric. But if Barton is a fool to his appetites, then so too, the backdrop suggests, would we all be, as we are all liable to the same stimulation of our "hungry senses."

Eliot's narrative style thus has implications for the ways in which she presents human experience in a more profound sense than might otherwise be appreciated. As Catherine Gallagher has noted, Eliot's works tend to follow a Malthusian script, which posits that humans are always subject to competing appetites for, on the one hand, nourishment, and on the other, sexual reproduction. This is seen most clearly in "Amos Barton": Barton's predicament—that he has too many children, and not enough resources to feed and clothe them—is a text book case in Malthusian economics (Gallagher 172–82). The privations of his family are exacerbated by his egotism and vanity, which lead him to satisfy his own appetites before those of his family, thus hastening his wife, Milly's, death.

The Malthusian imperative in this story, that he should better regulate his appetites, is nonetheless no more than implicit; and it is met by an equally strong sense that, despite his family's difficulties, they nevertheless exist in a world of "ample" (a favored word in "Amos Barton") resources, in which things are more likely to overflow than underflow. This plenitude is evident throughout the story—not just in Milby Vicarage. In the first chapter, for instance, we are introduced to a panoply of comfortable characters, including Mrs. Patten, who had "got rich . . . by the negative process of spending nothing" (10; ch. 1), and who is associated with "[q]uiescence in an easy-chair, under the sense of compound interest perpetually accumulating" (11; ch. 1). So too, Milly's heart "overflowed with love, she felt sure she was near a fountain of love that would care for husband and babes" (23; ch. 2); as does the tureen at the Countess's dinner party, from which spilt gravy ruins Milly's silk dress, triggering the gift of a new and better dress. The excessive materiality of the world of Shepperton is mirrored in the narrative by the superabundant, or "superogatory," detail (7; ch. 1). It is almost as though a Malthusian moral view is projected onto, but fails to connect with, a pre-Malthusian, plenitudinous world.

The distinction is all the more important in the fact that it references the difference between the then and now of the story. On a number of occasions we are reminded about the controversial New Poor Law, enacted in 1834, which was closely identified with Malthusian values, and for many represented a major assault on traditional notions of community and affiliation. "Remember, the New Poor Law had not yet come into operation," the narrator urges in chapter 2. "Mr Barton was not acting as paid chaplain of the Union, but as the pastor who had the cure of all souls in his parish, pauper as well as other"(25; ch. 2). Barton's visit to the workhouse is highly significant for establishing the positive values of an Old Poor Law community: here we encounter a harmonious assemblage of elderly and infirm eccentrics—"Old Maxum," Poll Fodge, "Silly Jim," Mr. Fitchett, and Mrs. Brick—and a "certain number of refractory children" (26–27; ch. 2). As if to underline their organic unity, we are shown Fitchett, sleeping to the sound of Barton's sermon: "in the recurrent regularity with which he dozed off until he nodded and awaked himself, he looked not unlike a piece of mechanism, ingeniously contrived for measuring the length of Mr Barton's discourse"(27; ch. 2). Under the Old Poor Law all hearts beat to the same rhythm. We are left to speculate on the consequences of the ministry of a "paid chaplain of the Union."

We have come full circle back to the village. In the history of the administration of poor relief, the New Poor Law is significant because it changed the unit of governance from the parish, or the village, to the Union, an assemblage of parishes more like a town. The importance of the single parish dwindled as administrative responsibilities for managing the poor shifted to Unions, and with it the village also declined in importance as the remnant of the parish system. It is therefore significant that many of Eliot's works, including *The Mill on the Floss*, *Felix Holt*, and *Middlemarch*, are set on the cusp of this legislative change. In "Amos Barton" the village depicted is the village of the Old Poor Law parish; yet it is remembered through the eyes of a narrator looking back on an old way of life, with a modern, town-based, and Malthusian—or New Poor Law—sensibility.

Printed Villages, Modern and Ancient

Eliot's imagined localities are highly complex literary constructions and never simply autobiographical recollections or unmediated reflections on the past. As we have seen, they incorporate historical and sociological depictions of change, and discuss the very factors that had shaped communities and their relationship to environments then, and in the past. She knits these reflections into the form of her representations so that her very style embodies a commentary on modes of life and living. But Eliot's work also owes much to other literature that circulated in the print culture of the time, which provided alternative ways of imagining locality and affiliation, often in the form of a village. Two contrasting visions of the village stand out, and both find their way into Eliot's literary topography. The first is a literary form of the village, mediated by Mary Russell Mitford in her highly successful, light-hearted serial, *Our Village*. The second is the primitive or archaic village, which came to Eliot in the weightier tomes of the legal historian Henry Maine. The influence of both of these visions is particularly evident in *Middlemarch*—paradoxically, as this is the novel principally concerned with towns rather than villages.

The genre of the "village tale" was made famous by Mitford in a popular series of village stories published initially in the *Ladies' Magazine* in the 1820s, and quickly reprinted in volume form (Moretti 35–42). These stories set the terms for an influential genre of provincial writing emulated by later women writers, including Eliot. *Our Village* was a series of loosely connected short stories all set in or around Mitford's home village of Three Mile Cross in Berkshire. They comprised anecdotes about local characters, alongside loco-descriptive narratives describing flora and fauna in the changing seasons of the year, in the form of "walks in the country." The narrator was Mitford herself, adopting the voice of a confidential and gossipy friend, who addressed her readers as though they were personal acquaintances. The "walks in the country" were particularly popular; their ground-level viewpoint emphasized that the landscape was inhabited and familiar, despite the fact that the narrative stance often looked from above, and viewed the terrain as though it were a map or a plan.

The stories were notoriously uneventful, and relentlessly saccharine in tone, seeing even rural poverty in an optimistic light (Helsinger 121–23). Nevertheless, they described the changing conditions of country life, depicting a highly mobile population and a landscape subject to the changes wrought by agrarian capitalism. The village in Mitford was far from a nostalgic category, but a social unit plugged into networks of modern communications, including roads, print, and the post. Such features helped these tales of English rural life to become internationally successful commodities, pirated in the United States, and enthusiastically consumed across the colonial world. The form was readily adaptable, appropriated by a range of writers in a diversity of contexts in Britain and beyond.

When Eliot sat down to write a "village story," as she records in her journal, it is likely that, despite her contempt for literature by "silly ladies," she had Mitford's *Our Village* in mind as a successful and lucrative genre well suited to women writers. Indeed, many of the characteristics of *Our Village* are evident in *Scenes of Clerical Life*. Published initially in serial form in *Blackwood's Edinburgh Magazine*, the stories are only loosely connected, joined together by their common location, in and around Shepperton; and as in *Our Village*, the narrator (in *Scenes* personified as a rural clergyman) assumes an easy familiarity with readers, who are addressed as friends and companions. As in *Our Village*, the stories highlight everyday, ordinary occurrences and people, and adopt bathos as the dominating mode (Hardy 28–30). In each story, local people tend to imagine situations that are more scandalous than the narrative suggests they are, and the plot is in part concerned with the intrigues that are caused by the overactive imaginations and speculation of others. Like Mitford, in *Scenes of Clerical Life*, Eliot presents a progressive view of society only partially tinged with nostalgia for a lost world.

These characteristics persist in Eliot's later work. In common with *Our Village* her narrative voices oscillate between the ground level of shared experience and the higher view of an omniscient narrator. In *Middlemarch* especially, the narrator famously mediates between expressions of sympathetic identification with characters and situations, and judgments on individual characters, measuring their behavior against universal standards. Even though its tone is now more serious, even the omniscient narrative of *Middlemarch*, moving stealthily in and out of the characters' interior thoughts, owes something to the free-roaming, confidential narrator of *Our Village*. Moreover, *Middlemarch* takes to new lows the bathetic mode found in *Our Village* in the stories of Dorothea, "foundress of nothing," and Lydgate, whose high ambitions are spectacularly thwarted by personal weakness and social interference (*Middlemarch* 4; Prelude). Above all, and much in the mode of the village story, *Middlemarch* is a novel about gossip, and the ways in which circulating stories both falsify realities and derail intended outcomes.

Given the broader and more ambitious canvas of *Middlemarch*, and the range and scope of the novel's vision, these resemblances to the village tale are surprising. Indeed, *Middlemarch* is usually read as a national novel, in which Middlemarch, the town, stands as a metonymic representation of the whole of Britain (Helsinger 224). As Ian Duncan has written, it is the "authentic site of an imperial England able to select and absorb the forces of change, renewing rather than surrendering its traditional properties" (Duncan 331). By focusing on a small provincial community during the period leading to the Reform Act of 1832, *Middlemarch* demonstrates how local occurrences and concerns were both representative of, and instrumental in making, the new national map. With its emphasis on evolutionary change, and the slow processes of adaptation, the novel made Middlemarch, the town, a small but eloquent node in a larger system of slow-paced national development. As such, it had much wider reach and weightier concerns than the seemingly inward-looking and light-hearted village tale.

Yet it is important to remember that the village tale, as developed by Mitford, always views the village as an outward-looking social unit. It was connected to the wider world, and participated in the same processes of modernization as metropolitan centers. In a stronger sense than is usually presumed, the village tale provides the model for the more ambitious provincial novel like *Middlemarch*. For instance, the emphasis on networks of communication that is found in Mitford's village is taken to an extreme in *Middlemarch* in which images of nets, and mesh-like woven objects like webs, textiles, and even human tissue, have an important imaginative position (Miller). They provide the central models for social relations in the novel, which are conceived as organisms in which individuals are knitted together by the "stealthy convergence of human lots" (93; ch. 11), that is to say, overlapping interests that operate in both positive and negative ways. Eliot extends this model to whole communities, and the relationships between communities. As she writes:

> [m]unicipal town and rural parish gradually made fresh threads of connection – gradually, as the old stocking gave way to the savings-bank, and the worship of the solar guinea became extinct; while squires and baronets, and even lords who had once lived blamelessly afar from the civic mind, gathered the faultiness of closer acquaintanceship. (94; ch. 11)

Thus, rather than positing the village as the forerunner or origin of the town, Eliot instead maintains the village intact, as a separate and independent social unit that becomes newly connected to the town. Eliot uses the very same metaphors of threads and knitted textiles to describe the relationships between communities as those within them. The village is presented here as a point of connection in a network of fiscal relations, alongside, but not necessarily subordinate to, the town.

The village tale does not account for all representations of villages in *Middlemarch*. Quite often, contrary to this, villages are presented as separate and self-sufficient, and out of step with modernity. Sometimes they appear as residual formations, cut off from the rest of the world: Mr. Farebrother's goats in Lowick, for instance, which "walk at large . . . as sacred animals," give the impression that Lowick is an otherworldly place. Although goats rather than cows, the sacred beasts give Lowick the look of ancient India rather than an English Midlands village. On other occasions, however, the idea of the village is presented as a laboratory for utopian experimentation, such as for instance Dorothea's proposed "village of industry," and her ill-fated cottages. Elsewhere the village appears as the ideal social organism of the past, epitomizing relations of cooperation and dependency that the novel values so highly and sometimes laments having lost.

A good deal of Eliot's thinking about villages as social units was derived from the work of Henry Maine, whose *Ancient Law* (1861) was an important source for the portrayal of inheritance in *Middlemarch*. Maine put forward the notion that the origins of modern concepts of law, including the idea of property, could ultimately be traced back to primitive villages, such as existed in feudal times in Europe, but which had been preserved in India. In *Ancient Law* and subsequent works, Maine traced an evolution from "status" societies, in which social structures, and laws, were ruled by customary relations between people, to "contract" societies, in which written legal codes governed social structures (Fleishman 172–73). The Indian village—as referenced by Mr. Farebrother's sacred goats—was a "status" society, which contained a privileged source of information about this evolution. Maine was a comparative historian of the law, who drew his ideas from an extraordinary range of sources from ancient and modern literatures of the world.[3] His methodology had been influenced by German historical scholarship, in particular the writings of the legal historian G. L. von Maurer, whose work in understanding the evolution of modern institutions he emulated. Maine and Maurer produced the kind of study that Will Ladislaw held as a scholarly rebuke to the myopic Casaubon, whose search for the "Key to all Mythologies" he criticizes in particular for Casaubon's failure to read German historical works. As Ladislaw notes, and as Maine's work demonstrates, there is no single key to all mythologies. Rather, a wide-ranging and eclectic study of all world mythologies would yield extraordinary gains in seeking to understand the multiple origins of modern society.

Eliot eagerly read *Ancient Law* in the winter of 1869, while she was preparing *Middlemarch*, and her notebooks give some clues as to the ways in which it engaged her imagination. She was fascinated by his account of primitive patriarchal societies and early practices regarding property and inheritance, and this fed directly into her critique of women's unfortunate lot in Middlemarch society (Graver 217). Most important however, it presented a new way of thinking about ownership that related specifically to the idea of the primitive village. For Maine, the primitive village was "an assemblage of joint proprietors, a body of kindred holding a domain in common" (Maine, *Ancient Law* 272). As Eliot records in her notes, this conception of the village derived from "Hindoo laws" of inheritance: "a son as soon as born acquires a vested right in his father's property. On the son's attaining full age, he can force a partition: this did not occur in practice & thus the family expands into the village community" (Pratt and Neufeldt 205–06). The village, therefore, is the social unit that emerges specifically when the possibility of individual ownership, or "partition," is declined.

The imaginative possibilities of this idea for Eliot are immense. *Middlemarch* opens with the scene in which Dorothea refuses to accept her share of the family jewels, and this provides something of a benchmark against which other acts of inheritance and attitudes to property are measured. The emphasis in the novel on wills, and the efforts of individuals to control the future posthumously through the division of their property, for instance, relates directly to Maine's claim that "the view of a Will which regards it as conferring the power of diverting property from the Family, or of distributing it in such uneven proportions as the fancy or good sense of the Testator may dictate, is not older than that later portion of the Middle Ages in which Feudalism had completely consolidated itself." (Maine, *Ancient Law* 132). In the case of Dorothea, only by relinquishing her claims to Casaubon's property altogether can she escape her husband's "dead hand." The idea of shared property, on the other hand, reveals to Eliot the notion that "Society consists of Families, not of individuals," and that "Guilt is corporate, merit is corporate" (Pratt and Neufeldt 204). "A man was not regarded as himself—as an individual; his individuality was swallowed up in the group to which he belonged" (205). Ideas of shared, or "corporate guilt" recur throughout the novel in episodes in which the actions of individuals impact in unintended ways on the lives of others: for instance Fred Vincy and his indebtedness to the Garth family or, worse, Bulstrode in relation to Ladislaw's relatives. Both are examples of "the stealthy convergence of human lots." Eliot's work exposes both their positive and negative aspects.

The idea of an Indian Village is only faintly evident in *Middlemarch*. Nevertheless, it offers Eliot an important model of affiliation that she engages with throughout the novel, and, despite its exotic origins, it also provides a locality of sorts. Maine argued that the vestiges of a primitive village—like the Indian Village—could be traced in the ancient customary laws of rural England, in the "common and common-able fields, Lammas lands, common meadows, and limited rights over Wastes" (Maine, *Village Communities* 200). Eliot, acutely conscious of England's medieval history, makes these traces real in her depictions of rural landscape. As they drive across the Midlands countryside, Fred and Rosamond Vincy see a landscape "almost all meadows and pastures, with hedgerows still allowed to grow in bushy beauty and to spread out coral fruit for the birds. Little details gave each field a particular physiognomy . . . the sudden slope of the old marl-pit making a red background for the burdock; . . . the stray hovel," and so on (102; ch. 12). The details in the landscape provide evidence of a medieval past in both its features and its language: the "old marl-pit" is perhaps the same marl pit of Chaucer's "Miller's Tale" (which is referenced in the head note to the chapter).[4] This is a landscape with a history, and with it for Eliot imaginative variations on the present.

Eliot's engagement with Maine is a larger topic than we can do justice to in this essay. Yet to acknowledge it gives an indication of the range and depth of her thinking about locality and affiliation, and the centrality of this within the imaginative world that she constructed. Her depictions of landscape that seem at first sight merely documentary are nevertheless, through her rendering, locked into a complex fabric of debates about place and personhood. Cross was not wrong to characterize his deceased wife as an archivist of the English past; but he was wrong to sentimentalize her work as parochial documentation or nostalgia. To understand her representations of locality, one needs to take into account the full range of influences and references that pressed on her work, and moreover, to recognize the ways in which her conception of place was embedded in the very form of realism that she developed.

NOTES

1 On villages, see Williams, *The Country and City*, 18–22 and throughout. For a contemporary view, see Matless.

2 The philosophical context of Eliot's organicism is discussed by Graver, and by Dentith (9–29); the classic account of its ideological commitments is Williams, *Culture and Society* (110–18).

3 Sir Henry Sumner Maine (1828–88) was a lawyer and writer. After the success of *Ancient Law* he spent a seven-year period in Calcutta as legal member of the Governor General's Council of India, and Vice-Chancellor of Calcutta University. On his return to Britain he was elected Professor of Jurisprudence at Oxford in 1869. Eliot records reading *Village Communities* (1871), which was based on his Oxford lectures, in her Pforzheimer Notebook (Irwin 251). In the 1870s, Maine contributed to the *Saturday Review*, and came into contact with Lewes. He attended gatherings at the Lewes-Eliot household, corresponded with the couple, and was present at Eliot's funeral.

4 A marle pit is a clay pit, and, according to the OED, appropriated in English place names in medieval times. Eliot silently underlines the medieval associations of the landscape through a subtle pattern of allusion: the head note to the chapter is a quotation from Chaucer's *Miller's Tale*, in which a character falls into a marle pit, distracted by learning.

References

Anderson, Amanda. *The Powers of Distance: Cosmopolitanism and the Cultivation of Distance.* Princeton: Princeton UP, 2001.

Baucom, Ian. *Out of Place: Englishness, Empire, and the Locations of Identity.* Princeton: Princeton UP, 1999.

Belich, James. *Replenishing the Earth: The Settler Revolution and the Rise of the Anglo- World, 1783–1939.* Oxford: Oxford UP, 2009.

Blind, Mathilde. *George Eliot.* London: W. H. Allen, 1883.

Bodenheimer, Rosemarie. *The Real Life of Mary Ann Evans: George Eliot, Her Letters and Her Fiction.* Ithaca: Cornell UP, 1994.

Cooke, George Willis. *George Eliot: A Critical Study.* London: Sampson Low, Marston, Searle, & Rivington, 1883.

Cross, John. *George Eliot's Life as Related in her Letters and Journals.* 3 vols. Edinburgh: Blackwood, 1885.

Dentith, Simon. *George Eliot.* Brighton: Harvester, 1986.

Duncan, Ian. "The Provincial or Regional Novel." *A Companion to the Victorian Novel.* Ed. Patrick Brantlinger and William B. Thesing. Oxford: Blackwell, 2002. 318–34.

Eliot, George. *Adam Bede.* Ed. Stephen Gill. London: Penguin, 1980.

Eliot, George. *Daniel Deronda.* Ed. Barbara Hardy. London: Penguin, 1967.

Eliot, George. *The George Eliot Letters.* Ed. Gordon S. Haight. 9 vols. New Haven: Yale UP, 1954–78.

Eliot, George. *Middlemarch.* Ed. David Carroll. Oxford: Oxford UP, 1996.

Eliot, George. *Scenes of Clerical Life.* Ed. Jennifer Gribble. London: Penguin, 1997.

Eliot, George. *Selected Essays, Poems and Other Writings.* Ed. A. S. Byatt and Nicholas Warren. London: Penguin, 1990.

Eliot, George. *Silas Marner.* Ed. Q. D. Leavis. London: Penguin, 1967.

Feldman, David. "Migration." *The Cambridge Urban History of Britain.* Ed. Martin Daunton. Vol. 3. Cambridge: Cambridge UP, 2001. 185–206.

Fleishman, Avrom. *George Eliot's Intellectual Life.* Cambridge: Cambridge UP, 2010.

Gallagher, Catherine. *The Body Economic: Life, Death, and Sensation in Political Economy and the Victorian Novel.* Princeton: Princeton UP, 2006.

Graver, Suzanne. *George Eliot and Community: A Study in Social Theory and Fictional Form.* Berkeley: U of California P, 1984.

Haight, Gordon S. *George Eliot: A Biography.* Oxford: Clarendon, 1968.

Hardy, Barbara. *The Novels of George Eliot: A Study in Form.* London: Athlone, 1959.

Helsinger, Elisabeth. *Rural Scenes and National Representation: Britain, 1815–1850.* Princeton: Princeton UP, 1997.

Henry, Nancy. *George Eliot and Empire.* Cambridge: Cambridge UP, 2002.

Irwin, Jane, ed. *George Eliot's* Daniel Deronda *Notebooks.* Cambridge: Cambridge UP, 1996.

McDonagh, Josephine. "Space, Mobility and the Novel: 'The Spirit of Place is a Great Reality'." *Adventures in Realism.* Ed. Matthew Beaumont. Oxford: Wiley-Blackwell, 2007. 50–67.

McDonagh, Josephine. "On Settling and Being Unsettled: Legitimacy and Settlement around 1850." *Legitimacy and Illegitimacy in Nineteenth-Century Literature and History.* Ed. Margot Finn, Michael Lobban, and Jenny Bourne Taylor. Basingstoke: Palgrave, 2010. 48–66.

McDonagh, Josephine. "*Adam Bede* and Emigration." *The George Eliot Review: Journal of the George Eliot Fellowship* 41 (2010): 35–43.

Maine, Henry. *Ancient Law.* 1861. London: Dent. Rpt. 1917.

Maine, Henry. *Village Communities in the East and West: Six Lectures Delivered at Oxford.* London: John Murray, 1871.

Matless, David. "Villages." *Patterned Ground: Entanglements of Nature and Culture.* Ed. Stephan Harrison, Steve Pile, and Nigel Thrift. London: Reaktion, 2004. 161–64.

Miller, J. Hillis. "Optics and Semiotics in *Middlemarch.*" *The Worlds of Victorian Fiction.* Ed. Jerome H. Buckley. Cambridge: Harvard UP, 1975. 125–45.

Moretti, Franco. *Graphs, Maps, Trees*. London: Verso, 2005.

Plotz, John. *Portable Property: Victorian Culture on the Move*. Princeton: Princeton UP, 2008.

Pratt, John Clark and Victor A. Neufeldt, eds. *George Eliot's "Middlemarch" Notebooks: A Transcription*. Berkeley: U of California P, 1979.

Price, Leah. "George Eliot and the Production of Consumers." *Novel* 30.2 (1997): 145–69.

Wah, Sarah. "'The Most Churlish of Celebrities': George Eliot, John Cross and the Question of High Status." *Journal of Victorian Culture* 15.3 (2010): 370–87.

Williams, Raymond. *Culture and Society, 1780–1950*. London: Chatto, 1958.

Williams, Raymond. *The Country and the City*. 1973. London: Paladin, 1975.

26
George Eliot's Liberalism

Daniel S. Malachuk

Modern commentators have long pursued in George Eliot's novels a tension "between the legitimate claims of individualism and the imperative need for a 'coherent social faith and order'" (113), as Tim Dolin puts it with reference to the Prelude from *Middlemarch*. Many, like Suzanne Graver and Bernard Semmel, have used Ferdinand Tönnies's 1887 thesis to expand this tension into a central drama of Eliot's novels, which require us to "choos[e] between" (Semmel 5) the new self-interested individualism of urban industrial society (*Gesellschaft*) and the old agrarian communal order (*Gemeinschaft*). Those who believe Eliot chooses the latter label her a "conservative." Those who believe Eliot sides with the new individualism label her a "liberal" in the pejorative sense of elites who "take themselves to be something like the voice of society itself" (Cottom 8). Both groups of scholars often reach their conclusions by construing Eliot's skepticism about the civic virtue of representative democracy as proof of her allegiance to either the ancien régime or the new liberal elite.

In pursuit of George Eliot's liberalism, this chapter begins by questioning the existence of this tension in her work. Consider again Dolin's way of putting it. While Eliot did indeed consistently champion "the legitimate claims of the individual," she upheld no corresponding imperative for a "coherent social faith and order." Whatever might have been the case long ago, Eliot explains in the *Middlemarch* Prelude, "later-born Theresas"—today's liberal reformers—are "helped by *no* coherent social faith and order which could perform the function of knowledge for the ardently willing soul" (25; Prelude; emphasis added). There is no old order to which we can return: this is the starting point for Eliot's liberalism. As one gentleman reminds another in an

A Companion to George Eliot, First Edition. Edited by Amanda Anderson and Harry E. Shaw.
© 2013 John Wiley & Sons, Ltd. Published 2016 by John Wiley & Sons, Ltd.

epigram early in *Middlemarch*, the land of "order and a perfect rule" exists only "in human souls" (98; ch. 9).

As these quotations suggest, Eliot's novels are driven by a different tension, one between the ardent but vague visions in human souls and the world in which we must live together. In the very last paragraph of *Middlemarch*, Eliot describes Dorothea as "a new Antigone," her "young and noble impulse struggling amidst the conditions of an imperfect social state" (896; Finale). Eliot formulated her liberalism exactly the same way sixteen years earlier in her essay on Sophocles's play. This "struggle between Antigone and Creon," she wrote, "represents that struggle between elemental tendencies and established laws"; it is a play about an "antagonism between valid claims," showing how our "inward needs" (or "moral sense") and "the outer life of man" (or "the rules which society has sanctioned") are "gradually and painfully being brought into harmony" (246). Eliot sought to do the same liberal work. Like Sophocles in his play, Eliot in her novels does not require us to choose. Instead, Eliot proposes a set of liberal practices that may enable us to cultivate the moral sense without forsaking a world full of other people trying to do the same. Most importantly, for Eliot, the most effective political practices will, somewhat paradoxically, no longer take inspiration from the ancient *polis* of Sophocles. The author of *Romola* understood that civic republicans had sought to revive that *polis* starting in the fifteenth century; Eliot also appreciated how contemporary liberals like John Stuart Mill were attempting to reengineer that *polis* for the nineteenth. But, in Eliot's view, the conditions—or, to use her word, "medium"—which enabled previous forms of political life had altered irrevocably (Middlemarch 896; Finale). Rather than continuing to restrict our focus to the *polis*, Eliot believed, liberals should reconsider realms and practices outside the *polis*: indeed, though she does not use the term, it is useful to see Eliot as promoting the neglected *oikos*, disdained by the ancients, most republicans, and even most nineteenth-century liberals as the sphere of "necessity" opposite the *polis*'s "freedom," as Hannah Arendt styled it in *The Human Condition* (30). Eliot's body of work suggests that for liberals the *oikos* could prove to be the key domain of those "unhistoric acts" upon which "the growing good of the world is partly dependent" (896; Finale).

In her two other elaborations upon the civic republican tradition inherited from the ancient Greeks, Eliot's work was less original but certainly important. Many other nineteenth-century liberals believed, like her, that civic virtues should be cultivated for the sake of progress and not just order, and that such virtues are justified not by metaphysical or religious systems but by an intuited cosmic order. Including her distinctive focus on the *oikos*, all three of these nineteenth-century liberal elaborations upon republicanism are explained in the first half of this chapter. However, because it is her most remarkable contribution to the liberal tradition, Eliot's attention to the *oikos* will organize the second part of this chapter, which examines three of the liberal practices of the *oikos* developed in her novels: practices of place, work, and marriage. In appealing to an expanded conception of *oikos* which will cover the various sites and practices of interest to Eliot, I will draw on new explorations of this term within ecocriticism. Throughout this chapter, the focus will be on two of Eliot's later novels:

Felix Holt (1866) and *Middlemarch* (1872). As I have argued elsewhere, Eliot only really came to understand the republican tradition when writing *Romola* (1863) (Malachuk, "*Romola* and Victorian Liberalism"). Her last novel, *Daniel Deronda* (1876), makes the case against a *polis*-oriented liberalism in a different way (Malachuk, "Nationalist Cosmopolitics"), considered briefly in conclusion.

***

When they recovered the civic republican tradition in the 1970s, historians recovered that tradition's mythology along with it. This was a mythology largely shared by nineteenth-century liberals though not usually their twentieth-century commentators. In Eliot's case, this critical disconnection is evident in the reception of *Romola*, a novel Eliot understood to be examining the most important early modern passage in that republican mythology: the collapse of the Florentine Medici oligarchy in 1492, the revival of that city's fabled republic as a new Jerusalem by the radical Dominican priest Girolamo Savonarola, and his execution in 1498. Only recently, though, have critics also understood this (Malachuk, "*Romola* and Victorian Liberalism," Wihl). As J. G. A. Pocock explained in the 1975 book that initiated the recovery of the republican tradition, *The Machiavellian Moment: Florentine Political Thought and the Atlantic Republican Tradition*, Savonarola's republic was the first modern republic to attempt "to realize a universality of values within a particular . . . political structure" by making "the final phase of a republic's existence . . . coincide with the millennium" (84). For Pocock, the real importance of Savonarola's millennialist republicanism was to inspire Machiavelli to revive the ancient alternative: the merely prudential republic, provisionally stabilized against *fortuna* through the vigorous and imaginative exercise of civic virtue. Reviving a host of ancient institutions for cultivating virtue, Machiavelli and a handful of other post-Savonarolan Florentines transmitted the ancient crafts of republicanism to the architects of the modern republics of the seventeenth and eighteenth centuries, including the English, the American, and the French.

The ideological tenor of the late 1970s and 1980s was such that this recovered republicanism was too often enlisted by "communitarians" engaged in a squabble with liberals, which delayed the recognition of important continuities between early modern civic republicanism and the nineteenth-century liberalism that followed. Today, though, the continuities are obvious to readers who familiarize themselves with the republican historiography. Even in the most preeminent nineteenth-century defense of individual liberties, *On Liberty* (1859), one finds the old republican insistence that a citizen should "rightfully be compelled to perform" such acts of civic virtue as jury duty, military service, and "any other joint work necessary to the interest of the society of which he enjoys the protection" (81–82).

Remembering this continuity between republican and liberal traditions also enables us, however, to see that the Machiavellian moment was in truth a Savonarolan moment, too. For all the lessons about *virtù* and prudence and stability that were passed on to liberals, other lessons were too, including the desirability of cultivating virtue for moral progress as well as political order, the first of the three liberal elaborations to be considered here. As Mill recognized in his 1861 *Considerations on Representative Government*, "[w]e cannot say that in constituting a polity certain provisions ought to be made for Order and certain others for Progress" because "the agencies which tend to preserve the social good which already exists are the very same which promote the increase of it" (201). That civic virtue both stabilizes and improves polities was recognized by Eliot, too. She, like Mill and many other nineteenth-century liberals, listened carefully to the lessons of Machiavelli and Creon and also to Savonarola and those "nasty little Antigones," as Pocock put it (in a 1973 essay indicating the kind of bias that required a few decades to overcome [40]).

A second elaboration some nineteenth-century liberals made to the republican tradition was to look beyond the *polis* for the means of cultivating civic virtue. There is no denying the centrality of the *polis* to most nineteenth-century liberals, including Mill (deeply influenced by his friend George Grote's sparkling tribute to the Athenian *polis* in *History of Greece* (1845–46), and of course Matthew Arnold (with his heady tributes to "the State" as liberalism's foremost tool). But at least a few late republicans and early liberals looked to the *oikos* as a locus for civic virtue, too. This is one way, for example, to understand what we now call republican womanhood theory, which is so central to *Romola* (Malachuk, "*Romola* and Victorian Liberalism" 92–94). An important text that promoted such a shift to the *oikos* was the 1819 lecture "The Liberty of the Ancients Compared with the Moderns" by Benjamin Constant (whose novel *Adolphe* Eliot adored). "[W]e can no longer enjoy the liberty of the ancients, which consisted in an active and constant participation in collective power," Constant announced; rather "[o]ur freedom must consist of peaceful enjoyment and private independence." Eliot's research for *Romola* taught her the same lesson. As Constant noted, in the ancient *polis* the citizen could "feel with pride all that his suffrage was worth," for "the will of each individual had real influence" and "the exercise of this will was a vivid and repeated pleasure." But the modern *polis*, as Romola bitterly notes, had "disappointed her trust" (650; ch. 69). However, neither Constant nor Eliot concluded that civic virtue was unnecessary. Instead, Constant urged modern citizens to find new ways to align our "desire to broaden our knowledge and develop our faculties" (327)—Goethe's ideal of *Bildung*, central to Eliot's vision as well—with the exercise of "political liberty" which for citizens "enlarges their spirit, ennobles their thoughts, and establishes among them a kind of intellectual equality which forms the glory and power of a people" (327). Eliot shared with Constant this politicized understanding of *Bildung* as well as a skepticism about how much of this could actually occur in the *polis*; a text like the 1868 "Address to Working Men, by Felix Holt" makes that perfectly clear. But it must be noted—given the unfortunate tendency for scholars to point to this text as proof Eliot was a Tory—that virtually every nineteenth-century liberal shared her doubts about the civic virtue of the *polis*: from Tocqueville's chapters on the "tyranny of the majority" in *Democracy in America* (1835) to Thoreau's "[i]s democracy . . . the last improvement possible in government?" in "Resistance to Civil Government" (1849) to Mill's own scheme of plural voting in *Considerations on*

Representative Government (1861) to Arnold's "Numbers, or The Majority and the Remnant" (1883). Nineteenth-century liberals were generally wary of democracy, but only a few, like Constant and Eliot, imagined the *oikos* as an alternative.

Finally, in addition to these two elaborations upon the republican tradition—to not merely sustain but cultivate citizen virtues, and to do so both in and out of the *polis*—the nineteenth-century liberals developed new justifications for those virtues, or at least a facility for drawing less dogmatically upon traditional metaphysical and Judeo-Christian—Hellenic and Hebraic—justifications. Eliot's fluent command of this general tension in Victorian culture is well known, and, more specifically, her ability in *Romola* to reconcile these two philosophical justifications has been noted (Malachuk, "*Romola* and Victorian Liberalism" 85, 95n). The two novels that follow *Romola*, though, also pursue modes of justification that eschew the sectarianism of Hebraism and Hellenism alike. In *Middlemarch*, for example, Eliot dramatizes how Dorothea Brooke and Will Ladislaw shifted from Hebraic and Hellenic extremism to more nuanced defenses of civic virtue (as explored below as an aspect of their premarital relationship). *Felix Holt* is even more thorough in its critique of Hebraic and Hellenic sectarianism and in its articulation of an alternative justification. Noting in the first chapter that Hellenic fatalism is antiquated, since we now can "discern between will and destiny" (10; Introduction), Eliot is careful to trace Mrs. Transome's tragic sufferings to her own bad choices, for (as chapter 39's epigram puts it) "a mortal's happiness . . . is mainly a complex of habitual relations and dispositions not to be wrought by . . . any whirling of fortune's wheel" (371; ch. 39). Eliot likens the Transomes to a Greek tragedy often but always rejects the Greeks' fatalism, a subtlety in her work illuminated by contrast with a contemporaneous true believer like Friedrich Nietzsche in his 1872 *The Birth of Tragedy*. Eliot's humorous portrait of the dim-witted Mrs. Holt, confusing a statue of the satyr Silenus for a Transome patriarch (she politely remarks "it was odd he should have his likeness took without any clothes" [422; ch. 43]), should be read alongside Nietzsche's unabashed reverence for "the wisdom" of this wood-god, companion to Dionysus, who teaches us (as Nietzsche repeats like a mantra through this book) that "[t]he very best thing is . . . not to have been born, not to *be*, to be *nothing*. However, the second best thing for you is: to die soon'" (23).

Eliot shrugs off Hebraic piety, too; in *Felix Holt* this is most obvious in her rough handling of the Reverend Lyon, whose sectarianism, comical at first, ultimately disfigures his guidance to his daughter Esther as she contemplates a life where "one bears and does everything because of some great and strong feeling" ("but the feeling that should be thus supreme is devotedness to the Divine Will," he chides [253; ch. 26]), and questions an inheritance that would benefit her but hurt the Transomes (it's a "providential arrangement," he insists, thinking of her future donations to his sectarian cause [390; ch. 41]). Eliot's skepticism arguably extends to even more mild versions of Hebraism, too, a subtlety in her work again coaxed forth by means of comparison. For example, while Eliot's convictions about her conscientious "Christian Antigone" (as one character calls Dorothea in *Middlemarch*) are in earnest (for is there a nineteenth-century novel that uses the word "ardent" more?), Eliot's reverence for her heroine is quite mild compared to, say, American abolitionists whose lavish praise of Antigone's fealty to "unwritten laws" over "man's laws" made her a spiritual sister to John Brown. Or compare the defenses of civil disobedience one finds in Emerson's addresses on behalf of Brown following the 1859 raid on Harpers Ferry with the conditional, post-sectarian language Eliot in 1866 allows Felix in defense of his accidental killing of a constable during the riot: "I hold it blasphemy to say that a man ought not to fight against authority: there is no great religion and no great freedom that has not done it, in the beginning" (442; ch. 46). While a younger Eliot may have relied upon Emerson to move beyond her Biblical literalism in the early 1840s (Cross 82) and admired him during his 1848 visit to England as "the first *man* I have ever seen" (164), Emerson's faith in the moral sense—yielding access to "the Over-Soul" and "Self" and other words he preferred to capitalize—is wildly uninhibited compared to Eliot's, who uses phrases more like Esther's "some great and strong feeling."

Still, Eliot's relative hesitation to transcendentalize our moral intuitions does not mean she's a "political liberal" in John Rawls's sense, content to overlook private motives so as to reach public "overlapping consensus" (Sandel). If Eliot dispenses with the "wisdom of Silenus," the Reverend's Hebraism, and even Emerson's transcendentalism, she still cannot deny that Felix's actions during the riot were (in his words) "urged . . . by what I hold to be sacred feelings, making a sacred duty either to my own manhood or to my fellow-man" (442; ch. 46). One of the major themes of the novel is that not only actions but motives matter: Matthew Jermyn's virtuous revelation of himself as Harold's father was viciously motivated by a desire to control him (400–01; ch. 42); Harold's virtuous confession to Esther of his conflicting interests as lover and heir was viciously motivated by his desire to woo her in the process (460–61; ch. 49). For Eliot, virtuous motives seem to require more than human guidance. As she delicately implies in her 1867 poem "O May I Join the Choir Invisible," there is "a beauteous order that controls / With growing sway the growing life of man" (11–12). Intuitions of that "beauteous order" justify the virtuous motives of Felix. As he puts it to Esther during her visit to his cell, he "cleav[es] to the purpose [he] sees to be best," knowing that if he suffers in consequence "the universe has not been arranged for the gratification of his feelings" (434; ch. 45). Has the universe been arranged, though, to support his virtuous motives? It appears so. When those virtuous motives lead to their marriage in the Epilogue, witnesses are "affected somewhat in the same way as happy-looking Mr Wace, who observed to his wife . . . 'It's wonderful how things go through you—you don't know how. I feel somehow as if I believed more in everything that's good'" (476; Epilogue).

***

A student of the ancient republics and the revival of that tradition by Savonarola and Machiavelli in the fifteenth century, Eliot like many nineteenth-century liberals nonetheless contended that civic virtues ought to be cultivated for progress as well as order, and that these virtues ought to be justified without recourse to sectarian philosophies or religions but instead as intuitively part of "a beauteous order." Eliot's liberalism, however, is most important for its third and most distinctive characteristic, its careful attention to liberal practices of the *oikos*. This part of my chapter examines three of those practices—of place, work, and marriage—as they are developed in the two novels most invested in a liberalism of the *oikos*, *Felix Holt* and *Middlemarch*.

Nineteenth-century literature about the English countryside has of course long been productively read by critics through the lens of the pastoral tradition (including the georgic). More recently, ecocritics have shown how the work of Romantic poets effectively validated the *oikos* as a specific place for the achievement of human wholeness; in his groundbreaking *Romantic Ecology* (1991), Jonathan Bate, reminding us that "ecology" is ultimately derived from the Greek oikos and logos," points out that "Wordsworth achieves a truly ecological poetry" in many of his place-specific poems (103). This recovery of the *oikos* as a specific ecological place was not only a moral project for the Romantics but sometimes a political one, too, as when they represented the *oikos* as a viable "counterpublic" to the corrupted discourses of the urban demos. In his 1798 "Fears in Solitude," for example, Coleridge turns from the war-mongering demos in town, where the "fluent phraseman" proffers "dainty terms for fratricide," to the Quantock Hills; its "huge amphitheatre of rich / And elmy fields seems like a society," he proposes, "[c]onversing with the mind, and giving it / A livelier impulse and a dance of thought!" (111, 113, 217–20). As these lines suggest, this poem is not only paradigmatic of a "natural patriotism" common in Romantic poetry, as another important ecocritic, Karl Kroeber, has explained (85–93), but more specifically an exploration of nature as paradoxically more conducive than cities to the exercise of civic virtue, even of public reason.

As Michael Squires first demonstrated, Eliot drew in her early novels upon the Romantics to explore rural life as a pastoral locus of morality. This project continues in more explicitly political ways in her later novels. In chapter 68 of *Romola*, for example, Eliot deliberately contrasts Romola's exercise of civic virtue in a "green valley" (650; ch. 69) with the decadent and violent Florentine *polis* she fled. *Middlemarch*, Eliot's "study of provincial life," is notably careful at times to associate its protagonists' growing virtue with their rural place: for example, Lydgate's "glocal" ethic—"to do good small work for Middlemarch, and great work for the world" (178; ch. 15), for instance, and Dorothea's inspiration to be virtuous by the sight from her window of figures working in a field, including "perhaps the shepherd with this dog." Dorothea's pastoral vision—"the manifold waking of men to labour and endurance"— tints in green her "yearn[ing] towards the perfect Right" (846; ch. 80). The chapter is fittingly prefaced by lines from Wordsworth's *Ode to Duty* that contend that our virtuous actions preserve "the Stars from wrong; / And the most ancient Heavens, through thee, are fresh and strong" (842; ch. 80), which sounds like Eliot's linking of civic virtue and the "beauteous order."

But it is arguably *Felix Holt* that most intensively shows how a rural place might enable us, like its two major protagonists, to discern our duties in a liberal polity.

Early on Eliot signals her intention to recall the forgotten civic significance of English places: the novel's epigram, from Michael Drayton's *The Poly-Olbion or a Chorographicall Description of Tracts, Rivers, Mountains, Forests, and other Parts of this renownd Isle of Great Britaine* (1598–1622), praises "[m]y native country" for having "bred" other "brave spirits" as well as "breathd'st" (which Eliot alters to "bred'st" to emphasize the land as a cultivating force) "vertues" into the poet too (2). This rural tradition (like all modern traditions for Eliot) is in transition, as spelled out in the "Introduction," which contrasts "a rich and marly" land dotted with independent "homesteads" which "paid no rent" (5; Introduction) with a "land . . . blackened with coal-pits" and ruled by a dissenting population "not convinced that old England was as good as possible" (6; Introduction). Like Theocritus, the first pastoralist and Eliot's favorite, she does not simply side with country against city, but is concerned that some of the lessons of the former will be lost. When Eliot concludes this introduction with a reminder of Virgil's and Dante's "dolorous enchanted forest in the underworld," full of "thorn bushes" and "thick-barked stems" with "human histories hidden in them" like blood (10; Introduction), we are reminded of the hold upon us of not just history but the land.

Into this landscape, Eliot sends forth her two rival "Radicals." Harold Transome, seeking to "root . . . out abuses" by replacing "rotten timbers" with "fresh oak," reminds us, as Lynda Mugglestone notes, of that introductory warning about the living forest (xiii). Felix Holt, however, pursues society's roots in the land in a different spirit. Chapter 10, in which Felix first challenges Esther to "be kindled to a better ambition" (125; ch. 10), begins with an epigram from the eleventh Idyll of Theocritus, about a lover (the Cyclops Polyphemus) who "made love neither with roses, nor with apples, nor with locks of hair" (as cited by Eliot) but rather with song (Gordon 10). This is a fitting portrait of "the public-spirited, contradictory, yet affectionate Felix" (119; ch. 10), who in the next chapter, en route to the public space of a tavern in Sproxton, a manufacturing town, quietly composes his "song" for the workers while crossing a "common, broken here and there into red ridges below dark masses of furze." This description alludes to Wordsworth's and Coleridge's pastoral heroes as well as Emerson "crossing a bare common" in *Nature* (10). In the fine English tradition of complex pastorals, Eliot's story leads not to selfish leisure or frivolous romance, but to a union of purpose between Felix and Esther, realized in chapter 27 in a timberland dappled with sunlight. "See how beautiful those stooping birch-stems are with the light on them!" declares Felix. "Here is an old felled trunk they have not thought worth carrying away. Shall we sit down a little while?" Lounging against this log, the lovers converse, pledging their readiness to "never lose your best self" (262; ch. 27). Felix and Esther's pastoral project is an alternative to both the Hebraic and Hellenic worldviews described earlier, a cultivation of virtue justified by place even after Holt is removed from it by incarceration, as Eliot hints with two epigrams: a sonnet by Elizabeth Barrett Browning in which the lover pledges that while "[t]he widest land / Doom takes to part us . . . What I do / And what I dream include thee" (306; ch. 32), and a few lines from Tennyson's *In Memoriam* where the speaker imagines his beloved Hallam "So far, so near" (405; ch. 43).

Eliot's command of the pastoral is a likely reason that her most compelling portrait of liberal work—the second liberal practice of the *oikos* under consideration here—is Caleb Garth's in *Middlemarch*. One of the modern republican tradition's greatest conceptual reversals was its view of economic work as a virtue rather than a vice. Such a view is evident in Montesquieu as well as Scottish Enlightenment figures, who focused on commerce and, like Rousseau and Thomas Jefferson, relied upon the pastoral (including the georgic) to describe the virtuous work of the citizen-farmer. Eliot signals her intentions in this regard with a classical reference, associating Garth with Cincinnatus. So intent is Eliot to make this association that in chapter 24 she introduces into the Garth children's lessons this exemplary Roman farmer and patriot (277–79; ch. 24) so that in chapter 40 she can have one of these children liken their father to him, when he is invited to manage the estates of the local Baronet (437; ch. 40). The analogy is amusingly off, of course, but Eliot is also making the more serious point that a citizen-farmer might not, after all, need formally to leave his fields for the *polis* in order to exercise his civic virtue. The *oikos*, in other words, has become a specific place where not only "labor" occurs (to recall Arendt's terminology) but "action," those deeds that build "the world" (196–97). Garth's tribute to farming as not only sustainable—rotating crops, locally sourcing the bricks (438; ch. 40)—but as an action that "[gets] . . . solid building done" is described in even more consequential terms by his wife Susan as "good work [that] remains though his name may be forgotten" (438; ch. 40).

Eliot was certainly not alone among nineteenth-century liberals in paying tribute to the citizen-farmer as a source of "action" and not just "labor"; Thoreau's *Walden* is another such effort, for example. But Eliot seems determined to imagine other kinds of work as equally worthy of political praise. She allows the scientist Lydgate to wax classical on the civic essence of his work, as when he cites Samuel Daniel's "Musophilus, Containing a General Defense of Learning" (475; ch. 43). And yet, Lydgate's example is finally a cautionary one: far from cultivating virtues through his work, Lydgate "had two selves within him apparently" (182; ch. 15), his professional self and his private self, each suffering from their disconnection: where Garth's work is an expression of his "best self," Lydgate's is finally a "life away from home" (719; ch. 65). Eliot seems determined to show that the difference is *not* that Garth "labors in the earth" and is thus among "the chosen people of God" (217), as Jefferson proposed in *Notes on Virginia*, but rather that Garth's approach to his work is entirely liberal in the sense of cultivating the virtue of both the worker and society. Eliot's own poetic epigram to chapter 40 makes this explicit; what matters most is not farming or any specific profession but plying one's "utmost sense" "to fruits of diligence / And not to faiths or polity"; for in trusting one's "utmost sense" we do actions that are "[w]ise," and "[w]ithout them how could laws, or arts, / Or towered cities rise?" (434; ch. 40). Garth's work may be in the fields, but his acts of "utmost sense" could be replicated in any profession. The epigram to another chapter dedicated to Garth's liberal work is from Sir Henry Wotton's poem "The Good Man," which reminds us that he is "Lord of himself, though not of lands" (596; ch. 56). Garth's most compelling moments of civic action are expressions of his principled positions not his actual farming: dissuading farmers from violence against the railway surveyors (605; ch. 56) and declining to work for Bulstrode for fear of hurting others (748; ch. 69). In these ways, Eliot offers Garth as a model of liberal work for all of us, farmers and non-farmers alike.

Turning finally to Eliot's third liberal practice of the *oikos*, marriage, it's important first to grasp her liberal investment in individuality (as advocated by Mill in *On Liberty*, for example, as a "chief ingredient of individual and social progress" [124]) as opposed to individualism (as diagnosed by Tocqueville in *Democracy in America* as "willingly abandon[ing] society" [482]). Individuality involves sociability and was precisely the expression of "modern liberty" that Constant taught nineteenth-century liberals to appreciate: a self-regard that engages society's regard. Rousseau, the thinker who promulgated the cult of ancient liberties that Constant challenged (317–18), infamously dismissed individuality in the Second Discourse as "*amour propre*"; he preferred to fantasize about a return to the "*amour de soi*"—an individualism that relies on no one else's regard—once enjoyed in the state of nature (27n). Like Mill, Emerson, and virtually all other nineteenth-century liberals, Eliot sided with Constant, and in *Middlemarch* signals as much by having Lydgate—particularly when in dialogue with the aptly named Farebrother, a champion of sociable individuality—indulge in Rousseau's fantasy of retreating from the city to the country where "people . . . are less of companions" and one can "follow one's own course more quietly" (204; ch. 17). Eliot mocks this primitivism by having Lydgate botch the terminology—misidentifying this deliberate isolation as "affecting one's *amour-propre* less" (Lydgate meant *amour de soi*)—and thus draws attention to his unrecognized need actually to cultivate his *amour-propre* more, not less. This "improper pride," as Garth puts it (445; ch. 40), is a self-regard without regard for others.

Eliot illustrates the importance of sociability in individuality in other ways, some of which have been the focus of excellent scholarship: among these we might count Eliot's self-reflective *Bildung*, very much in the Goethean mode (Fleishman 76–79), Eliot's investigation of discursive intersubjectivity (Thomas; Bentley), and Eliot's nuanced practice of "detachment" (Anderson). One practice of sociable individuals in Eliot's novels that deserves more examination, however, is marriage, the quintessential *oikos* relationship. Perhaps the most important source for understanding Eliot's liberal theory of marriage is Margaret Fuller's *Woman in the Nineteenth Century*. In a very favorable 1855 review, Eliot praised the book's advocacy of individuality, noting it relies upon no homogenizing "exaggeration of woman's moral excellence" or "injudicious insistence on her fitness for this or that function hitherto engrossed by men" but instead offers "a calm plea for the removal of unjust laws and artificial restrictions, so that the possibilities of her nature may have room for full development" (*Selected Critical Writings* 180). The review, however, is a misleading gauge of the book's full influence on Eliot's novels. One might conclude from Eliot's review, for example, that Fuller's *Woman in the Nineteenth Century* makes basically the same point as Mill would make in his 1869 *The Subjection of Women*: namely, that "the legal subordination of

one sex to the other . . . is . . . now one of the chief hindrances to human improvement" (125). But Fuller's book is ultimately more focused on the civic potential of
marriage between equals; to this end, she examines four types of union: the basic
"household partnership"; an equitable but regrettable "mutual idolatry; an admirable
"intellectual companionship"; and "the fourth and highest grade of marriage union
. . . the religious which may be expressed as pilgrimage towards a common shrine"
(42, 48). This section of my chapter will conclude by highlighting four points of
similarity between Eliot and Fuller: (a) they are critical of marriages that do not rise
above mutual improvement, (b) they imagine marriages rising above mutual improvement through civic virtue, (c) they understand marital civic virtue as aligned with
the "beauteous order," and (d) they imagine men as well as women in premarital
relationships dedicated to civic virtue as "angels."

   Lynda Mugglestone observes that Eliot relies on Fuller's book to describe the burgeoning relationship of Felix and Esther as one of mutual improvement (xxiii), which
is how Mill, too, would describe marriage in his *The Subjection of Women*, where it is
"a school of moral cultivation" (173) and "the school of the virtues of freedom" (175).
But, what Fuller more distinctively explains in *Woman in the Nineteenth Century*—and
what Mill really does not explore in *The Subjection of Women*—is that these marriages
of mutual improvement can lapse into mutual idolatry; "[t]he parties weaken and
narrow one another," Fuller warns, "lock[ing] the gate against all the glories of the
universe, that they may live in a cell together" (42). Fuller argues instead that spouses
must engage in "public life," beginning with the man but "as the intellectual development of woman has spread wider and risen higher, they have, not unfrequently,
shared the same employment" (42–43). In *Middlemarch*, Lydgate and Rosamond's
marriage explicitly fails to engage public life. After meeting Dorothea, who frightens
him as a woman who "was about as relaxing as going from your work to teach the
second form," Lydgate thinks with satisfaction of marrying Rosamond and privately
"reclining in a paradise with sweet laughs for bird-notes, and blue eyes for a heaven"
(122; ch. 11). When Lydgate "had talked fervidly to Rosamond of his high hopes as
to the highest uses of his life," he selfishly "found it delightful to be listened to by a
creature who would bring him the sweet furtherance of satisfying affection—beauty—
repose" (391; ch. 37) but no more. This "total missing of each other's mental track,"
the narrator notes, "casts the blight of irony over all higher effort" (633; ch. 58). In
Felix Holt, though, the central marriage plot shifts precisely from (in Fuller's terms)
mutual improvement to intellectual companionship; Felix and Esther obviously
improve one another through the bulk of the book but then they go public: Esther
testifies in court in support of Felix's "great resolutions that came from his kind feeling
toward others" (449; ch. 56). Her "maidenly fervor" not only leads to their eyes
meeting "in one solemn glance" (449; ch. 56) but "a stirring of heart in certain just-
spirited men and good fathers among them" to assist Felix (451; ch. 57); Felix and
Esther's marriage brings both order and progress to society. In *Middlemarch*, similarly,
Dorothea sees that Will offers not just improvement for her but "a fuller sort of companionship"; trapped in her marriage to Casaubon, whose scholarship is destined to

have no public value, "[s]he longed for work which would be directly beneficent like the sunshine and the rain," but saw "Will Ladislaw receding into the distant world of warm activity and fellowship" (516; ch. 48) without her. As the novel draws to a close, Will tells Dorothea of his plans to use Bulstrode's money for "a public purpose," and in the teeth of a sublime thunderstorm Dorothea chooses to sacrifice private ease for shared public work with Will (868, 870; ch. 83). It is this focus on others that makes Caleb and Susan Garth's marriage admirable; he "would take no important step without consulting Susan," including not only working the Chettam land but helping Fred: "that young man's soul is in my hand" (610; ch. 56). And we learn in the Epilogue that Fred and Mary's marriage has yielded two important books, *Cultivation of Green Crops and the Economy of Cattle-Feeding* and *Stories of Great Men, taken from Plutarch* (890; Finale).

Fuller portrays this shared interest in the public as a transcendental venture, "keep[ing] steadily the higher aim in view" so that the betrothed are "religious students of the divine purpose with regard to man" (45). As discussed above, Eliot is a warier metaphysician than the American Transcendentalists, but she does find ways to signal that the public goods pursued in marriage are something more than our political constructions. After Esther witnesses Felix's conduct to his mother, she admires his "highest gentlemanliness" and senses "if Felix Holt were to love her, her life would be exalted into something quite new—into a sort of difficult blessedness, such as one may imagine in beings who are conscious of painfully growing into the possession of higher powers" (228; ch. 22). When Dorothea marries Will, "an ardent public man" (894; Finale), "her full nature, like that river of which Cyrus broke the strength, spent itself in channels which had no great name on the earth." Interestingly, Cyrus also appears in *Romola*, where Eliot ironically observes four times that Savonarola hoped Charles VIII of France would be a "new Cyrus" and return Florence to republicanism and God (267–75; ch. 21). The allusion to Cyrus in *Middlemarch* allows Eliot one last occasion to contrast classically political actions with Dorothea's civic virtue; her virtue may seem to be a form of waste, "[b]ut the effect of her being on those around her," Eliot explains, "was incalculably diffusive" (896: Finale). It is true that Eliot then signals twice that other powers than Dorothea's liberal practices of the *oikos* are at work: the good of the world is only "partly dependent" on her "unhistoric acts," and the goodness in our own lives is only "half owing" to Dorothea and her ilk (896; Finale). But are we really to conclude that the *polis* actions of Cyrus, Savonarola, and Charles VIII make up the difference?

That these civic actions of the *oikos* are in line with a "beauteous order" is suggested by a final facet of Eliot's marriage plots, her use of "the angel." This is of course a figure notoriously associated with Coventry Patmore's "angel of the house" and separate spheres ideology, but both Fuller and Eliot were up to something more interesting. In her *Woman in the Nineteenth Century*, Fuller draws explicitly upon Goethe's suggestion in his 1790 drama *Torquato Tasso* that there (in Fuller's words) "should be a senate of the matrons in each city and town, who should decide what candidates were fit for admission to their houses and the society of their daughters" (90). Fuller endorses this idea, exclaiming that "one such Senate in operation would affect the morals of the civilized world." However, "[a]s preparatory to the Senate, I should like to see a society of novices" who "should have a religious faith in the capacity of man for virtue" and "wear in the heart a firm resolve not to stop short of the destiny promised him as a son of God." Fuller proposes they be called "Los Exaltados," or "the exalted ones," after a radical Spanish political party of the 1820s: "Los Exaltados, Las Exaltadas" (91). In the opening pages of *Woman of the Nineteenth Century*, long before she introduces her Exaltados/as, Fuller had already referred to those people who "ascertain and fulfill the law of [their] being" as "angels[s] or messenger[s]" to the rest of us (5). Now, having introduced the Exaltados/as, Fuller looks at her nation (which had recently annexed Texas "for the expansion of slavery") and cries out specifically for the intervention of "Women of my country!—Exaltadas! If such there be,—Women of English, old English nobleness" (98). Giuseppe Mazzini, a leader of the Italian *Risorgimento* and an important liberal visionary for both Fuller and Eliot, had urged through the 1830s and 1840s a similar process of "angelification;" as he explained in his 1844 "The Duties to Man," "in the midst of a society rotten as that of the Roman Empire, [we] feel in our souls the need of reviving and transforming it, of associating all its members . . . in one single faith" that will enable "the free and progressive development of all the faculties which God has planted in His Creatures" (19). But Eliot's vision of such angelic figures rising from premarital relationships seems closest to Fuller's. In *Felix Holt*, it is Felix who first achieves angelic status, pushing Esther (as cited earlier) to "painfully grow . . . into the possession of higher powers." Felix is thus initially "an influence above her life . . . as if he belonged to the solemn admonishing skies, checking her self-satisfied pettiness with the suggestion of a wider life" (356; ch. 37), but she in turn joins him: during the cell visit, when Felix intuits that Esther shares both his love and his sense of purpose, "[t]hey looked straight into each other's eyes, as angels do when they tell some truth" (434; ch. 45). When Esther speaks at Felix's trial, she becomes one of the "maidens of heroic touch" (437; ch. 46) that Eliot describes in that chapter's epigram. "I think I am getting that power Felix wished me to have: I shall soon see strong visions," Esther says to herself a few pages later just before declining Harold's offer of marriage "with an angel's tenderness in her face" (462; ch. 49). Early in *Middlemarch* Eliot is notably interested in these premarital relationships, albeit critically: "[h]as anyone ever pinched into its pilulous smallness the cobweb of pre-matrimonial acquaintanceship?" (45; ch. 2). However, like Fuller, Eliot seems increasingly intrigued by the civic potential of this overlooked relationship. In chapter 21 Dorothea, like Felix and Esther, has begun to make her "higher powers" known, at least to Will, who revealingly views Dorothea in her current marriage as "an angel beguiled" (241; ch. 21). Dorothea then develops an exalted premarital relationship with Will, enabling both to come into their full civic powers. Dorothea's role as an Exaltada is particularly explicit; in chapter 80, after a sleepless night, she is moved by the pastoral morning (as described above) to lay aside her mourning weeds, put on a new dress and bonnet, and become (her maid anticipates) "like an angel" (847; ch. 80). Dorothea is appropriately launched in the next chapter by an epigram from *Faust* where the earth's morning work similarly "inspires" Faust "to the perfection of existence" (Fleishman 186). Dorothea's work that morning is—preparatory to the senate of matrons—to help Rosamond and Lydgate save their marriage, her intervention being "the saving influence of a noble nature," an act even of "divine efficacy" (861; ch. 82).

***

Bernard Semmel has contended that Eliot came to love the English "national inheritance" as Mazzini or Herder did: as "a liberal-conservative" who "love[s] the national tradition as one among many in a world of cultural pluralism" (142). But Eliot was not actually conservative about that national inheritance. As I have argued elsewhere, like many late eighteenth-century republicans and nineteenth-century liberals, including Mazzini, Eliot envisioned nations as indispensable stepping stones toward a world without them (Malachuk, "Nationalist Cosmopolitics"). *Romola* antici-pates this argument when Romola reflects on her work among stateless peoples as "a new baptism" (650; ch. 69), but it is not until *Daniel Deronda* that Eliot develops this nationalist cosmopolitanism, via Mordecai's claims that Israel, "the nation which has been scoffed at for its separateness, has given a binding theory to the whole human race" (802; ch. 61). *Romola* also anticipates Eliot's other great challenge to *polis*-oriented liberalism by emphasizing Romola's practices of the *oikos* while demytholo-gizing one of the key moments in the republican cult of the *polis*, Savonarola's Florentine republic. Eliot's sets her next two novels during the period of the First Reform Act with the same mischievous intent: in *Felix Holt* and *Middlemarch*, she contrasts her liberal practices of the *oikos* with the *polis* during yet another of its mythical moments. Mill and most other nineteenth-century liberals may have under-stood the First Reform Act to herald liberal nation-building for centuries to come, but Eliot read it differently, closer to Emerson's reading of the 1830s, which suggested to him (in his 1844 "Politics") that government will eventually give way to "the influence of private character" and thus shall "the principal supersede the proxy" (567). In her attention to the *oikos*, Eliot's later novels dramatize that supersession and imagine a new liberalism of the principals rather than the proxies.

REFERENCES

Anderson, Amanda. *The Powers of Distance: Cosmo-politanism and the Cultivation of Detachment.* Princeton: Princeton UP, 2001.

Arendt, Hannah. *The Human Condition*, 2nd ed. Chicago: U of Chicago P, 1998.

Bate, Jonathan. *Romantic Ecology: Wordsworth and the Environmental Tradition.* London: Routledge, 1991.

Bentley, Colene. "Democratic Citizenship in *Felix Holt*." *Nineteenth-Century Contexts* 24.3 (2002): 271–89.

Coleridge, Samuel T. "Fears in Solitude." *English Romantic Writers.* Ed D. Perkins. New York: Harcourt, 1967. 425–28.

Constant, Benjamin. "The Liberty of the Ancients Compared with that of the Moderns." *Political*

Writings. Trans. and ed. Biancamaria Fontana. Cambridge: Cambridge UP, 1988. 309–28.

Cottom, Daniel. *Social Figures: George Eliot, Social History, and Literary Representation*. Minneapolis: U of Minnesota P, 1987.

Cross, J. W. *George Eliot's Life as Related in Her Letters and Journals*. Vol. 1. Boston: Houghton, 1908.

Dolin, Tim. *George Eliot*. Oxford: Oxford UP, 2005.

Eliot, George. *Daniel Deronda*. Ed. Barbara Hardy. London: Penguin, 1967.

Eliot, George. *Felix Holt*. Ed. Lynda Mugglestone. London: Penguin, 1995.

Eliot, George. *Middlemarch*. Ed. W. J. Harvey. London: Penguin, 1965.

Eliot, George. "O May I Join the Choir Invisible." *The Writings of George Eliot: Poems*. Ed. J. W. Cross. Boston: Houghton, 1908. 271–73.

Eliot, George. *Romola*. Ed. Andrew Sanders. London: Penguin, 1980.

Eliot, George. *Selected Critical Writings*. Ed. Rosemary Ashton. Oxford: Oxford UP, 1992.

Emerson, Ralph Waldo. *Essays and Lectures*. New York: Library of America, 1983.

Fleishman, Avrom. *George Eliot's Intellectual Life*. Cambridge: Cambridge UP, 2010.

Fuller, Margaret. *Woman in the Nineteenth Century: An Authoritative Text, Backgrounds, Criticism*. Ed. Larry J. Reynolds. New York: Norton, 1998.

Gordon, Lesley. "George Eliot and Theocritus." *George Eliot-George Henry Lewes Studies*. 26–27 (1994): 6–14.

Graver, Suzanne. *George Eliot and Community: A Study in Social Theory and Fictional Form*. Berkeley: U of California P, 1984.

Jefferson, Thomas. *Notes on the State of Virginia. The Portable Thomas Jefferson*. Ed. Merrill Peterson. London: Penguin, 1975. 23–232.

Kroeber, Karl. *British Romantic Art*. Berkeley: U of California P, 1985.

Malachuk, Daniel S. "*Romola* and Victorian Liberalism." *Victorian Literature and Culture* 36.1 (2008): 83–99.

Malachuk, Daniel S. "Nationalist Cosmopolitics in the Nineteenth Century." *Cosmopolitics and the Emergence of a Future*. Ed. Diane Morgan and Gary Banham. Basingstoke: Palgrave, 2007. 139–62.

Mazzini, Joseph [sic]. *The Duties of Man and Other Essays*. London: Everyman, 1966.

Mill, John Stuart. *The Subjection of Women*. In John Stuart Mill and Harriet Taylor Mill. *Essays on Sex Equality*. Ed. Alice S. Rossi. Chicago: U of Chicago P, 1970.

Mill, John Stuart. *Utilitarianism, On Liberty, and Considerations on Representative Government*. London: Everyman, 1972.

Mugglestone, Lynda. "Introduction." Eliot, *Felix Holt* vii–xxx.

Nietzsche, Friedrich. *The Birth of Tragedy and Other Writings*. Ed. Raymond Geuss and Ronald Speirs. Cambridge: Cambridge UP, 1999.

Pocock, J. G. A. *The Machiavellian Moment: Florentine Political Thought and the Atlantic Republican Tradition*. Princeton: Princeton UP, 1975.

Pocock, J. G. A. "Verbalizing a Political Act: Toward a Politics of Speech." *Political Theory* 1.1 (1973): 27–45.

Rousseau, Jean-Jacques. "Discourse on the Origin and Foundations of Inequality among Men." *Rousseau's Political Writings*. Ed. Alan Ritter and Julia Conaway Bondanella. New York: Norton, 1988. 3–57.

Sandel, Michael J. "A Response to Rawls' Political Liberalism." *Liberalism and the Limits of Justice*. 2nd ed. Cambridge: Cambridge UP, 1998.

Semmel, Bernard. *George Eliot and the Politics of National Inheritance*. Oxford: Oxford UP, 1994.

Squires, Michael. *The Pastoral Novel: Studies in George Eliot, Thomas Hardy, and D. H. Lawrence*. Charlottesville: UP of Virginia, 1974.

Thomas, David Wayne. *Cultivating Victorians: Liberal Culture and the Aesthetic*. Philadelphia: U of Pennsylvania P, 2004.

Tocqueville, Alexis de. *Democracy in America*. Trans. Harvey Mansfield and Delba Winthrop. Chicago: U of Chicago P, 2000.

Wihl, Gary. "Republican Liberty in George Eliot's *Romola*." *Criticism* 51.2 (2009): 247–62.

27

George Eliot: Gender and Sexuality

Laura Green

George Eliot wrote in the inescapable context of the Victorian Woman Question of the second half of the nineteenth century; the most recent, focused renewal of interest in her work occurred in the context of the second-wave feminism of the last decades of the twentieth century. These contexts have amplified the ambivalence that marks Eliot's relationship to her own position as a woman intellectual and the representation of women in her work. For much feminist scholarship on Eliot in the twentieth century, the focus was not on gender broadly conceived but on her representation of women, and its relationship to her own experience, and it is with this focus that this essay begins. A variety of critical turns and developments of the last decades, however—toward integration of formal with cultural or historical concerns; toward broader conceptions of gender studies and queer theory—have brought into view a more expansive set of questions about how Eliot's work grapples with questions of gender and sexuality, toward which this essay will move.

At its most fundamental, the "woman question" centered on the conflict of women's vocational needs and ambitions, in relation to an increasingly rich and complex public sphere, with cultural expectations that confined the vocation of woman to the home. This conflict was one that Eliot had begun to experience while she was still Mary Ann Evans, a dutiful daughter. By the time she left home, at the age of thirty, she had been running her widowed father's household for thirteen years and had cared for him devotedly through the illness that led to his death. After the Evangelical piety of her school years, she created a brief but intense household crisis in her teens by refusing to accompany her father to church; though she later regretted her intransigence, her

A Companion to George Eliot, First Edition. Edited by Amanda Anderson and Harry E. Shaw.
© 2013 John Wiley & Sons, Ltd. Published 2016 by John Wiley & Sons, Ltd.

translation of Friedrich Strauss's *The Life of Jesus* (1846) in her twenties completed her abandonment of Christian orthodoxy. These years suggest an identity already divided between the domestic role of the dutiful daughter and the more publicly participatory role of the "strong-minded woman" that Thomas Carlyle disapprovingly pronounced her on learning of her extramarital union with the already-married George Henry Lewes (qtd. in Haight 160–61).

Certainly, when she arrived in London in the 1850s, as a *femme émancipée*, translator, essayist, and reviewer, and editor (in all but name) of the liberal *Westminster Review*, Eliot seemed on the brink of a "strong-minded," if not radically feminist, career. By 1857, when her first work of fiction, *Scenes of Clerical Life*, appeared in volume form, most of her closest friends were feminist activists, such as Barbara Bodichon and the suffragist Clementia (Mrs. Peter) Taylor. That year itself was a significant one for feminist activism, with the passage of the Matrimonial Causes Act and a failed but hard-fought effort to pass a Married Women's Property Bill, in both of which efforts Bodichon was involved. Gillian Beer observes that "The people to whom George Eliot offered energy prove almost to a woman to have been" in sympathy with the women's movement (183). Yet as so many scholars have noted, Eliot's practical support for such feminist efforts as the founding of what became Girton College, and for the feminist *English Woman's Journal*, begun by Bodichon and Bessie Rayner Parks in 1858, was tepid. She contributed £50 to the foundation of the college and subscribed to, but claimed to be too busy write for, the journal.

Throughout her career, Eliot tended to emphasize not her connections to women's activism but her exceptionality as a woman and an artist, and the extent to which this exceptionality exempted her from certain kinds of political involvement. In an often quoted 1867 letter to John Morley, addressing the topic of "Female enfranchisement," she asserts that "the peculiarities of my own lot have caused me to have idiosyncrasies rather than an average judgment" (*Letters* 8:402). The inescapable, shaping features of her "lot" as an intellectual, socially emancipated woman in Victorian society form the basis for a disconnection from the "lot" of Victorian women generally. Similarly, as a novelist, she represents herself as standing above or to the side of political or ideological questions: "My function," she claimed in an 1878 letter to Taylor, "is that of the aesthetic, not doctrinal teacher . . . the rousing of the nobler feelings which make mankind desire the social right, not the prescribing of special measures" (*Letters* 7:44). The adjective "doctrinal" here hovers between a political and a theological sense. That ambiguity allows Eliot to disavow political action ("the prescribing of special measures") and embrace instead a quasi-hieratical, but also quintessentially female, function—"the rousing of the nobler feelings."

Similarly, as Eliot began to conceptualize her role as a novelist, her initial concern was to distance herself from the triviality associated with popular women's writing. As many critics have noted, Eliot's *Westminster Review* essays of the 1850s function as manifestos for the ideas about fictional realism that she was developing. Two— "Woman in France: Madame de Sablé" (1854) and "Silly Novels by Lady Novelists" (1856)—focus specifically on the gender of authorship. In "Woman in France," Eliot attempts a transvaluation of the apparently trivial, domestic matter of women's writing: "One might say, at least with regard to the [French] women of the seventeenth century, that their writings were but a charming accident of their more charming lives, like the petals which the wind shakes from the rose in its bloom" (*Selected Essays* 9). But such floral emanations from seventeenth-century aristocratic women in France, who "were not trying to make a career for themselves [and] . . . thought little, in many cases not at all, of the public" (*Selected Essays* 9) could hardly serve as a model for Eliot's needs and ambitions as a middle-class Victorian woman earning a living by her pen.

Models closer to home, however, were more threatening in their very proximity, and evoked not Eliot's admiration but her scorn. In "Silly Novels," Eliot mounts a coruscating attack on the "mind-and-millinery" genre. She mocks the genre's frank wish-fulfillment, its unapologetic mingling of worldly and ethical pretensions: "The fair writers . . . think £500 a miserable pittance; Belgravia and 'baronial halls' are their primary truths; and they have no idea of feeling interest in any man who is not at least a great landed proprietor, if not a prime minister" (*Selected Essays* 142); at the same time, these women writers appear to "think that an amazing ignorance, both of science and of life, is the best possible qualification for forming an opinion on the knottiest moral and speculative questions" (*Selected Essays* 149). What is striking about Eliot's humorous anatomization of women novelists—the "*oracular* species" (High Church), the "*white-neck-cloth* species" (Evangelical), and the "*modern-antique* species" (historical)—is less its lack of sisterly solidarity, how sharply Eliot draws the line between "lady novelists" and her own incipient fictional practice, than how close to that line the novels she writes will prove to fall (148, 156, 159). What is Dorothea Brooke—possessed of "that kind of beauty which seems to be thrown into relief by poor dress" (*Middlemarch* 7; ch. 1)—if not a version of "the ideal woman in faculties and flounces" (141)? Do *Romola* and *The Spanish Gypsy* avoid the anachronism of the modern-antique species, "which unfold to us the domestic life of Jannes and Jambres, the private love affairs of Sennacherib, or the mental struggles and ultimate conversion of Demetrius the silversmith" (159)? The *Westminster Review* critic was far from alone in noting that "We cannot escape the feeling that the chief interest of *Romola* reposes on ideas of moral duty and of right which are of very modern growth, and that they would have been more appropriately displayed on the modern stage" (Carroll 217). Rather than break with the feminine tradition of the "mind-and-millinery" novel, Eliot attempts to revise it. She replaces its trumped-up conflicts—"as often as not [the heroine] marries the wrong person to begin with, and she suffers terribly from the plots and intrigues of the vicious baronet . . . [but] whatever vicissitudes she may undergo, from being dashed out of her carriage to having her head shaved in a fever, she comes out of them all with a complexion more blooming and locks more redundant than ever" (*Selected Essays* 141)—with ethical crises of vocation and desire. But the heroines, the mistaken marriages, and the social "vicissitudes" remain—they are as much the stuff of High Realism as of silver fork and sensation novels. The very proximity of her own narratives to those of her sister-novelists, not the distance between them, surely underlies the intensity—barely masked by its wit—of Eliot's disavowal of kinship.

In remaking the society novel as not silly but serious, not materialistic but moralistic, Eliot grounds her aesthetic in the suffering of women, which becomes for her a test of realism. In her own case, the choice to follow the promptings of intellectual and romantic ambition was in fact marked by loss. Her decision to live with Lewes effected a total breach with her brother Isaac, the head of the family, that was not healed until just before her death, on the occasion of her late, brief marriage to John Cross. Meanwhile, a gulf opened between herself and female peers who valued their respectability. One of the less edifying records of Victorian feminism is the consternation of several redoubtable activists for women's higher education over the propriety of visiting Eliot: "Mrs. Gurney takes the same view that you do," wrote Emily Davies to Adelaide Manning, "that it is justifiable to go and see Mrs. Lewes herself, but not to meet people at her house" (Stephen 171). Certainly, Eliot outwrote and outlasted the social repercussions of her transgressions; in her later life, no less unimpeachably respectable an admirer than Queen Victoria collected her autograph along with that of Lewes (Haight 481). The image of Eliot as marmoreal sybil, fostered by herself, by Lewes, and by Cross's *Life and Letters* buried the traces of Eliot's lifelong ambivalence, questioning, and testing of convention beneath its weight.

Reading Cross's *Life and Letters*, the popular, prolific, but less celebrated novelist Margaret Oliphant could observe enviously that Eliot had "no trouble in all her life as far as appears, but the natural one of her father's death—and perhaps coolnesses with her brothers and sisters, though that is not said" (7). This startlingly inaccurate judgment testifies to how much had to be "not said" to allow Eliot, an unmarried "wife" (who requested that her friends address her as "Mrs. Lewes"); a step- rather than biological mother (whose earnings helped to support Lewes's sons); and, in T. H. Huxley's phrase, "a person whose life and opinions were in notorious antagonism to Christian practice in regard to marriage, and to Christian theory in regard to dogma" (qtd. in Haight 548–49), to become a prominent, celebrated voice of secular morality. But the closet, as Eve Sedgwick reminds us, is a particularly uncomfortable and porous shelter. Though Eliot scaled remarkable heights as Victorian woman intellectual, she could hardly forget that from one culturally non-negotiable point of view, instantiated by her brother, she had not risen but fallen. "There is no question on which I am more inclined to hold my peace and learn," she wrote in a famously opaque pronouncement, "than on the 'Women Question.' It seems to me to overhang abysses of which even prostitution is not the worst" (*Letters* 5:58). Eliot's proximity to these gothic, unspecified abysses, and the real losses that it brought (of connection to or reproduction of biological family, of ordinary sociality), create a lasting connection in her work between desire and loss, a connection experienced not exclusively, but most intensely, by women.

Eliot continually imagines women as intellectual and aesthetic subjects, motivated by desires for thought, utterance, art. As continually, she narrates the frustration or abandonment of their vocations: from the Methodist preacher Dinah Morris, who at the end of *Adam Bede* embraces her church's ban on women's ministry; to the "ardent, theoretic, and intellectually consequent" Dorothea Brooke (*Middlemarch* 24; ch. 3), who reads theological treatises, longs to learn classical languages, and plans utopian communities, but by the end of *Middlemarch* is "known only in a certain circle as a wife and mother" (680; Finale); to the paired singers of *Daniel Deronda*, the Princess Halm-Eberstein, whose career has severed her from all religious and familial ties, and Mirah Lapidoth, who avoids such isolation by eschewing musical performance for Deronda and Zionism; and to Armgart, in the poem of that title, who chooses per-formance over marriage, only to lose her voice and resign herself to teaching others.

If vocational passions are thwarted, romantic ones are not guaranteed fulfillment. In *The Mill on the Floss*, Maggie's renunciation of her love for Stephen does not obviate the apparent necessity for her death; as she turns in despair to "the Unseen Pity that would be with her to the end," the floodwaters have already begun to rise about her, and she drowns in her brother's arms (515; bk. 7, ch. 5). Like Maggie choosing between loyalty to her clan and loyalty to her desire, Fedalma, the half-gypsy heroine of *The Spanish Gypsy*, must choose between her Spanish betrothed, Duke Silva, and her gypsy father, his captive enemy; Romola de' Bardi's love for Tito Melema ends definitively when he betrays her father by selling his books. Women's desires, whether artistic or romantic, historical or contemporary, end in loss, renunciation, or the transformation of a suffered loss into a chosen renunciation. This connection is present from the beginning of Eliot's career as a writer of fiction. Despite its apparent remove from scenes of activism or questions of women's rights, *Scenes of Clerical Life* features in its three novellas as many suffering wives: in "Amos Barton," domestically angelic Milly Barton, a "large, fair, gentle Madonna" (15; ch. 2), whose death sanctifies her otherwise ordinary, bumbling husband; in "Mr. Gilfil's Love Story," childlike Caterina Sarti, the first of Eliot's female singers and also the first of many fantasied or actual uxoricides; and most strikingly, Janet Dempster, the abused, alcoholic, and ultimately redeemed wife of "Janet's Repentance." Following the paths laid by this initial gallery, Eliot's major female protagonists, doomed (Maggie Tulliver), ultimately conventional (Dinah Morris, Esther Transome, Dorothea Brooke), or disillusioned (Gwendolen Harleth, Romola), struggle to forge significant lives against social restrictions and demands always tied to their identities as women. It is these struggles that anchor the realism of their narratives.

In a review in the *Westminster Review* of popular author Geraldine Jewsbury's novel *Constance Herbert*, Eliot protested "the moral . . . illustrated in the novel by the story of three ladies who, after renouncing their lovers, or being renounced by them, have the satisfaction of feeling in the end that these lovers were extremely good-for-nothing and that they (the ladies) have had an excellent riddance." Such a pleasing outcome, Eliot asserts, reflects neither "the true doctrine of renunciation, nor a true representa-tion of the realities of life." Any true representation of "the realities of life" must confront the reality of loss. The best that Eliot's heroines can hope for is that loss will be transmuted into the heroism of renunciation: "It is the very perception that the thing we renounce is precious, is something never to be compensated to us, which constitutes the beauty and heroism of renunciation" (*Selected Essays* 321). Maggie's fate represents perhaps Eliot's most direct rebuke to Jewsbury's false doctrine. Tempted first to run away with Stephen, and then to return to him, Maggie conquers her temptation by clinging to "the memories that no passion could long quench: the long past [that] came back to her, and with it the fountains of self-renouncing pity and affection" (515; bk. 7, ch. 5). Maggie chooses a return to her family of origin over an exogamous desire. "Women, very properly, don't change their views, but keep to the notions in which they have been brought up; it doesn't signify what they think—they are not called upon to judge or to act" (*Felix Holt* 117; ch. 2), asserts Harold Transome loftily. Harold is arrogant and ignorant; like Lydgate, he will pay for the "spots of commonness" (*Middlemarch* 123; ch. 15) that make him conventional in his social judgments and therefore blind to the significance that women's actions will come to have for him (in particular, those of his mother, in bearing him out of wedlock). But if Eliot reveals the cost, to men as well as to women, of such assumptions, she nevertheless retains at the center of her project a Victorian belief in the association of the figure of Woman with social reproduction, continuity, and instinct, and of the association of creativity, change, and invention with masculinity.

A version of Maggie's choice is repeated by Romola de' Bardi in *Romola*, who leaves her husband Tito when she discovers that he has sold her father's scholarly library, only to return at the direction of Savonarola: "My daughter, if the cross comes to you as a wife, you must carry it as a wife. You may say, 'I will forsake my husband,' but you cannot cease to be a wife" (435–36; ch. 40). Although Romola pleads that her father's death as well as Tito's betrayal have released her from her loyalties, Savonarola frames Romola's necessary return as a daughterly as much as a wifely duty: "If you held that [Christian] faith, my beloved daughter, . . . you would feel that Florence was the home of your soul as well as your birthplace, because you would see the work that was given to you to do there" (433; ch. 40). Even in cases, such as that of Eppie in *Silas Marner* and Esther Lyon in *Felix Holt*, in which the daughter chooses an elective over a biological family tie, and weds the man of her choice, the happy ending is framed as both a renunciation and a return. In rejecting her status as heiress to Transome Court and, at the same time, the hand of Harold Transome, Esther Lyon gives up a wealth and ease to which she is not indifferent, for marriage to a man determined to remain (relatively) poor. Eppie, too, in rejecting Godfrey Cass's claim of fatherhood, gives up the opportunity to become a "lady," and marries a working man instead. In both cases, the marriages are to men warmly approved of by the foster-fathers, who are included in the subsequently formed households; thus in feeling, if not in biological fact, the daughter's choice is one that entails a return to the family fold.

This necessity of choice, often between the family of origin and a new romantic or vocational direction, and always involving some moment of renunciation, that Eliot imposes on her female protagonists is central to her conception of fictional realism. Her aesthetic practice is built around her Victorian conception of the differential in experience between men and women and its consequences: "As a fact of mere zoological evolution, woman seems to me to have the worse share in existence. But for that very reason I would the more contend that in the moral evolution we have an 'art that does mend nature.' And in the thorough recognition of that worse share, I think there is a basis for a sublimer recognition in women and a more regenerating tenderness in man" (*Letters* 4:364). It is in the representation of the operation of that "thorough recognition" that the triviality of "silly novels" is transmuted, in Eliot's imaginative effort, into her own "art that does mend nature."

While Eliot's interpretation of Victorian domestic ideology was hardly unconventional, both the bleakness of its fictional application, and its tension with Eliot's own life and career, were nevertheless puzzling to Eliot's contemporaries and almost scandalous for twentieth-century feminist criticism. In 1861, for example, Dinah Mulock (later Craik) reviewed *The Mill on the Floss* in *Macmillan's* magazine. Like Eliot a woman of letters (author, among other novels, of the bestselling *John Halifax, Gentleman* [1856], and *A Woman's Thoughts About Women* [1857–58], which offered advice and support for single women), Mulock finds sympathetic the question the novel poses: "What is to become of the hundreds of clever girls, born of uncongenial parents, hemmed in with unsympathizing kindred, . . . blest with no lover on whom to bestow their strong affections, no friend to whom to cling for guidance and support?" (Carroll 157). Yet Mulock cannot reconcile herself to what she sees as Eliot's failure to inculcate a Christian resignation that might "lighten any burdened heart, help any perplexed spirit, comfort the sorrowful, succour the tempted, or bring back the erring into the way of peace" (Carroll 156). She concludes unhappily that "uncertainty is the prevailing impression with which we close *The Mill on the Floss*" (159). Similarly, Sidney Colvin, reviewing *Middlemarch* in 1873, takes its topic to be "the necessary disappointment of a woman's nobler aspirations in a society not made to second noble aspirations in a woman," and also feels "uncertainty" in the face of the novel's "chastened and subdued . . . conclusion." Colvin, like Mulock, locates this deficit in Eliot's implicitly post-Christian worldview: "Is [the problem] . . . that a literature which confronts all the problems of life and the world . . . and all the importance of one life for the mass,—is it that such a literature must be like life itself, to leave us sad and hungry?" (Carroll 338). Ending with this rhetorical question, Colvin suggests an affirmative answer to his negative query. Like Thomas Hardy only a few years later, Colvin here proposes a female protagonist as the aptest representative of a troubling, secular, modernity. It is Tess Durbeyfield who, in *Tess of the D'Urbervilles* (1878), experiences those "feelings that might almost have been called those of the age—the ache of modernism" (105; ch. 19)—feelings already legible in Maggie Tulliver, Dorothea Brooke, and Eliot herself.

In the framework of the powerful feminist scholarship that developed around Victorian women novelists beginning in the 1970s, the ache sometimes threatened to overwhelm the modernism outright. Kate Millett in *Sexual Politics* (1968) lamented that "'Living in sin,' George Eliot lived the revolution as well, perhaps, but she did not write of it" (192). Zelda Austen, in the resonantly titled article "Why Feminist Critics Are Angry at George Eliot" (1976), came to Eliot's defense against this and similar reproaches by emphasizing Eliot's "fidelity to the actual" (552) and her "pity for both men and women in their suffering [that] transcended anger" (561). In the 1980s, readings of Eliot's representations of women began to produce more ambivalent and less polarized interpretations. As Tracey Rosenberg observes in her useful summary of feminist responses to Eliot, in the 1980s "the 'traditional' modes of womanly behavior that she allegedly perpetuated began to be viewed as astute analyses of the position of women" (par. 20). The fates of Eliot's heroines, in particular Maggie Tulliver's drowning and Dorothea's diminishment into domesticity, became critical cruxes around which claims about Eliot's attitudes toward women and gender were negotiated. In Mary Jacobus's Irigarayan analysis, for example, Maggie's drowning becomes "[the] moment in the novel [at which] we move most clearly into the unbounded realm of desire, if not of wish fulfillment. It is at this moment of inundation, in fact, that the thematics of female desire surface most clearly" (78). Deirdre David concludes a book that argues for Eliot's generally "strong ideological bond to patriarchal culture and to certain conservative modes of thought" (185) with a moment of mourning for Maggie and Eliot: "Lastly, [Maggie] dies, perhaps, as an emblem of irresolvable contention between the Victorian containment of woman to an undeveloped intellectual life and the elevation of one woman intellectual to iconic sagehood" (224).

Since the 1990s, with the rise of gender and sexuality studies and the partial absorption of the methods and insights of feminist theory into a broader range of methods and inquiries, debates over the representation of women have become a less defining feature of scholarship on Eliot. In Rosenberg's account, this development is not entirely a gain; on the one hand, Eliot is "releas[ed] from the obligation to meet specific requirements in order to fulfill a position as a feminist heroine," on the other, the corollary is that "feminist research on Eliot—work which defines itself in its title or main thesis as 'feminist'—has slowed to a crawl" (par. 22). To the extent that this claim is accurate, it might not have been altogether unwelcome to Eliot, who insisted, in a letter to Jane Senior, that "I know very little about what is specially good for women—only a few things that I feel sure are good for human nature generally, and about such as these last alone, can I ever hope to write or say anything worth saying" (*Letters* 5:58). Indeed, the tension in Eliot's work between the "special" or particular situation of women, which Senior seems to be soliciting Eliot to address, and the situation of a more general "*human* nature" (italics added) is itself an area of inquiry that can open onto broader questions of gender and representation.

That tension between the female particular and the human general is perhaps a particularly salient iteration of what Catherine Gallagher calls "the strife between type and instance" (67) that, she suggests, characterizes fictional realism as Eliot developed it. Gallagher argues that Dorothea Brooke's struggles, and the reader's response to her character, exemplify a *general*, rather than gendered, relationship to human corporeality made vivid by fictional realism: "George Eliot is the greatest English realist because she not only makes us curious about the quotidian, not only convinces us that knowing its particularity is our ultimate ethical duty, but also, and supremely, makes us want it" (73). To the extent, however, that the constricting "type" against which

Dorothea presses as an "instance" is what was for Victorian culture the type of types—Woman—her struggle, and potentially the reader's relationship to her, remain over-determined by gender.

Certainly thwarted vocational and romantic aims shape men's as well as women's careers in Eliot's novels. With some justice, Tom Tulliver reproaches Maggie: "Yes! I have had feelings to struggle with [in his unrequired love for Lucy Deane]; but I conquered them. I have had a harder life than you have had: but I have found my comfort in doing my duty" (*The Mill on the Floss* 485; bk. 7, ch. 1). *Middlemarch* is full of failed male vocations: Casaubon's as a scholar, Lydgate's as a medical researcher, even the Reverend Farebrother's passion for natural history, checked by the need to support a family of women. High-minded men—Bardo de' Bardi in *Romola*, Philip Wakem in *The Mill on the Floss*, and Mordecai Cohen in *Daniel Deronda*—are thwarted by physical infirmity. In "Silly Novels," Eliot mocks the way in which "The men play a very subordinate part by [the heroine's] side. . . . The final cause of their existence is that they may accompany the heroine on her 'starring' expedition through life" (*Selected Essays* 141). Eliot strives to avoid such partisanship; a social canvas on which the struggles of both men and women are given equal weight—on which, to adapt *Middlemarch's* famous phrase, men and women show "equivalent centre[s] of self, whence the lights and shadows must always fall with a certain difference" (*Middlemarch* 173; ch. 21)—remains one of the defining features of her novels. "She seems to have what I never saw in any woman before—a fountain of friendship toward men" (*Middlemarch* 629; ch. 76), reflects Lydgate wistfully, when Dorothea offers him financial and emotional support in the face of suspicion and self-doubt. Deronda eases Gwendolen's conscience after Grandcourt drowns; Dolly Winthrop reaches out to Silas Marner when he finds himself unexpectedly the guardian of infant Eppie.

But as frequent as such connections between women and men are moments of profound division, such as Lydgate's despairing reflection that Rosamond "no more identified herself with him than if they had been creatures of different species and opposing interests" (487; ch. 58). The very titles of her novels hint at the tension between these two poles. The masculine eponyms of *Adam Bede, Silas Marner, Felix Holt,* and *Daniel Deronda* have seemed to many readers priggish and unreal, while the novels' erring women (Hetty Sorrel, Mrs. Transome, Gwendolen Harleth) offer the complexity the masculine protagonists lack. Conversely, those novels most clearly centered on female protagonists are named instead for locales—*The Mill on the Floss, Middlemarch*—as if to insist on the public and general, not merely domestic and personal, significance of women's lives. A telling division of structure, too, haunts many of the novels. *Middlemarch* enfolds an originally separate tale entitled "Miss Brooke" (*Middlemarch* xii); *Daniel Deronda* notoriously elicited from F. R. Leavis the opinion that the Deronda plot should be excised altogether; *Felix Holt,* as Bonnie Zimmerman observes, "seems to be sundered into parts corresponding to the traditional male and female spheres of interest. . . . George Eliot is forced into flimsy attempts at unification by means of complicated plot resolutions and coincidences" (447). Uniting the "separate spheres" of masculine power and feminine influence is an aspirational as much as an achieved goal of Eliot's work. Most significantly, men's suffering in Eliot's novels lacks the conclusive significance of women's renunciation and loss. It is Maggie's death, not Tom's, that constitutes the fatality of the ending of *The Mill on the Floss*; it is Gwendolen Harleth's parting from Deronda, not the death of Ezra Cohen, that gives the close of *Daniel Deronda* its poignancy. The conflicts Eliot stages between vocation and renunciation, duty and desire, remain saturated with gendered significance.

Finally, gothic shards of murderous intent, most frequently directed against male characters, occasionally break the surface in the novels to mitigate her heroine's fates and to make room, however briefly or covertly, for wishes entirely the opposite of renunciatory. In *Middlemarch* we meet very briefly the actress Madame Laure, who repeats, in Eliot's own italics, "*I meant to do it*" as she confesses to Lydgate that she murdered her husband on stage under the cover of dramatic action (126; ch. 15). This direct linkage of aggressive motive to fatal effect is, however, unusual; usually it is a half-formed wish that precedes an apparently unconnected fatality. As Carol Christ memorably summarizes:

> People die conveniently in George Eliot's novels. Grandcourt falls off a boat and drowns at the moment when Gwendolyn finds her murderous fantasies unbearable. In "Mr. Gilfil's Love Story," Anthony collapses immediately before Caterina comes to the Rookery with the intention of killing him. Casaubon dies immediately before Dorothea comes to the garden to promise against her will to obey her husband's wishes after his death. By dying at the right moment, Robert Dempster saves Janet, and Tito saves Romola from their decisions to rededicate their lives to their marital duties. (131)

It is almost always men who suffer these convenient fates, and often women whose aggressive fantasies they fulfill, clearing the way for a turn from renunciations toward ends that, if disappointing in relation to earlier ambitions, still make room for a modicum of happiness. Romola, for example, becomes the head of the thriving little family consisting of herself, Tessa, Tessa's mother, and the children of Tessa and Tito. As Gillian Beer observes, calling it a "weakness. . . . The conclusion of *Romola* is [Eliot's] one conformity to that possible ending which she had resisted in [Frederika] Bremer and Jewsbury: the woman on her estate, exempted from passion and passed into wisdom" (124–25).

Beer's phrase "exempted from passion" in this context suggests that sexual desire, an erotic attraction to beauty and vitality of the kind that Romola initially feels for Tito Melema, Maggie for Stephen Guest, and Dorothea for Will Ladislaw, is as troublesome as the vocational kind. The most conventionally desirable male characters often spell trouble for the women they attract: Stephen Guest, Will Ladislaw, with his "smile [that] was delightful . . . a gush of inward light illuminating the transparent skin as well as the eyes, and playing about every curve and line as if some Ariel were touching them with a new charm" (168; ch. 21), Tito Melema, whose "bright face show[ing] its rich tint of beauty" bursts on Romola's Miranda-like innocence "like a wreath of spring" (105; ch. 6). Dorothea's happy union with Ladislaw offers a counter to the disasters wreaked by the fickle Stephen and Tito, but before it can occur he deeply wounds both Rosamond and Dorothea by his flirtations, causes scandal for Dorothea by making their relationship the subject of Casaubon's codicil, and necessitates the renunciation of her fortune in order that they may wed.

In fact, the fates of women who experience or even imagine sexuality outside of marriage in Eliot's novels suggest that she shared Victorian mainstream culture's distrust of the disruptive energies of eros and the localization of that distrust in a stringent demand for female "purity," as well as a perhaps more sympathetic apprehension of the consequences of women's "worse share in existence," the physical as well as social burdens of pregnancy and maternity. The elaborate construction of marriages where the plot clearly calls for extramarital unions (the mock marriage into which Tito inveigles Tessa in *Romola*; the secret marriage between Godfrey Cass and Molly Farren in *Silas Marner*), and the fates of unmarried mothers are among the more conventional features of Eliot's novels. Lydia Glasher, the about-to-be-discarded lover of Grandcourt, confronts Gwendolen Harleth to tell her that "Mr. Grandcourt ought not to marry anyone but me. I left my husband and child for him nine years ago. Those two children are his." To Gwendolen, she appears as a gothic apparition, "as if some ghastly vision had come to [Gwendolen] in a dream and said, 'I am a woman's life'" (128; ch. 15). That ostentatiously admonitory scene recurs at the end of *Felix Holt*, when Esther encounters the revelation of Mrs. Transome's long-hidden affair with Jermyn: "The dimly suggested tragedy of this woman's life, the dreary waste of years empty of sweet trust and affection, afflicted her even to horror" (597; ch. 50). Horror too is what Dorothea imagines, warning Rosamond off an affair with Ladislaw: "I mean, marriage drinks up all our power of giving or getting any blessedness in that sort of love. I know it may be very dear—but it murders our marriage—and then the marriage stays with us like a murder—and everything else is gone" (651; ch. 81). As Hina Nazar observes, writing of Dorothea's marriage to Casaubon, "In her repeated attempts to draw her estranged husband into relationship, to make a disembodied marriage a real marriage, Dorothea transforms marriage into ethics" (307). To "murder" marriage, "the bourne of so many narratives" that "is still a great beginning" (*Middlemarch* 677; ch. 86) is, in Eliot's vision, to sever some of the strongest ties that bind, not only men and women, but realism and ethics.

Eliot's invocations of marital intimacy can be equally reverential, as when she describes "that quiet mutual gaze of a trusting husband and wife that is like the first moment of rest or refuge from a great weariness or a great danger" shared by Nancy and Godfrey Cass in *Silas Marner* (174; ch. 20). Yet Eliot's representation of erotic feeling, if not of sexual experience, is more unsettlingly vivid than such conventional moments might suggest. Notably, it is not Eliot's obviously "bad" women, such as Hetty Sorrel and Rosamond Vincy, who are most susceptible to sensual pleasure. Hetty and Rosamond, in fact, are rather cold; they feel their own attractions keenly, and enjoy being looked at (always a sign of flawed morality), but their affective relationship to their masculine suitors is essentially functional: admiration feeds their egos.

Rather, it is Eliot's most heroic and monumental heroines—Maggie, Dorothea, Romola—who are unselfconsciously, vividly embodied. Dorothea, for example, found by men "bewitching when she was on horseback," enjoys riding in "a pagan sensuous way" that makes her "[look] forward to renouncing it" (9; ch. 1). Her final reunion with Ladislaw, which causes her a "throbbing excitement," takes place in a thunderstorm, culminating with "the flood of her young passion bearing down all the obstructions" of money and parentage that have parted them (663; ch. 83). For Gallagher, Dorothea's awakening to her erotic attraction to Ladislaw embodies the erotic energy of narrative itself. When Dorothea awakens to her "yearning" for Ladislaw, which occurs after she learns of Casaubon's codicil, she "experiences not just a reorganization of her consciousness but its annexation of a desiring body. . . . She stands for all novel characters in their demand for realization" (71–72). If she does, she embodies that demand not, like Rosamond or Hetty, by a claim for recognition *from* the masculine other, but by an overmastering impulse *toward* him.

If Dorothea comes to feel her own need for embodiment, it is Maggie whom Eliot represents as most fully embodied throughout her narrative: from her hungry, muddy, curly-haired childhood, through her queenly emergence into young adulthood, with a "broad-chested figure . . . the eyes [that] are liquid, the brown cheek [that] is firm and rounded, the full lips [that] are red," to the climactic moments of her erotic life, the mutual attraction to Stephen (299; bk. 5, ch. 1). That attraction is located most specifically, as many critics have noted, in the fleshly reality of Maggie and Stephen's arms. Their physical relationship begins with Stephen's "offer of a firm arm"; "There is something strangely winning to most women," the narrator reflects, "in that offer of the firm arm: the help is not wanted physically at that moment, but the sense of help—the presence of strength that is outside them and yet theirs—meets a continual want of the imagination" (408; bk. 6, ch. 6). This moment is one of the few exceptions to the implicitly masculine tone that characterizes Eliot's generalizing narrative comments; here, the narrative seems to identify with the feminine desire that it describes. It is perhaps as a way of minimizing this unaccustomed identification that the narrative voice, in the next sentence, suddenly distances itself from the awareness it has just expressed: "Either on that ground or some other, Maggie took the arm" (408; bk. 6, ch. 6). The sudden swerve from claiming intimate knowledge to waiving certainty is startling, but—for us as for Maggie—the sense of intimacy, the remembered pressure of that arm, remains.

The power of such a frank representation of female desire to disturb is attested, perhaps, by the fulminant responses that Stephen Guest, and Maggie's attraction to him, elicited from some male Victorian critics, of whom Swinburne is only the most energetic example:

> If we are really to take it on trust, to confront it as a contingent or conceivable possibility, resting our reluctant faith on the authority of so great a female writer, that a woman of Maggie Tulliver's kind can be moved to any sense but that of bitter disgust and sickening disdain by a thing—I will not write, a man—of Stephen Guest's [*sic*]; if we

are to accept as truth and fact, however astonishing and revolting, so shameful an avowal, so vile a revelation as this; in that ugly and lamentable case, our only remark, as our only comfort, must be that now at least the last word of realism has surely been spoken, the last abyss of cynicism has surely been sounded and laid bare. (Carroll 164)

That the proudly Decadent author of "Anactoria," among other works, should find so "astonishing and revolting" the attraction of a warm-blooded and naïve young woman for a handsome, admiring young man is hardly credible—unless, as his negative invocation of "realism" suggests, it is precisely the prosaic nature of the case that alarms him. Lush couplets in the voice of a lover of Sappho only serve to bring that earlier "great female writer" within the purview of a male homosocial, Hellenistic aesthetics; the contemporary expression of the desires of living women for ordinary men loudly disturbs those quiet Oxbridgean precincts.

Even more disturbing, perhaps, is the possibility that the "realism" of women's desire might dispense altogether with a masculine object. Shortly after Maggie takes Stephen's arm, the situation is reversed: it is Maggie's arm that becomes the object of Stephen's yearning:

Who has not felt the beauty of a woman's arm? —the unspeakable suggestions of tenderness that lie in the dimpled elbow, and all the varied gently lessening curves down to the delicate wrist, with its tiniest, almost imperceptible nicks in the firm softness.
A mad impulse seized on Stephen; he darted towards the arm, and showered kisses on it, clasping the wrist. (441–42; bk. 6, ch. 10)

Here, the narrative voice seems indicatively, or at least normatively, masculine, in its identification with the position of Stephen's "mad impulse." But we might ask here what Kathryn Bond Stockton asks of the narrative voice of *Middlemarch*: "Why should the narrator's desire for a woman necessarily mark the narrator as a man?" (169). After all, Stockton points out, *Middlemarch* "comes to a climax in a scene between women [Dorothea and Rosamond]. Their erotic dynamics—an orgasmic encounter between saint and supplicant—conveys the possibility that a woman might (unconsciously) desire another woman. . . . The narrative could be read as *functioning autoerotically for a narrator* who, within the text and through the telling, takes the place of a desiring woman" (170).

Stockton is one of the few critics to have undertaken a sustained queer reading of Eliot's fiction. If we consider the concept of "queer" representation in the expanded sense in which it is sometimes currently used—as denoting representation that falls outside of, or athwart, heterosexual norms, even if not committing itself fully to a representation of same-sex desire—then Eliot's oeuvre certainly invites such attention. We might consider the spillover of intimacy and attachment beyond the boundaries of the officially heterosexual couple: the nonerotic friendships between men and women; the multiplication of passionate or supportive, if not always orgasmic, encounters and connections between women (Dinah and Hetty, Lucy and Maggie, Romola, and Tessa); the characters whose vocational devotion trumps thoughts of marriage. But if Eliot invites such readings, she also resists them. Stockton's question—"Why should the narrator's desire for a woman necessarily mark the narrator as a man?"—is not entirely, in the context of Eliot's own affectional life, a rhetorical one. As Eliot's sage persona developed, particularly following the publication of *Middlemarch*, she attracted correspondence and visits from devoted readers, male and female. While she and Lewes called her female admirers "spiritual daughters," her relationships to them could be equivocal. In the case of the most devoted and frank in her acknowledgment of desire, the activist and journalist Edith Simcox, "Eliot was," as Ellen Rosenman writes, "more than willing to keep [Simcox's] desire in tension, never accepting but subtly encouraging it" (321). When Simcox pushed at the boundaries of subtlety after Lewes's death, however, Eliot reaffirmed them sharply: "She said—expressly what she has often before implied to my distress—that the love of men and women for each other must always be more and better than any other and bade me not wish to be wiser than 'God who made me'—in pious phrase" (qtd. in Vicinus 124). Eliot then allows a thrilling kiss before parting, but, as Martha Vicinus sums up the sequel:

> Simcox knew exactly what she wanted—those passionate kisses by the fire came from a pent-up fire within. But Eliot knew what she did not want, and deftly pushed her aside by telling her she wanted only her "beautiful affection." Two months later Eliot, reverting to her original name, Mary Ann Evans, married the young Johnny Cross, who had earlier called her Aunt. She left it to her stepson Charles Lewes to tell Simcox. (124)

Eliot's capacity for both the experience and the representation of forms of desire and intimacy, as well her attachment to the signifying power of gender difference, were shifting, various, sometimes playful and generative, at others painful and even cruel—to her protagonists, to her acolytes, and perhaps to herself. Vicinus's barely muffled indignation on behalf of Simcox, who "knew exactly what she wanted," suggests that now that feminist critics have stopped being angry with George Eliot, queer critics may be tempted to step into a similar affective role. So many of us think we know what we want from Eliot, and it may be that none of us will ever quite have it.

References

Austen, Zelda. "Why Feminist Critics Are Angry with George Eliot." *College English* 37.6 (1976): 549–61.

Beer, Gillian. *George Eliot*. Bloomington: Indiana UP, 1986.

Carroll, David, ed. *George Eliot: The Critical Heritage*. New York: Barnes & Noble, 1971.

Christ, Carol. "Aggression and Providential Death in George Eliot's Fiction." *Novel* 9.2 (1976): 130–40.

David, Deirdre. *Intellectual Women and Victorian Patriarchy: Harriet Martineau, Elizabeth Barrett Browning, George Eliot*. Ithaca: Cornell UP, 1987.

Eliot, George. *Adam Bede*. Ed. Valentine Cunningham. Oxford: Oxford UP, 1996.

Eliot, George. *Daniel Deronda*. Ed. Graham Handley. Oxford: Oxford UP, 1988.

Eliot, George. *Felix Holt*. Ed. Peter Coveney. London: Penguin, 1987.

Eliot, George. *The George Eliot Letters*. Ed. Gordon S. Haight. 9 vols. New Haven: Yale UP, 1954–78.

Eliot, George. *Middlemarch*. Ed. David Carroll. Oxford: Oxford UP, 1988.

Eliot, George. *The Mill on the Floss*. Ed. Gordon S. Haight. Oxford: Oxford UP, 1996.

Eliot, George. *Romola*. Ed. Andrew Sanders. London: Penguin, 1980.

Eliot, George. *Scenes of Clerical Life*. Ed. Thomas A. Noble. Oxford: Oxford UP, 1988.

Eliot, George. *Selected Essays, Poems, and Other Writings*. Ed. A. S. Byatt and Nicholas Warren. London: Penguin, 1990.

Eliot, George. *Silas Marner*. Ed. David Carroll. London: Penguin, 1996.

Gallagher, Catherine. "George Eliot: Immanent Victorian." *Representations* 90 (2005): 61–74.

Haight, Gordon S. *George Eliot: A Biography*. New York: Penguin, 1985.

Hardy, Thomas. *Tess of the D'Urbervilles*. Ed. Juliet Grindle and Simon Gatrell. New York: Oxford UP, 1983.

Millett, Kate. *Sexual Politics*. New York: Avon, 1969.

Nazar, Hina. "Philosophy in the Bedroom: *Middlemarch* and the Scandal of Sympathy." *The Yale Journal of Criticism* 15.2 (2002). 293–314.

Oliphant, Margaret. *The Autobiography of Mrs. Oliphant, Arranged and Edited by Mrs. Harry Coghill*. Chicago: U of Chicago P, 1988.

Rosenberg, Tracey. "The Awkward Blot: George Eliot's Reception and the Ideal Woman Writer." *Nineteenth Century Gender Studies* 3.1 (2007). 23 pars. <http://www.ncgsjournal.com/issue31/rosenberg.htm>.

Rosenman, Ellen Bayuk. "Mother Love: Edith Simcox, Maternity, and Lesbian Erotics." *Other Mothers: Beyond the Maternal Ideal*. Eds. Ellen Bayuk Rosenman and Claudia Klaver. Columbus: Ohio State UP, 2008.

Stephen, Barbara. *Emily Davies and Girton College*. London: Constable, 1927.

Stockton, Kathryn Bond. *God Between Their Lips: Desire Between Women in Irigaray, Brontë, and Eliot*. Stanford: Stanford UP, 1994.

Vicinus, Martha. *Intimate Friends: Women Who Loved Women, 1778–1928*. Chicago: U of Chicago P, 2004.

Zimmerman, Bonnie. "Felix Holt and the True Power of Womanhood." *ELH* 46.3 (1979): 432–51.

28

The Cosmopolitan Eliot

Bruce Robbins

"If there is one Victorian writer for whom the term *cosmopolitanism* seems inescapably appropriate," David Kurnick writes, "it is George Eliot" (Kurnick 489). This judgment does indeed seem inescapable. At the beginning of her career Eliot acquired a quite exceptional knowledge of European languages, lines of thought, and national histories, and she deployed that knowledge to impressive effect as an intellectual journalist and translator. Her quest to deprovincialize herself and her readers did not end when she began publishing fiction. A fundamental goal of that fiction was to achieve a larger, more comprehensive view of matters that might seem petty, domestic, or provincial. Often this meant nurturing empathy with people who stood outside the invisible circle that separated significant from insignificant lives. Nothing is more obviously cosmopolitan than the aim of making that circle visible, inducing readers to see and feel its restrictedness, generating impatience with the selfishness, stupidity, and provinciality that kept it in place.

Still, to make use of a title that attaches to Eliot the honorific adjective "cosmopolitan," as I do here, might seem to prejudge the degree of eagerness with which she in fact embraced that concept, while also skirting the possibility that her version of it might involve something other than self-evident virtue and achievement. What sort of boast is this? The question needs to be asked, and how one answers will depend on judgments of what exactly cosmopolitanism was for her and how far in its direction she was willing to go.

Where cosmopolitanism is concerned, many readers will recognize Eliot's reluctance (I paraphrase Mr. Brooke) to go "too far." Will Ladislaw's dream, remembered

A Companion to George Eliot, First Edition. Edited by Amanda Anderson and Harry E. Shaw.
© 2013 John Wiley & Sons, Ltd. Published 2016 by John Wiley & Sons, Ltd.

in the wake of Brooke's disastrous election speech, has been that "now public life was going to be wider and more *national*" (351; ch. 51; emphasis added). The dream was never that public life would be *inter*national, though Ladislaw's own perspective of course is, and much of the authority of his character depends on the fact that it is. It's as if the historical events of the 1830s, momentous as they were, could not make room for an intellectual internationalism that Eliot is nonetheless impelled to register. This divergence touches upon one of the salient ambiguities of the term cosmopolitanism: the scale at which it should be taken to apply. In ordinary usage, it does not always apply to the scale of the world. (What "world" meant at the linguistic moment of origin, when *kosmo-polites* or "citizen of the world" emerged both in mimicry of and by contrast to the Greek *polis*, which was not a modern nation, is in any case a complicated story.) The term is of course sometimes defined as detachment from national loyalty in favor of loyalties and principles that are universal, but it can also refer (as it does sometimes in the United States) to the transcendence of smaller, potentially separatist loyalties (to locality, race, ethnicity, and so on) in the name of the nation itself.[1] As far as attitude toward the nation is concerned, cosmopolitanism can therefore count as both pro-nationalist and anti-nationalist.

Eliot herself tends to be pro-nationalist. Writing in the era of heroes like Giuseppe Mazzini and movements like Italian unification, she is deeply appreciative of self-sacrifice in the name of the larger national cause. Ambivalent about her own liberalism, she seems suspicious of anyone who would seriously entertain a larger-than-national dream (though Mazzini himself did) or, as we see more often in her novels, who would think about the world in the sort of abstract, universalistic way that would encourage such dreaming. Anti-cosmopolitanism in this specific sense lies at the very beating heart of *Middlemarch*. Why else does Mary Garth express an ultimate preference for Fred Vincy over the Reverend Farebrother, who is clearly (at least at first) the better man? When Mary chooses in favor of local loyalties, she is choosing in effect to pretend that she had no choice. Affection rooted in childhood memories is absolute; it justifies a refusal of all comparison. It's as if Eliot feared that feeling itself could not survive a weighing and measuring of sympathy by universal or rational or merely non-local standards. What else is the novel's single most famous passage about than a reluctant restraining of imaginative sympathy even though ethics would seem to require precisely that one's sympathies be universal and unrestrained? I refer of course to the sublime vision of the squirrel's beating heart, the growing grass, the fatal roar on the other side of silence (135; ch. 20). Trying to take in the world's neglected subjectivities is both morally obligatory for Eliot and, she seems to suggest, emotionally or imaginatively unlivable. It's like the task of making space in one's feelings for the inhabitants of distant countries.

Eliot's most explicit and most negative statement on the subject of cosmopolitanism appears in her essay "The Modern Hep! Hep! Hep!" from *Impressions of Theophrastus Such*: "The time is not come for a cosmopolitan to be highly virtuous. . . . I am not bound to feel for a Chinaman as I feel for my fellow-countryman." This judgment of the limits of her time is immediately and seriously qualified:

I am bound not to demoralize him with opium, not to compel him to my will by destroying or plundering the fruits of his labor, on the alleged ground that he is not cosmopolitan enough, and not to insult him for his want of my tailoring and religion when he appears as a peaceable visitor on the London pavement. (147)

In adding these important qualifications, especially concerning the economic dimensions of England's international bad behavior, Eliot is speaking as a cosmopolitan in the largest, most international sense. She certainly cannot be accused of flattering the complacency or common sense of her compatriots. But she quickly comes back to a sort of solidarity with those compatriots, an inevitable re-centering of perspective in their concerns, values, and interests: "Affection, intelligence, duty radiate from a center, and nature has decided that for us English folk that center can be neither China nor Peru" (147).

Here Eliot seems to choose a pragmatic nationalism whose potential overlap with cosmopolitanism is worthy of further attention. With the mention of China and Peru, however, she also aligns herself somewhat surprisingly with the Tory crowd that mocks Brooke's campaign speech. The liberal, free-market cosmopolitanism of this speech has naturally been upstaged by its other qualities, but it too may be worth a second look.[2]

"I've always gone a good deal into public questions—machinery, now, and machine-breaking—you're many of you concerned with machinery, and I've been going into that lately. It won't do, you know, breaking machines: everything must go on—trade, manu-factures, commerce, interchange of staples—that kind of thing—since Adam Smith that must go on. We must look all over the globe:—'Observation with extensive view,' must look everywhere, 'from China to Peru,' as somebody says—Johnson, I think, 'The Rambler,' you know. That's what I have done up to a certain point—not as far as Peru; but I've not always stayed at home— I saw it wouldn't do. I've been in the Levant, where some of your Middlemarch goods go—and then, again, in the Baltic. The Baltic, now" (349; ch. 51).

It's when he passes from the Levant to the Baltic that Brooke is interrupted by a laugh-creating echo from the crowd, an echo which, "by the time it said, 'The Baltic, now'" (350; ch. 51), has become fatal.

Brooke is of course punished by the crowd first of all because of his signature inability to keep to the point, any point. The crowd wants to hear about his support for the Reform Bill, not about Peru or China or the Baltic, and rightly so. But Brooke has been presented from the first chapter on as "a man who had traveled in his younger years, and was held in this part of the country to have contracted a rambling habit of mind" (2; ch. 1). If you think of the rambling mind as a product or stylistic expression of his physical ramblings (a connection accentuated by the mistaken allusion to Johnson's *Rambler*), it's not just his incoherence that is repudiated, but his cosmopolitanism. And if so, then Eliot's own echoing of the interruption becomes a bit harder to interpret. After all, there is nothing self-evidently incorrect about the idea that knowledge of the countries where the goods produced in Middlemarch are sold is relevant to the town's welfare and ought to be of interest to its inhabitants. Brooke is right to insist on the significance of distant places for his constituents-to-be, even if the Middlemarchers themselves don't see the connection. This is, recall, a novel of *provincial* life. Provinciality is one of its problems. From this angle, Brooke's incoherence could be presented with a little ingenuity as less a portrait of the cosmopolitan as such than a portrait of the cosmopolitan as seen with impatience by a local or provincial. Of course any mention of Peru or the Baltic or the Levant will look tactless and incoherent if your standards of tact and coherence are determined exclusively by local spaces and provincial loyalties. But should they be? In setting the crowd up to interrupt Brooke, it's as if Eliot were herself channeling him in his self-correcting, self-restraining mode: "It is easy to go too far, you know. You must not let your ideas run away with you" (508; ch. 72).

China and Peru seem to be there largely because Johnson had melodiously joined them in verse, yet it would not be difficult to fill in some hard facts about all of the countries mentioned, those two included, which would bring out important causal links between the Middlemarch economy and the countries Brooke never gets to talk about. Even a couple of hours of cursory digging turn up some promising hints both in the lead-up to the Reform Act and in the years when Eliot was writing *Middlemarch*. China: In the early 1830s, the East India Company's massive smuggling of opium into China, which would soon lead to the First Opium War, was gearing up in a big way. In 1829, the first opium clipper was built, speeding up the trade considerably by beating the monsoon winds; in 1830, permission was granted to grow poppies in India, enormously expanding production, and the Chinese authorities sent a letter of protest to Queen Victoria; in 1832, the opium trading house of Jardine Matheson and Company was registered, which made huge profits from the trade and remains "one of the foremost trading multinationals in South-east Asia" (Booth, 114). As we have seen, Eliot was still upset by the opium trade when she wrote *Impressions of Theophrastus Such* at the very end of her writing life. The Baltic: in 1857 the abolition of the "Sound Tolls" that had discouraged shipping from entering the Baltic led to the rapid development of Copenhagen and no doubt to consequences for British trade as well, for example in Russian timber and precious stones. (One thinks of *Middlemarch*'s jewels and furniture.) By 1879, ships carried as much tonnage through the Baltic as through the western Mediterranean. Peru: Peruvian mines, which are mentioned as a site of investment in Dickens's *Dombey and Son*, were at issue when Britain backed Chile against Peru in a war over nitrates. With respect to Peru, the middle of the nineteenth century saw a paradigmatic investment curve, rising with the sudden importance of guano for fertilizer (a determining element in international food prices, and for that matter in the Irish famine), and then falling dramatically with the exhaustion of Peru's reserves.[3]

Even these very provisional findings are enough, I think, to suggest that Brooke had a case, whether or not he himself was capable of making it.[4] This case gives greater interest both to Eliot's smack-down of cosmopolitanism on the hustings, assuming this episode can be so described, and to the role played in Eliot's fiction and in the Victorian period generally by what might be called "free-trade cosmopolitanism"—an impulse, unexpectedly produced by fidelity to Adam Smith and laissez-faire, not to erect racial and imperial stereotypes but on the contrary to tear them down. Established scholarship on the subject of cosmopolitanism would suggest that the concept's great century is the eighteenth, while the nineteenth century sees an exponential growth in nationalism and racism. In the late eighteenth and early nineteenth centuries, champions of anti-slavery consumer boycotts argued, not without reason, that to add sugar to your tea was to spill the blood of slaves. To read Charlotte Sussman on the sudden decline of these boycotts after emancipation in the 1830s— the period covered by *Middlemarch*—is to be instantly convinced that there has been no steady progress toward cosmopolitanism.

> After 1838, appeals to a universal sensibility—mutual emotions discovered in sympathy and tears across vast distances—began to disappear from British conceptions of cultural difference, to be replaced by a more essentialist and 'scientific' understanding of 'race' . . . by the mid-nineteenth century, these views had given way to a more pessimistic, deterministic belief in the ineradicable savagery of inferior nations. (Sussman 193)

Once slavery was gone, there were few if any boycotts, though the coercive exploitation and physical abuse of colonial labor had not of course disappeared. Imperialism encouraged a "deterministic belief" in "ineradicable savagery." And yet, given the example of the boycotts, the hypothesis emerges here that there nevertheless existed a nineteenth-century cosmopolitanism that can be disengaged from imperialism, if not completely, and that might have led to a different sort of British knowledge of the non-European world, even if George Eliot herself had mixed feelings about it.

Eliot has been described as cosmopolitan on the grounds of her valiant attack on anti-Semitism in *Daniel Deronda* and her endorsement of Jewish nation-building, a project which is not deferential to the English national perspective and indeed propels her hero and the novel itself far outside England. But on the evidence of the same novel she can equally well be called anti-cosmopolitan. We are told in chapter 3 what a pity it is that Gwendolen Harleth, who has wandered so much, has no real home to return to, no special place endeared to her by childhood memories. "A human life, I think, should be well rooted in some spot of a native land, where it may get the love of tender kinship for the face of the earth, for the labors men go forth to, for the sounds and accents that haunt it, for whatever will give that early home a familiar unmistakable difference amidst the future widening of knowledge" (50; ch. 3). The suggestion is that without the "sweet habit of the blood" imposed by accident of birth and acquired before there is choice or knowledge, all subsequent knowledge may suffer from a fatal and mysterious defect. Knowledge may widen, but without leading to empathy; no amount of "effort and reflection" will be able to make it do so. "At five years old, mortals are not prepared to be citizens of the world, to be stimulated by abstract nouns, to soar above preference into impartiality; and that prejudice in favor of milk with which we blindly begin, is a type of the way body and soul must get nourished at least for a time" (50). This "at least for a time" may be only what it seems, an account of how ethics develop in early childhood, and (as it seems to me) it may be somewhat disingenuous: a way of presenting partiality not merely as necessary in childhood, but as necessary to human life as such.

The point is underlined in the novel's plot. Deronda too is a kind of rootless cosmopolitan, and though he knows more about others than Gwendolen and feels more for them—he knows and feels too much rather than too little—he is threatened by much the same pathology: a paralyzing absence of locally-rooted partiality. "A too reflective and diffusive sympathy was in danger of paralyzing in him that indignation against wrong and that selectness of fellowship which are the conditions of moral force" (413; ch. 32). What he is looking for is an "event" or "influence that would justify partiality . . . making him what he longed to be yet was unable to make himself—an organic part of social life, instead of roaming in it like a yearning and disembodied spirit, stirred with a vague social passion, but without fixed local habitation to render fellowship real" (413; ch. 32). As the representative at once of an ideal and a pathology, the cosmopolitan for Eliot seems to be just this "yearning and disembodied spirit," knowing a lot and vaguely stirred by that knowledge, but without local fixity and partiality, hence merely a kind of ghost. Daniel's miraculous discovery of his Jewish blood cures this disease in him. But it does so only by suggesting that nothing less outlandish and improbable would restore him to health—by suggesting, in other words, that in most cases there will be no treatment at all. This leaves Gwendolen rather than Daniel to stand for the modern or cosmopolitan norm, a norm which is also a malaise.

Mary Wilson Carpenter, who joins cosmopolitanism to the discourse of disease, uses cosmopolitanism's most negative sense, "the 'riff-raff' of the world or those who were—like the cholera itself—without local attachment and, therefore, entirely lacking in the capacity for fellow-feeling" (512), as a link between Gwendolen and Bulstrode, the relatively straightforward villain of *Middlemarch*.[5] But Gwendolen resembles Daniel more than she does Bulstrode. As the resonance between the two protagonists suggests, Eliot could not extricate herself from this dilemma by means of an ethical discrimination between good and bad characters. The problem was much too intimate for that. Like liberalism itself, Eliot worried that comprehensive knowledge and rational principles, valued and eagerly sought as the key to progress and righteousness, might somehow be antithetical to feeling and action, or that feeling and action might themselves be fundamentally partial and unfair.

In one of the most influential arguments about Eliot's cosmopolitanism, Amanda Anderson defends *Daniel Deronda* against charges like Terry Eagleton's "that the utopianism of the Jewish plot, with its accompanying ideal of organic totality, disavows the unstable conditions of modernity so vividly depicted in the Gwendolen Harleth plot" (Anderson 119). Anderson's counter-argument is that "Eliot seeks to elaborate through her ideal of cosmopolitan Judaism a critical and nondogmatic way of relating to one's cultural heritage" (120). Partiality is good and necessary; in effect, it is not a problem so long as Eliot can ensure that it will be a "cultivated partiality" (121), thoughtful, critical, and not "an attempt to flee . . . instabilities by constructing Jewish identity as an absolute ideal or ground" (121). The hinge of this argument is the difference Anderson establishes between Mordecai's and Daniel's conceptions of Jewish identity, the first based on the absoluteness of blood and fate and the second more self-conscious and self-critical—in short, more detached.[6] In pursuing this logic Anderson suggests that "Eliot goes a long way toward balancing the claims of the particular against those of the universal" (122). It is this proposition that Kurnick queries in his reading of *The Spanish Gypsy* in parallel with *Deronda*. In fact, Kurnick says, Eliot had doubts "that ethnic nationalism can be easily squared with universal justice" (490). Being what he calls "a *sanguine* cosmopolitan writer" means being "one who believes firmly in the possibility of honoring both local and global claims without ethical contradiction" (490). Eliot may be a cosmopolitan, but she is not a credulously optimistic one.

Kurnick gives *The Spanish Gypsy* credit for acknowledging "that the project of establishing gypsy *Lebensraum* on settled territory will necessarily entail the 'blight[ing]' of another people" (502), an acknowledgment that as he says is "missing from the proto-Zionism of *Daniel Deronda*" (502). He is careful not to imply (as others, less scrupulous, might well have done) that injury to those it excludes is the universal, implacable, and bitterly unacceptable truth of the nation. For him this "zero-sum logic" follows not from the nation as such but more precisely from "any territorially-based ethnic nationalism" (502). At least in theory, then, the possibility remains open for a civic nationalism, not based on exclusive claims to territory, that would also not contradict cosmopolitanism's universal principles. Kurnick and Anderson could presumably find common ground, therefore, in something like the following line of thought: contradiction between the national and planetary scales of cosmopolitanism is not necessary, but it is certainly possible, and no cosmopolitanism can afford to ignore the possibility of such a contradiction, the possibility of a collision and an unavoidable choice between local loyalties and more expansive ones. Anyone who pushes for the highest, most restrictive understanding of cosmopolitanism will demand accordingly that in the event of such a choice, the word will apply to the larger and not the smaller loyalty. But the case that here and now the choice is indeed unavoidable cannot be taken for granted; it must be made.

If cosmopolitanism means nothing more than being nice to foreigners, if it does not entail the possibility of having to choose the welfare of foreigners over one's own interests and those of one's fellow nationals, then the term offers precious little to boast about. Facing the risk that it will lend itself to easy self-congratulation, Kurnick tries to give the concept more backbone by demanding from it "a willingness to endure the trauma of the encounter with the other." He judges that by this standard, "Eliot simply never seems traumatized enough" (489). The standard itself is open to question. Perhaps it's not enough to be nice; the price of admission to the cosmopolitan club should be higher. But must the cost be paid in the currency of trauma? Or, as Christopher Herbert suggests, is trauma merely a counterfeit piece of secularized theology, familiar enough to escape detection but finally of questionable value?

> The cultural anthropologist's idea of the necessity of undergoing 'an extremely personal traumatic kind of experience' as the prerequisite of shedding prejudice and thus attaining ethnographic truth (defined as entering into another conceptual world) reproduces closely the Evangelical salvation narrative in which an awareness of sin is imagined to be the prerequisite of the shedding of egoistic selfhood and the spiritual new birth which follows. (174) [7]

If trauma is indeed a prerequisite for cosmopolitanism, the paradigmatic scene in Eliot's fiction would have to be Dorothea's honeymoon in Rome. It is not often noted that the famous passage about hearing the grass grow and the squirrel's heart beat comes in the brief Roman chapters. In that context, the notion that the world's subjectivities are too vast and manifold to take in without extreme discomfort does not refer only to Dorothea's wifely unhappiness, which Eliot suggests is too common to notice. Less obviously, it also refers to Dorothea's own inability to take in the historical unhappiness embodied in the paintings, sculptures, and ruins of Rome. Recall that even her own unhappiness is not merely the result of a bad marriage choice. "There are few paintings," Dorothea confesses to Will, "that I can really enjoy . . . when I begin to examine the pictures one by one, the life goes out of them, or else is something violent and strange to me" (143; ch. 21). The strangeness and the violence could be read as a displacement onto the paintings of the disappointing discoveries of married life, but Eliot takes some trouble to insist that they are what they seem, products of "the weight of unintelligible Rome" (134; ch. 20).

> Ruins and basilicas, palaces and colossi, set in the midst of a sordid present, where all that was living and warm-blooded seemed sunk in the deep degeneracy of a superstition divorced from reverence; the dimmer but yet eager Titanic life gazing and struggling on walls and ceilings; the long vistas of white forms whose marble eyes seemed to hold the monotonous light of an alien world: all this vast wreck of ambitious ideals, sensuous and spiritual, mixed confusedly with the signs of breathing forgetfulness and degradation, at first jarred her as with an electric shock, and then urged themselves on her with that ache belonging to a glut of confused ideas which check the flow of emotion. (134; ch. 20)

Dorothea is traumatized in a fairly uncontroversial sense: she suffers a radical interruption in her ability to continue within the patterns of emotion to which she is accustomed—an interruption in her ability to feel.

In effect, Rome and Casaubon fuse together into a single traumatic cause. Thanks to his ignorance of German, his inability to feel any personal enthusiasm for the glories of Rome, and his desire to defend the Christian faith against the threats of an emergent social science, Casaubon may seem an archetypal anti-cosmopolitan, but the subject of his research is after all comparative mythology, and it is comparative mythology that Dorothea is trying and failing to assimilate when she makes her dutiful rounds of Rome's ruins, museums, galleries, and churches. To see so much of the past on display, especially a past that is at once pagan, Catholic, and aesthetically magnificent, is to have just the experience that Mary Garth successfully rejects: the distressing, self-subverting experience of pure comparison. It is no simple thing to open one's eyes to the full range of lives and cultures, joys and sufferings that have flourished on this planet. The event cannot leave one unaltered. Dorothea takes comparison as a threat to the ethical core of her being. Choosing "to drive out to the Campagna where she could feel alone with the earth and sky, away from the oppressive masquerade of ages, in which her own life too seemed to become a masque with enigmatical costumes" (134; ch. 20), she flees what the display of Rome seems to reveal to her about herself.[8]

In a sense, Rome merely stands in for ambiguities of cosmopolitanism that were already visible elsewhere in Eliot's fiction. As a self-declared novelist of provincial life, Eliot aimed to stretch the social circle by inducing in her readers (assumed to be largely metropolitan) a sympathetic interest in provincials. As her critics have often commented, much of her own sympathy went out however to the provincials and their quaint traditions. These made up a large part of her literary capital, so to speak, in addition to being the objects of her own early and formative fondness. When she expresses that fondness in a sly Toryism, stubbornly appreciative of tradition that she might elsewhere judge to be backward, she is facing one classic paradox of cosmopolitanism: should one be tolerant of those who, given a choice, would not themselves show tolerance? A similar paradox haunts the question of a proper cosmopolitan attitude to the nation: does solidarity with *someone else's* national movement (for example, the Italian *Risorgimento*, from which Eliot clearly borrowed for her account of Deronda's proto-Zionism) count as a bold cosmopolitan transgression of one's own national loyalty? Or should it be taken on the contrary as a regressive fidelity to the nation-form and evidence of an inability to see from an international or trans-national perspective?

In short, Dorothea did not have to travel or even to marry badly in order to be so traumatically disoriented. She achieves a sense of disorienting connection to a distant world as early as the first chapter of *Middlemarch* when she and her sister make their choices from among their mother's jewels. For Dorothea, this means inquiring into the ethical status of a commodity that has a foreign source. Declaring that if she were to wear her mother's emeralds, she would feel like she was "pirouetting," Dorothea decides after all not to give them up—and immediately afterwards, she thinks of the labor behind them.

> "Yes! I will keep these—this ring and bracelet," said Dorothea. Then, letting her hand fall on the table, she said in another tone—"Yet what miserable men find such things, and work at them, and sell them!" She paused again, and Celia thought that her sister was going to renounce the ornaments, as in consistency she ought to do. (6; ch. 1)

Dorothea doesn't renounce them. Neither moral consistency nor moral clarity seems easily available. What does "miserable" mean here? Does it invoke misery in the economic sense? Mere unhappiness? Moral deficiency? One might think that it's the hard and physically deforming labor of producing the jewels that makes these workers unhappy, but that reading seems undercut when Dorothea equates finding and working on the jewels, which seem strenuous occupations, perhaps underpaid and perhaps bad for the health, with merely selling them, which presumably is no worse in these respects than selling anything else. One could read this scene as evangelical-ism, or as a vestigial expression of the casual contempt that the landowning class had for retailers, or as foreshadowing the anti-sweatshop discourse that would remind jewelry-wearers of, say, the eight-year-old Indian children at risk of an early silicosis death from grinding agate.[9]

These are the ambiguities that cluster at the intersection of cosmopolitanism and free-market capitalism. The intersection had been noted. The Oxford English Dictionary's first reference for "cosmopolitan" is from John Stuart Mill's *Political Economy* (1848): "Capital is becoming more and more cosmopolitan." There has been no lack of attention to the limits and distortions that cosmopolitanism was likely to suffer from its dependence on this energy source, or for that matter to the value that Eliot's occasional Toryism acquires by its conjunctural resistance to Whig arrogance. But the topic of Eliot and cosmopolitanism cannot afford to neglect the possibility that she learned something worth learning from its capitalist adherents. Why did Disraeli attack the Liberals as cosmopolitans in his Crystal Palace speech of June 1872, while Eliot was writing *Middlemarch*? He might have been inventing a convenient straw man, but it appears he was not. Not only were some Liberals indeed willing to jettison the empire as too expensive, they were willing to ask inconvenient ethical questions about it. John Bright, whose speeches on India from the late 1850s Eliot was reading in the late 1860s while preparing for *Middlemarch*, was interested in India's potential to grow cotton as an alternate source to the slave-holding American south (Henry 104). That is, he was still thinking morally, if imperfectly, about the conditions of labor that produced English commodities—as Dorothea comes so close to doing when she considers the labor that produced the inherited jewels she is inspecting in the novel's first scene.

Bright favored investment in public works projects in India, including transportation, while he also complained that there had been no progress there. Whose fault was that? Consider:

I hope that no future historian will have to say that the arms of England in India were irresistible, and that an ancient empire fell before their victorious progress,—yet that finally India was avenged, because the power of her conqueror was broken by the intolerable burdens and evils which she cast upon her victim, and that this wrong was accomplished by a waste of human life and waste of wealth which England, with all her power, was unable to bear. (qtd. in Henry 105)

Bright is clearly worried about the expense. He never says England was wrong to
conquer India. But he does say, and quite clearly, that the English are mistreating the
Indians, and that this fact may determine the eventual judgment of history upon
the British Empire as a whole.

George Eliot was one of those who did invest in Indian public works, including
transportation. In this she was representative of the large numbers of middle-class
Englishmen who, thanks to new financial instruments, were for the first time able to
participate in overseas investment in the 1850s and 1860s. In a sense this was indirect
participation in colonialism itself. In 1860, while finishing her "sugar" story, "Brother
Jacob," and receiving the first profits from *The Mill on the Floss*, Eliot was investing
a lot of money (two thousand pounds) in "East Indies" railway stock. She was reassured
that her return of 5% was "guaranteed." What this meant was that if the Indian
railway didn't make enough profit to pay the 5%, the money would be raised by
Indian taxes. In other words, the money would be taken forcibly from the Indians.
That's exactly what happened. By 1869, something like 15 million pounds had been
paid to investors under the guarantee system. In a letter in 1879, Eliot acknowledged
that this logic was not foreign to her when she wrote that the disastrous failure of the
Second Afghan War would be "a black day of Indian finance, which means alas a great
deal of hardship to poor Hindus" (qtd. in Henry 78). Nancy Henry, from whom I
take all this information, uses it to argue very usefully that Eliot derived her concept
of realism in part from her skepticism about unscrupulous accounts of Empire intended
to encourage investment.

At the same time, cosmopolitan knowledge enters into this picture in a potentially
different way than it would in the case of, say, missionary work or imperial conquest.
In order to feel confident enough to invest in a place, what would one want to know?
One would want to know that the investment will turn a profit. If that's the goal,
then the degrading stereotypes of the native that we associate with nineteenth-century
imperialism may be counter-productive. Yes, there is the myth of the lazy native. But
that myth does not fill the entire field of representation. It would be shocking if it
did, for the motive of encouraging investment was a strong incentive to brighten the
picture, and even to pay attention to various sorts of abuses. The Indian railway in
which Eliot invested was built in 1853 by the cousin of the publisher John Chapman,
for whom Eliot edited the *Westminster Review*. Also called John Chapman, he published
"Our Colonial Empire" in the *Westminster Review*, on Eliot's watch, and in it "rejected
Britain's right to rule" (100). "We are not lords of India in any other than a present
practical sense. We do not and cannot rule it by force. We cannot colonize it nor
ought we" (101). This was of course not the dominant view, but it's obviously one
direction in which thinking about investment in India could lead. The piece, which
was republished by *Westminster Review* in 1870, sixteen years after the author's death,
would have to count as a sample of Victorian cosmopolitanism. Chapman and Bright
have none of Brooke's spectacular incoherence, but they deepen the portrait of Brooke
on the hustings, hinting at the existence of a vision on the other side of the interruption and the novel's geo-political silence. At a minimum, they help explain Eliot's

cosmopolitan resistance both to stereotypes about foreigners and to the cruder forms of colonial exploitation.

In his stump speech Brooke declares himself a follower of Adam Smith, a free trader. Smith has much to answer for. For example, he did not believe that poverty was an injury to the worker's dignity or, therefore, that the fact that capitalism might produce poverty should count as a damning argument against it. But he was of course opposed to the acquiring of colonies. He makes it clear that the impulse to legitimate colonialism can by no means be equated with the impulse to legitimate the so-called free market. The space between the free market and colonialism is a reminder that one did not have to get outside England in order to achieve detachment from its culture. Culture should never be defined as if taking distance from it is impossible. On the contrary, distance from cultural belonging is a fact about cultural belonging. Cosmopolitanism is an example: it was a potential that emerged from England's own contradictions. It should be no surprise that Eliot, whose greatness is inseparable from her own contradictions, should have represented cosmopolitanism with such passion or with such ambivalence.

NOTES

1   In the United States, cosmopolitanism is often a way of characterizing a proper sort of patriotism in which the nation is valued (inevitably, valued to some extent over other nations) because of the degree to which it itself values heterogeneity within it.

2   This section of the essay is adapted from my "Victorian Cosmopolitanism, Interrupted."

3   According to Poovey, one moral seems to be, as far as Peru is concerned, that the bottom dropped out of the market when it was discovered that there was a bottom to the guano deposits.

4   One page before the fatal encounter on the hustings that ends his career, Brooke has another failed exchange, this one with a local merchant who sells tea, sugar, and spices. The foreign origins of those commodities are not alluded to, and it's not clear that Brooke himself is conscious of the ways in which his election or the passage of the Reform Bill might connect with those countries. (346–47). "Such a thing as a vote, now: why, it may help to make men's fortunes at the Cape—there's no knowing what may be the effect of a vote," Mr Brooke ended, with a sense of being a little out at sea" (347).

5   It seems worth mentioning that as a cosmopolitan disease, cholera defied the received opinion that climate is determining as well as the moralizing of disease in terms of drunkenness, prostitution, and so on. Anyone drinking contaminated water, including the most pious and well-regulated of citizens, would fall ill.

6   Anderson complicates her argument interestingly in her discussion of Leonora Halm-Eberstein, Deronda's "bad mother." On the one hand, Anderson says, Halm-Eberstein's "deracinated cosmopolitanism" (139) represents "the threat of absolute detachment from the affective ground of community" (139–40). On the other hand, art becomes another community for her, and one that also offers a mode of affect. "I cared for the wide world, and all that I could represent in it" (693). As Anderson comments, this statement does not merely claim personal freedom but also "redefines a central term in Eliot's ethic of sympathy and duty" (141). "[A] recuperation of Daniel's character should not be made at the expense of Leonora, who represents a viable and deeply felt response to her own cultural context and personal past" (143).

7   Herbert, 174.

8   Is it a coincidence that, like Henry James
    in *Portrait of a Lady*, Eliot made the threat
    of cosmopolitanism in deep time—that's
    one way of describing what Rome meant to
    her—coincide with the heroine's perception
    of a marriage that was not working, her
    disappointment in the expectation of what
    marriage would mean? Marriage was of course
    the conventional happy ending of novelistic
    plot. In that sense, it makes sense that open-
    ing up the temporal scale of novelistic plot
    should overlap dramatically with a vision
    in which those present principles which
    seem so peremptory and absolute should be
    exposed to a long history that exposes their
    relativity.

9   What knowledge lies behind this exclamation?
    Emeralds were largely mined in Colombia and
    Africa, though some came (perhaps through
    the Baltic) from Russia and Austria. The
    largest source of diamonds had been India, but
    in the nineteenth century excited attention had
    turned to Brazil. And then in 1866, the dis-
    covery of diamonds in South Africa led to a
    diamond rush. Amethysts, which Dorothea
    does not choose, could also be found in Russia
    and Austria though Brazil and Uruguay and
    Mexico were more prominent sources. The
    exhaustion of the German deposits of agate
    in the nineteenth century had led to mining in
    Brazil, hence to the discovery of amethyst
    deposits there. See also Freedgood 126–28.

References

Anderson, Amanda. *The Powers of Distance: Cosmopolitanism and the Cultivation of Detachment.*
Princeton: Princeton UP, 2001.

Booth, Martin. *Opium: A History.* New York: St.
Martins, 1996.

Carpenter, Mary Wilson. "Medical Cosmopolitanism: *Middlemarch*, Cholera, and the Pathologies
of English Masculinity." *Victorian Literature and
Culture* 38.2 (2010): 511–28.

Eagleton, Terry. *Criticism and Ideology: A Study in
Marxist Literary Theory.* London: Verso, 1978.

Eliot, George. *Daniel Deronda.* Ed. Barbara Hardy.
London: Penguin, 1967.

Eliot, George. *Impressions of Theophrastus Such.* Ed.
Nancy Henry. Iowa City: U of Iowa P, 1994.

Eliot, George. *Middlemarch: An Authoritative Text,
Backgrounds, Reviews, and Criticism.* Ed. Bert G.
Hornback. New York: Norton, 1977.

Freedgood, Elaine. *The Ideas in Things: Fugitive
Meaning in the Victorian Novel.* Chicago: U of
Chicago P, 2006.

Henry, Nancy. *George Eliot and the British Empire.*
Cambridge: Cambridge UP, 2002.

Henry, Nancy. "George Eliot and Politics." *The
Cambridge Companion to George Eliot.* Ed. George

Levine. Cambridge: Cambridge UP, 2001.
138–58.

Herbert, Christopher. *Culture and Anomie: Ethnographic Imagination in the Nineteenth Century.*
Chicago: U of Chicago P, 1991.

Kurnick, David. "Unspeakable George Eliot."
Victorian Literature and Culture 38.2 (2010):
489–509.

Levine, George. "*Daniel Deronda*: A New Epistemology." *Knowing the Past: Victorian Literature
and Culture.* Ed. Suzy Anger. Ithaca: Cornell UP,
2001. 52–73.

McCaw, Neil. "'The Most Ordinary Prompting of
Comparison'? George Eliot and the Problemat-
ics of Whig Historiography." *Literature and
History*, third series 8.2 (2004): 18–33.

Poovey, Mary. *The Financial System in Nineteenth-
Century Britain.* Oxford: Oxford UP, 2003.

Robbins, Bruce. "Victorian Cosmopolitanism,
Interrupted." *Victorian Literature and Culture*
38.2 (2010): 421–25.

Sussman, Charlotte. *Consuming Anxieties: Consumer
Protest, Gender, and British Slavery, 1713–1833.*
Stanford: Stanford UP, 2000.

29
The Continental Eliot

Hina Nazar

Six days after her father's funeral in 1849, a thirty-year-old Marian Evans—not yet "George Eliot"—left England for an extended stay on the Continent, thereby initiating a tradition of long European visits that was to last until just before her own death in 1880. These trips often coincided with momentous personal events—most notably, Evans's elopement to Germany with G. H. Lewes in 1854—but they were also always times of sustained study and intellectual exploration. The nineteenth century's most learned autodidact, who read German, Italian, French, Greek, and Latin, had wide-ranging cultural engagements with the Continent. She translated into English some of the most sensational philosophical works of the Enlightenment and its immediate aftermath: Benedict de Spinoza's *Ethics*, David Friedrich Strauss's *The Life of Jesus, Critically Examined*, and Ludwig Feuerbach's *The Essence of Christianity*.[1] Her letters, notebooks, and essays for the *Westminster Review* reveal extensive familiarity with a mind-boggling number of European writers, including Dante, Auguste Comte, Jean-Jacques Rousseau, George Sand, Johann Wolfgang von Goethe, Gottfried Ephraim Lessing, and Heinrich Heine. Reciprocally, she enjoyed a strong reputation on the Continent, even at the beginning of the twentieth century when the British modernists decried her fiction as a dusty relic of bygone times. Marcel Proust identified *The Mill on the Floss* as a crucial shaper of his vision of temporality, and Simone de Beauvoir found in Maggie Tulliver's struggles an enabling prototype of her own need for the life of the mind. Even Nietzsche's summary dismissal of the "English bluestocking" in *The Twilight of the Idols* speaks to Eliot's place in fin de siècle Europe's self-understanding. More than any other Victorian novelist, George Eliot must be regarded as a major figure in a European history of ideas.

A Companion to George Eliot, First Edition. Edited by Amanda Anderson and Harry E. Shaw.
© 2013 John Wiley & Sons, Ltd. Published 2016 by John Wiley & Sons, Ltd.

Obviously, no one essay can do justice to Eliot's claims in this regard. Fortunately for her readers, a spate of recent studies has vivified her connections with particular European authors, illuminating especially the influence of Goethe, Dante, and the French realists (Guth; Rignall; Röder-Bolton; Thompson). This essay interprets "the continental Eliot" complementarily but differently: it situates her work in an ongoing tradition of continental philosophy that has profoundly shaped recent debates in critical theory and literary studies—especially debates about the value of the Enlightenment project and liberal modernity.[2] The tradition at stake can be broadly characterized as "Hegelian," and extends from G. W. F. Hegel and the Young or Left Hegelians in the nineteenth century to such strands of postwar moral and political theory as communicative ethics, pragmatism, and communitarianism.[3] It is informed by Hegel's critique of the dualism underpinning Immanuel Kant's idealism, its radical separation of noumena and phenomena, freedom and nature, universality and social history. Kant, Hegel argued, liberated man by asserting the right of all to think for themselves and to exercise autonomy. But the freedom he upheld remained in the thrall of a mystifying otherworldliness: it diminished the interdependence of mind and world, and especially of self-consciousness and consciousness of another—an argument that received one memorable instantiation in the "Lordship and Bondage" section of the *Phenomenology of Spirit*. On this reading then, Kant was right to make self-reflective agency the centerpiece of the discourses of modernity but wrong to identify such agency with the exercise of supersensible reason.

Hegel's vision of situated subjectivity resonates powerfully with the contemporary humanities' widespread discomfort with rationalist projects of self-making and the claims of pure reason. Indeed, in *The Philosophical Discourse of Modernity*, Jürgen Habermas suggests that today we are all Young Hegelians, in that critical theorists of all stripes seek to contextualize reason by exploring its embedment in history and sociality. Habermas's argument finds support in Judith Butler's recent writings on ethics, which are self-identified as "post-Hegelian" rather than poststructuralist or postmodernist because they begin with an understanding of subject constitution that is reminiscent of Hegel's. But whereas for Habermas, Hegelianism helps us refresh and ultimately reaffirm ideals first charted out by Hegel's great Enlightenment predecessor, Kant, for Butler it leads more tellingly in the direction of Michel Foucault's poststructuralist critique of Enlightenment reason, as developed in works like *Discipline and Punish* and *The History of Sexuality*.

Does the premise of the subject's social embedment, or the attempt to complicate the dualism of freedom and nature, entail a rejection of the claims of reason? What does a context-sensitive account of agency and autonomy look like? This essay considers some ways in which Eliot and the Hegelians most relevant to her thinking might be interpreted as engaging these questions of contemporary theory (I will refer in passing also to Comte, another continental philosopher important to Eliot). Their engagement is implicit in the critique of religion begun by Left Hegelians like Strauss and Feuerbach, and reworked by Eliot in fiction that is best described as the novel of ideas. The critique of religion brought into focus the characteristically religious gesture of looking to a superhuman being or God for an explanation of worldly goals and individual striving. It aimed to make individuals capable of scrutinizing unexamined assumptions—that which is taken on faith—not necessarily with the goal of desacralizing the world, but certainly with that of expanding the agency of individuals. Above all, it understood agency in social and practical terms, as a development of intersubjective life and specific social practices.

The social-theoretical aspects of the critique of religion become obscured, however, when Eliot's readers align her Hegelian inheritance with a secular humanism that transformed God into man and religion into a secular ethics of love and fellow-feeling.[4] The word "humanism" flourishes today in literary and cultural studies as a legacy principally of poststructuralist critiques of so-called Enlightenment humanism (as opposed to the project of Renaissance learning that constituted humanism's original meaning), and it carries the negative charge of totalizing belief in an unchanging human essence and sovereign paradigms of subjectivity. To describe either Eliot or the Left Hegelians as humanist in this sense is to elide what is most innovative about their social criticism: the challenge it posed to the very idea of a human essence, a challenge that Feuerbach succinctly characterized in *The Essence of Christianity* as the attempt to complicate essence by reference to existence.

Eliot herself is explicit on this point. The question of "the human" looms large in her fiction, and nowhere more clearly than in *Silas Marner*, a slim early novel that interrupted her work on the magisterial *Romola*, a story about Renaissance Florence. *Silas Marner* begins with its eponymous hero, a weaver, as a recluse, whose profession of binding threads together stands in ironic contrast to his social isolation. Tied to the community at the significantly named "Raveloe" only in a professional capacity, Marner is represented as having fallen off the path of humanity altogether. In imagery taken from his work, the narrator figures him as a spider that "seemed to weave . . . from pure impulse without reflection" (16; ch. 2), as "a spinning insect" (16; ch. 2), and even as "a handle or a crooked tube, which has no meaning standing apart" (20; ch. 2).

The inability to stand apart or exercise autonomy is, Eliot suggests, the ironic consequence of Silas's too-great isolation. The unraveled weaver is woven back into shape as a reflective and purposeful agent—as opposed to that seemingly unreflective spinner of webs, the spider—through his adoption of a young child who integrates him into the community. A revision of the New Testament story of Lazarus, the man Christ awakened from the dead—Marner, the narrator observes at one point, is like a "dead man come to life again" (8; ch. 1)—*Silas Marner* suggests that humanity is not a biological given, or conferred by birth, but a development of shared life. While Lazarus's awakening highlights God's power and agency (as this is made manifest in the world through the Son), Marner's endorses a profoundly intersubjective and practical conception of subjectivity. The narrator observes of his relationship with his daughter: "As the child's mind was growing into knowledge, his mind was growing into memory: as her life unfolded, his soul, long stupefied in a cold narrow prison, was unfolding too, and trembling gradually into full consciousness" (126; ch. 14).

The full consciousness cited here is not the masterful reflexivity of a sovereign humanist subject but a contingent and fragile construction of social life.

A fuller consideration of Eliot's contributions to the Left Hegelian critique of religion requires first a reframing of that critique. Neither Strauss nor Feuerbach, the Left Hegelians Eliot brought to England through her translations of their work, was practicing close readings of the scriptures of the sort affiliated with the Biblical criticism of Friedrich Schleiermacher or Johann Gottfried Eichhorn. In their own day they were regarded first and foremost as interpreters of Hegel, who radicalized his thesis of the subject's social embedment in ways that promised far-reaching social and political reform. We have no less an authority for this interpretation than Karl Marx himself. "For Germany, the criticism of religion has been essentially completed," announced the young Marx in *A Contribution to the Critique of Hegel's Philosophy of Right*, adding that "the criticism of religion is the prerequisite of all criticism" (*Early Writings* 243). The story of how Marx and Engels subsequently distanced themselves from the older generation of Left Hegelians has been extensively told, including by Marx and Engels themselves (see also Breckman; Brudney). The crux of their critique, encapsulated in Marx's *Theses on Feuerbach*, was that Hegel's students fell into the same subjectivist trap as Hegel himself, whose desire to embed consciousness in history ultimately devolved into the celebration of consciousness alone.[5] In recent times, however, historians and philosophers of Left Hegelianism have substantially complicated the idea of a neat break between Marxism and an earlier Left Hegelianism—especially Feuerbachian anthropology (Toews; Breckman; Brudney). In Feuerbach's writings, Warren Breckman has argued, "we find in embryo not only the politics of Young Hegelianism but also the philosophical basis for the 'philosophy of the deed' and, indeed, for Marxism" (104). It is to the Left Hegelian philosophy of the deed that I now turn.

The Real God-Man

Hegel himself first charted the connections between religion and social theory, placing the Christian doctrine of the Incarnation at the center of his speculative philosophy or absolute idealism. Through its symbolism of the God-man, Christianity, he argued, first revealed to the world the necessary coexistence of infinite and finite, Spirit and world.[6] God became man because Spirit has no meaning except through the encounter with its other. Hegel builds here on Spinoza's substance monism, which placed God and nature on a single continuum, but he is more interested than the latter in the subject-like structure of the continuum and its ability to incorporate internal differentiation and individuation.[7] The Christ figure of Christianity is important to him not least because it designates an individual permeated by the universal but not destroyed by it.

Attitudes to Hegel's Christology were crucial in determining party lines in the post-1820 German political landscape and led to the eventual splitting up of Hegelianism into an Old or Right Hegelianism and a Young or Left Hegelianism (Breck-man; Brudney; Massey; Toews). The first group saw Hegel's writings on religion as fully supportive of the messianic claims of the historical Jesus of Nazareth, and hence of the top-down model of authority embodied by the Prussian state. The second group argued that Hegel had been far too reverential toward the historical Jesus, in ways that prohibited an extensive revision of the Christ symbol into a theory of socially-situated agency.

Strauss's *Life of Jesus* was at the vanguard of challenges to right-wing Hegelianism. It was received in Germany with "panic-stricken terror" (F. C. Baur, qtd. in Massey 11), even though its conclusion was by no means novel—or at least the conclusion that the seemingly miraculous incidents of Jesus's life are best understood as mythical constructions of the early Christian community, and in the light of expectations established by the Old Testament.[8] Its stormy reception, which led to Strauss being disbarred from academia, is explained instead by its thesis that the historical meaning of the Incarnation rests in the collectivity rather than in any one particular individual. As Strauss put it, "In an individual, a God-man, the properties and functions which the church ascribes to Christ contradict themselves; in the idea of the race they perfectly agree" (780). On this reading, it is not Jesus but individuals collectively who undergo the cycle of birth, death, and resurrection ascribed to Christ. It is individuals who claim divinity through every day morality, and in the achievements of science and culture. God becomes man through time, in the "multiplicity of exemplars which reciprocally complete each other—in the alternate appearance and suppression of a series of individuals" (779–80).

If Strauss's *Life of Jesus* shook the German political and academic establishments by disabling revealed religion, Feuerbach's *The Essence of Christianity* offered itself as an all-encompassing new creed for the activist left. As Engels put it, "enthusiasm was general" and we all became at once Feuerbachians" (18). The book's inspirational quality—its effect of baptism by fire ("Feuer-bach," fiery brook)—derived from the importance it attached to autonomous individuality, in addition to the species consciousness foregrounded by Strauss. Anticipating key terms from Marxism and Freudian psychoanalysis, Feuerbach identifies Christianity as a program of self-alienating projection, as a kind of self-help gone awry. Under Christianity, he argues, man projects his own capacities onto a God, who serves as the Subject to which the individual then becomes an abject object: "Man—this is the mystery of religion—projects his being into objectivity, and then again makes himself an object to this projected image of himself" (29–30). This truncation of individual potential is ascribed by Feuerbach, moreover, also to Hegel's idealism, which is described in *The Principles of the Philosophy of the Future* as a theology, not unlike Christianity, in that it too mystifies human nature: in its case, by reducing human nature to rational capacity alone. Through his critique of the two theologies, Christianity and absolute idealism, Feuerbach aims to effect a twofold revolution: to restore to individuals their alienated human nature; and further, to restore to them a nature that is constituted not only by reason but by what is described in *The Essence of Christianity* as the real secular content of the Christian Trinity: the human "essence" as "thinking, loving, willing *existence*" (3; my emphasis). The move from essence to existence under Feuerbach's "new philosophy" or anthropology institutes what the Left Hegelian himself described as a new categorical imperative: "Think in existence, in the world as a member of it, not in the vacuum of abstraction as a solitary monad, as an absolute monarch, as an indifferent, superworldly God" (*Principles* 67).

One way of approaching the somewhat cryptic injunction to "think in existence" is to follow Feuerbach's argument about feeling, to unpack his claim that "the essence of Christianity is the essence of human feeling" (*Essence* 140). Feeling is a highly valued term in the Feuerbachian corpus and accounts for the intensity of Feuerbach's interest in religion, which is perceived by him to be both at best and worst principally a matter of feeling. The true anthropological meaning of the Incarnation, Feuerbach argues, is the principle of love, since God sent into the world a Son who died out of love of humanity. But religion perverts this affective principle by mobilizing feeling at its lowest levels, as cheap fantasy and wish fulfillment. On Feuerbach's reading, the Christian (qua subject) eliminates the world (qua object) by the force of her projected desires, and especially through her belief in the reality of a personal God, a guardian who renders superfluous all reasoning about means and ends—and indeed moral choice itself. Christianity, in other words, denotes a pathological subjectivism or egotism which is opposed not only to ethics but also to science's vision of a lawful world: "In Christianity, man was concentrated only on himself, he unlinked himself from the chain of sequences in the system of the universe. . . . Because he no longer regarded himself as a being immanent in the world, because he severed himself from connection with it, he felt himself an unlimited being . . . he had no longer any reason to doubt the truth and validity of his subjective wishes and feelings" (150).

Feuerbach asserts, however, that feeling carries the cure for its own excesses since feeling also connects the individual to the world of other subjects. Hence the centrality of love, including sexual love, to Feuerbach's anthropology: love alerts individuals to their necessary interdependence with others, to the idea that "the *thou* belongs to the perfection of the *I*, that *men* are required to constitute humanity, that only men taken together are what man can and should be" (155). Feuerbach's suggestion that "only men taken together are what man can and should be," and elsewhere in *The Essence of Christianity* that "only community constitutes humanity" (158), is the most innovative aspect of his anthropological revisionism. It anticipates what Seyla Benhabib has described as the decisive shift from *"legislative to interactive rationality"* (6; emphasis in original) characteristic of postmetaphysical philosophies of the second half of the twentieth century. And it does so by "socializing" reason, so to speak. Feuerbach argues, for example, that "only where man communicates with man, only in speech, a social act, awakes reason. To ask a question and to answer are the first acts of thought" (*Essence* 83). In the moral domain, the other-directedness of reason translates into an understanding of laws or principles as constructions of shared life, an argument that links the Left Hegelians back in time to the British sentimentalists and forward to neo-Kantians such as John Rawls and Habermas. Feuerbach asserts, for example, that "The consciousness of the moral law, of right, of propriety, of truth itself, is indissolubly united with my consciousness of another than myself" (158). A "judicious friend," he adds, is imperative to moral discrimination since "I cannot so abstract myself from myself as to judge myself with perfect freedom and disinterestedness; but another has an impartial judgment; through him I correct, complete, my own judgment, my own taste, my own knowledge" (159).

In other words, "humanity," as conceived by anthropology, is not one undifferentiated species but is constituted by particular individuals exercising their reason at particular times and in particular places. As Feuerbach explains, "Doubtless the essence of man is *one*, but this essence is infinite. . . . Unity in essence is multiplicity in existence" (158). The move from essence to existence, as depicted here, is a move to a fundamentally practical conception of rationality. Feuerbach's, and also Marx's, emphasis on practice, Daniel Brudney has argued, is the most distinctive aspect of their immanent critique of their idealist precursors. Brudney contends that "Both Feuerbach and Marx rejected the goal of a professor's chair, yet neither rejected reason. When they proceed by means opposed to that of many a professor, they do so with the belief that reason itself is better served thereby. Their goal is to make *thought* practical" (11; emphasis in the original).

However, if one consequence of the Feuerbachian dictum that "only community constitutes humanity" is a new individualism that contests the binary opposition of autonomy and sociability established by Kant, another, less salutary, one, is that all thinking must be dedicated to social ends. This instrumentalism—implicit, for example, in Feuerbach's repeated depiction of the philosophical life as a fundamentally egotistical one—stands in unattractive contrast to Hannah Arendt's memorable (and Kantian) representation of thinking in *The Life of the Mind* as "the habit of examining whatever happens to come to pass or to attract attention, regardless of results and specific content" (5). Feuerbach's, and also Marx's, often suspicious stance toward contemplation needn't follow from the turn they institute to existence, and away from essence, since thinking, as Arendt clarifies, is itself an activity, and one that can never fully leave behind the world. Instead, it "permits the mind to withdraw from the world without ever being able to leave it or transcend it" (45). Withdrawal, however, tends to have a negative charge in Feuerbach's writings—not least because of the highly optimistic picture of community they develop, one that links Feuerbach's Left Hegelianism more explicitly to the traditionalist communitarianism of Alisdair MacIntyre than the discourse ethics of the Habermasian school.

The risks of the emphasis on community are still more pronounced in Auguste Comte's positivism, which is linked to Left Hegelianism on multiple levels, including through its critique of religion.[9] Comte's critique, however, delineates a hierarchical positive polity, in which duty supplants rights, with duty itself conceived of as submission to necessity—as determined by a structured universe of cause and effect—and as service to Humanity or the Great Being, the Comtean equivalent of the Left Hegelians' species. Because Humanity is, by definition, composed of more dead than living people, "The living are, by the necessity of the case, always and more and more, under the government of the dead" (*Catechism* 54). Comte suggests that a principle of Continuity (love of past and future humanity) overrides the claims of autonomous individuality and even solidarity with living human beings. The purpose of life, as positivism understands it, is less the dignity of self-reflective choice than "to transmit, improved to those who shall come after, that increasing heritage, we received from those who went before" (63).

Comte's writings remind us very clearly of the post-revolutionary cultural context of the development of ideologies such as positivism and Hegelianism, both of which were propelled in significant ways by the desire to completely reorder a world disordered by, on the one hand, a political rhetoric of the rights of man, and, on the other hand, by science and philosophy's growing disenchantment with final causes and metaphysical explanations. Fear of the unknown, like the cautious rhetoric surrounding today's Arab spring, permeates the writings of intellectuals like Comte and produces unlikely bedfellows. Especially noteworthy are the intersections between Comte's utopian socialist thought and Edmund Burke's traditionalism, as espoused in *The Reflections on the Revolution in France*: this too upholds a conception of duty that entails submission to ancestral wisdom.[10]

For Eliot as well, the past and inherited traditions weigh heavily upon the claims of the individual.[11] Marian Evans's enthusiastic review of the pioneering German sociologist Wilhelm Heinrich von Riehl's *Die Bürgerliche Gesellschaft* and *Land und Leute* in "The Natural History of German Life" (*Westminster Review*, 1856)—an essay that appeared on the cusp of Evans's transformation from journalist and translator to novelist—is revealing in this regard. Attributing to Riehl an understanding of society as "incarnate history" (*Selected Essays* 127), Evans endorses a developmental view of individuals and societies that is suspicious of sweeping social and political reforms. Like Burke, she contends that individuals are ill-prepared to use their reason without the crutch of tradition: "The nature of European men has its roots intertwined with the past, and can only be developed by allowing those roots to remain undisturbed while the process of development is going on, until that perfect ripeness of the seed which carries with it a life independent of the root" (128–29).

And yet it is the special task of the novelist, Evans observes in the same essay, to make the claims of the individual vivid to even the most obtusely self-centered: "Appeals founded on generalizations and statistics require a sympathy ready-made, a moral sentiment already in activity; but a picture of human life such as a great artist can give surprises even the trivial and the selfish into that attention to what is apart from themselves, which may be called the raw material of moral sentiment" (*Selected Essays* 110). Eliot's narrators are still more emphatic about the value of individuality, as in *Middlemarch*'s narrator's observation that "There is no general doctrine which is not capable of eating out our morality if unchecked by the deep-seated habit of direct fellow-feeling with individual fellow-men" (619; ch. 61). This narrator, like Eliot's other narrators, sees his/her special task to be giving voice to the many mute inglorious Miltons of the world, those who "found no sacred poet and sank unwept into oblivion" (*Middlemarch* 3; Prelude).

Eliot's self-identified "sacred" vocation as a novelist entailed far more than a celebration of the past. It sought also to sanctify individuals as the locus of situated agency. In doing so, Eliot drew especially upon Feuerbach's writings. "With the ideas of Feuerbach I everywhere agree" (*Letters* 2:153), she wrote Sara Hennell, who advised her on the translation of *The Essence of Christianity*. Her admiration of Strauss was more qualified. While she described Strauss to Hennell as "so klar und ideenvoll" (*Letters* 1:218), she found the massive Strauss translation emotionally and physically exhausting. This is testified to by Cara Bray, Sara's sister and Eliot's Coventry neighbor. "We have seen more of M.A. than usual this week," Bray writes to Hennell on 14 February 1846. "She said she was Strauss-sick—it made her ill dissecting the beautiful story of the crucifixion, and only the sight of her Christ-image and picture made her endure it" (206).

Eliot's discomfort with Strauss's method indicates why she turned to fiction to further the critique of religion begun by the Left Hegelians: fiction tempers criticism with sympathy. It helps us understand how things came to be in addition to what is wrong with them. By permitting a high degree of individuation, fiction produces sympathy for the many individuals whose struggles are obscured by a judgmental posterity—individuals who, according to *Middlemarch's* narrator, are victims of "an imperfect social state, in which great feelings will often take the aspect of error, and great faith the aspect of illusion" (*Middlemarch* 838; Finale). As the eponymous hero of *Daniel Deronda* vivifies, one is less disposed to judge the actions of others harshly when these others are seen as particular individuals with particular histories: Deronda, we are told, "hated vices mildly, being used to think of them less in the abstract than as a part of mixed human natures having an individual history, which it was the bent of his mind to trace with understanding and pity" (364; ch. 32).

The individuals whose life stories Eliot seeks to illuminate are predominantly female—latter-day Santa Teresas rather than mute inglorious Miltons. And in their narratives we find the seeds of a wide-ranging social critique.

From God-Man to Historical Women

Eliot's novels are all, in one way or another, stories of conversion, in which one or more characters rise from the hypersubjectivism associated with religion by the Left Hegelians to some larger vision of relatedness and their place in the world. *Daniel Deronda* best articulates the goal of the awakening these characters experience through his desire to be "an organic part of social life, instead of roaming in it like a yearning disembodied spirit, stirred with a vague social passion, but without fixed habitation to render fellowship real" (365; ch. 32). The more complex narrative of conversion Eliot documents in *Daniel Deronda* is, however, Gwendolen Harleth's, which lacks the clarity of Deronda's world-historical mission to create a Jewish homeland—a mission cemented by Eliot's hero's newfound identity as a Jew and by his marriage to a Jewess. Something of a composite of the long line of female characters preceding her, mingling traits of Rosamond Vincy with those of Janet Dempster, Gwendolen, like Feuerbach's Christian, begins the novel with a false sense of freedom, articulated as her faith in a limitless will. She believes that she can "move the world without [a] precise notion of standing-place or lever" (250; ch. 23). Gwendolen first begins to perceive limits to her will through her friendship with Deronda, which encourages at once a sense of dependence on another and a growing habit of self-scrutiny. For Eliot, as for Feuerbach, the individual's capacity to reflect upon her own actions is not independent of her relations with others. From Janet and Tryan's relationship in *Scenes of Clerical Life* to Gwendolen and Deronda's, lovers or potential lovers play a crucial role in the development of self-consciousness and hence of conscience. Fred Vincy's love for Mary Garth proves his salvation in *Middlemarch*, the narrator of which observes that "Even much stronger mortals than Fred Vincy hold half their rectitude in the minds of the being they love best . . . and they are fortunate who get a theatre where the audience demands their best" (242; ch. 24). Other people are represented in Eliot's fiction not only as a theatrical audience witnessing the drama of their friends' and neighbors' lives but also as more or less impartial mirrors for them. The minds of others, Eliot's narrators tirelessly remind us, are the medium though which the self learns to take itself as an object of thought. It becomes imperative, therefore, that the mirror we offer others enables rather than disables their sense of self as active beings. Even Milton, *Middlemarch*'s narrator humorously notes, "must submit to have the facial angle of a bumpkin" (84; ch. 10) if he looks for his portrait in a spoon.

In the context of Gwendolen's conversion, Deronda initially serves less as a mirror than a personal God or Christ, who stands in a special relation of care to the self. He becomes a comforting "outer conscience" (763; ch. 64) that prohibits the development of an inner conscience. Gwendolen's institution of Deronda as Christ diminishes them both: him, because she is uninterested in the particulars of his life (except as they touch her life), and her, because she feels no need to take charge of her own actions. It is through the shocking recognition that he has goals and desires apart from her that she comes to accord both him and herself the status of ethical agents. From being a mere acolyte, Gwendolen progresses to the status of an equal; she becomes a "friend" in Feuerbach's sense. Gwendolen's last gesture in the novel is one of concern for a friend she had treated instrumentally. In the letter she sends Deronda on his wedding day, Gwendolen assumes responsibility for herself in a new way: "I only thought of myself, and I made you grieve. It hurts me now to think of your grief. . . . It is better—it shall be better with me because I have known you" (810; ch. 70).

By becoming a reflective agent in her own right, Gwendolen joins the ranks of the many Eliot heroines who must cease to treat the men in their lives as personal saviors. Her story finds precedents in Romola's, whose quest for faith cannot be answered by a flawed Savonarola; in Maggie Tulliver's, who is thwarted in her attempts to model her life on the saintly paradigm outlined by Thomas à Kempis's *Imitatio Christi*; and in Dorothea Brooke's, who must learn to see her marriage to Casaubon as something other than the key to the mythological "provinces of masculine knowledge" (64; ch.

7). In a well-known passage in *Middlemarch*, describing Dorothea's shift from her earlier instrumentalism, Eliot identifies self-recognition as an active being to be one crucial endpoint of conversion:

> We are all of us born in moral stupidity, taking the world as an udder to feed our supreme selves: Dorothea had early begun to emerge from that stupidity, but yet it had been easier to her to imagine how she would devote herself to Mr. Casaubon, and become wise and strong in his strength and wisdom, than to conceive with that distinctness which is no longer reflection but feeling—an idea wrought back to the directness of sense, like the solidity of objects—that he had an equivalent centre of self, whence the lights and shadows must always fall with a certain difference. (211; ch. 21)

While the passage is most explicitly about the recognition others demand, it indicates that no such recognition is possible without respect for one's own individuality. Dorothea assumes an ethical posture toward her husband only when she distinguishes herself from him, when she recognizes that they both have "centres of self, whence the lights and shadows . . . always fall with a certain difference." Such a center of self or perspective on the world, Eliot's novels suggest, is not a substantive or innate essence but is shaped by the individual's social experiences. Dorothea and Casaubon are at once like and unlike one another: they are different because both have standpoints of their own from which to view themselves and others, and they are alike by virtue of this difference—because both have such a centering perspective.

Of course the newfound agency of heroines like Dorothea and Gwendolen remains a highly circumscribed domestic one, since it is realized in the context of the constricting gender conventions of their times. Unlike Feuerbach, however, Eliot foregrounds how disabling the community that constitutes humanity can be when Feuerbach's generic "man" is particularized as women. While intersubjective relations cultivate moral competence, the circuit of others that society presents to women is too often composed of "various small mirrors" (*Middlemarch* 84; ch. 10) that reflect back a highly diminished self. The community, as in the "world's wife" of *The Mill on the Floss*, too often judges without sympathy and through an ugly consequentialism, whereby a woman's worth, equated with her social status, is determined by her marriage. Women like Dorothea Brooke and more tragically, Maggie Tulliver, have virtually no others who can reflect back to them an adequate sense of their own potential outside of domestic ties. In a closing salute to the heroine of *Middlemarch*, its narrator wryly observes: "Many who knew her, thought it a pity that so substantive and rare a creature should have been absorbed into the life of another, and be only known in a certain circle as a wife and mother. But no one stated exactly what else that was in her power she ought rather to have done—not even Sir James Chettam, who went no further than the negative prescription that she ought not to have married Will Ladislaw" (836; Finale). The paradox of female conversion, as Eliot amply recognizes, is that a woman's growing sense of her own independence is too often accompanied by "absorption into the life of another," an absorption so widely accepted that the world can only judge women's actions in the context of their marital choices.

As already noted, the conservatism that creeps into Eliot's otherwise searing social commentary derives from the other aspect of the historicism she shares with the various contextualizers of reason of the first half of the nineteenth century: the emphasis on the past and inherited traditions. Maggie Tulliver represents a particularly telling case in point. Positioned by her abilities to be a critic of her unreflective community—the provincial Dodsons and Tullivers sound very much like Riehl's German peasantry for which custom *"holds the place of sentiment, of theory, and in many cases of affection"* (*Selected Essays* 119; emphasis in original)—Maggie cannot become a social exile. This is so, however, not only because of the gender conventions of her time but also because of her repeated prioritizing of duty over right, and her interpretation of duty, ultimately, as the affirmation of long-standing affiliations. Articulating this understanding, she observes to Stephen Guest, "If the past is not to bind us, where can duty lie? We should have no law but the inclination of the moment" (496; bk. 6, ch. 14). Here Eliot's desire to situate the individual in a communal and historical context has the effect of folding the individual wholly into the community—unlike as in *Silas Marner*, where the ability to stand apart from others is represented as one crucial endpoint of shared existence.

Significantly, this conservative aspect of Hegelianism reproduces itself in poststructuralism, insofar as the latter interprets the thesis of the subject's social embedment as disabling the ethics of autonomy. Judith Butler argues, for example, that the self-other relationship makes it impossible to summon an "I" in isolation from a "you." It constitutes "an exchange that cannot be assimilated into the schema in which the subject is over here as a topic to be reflexively interrogated, and the Other is over there, as a theme to be purveyed" (129–30). In *Precarious Life*, Butler identifies inarticulate tokens of connectedness to others—like the grief we feel at the loss of a loved one—to be most fully indicative of our ethical potential: "What grief displays . . . is the thrall in which our relations with others hold us, in ways that we cannot always recount or explain, in ways that often interrupt the self-conscious account of ourselves we might try to provide, in ways that challenge the very notion of ourselves as autonomous and in control" (23).

My argument here has been that such thralldom to relationship is one that Eliot and the Left Hegelians mostly contest, even as they situate individual agency in the context of intersubjective relations. Their writings reveal that the attempt to be respectful at once of the individual and of the social and material contexts of agency is a difficult one. But their critique of transcendental mindsets, beginning with religion, identifies them as important initiators of the social critique that, according to Marx, must be preceded by the criticism of religion. Insofar as Eliot's fiction has vivified for many generations the moral dignity of individuals, we must see her as a remarkable representative of the nineteenth century's broadly liberal desire to bring God down into the world through the affirmation of self-reflective agency.

NOTES

1 Eliot also began but never completed a translation of Spinoza's *Theological-Political Treatise*.

2 For an outline of, and crucial intervention, in these debates, see Anderson.

3 For a wide-ranging discussion of Hegel's legacy, including its connections to poststructuralism, see Benhabib.

4 For readings of Eliot's Hegelian inheritance deploying the organizing rubric of humanism, see Fleishman; Knoepflmacher; Kucich; Paris. In his recent intellectual biography, Fleishman, for example, pits Eliot against contemporary theory, arguing that she believes "in a human essence, another tenet at odds with the postmodern belief in the almost exclusive influence of culture. rather than human nature in determining what we are and do" (9). Kucich makes a similar argument about Feuerbach: "For Feuerbach, human nature is an unchanging force within us, unmodified by direct external influences of any kind" (127).

5 Hence Marx's contention in the *Theses on Feuerbach* that "The chief defect of all hitherto existing materialism (that of Feuerbach included) is that the thing, reality, sensuousness, is conceived only in the form of the object or of contemplation, but not as sensuous human activity, practice" (*Early Writings* 421).

6 For Hegel on religion, see especially Hodgson.

7 In the *Phenomenology of Spirit*, Hegel declares his break with Spinoza when he suggests that "everything turns on grasping and expressing the True, not only as Substance, but equally as Subject" (10). On this reading, Spinoza's concept of Substance doesn't accord sufficient weight to consciousness. "Human beings," Hegel argues, "are truly human through consciousness—by virtue of the fact that they think and by virtue of the fact that they are spirit."

8 An excellent account of the mythical school of Biblical criticism and its implications for British literature is provided by Shaffer.

9 Like the Left Hegelians, Comte was highly critical of revealed religion. He depicts religion as an infantile phase in the life of individuals and of humanity as a whole, one that should give way to "positivist" maturity—by which Comte means the developmental stage where the mind ceases to look for final causes and is content with tracking laws in the observable world. Moreover, for Comte, as for Feuerbach, feeling has special importance in a tripartite human nature composed of reason, will, and feeling: "this only . . . gives a stimulus and direction to the other two parts of our nature" (*General View* 10). But whereas for Feuerbach, the emphasis on feeling leads to a refurbishment of reason, for Comte, feeling's importance derives from the submission to necessity it engenders. Women are accorded great significance in the positive polity because they are associated with the principle of love. Woman, Comte contends, "personifies in the purest form the principle of Love upon which the unity of our nature depends; and the culture of that principle in others is her special function" (*General View* 253).

10 For an insightful reading of Comte's and Eliot's treatments of the Burkean principle of inheritance, see Semmel.

11 T. R. Wright offers an extensive discussion of the Eliot-Comte relationship. As Wright notes, the question of Eliot's affinity to Comte is a complicated one, since strong personal relationships mediated her approach to positivism. Together with John Stuart Mill, G. H. Lewes was one of Comte's first English disciples, although, like Mill, he eventually became alienated by the Religion of Humanity. Also important in shaping Eliot's stance toward positivism was her long-standing friendship with Maria Congreve, whose husband, Richard Congreve, headed the Positivist Society in England. Eliot writes to Mrs. Congreve of her "gratitude . . . for the illumination Comte has contributed to my life" (*Letters* 4:333), and her notebooks and letters indicate extensive familiarity with Comte's writings.

REFERENCES

Anderson, Amanda. *The Way We Argue Now: A Study in The Cultures of Theory*. Princeton: Princeton UP, 2006.

Arendt, Hannah. *The Life of the Mind*. Ed. Mary McCarthy. New York: Harcourt, 1978.

Benhabib, Seyla. *Situating the Self: Gender, Community, and Postmodernism in Contemporary Ethics*. London: Routledge, 1992.

Breckman, Warren. *Marx, the Young Hegelians, and the Origins of Radical Social Theory*. Cambridge: Cambridge UP, 1999.

Brudney, Daniel. *Marx's Attempt to Leave Philosophy*. Cambridge: Harvard UP, 1998.

Butler, Judith. *Precarious Life: The Powers of Mourning and Violence*. London: Verso, 2004.

Comte, Auguste. *The Catechism of Positive Religion*. Trans. Richard Congreve. London: John Chapman, 1858.

Comte, Auguste. *A General View of Positivism*. Trans. J. H. Bridges. New York: Speller, 1957. Trans. of *Discours sur l'ensemble du positivism*. 1848.

Eliot, George. *Daniel Deronda*. Ed. Terence Cave. London: Penguin, 1995.

Eliot, George. *The George Eliot Letters*. Ed. Gordon S. Haight. 9 vols. New Haven: Yale UP, 1954–78.

Eliot, George. *Middlemarch*. Ed. Rosemary Ashton. London: Penguin, 1994.

Eliot, George. *The Mill on the Floss*. Ed. A. S. Byatt. London: Penguin, 1985.

Eliot, George. *Selected Essays, Poems, and Other Writings*. Ed. A. S. Byatt. London: Penguin, 1990.

Eliot, George. *Silas Marner*. 1861. Ed. David Carroll. London: Penguin, 1996.

Engels, Friedrich. *Ludwig Feuerbach and the Outcome of German Classical Philosophy*. Ed. C. P. Dutt. New York: International Publisher, 1941.

Ermarth, Elizabeth Deeds. "George Eliot's Conception of Sympathy." *Nineteenth-Century Fiction* 40 (1985): 23–42.

Feuerbach, Ludwig. *The Essence of Christianity*. 1854. Trans. George Eliot. Buffalo: Prometheus, 1989. Trans. of *Das Wesen des Christentums*. 1841.

Feuerbach, Ludwig. *The Principles of the Philosophy of the Future*. Trans. Manfred Vogel. Indianapolis: Hackett, 1986. Trans. of *Grundsätze der Philosophie der Zukunft*. 1843.

Fleishman, Avrom. *George Eliot's Intellectual Life*. Cambridge: Cambridge UP, 2010.

Guth, Deborah. *George Eliot and Schiller: Intertextuality and Cross-Cultural Discourse*. Warwick Studies in the European Humanities. Farnham: Ashgate, 2003.

Habermas, Jürgen. *The Philosophical Discourse of Modernity: Twelve Lectures*. Trans. Frederick G. Lawrence. Cambridge: MIT P, 1987.

Hegel, G. W. F. *Phenomenology of Spirit*. Trans. A. V. Miller. Oxford: Oxford UP, 1977. Trans. of *Phänomenologie des Geistes*. 1807.

Hodgson, Peter C. "Hegel's Philosophy of Religion." *The Cambridge Companion to Hegel and Nineteenth-Century Philosophy*. Ed. Frederick C. Beiser. Cambridge: Cambridge UP, 2008. 230–52.

Knoepflmacher, U. C. *Religious Humanism and The Victorian Novel: George Eliot, Walter Pater, Samuel Butler*. Princeton: Princeton UP, 1966.

Kucich, John. *Repression in Victorian Fiction: Charlotte Brontë, George Eliot, and Charles Dickens*. Berkeley: U of California P, 1987.

Marx, Karl. *Early Writings*. Trans. Rodney Livingstone and Gregor Benton. Introd. Lucio Colletti. London: Penguin, 1975.

Marx, Karl and Friedrich Engels. *The German Ideology*. Amherst, NY: Prometheus, 1998.

Massey, Marilyn Chapin. *Christ Unmasked: The Meaning of the Life of Jesus in German Politics*. Chapel Hill: U of North Carolina P, 1983.

Paris, Bernard J. *Experiments in Life: George Eliot's Quest for Values*. Detroit: Wayne State UP, 1965.

Rignall, John, ed. *George Eliot and Europe*. Coventry: Scolar, 1997.

Rignall, John, ed. *George Eliot, European Novelist*. Farnham: Ashgate, 2011.

Röder-Bolton, Gerlinde. *George Eliot and Goethe: An Elective Affinity*. Amsterdam: Rodopi, 1998.

Semmel, Bernard. *George Eliot and the Politics of National Inheritance*. Oxford: Oxford UP, 1994.

Shaffer, Elinor S. *Kubla Khan and the Fall of Jerusalem: The Mythological School in Biblical Criticism and Secular Literature, 1770–1880*. Cambridge: Cambridge UP, 1975.

Spinoza, Benedict de. *Ethics of Benedict Spinoza*. 1856. Trans. George Eliot. Salzburg Studies in Romantic Reassessment. Mellen, 1981.

Strauss, David Friedrich. *The Life of Jesus, Critically Examined.* 1846. Trans. George Eliot. Ed. Peter C. Hodgson. Philadelphia: Fortress, 1972 Trans. of *Das Leben Jesu kritisch bearbeitet.* 1835.

Thompson, Andrew. *George Eliot and Italy: Literary, Cultural, and Political Influences from Dante to the Risorgimento.* New York: Palgrave, 1998.

Toews, John Edward. *Hegelianism: The Path to Dialectical Humanism, 1805–1841.* Cambridge: Cambridge UP, 1980.

Wright, T. R. *The Religion of Humanity: The Impact of Comtean Positivism on Victorian Britain.* Cambridge: Cambridge UP, 1986.

30

George Eliot and Secularism

Simon During

What might George Eliot's work mean to a reader who knows nothing about the academic criticism that has accrued around it, and nothing about her life either? From such an innocent position, what would her oeuvre's main concerns look like?

One plausible answer might be: Eliot wishes to describe various kinds of Anglican churchmanship in order to promote an atmosphere where vicars might become more effective parish leaders. Let us not forget that, when George Henry Lewes sent her first fiction ("Amos Barton") to John Blackwood's Tory-inclined *Blackwood's Magazine,* he pretended that it was in fact written by an Anglican country parson (Haight 214–15). Later Marian Evans concealed her authorship to her sister Fanny by passing off the same pretense (Haight 231). Certainly many early readers believed *Scenes of Clerical Life* to be written by a clergyman, or if not, like Jane Carlyle, at least "a brother or first cousin to a clergyman" (Haight 251). Leaving *Romola* and *Daniel Deronda* aside, even the later novels have Anglican vicars as central characters whose pastoral success or failure is a crucial element in the story.

Another answer might be this. Eliot's fictions mount an ambitious attempt at spiritual and intellectual invigoration and elevation, but one which does not adhere to revealed Christianity. And of course no careful reader is likely to dispute this: all Eliot's novels do indeed promulgate such a purpose. Indeed, when she embraced this non-Christian re-vitalizing project in her late twenties, she joined a group of heterodox intellectuals and activists who thought of their movement either as "spiritualism" (a word that changed its meaning to the now familiar one only later) or as the "New Reformation" (see Francis 142–45; Stedman Jones). This politico-spiritualist

A Companion to George Eliot, First Edition. Edited by Amanda Anderson and Harry E. Shaw.
© 2013 John Wiley & Sons, Ltd. Published 2016 by John Wiley & Sons, Ltd.

movement in effect replaced the Christian God as revealed in the Scriptures by religious feelings and beliefs which retained their sacral quality while being focused on this world—for instance on hope for, and action toward, a social future in which human sympathies are enlarged. This line of thought is already apparent in Eliot's first novel, *Adam Bede*, whose narrator tells us that, in the cases of laborers like Dinah and Seth Bede, Methodism "linked thoughts with the past, lifted their imagination above the sordid details of their own narrow lives, and suffused their souls with the sense of a pitying, loving, infinite Presence" (34; ch. 3). We can note that here, notwithstanding Dinah and Seth's Methodism, this "infinite Presence" exists in the world, not outside it, even if its qualities—pity, love and infiniteness—are traditional features of the Christian God.

So we might call Eliot's larger mission an *immanentization or naturalization of the Christian transcendent*, or to use a vocabulary closer to that of her own time, an *accessing of the infinite by human finitude*. And in her fictions, if rarely anywhere else, this access is often channeled through a simultaneously sexual and spiritual personal charisma, granted only to exceptional—usually male—characters: Felix Holt and Daniel Deronda most of all. That, as even an innocent reader might surmise, is what in the end replaces God's grace in the human world.

Of course an untrained reader might have many other ideas about Eliot's fiction. She might suggest, for instance, that Eliot is drawing attention to the small-mindedness of provincial middle-class life, as in the just cited passage which thinks of Dinah and Seth's lives as mainly sordid and narrow. And (although this is a reading that perhaps only a university-educated reader would conjecture), she might equally propose that this picture of provincial life is also a depiction of linguistic diversity—after all, in Eliot's novels, characters from different classes usually speak and think differently from one another. How you speak is who you are, even if like Adam Bede himself some people speak in different idiolects in different situations. And so, at least implicitly, her novels also describe how linguistic diversity maps onto social hierarchies. Class maps onto language all the more tenaciously in her fictions, because their omniscient, extra-diegetical narrator has, or is reaching for, her own, more universal language, one that becomes progressively more subtle, more conceptually rich, more psychologically attuned, more spiritually inspirational, as Eliot's career progresses. This is the language which becomes the measure against which mundane discourse is to be judged, even if, obviously, it belongs to literature not to ordinary life. In fact as Eliot's career progresses her novels deploy this language, and its invocation of concepts like "infinite Presence," to make subtle judgments of all kinds of characters who may be social or moral or religious types but who are also individualized products of thickly and concretely described social environments. In the end, this judging, imaginative intelligence (and the wisdom and security that it promises) is what many readers, academic or not, have valued in her work.

These more or less innocent readings of Eliot's fiction pose a problem insofar as their interest in Anglicanism and their interest in secular spirituality seem to contradict one another. Why should a body of work that aims to disseminate an elevated natural spirituality against the Christian faith also be interested in the practicalities of Anglican churchmanship? Part of the answer, as we shall see, turns out to be that the particular mode of secularism in which Eliot refused Christianity did not actually lead her away from thinking about the Church, but toward it. It led to a positive reengagement with the actual ecclesiastical organization in place, even if that positive engagement with the Church does not try to revitalize Christianity. Indeed the actual Christian effort to intensify feeling and belief in her time—the movement then (as now) known as Evangelicalism—is often especially dangerous as far as Eliot is concerned precisely because for her the church is important for its secular, not its religious, work. As I say, the impulsion for spiritual elevation happens elsewhere—in and through the novels themselves, that is, in *literature*, where literature, admittedly, is an articulation of a wider, if informal, social movement.

This brief conspectus of Eliot's purposes in her fiction should make it clear that her novels are not really secular at all. Or rather, as we might say, they are simultaneously secular and not secular. They involve what we can (clumsily) call a literary and secular de-secularization of the secular, in which the Anglican—or any other—church is thought of historically and socially rather than as a guarantor of faith and truth.

***

In order to make sense of these perhaps rather enigmatic propositions, it helps to have a stronger sense of what secularization is. This is difficult since, as many have noted, it denotes several quite distinct things. Three of these are especially pertinent to understanding Eliot.

Most usually, secularization means the successful critique of revealed religion and supernaturalisms. From this point of view, secularism is the intellectual movement that disproves and delegitimizes religious faith and thought. Intellectual irreligion (as we may call it) takes many forms. In particular, in the European Enlightenment, it could be either philological or philosophical, although it was also often both at once. Philological secularism discounted the textual evidence upon which the claims for the truth of Christian revelation were made, thereby transforming them into mere untruth or into myth or into the object of a rationally groundless faith. Philological criticism was established in the seventeenth century, and was reinvigorated in Eliot's time through figures like David Friedrich Strauss who critically examined the archives to argue that Christianity might not actually be a revealed or even a historical truth (indeed Christ might not have really lived) but remains a spiritual truth. This of course would make Christ not ontologically different from, say, Daniel Deronda: he becomes a fictional hero even if not usually recognized as such.

Rather differently, philosophical secularism offered a non-supernatural account of nature, human and otherwise, often by arguing that all knowledge is grounded in experience. For this way of thinking there can be no good evidence for knowing that God exists, let alone what kind of entity he (she? it?) might be. Our senses, and the ideas based on them, can tell us nothing certain about God. In its modern forms, philosophical secularism was also established in the seventeenth century, by Benedict de Spinoza, Thomas Hobbes, John Locke and others, but its dominant figure was the eighteenth-century skeptic, David Hume. With Hume it becomes clear that intellectual irreligion's object of critique is larger than any particular religion. Hume denies that we can be certain of anything that exists outside nature's regularities. The transcendental, as such, cannot be knowable to us. It actually belongs to the natural, that is to say, to the human, world. This is the philosophy that grounds the politico-spiritualist movement that Marian Evans joined in the early 1850s.

Thinking like this also inspired a widespread conspiracy theory of history. From this point of view, God lived so long in Western societies despite his being a fiction or myth because his existence is helpful to the powerful—to kings and priests—who often "esoterically" concealed their private disbelief and encouraged faith for their own ends, namely to keep "down the obtrusiveness of the vulgar and the discontent of the poor" as *Felix Holt's* Mrs. Transome, who holds this view, puts it (105; ch. 7). This mode of enlightened thought was softened by the secular spiritualist movement of the1840s and 1850s although traces of it are still to be found in, for instance, a work like Robert Mackay's *The Progress of the Intellect, as Exemplified in the Religious Development of the Greeks and Hebrews* (1850) which Eliot reviewed quite favorably for the *Westminster Review* in 1851, drawing particular attention to its picture of Christianity nonetheless as "prophetic spiritualism" (*Essays* 44). Indeed Eliot's own view of Anglicanism is esoteric insofar as she provisionally supports it as an institution not because its doctrines are true but because it is socially and ethically useful. So there is a sense in which she agrees with Mrs. Transome, despite this passage's irony.

Eliot was herself a far from negligible figure in the history of intellectual irreligion. Before becoming a fiction writer, she worked on translations of some of its key texts: first Spinoza's *Tractatus Theologico-Politicus,* then Strauss's path-breaking *Das Leben Jesu,* next, Ludwig Feuerbach's *Das Wesen des Christentums,* and finally Spinoza's *Ethics.* This was the work through which she gained entry into London's heterodox intellectual world.

The second important mode of secularization is not intellectual or critical at all. It involves granting legal and parliamentary autonomy to religion, and, in particular, the Church's separation from the state. Secularization of this kind occurred slowly and conflictually across Europe from the mid-seventeenth century, when following the Peace of Westphalia (1648), subjects were permitted to hold different religious faiths from their sovereign's. But at least until the 1820s England was itself a confessional state, that is, a state with an official religion (Anglicanism) in which the monarch's sovereignty was sacral (he or she was head of the Church) and important civil rights were reserved for Anglicans—only Anglicans could, for instance, attend English universities or work for the government. Indeed, marriages and burials were only recognized by the state if they had been solemnized under Anglican ritual. Most importantly, civil administration was fundamentally parochial: its basic geographical unit was the parish and it was administered in large part by church vestries led by clergymen who usually doubled as magistrates. (*Adam Bede* provides a good description of a country clergyman's various governmental responsibilities [131–34; ch. 14]).

In 1829 a Tory government under the Duke of Wellington passed the Catholic Emancipation Act which, for the first time, permitted Roman Catholics to become members of parliament, enabled non-Anglicans to take government and juridical posts, and opened the way for the secular state and private interests to replace the parochial system of administration. This shift began to happen in the aftermath, first, of the New Poor Law (1834) which amalgamated parishes into unions, and then of the ground-breaking Municipal Corporations Act (1835) which set up town councils on bureaucratically-rational, relatively democratic lines. As the confessional state fell apart, a way to a new social, legal, intellectual, and spiritual regime was opened.

Three of Eliot's novels—*The Mill on the Floss, Felix Holt,* and *Middlemarch*—are set in the period of the confessional state's collapse. The 1829 passing of the Catholic Emancipation Act is quite as important to them as the now more famous 1832 Reform Act, which mandated mere electoral reform. As a character in *Felix Holt* puts it, "when Peel and the Duke turned round about the Catholics in '29 . . . it was all over for us" (302; ch. 20). This transformation was dangerous as well as liberating at least from a Tory point of view. It seemed to break the fabric of English life. And the rural Anglican vicars who populate Eliot's novels remind us that Anglican pastoral work, whatever its failings, had been, and perhaps even remained, crucial to English society's coherence and inherited sense of itself.

 The third mode of secularization involves religion's more informal displacement from society's center. More specifically, as trade and industrialization expanded, as London became an imperial world center, new nonreligious social and cultural zones proliferated. Under urbanization and commercialization, life could increasingly be lived without reference to religion; and culture and knowledge could increasingly be disseminated outside the Church. Furthermore, this mode of secularization was underpinned by what we can call vernacular mundaneity—the "timeless" business of routine everyday life whose calculations and values have no relation to religion or even to supernature. Eliot has an abiding interest in vernacular mundaneity as does the novel form as such, and she often emphasizes ordinary life's sheer secularity, perhaps most insistently in those passages of *The Mill in the Floss* focused on the world of Mrs. Tulliver's sisters. But, in her work, vernacular mundaneity is usually treated archly because of its sheer worldliness, its lack of spiritual intensity and aspiration. It signals triviality as well as an elemental secular vitality.

***

Secularism remains a topic of interest, and not just to academics, because its progress is still debated and resisted by many. For all that, most scholars today accept a version of what is often called the "disenchantment of the world" thesis. They agree that in the modern period, society and culture have become increasingly secularized, both institutionally and intellectually. Or, to put the case somewhat more carefully, they agree that, as Charles Taylor puts it, we in the West now live in, "a secular age," which Taylor himself rather disconsolately defines "as a move from a society where belief in God is unchallenged and indeed, unproblematic, to one in which it is understood to be one option among others, and frequently not the easiest to embrace" (Taylor 3). But if we are correct in regarding Eliot as involved in a secular desecularization of the secular, then this disenchantment of the world narrative is not quite adequate to her. After all, in her work the secular productively re-engages the non-secular, and vice-versa. She seems to be a secular and a non-secular writer simultaneously. This doubleness is not unusual in the history of modernity (today we find new versions of it under the rubric "post-secular") but rarely has it reached the degree of intellectual power and literary accomplishment that it did in Eliot. Why? What motivated this extraordinary literary conjunction of the secular with the non-secular? To answer this we need to explore in a little detail the context out of which her writing developed.

***

As is well known, the young Eliot experienced an intensely religious, Evangelical phase as an adolescent, but around the age of twenty-one through her Coventry friends Charles and Cara Bray, she met a group of secular, progressive intellectuals and lost her faith. The Brays were associated with radical politics (especially with Robert Owen's cooperative movement) as well as with intellectual irreligion, and had friendships and contacts across London's radical literary-intellectual avant-garde. After her father's death, Marian Evans moved to London and joined this avant-garde, working as a translator and magazine editor. This was when she formed the intellectual and spiritual beliefs that would motivate her across the next twenty-five or so years of her career as a novelist. Her narrative techniques and style changed as she became increasingly famous but her core beliefs and purposes were in place from the beginning.

The circles in which Eliot moved in the late 1840s and early 1850s were not, of course, committed to a single project. They were divided, politically, intellectually, and spiritually. But still, some general points about them can be made. Thinking first institutionally, this world was centered on a small number of publishers and magazines, none of which was closely associated with any organized intellectual or political formation. Of these, the most important was the weekly journal the *Leader,* which G. H. Lewes co-edited before he became Marian Evans's partner. The other important print venture was John Chapman's publishing house which owned the quarterly, the *Westminster Review*, and which employed Evans as an editor in 1852. Chapman also hosted a weekly salon for local and visiting radical intellectuals which formed the group's meeting place. Because of their secularism, many in the group were disbarred from working in the universities and professions, or for the Church or state—indeed they could be under some legal jeopardy under blasphemy laws. So they typically lived hand to mouth. Occasional acts of patronage were required to maintain opportunities for disseminating their views: for instance the *Leader* was at first underwritten by a rich Anglican parson; Charles Bray, who inherited a manufacturing business, funded Evan's first translation of Spinoza; the radical political fixer, Joseph Parkes, paid for the *Das Leben Jesu* translation. And so on. It was from this precarious entrepreneurial world that the various postulates of the New Reformation were formulated in a series of texts between 1849 and 1855, all published by Chapman. Of these the most notable were Francis Newman's *The Soul: Its Sorrows and Aspirations* (1849) and *Phases of Faith* (1850); Robert Mackay's *The Progress of the Intellect* (1850); Herbert Spencer's *Social Statics* (1851), and Leigh Hunt's *The Religion of the Heart: A Manual of Faith and Duty* (1853). The tone of these works' reception can be gauged from a statement in Lewes's review of Newman's *Phases of Faith* in the *Leader*: "No work in our experience has yet been published . . . so capable of making a path for the New Reformation to tread securely. . . . Modern spiritualism has reason to be deeply grateful to Mr. Newman" (qtd. in Francis 116).

Politically, the group was formed around Chartism's decline after 1848. Two of the *Leader*'s founders (G. J. Holyoake and Thornton Hunt) were members of the Chartist Executive. The Chartists had agitated for constitutional reform that would allow the (male) working class to participate in politics. Their movement had come adrift largely because it was not able to negotiate a compromise with the liberal bourgeoisie. It had also been unable to reconcile its Paineite "radical red" members to Christian socialism (Finn 156–57). And so it slowly drifted toward popular nationalism, in part as a result of enthusiasm for the Italian Risorgimento. In the aftermath of Chartism's failure, those middle-class radicals clustered around Chapman and *The Leader* concluded that social reform was not reducible to political reform, that is, to extending the franchise to workers. As a result, the radicalism which in Paineite Chartists like Richard Carlisle had been attached to a militant anti-Christianity was moderated. It was displaced by two disparate terms or concepts: growth or adaptation (key terms for Herbert Spencer) and aspiration (a key term for Francis Newman). The first of these—"growth"/"adaptation"—acceded to an understanding of historical processes as natural, determined, "necessary" in the philosophic jargon of the time. When applied to political theory and policy, this meant that reform would have to occur as it were "naturally" as a slow development from structures in place—namely, as "improvement." The second key term—"aspiration"—acceded to a sense that, while necessity ruled the material world and the material world governed the spiritual world, the future was, for us, contingent and open to will and imagination's shaping powers. When this in turn was applied to politics it meant that spiritual hope could itself become an agent of social change. Otherwise put, aspiration acknowledged the motivating political power of a hope (connected to love, pity, sympathy), which reached beyond the world that we know and live in. Under this way of thinking, social transformation would involve a new spirit of community able to trump both class warfare and the new forms of secular statism that were emerging among the Benthamite intellectuals known as the philosophical radicals and who had found some welcome in the post-1832 parliament and state bureaucracy. In sum, this new anti-statist, anti-individualist social reform, bound to growth and aspiration, entailed a general moral and spiritual renovation, which in turn required a realignment of radical secularism's relation to Christianity.

This realignment could be based on God's immanentization and naturalization. It drew on a theology for which God exists in this world not in any other, and is not knowable through revelation or through reason but indirectly through feeling and practical action in the world, and for which the substance of religious feeling—love, compassion, charity, pity, and so on—was largely derived from Protestantism. This immanent God, who exists in the world in movement not in representation, can be understood as belonging to an anti-theology for which nature's chain of determined or necessary event, its vital animation and futurity's infinite mystery, could all be relabeled as "God" by those who wished. The philosophy that underpinned this inverted theology was widespread in the period. The Anglican Church itself harbored versions of it in Sir William Hamilton and Henry Mansel's metaphysics. And in Europe it was being developed with incomparable sophistication by Ludwig Feuerbach, as well as by utopian social theorists like Auguste Comte. Indeed, as we have seen, Eliot's original point of entry into London's advanced progressive world was as a translator of such post-secular treatises.

It is not as though this communitarian spiritual reformist movement in England came out of nowhere. It can be usefully thought of as combining two separate lineages, one literary, the other laborist. The literary lineage was English Romanticism, both in its Wordsworthian and its Shelleyan forms. In his great lyrics, as well as in *The Prelude* (not coincidently first published in 1850), William Wordsworth articulated the poetic language in which immanent naturalist spirituality could be most powerfully expressed. And Shelley connected a transcendental metaphysics to a politics which was at once "atheist," spiritualist, and emancipatory. Shelley in particular was important to the politico-spiritual avant-garde of the early 1850s: it is no accident, for instance, that Lewes began his career by wishing to write the poet's biography (that was how he met Thornton Hunt with whom he edited *The Leader*), and his path-breaking 1841 essay on Shelley in the *Westminster Review* compared Shelley to Jesus, Luther, and Mahomet because his atheism was a "faith" attached to the politics of passionate "friends of liberty."

The laborist lineage was established by Robert Owen, the progenitor of English socialism and the cooperative movement. Owenism was everywhere in Eliot's milieu of the early 1850s. To take two instances: the Owenist leader George Jacob Holyoake was one of *The Leader's* founders (after finishing a prison sentence for blasphemy), and Eliot's best friend, Barbara Leigh Smith, ran an Owenist school. Indeed in 1851, under Holyoake's leadership, the Owenist movement reconfigured itself into a number of Secular Societies, as a result of which "secularism" under that name became a political movement.

As Karl Polyani has argued, Owenism marks a profound shift in modern politics and intellectual history. Owen was the first person to grasp the full implications of the theory that individuals are social products: that, as Eliot put it in *Felix Holt*, "there is no private life which has not been determined by a wider public life" (129). For he also grasped that what binds individuals together is not simply sympathy, as apostles of polite, individualistic, commercial society like Adam Smith and Hume had proposed, but material institutions which join people collectively in labor and production. It is for that reason that markets, competition, and possessive individualism pose a real threat to communal society. In Polyani's words, Owen argued that "only in co-operative commonwealth could all that is truly valuable in Christianity cease to be separated from man. . . . The post-Christian era of Western civilization had begun, in which the Gospels did not any more suffice, and yet remained the basis of our civilization" (Polanyi 258).

By the 1850s this program itself had become attached to spiritualism of the kind I have outlined. Thus, for instance, Holyoake's journal the *Reasoner*, the house journal of Secular Societies, routinely reprinted politico-spiritual texts from Chapman's various publications as well as from *The Leader*. Holyoake lent out Strauss's *The Life of Jesus* at two pence a time. And the journal often turned itself to the non-secular language of immanent spiritualism, which had been commandeered by the bourgeois radicals attached to Chapman and *The Leader*. In sum, Owenism's sense (shared in one form or other by European utopian movements like Comte's positivism) that Christianity remains the basis of a society to which, however, it is ethically and intellectually inadequate, grounds Eliot's literary effort to evoke Anglicanism's parochial functions in the interests of a non-Christian political spirituality.

***

Let us now turn more closely to Eliot's work. I will do so first by sketching a general account of how the spiritual politics that I have been describing is transformed when it is articulated by her as the narrator of novels which imagine the lives of individuals who live during the English confessional state's end-time, but do so inside generic conventions established by Samuel Richardson and Henry Fielding around 1750. And then I will offer a description of how Anglicanism in particular works in her fiction.

In Eliot's novels, the confessional state's collapse breaks England's moral and spiritual mooring. Neither the now wholly Erastian Church, nor the state, nor new zones of secularity, nor vernacular mundaneity, can recenter it. Certainly the education system cannot: let young Tom Tulliver's useless education under the Anglican parson Mr. Stelling, or Arthur Donnithorne's in *Adam Bede*, or Fred Vincy's no less useless education at Oxford in *Middlemarch* stand for this. And commonplace ideals of gentility and even "character" are too superficial, too merely worldly, to provide the sustenance and authority that society requires. In the novels, all this is often figured, quasi-allegorically, at the level of family. Eliot's fictions (like Jane Austen's) are remarkable for the rarity with which biological fathers and even more so mothers, are wise, or even emotionally and intellectually to be depended upon. (The Garths in *Middlemarch* are an exception to this: but they merely preach the religion of work and business.) It as if the secularization of society in which weak ideals and confusion proliferate, also destroys good parents. Nor does society provide extra-familial offices in which fully rewarding lives can be lived. In particular, what career is adequate to those who wish to join the new politico-spiritual project? That is the problem that confronts Will Ladislaw and Daniel Deronda. And what such office is available to upper-class women? None really: there is only unease, aspiration, or submission.

In this society, life is lived by individuals through daily experiences which are more formative than learned values or abstract knowledge. On rare occasions, as *Middlemarch* puts it, experiences can be imaginative and prophetic as well as actual (461; ch. 42). At such moments aspiration may become vivid: take Adam Bede's feelings in the Anglican Church during his father's burial service as an example. Or, on the other hand, dread may irrupt, as it does for Gwendolen Harleth in *Daniel Deronda* when she suddenly sees a painting of an "upturned dead face" behind a panel at Offendene (20; ch. 3).

Furthermore, and especially in the last two novels, because society is losing its coherence, individuals relate to one another somewhat indirectly, by *interpreting* one another, whether emotional or morally. These readings offer only a limited knowledge of other people since they rely on what is already familiar, and hence express the interpreter's own sensibility. Because we necessarily tend to read others in the light of our own desires and experiences, we tend to misread them as Lydgate (in the grip of sexuality and vernacular sexism) does Rosamund, or Gwendolen (under financial pressure) does Grandcourt. As the later, more pessimistic, novels imply, this distance between people becomes problematic to the degree that society does not provide shared or common purposes and values to its members.

For all that, however, an individual's life is not autonomous. It cannot be, since we all live our lives on terms that are not our own. At its very best, an individual life may be formed in inherited knowledge which "breathes a growing soul" into it (*Middlemarch* 225; ch. 20), that is, by means of a non-secular transmission of spiritual vision, especially from a charismatic guide to a neophyte or waverer. This happens, most notably, in Deronda's relation to Mordecai, but also more casually in cases like Janet Dempster's submission to the Reverend Tryan in "Janet's Repentance."

At any rate the value of an individual's life is in large part to be measured by its capacity to abnegate itself. It may do so productively on two levels, one of which is more available to the middle classes, the other to the upper classes. Validated middle-class individuals may dedicate themselves to work or business as Adam Bede and Mr. Garth do. But among the upper classes, they may have a "higher" commitment than this: they may aim to de-individuate themselves by attaching themselves to a hidden flow of spiritual sympathy and hope which gives access to, and enacts, the immanentized infinite. (For an early articulation of this theory, see *Scenes of Clerical Life* ["Mr. Gilfil's Love-Story" 159; ch. 19]). This model of self-abnegation reaches back to Christian mystical quietism in which the faithful, characteristically after experiencing suffering, empty themselves in order to let God enter their souls. Maggie Tulliver, Dorothea, and Daniel Deronda all read Judeo-Christian mystics who describe such a connection to the divine. But Eliot's is a secularized mysticism. Her most favored characters disappear not into God but into that historical flow in which spiritual and social reform will come together in the future, and they do so by concrete acts of altruism. As *Felix Holt's* narrator puts it, we are to aim for "a wider vision of past and present realities—a willing movement of a man's soul with the larger sweep of the world's forces—a movement toward a more assured end than the chances of a single life" (382; ch. 16). Importantly, such self-abnegation may enable an individual's life and experience to express a tradition, as Mordecai and Deronda's do. Yet in Eliot, valued traditions will never be completed, since in history the real constantly tests the ideal, and growth checks aspiration. Self-abnegation joins Eliot's characters to a lineage and a process, not to a (divine) fullness.

What limits and slows spiritual growth is reality. Likewise reality is what turns aspiration into mere fantasy and our interpretations of one another into misinterpretations. In Eliot, reality, then, is conceived not so much as the realm of objectivity but as what resists desire and will. It may exist as a limit encountered in the form of another's obdurate will: in the pressure that brutal characters like Robert Dempster, Harold Transome, Grandcourt, or even Casaubon, bring to bear on those around them. Their hardness leads those under their sway to depression and fantasy. Metaphysically, however, reality is understood as necessity, the iron chain of cause and effect that nothing can wish away. Socially, the real is largely encountered through poverty and money as by the Lydgates, the Tullivers, and Gwendolen Harleth, all of whom cannot live the larger lives they dream of because they don't have the funds to do so. By the same stroke, to refuse wealth—its inheritance or pursuit—as Esther in *Felix Holt* or Dorothea in *Middlemarch* do, is a sign that exceptional characters may sometimes reconcile aspiration to reality.

But there is an unforeseen, unaccommodated, self-referential twist in this understanding of the relation between aspiration, fantasy, and reality. After all, Eliot's novels' own politico-spiritual aspirations may lapse into fantasy, as becomes especially apparent in *Daniel Deronda* where Daniel's trip to Palestine as a somewhat Messianic figure with Zionist objectives (inspired both by the Jewish mystical heritage and Mazzini-style popular nationalism) breaks with realism. Here, at the end of Eliot's career, it becomes quite apparent that social reality cannot accommodate her generation's avant-garde politico-spiritual project.

What then of Anglicanism? In the novels, it is still embedded in English social reality as a long-established pastoral institution. Indeed, at least up until the 1830s it was where English spiritual aspiration and growth (albeit in its now intellectually exploded Christian form) is firmly bound to historical reality. This is not itself a nostalgic fantasy: Robert Lee's *Rural Society and the Anglican Clergy, 1815–1914* (2006) provides the most recent evidence for the argument that Anglicanism did indeed lose touch with rural life's deeper structures only as late as the early nineteenth century. And the Anglicanism of Eliot's novels is a complex, frictional institution. First of all, it is internally divided into its Evangelical and what we might call its Tory wings, and many of her novels are interested in describing and judging relations between these. Evangelicalism, of course, was a movement committed to revitalizing Christian faith. For it, faith became fixed to an overwhelmingly emotional sense that one had been saved, a moment of conversion which was thought only likely to last when motivated by suffering and remorse for past sins, as well as by continuing close inspection of the state of one's soul. This structure, which downplayed the Church as an ecclesiastical institution, organizes the lives of many of Eliot's most ethico-spiritually privileged characters in one form or other: most notably, Janet Dempster, Dorothea Brooke, and (more arguably) Gwendolen Harleth—although only the first of these is actually Evangelical. This is to say that Anglican Evangelicalism provides one model for the ethics of Eliot's de-secularizing of the secular.

No doubt for that very reason Evangelicalism is also under sustained critique in the novels. It is too exclusive and intolerant. By dividing society up into sinners and saved, it destroys social interconnections and totality. It is too individualistic and personal: because it is so focused on individual salvation, it encourages people to read their lives providentially and, especially, to read their material success as signs of grace, as Bulstrode in *Middlemarch* does for instance. Then too its emphasis on conversion breaks with Eliot's insistence on growth. And lastly, despite its emphasis on faith, it in fact tends to reduce spiritual energy to conformity, and, in so doing, as Bulstrode's career again demonstrates, it can be used as an instrument of power, to foster patronage and support networks against the larger social interest.

Evangelicalism's opponent within Anglicanism—Tory Anglicanism—is marked most of all by its connection with upper-class gentility. In fact, Eliot's understanding of it is a more radical version of the innovative account of recent Church history put forward by Mark Pattison (an old *The Leader* colleague) in his contribution to the controversial collection, *Essays and Reviews* (1860). In "The Tendencies of Religious Thought, 1688–1750," Pattison argued that in resisting both Catholic orthodoxy and dissenting enthusiasm, eighteenth-century Anglicanism turned to polite commonsense for support. Thus it became increasingly genteel and aristocratic. And, as Eliot's novels see it, this cut the Church off both from renovating spiritual energies and from advanced philosophical thought. Anglicanism's grasp on philological and philosophical enlightenment was so weakened that it lost the means to ground the church in truth. Mr. Sherlock's cowardly running away from a debate on ecclesiology with Rufus Lyon in *Felix Holt* can stand as an emblem of this. In broader terms, in *Middlemarch,* the genial, *fait néant,* aristocratic rector, Cadwallader, as well as Casaubon with his obsolete scholarship, represents Pattison's thesis in action as late as the 1830s. Fred Vincy is right to prefer farm management to the Church as a career. And certainly the Church provides no office for those who would join the New Reformation.

Nonetheless, the novels basically support Tory Anglicanism. Non-evangelical clergyman like Mr. Gilfil in *Scenes of Clerical Life,* Mr. Irwine in *Adam Bede*, Dr. Kenn in *The Mill and the Floss* and Mr. Farebrother in *Middlemarch* are just about the only upper-class characters who live useful lives, helping and encouraging others. That is because they live at the dynamic centre of the only unified, coherent, "organic" society that exists within recent English historical memory—namely, the confessional state's rural parish. Religious beliefs are all but irrelevant to this: most of Eliot's best clergymen barely have them. What matters instead is how a vicar's various offices, capacities, and responsibilities come together—their governmental role (e.g. as magistrates); their charge of the rituals of life passage as ordained ministers (baptism, marriage, burial); their private acts of charity; their intimate knowledge of their parishioners; their living out the daily rhythms of rural life; their relative ease at crossing class hierarchies; their casuistical judgments of particular moral situations and difficulties; their shrewd skepticism with regard to theory and enthusiasm. The ideal parson combines all these, and draws them into a mutually supportive instrument of pastoral care and moral acuity. Take Mr. Farebrother, for instance, who, hard up, dissolutely plays whist and billiards for petty cash, but who is the only person who can offer real emotional support and provide sound judgment to Fred Vincy (his love rival), to Lydgate, and even to Dorothea after she gives him Casaubon's living. That is just because of his disabused but loving and practical understanding of life in the parish, as well as his independence from particular party interest—unlike his Evangelical rival, Mr. Tyke.

The novels are aware that the internally divided, over-gentrified Anglican Church rarely delivers on its ethical capacities. Mr. Irwine, for instance, is one of Eliot's most effective and intelligent clergymen, but even he cannot influence Arthur so as to prevent Hetty's tragedy, just as he does not reach those who come to hear Dinah Morris's Methodist preaching either. It is also the case that, whatever its historical grounding, Eliot's representation of the early nineteenth-century parish is rose-tinted. She underplays the period's agricultural immiseration, and fails in particular to mention the Swing riots, the organized violence that rural laborers organized in the 1830s, partly against the tithe system, which paid for the Anglican Church. What is important to her is that the Anglican rural parish is not just the favored setting of the English novel lineage in which she wrote, but the basis, grounded in the real, from which growth and adaptation toward a more universal and just society (adequate to her novel's literary wisdom) might begin. Urban, commercial life offered no such promise.

Historically, Eliot's localized project of de-secularizing liberal-democratic secularity would be displaced by two main rivals. The first, already implicit in Owenism and today almost exhausted, was socialism, usually in its Marxist forms. The second was the culture idea as developed mainly by Matthew Arnold: the idea that "culture," considered as an ethic informed by a selected aesthetic heritage, might provide the basis of a modern organic society through the state-managed education system. That idea, of course, underpinned the literary humanities in the period of their greatest confidence, and so was to help transmit Eliot's novels into the future. But she herself did not share Arnold's hopes for culture, even if its rudiments do appear in her work. Will Ladislaw, who, tellingly, was educated at Rugby like Arnold, goes through a culture phase before giving it up for a political career as a radical. (A fate we can read, in context, as faintly tragic.) Deronda, who seems ripe for Arnoldianism, chooses (fantastically) mysticism and nation-building instead.

Given the account of Eliot's project presented here, it is also fair to say that she held back from the culture idea because it was both too secular and not secular enough. It was too secular in that it abandoned the notion that an immanent divine Presence might itself be at work in ambitious social aspirations and actions. It was not secular enough because it failed to ground itself in what was still society's most solid institution—the established Church—and placed its hope instead in the merely secular centralized, politicized state and/or private interests. But of course the social movement whose object was to desecularize secularity that she joined as a young woman survives now almost nowhere except in her novels, that is, in a literary form maintained by the academic humanities largely in memory of the culture idea.

References

Eliot, George. *Adam Bede*. Ed. Carol A. Martin. Oxford: Oxford UP, 2008.

Eliot, George. *Daniel Deronda*. Ed. Graham Handley. Oxford: Oxford UP, 2009.

Eliot, George. *Essays of George Eliot*. Ed. Thomas Pinney. New York: Columbia UP, 1963.

Eliot, George. *Felix Holt*. Ed. Peter Coveney. London: Penguin, 1972.

Eliot, George. *Middlemarch*. Ed. W. J. Harvey. London: Penguin, 1965.

Eliot, George. *Scenes of Clerical Life*. Ed. Thomas Noble. Oxford: Oxford UP. 2009.

Finn, Margot C. *After Chartism: Class and Nation in English Radical Politics 1848–1874*. Cambridge: Cambridge UP, 2004.

Francis, Mark. *Herbert Spencer and the Invention of Modern Life*. Ithaca: Cornell UP, 2007.

Haight, Gordon S. *George Eliot: A Biography*. Oxford: Oxford UP, 1968.

Lee, Robert. *Rural Society and the Anglican Clergy, 1815–1914*. Woodbridge: Boydell, 2006.

Lewes, George Henry. "Percy Bysshe Shelley." *The Westminster Review* 35 (1841): 30344.

Polanyi, Karl. *The Great Transformation: The Political and Economic Origins of Our Times*. New York: Beacon, 1957.

Stedman Jones, Gareth. "Religion and the Origins of Socialism." *Religion and the Political Imagination*. Eds. Ira Katznelson and Gareth Stedman Jones. Cambridge: Cambridge UP, 2010. 171–89.

Taylor, Charles. *A Secular Age*. Cambridge: Harvard UP, 2007.

31
Living Theory: Personality and Doctrine in Eliot

Amanda Anderson

Throughout George Eliot's writings a persistent concern is registered over the distortions and even moral dangers of abstract, schematic, or doctrinaire thinking. In "The Natural History of German Life," which bears the marks of her increasing attention to realist fiction as a vehicle for rendering life's complexity, Eliot critiques forms of abstraction and objective social science, promoting in their stead ethnographic sociology and aesthetic realism, both of which are seen to better capture the lived experience of ordinary people. Ten years later, in a letter to Frederic Harrison in August of 1866, she characterizes her work as "the severe effort of trying to make certain ideas thoroughly incarnate, as if they had revealed themselves to me first in the flesh and not in the spirit." She continues, "I think aesthetic teaching is the highest of all teaching because it deals with life in its highest complexity. But if it ceases to be purely aesthetic—if it lapses anywhere from the picture to the diagram—it becomes the most offensive of all teaching" (*Letters* 4:300).

A number of well-known passages from the novels underscore the negative consequences of abstraction. Chapter 17 of *Adam Bede*, which famously contains an interlude elaborating aesthetic views similar to those put forth in "The Natural History of German Life," concludes with a conversation between the narrator and Adam Bede ("in his old age") about the limited value of "doctrines and notions," and the greater importance of feelings, practical knowledge, and human fellowship (198, 200; ch. 17). The passage about "men of maxims" in *The Mill on the Floss* underscores that "moral judgments must remain false and hollow, unless they are checked and enlightened by a perpetual reference to the special circumstances that mark the individual

A Companion to George Eliot, First Edition. Edited by Amanda Anderson and Harry E. Shaw.
© 2013 John Wiley & Sons, Ltd. Published 2016 by John Wiley & Sons, Ltd.

lot" (517; bk. 7, ch. 2). The effects here are not simply on soundness of judgment, but on the moral development of the individual: "to lace ourselves up in formulas of that sort is to repress all the divine promptings and inspirations that spring from growing insight and sympathy" (518; bk. 7, ch. 2). Similarly, *Middlemarch* contains a significant passage, in the context of Bulstrode's fall, which insists, "There is no general doctrine which is not capable of eating out our morality if unchecked by the deep-seated habit of direct fellow-feeling with individual fellow-men." (619; ch. 61).

Perhaps Eliot felt the dangers of abstract or general thinking so keenly because of her own strong philosophical inclinations, her interest in theories that could help her to make sense of the forms of life she wished to render in their full complexity. The philosophical frameworks that particularly compelled Eliot included the moral law of consequences (derived largely from Charles Bray's *The Philosophy of Necessity*), evolutionary understandings of individual and societal development (drawn from Auguste Comte), and, not least, the Feuerbachian critique of Christianity. Eliot was therefore in no sense anti-theoretical. Rather, she was concerned with the profound challenges of creating a novelistic world expressive of her philosophical views or, as she puts it in the letter to Harrison, making ideas incarnate. But to characterize her project in this way does not fully capture the situation, since Eliot was interested not only in illustrating theories through art, but in capturing the existential challenges of a morally committed existence, which is to say, the challenges of *living* theory. Beyond her critique of undesirable forms of theory and abstraction, then, stands a far more demanding attempt to represent her moral-philosophical views as a consciously enacted form of life. This is where we see the markings of a "severe effort," to recur once more to the letter to Harrison. Across the novels, a number of individual characters represent not simply forms of moral exemplarity but rather a significant moral struggle to enact ideals, one punctuated by errors or lapses. In certain instances, most dramatically in *The Mill on the Floss*, Eliot emphasizes the outright failure of these attempts. And even where we see clear indications of redemptive modes of thinking and acting, Eliot often insists upon tragic belatedness or compromised results. These darker emphases have to do precisely with her own apprehension of the gap between life and doctrine.

My analysis will focus on the novels' ways of registering this difficulty, as well as emerging attempts to mitigate or address it. At the center of Eliot's thinking on these issues, I will suggest, is a reworking of Feuerbach in a fictional realist context, with special attention to the force of personality in mediating belief. In *The Essence of Christianity*, which Eliot translated, Feuerbach stresses the psychological dimensions of religious belief, including the need for a personal God (as demonstrated through the Christian Incarnation). In the novels, Eliot adapts this theory to explore the ways in which *other people* can come to mediate this need, as in the case of charismatic religious visionaries, or serve it outright, as exemplary moral personalities within a secular framework. More generally, Eliot is interested in shifting the ground of moral thinking from religious doctrine and divine being to human aspiration and intersubjective inspiration. The existential problematic of living theory becomes, in Eliot's oeuvre, a broadly secularizing project that includes conscious awareness of personality as enchantment.

The account of Eliot offered here revisits a longstanding dissatisfaction with ideal-ized characters in Eliot's novels, and re-describes the dynamic in which Eliot is seen to lose distance from certain of her moral exemplars, a criticism advanced most influ-entially by F. R. Leavis in *The Great Tradition*. To begin with, Eliot's investment in exemplary personality is best understood not as a personal idiosyncrasy but rather as part of a broader historical focus on character and charisma as forms of moral energy in the post-sacred age. Character was for the nineteenth century a site of charged meaning-giving force, emerging as a value-laden secular concept in the face of the diminishment or demystification of religious frameworks of moral orientation (Ander-son). The example of Eliot is somewhat special, however, insofar as she does not merely reflect this tendency but also actively diagnoses it in her treatment of the psychology and sociology of enchantment across the sacred/secular continuum. Beyond her focus on the internal struggles of individual characters, and the specific dramas of moral consciousness they present, Eliot uses a range of dyadic character relations to explore the deeply personalized way in which actors engage the tension between theory and practice. As the narrator writes of Deronda's effect on the erring Gwendolen, "It is one of the secrets in that change of mental poise which has been fitly named conversion, that to many among us neither heaven nor earth has any revelation till some personality touches theirs with a peculiar influence, subduing them into recep-tiveness" (430; ch. 35). Apart from the case of Deronda and Gwendolen, there are numerous situations in which exemplary moral personalities—Dinah, Adam Bede, Romola, Felix Holt, Dorothea—positively affect the lives of more mixed and erring characters. The point about the need for incarnate teaching, made so explicitly in the quote from *Daniel Deronda*, animates much of the larger oeuvre in the portrayal of inspirational moral exemplars. Moreover, as her novel-writing career progresses Eliot becomes increasingly interested in staging dynamic relations between exemplary personalities (heroic protagonists) and charismatic visionaries who still remain within religious frameworks of belief (the key examples here are Romola/Savonarola and Deronda/Mordecai). As I will suggest, these relationships dramatize with lucidity the psychological and existential components involved in living a life that is both deeply examined and morally felt.

The analysis pursued here will pay close attention to forms of characterization in Eliot, as well as to the larger character system at play in the works, including the persistence of dyadic tutelary relations. But the tension between theory and existence, or doctrine and personality, plays out in relation to the narrative voice as well, espe-cially as it departs from or veers toward the voice of specific characters. Insofar as the narrative voice remains at a remove from the conditions of embodied and embedded existence, it can give untroubled expression to some of the theories animating the presentation, but when the gap between the narrator's own philosophical doctrines and the conditions of existence facing the characters is lit up, then the particular struggles animating Eliot's project are also exposed.

It is important to situate the analysis that follows in relation to existing criticism of Eliot. Many readings of Eliot, especially over the past several decades, have identified her ideals of moral development and of sympathy as either ideologically suspect, insofar as they displace politics with ethics, or internally nonviable, because undermined by egotism, power, or indeterminacy (see Kucich; Cottom; Cvetkovich; Miller). In analyzing Eliot's keen awareness of the difficulty of the moral life, this essay does not aim to contribute to a sense that Eliot's project is suspect or productively undermined in its core aims. Eliot's own internal divisions and doubts are best understood as a feature of her ongoing, considered struggle with the very project of imagining her philosophical views as a way of life, a struggle that arguably shapes her realism. One central difficulty that Eliot emphasized, as will be seen, has to do with the limits of human control, including the impossibility of effectively foreseeing consequences or redressing harms that have already occurred. There are also extravagant burdens of consciousness associated with moral vigilance or a doctrine-driven life. Moreover, as Eliot's novels begin increasingly to stress the importance of reflective endorsement, or conscious avowal of belief, we begin to see a strain introduced precisely by the forms of sociological and psychological knowledge that the higher criticism, and Feuerbach's psychology in particular, induce (for a related discussion, see Myers 128–32). Specifically, an informing awareness of the psychological pull of charisma and moral personality leads to the contextualization, and even deflation, of a force that is elsewhere more immediately valorized as the expression of an immanently felt need. The fact that Eliot's texts can at once enact and expose what we might call the "natural attitude" diagnosed by Feuerbach thus helps to refute the idea that Eliot fails to gain distance from her idealized characters: the problem is a genuine one, that is to say, and the aesthetic achievement arguably profound rather than confused.

Eliot's registration of the limits of human control have of course drawn significant attention from critics interested in tracing the relation between her determinism and her moral vision. Since this element of her thought subtends the other concerns that will be explored here, it is important to rehearse them. Her conception of subtle accretions of habit and determining actions often results in diminished claims for the powers of deliberate intention, which in moments of crisis often cannot supersede the accumulated effects of earlier choices or the developing bias of character. There is nothing blunt about Eliot's determinism, and yet its fine-grained attention to elements internal and external, conscious and unconscious, produces in some ways a more constricting world, best captured in the negative web imagery (or "hampering threadlike pressures") Eliot favors than in any billiard ball cause-and-effect-model (*Middlemarch* 180; ch. 18). There are forms of moral heroism keyed to this view of the world: most centrally, a form of watchfulness born of conscious awareness (and experience) of the law of consequences (G. Levine). But of course Eliot's view of the world extends beyond a no-harm principle: her secular humanism stresses the importance of sympathy, fellowship, and moral assistance, all of them rendered most poignant when extended to the erring or the morally stunted. Eliot takes pains to highlight, more generally, the ways in which individuals can undergo a development from blind egotism to forms of sympathy and insight. And given her profound investment in pre-reflective forms of rootedness and belonging—in those primary affections and communities which ground our moral nature—she also highlights the exceptionalism of those who manage, against the pull of outside forces and desires, to affirm the importance of early ties (Maggie Tulliver and Mary Garth are two very different instances of this form of moral exemplarity, the former post-lapsarian, the latter non-lapsarian).

None of these forms of endorsed moral orientation is easy to achieve, and Eliot constantly reminds her readers of the forces and conditions struggling individuals are up against. The precise difficulties involved, as well as Eliot's response to them, can be traced in part through the developing forms of characterization in the novels. In the relatively early *Adam Bede*, for example, the eponymous hero not only advocates but seems to personify the law of consequences, serving as an unyielding mouthpiece for the harshest expression of the moral law. However great his rectitude, he has a shadow-casting implacability about him, and the narrator reveals him to be too harsh in his expectation that everyone should have always already internalized the law of consequences. Even though there is justification for his early wisdom (he has watched the moral decline of his father), he is a contradictory emblem of moral rectitude: his very insistence on, and submission to, the law of consequences means that he is unable to sympathize with those who err, and thus, unable to truly represent the Eliotic moral ideal. The embodiment of moral law here fundamentally disables the possibility of a refined moral response to human limits.

Adam does come to realize that he has been too harsh, and this is one of the powerful moral lessons given expression in the novel. We are therefore invited to notice the moral importance of an unyielding law, but cautioned against adopting its harshness as a feature of our personality. It must be tempered by charity for human weakness. And yet there is a further twist to the lesson that Adam learns, one that reveals the fundamentally tragic form of learning that even the most sensitive moral actors are condemned to: it is necessarily post-hoc. As Adam himself says, in a strikingly bleak formulation, "Perhaps nothing 'ud be a lesson to us if it didn't come too late" (220; ch. 18). The desperate accompaniment to such belatedness is dread, as we learn from the far more psychologically developed moral drama in *Daniel Deronda*: "Take your fear as a safeguard," says Deronda to Gwendolen. "It is like quickness of hearing. It may make consequences passionately present to you. Try to take hold of your sensibility, and use it as if it were a faculty, like vision" (452; ch. 36). A haunting temporal disconnection between moral certainty and blind existence is revealed in this strained exhortation to Gwendolen to cultivate an affective, corporeal intellection. Fundamentally, tragic regret and anticipatory dread are the living consequences of trying to avow the law of consequences, unless you are lucky enough to be the narrator. It is not a simple matter of a lesson to be learned, but rather a condition to be persistently, wakefully endured.

In light of the characterization of Adam, it is worth pondering the fact that *Adam Bede* also contains another highly favored character, Mr. Irwine, who is praised pre-

cisely for being nondoctrinal, even though he is a rector. Mr. Irwine embodies an
expansive sympathetic fellowship that affects others like benign nature: repeatedly
associated with radiance and freshness, he is said to harmonize extremely well with
the landscape, even if he is lax about doctrine and the souls of his parishioners. He
manages to wear his moral wisdom lightly, so lightly, in fact, that one doesn't know
whether the knowledge is reflective or intuitive. "If I were closely questioned," the
narrator says, "I should be obliged to confess that he felt no serious alarms about
the souls of his parishioners. . . . If he had been in the habit of speaking theoretically,
he would perhaps have said that the only healthy form religion could take in such
minds was that of certain dim but strong emotions, suffusing themselves as a hallow-
ing influence over the family affections and neighborly duties" (76; ch. 5). This
passage distances itself from theoretical knowledge twice over, by making it something that doesn't flow glibly from the tongue of the rector ("If he had been in the
habit of speaking theoretically") nor, presumably, from the narrator, who is suggesting
the pearl has been extracted under pressure ("If I were closely questioned"). And
then the knowledge shared is about how very limited the positive powers of doctrine
truly are. Of course both the narrator and the rector are able to dispense wisdom
about deeds and consequences, but the rector's nondoctrinal tendencies here honor-
ifically align him with life and nature, which are in turn associated with benign
fellowship.

The fact that the rector is constructed so that he can sound at times as though he
is very much in the habit of speaking theoretically and yet also—in key descriptive
moments—represent an intuitive ethical responsiveness and easy fellowship is not
merely a result of Eliot's desire to differentiate between a practical morality responsive
to living communities and a doctrinal approach that is imposed bluntly. It is also, I
would suggest, the symptom of a more general concern about the distinctly alienating
effects of theoretical language. Interestingly, when Arthur visits Mr. Irwine intending
to confess his susceptibility to Hetty, the turn to philosophical discussion (Mr. Irwine
speaks a version of the narratorial rhetoric about character, deeds, and consequences)
is precisely what effects Arthur's decisive turn away from confession. When Mr. Irwine
asks, "But I never knew you so inclined for moral discussion, Arthur? Is it some danger
of your own that you are considering in this philosophical, general way?," Arthur
shrinks from confessing, concerned that somehow the content of the confession would
carry more weight because the conversation is so serious in tone and substance (188;
ch. 16). Without going the length of saying philosophy is to blame here, one can note
the apparent gulf between psychologically delicate moral situations and those forms
of theorizing that would seem to capture the dangers at play. The novel here shows
how hard it is to make even a nuanced moral philosophy meet or appropriately guide
real-life situations. This is especially evident in a moment like this, where the narrator's voice and perspective seem to enter that of a character within the story.

The tellingly uneven relation of personality to doctrine, in the case of Adam and
the Rector, is accompanied by a series of moments, in the earlier novels, in which
Eliot seems to suggest an effective mediation of *written* doctrine by living voice or

personality. In this transmutation of the Christian form of the Gospel, charismatic religious personality is central. In *The Mill on the Floss*, for example, within the passage describing Maggie's transformative reading of Thomas à Kempis, we see a marked instance of living doctrine, conceived as a direct transmission, soul to soul, of the importance of sorrow and renunciation. "[Maggie] knew nothing of doctrines and systems—of mysticism or quietism: but this voice out of the far-off middle ages, was the direct communication of a human's soul's belief and experience, and came to Maggie as an unquestioned message" (384; bk. 4, ch. 3). An interesting scene in *Adam Bede* reflects a similar privileging of individuating presence: Adam reads a doctrine-suffused letter written from the Methodist Dinah to his brother Seth, remarking that he doesn't know what he would have thought if he had read the letter but never seen the writer. He then states, "But she's one as makes everything seem right she says and does" (359; ch. 30).

A conception of living doctrine informs Eliot's own investments in the possible effects of narratorial personality on the reader. Philip's powerful letter to Maggie at the end of *The Mill on the Floss* begins with a direct intersubjective appeal ("Maggie, I believe in you") but ends by giving voice to the narratorial wisdom: "The new life I have found in caring for your joy and sorrow more than for what is directly my own, has transformed the spirit of rebellious murmuring into that willing endurance which is the birth of strong sympathy"—so that that the novel itself suddenly feels like a personal letter to the reader (523; bk. 7, ch. 3). While many critics have emphasized Eliot's use of tutelary scenes of sympathetic fellowship (Dinah and Hetty, Dorothea and Rosamond, Maggie and Lucy, Deronda and Gwendolen), there is also a repeated impulse to transfer the power of living sympathy to the interaction between text and reader. These moments illuminate a motivating anxiety not only, as it might at first glance appear, about the potential distance between life and fiction, but also about the gap between character and doctrine.

The Mill on the Floss gives the strongest expression to Eliot's doubts about the successful living out of doctrine. A serious challenge to the doctrine of moral development, it insists on a seemingly endless cycle of lapse and regret, one halted only through the apocalypse of its ending. The novel foregrounds in all manner of ways the impulse to flee the demands of conscious moral life, from the daydreaming of the narrator in the opening chapter, to the lapses in consciousness of Mr. Tulliver after his fall, to the tendency of Maggie to forget where she is, to daydream, to drift without any awareness that she is drifting. In Maggie's case, the problem of a viable translation of doctrine into existence is extreme. After her fall, the novel seems to give precedence to the corrective action of renunciation and regret, and its accompanying reaffirmation of stronger duties and earlier ties. But there remains a sense that such a position will always be at war with the conditions of life. As Maggie says to Stephen, after she has decided against yielding to him,

> If we—if I had been better, nobler—those claims would have been so strongly present
> with me, I should have felt them pressing on my heart continually, just as they do now

in the moments when my conscience is awake—that the opposite feeling would never have grown in me, as it has done—it would have been quenched at once—I should have prayed for help so earnestly—I should have rushed away, as we rush from hideous danger. (496; bk. 6, ch. 14)

What is striking here is the conception of constant moral wakefulness, which might be seen to give a painful embodiment to the moral ideal of sympathy. To live the doctrines that animate Eliot's narrative translates here into a form of strained, hypersensitive consciousness—as in Deronda's advice to Gwendolen to try to turn her moral fear into a faculty like vision or hearing—one best eluded by the obliteration of consciousness through sleep, drifting, or death. It is no surprise, in view of passages such as this, that Eliot interrupted the composition of *The Mill on the Floss* to compose her gothic tale, "The Lifted Veil," which represents sympathetic insight as a nightmarish capacity to hear the thoughts of others and to foresee one's own death.

It is especially interesting to note the way the burden of acute moral consciousness is gendered, as in the famous passage invoking Hector and Hecuba:

While Maggie's life-struggles had lain almost entirely within her own soul, one shadowy army fighting another, and the slain shadows forever rising again, Tom was engaged in a dustier, noisier warfare, grappling with more substantial obstacles, and gaining more definite conquests. So it has been since the days of Hecuba, and of Hector, Tamer of horses: inside the gates, women with streaming hair and uplifted hands offering prayers, watching the world's combat from afar, filling their long, empty days with memories and fears: outside the men in fierce struggle with things divine and human, quenching memory in the stronger light of purpose, losing the sense of dread and even of wounds in the hurrying ardour of action. (320; bk. 5, ch. 2)

In the conceptual economy of this novel, men get the clarity of action and of reductive maxims. In aesthetic and moral terms, what men are allotted is primitive, but it is also cast as a less punishing form of consciousness. Throughout the novel, Maggie oscillates between attenuated consciousness (yielding, drifting) and then a nightmarish awakening to the implications of her lapse.

The Mill on the Floss is revelatory of the darker implications of moral consciousness in Eliot. Difficulties beset not only the actor caught up in the conflicting pull between surging personal desires and longstanding emotional ties, but also the more detached form of consciousness associated with the narratorial perspective itself. If Maggie reveals a morally committed life to be a kind of torture, that is, Philip reveals that a morally discriminating judgment, such as an omniscient narrator needs, is itself problematic to live. Neil Hertz has written compellingly of a certain transfer within *The Mill on the Floss* between the narrator and the characters, and points to the interesting fact that the narrator, like Mr. Tulliver within the novel, dozes off. But whereas Hertz sees the narrator as borrowing authority from the characters in what is ultimately a drama of authorship based on anxieties about writing, contingency, and differentiation, such transfers might be better understood as an acute rendering of the existential challenge of actually living the narratorial perspective. The dozing narrator at the beginning of *The Mill on the Floss* is both a symptom of, and compensation for, the sharper problems of staying morally awake on the plane of lived existence.

We can pursue this claim by more closely examining the trajectory of Philip Wakem, who by the end of the novel, as the example of his letter attests, functions as a kind of narrator surrogate, someone within the novel who is able to dispense the wisdom of the novel. One might imagine that this is meant to be seen as a form of moral growth, grounded on an ability to understand Maggie's character—specifically, the fact that she can be at once sincere but self-deceived or self-divided. The moral sophistication and understanding required to comprehend this without condemning Maggie for running off with Stephen Guest is evidenced in Philip's letter, when he refers to "that partial, divided action of our nature which makes half the tragedy of the human lot" (522; bk. 7, ch. 3). Philip has some distance to travel before he arrives at this more capacious view; indeed, his very ability to understand Maggie's complexity is initially motivated, and compromised, by the force of his own desire. After the unsettling encounter with her at the bazaar, we read: "Philip felt that he ought to have been thoroughly happy in that answer of hers: she was as open and as transparent as a rock pool. Why was he not thoroughly happy? Jealousy is never satisfied with anything short of an omniscience that would detect that subtlest fold of the heart" (463; bk. 6, ch. 10).

And yet, there remains a problem, at once epistemological and moral, with the ostensibly more forgiving form of omniscience that Philip ultimately achieves, and that Dr. Kenn models as well. Toward the end of the novel, when defending Maggie— or rather, Dr. Kenn's deep understanding of Maggie—against the hasty judgment of others, the narrator writes: "The casuists have become a by-word of reproach; but their perverted spirit of minute discrimination was the shadow of a truth to which eyes and ears are often fatally sealed: the truth, that moral judgments must remain false and hollow, unless they are checked and enlightened by a perpetual reference to the special circumstances that mark the individual lot" (517; bk. 7, ch. 2). This moral principle is offered in some sense as the beginning of a contrast to the "men of maxims," who are described and critiqued directly afterwards. But what is of particular interest here is Eliot's linking of moral omniscience to a practice not so much of practical or relative judgment but of infinite moral and intellectual discrimination. And again, as with the Maggie's torturing form of constant moral wakefulness, we have here a sense of a bad infinite in the notion of "perpetual reference." This is a disabling condition, as Eliot takes pains to demonstrate in her portrayal of the condition that Daniel Deronda must overcome in his aimless youth: he is so alive to sympathy that all capacity for action or partiality is neutralized. Things are more chilling in *The Mill on the Floss*, insofar as this position is the endpoint for Philip Wakem, and he is left not only "enlightened," but cloistered.

Eliot does not rest with the bleakness of view that marks *The Mill on the Floss*, though it is important to recognize that its driving fears importantly subtend her work, even as she moves toward more hopeful scenarios. As I suggested at the begin-

ning of the essay, Eliot's novels offer more than one response to the pressures of the
examined life, and I now want to turn to Eliot's use of dyadic relations to restage
the problem of incarnate doctrine. It is certainly the case that the greatest forms of
moral heroism in Eliot are reserved for those who attempt reflectively to affirm the
modes of embedded existence that serve as the ground of moral development. But
there is another type of character in Eliot that plays a crucial role in answering to the
punishing constraints of moral awareness: the charismatic visionary protagonists,
specifically Savonarola in *Romola* and Mordecai in *Daniel Deronda*. These characters
live a life so dedicated to doctrine that they seem not quite of this world, and they
are associated with animating forms of belief that are asserted to be themselves capable
of determining consequences. They thus elude the more naturalistic law of consequences in their visionary capacity to alter states of affairs through the power of their
belief and visions. There is always the danger that visionary figures will fall into the
hubris of thinking they can transcend the limits laid down by scientific and moral
law; but they are also seen as vital to the progress of moral ideals and to the expression of that which has not yet, and perhaps never can be, actualized.

Unlike Adam Bede, who too rigidly represents—or personifies—the law of consequences, and thus despite his morally privileged place in the novel is closer to a figure
like Tom Tulliver than to Dorothea, the charismatic figures represent a life spiritual-
ized by doctrine. But in doing so they also must in some sense separate themselves
from ordinary existence, and deny themselves the pleasures of private and family life.
"In brilliant Ferrara, seventeen years before," the narrator writes of Savonarola, "the
contradiction between mens' lives and their professed beliefs had pressed upon him
with a force that had been enough to destroy his appetite for the world, and at the
age of twenty-three had driven him to the cloister" (209; ch. 21). Dinah, an early
version of the charismatic, has to give up her preaching when she yields to her all-
too-human love for Adam.

Eliot's portrayal of these characters typically shifts back and forth between admiration, often routed through the consciousness of the heroic protagonists, and skepticism
or sociological diagnosis. In this, her presentation plays out Feuerbachian elements:
inhabiting the projection of a human ideal, and then deflating it through analysis
(exposing not only the all-too-human character of the idealized figure, but also the
projective idealizations of the heroic protagonist). It is worth noting, moreover, that
even while the heroic protagonists of Eliot's fiction are typically drawn to these visionary figures, their attitude toward them is fundamentally a disenchanted one, even as
they display ongoing impulses to idealize. The heroic protagonists have themselves
often been the subject of exasperated critique: they are overly idealized, the criticism
asserts, or Eliot is too identified with their idealizing tendencies. But the crucial thing
to recognize is that these characters have a post-Feuerbachian relation to the visionary
protagonist figures, not disenchanted in the sense of disillusioned, but rather understood as an effort of belief, as an aspiration in the midst of an alert skepticism. And
this is precisely where a more interesting Eliotic resolution begins to take place, one
that manages to avoid both the tragic and casuistic forms evident elsewhere. In the

relation between the prophetic figures and the striving protagonists, we see a relation that must be described in terms of a long argument, one that is typically re-figured, moreover, in terms of a hermeneutic scene of reading.

Thus, there is a fundamental shift in the terms through which Eliot presents the central problem of living doctrine. What seems to break the various impasses associated with unmediated embodiment of doctrine, either in its visionary or hyper-vigilant forms, is the move to understand, and enter in a relation with, a figure who represents a form of extreme embodiment. Such figures thereby become the object of a form of careful devotion and study that does not preclude interrogation and challenge. We see this powerfully in evidence in *Romola*, which works through the whole problematic with extraordinary subtlety. When at the cloister Romola hears from her brother Dino's lips the harsh prophecy about her proposed marriage, she rejects the shadowy world he inhabits, and the narrator makes clear that Dino has no access to the fuller understanding of life, motive, action, and conscience that living fellowship and everyday familial exchange would provide. What is implied here is not only that true knowledge relies on sympathetic fellowship, but that the novel itself, drawing on such forms of understanding, can provide the fuller forms of wisdom that can comprehend and predict character and action (C. Levine).

And yet, even as Romola rejects Dino's prophetic mode and the threat to trusting openness that it carries, she is still drawn, in the wake of her inward debate over his warning, to the project of understanding, in their full embeddedness, lives that are dedicated to vision, mysticism, martyrdom, and prophecy. She is interested in such lives, even as she judges them to distort the complexity of human existence and to deny the primacy of human fellowship. Indeed, in her conversation with Tito about Dino's prophecy, she speaks "meditatively" of the "life of men possessed with fervid beliefs that seem like madness to their fellow beings," adding that Savonarola's voice "seems to have penetrated me with a sense that there is some truth in what moves them: some truth of which I know nothing" (176; ch. 17). Interestingly, it is the act of being moved, the act of belief, that itself partakes of the truth she senses. The impulse rather than the content of the belief is what is true, as it were, and she wants to understand the impulse. This is of course a deeply Feuerbachian moment: it represents a desire to understand the religious life, and it registers also the great power of personality (here, "voice") through which Romola gains access to this insight.

Romola encounters an extended opportunity to study such a life, while also experiencing its profound charisma, in her developing relation with Savonarola. It is significant that despite the intense power that Savonorola's personality has for her, and his influence over her actions, Romola always has a selective and ambivalent relation to him and his preaching. The force of his personality—his charisma—mediates their relation, and in essence compensates for or covers what is always an attitude of incomplete belief on Romola's part, of fundamentally skeptical inquiry that echoes her original reaction to Dino. Her skepticism transmutes into outright resistance when she challenges Savonarola to appeal the sentence against her godfather. The argument is tense: she accuses him of a kind of sophistry and strongly opposes the idea that the cause of his party is the cause of God's kingdom. But the narrative itself maintains a dual perspective on this point: later, we are told that despite her analytic insight at that moment, she is herself blind, since the Frate's notion about his party is "the implicit formula of all energetic belief" (501).

In the relation of Romola to Savonarola, the novel presents disenchantment as the necessary counterforce to religion as myth or "false certitude" (234; ch. 25). *Romola* is centrally about the profound existential struggle that this disenchantment causes as it becomes a burden of consciousness, especially given the ineluctable force of the religious impulse. Romola finds herself constantly trying to discard part of what Savonarola is saying. And she tries to secularize the message, to render it as a humanism. But the problem is exacerbated by the very strong interpersonal need vis-à-vis Savonarola, one that originates in the function he plays as what we might call Eliot's resolutely human adaptation of the Feuerbachian personal God. In the moment of Romola's encounter with Savonarola during her flight from Florence, at which point he persuades her to return to the city and her existing sphere of duty, the determining check to her resistance comes with a specific effect of solicitous care that his eyes communicate: "The source of the impression his glance produced on Romola was the sense it conveyed to her of interest in her and care for her apart from any personal feeling. It was the first time she had encountered a gaze in which simple human fellowship expressed itself as a strongly felt bond" (356; ch. 40). Eliot goes on to characterize this type of gaze as a prevalent feature of priests and spiritual guides, but there is clearly a strong emphasis on the more general medium of intersubjective influence, at once personal and impersonal, which subtends this and many other moments of moral awakening in Eliot. Aspiration and a kind of raw psychological need often accompany each other in such moments, and both elements typically remain in a tense relation with Romola's skepticism toward Savonarola.

After failing to convince Savonarola of the need to intercede on behalf of her imprisoned godfather, Romola leaves not only Florence but also the demands of conscious moral life, setting herself adrift in a boat and falling into a deep sleep. As in the case of Maggie, it is the strain caused by a concrete existential challenge that produces flight and drifting, which is then followed by a re-awakening to an immediate form of active charity. The cause of flight in Romola's case is the loss of faith in Savonarola after the execution of her godfather, but one might generalize the situation to a larger problem of negotiating the profound challenge of a charismatic humanism dependent on effects of personality—and social relation—that result in forms of strained commitment. It is no accident, it seems, that what Romola escapes are the very demands of reflective consciousness. In a key passage, the narrator reflects back on Romola's eventual awakening (to the sound of a cry of help), and the subsequent phase of time she devotes to the urgent needs of the plague-stricken village upon whose shore she lands: "From the moment after her waking when the cry had drawn her, she had not even reflected, as she used to do in Florence, that she was glad to live because she could lighten sorrow—she had simply lived, with so energetic an impulse to share the life around her, to answer the call of need and do the work which cried aloud to be done, that the reasons for living, enduring, labouring, never took the form of argument" (560; ch. 69).

This condition of unreflective commitment is transient, it must be stressed, and is followed by a period of contemplation and then profound hermeneutic engagement, on Romola's part, with the transcript of Savonarola's confession after his arrest and imprisonment for heresy. Her interpretive study produces a clear reiteration of what the narrative has often invited the reader to recognize in Savonarola; a combination of excess, self-deception, and profound nobility. Moreover, there is a speculation that the confession gives expression to an ennobling wavering of belief on Savonarola's part. Savonarola's doubts about God are, as a parallel to Romola's doubts about him, part of what ennobles him and makes him an object worthy of devoted study. Indeed, ultimately Savonorola refuses the name of martyr, and the narrator writes, "But therefore he may the more fitly be called a martyr by his fellow-men to all time" (575; ch. 71).

Interpretive study here allows one more fully to understand the psychological and moral conditions of the spiritual life, without the seductive pressure of live personality. A similar dynamic is at play in Daniel Deronda's relation to Mordecai, in the scene in which Daniel gently resists Mordecai's insistence on a Kabbalistic merger of their two souls: "You must not ask me to promise that," said Deronda, smiling. "I must be convinced first of special reasons for it in the writings themselves" (751; ch. 63). Unlike those moments, discussed earlier, in which the written word was seen to transmit the force of personality, here a studied hermeneutic practice can diminish the potentially excessive effects of charisma. By contrast, the more immediate effects of personality are quite strongly at play in the relation of Deronda to Gwendolen. Indeed, for Gwendolen, the desire for intersubjective intensity is paramount: "It had been Gwendolen's habit to think of the persons around her as stale books, too familiar to be interesting. Deronda had lit up her attention with a sense of novelty: not by words only, but by imagined facts, his influence had entered into the current of that self-suspicion and self-blame which awakens a new consciousness" (430; ch. 35). Despite the promise of moral awakening, we should be wary of what is here described, insofar as Gwendolen appears to have no capacity for the forms of interrogation and interpretive practice that define the heroic protagonists' own engagements with moral exemplars. Gwendolen implores Deronda, in scene after scene, to tell her what she should think and do: her only challenge to him is to insist that he is not being explicit enough in telling her how to live her life. This is psychological need undercutting the movement of growth through reflective interrogation.

***

One of the interesting aspects of Feuerbach's thought, as of Weber's after him, is the enduring significance he assigns to psychology in his treatment of religion. Even as he calls for the demystification of religion, Feuerbach holds not only to the human tendency to project ideal human qualities outward, but also to the human desire for recognition from a personal God; Weber insists on a flexible interplay between doctrine and psychology, attributing it to varying social, historical, and economic forces. There is, in neither of these thinkers, any ultimate disenchantment of religion, if disenchantment means a complete supersession of the need for, or aspiration toward, the forms of intensified meaningfulness provided by the religious life and its various secular iterations. This need obtains even as charisma migrates from traditional religious sites to more secular ones: there would be no need for migration were this not the case. In Eliot, the treatment of projected ideals and charismatic power is treated existentially, philosophically, and sociologically—when treated existentially, it could be said to remain blind to the very sociological and philosophical analysis that should logically deflate it. But to react to Eliot's investment in charismatic personality as a kind of blind idealism seems a narrowly conceived critique. One could say that Eliot lacks the courage of her disenchantment. But Eliot has an interestingly divided relation to charisma. On the one hand there is a firm critique of the attempt to use charisma to sidestep the demands of moral argument (in the case of both Savonarola and Mordecai). On the other hand there is a sociological and psychological understanding of the importance of charisma. So one could also say that Eliot avoids the deeper cynicism of disenchantment, in her recognition of the ineluctable force of personality as that which breathes life into doctrine. Two extremes must be avoided, however. It is imperative that doctrine not define personality: such a formation issues in a fatal compression of life into doctrine, producing either asceticism or rigid harshness. Equally problematic is the use of the power of personality to impose doctrines that should be reflectively endorsed. To avoid both problems, but also to bring theory to life, Eliot projects through her heroic protagonists versions of what might be called the proximate visionary, the second-generation idealist, the reader and interpreter, as a way to simultaneously acknowledge and mediate the relation between doctrine and personality. We might measure what she achieves here by noticing what happens in *Middlemarch*, where the *deluded* investment in the scholar as visionary (Casaubon) results in a compensatory overinvestment in the proximate visionary, or rather, produces a character (Dorothea) who is the conflation of the visionary and the heroic. In other words, there is not the same possibility for a productive skeptical relation, since all we are given is a collapsed delusion and then an ardent idealist with nothing to work against. This conflation does arguably tip the scales toward an immoderate idealism—in this case Leavis's reaction is warranted—and it indicates by contrast what is accomplished in the skeptical, dialogical scenarios we see elsewhere in Eliot.

References

Anderson, Amanda. *The Powers of Distance: Cosmopolitanism and the Cultivation of Detachment.* Princeton: Princeton UP, 2001.

Cottom, Daniel. *Social Figures: George Eliot, Social History, and Literary Representation.* Minneapolis: U of Minneapolis P, 1987.

Cvetkovich, Ann. *Mixed Feelings: Feminism, Mass Culture, and Victorian Sensationalism*. New Brunswick: Rutgers UP, 1992.

Eliot, George. *Adam Bede*. Ed. Margaret Reynolds. London: Penguin, 2008.

Eliot, George. *Daniel Deronda*. Ed. Terence Cave. London: Penguin, 1995.

Eliot, George. *The George Eliot Letters*. Ed. Gordon S. Haight. 9 vols. New Haven: Yale UP, 1954–78.

Eliot, George. *Middlemarch*. Ed. Rosemary Ashton. London: Penguin, 1994.

Eliot, George. *The Mill on the Floss*. Ed. A. S. Byatt. London: Penguin, 2003.

Feuerbach, Ludwig. *The Essence of Christianity*. Trans. George Eliot. Buffalo: Prometheus, 1989.

Hertz, Neil. *George Eliot's Pulse*. Stanford: Stanford UP, 2003.

Kucich, John. *Repression in Victorian Fiction: Charlotte Brontë, George Eliot, and Charles Dickens*. Berkeley: U of California P, 1987.

Leavis, F. R. *The Great Tradition*. New York: Doubleday, 1954.

Levine, Caroline. *The Serious Pleasures of Suspense: Victorian Realism and Narrative Doubt*. Charlottesville: U of Virginia P, 2003.

Levine, George. "Determinism and Responsibility in the Works of George Eliot." *PMLA* 77.3 (1962): 268–79.

Miller, D. A. *Narrative and Its Discontents: Problems of Closure in the Traditional Novel*. Princeton: Princeton UP, 1981.

Myers, William. *The Teaching of George Eliot*. Totowa: Barnes & Noble, 1984.

32

George Eliot and the Sciences of Mind: The Silence that Lies on the Other Side of Roar

Jill L. Matus

The period in which George Eliot came of age as an intellectual and rose to a position of eminence among Victorian novelists was also the great age of nineteenth-century science. Indeed historians have described the years 1850–90 as "an age of the cult, or worship, of science" (Lightman 17).[1] From the Great Exhibition and museums featuring full-size dinosaurs to undersea cables and evolutionary theory, the public imagination was fired by science and technological inventions of all kinds. Science became part of culture as Victorians flocked to museums, attended lectures and *"conversazione,"* and read avidly about scientific advancements in the newspapers and periodicals. Although science was being professionalized in this period, it was still largely accessible to lay readers.[2]

At the mid-century, a new generation of scientists sought to wrest both scientific and cultural authority from the hands of largely Oxbridge-educated gentlemen scientists and the Anglican clergy. Scientific naturalism, as T. H. Huxley termed it, was arguably the most important intellectual phenomenon of the period. The vision that the scientific naturalists promoted for both science and culture in a modern industrial Britain was avowedly liberal, secular, and middle class (Lightman 17, 20). Whereas the previous generation (John Herschell, Charles Babbage, Charles Lyell, and Richard Owen) had endorsed natural theology and divine order, their challengers and successors (amongst others, Charles Darwin, T. H. Huxley, Herbert Spencer, John Tyndall, and George Henry Lewes) were committed to the secularization of nature. According to Huxley, science was not in the business of proving or denying the existence of a deity, though it certainly might lead to denying the validity of evidence in support

A Companion to George Eliot, First Edition. Edited by Amanda Anderson and Harry E. Shaw.
© 2013 John Wiley & Sons, Ltd. Published 2016 by John Wiley & Sons, Ltd.

of such claims. Science was not about anything but observable causes and effects (Lightman 17). Positivism, the philosophy of social life built on the tenets of this scientific spirit, and championed initially by Auguste Comte, was similarly influential and sought nothing less than to establish a religion of science (Dale 7).

If any novelist was poised to understand the rapid and wide-ranging developments shaping mid- to late-nineteenth-century science and to reflect deeply on their meanings in her fiction, it was George Eliot. In his posthumous tribute to her, the psychologist James Sully rightly described her as "touched by the scientific spirit of her age" (Sully 393). A self-educated generalist, she was intellectually the most impressive of Victorian novelists and demonstrated an extraordinary capacity for grasping the import of a range of scientific enterprises. Eliot was, furthermore, closely acquainted with key figures in the circle of avant-garde science—George Henry Lewes was her common-law spouse and Herbert Spencer a long-time friend. The Leweses were on visiting terms with the Darwins, Huxley, and Tyndall. And like the scientific naturalists, Eliot saw observable causes and effects as the basis of a new, secular, social order. It was to be the foundation for moral law and ethical conduct, imperatives previously sanctioned by conventional religion.

Yet even as Eliot's work reveals a commitment to positivism and secularization, it also implicitly addresses the significance of belief and value systems and asks what role religion is to continue to play in a world of material causes and effects increasingly enlightened by science. Her well-known response to *The Origin of Species* (1859) aptly illustrates both excitement about scientific advancement and attentiveness to broader implications, not least the effect of scientific theories and discoveries on social attitudes and affective beliefs:

> We have been reading Darwin's Book on the "Origin of the Species" just now: it makes an epoch, as the expression of his thorough adhesion, after long years of study, to the Doctrine of Development. . . . [It] will have a great effect in the scientific world, causing a thorough and open discussion of a question about which people have hitherto felt timid. So the world gets on step by step towards brave clearness and honesty! But to me the Development theory and all other explanations of processes by which things came to be, produce a feeble impression compared with the mystery that lies under the processes. (*Letters* 3: 227)[3]

Eliot's wide-ranging knowledge of contemporary sciences has prompted exploration of the fiction in relation to a host of scientific fields and topics: Darwinism, positivism, organicism, psychology, neurology, medicine, wave theory, thermodynamics and the "new physics," mathematics, optics, audiology. While it will not be possible to survey work in all of these, I want to provide in the next few pages a very brief conspectus of some key aspects of this criticism. This will serve also to introduce my discussion in the second part of the essay, which will focus on Eliot's engagement with the sciences of mind and consciousness.[4] Over the past three decades, sustained critical attention has been paid to Eliot's complex responses to Darwin's epoch-making book and evolutionary theory as it developed in the years after the publication of *On the Origin of Species*. It is appropriate therefore to begin with Darwinism, clearly the dominant topic in critical work on Eliot and science. Abidingly influential in this field is Gillian Beer's *Darwin's Plots* (1983), which examines both the narrative means by which Darwin mediated his ideas about evolution and the effect of Darwin's work on a range of novelists. The sections on Eliot explore his influence on her ideas and narrative structures, drawing on evidence from her journal entries, letters, and published reviews and also exploring the work of Lewes. A chapter on *Middlemarch* looks at Eliot's use of the web image and her "insistence on structure as the bearer of signification" in relation to *On the Origin of Species* (142). Applying a strong Darwinian lens, Beer is able to reveal the implications of Eliot's language of species and variation in the Prelude and to show how the novel grapples with the notion of "the single progenitor" through the fruitless academic quests of Lydgate and Casaubon. As with Darwin, questions of relation and origin occupy Eliot throughout (143).

Well before Darwin published his epoch-making book in 1859, Eliot and Lewes were already conversant with what was called the development hypothesis or developmental theory.[5] Sally Shuttleworth notes that "many of the issues crystallized by Darwin were already current in the cultural and scientific discourse of the era." *The Mill on the Floss*, which was one-third complete at the time of the *Origin*'s publication, "was already 'Darwinian' in conception" in its preoccupation with "breeding, development and survival" ("Darwinism" 87). According to Shuttleworth, Eliot may not initially have fully understood the implications of Darwin's theory of natural selection because Darwin's text is itself uncertain in the way it offers two opposing views of development. A progressive narrative of development occurs alongside statements about the relativity of perfect adaptation, which could become "maladaptation . . . if the climate changes or new competitors emerge." Evolving perfection is set against "chance, warfare and extermination" (88).

The important question of whether evolution could be consciously influenced is more fully explored in Peter Allan Dale's *In Pursuit of a Scientific Culture* (1989), which shows that Lewes held firmly to the idea that evolution for intelligent sentient beings was under control and could be directed and structured. As "man" developed, moral ideals represented in civilized societies were themselves instantiated in mind and "acquired," to be then transmitted through heredity. They may not have been "original biological structures," but they became so (118–19). Whereas Darwin does not give any sense that environment plays a part in variation, "Lewes is adamant in his insistence on environment or 'conditions' as the principal cause of variation" (119). That is, Eliot and Lewes remain supportive in some way of Lamarkianism and adopt a "melioristic" view of evolution in which mind is capable of improving and developing by "gradual adaptation to cultural structures."[6] Forms of later neo-Darwinism articulated more explicitly than Darwin the "fully pessimistic concept" of "the mind as an accident of evolution spawned on a universe to whose workings it may well be at once irrelevant and unadaptable" (Dale 25). Dale's study is usefully explanatory on these Darwinian issues, but its scope is broader yet—the development of the positivist project—and it positions the work of Eliot and Lewes in relation to Comte and the positivist scientific culture of the century.

In her own day and after her death, Eliot was considered a disciple of Herbert Spencer rather than Darwin. On its publication, she praised Spencer's *Principles of Psychology* (1855), which was a pioneering attempt to apply the developmental theory to the study of the mind and which argued that the transmission of innate mental characteristics was hereditary. Nancy L. Paxton's *George Eliot and Herbert Spencer: Feminism, Evolutionism, and the Reconstruction of Gender* (1991) charts the pervasive role that Spencer played throughout Eliot's life and career and explores the extent of Eliot's feminist resistance to evolutionary theory. Paxton also draws attention to the reciprocal nature of influence in the relationship: "Spencer's debts to Eliot have been even more difficult to recognize, because, first of all, he seemed incapable of acknowledging intellectual influences of any kind" and seems also to have felt an "anxiety of influence" with respect to his female contemporary and friend (7). Paxton argues that Spencer's position on gender and ethics shifted in part as a result of her effect on his thinking. Evidence for this influence lies in the obvious parallels between his *The Principles of Ethics* (1879–93) and her *Middlemarch*, which show that he eventually developed a "new and deeper appreciation for the social value of . . . compassion" (232).

As her essays for the *Westminster Review* reveal, Eliot was early committed to Comte's positive philosophy and its application to the analysis of social life. The laws of cause and effect underpin her moral credo: what enjoins a set of behaviors in a secular society is not reward or punishment in a world hereafter but a keen sense of consequence—what it means to harm or impinge on others by our actions in this world. The interconnection and interdependence of all parts of the social web, so powerfully demonstrated in *Middlemarch*, depend on organic conceptions of society. In *George Eliot and Nineteenth Century Science* (1984), Sally Shuttleworth undertakes a thorough analysis of Eliot's complex and ambivalent responses to nineteenth-century organicism, which is at base a belief in the interconnection of part and whole, and which was the undergirding for many branches of science. Eliot's organic conception of society and moral theory of organic unity have close connections to nineteenth-century physiological theory, but, as Shuttleworth shows, an organic conception of society did not offer a single consistent image; it depended largely on what physiological assumptions the theory adopted (xi). Eliot's ambivalent views about natural history, organicism, and the Comtean positivist model of history evolved during her career as a writer and ultimately moved her away from the literary realism of her early novels. We see this in the more open narrative form of Eliot's last novel, which continues to affirm the values of organic unity even as it demonstrates the conditions of their impossibility (201).

At the time Eliot began writing fiction, there were several important contributions to the emerging field of scientific psychology: Lewes published *The Physiology of*

Common Life in 1859; Alexander Bain's *The Emotions and the Will* also appeared in 1859, the companion volume to his earlier *The Senses and the Intellect* (1855). Herbert Spencer had recently published the monumental *Principles of Psychology* (1855). Darwin's *On the Origin of Species* was not initially a primary influence in shaping ideas about the mind, and the nature and origin of mind was not central to the polemic of evolutionary theory. According to Roger Smith, it was somewhere between 1868 and 1875 that physiology and Darwinian evolutionary theory became more closely engaged with each other and "a greater integration of debates was achieved" on questions about the human mind and the theory of evolution (see Smith 84; Matus, *Shock* 26). The new scientific psychology of the period occasioned a shift in mental science from philosophy and metaphysics to physiology, and explored—not without vigorous controversy—the material and physical basis of mind.

The aim of Rick Rylance's *Victorian Psychology and British Culture 1850–1880* (2000) is to map out the constituent discourses of psychology (religion, medicine, philosophy and physiology). The book is also in some way a parallel study of Eliot in that it is her work primarily that provides examples of fiction's engagement with psychological discourse. In the first full-length study of Eliot's representations of mind, *George Eliot and Nineteenth Century Psychology* (2006), Michael Davis charts the centrality of mind to Eliot's ethical and aesthetic vision, showing her emphasis on the role of language in shaping the conscious self and arguing that she uses the scientific language of mind to formulate a new spirituality. An array of recent articles and chapters have dealt with Eliot in relation to phrenology, mesmerism, and other forms of altered consciousness, memory and amnesia, emotion and the effect of shock on the mind, agency, automatism, and the will.[7]

***

When Gillian Beer revised her influential *Darwin's Plots* for a third edition in 2009, she included a new chapter on "Darwin and the Consciousness of Others," a choice that seems in some measure a reflection of the critical interest recently shown in Victorian psychology and theories of consciousness and emotion. While many regarded Darwin as the "man who banished mind from the universe," Beer argues that from his early speculative notebooks to his major late works, *The Descent of Man* (1871) and *The Expression of the Emotions in Man and Animals* (1872), "Darwin is fascinated by the shifting boundaries between awareness, intent, and reason on the one hand—which together make up much of what we commonly call consciousness—and instinct, reflex action, and unconsciousness on the other. He is by no means satisfied with the hierarchies implicit in this sorting" (251). Darwin's questioning of hierarchies in this regard was shared by several others, not least George Henry Lewes and George Eliot. Over the course of twenty years as an increasingly respected amateur scientist in physiological psychology, Lewes developed the idea that consciousness is just the tip of the iceberg of psychical life. In *The Physiology of Common Life* (1859–60) and *Problems of Life and Mind* (1874–79) he set out and elaborated the view that "Mind" is not equivalent to brain, and does not designate intellectual operations only. It includes "all Sensation, all Volition, and all Thought: it means the whole psychical Life; and this psychical Life has no one special centre, any more than the physical Life has one special centre" (*Physiology* 2:12). The brain, he argued, is only one of the organs of mind, and by no means the "exclusive centre of Consciousness" (*Physiology* 2:11). Rather than reducing mind to body, he sought to bring the bodily into the conception of mind. The resultant interpenetration of neural and psychical processes meant that previous distinctions between mind and body were neither clear nor useful.

For the remainder of this chapter, I want to explore Eliot's understanding of what Lewes terms "the psychical Life" and the role of consciousness in it. In particular, I will discuss one of her final essays, a darkly ironic response to a controversial aspect of later nineteenth-century mental physiology—the epiphenomenalist dethroning of consciousness. A perfunctory word-scan reveals that Eliot's use of the term "consciousness" in her fiction rose dramatically over the course of her career. There are twenty-three instances of its occurrence in *Scenes of Clerical Life* and twenty-five in *Adam Bede*; forty-four in *The Mill on the Floss;* sixty in *Romola*; thirty-five in *Felix Holt*; ninety in *Middlemarch* and one hundred ten in *Daniel Deronda*. ('The shorter works, *Silas Marner* and "The Lifted Veil," contain sixteen and fifteen instances respectively.) This trajectory can be accounted for by the fact that "consciousness" becomes increasingly part of nineteenth-century discourses on the mind, a cultural shift that is manifested in Eliot's work. Concurrently, she becomes increasingly interested in (self-conscious about) consciousness and the various states of mind to be distinguished from it—unconsciousness, for example—and thus engages in more explicit discussions of it in her later novels. *Felix Holt* is the anomaly in the group, perhaps because it is far more concentrated on external than internal action.[8]

In the mid-1870s, Thomas Huxley's pronouncements about consciousness seem to have ignited discussion around questions of agency and automatism. His avowedly epiphenomenalist position proposed that mental states were dependent on physical states and that consciousness was merely a side-effect of the main activity going on elsewhere:

> The consciousness of brutes would appear to be related to the mechanism of their body simply as a collateral product of its working, and to be as completely without any power of modifying that working as the steam-whistle which accompanies the work of a loco-motive engine is without influence upon its machinery. (240)

He also analogized the soul's relationship to the body as the bell of a clock to its works—consciousness is merely the sound the bell makes when struck (242). Many respondents picked up on Huxley's use of the steam-engine analogy in his relegation of consciousness to a subsidiary and essentially powerless position. While the locomotive had long been a favored analogy for automatism, representing consciousness as the steam-whistle—a mere epiphenomenon—seemed to strike a nerve. Pre-eminent in the field of mental physiology, William Carpenter addresses Huxley's views on automatism directly in the preface to his 1876 edition of his *Principles of Mental Physiology*, arguing against the doctrine that "Man is only a more complicated and variously-endowed Automaton" (vii). In opposition, Carpenter emphasized the phenomenology of agency and the importance of disciplining and educating the will. As Dale has noted, Lewes, too, regards "Animal Automatism" as one of the problems in his *Problems of Life and Mind* and is concerned to refute the reduction of mind to physical causes—the position taken by Huxley and other contemporary materialists. Lewes is not refuting Huxley from an idealist point of view, because he too accepts that mind is dependent on matter. "What he denies is that consciousness, once evolved, lacks an independent causality of its own, that it is unable to turn back upon and modify the physical structures (Huxley's 'locomotive') from which it has evolved" (Dale 120). Like Carpenter, Lewes emphasized social conditioning, mental habits, moral and religious teachings, so that modes of reaction become virtually automatic.

If an epiphenomenalist position challenged cherished ideas about consciousness and agency, it was similarly contentious in other areas of psychology where the once sovereign province of mind was threatened with encroachments from the territory of the unthinking, the body. There was a growing tendency through the century, as Thomas Dixon has shown, to replace "passion" with "emotion," a terminology that enabled a secularizing psychology to assert that emotions were automatic bodily changes, non-assessing and non-cognitive. The passions of the *soul* became the emotions of the *body* (Dixon 3). But, like Lewes, Eliot understood emotion as part of an expanded notion of mind, part of "psychical Life," which included all sensation. Feelings (emotions, sense impressions, perceptions) inform ideas through their connection to the world outside of the self. Abstract thought and reflection, on the other hand, may prohibit one from being *in touch* with the real rather than imagined other. The following passage about Dorothea's painful growth to understand the real rather than ideal Casaubon exemplifies the importance of apparently non-cognitive sensation in shaping thought:

> [I]t had been easier to her to imagine how she might devote herself to Mr Casaubon, and become wise and strong in his strength and wisdom than to conceive with that distinctness which is no longer reflection but feeling—an idea wrought back to the directness of sense, like the solidity of objects—that he had an equivalent centre of self, whence the lights and shadows must always fall with a certain difference. (*Middlemarch* 198; ch. 21)

Feeling is distinguished from reflection or thought, and is to be valued in the development of clear (as opposed to vague) knowledge, dependent as it is on the direct evidence of the senses.[9] Rather than a line between mental or cognitive and bodily processes, or a hierarchy in which the cognitive is paramount, Eliot posits a web of interconnecting informants. And she reiterates in a variety of ways that consciousness may be the last to know what begins much earlier at the level of nerve and feeling: "Our consciousness rarely registers the beginning of a growth within us any more than without us: there have been many circulations of the sap before we detect the smallest sign of the bud" (*Silas Marner* 194; ch. 7). Unconsciousness, or what is not conscious, is thus an integral part of the psychic process. While motives and feelings may operate unawares, they shape and inform moments of decision and conscious thought. The narrator in *Adam Bede* warns that "Our mental business is carried on in much the same way as the business of the State: a great deal of hard work is done by agents who are not acknowledged. In a piece of machinery, too, I believe, there is often a small unnoticeable wheel which has a great deal to do with the motion of the large obvious ones. . . . The human soul is a complex thing" (189; ch. 16).

Arthur Donnithorne's secret motives are certainly acknowledged in *Adam Bede*, but it is their external consequences that are forcibly brought home in his dalliance with the pretty dairymaid, Hetty. Looking at the trajectory from the early to late fiction, and the emphasis in Eliot's final novels on unconscious processes, one might say that the laws of cause and effect are less externally insistent in the later work where the emphasis shifts to "how things came to be" in a psychological sense and the role of the hidden components of consciousness is more fully explored. In *Daniel Deronda*, for example, there is nothing externally significant about Gwendolen's ultimate realization of her own insignificance. It is, however, internally momentous and forcibly conveyed through images of a consciousness shifting vertiginously: "The world seemed getting larger round poor Gwendolen, and she more solitary and helpless in the midst. The thought that he might come back after going to the East, sank before the bewildering vision of these wild-stretching purposes in which she felt herself reduced to a mere speck" (689; ch. 59). Much earlier in the novel, the narrator contrasts the large, historic movements taking place in the world with Gwendolen's trivial self-involvement, foreshadowing the relegation she will suffer: "Could there be a slenderer, more insignificant thread in human history than this consciousness of a girl, busy with her small inferences of the way in which she could make her life pleasant?" (102; ch. 11). When Daniel's departure causes a disruption of Gwendolen's narrow perception of the world, it elicits the narrator's most heroic, sonorous, and indeed sternly punitive prose:

> There comes a terrible moment to many souls when the great movements of the world, the larger destinies of mankind, which have lain aloof in newspapers and other neglected reading, enter like an earthquake into their own lives—where the slow urgency of growing generations turns into the tread of an invading army or the dire clash of civil war. . . . Then it is as if the Invisible Power that has been the object of lip-worship and lip-resignation became visible, according to the imagery of the Hebrew poet. . . . Then it is that the submission of the soul to the Highest is tested, and even in the eyes of frivolity life looks out from the scene of human struggle with the awful face of duty, and a religion shows itself which is something else than a private consolation. (689; ch. 59)

By the time we read the last rolling cadences of the passage, it may be difficult to recall that the cataclysm Gwendolen suffers is not in fact a world-shaking catastrophe like civil war, demanding widespread renunciation and courage. It is a largely internal event, a shift in perspective about her inconsequentiality in the world. But as Daniel's mother, Princess Halm-Eberstein, knows all too well, internal events can be as momentous as external. "[E]vents come on us like evil enchantments: and thoughts, feelings, apparitions in the darkness are events—are they not?" (540–41; ch. 52). In a novel that dwells on Gwendolen's shadowy dread, terror, and the trauma of guilt and conscience after Grandcourt's death, Eliot explores the unconscious components that accumulate to produce a tormented consciousness.

In *The Descent of Man*, Darwin had put forward the view that man and the higher animals do not differ fundamentally in their mental faculties. Huxley extended that view, as we have seen, by arguing that all animals, human beings included, are essentially automata. Lewes and Eliot, however, regarded human psychology as distinctive, a position which flowed in large measure from their conviction that the mind was shaped and modified over time by social experience as a form of inheritance. The complexity of human experience, Lewes argued, has as its consequence the evolution of consciousness, the principle of reflection. In *The Study of Psychology*, edited by Eliot for publication after Lewes's death, we encounter a section on the differences between animal and human, which notes that what distinguishes the human is "Consciousness, that Inner Sense which Kant marks as the distinguishing attribute of man when it makes its own affections objects of thought" (135).[10] In *The Mill on the Floss*, Eliot describes Maggie, stung by Tom's accusations of selfishness, as "gifted with that superior power of misery which distinguishes the human being, and places him at a proud distance from the most melancholy chimpanzee" (47; ch. 6). Throughout the fiction, animals feature analogically to comment on human motive, intention, and agency and are often treated with humorous anthropomorphism, as in the descriptions of Bartle Massey's dog Vixen in *Adam Bede*, whose loose morals have put her in the family way. The humor depends largely on the unwarranted equivalence implied between human consciousness and that of other animals.

When it comes to contrasting purposive agency with automatic activity and the narrowing of consciousness, however, the insect order is Eliot's favored comparator: "But were not men of ardent zeal and far-reaching hope everywhere exceptional?—the men who had the visions which, as Mordecai said, were the creators and feeders of the world—moulding and feeding the more passive life which without them would dwindle and shrivel into the narrow tenacity of insects, unshaken by thoughts beyond the reach of their antennae" (*Daniel Deronda* 586; ch. 55). The most sustained usage of this kind appears in *Silas Marner*, whose spinning activity is repetitive and mindless: "Then there were the calls of hunger; and Silas, in his solitude, had to provide his own breakfast, dinner, and supper, to fetch his own water from the well, and put his own kettle on the fire; and all these immediate promptings helped, along with the weaving, to reduce his life to the unquestioning activity of a spinning insect." Narrow tenacity and unquestioning activity are symptoms of automatic behavior.

While their opposite would seem to be an "active" life of choice and reason, if we think of the novel's drift, it is not the capacity to reason but the emotional life which makes the difference. In *Silas Marner*, the shock of betrayal and false accusation prompts a withdrawal from community life and affective bonds. Though Silas suffers from lapses in consciousness, it is not his cataleptic trances that are the cause of his reduced life. "Stunned" by despair, his faith "benumbed," Marner's consciousness narrows and habitual, repetitive, mechanical behavior replaces conscious activity: "He seemed to weave, like the spider, from pure impulse, without reflection." "Thought was arrested by utter bewilderment, now its old narrow pathway was closed, and affection seemed to have died under the bruise that had fallen on its keenest nerves" (15; ch. 2). Both emotion and cognition suffer as a result of the shock of betrayal. The novel proceeds by way of chiasmic substitutions and withdrawals, the gold Silas is accused of stealing becoming the gold he amasses through his insect-like weaving activity, which is then replaced by the golden-haired child. When the theft of his hoarded gold propels him to the town's tavern to seek help from the inhabitants of Raveloe, his slow integration into the community begins. The primary role of affect in his expanding consciousness of himself as a community member, friend, and father is repeatedly emphasized.

Eliot's faith in affective growth and expanded consciousness has a darker and more pessimistic underside, which is the ironic contemplation of consciousness as a burden or curse. "The Lifted Veil" explores what she calls superadded or diseased consciousness—that "double consciousness" of knowing what is in other people's minds as well as one's own. This work goes beyond contemporary physiologists' interest in altered states, and in particular beyond Henry Holland's theories of double consciousness, to explore the loss of protection from our own dullness or what she refers to in *Middlemarch* as a well-wadded stupidity.[11] In her well-known pronouncements about the roar on the other side of silence, she echoes similar remarks by Huxley (*Middlemarch* 182; ch. 20; see Davis 142; Beer 142). Both see the "dullness" of consciousness as a form of protection and survival. Considered in this context, "The Lifted Veil," her "*jeu de melancholie*," is a way of exploring the effect of excessive exposure and the inability to regulate stimuli and hence the sheer onerousness of an over-attuned consciousness. Through the medium of an unsympathetic narrator to whom this extraordinary ability is wearying and tedious, she touches on the way consciousness may be experienced as a curse. While the peculiar sensitivity of the narrator renders him privy to the stream of other people's consciousness, the result is not a heightened compassion for the exposed suffering of others, but a sense of intolerable and painful invasion. Furthermore, the working of Latimer's extraordinary consciousness is rendered in terms of auditory images—an amplification and cacophony that is like "the loud activity of an imprisoned insect" (11). Consciousness in this story is a form of noise pollution.[12]

Going much further down this track in one of her last satiric essays, "Shadows of the Coming Race," in *Impressions of Theophrastus Such* (1879), Eliot imagines what it would be like if this planet were filled with evolutionarily superior beings who are "blind and deaf as the inmost rock" (142). The essay echoes the title of Edward Bulwer-Lytton's novel, *The Coming Race* (1871), and, like Samuel Butler's *Erewhon* (1872), imagines a world in which machines have superseded humans not only by being able to do the work that human beings currently do, but by developing in such a way as to eliminate consciousness altogether.[13] This essay elaborates a wonderfully cynical view of consciousness and allows Eliot to dilate, with some gusto, on the implications of ephiphenomenalism.

Consciousness in the essay is not only a nuisance; it is (worse) merely incidental and peripheral. It is a "futile cargo" like "a fowl tied head downmost to the saddle of a swift horseman," "screeching irreverently" (141). We may need consciousness to bring reflection and conscience to bear on what we experience, but its inner demands can be inhibiting and annoying. In this fantasy of evolving technology, inventions such as micrometers, tasimeters, thermopiles, and microphones will be able to do everything better than us but with the advance of banishing "screaming conscious-nesses" which make an intolerable noise and fuss to each other about every petty ant-like performance. Whereas now a microphone might detect and discriminate "the noises of our various follies as they soliloquise or converse in our brains" (138), in the future, we will produce a coming race that is free of such soliloquizing: "free from the fussy accompaniment of that consciousness to which our prejudice gives a supreme governing rank, when in truth it is a parasite on the grand sequence of things" (139); free from "a maniacal consciousness which imagined itself moving its mover." Humans, as a race enfeebled by consciousness, "will have vanished, as all less adapted existences do before the fittest—i.e. the existence composed of the most persistent groups of movements and the most capable of incorporating new groups in harmonious relation" (141). Consciousness is a superfluity and will not be evolution's choice as it does not fit us for survival. Why not then imagine an evolved machine that supersedes us in this and all other regards?

> Who—if our consciousness is, as I have been given to understand, a mere stumbling of our organisms on their way to unconscious perfection—who shall say that those fittest existences will not be found along the track of what we call inorganic combinations, which will carry on the most elaborate processes as mutely and painlessly as we are now told that the minerals are metamorphosing themselves continually in the dark laboratory of the earth's crust? . . . Thus this planet may be filled with beings who will be blind and deaf as the inmost rock, yet will execute changes as delicate and compli-cated as those of human language and all the intricate web of what we call its effects, without sensitive impression, without sensitive impulse: there may be, let us say, mute orations, mute rhapsodies, mute discussions, and no consciousness there even to enjoy the silence. (142)

Eliot and Lewes were certainly not epiphenomenalists, and though they might have been prepared to take consciousness down a peg or two by insisting on its insepa-rability from lowlier forms of sentience, they were not prepared to relegate it to the sidelines as a superfluity. It is therefore worth pausing to consider the zest and enjoyment with which Eliot allows her narrator to play devil's advocate and to dilate lyrically on the demise of consciousness. She seems to relish her parody of Huxley, venting playfully about our hubris in imagining consciousness as a prime mover and indulging perhaps her own wish for the silencing of incessant and clamouring inner voices. Gone would be the endless engagement with one's own thoughts, the fret, the headaches, the neurotic concerns. Whereas in "The Lifted Veil" it was the consciousness of others that intruded loudly on Latimer and poisoned his experience of life, in this essay, Eliot considers the silencing of one's *own* internal voices and the erasure of the distinctively human capacity to make one's thoughts the objects of reflection. If the power of the prose is any indication, that prospect is in some respects a heady and delightful one. Even as it parodies epiphenomenalism, the essay gleefully predicts a silent world where the demands of consciousness, and with it conscience and the moral sense so essential to George Eliot's vision, have been eliminated. If *Middlemarch* has already sounded the note of warning that without our protective wadding we might die of the roar that lies on the other side of silence, this final essay imagines the obliteration of consciousness and the blessed silence that lies on the other side of roar.

Notes

1 My summary of the great age of science in these first two paragraphs is indebted to Lightman's essay, which provides an excellent introduction to the cultural authority sought by the scientific naturalists.

2 See Postlethwaite (99), who traces the shifting definitions of professional and lay science in the period.

3 This last observation sounds a cautionary note characteristic of Eliot. But this is not to suggest that preservation of a sense of wonder and mystery is the role solely of the novelist. The scientific naturalists expressed similar reverence for nature's mysteries and wonders. Both Tyndall and Huxley revered Goethe and the latter praised Goethe's poetic vision as containing a "truthful and efficient symbol of the wonder and mystery of Nature" (see Lightman 22).

4 I am grateful to my research assistant Andrea Day for assistance in preparing the overview of critical work. On Eliot and thermodynamics, see Dale; on sound, see Picker; on optics and microscopy, see Miller and Wormald; on the role of geometry, and the absence of mathematics from considerations of literature and science, see Jenkins; on medicine and doctors see Logan, Rothfield, and Sparks.

5 See also Levine, who does not discuss Eliot's novels in detail but holds them up as the gold standard of engagement with Darwinian thought.

6 Dale argues that Lewes's Lamarkianism shifted in the course of his fourth volume of *Problems, The Study of Psychology*, in the 1870s, which in turn must have affected his progressive view of history and positive change; see his discussion 121–26.

7 See Taylor; Matus; Dames; Wood; Vrettos; Ryan; Palmer.

8 The incidence of the term "unconscious" is, however, erratic, ranging from high in *Adam Bede*, *Romola*, and *Daniel Deronda* to relatively low in *The Mill on the Floss* and *Middlemarch*.

9 See the discussion of this passage in Matus, "George Eliot" 230.

10 Lewes does elsewhere draw on other definitions of consciousness and notes that consciousness in its general sense as "sentience" should be distinguished from consciousness in its special sense as a reflected feeling of

attention, which is how he is using it here. See Lewes, "The Physical Basis of Mind" 357.

11   Holland writes about the exceptional condition in which "the mind passes by alternation" from one set of ideas and impressions to another without the usual linking of "mutual memory" or normal gradation (Holland 187).

Altered states of mind (such as somnambulism, trance, double consciousness, alternating memory) were widely discussed in the period. See Taylor.

12   See Matus, *Shock, Memory and the Unconscious* 121–41.

13   On the genesis of the essay, see Haight 522.

REFERENCES

Beer, Gillian. *Darwin's Plots: Evolutionary Narrative in Darwin, George Eliot, and Nineteenth-Century Fiction*. 3rd ed. Cambridge: Cambridge UP, 2009.

Carpenter, William Benjamin. *Principles of Mental Physiology*. 1876. 4th ed. New York: Appleton, 1890.

Dale, Peter Allan. *In Pursuit of a Scientific Culture: Science, Art, and Society in the Victorian Age*. Madison: U of Wisconsin P, 1989.

Dames, Nicholas. *Amnesiac Selves: Nostalgia, Forgetting, and British Fiction, 1810–1870*. Oxford: Oxford UP, 2001.

Davis, Michael. *George Eliot and Nineteenth-Century Psychology: Exploring the Unmapped Country*. Farnham: Ashgate, 2006.

Dixon, Thomas. *From Passions to Emotions: The Creation of a Secular Psychological Category*. Cambridge: Cambridge UP, 2003.

Eliot, George. *Adam Bede*. 1859. Ed. Margaret Reynolds. London: Penguin, 2008.

Eliot, George. *Daniel Deronda*. 1876. Ed. Graham Handley. Oxford: Oxford UP, 1998.

Eliot, George. *The George Eliot Letters*. 9 vols. Ed. Gordon S. Haight. New Haven: Yale UP, 1954–78.

Eliot, George. *Impressions of Theophrastus Such*. 1879. Ed. Nancy Henry. Iowa City: U of Iowa P, 1994.

Eliot, George. *The Lifted Veil* and *Brother Jacob*. Ed. Helen Small. Oxford: Oxford UP, 2009.

Eliot, George. *Middlemarch*. Ed. David Carroll. Oxford: Oxford UP, 1997.

Eliot, George. *The Mill on the Floss*. Ed. Gordon S. Haight. Oxford: Oxford UP, 2008.

Eliot, George. *Silas Marner*. 1861. Ed. Terence Cave. Oxford: Oxford UP, 1998.

Haight, Gordon S. *George Eliot: A Biography*. Oxford: Clarendon, 1969.

Holland, Henry. *Chapters on Mental Physiology*. London: Longman, 1852.

Huxley, T. H. "On the Hypothesis that Animals are Automata and Its History." *The Collected Essays of T. H. Huxley*. Vol 1. London: Macmillan, 1894. 199–250.

Jenkins, Alice. "George Eliot, Geometry, and Gender." *Literature and Science*. Essays and Studies Collected on Behalf of the English Association 61. Ed. Sharon Ruston. Cambridge: D. S. Brewer, 2008. 72–90.

Levine, George. *Darwin and the Novelists: Patterns of Science in Victorian Fiction*. Cambridge: Harvard UP, 1988.

Lewes, George Henry. *The Physiology of Common Life*. 2 vols. New York: Appleton, 1859–60.

Lewes, George Henry. *Problems of Life and Mind*. 5 vols. London: Trübner, 1874–79. First Series: [1] The Foundations of a Creed (1874); [2] The Foundations of a Creed (1875). Second series: [3] The Physical Basis of Mind (1877). Third series [4] The Study of Psychology: Its Object Scope and Method (1879); [5] Mind as a Function of the Organism; The Sphere of Sense and Logic of Feeling; The Sphere of Intellect and Logic of Signs.

Lightman, Bernard. "Science and Culture." *The Cambridge Companion to Victorian Culture*. Ed. Francis O'Gorman. Cambridge: Cambridge UP, 2010. 12–42.

Logan, Peter Melville. "George Eliot and the Fetish of Realism." *Studies in the Literary Imagination* 35.2 (2002): 27–51.

Matus, Jill L. "George Eliot." *The Cambridge Companion to English Novelists*. Ed. Adrian Poole. Cambridge: Cambridge UP, 2009. 225–41.

Matus, Jill L. *Shock, Memory and the Unconscious in Victorian Fiction*. Cambridge: Cambridge UP, 2009.

Miller, J. Hillis. "Optic and Semiotic in *Middle-march*." *New Casebooks: Middlemarch*. Ed. John Peck. Basingstoke: Macmillan, 1992. 65–83.

Palmer, Alan. *Fictional Minds*. Lincoln: U of Nebraska P, 2004.

Palmer, Alan. "Intermental Thought in the Novel: The Middlemarch mind." *Style* 39.4 (2005): 427–39.

Paxton, Nancy L. *George Eliot and Herbert Spencer: Feminism, Evolutionism, and the Reconstruction of Gender*. Princeton: Princeton UP, 1991.

Picker, John. *Victorian Soundscapes*. Oxford: Oxford UP, 2003.

Postlethwaite, Diana. "George Eliot and Science." *The Cambridge Companion to George Eliot*. Ed. George Levine. Cambridge: Cambridge UP, 2001. 98–118.

Rignall, John, ed. *The Oxford Reader's Companion to George Eliot*. Oxford: Oxford UP, 2000.

Rothfield, Lawrence. "'A New Organ of Knowledge': Medical Organicism and the Limits of Realism in *Middlemarch*." In Rothfield, *Vital Signs: Medical Realism in Nineteenth-Century Fiction*. Princeton: Princeton UP, 1994. 84–119.

Ryan, Vanessa. "Reading the Mind: From George Eliot's Fiction to James Sully's Psychology." *Journal of the History of Ideas* 70 (2009): 615–35.

Rylance, Rick. *Victorian Psychology and British Culture 1850–1880*. Oxford: Oxford UP, 2000.

Shuttleworth, Sally. *George Eliot and Nineteenth-Century Science: The Make-Believe of a Beginning*. Cambridge: Cambridge UP. 1984.

Shuttleworth, Sally. "Darwinism." Rignall 87–89.

Shuttleworth, Sally. "Science." Rignall 365–69.

Smith, Roger. "The Physiology of the Will: Mind, Body and Psychology in the Periodical Literature, 1855–1875." *Science Serialized: Representations of the Sciences in Nineteenth-Century Periodicals*. Ed. Geoffrey Cantor and Sally Shuttleworth. Cambridge: MIT P, 2004.

Sparks, Tabitha. *The Doctor in the Victorian Novel: Family Practices*. Farnham: Ashgate, 2009.

Sully, James. "George Eliot's Art." *Mind* 6.23 (1881): 378–94.

Taylor, Jenny Bourne. "Obscure Recesses: Locating the Victorian Unconscious." *Writing and Victorianism*. Ed. J. B. Bullen. London: Longman, 1997, 153–58.

Vrettos, Athena. *Somatic Fictions: Imagining Illness in Victorian Culture*. Stanford: Stanford UP, 1995.

Wood, Jane. *Passion and Pathology in Victorian Fiction*. Oxford: Oxford UP, 2001.

Wormald, Mark. "Microscopy and Semiotic in *Middlemarch*." *Nineteenth-Century Literature* 50.4 (1996): 501–24.

33

George Eliot and the Science of the Human

Ian Duncan

We Belated Historians

"Who that cares much to know the history of man, and how the mysterious mixture behaves under the varying experiments of Time, has not dwelt, at least briefly, on the life of Saint Theresa" (Eliot, *Middlemarch* 3; Prelude): *Middlemarch* opens with an affirmation of its place in the main tradition of the English novel. "The provision . . . which we have here made," Henry Fielding had announced in the introduction to *Tom Jones*—the manifesto of the genre's mid-eighteenth-century "rise"—"is no other than *Human Nature*" (30; emphasis in original). Seeking to justify "a new province of writing," Fielding invoked the ascendant philosophical discourse that David Hume, ten years earlier, had called "the science of man." "In pretending . . . to explain the principles of human nature," Hume declared, "we in effect propose a compleat system of the sciences built on a foundation almost entirely new, and the only one upon which they can stand with any security" (42–43). The science of man would also provide a new, secure foundation for that modern, post-metaphysical literary form, the novel.

By the 1870s the novel had risen to the summit of the genre system, and Fielding had acquired classical stature. George Eliot invokes him as such—a towering forebear—in one of the essayistic reflections on her art that punctuate *Middlemarch*:

> A great historian, as he insisted on calling himself, who had the happiness to be dead a hundred and twenty years ago, and so to take his place among the colossi whose huge legs our living pettiness is observed to walk under, glories in his copious remarks and

A Companion to George Eliot, First Edition. Edited by Amanda Anderson and Harry E. Shaw.
© 2013 John Wiley & Sons, Ltd. Published 2016 by John Wiley & Sons, Ltd.

digressions as the least imitable part of his work. . . . But Fielding lived when the days were longer (for time, like money, is measured by our needs), when summer afternoons were spacious, and the clock ticked slowly in the winter evenings. We belated historians must not linger after his example. . . . I at least have so much to do in unravelling certain human lots, and seeing how they were woven and interwoven, that all the light I can command must be concentrated on this particular web, and not dispersed over that tempting range of relevancies called the universe. (141; ch. 15)

The author of *Middlemarch* (this is no mere narrator) articulates the difference between herself and the author of *The History of Tom Jones*, and between his age and hers, as a difference of temporal and spatial scales. Fielding was greater than us because he had more time. The diminished condition of human life in the present is measured by an accelerated temporal economy. Conversely, "the universe," the potential totality of "human lots," has expanded beyond our field of vision.

Time makes the difference. Fielding called his work a "history" while affirming the uniformity of his topic, "human nature." Eliot, with keener urgency, addresses "the history of man" as a "mysterious mixture," no longer uniform or stable, subject to "the varying experiments of Time." History became the chief discourse for understanding human nature in the half-century after Fielding, in the conjectural anthropologies and social histories of the late Enlightenment. The scientific revolution that issued in Charles Lyell's *Principles of Geology* in the early 1830s (the period at which *Middlemarch* is set) extended the history of the world, considered as a physical object, to an inconceivable magnitude: splitting it apart from the timescale of human history, the recorded history of nations, and throwing the natural history of man into categorical crisis. Fielding could enjoy longer days, more spacious summer afternoons, in a universe that was less than six thousand years old. A brisk scientific debate about the age of the earth attended the conception of *Middlemarch*: in 1869 T. H. Huxley refuted William Thomson's (the future Lord Kelvin's) 1862 calculation, of between 20 million and 400 million years, as insufficient to accommodate the operations of random individual variation and natural selection that Charles Darwin's new theory prescribed for the transmutation of species.

The "belated historian" is writing, in short, in an age when her theme, the history of man, has undergone radical change: preceded, and dwarfed, by unimaginable stretches of geological time, untenanted by human life or (indeed) by any life at all; followed, hypothetically, by a no less immense, indeed potentially infinite, duration—in which the human, just as it has evolved out of some other biological form, will continue to mutate into forms that are scarcely if at all conceivable to our present way of life. The prospect of a dispersal of interwoven human lots across the universe appalls in its character as a temporal more than as a spatial contingency. (Eliot is not thinking of life on other planets.) Eliot came to understand the novelist's task as a shoring up of human nature, a defense of its coherence and integrity, against the abysmal wastes of cosmic time—until her last writings, in which we find her dissolving the stabilizing figures of provincial and national life, and even of "man" and of organic form altogether, to imagine posthuman futures which extend outside the domain of the novel as we have known it.

Involuntary, Palpitating Life

Near the end of *Middlemarch*, after her night of spiritual trial, Dorothea Casaubon looks out on the world:

> She opened her curtains, and looked out towards the bit of road that lay in view, with fields beyond outside the entrance-gates. On the road there was a man with a bundle on his back and a woman carrying her baby; in the field she could see figures moving— perhaps the shepherd with his dog. Far off in the bending sky was the pearly light; and she felt the largeness of the world and the manifold wakings of men to labor and endurance. She was a part of that involuntary, palpitating life, and could neither look out on it from her luxurious shelter as a mere spectator, nor hide her eyes in selfish complaining. (788; ch. 80)

The prose reaches beyond the archetypal human realms (economic, biological) of work and the family to affirm Dorothea's membership in a greater organic entity, "involuntary, palpitating life"—an entity that is at once subhuman and superhuman, internal to each individual body and enfolding all of them.

The historicization of human nature, the shift from the science of man (a synonym for moral philosophy) to the history of man, accompanied the breakup of the category— the putatively universal platform for all knowledge—into a throng of contending disciplines and ideologies by the early decades of the nineteenth century. As human history came under the aegis of natural history, the Enlightenment figure of "man" was subsumed into the grander category of "life." The Victorian social and natural sciences recalibrated life beyond the once absolute standards of the individual human body and lifespan, outwards and inwards, to scales both macroscopic and microscopic. Political economy "increasingly became a kind of life science" in the work of David Ricardo and—decisively—Thomas Malthus, as they made life the ground of value (Gallagher 22). On the one hand, the human was absorbed into the macroeconomic scale of the life of populations and, in Darwin's application of Malthus's argument to natural history, the life of species. On the other hand, cell theory—pioneered by Theodor Schwann and Matthias Schleiden in the 1830s, developed by Rudolf Virchow in the 1850s—relocated life to the cellular level: a human body was not a self-enclosed, integral being but an aggregate of living units at the level of the cell.

Eliot paid close and sophisticated attention to political economy and its disciplinary offshoots, such as the emergent science of society, through her association with the *Westminster Review* and, in particular, with Herbert Spencer and George Henry Lewes. Spencer introduced Eliot and Lewes to the positivist philosophy of Auguste Comte, which asserted a doctrine of inevitable social progress articulated through a homological or organic relation between individual and social life. In her first article for the

Westminster Review, on Robert Mackay's *The Progress of the Intellect* (1851), Eliot affirms basic Comtean principles:

> [The key to knowledge] is the recognition of the presence of undeviating law in the material and moral world—of that invariability of sequence which is acknowledged to be the basis of physical science, but which is still perversely ignored in our social organization, our ethics and our religion. It is this invariability of sequence which can alone give value to experience and render education in the true sense possible. (*Essays* 30)

Lewes's monograph, *Comte's Philosophy of the Sciences*, appeared in 1853, the same year that he and Marian Evans began their relationship. Spencer developed the "organic" principle of universal development still further. In Eliot's summary (writing in 1856):

> The external conditions which society has inherited from the past are but the manifestation of inherited internal conditions in the human beings who compose it; the internal conditions and the external are related to each other as the organism and its medium, and development can take place only by the gradual consentaneous development of both. (*Essays* 286)

Synthesizing developmentalist theory in a series of essays for the *Fortnightly Review*, "Mr. Darwin's Hypothesis" (1868), Lewes would designate the "relation of Organism and Medium" as "the most fundamental of biological data" (63).

Eliot was no less conversant with advances in biology and physiology, including the new histology (the term was coined in 1847). Lewes invokes Schwann and Schleiden, and more recent developments, in his Darwin essay, published the year before Eliot began working on *Middlemarch* (61–62). Eliot lists Schwann and Schleiden in her notes for the novel, along with Huxley's 1853 essay "The Cell-Theory" (*Quarry* 131). Lewes and Eliot also knew Virchow's work, and owned several of his books (Blair 151–52). Famously, they read Darwin's *On the Origin of Species* together when it first appeared in 1859. "It is an elaborate exposition of the evidence in favour of the Development Theory, and so makes an epoch," Eliot wrote—assimilating Darwin's argument to the more diffuse evolutionism propounded by Spencer, and not yet appreciating the full force of the theory of natural selection, although she would come to do so (*Letters* 3:214; see Beer 146).

Recent scholarship has been alert to these aspects of Eliot's career. If an early strain of commentary exaggerated her debt to Comtean positivism, Sally Shuttleworth tracks Eliot's divergence from Comte's determinism by way of Spencer's more thoroughgoing developmentalism and, especially, Lewes's application of biological and physiological models to social science (4–23). For Shuttleworth, these models—Comte's, Spencer's, Lewes's—all negotiate a tension between the conservative force of the collective and a progressive drive toward individuation. Lawrence Rothfield reads Eliot's exploitation of growing contradictions within the ideology of organic form as it splits into rival sciences of the body: clinical pathology and cell biology (92–119). Gillian Beer, in her by now classic *Darwin's Plots*, considers not only the impact of Darwinian evolutionism on Eliot's narrative art—for example, in the interplay between organic affinity and variability in *Middlemarch*—but its relation to other scientific disciplines, notably the rise of Victorian myth criticism in comparative religion and philology, and astronomical reckonings of irreversible, illimitable time in *Daniel Deronda* (139–95). Catherine Gallagher considers Eliot's use of a sensation-based political economy, from Malthus to William Jevons, as well as Malthus's legacy in debates about the biopolitical origins of culture that were foundational to Victorian anthropology (118–84). One currently thriving line of critical inquiry attends to Eliot's interest—via Lewes and Alexander Bain—in the physiology of mental life, and the biological as well as social infrastructures of consciousness (Dames 50–56, 123–65; Matus 121–59).

This essay will take seriously Eliot's claim on the novel as a genre uniquely fitted to render "the history of man," at the crisis of that history's conceptual revolution. In her engagement with the new human sciences of the nineteenth century—sociology, biology, and cultural anthropology—Eliot proposes the novel as their queen rather than their handmaid.

The Natural History of Human Life

In "The Natural History of German Life" Eliot addresses the insufficiency of the abstractions of political economy to produce "a real knowledge of the People," one which would comprise

> the natural history of our social classes, especially of the small shopkeepers, artisans, and peasantry,—the degree in which they are influenced by local conditions, their maxims and habits, the points of view from which they regard their religious teachers, and the degree in which they are influenced by religious doctrines, the interaction of the various classes on each other, and what are the tendencies in their position towards disintegration or towards development. (*Essays* 272–73)

Eliot will choose the novel as even better able to provide such a natural history than the synthesis of ethnography and cultural criticism accomplished in the work under review, W. H. von Riehl's *Naturgeschichte des Volks*. For novels can do more than describe and analyze the influences and interactions that make up social life. They can join the reader affectively to that life through "the extension of our sympathies," "amplifying experience and extending our contact with our fellow-men beyond the bounds of our personal lot" (*Essays* 271, 270)—even if too few novelists have risen to the task. The seventeenth chapter of *Adam Bede* outlines a novelistic aesthetic in which "the faithful representing of commonplace things" is enhanced by "the secret of deep human sympathy" (224; ch. 17); while the narrator of *Middlemarch* acclaims "the deep-seated habit of direct fellow-feeling with individual fellow-men" that can check the deadening tendency of "general doctrines" (619; ch. 60).

The peasant Vs
The city man

The novel's capacity to move sympathy is founded on its attention to the lives of individuals within the "social medium." Individual variation has an ambiguous status, however, within the representational field of natural history. Eliot emphasizes the pre-modern character of Riehl's subject, the German peasantry, bound by an organic temporality of the race or nation that is anterior to—and resistant to—individual development:

> In Germany, perhaps more than in any other country, it is among the peasantry that we must look for the historical type of the national physique. In the towns this type has become so modified to express the personality of the individual, that even "family like-ness" is often but faintly marked. But the peasants may still be distinguished into groups by their physical peculiarities. In one part of the country we find a longer-legged, in another a broader-shouldered race, which has inherited these peculiarities for centuries. . . . [T]he cultured man acts more as an individual; the peasant, more as one of a group. Hans drives the plough, lives, and thinks just as Kunz does; and it is this fact, that many thousands of men are as like each other in thoughts and habits as so many sheep or oysters, which constitutes the weight of the peasantry in the social and political scale. (*Essays* 274–75)

Late Enlightenment philosophical history had characterized the peasantry as a residual mass in the uneven progress of nations toward modernity. Riehl's "natural history" consigns them to a prehistoric timescale regulated by biological laws of inheritance, the cycle of seasons, and the inertial force of custom. The temporality of "culture," of human historical progress and of individual development, belongs to urban life. Here we glimpse the classic formula of the nineteenth-century *Bildungsroman*, in which characters must escape from rural stagnation to enter the accelerated time of modernity—the time of the city, of human history as change rather than continuity, of individual experience as growth and choice. A central paradox takes shape. Human nature resides with the organic, communal life of the people; yet one becomes fully human by quitting that life, struggling into individuation, into historical and ethical identity.

The aesthetic imperative of a natural history of human life governs the fictions Eliot wrote after she reviewed Riehl—*Scenes of Clerical Life* (1858), *Adam Bede* (1859), and *The Mill on the Floss* (1860)—with, as Shuttleworth notes, increasing play being given to the tension between organic continuity at the level of collective life and differentiation at the level of the individual. If the organic social medium generates idyllic set pieces in *Adam Bede*, its dragging, thwarting force predominates in *The Mill on the Floss*. The novel tracks the painful growth of the Tulliver children ("still very much like young animals": 39; bk. 1, ch. 5) into the sexual, social, and ethical differentiations of adulthood. Eliot amplifies the rhetoric of natural history in her evocation of the provincial setting:

> It is one of those old, old towns which impress one as a continuation and outgrowth of nature, as much as the nests of the bower-birds or the winding galleries of the white

ants; a town which carries the traces of its long growth and history like a millennial tree, and has sprung up and developed in the same spot between the river and the low hill from the time when the Roman legions turned their backs on it from the camp on the hillside, and the long-haired sea-kings came up the river and looked with fierce, eager eyes at the fatness of the land. (115–16; bk. 1, ch. 12)

This deep historicity is inaccessible, however, to the town's inhabitants, or rather, to the organic mentality they collectively constitute: "The mind of St. Ogg's did not look extensively before or after. It inherited a long past without thinking of it, and had no eyes for the spirits that walk the streets."

Halfway through the novel, the narrator pauses to reflect upon "the mental condition of these emmet-like Dodsons and Tullivers," with their custom-bound, unreflective, "semi-pagan" lives:

> I share with you this sense of oppressive narrowness; but it is necessary that we should feel it, if we care to understand how it acted on the lives of Tom and Maggie,—how it has acted on young natures in many generations, that in the onward tendency of human things have risen above the mental level of the generation before them, to which they have been nevertheless tied by the strongest fibres of their hearts. The suffering, whether of martyr or victim, which belongs to every historical advance of mankind, is represented in this way in every town, and by hundreds of obscure hearths; and we need not shrink from this comparison of small things with great; for does not science tell us that its highest striving is after the ascertainment of a unity which shall bind the smallest things with the greatest? In natural science, I have understood, there is nothing petty to the mind that has a large vision of relations, and to which every single object suggests a vast sum of conditions. It is surely the same with the observation of human life. (272–73; bk. 4, ch. 1)

Suffering attends human progress, which the novel reckons in the scale of individual development. Thus Eliot derives a tragic ethos from the "large vision of relations" proper to "natural science." Early on she awards her heroine "that superior power of misery which distinguishes the human being, and places him at a proud distance from the most melancholy chimpanzee" (46–47; bk. 1, ch. 6): an irony that saddens into truth as Maggie grows older. To suffer is to be human; still more, following the Romantic female *Bildungsroman* of Germaine de Staël and Charlotte Brontë, it is to be a woman, entangled more deeply than men are in the thickets of custom. By virtue of their suffering—their relegation to the sacrificial role of "martyr or victim"— women earn their status as the most fully human beings in Victorian fiction.

The Limits of Variation

In *Middlemarch*, subtitled *A Study of Provincial Life*, Eliot brings the mid-Victorian *topos* of provincial life to its fullest development as the ground of a human natural history. The narrator reflects upon the "subtle movement" that characterizes "old provincial society":

> Municipal town and rural parish gradually made fresh threads of connection—gradually, as the old stocking gave way to the savings-bank, and the worship of the solar guinea became extinct. . . . In fact, much the same sort of movement and mixture went on in old England as we find in older Herodotus, who also, in telling what had been, thought it well to take a woman's lot for his starting-point. (95; ch. 11)

The narrative traces the involvement of the "woman's lot," Dorothea's, and that of a secondary, male protagonist, Lydgate, with "the hampering threadlike pressure of small social conditions, and their frustrating complexity" (180; ch. 18). The narrative also mobilizes the Darwinian language of a drive toward variation, dynamically at odds with the retentive, reiterative force of organic continuity, for which the relation between "the natures of women" and their "social lot" provides a test case:

> [T]he limits of variation are really much wider than anyone would imagine from the sameness of women's coiffure and the favourite love-stories in prose and verse. Here and there a cygnet is reared among the ducklings in the brown pond, and never finds the living stream in fellowship with its own oary-footed kind. (4; Prelude; see Beer 139–40)

The taxonomic status of the "new Theresa" (838; Finale)—mere sport, or type of a future species—remains cloaked in melancholy ambiguity.

Eliot thematizes dominant modes of scientific inquiry in both plots: Casaubon's quest for "the key to all mythologies" (comparative religion and philology) and Lydgate's for "the original tissue" (clinical pathology and histology). The failure of both projects sets off the subtler issue of Dorothea's *Bildung*. As Ladislaw points out, Casaubon's ignorance of German has barred him from current research in his field. It is not that it is the wrong field. Eliot regarded comparative religion as among the foremost of the human sciences; it informed her earliest published works, her translations of David Friedrich Strauss and Ludwig Feuerbach, and her *Westminster Review* essay on *The Progress of the Intellect*:

> Mr. Mackay holds, with [Georg Friedrich] Creuzer, that the basis of all mythology was a nature-worship; that "those interpreters are in the main right, who held that the heathen Pantheon, in its infinite diversity of names and personifications, was but a multitudinous, though in its origin, unconscious allegory, of which physical phenomena, and principally the heavenly bodies, were the fundamental types." (*Essays* 37)

By the 1870s the dominant proponent of this thesis was the philologist Max Müller, who argued that the sun held the key to all mythologies, since all religious systems were declensions of a primal solar myth. In her review of Mackay, Eliot pinpoints the error she will dramatize in Casaubon: lured into allegory by "the many-sidedness of all symbols," he is one of those who "acquire a . . . fanatical faith in their rule of interpretation, and fall into the mistake of supposing that the conscious allegorizing of a modern can be a correct reproduction of what they acknowledge to be unconscious allegorizing in the ancients" (*Essays* 38–39).

The narrator renders the growth of Lydgate's "intellectual passion" (144; ch. 15) with lively sympathy:

> he was enamoured of that arduous invention which is the very eye of research, provisionally framing its object and correcting it to more and more exactness of relation; he wanted to pierce the obscurity of those minute processes which prepare human misery and joy, those invisible thoroughfares which are the first lurking-places of anguish, mania, and crime, that delicate poise and transition which determine the growth of happy or unhappy consciousness. (164–65; ch. 16)

The synthesis of invention and analysis accords with Eliot's own representational project in *Middlemarch*, making fiction the precision instrument of science. Lydgate has studied in Paris, the center of advanced physiology in the first quarter of the nineteenth century, and—on the eve of the development of cell theory in Germany in the 1830s—he devotes himself to the clinical pathology pioneered a generation earlier by Xavier Bichat. Schwann recognized Bichat's tissue theory as laying the foundation for his own identification of the cell as the fundamental unit of life. Schwann's and Schleiden's work won immediate acceptance in Britain; however Huxley, after initial enthusiasm, criticized it in his influential review of the field, "The Cell-Theory," which Eliot used as a source for *Middlemarch*. The narrator observes that Lydgate has formulated his research question—"What was the primitive tissue?"— "not quite in the way required by the awaiting answer" (148; ch. 15). Although commentators have diagnosed Lydgate's error as a failure to grasp the nascent cell theory (Rothfield 92–99; Blair 147), it is possible that Eliot was bringing Huxley's critique to bear on his attunement to the emergent paradigm, which would designate the nucleated cell as "the primitive tissue," a generative and autonomous "centre of force"—as opposed to a more thoroughly developmental understanding of the organism as an evolving "interconnection of parts" (Richmond). The mistake lies not in the identification of the primitive tissue (or of the key to all mythologies), but in the idea that a complex system, developing over time in interaction with its environment, can be contained in a unitary origin.

The novelist offers herself as a better scientist and a better mythographer than Lydgate or Casaubon. The novel's sympathetic attention to the individual case allows it to model the complex interdependencies between inward and outward life which comprise the social medium in all its fluidity:

> Young love-making—that gossamer web! Even the points it clings to—the things whence its subtle interlacings are swung—are scarcely perceptible: momentary touches of fingertips, meetings of rays from blue and dark orbs, unfinished phrases, lightest changes of cheek and lip, faintest tremors. The web itself is made of spontaneous beliefs

and indefinable joys, yearnings of one life towards another, visions of completeness, indefinite trust. And Lydgate fell to spinning that web from his inward self with wonderful rapidity. . . . (346; ch. 36)

The novel shows us the moral causes, the "spots of commonness," that attend Lydgate's failure, as much as the constitutional morbidity that attends Casaubon's.

The novel also mobilizes mythic schemes and patterns over and against Casaubon's futile project (see Beer 162–67). Eliot anticipates her own mythological method, in terms reminiscent of Coleridge's distinction between allegory and symbol, in her review of Mackay: "We do not see what unconscious allegory can mean, unless it be personification accompanied with belief, and with the spontaneous, vivid conception of a symbol, as opposed to the premeditated use of a poetical figure" (*Essays* 38–39). In *Middlemarch* the spokesman for this organicist aesthetic is Ladislaw, who defines the poet as one who possesses "a soul in which knowledge passes instantaneously into feeling, and feeling flashes back as a new organ of knowledge" (223; ch. 22). The narrator adorns him with symbolic highlights from Müller's solar mythos (Beer 166–67):

> The first impression on seeing Will was one of sunny brightness, which added to the uncertainty of his changing expression. Surely, his very features changed their form, his jaw looked sometimes large and sometimes small; and the little ripple in his nose was a preparation for metamorphosis. When he turned his head quickly his hair seemed to shake out light. . . . (209; ch. 21)

The trope of incipient metamorphosis points to an Ovidian register—but also a Darwinian (or Lamarckian) one, in which Ladislaw quivers on the brink of mutation into some new organic form. The combination of registers, mythological and biological, typifies Eliot's synthetic project in *Middlemarch*—as well as leaving vague what future type Ladislaw's physiognomy might be preparing.

Ladislaw is an outsider in Middlemarch, less conformable to the retentive, stabilizing pressure of its "threads of connection." Another interloper (also a son at odds with legitimacy and inheritance) stands as his symbolic opposite: the "alien and unaccountable" (472; ch. 47) Joshua Rigg, who appears at old Featherstone's funeral "as if from the moon":

> This was the stranger described by Mrs Cadwallader as frog-faced: a man perhaps about two or three and thirty, whose prominent eyes, thin-lipped, downward-curved mouth, and hair sleekly brushed away from a forehead that sank suddenly above the ridge of the eyebrows, certainly gave his face a batrachian unchangeableness of expression. (332; ch. 35)

If Ladislaw embodies the Apollonian promise of a future human type, Rigg exhibits what the American pulp modernist master H. P. Lovecraft will call the "Innsmouth look" (603)—hinting at a more sinister evolutionary path.

Shadows of the Coming Race

Eliot develops such hints more forcefully in her last novel, *Daniel Deronda*. The case of Juliet Fenn, "underhung and with receding brow resembling that of the more intelligent fishes," prompts the narrator to hold up the mirror to marriageable men, "since their natural selection of a mate prettier than themselves is not certain to bar the effect of their own ugliness" (114; ch. 11). The description of the Cohen children, "looking more Semitic than their parents, as the puppy lions show the spots of far-off progenitors" (389; ch. 33), alludes to Darwin's hypothesis "that there is a *tendency* in the young of each successive generation to produce the long-lost character, and that this tendency, from unknown causes, sometimes prevails," as in "the stripes on the whelp of a lion, or the spots on the young blackbird" (*Origin* 126, 323; emphasis in original). The novel invokes the recurrence of ancestral characteristics as at once a biological and a cultural theme. The narrator speculates that the Cohens' assignment of "the thin tails of the fried fish" to their poor relation Mordecai may be "a 'survival' of prehistoric practice, not yet generally admitted to be superstitious" (397; ch. 34). An instance of the technical scientific usage complained about by Eliot's reviewers (Beer 139–40), "survival" is a key concept in E. B. Tylor's *Primitive Culture* (1871), one of the foundational works of Victorian cultural anthropology (the disciplinary heir to comparative religion).

Daniel Deronda combines biological and cultural registers under the umbrella of organic development, but—more than the earlier novels—it problematizes the combination. We are made aware of tensions between the registers (as well as within them, e.g. "between pathological and embryological-evolutionary perspectives" [Rothfield 119]), and of the outright strangeness of the combination, which yields the novel's most challenging thematic and formal effects.

Grandcourt and his bride-to-be, Gwendolen Harleth, are separately figured as reptilian. She exhibits "a sort of Lamia beauty" (12; ch. 1), "attractive to all eyes except those which discerned in them too close a resemblance to the serpent, and objected to the revival of serpent-worship" (19; ch. 2); he is likened to "a handsome lizard of a hitherto unknown species" (137; ch. 13), "[looks] as neutral as an alligator" (157; ch. 15), and exerts "a will like that of a crab or a boa-constrictor, which goes on pinching or crushing without alarm at thunder" (423; ch. 35). The zoological language, with its Darwinian cladding, encourages a literal reading of Grandcourt's case as one of genetic reversion to a remote, organically latent, pre-mammalian ancestry: as though, his will-to-power unchecked by the higher faculties of reason or sympathy, he is part saurian. Tylor included a discussion of "serpent-worship" in *Primitive Culture* (2:240–42). The cultural-anthropological register makes Gwendolen's case seem less biologically fixed, still capable of evolving into full humanity, thus available for the reader's sympathy.

Commenting on "the undefinable stinging quality—as it were a trace of demon ancestry—which made some beholders hesitate in their admiration of Gwendolen"

(68; ch. 7), the narrator adumbrates hints about her Celtic ancestry, her "streak of superstition" (276; ch. 24), affinity for second sight, and other regressive mental habits. She suffers "fits of spiritual dread" at the sublime enlargement of her horizon:

> Solitude in any wide scene impressed her with an undefined feeling of immeasurable existence aloof from her, in the midst of which she was helplessly incapable of asserting herself. The little astronomy taught her at school used sometimes to set her imagination at work in a way that made her tremble: but always when some one joined her she recovered her indifference to the vastness in which she seemed an exile; she found again her usual world in which her will was of some avail. . . . (63–64; ch. 6)

The prospect of a vertiginous unworlding is not Gwendolen's alone. In a striking departure from the preceding novels, *Daniel Deronda* unmoors its characters from the stabilizing customary networks of provincial life, and from provincial life's synecdochic container, national life. A lyrical and hortatory evocation of the topos, early in the novel, echoes *The Descent of Man* (sympathy for dogs and donkeys) as well as Wordsworth's "Tintern Abbey" ("sweet habit of the blood" [see Buzard 295–96]):

> A human life, I think, should be well rooted in some spot of a native land, where it may get the love of tender kinship for the face of earth, for the labors men go forth to, for the sounds and accents that haunt it, for whatever will give that early home a familiar unmistakable difference amid the future widening of knowledge: a spot where the definiteness of early memories may be inwrought with affection, and—kindly acquaintance with all neighbors, even to the dogs and donkeys, may spread not by sentimental effort and reflection, but as a sweet habit of the blood. (22; ch. 3)

The elegiac mood suggests that the ideal of a "spot of native land" that may root human life in tender kinship is already overwhelmed, in a "widening of knowledge" that must include—the novel's networks of allusion tell us—Darwinian natural history. Gwendolen's spiritual agoraphobia intuits not only the ethical overthrow of her egoism, or the dissolution of the literary forms of an English national narrative (domestic fiction, provincial life, the marriage plot) for a world-historical destiny: but sublime reaches of evolutionary drift in which human life as such is no longer stable.

The cosmopolitan theme of *Daniel Deronda* (Anderson 119–46; Buzard 293–98) also resonates within this natural historical field. Its major proponent, Deronda himself, embodies the possibility of a future human type around whom the collapsing formations of national life might be reintegrated. Deronda is a stronger development of Ladislaw, a New Man whose metamorphic potential expresses itself in a "feminine" sympathetic receptiveness to the lives of others. Ladislaw was "a creature who entered into every one's feelings, and could take the pressure of their thought instead of urging his own" (*Middlemarch* 496; ch. 50); Deronda possesses a "many-sided" and "plenteous, flexible sympathy" that expresses itself in "a half-speculative, half-involuntary identification of himself with the objects he was looking at" (364; ch. 32; 189; ch. 17). Darwin identified sympathy as one of the (pre-human) "social instincts," the expansion of which marks a higher, fully human moral development: "that disinterested love for all living creatures, the most noble attribute of man . . . seems to arise incidentally from our sympathies becoming more tender and more widely diffused, until they are extended to all sentient beings" (*Descent* 159). Deronda's sympathy, however, has hypertrophied: "too reflective and diffusive," unanchored to a "fixed local habitation," it blocks him from being "an organic part of social life" (364–65; ch. 32).

Deronda reclaims an "organic centre" in the discovery of his Jewishness, which supplies him, and the novel, with the future-directed national destiny that England no longer affords. The language of organic life clusters around the Jewish theme of the second half of the novel, and comes to fruition in Daniel's embrace of his heritage, in which cultural and biological determinants are richly mixed. Amanda Anderson argues that Deronda's "reflective dialogism," the rational and critical analogue to his sympathetic faculty, counterbalances the "blind" organicism preached by Mordecai (121, 129–38). Deronda promises a renewal of Enlightenment principles of critical reason, dialectically combined with Romantic organicism, which will secure the future humanity for which "Israel" stands as utopian centre. The formal weirdness of the solution—and its implications for the current topic—should not be overlooked. The novel's interest in the recurrence of ancestral identities as the organic matrix for future development yields startling narrative symptoms: in a full-scale activation of the trope of metalepsis, or of the transference of effects into causes, and metaphors into events, as what were "gothic" shadows and omens in Gwendolen's story (her second sight) migrate into the literal register of plotting in Deronda's.

Its most scandalous instance comes with the fulfillment of Mordecai's Messianic vision of "the prefigured friend." Deronda's critical doubts, and the narrator's equivocations, scarcely mitigate the force with which "that wish-begotten belief in his Jewish birth, and that extravagant demand of discipleship," do actually turn out "to be the foreshadowing of an actual discovery and a genuine spiritual result" (512; ch. 41) —since these are endorsed by the novel's plot:

> The more exquisite quality of Deronda's nature—that keenly perceptive sympathetic emotiveness which ran along with his speculative tendency—was never more thoroughly tested. He felt nothing that could be called belief in the validity of Mordecai's impressions concerning him or in the probability of any greatly effective issue: what he felt was a profound sensibility to a cry from the depths of another and accompanying that, the summons to be receptive instead of superciliously prejudging. (496; ch. 40)

He does not believe, but he sympathizes; and sympathy can be ethically more powerful than belief, since the narrative does his believing for him.

> And since the unemotional intellect may carry us into a mathematical dreamland where nothing is but what is not, perhaps an emotional intellect may have absorbed into its passionate vision of possibilities some truth of what will be—the more comprehensive massive life feeding theory with new material, as the sensibility of the artist seizes combinations which science explains and justifies. (514; ch. 41)

Deronda's sympathetic receptivity marks his evolutionary fitness, while the recurrence of an ancestral narrative form—typological and prophetic—brings forth the narrative of the future.

The science informing these turns appears to be Darwin's controversial "pangenesis" hypothesis, mooted in *The Variation of Animals and Plants Under Domestication* (1868), which provides for the combination of biological and cultural developmental forces at work in *Daniel Deronda*. Lewes devoted the concluding pages of his Darwin essay to a defense of the hypothesis, and identified its central question as "how it is possible for a bodily or mental characteristic which distinguished a parent to reappear in the offspring—how the peculiarity of an ancestor suddenly reappears in a descendant after lying dormant through generations" (504). Darwin posited that all bodily cells secrete hereditary particles, "gemmules," which are carried in the blood to the reproductive organs; by this mechanism modifications acquired in the organism's lifetime could be transmitted to succeeding generations, where they might develop or lie dormant:

> Reversion depends on the transmission from the forefather to his descendants of dormant gemmules, which occasionally become developed under certain known or unknown conditions. Each animal and plant may be compared to a bed of mould full of seeds, most of which soon germinate, some lie for a period dormant, whilst others perish. (*Variation* 2:404)

Pangenesis authorizes Daniel's rebuke to his mother, "[t]he effects prepared by generations are likely to triumph over a contrivance which would bend them all to the satisfaction of self" (663; ch. 53), as well as his acknowledgment of Mordecai's "[having] given shape to . . . an inherited yearning—the effect of brooding, passionate thoughts in many ancestors—thoughts that seem to have been intensely present in my grandfather" (750; ch. 63).

In *Daniel Deronda* Eliot forges beyond the conventions of realism into a kind of science fiction. She would venture further. "Shadows of the Coming Race," originally meant as the final chapter of *Impressions of Theophrastus Such*, speculates on a post-human, indeed post-organic evolutionary pathway. (The title alludes to Edward Bulwer Lytton's fantasy of a subterranean superhuman civilization, destined to replace our own, in his 1871 novel *The Coming Race*.) The essay imagines a future in which machines designed to save human labour themselves develop ("by a further evolution of internal molecular movements") into self-reproducing organisms: "This last stage having been reached, either by man's contrivance or as an unforeseen result, one sees that the process of natural selection must drive men altogether out of the field" (*Impressions* 199). Eliot's closing evocation assumes an eerie, litotic lyricism, resonant with her own rhetorical repertoire of a now superseded organicism:

> Thus this planet may be filled with beings who will be blind and deaf as the inmost rock, yet will execute changes as delicate and complicated as those of human language and all the intricate web of what we call its effects, without sensitive impression, without

sensitive impulse: there may be, let us say, mute orations, mute rhapsodies, mute discussions, and no consciousness there even to enjoy the silence. (201)

REFERENCES

Anderson, Amanda. *The Powers of Distance: Cosmopolitanism and the Cultivation of Detachment.* Princeton: Princeton UP, 2001.

Beer, Gillian. *Darwin's Plots: Evolutionary Narrative in Darwin, George Eliot and Nineteenth-Century Fiction.* 3rd ed. Cambridge: Cambridge UP, 2009.

Blair, Kirstie. "Contagious Sympathies: George Eliot and Rudolf Virchow." *Unmapped Countries: Biological Visions in Nineteenth-Century Literature and Culture.* Ed. Anne-Julia Zwierlein. London: Anthem, 2005. 145–54.

Buzard, James. *Disorienting Fiction: The Autoethnographic Work of Nineteenth-Century British Novels.* Princeton: Princeton UP, 2005.

Dames, Nicholas. *The Physiology of the Novel: Reading, Neural Science, and the Form of Victorian Fiction.* Oxford: Oxford UP, 2007.

Darwin, Charles. *On the Origin of Species.* Ed. Gillian Beer. Oxford: Oxford UP, 2008.

Darwin, Charles. *The Descent of Man, and Selection in Relation to Sex.* Ed. James Moore and Adrian Desmond. London: Penguin, 2004.

Darwin, Charles. *The Variation of Animals and Plants under Domestication.* 2 vols. London: John Murray, 1868.

Eliot, George. *Adam Bede.* Ed. Stephen Gill. London: Penguin, 1985.

Eliot, George. *Daniel Deronda.* Ed. Terence Cave. London: Penguin, 1995.

Eliot, George. *Essays of George Eliot.* Ed. Thomas Pinney. New York: Columbia UP, 1963.

Eliot, George. *The George Eliot Letters.* Ed. Gordon S. Haight. 9 vols. New Haven: Yale UP, 1954–78.

Eliot, George. *Impressions of Theophrastus Such.* London: Blackwood, 1879.

Eliot, George. *Middlemarch.* Ed. Rosemary Ashton. London: Penguin, 1994.

Eliot, George. *The Mill on the Floss.* Ed. Gordon S. Haight. Oxford: Oxford UP, 1981.

Eliot, George. *Quarry for Middlemarch.* Ed. Anna Theresa Kitchel. Berkeley: U of California P, 1950.

Fielding, Henry. *Tom Jones, the History of a Foundling.* Ed. Simon Stern and John Bender. Oxford: Oxford UP, 1996.

Gallagher, Catherine. *The Body Economic: Life, Death, and Sensation in Political Economy and the Victorian Novel.* Princeton: Princeton UP, 2006.

Hume, David. *A Treatise of Human Nature.* Ed. Ernest C. Mossner. London: Penguin, 1984.

Lewes, G. H. "Mr. Darwin's Hypothesis, Part III." *Fortnightly Review* (New Series). 4 (1868): 61–80, 492–509.

Lovecraft, H. P. *Tales.* New York: Library of America, 2005.

Matus, Jill L. *Shock, Memory and the Unconscious in Victorian Fiction.* Cambridge: Cambridge UP, 2009.

Richmond, Marsha L. "T. H. Huxley's Criticism of German Cell Theory: An Epigenetic and Physiological Interpretation of Cell Structure." *Journal of the History of Biology* 33.2 (2000): 247–89.

Rothfield, Lawrence. *Vital Signs: Medical Realism in Nineteenth-Century Literature.* Princeton: Princeton UP, 1992.

Shuttleworth, Sally. *George Eliot and Nineteenth-Century Science: The Make Believe of a Beginning.* Cambridge: Cambridge UP, 1984.

Tylor, Edward Burnett. *Primitive Culture: Researches into the Development of Mythology, Philosophy, Religion, Language, Art and Customs.* 2 vols. London: John Murray, 1871.

34
Eliot, Evolution, and Aesthetics

Jonathan Loesberg

In the beginning, art was never enough for Eliot. And Darwin's theory of evolution was always just a bit too much. About the former, as Samuel Johnson said about Clarissa's attitude toward the truth, there was always something she preferred to it (Hill 297). About the latter, she could be both dismissive in her letters and obviously troubled in her novels (Beer 156–58). Both of these attitudes have been noticed before. The connection between the attitudes and the way her grappling particularly with sexual selection changed her implicit, though not explicit, attitude toward aesthetics, however, has not drawn much remark. Partly the connection goes unremarked upon because discussions not only of aesthetics in Eliot but of nineteenth-century aesthetics generally do not usually notice the ways ideas about art and ideas about evolution bumped into each other over the issue of design, specifically the question of whether design existed in nature and how one might explain its existence. Because neither evolutionary theorists nor aesthetic theorists and artists much noticed the connection, the effects of one theory upon the other are easy to miss. Nevertheless, Eliot's developing sense of marriage as an insufficient end (both in the sense of goal and of closure) in her final two novels and her clearly deeply reflective consideration of Darwin's theory of sexual selection in *Daniel Deronda* lead to an implicit openness to an aesthetic mode of justifying one's ends. That openness effectively revises her more usually commented on descriptions of her realism and its link with human sympathy as the moral justification of her art. Oddly, a short consideration of the recent movement toward an evolutionary theory of literature will help clarify this shift.

A Companion to George Eliot, First Edition. Edited by Amanda Anderson and Harry E. Shaw.
© 2013 John Wiley & Sons, Ltd. Published 2016 by John Wiley & Sons, Ltd.

Before wandering off into contemporary evolutionary literary theory, however, let us start with the original connection between evolutionary explanations of nature and aesthetic explanations of natural beauty, whose groundwork is in Kant. The Introduction to *The Critique of Judgment* explains the purpose of the book as establishing the validity of a teleological judgment of nature that does not make the error of natural theology in arguing that since nature appears to have design and purpose, it must have a designer. This argument has two stages. First Kant will establish that it is intellectually coherent to perceive purposive form in things without attributing purpose to them (hence the aesthetic judgment's apprehension, in objects it perceives as beautiful, of their having purposiveness without purpose). Second, in the book's second half, on the teleological judgment, he extends his argument from *The Critique of Pure Reason* against the argument from design, while outlining how one can still rationally consider nature as morally ordered. None of this has any direct bearing on a theory of evolution, obviously, and although Kant gives empirical reasons for being skeptical of such theories, he also declares his teleological theory neutral with regard to them. And the aesthetic judgment explicitly entails an indifference to the existence of the object, which includes an indifference to its functional properties: in judging a flower to be beautiful, for instance, Kant asserts that we do not attend to the reproductive function of the blossom (Kant 76). Still, Kant's detachment of the form of design—purposiveness—from the fact of design—purpose—and his use of this distinction in his argument against deducing a designer from the appearance of design in nature, resulted in a natural object that looked much like the one depicted by Darwin's explaining of function as deriving somewhat haphazardly from natural selection. As George Levine shows in his discussion of John Herschel's response to Darwin, one could object to Darwin's antiteleological view of nature by analogy to an implicit objection to Kant's unpurposed aesthetic object.[1]

Levine has also explained the effect of Darwin's antiteleology on the form of Victorian narrative, most fully with regard to Anthony Trollope (*Darwin and the Novelists* 177–209), and his reading there has clear relevance for Eliot's claim, in *Adam Bede*'s justification of unideal characters, that her narratives are determined by the world she represents. But one should also note that, while Eliot accepted Darwin's theory as a description of the working of nature, she does not accept absence of purpose, and particularly moral purpose, as an acceptable end of art. Her declaration that Walter Pater's aestheticism was "poisonous in its false principles of criticism and false conception of life" is a particularly sharp manifestation of this view (*Letters* 5:100). Her insistence on moral purpose throughout her novels surely has a lot to do with her decline in reputation in the modernist period, whose own formalism revolted against such moralism. Despite her declaration that Pater's principles were false, however, she would not have insisted on the moral purposes of her art if she had not thought that Pater might be right and that art in and of itself might not have moral purpose. And, as we will see, she regularly depicted admirers of art as perhaps not sufficiently morally directed, a depiction that makes sense not if Pater is wrong about art but only if art is wrong about life. So the troubling antiteleology of Darwin's theory could also be a troubling antiteleology in art. And that view of art, worked out in Kant, as well as influencing important figures who had read Kant, such as Pater, was held commonly by numbers who had not read him as well.

But art can be even more pointless than evolution, it turns out, and that very pointlessness became its point for Eliot in her later fiction. Evolution threatened to capture human beings in a process that made life explicable without making it meaningful. In particular, as we will see, the theory of sexual selection made courtship narratives, at least in Eliot's final two novels, look like entrapment in generation. And the pointlessness of art in *Daniel Deronda* could become the creation of a distance from which to choose heritage rather than be entrapped by it. In order to give a full significance to that reading of art's potentially positive role in Eliot's final fiction, we need to start with an understanding of the potentially destructive role it always played in the theory of sexual selection, which Darwin came to find a necessary addition to natural selection and which has recently played an enhanced role both in evolutionary psychology and in explanations of the role of art in human evolution. The problem with the theory of sexual selection, however, is that it has never quite found the life-or-death melodramatic outcome of natural selection to explain its basic causal process. This problem has led both to more nuanced evolutionary literary theory and a contradictorily persistent role for aesthetics as explaining evolutionary causation rather than being explained by it. And this dual role of aesthetics, as both an escape from evolutionary ends and, in sexual selection, as its driving cause, allows Eliot's use of it in her final fiction.

In order to understand the role of art, we must briefly explain Darwin's theory of sexual selection and its more recent refinements. The theory starts with Darwin's recognition that some aspects of some species do not seem explicable in terms of natural selection, notoriously, the peacock's tail, whose length and ornateness would seem to make the peacock more vulnerable to predation than would a shorter, lighter tail that aided rather than impeded flight. Famously, Darwin wrote to Asa Gray, "The sight of a peacock's tail, whenever I gaze at it, makes me sick!" (*Correspondence* 140). To solve the problem Darwin took advantage of the fact that natural selection for survival advantage was always instrumental to reproductive advantage (reproduction, not mere endurance, being the way one passes on traits). He thus posited that some traits led to direct advantages in access to reproduction, even at the cost of survival benefit. Some of these traits might provide aid in a competition that looked enough like the competition entailed by natural selection as to make the explanation not really look that different from natural selection (deer developing antlers to do battle over access to mates, the shaping of reproductive organs in plants to aid the dissemination of seeds). But to explain the peacock's tail, Darwin had to posit that the peahen was choosing peacocks with longer tails, regardless of its disadvantage to the peacock's survival, thus giving those peacocks, despite their increased vulnerability to predation, a reproductive advantage.

Critics frequently attribute the controversial quality of this aspect of Darwin's theory to its offense of Victorian gender expectations (see Miller 42–45). More to the point, though, is the question of why a peahen would choose a mate with a longer tail. If we assume that animals do not choose at all but act in accord with practices leading to survival and/or reproductive advantages for themselves and their offspring, the peahen's preference makes no sense as it endangers the survival of male offspring to whom the trait is passed on. Darwin attributed the female choice to aesthetic preference, which made his theory ready-made for extension into human courtship rituals, but which really still begged the question that started him on the quest for the theory (*Descent* 640). Now, instead of the peacock developing a trait that is a survival disadvantage, he has the female preferring a trait that leads to a survival disadvantage among her own offspring, which hardly solves the original problem. One could lessen the problem by attributing various female preferences to pure accident and arguing that as long as the accident doesn't lead to features that cause extinction (Miller 42), there is nothing to control for its occurrence. But one might have as well argued that the trait itself developed randomly as to argue that the preference developed randomly. Either way, one had built into the theory a place for aesthetic preference that the theory could not explain.

With regard to Eliot, one might leave the theory here since Darwin's articulation of it, with its claim that female birds expressed an aesthetic preference, would have been all she knew. But its further development and the ways that development both serves to ground an aesthetically complex evolutionary theory of literature while remaining, for better or worse, vexed with a remaining element of aesthetic pointlessness, so to speak, gives a deeper explanation of the role aesthetics came to play in Eliot's last work. Although there has been a fair amount of work on sexual selection in the twentieth century, the most important advance has been the development by Amotz and Avishag Zahavi of the much broader concept of costly signaling, by which an organism bears an excessive burden or undertakes a practice that seems to work against its own immediate interests in order to signal its ability to bear that cost and thus its general fitness: "the high cost that animal signaling often involves is clearly seen in the case of the peacock. Most people have seen and admired a peacock spreading and quivering his enormous tail. . . . But to be able to put on such shows, peacocks have to drag massive tails around most of the year. By managing to find food and avoid predators despite such a burden, a peacock proves that he is the high-quality mate that the peahen is seeking to father her future chicks" (ix). In other words, the peacock's ability to survive the disadvantage of bearing the tail, instead of being a theoretical problem, becomes a theoretical solution. Organisms that show how well they bear handicaps display their fitness. The handicaps function as external signs of an otherwise invisible, internal fitness. The concept obviously has broader applications than sexual selection. But its explanation of the mechanism of sexual selection, by doing away with the notion of aesthetic preference, turns the main problem of that theory, why the female selects, into its main strength.

From this theory, it's a short step to offer an explanation of the evolutionary development of artistic ability as a like kind of sexually selected fitness indicator. As long as one remembers that such an explanation tells us about how art came about and not what it can be or do, there is a good possibility that one such theory may sketch out something like what happened.[2] But such a theory will have little relevance in describing the capacities of art and literature. William Flesch's *Comeuppance* represents an important exception to these theories in its literary complexities and, since its strengths and weaknesses will highlight the role Eliot's later view of art played in her connected view of sexual selection, a brief discussion of that theory will bring us back to Eliot and aesthetics in its fullest context.

Since he wants to argue that literature ultimately satisfies a socially beneficial genetic preference for cooperation, Flesch's theory begins with the argument, frequently made, that selection in humans favors cooperation because, in a competition between two groups for survival, a cooperating group will always do better than a non-cooperating one. Thus, even though individuals may benefit by defecting from the cooperating system (free riding, on the analogy with the person who avoids paying a fare and still rides the subway), their long-term benefit will align with the cooperation that benefits the group (too many free riders and the subway goes broke and serves no one). The problem with the theory is that, according to arguments that calculate probabilities, any given individual will always benefit more from both getting benefits from a cooperating system and defecting from it when advantageous than he or she would from merely cooperating. And this defection benefit exists well past the point at which so many individuals would free ride as to destroy the cooperating system (Flesch 46).

To solve this problem, Flesch proposes a systemic policing system whereby altruistic punishers make defection more costly to free riders than cooperation. An altruistic punisher punishes defectors in excess of the benefit he or she receives as an individual from the punishment. And, indeed, for the altruistic punishing to function as an effective policing system, the punishment would have to cost the punisher more than it benefits him or her. Only if free riders stand more to lose from the possibility of threatened punishment than they stand to gain from defecting will the benefits of cooperation outweigh those of cheating, so only if the punishment exceeds the benefit it affords the individual punisher will it succeed in policing. Altruistic punishers, of course, will fare less well than a non-punishing cooperator, thus destabilizing the system again. But Flesch also posits that our evolved ability to understand other minds, to monitor the behavior of other human beings, allows a system of mutual monitoring of both cooperation and altruistic punishment that sufficiently rewards all forms of altruistic behavior so as to stabilize the system. But this system also works because we respond to altruistic behavior, and especially altruistic punishment, as we do to costly signaling. As a result of the monitoring system, the cost of punishment is then outweighed by the benefit the signaling accrues to the individual punisher. Flesch thus combines the theory of costly signaling with the theory that cooperation evolves from a combination of rewarding altruistic behavior with regulating free riders by also rewarding altruistic punishment. Altruistic punishment, he argues, operates by being a costly signal of the punisher's social cooperation, just as handicaps operate to signal their possessors' general fitness. Further, human beings, as a part of the general pleasure they take in tracking the workings of other minds, take pleasure in tracking displays of such altruistic punishment (it is not just the punishment, or even the punishment at all, but the altruistic intention of engaging in it that we respond to).[3]

Costly signaling, in this theory, starts to function in the manner of an aesthetic display. It signals an indirect value only by putting on a display in excess of utility. Altruistic punishers signal their altruism by the way their punishment exceeds any benefit they, or even the system, receives from it directly. They and the system receive the benefit from the response of the system to the excessive display. From here, Flesch can argue that we enjoy precisely the recounting of the activity of fictive characters because such recounting gives, in a pure and distilled form, the costly signaling entailed in altruistic punishment. It is important to note that literature doesn't merely display altruistic punishment, though it does do that frequently and significantly, nor can Flesch's argument be reduced to such an uninterestingly limited claim. Rather, the effects we frequently think of as constitutively literary—complex psychological interaction of characters, self-referential narrative effects, etc.—work because we experience a pleasure in seeing such signals without regard to what they signal. And we experience that pleasure because such costly signals do reliably signal the forms of strongly reciprocal behavior that protect our cooperation.

The strength of this argument, which explicitly means to bring poststructuralist readings of literature in accord with an evolutionary basis to the human valuings of what those readings show us, though, rests on the very unpoststructuralist notion that costly signals are always accurate. Taken from a very long, evolutionary perspective, that claim, made explicitly by the Zahavis in their explanation of the theory, should be accurate. If peacocks with low levels of fitness developed ornate tails as a way of attracting mates, even assuming that they would not fall victim to predation because they did not have the strength they advertised (accidents happen, organisms get lucky), the resulting offspring would also inherit those low levels of fitness along with continuing the burden of that tail. Either females would develop a taste for short, aesthetically uninteresting tails or, more efficiently, peacocks who signaled falsely would have a long-term—over many generations—lower survival rate than peacocks who signaled accurately (in the long term, accidents and luck come out in the wash), thus stabilizing the accuracy of the signal. But there's a large difference between an accuracy that will occur over the long term and an absolute accuracy. When the Zahavis discuss costly signaling in terms of dominance within the bands of babblers they observed over many years, they saw numbers of cases of signals being tested and found wanting in terms of battles between individuals for dominance. Moreover, it seems extraordinarily unlikely that in any situation in which animals reacted to signals as indicating something different from what they were (and this is what a signal is, after all), there would not be some benefit that would accrue to free riding, false signalers. Their numbers would be kept in control by long-term forces. But there would surely always be enough of them so that signals, like all signs, would work because they could be inaccurate and sometimes were.

And this situation is magnified when human beings signal each other. One sees this in the highly unlikely analogy the Zahavis set up between vocalizing prey and jeering children in a game of tag in which only children with excess strength will jeer at the child who is "it" and that child will only chase those who do not jeer (8). But the point of tag is competition, not merely whether one is tagged or not, and if one does not taunt the child who is "it," there is little point in playing, and if the child who is "it" does not chase the strongest taunters, he or she might as well go play marbles. The point, of course, is that tag is a game with very different ends then the practice of preying or avoiding predation, and inaccurate signaling, as well as the sometimes wasteful testing of such signaling, is an implicit part of the game. Evolution probably allows wayward false signaling.[4] But numbers of human activities absolutely depend on it. Fictive narratives begin with false signaling, telling us about people who don't exist, and if our pleasure in those narratives depends on taking the signals as accurate, as Flesch argues, more fools we.

I do not mean to attack the principle of costly signaling in evolutionary theory or its force as explaining how sexual selection might work, as long as one understands the obvious dangers of applying it too quickly to human activities where outcomes aren't protected even in the long-term by survival disadvantage. And with regard to Flesch's theory, I consider a literary critic who dispenses with an elegant theory merely because it might be empirically inaccurate to be guilty of wanton destruction. Rather, I mean to indicate the way artistic practices may mime with delusory accuracy precisely the processes that are meant to explain them. Just as Darwin posited an inexplicable, ornithological aesthetic preference to explain the evolutionary inexplicableness of the feature it oddly preferred, Flesch posits the absolute accuracy of costly signaling to explain the manifest inaccuracy—the fictiveness of characters—implicit in signaling, of which literature obviously takes advantage. His theory brings us so close to so many aspects of literature, I would argue, not because it explains how literature evolved but because literature can mime a posited process with such dazzlingly inaccurate signaling. The striking factor in both Darwin's posited aesthetic response in birds and in Flesch's costly signaling is that they bring back as driving cause the form of aesthetic pointlessness (there is no reason for the female bird's aesthetic preference; the costly signal only works to the extent that it may not signal directly) that conflicts with what is often taken to be the reductive determinism of evolutionary explanation. Put with crude simplicity, for instance, the theory of sexual selection tells us that that which we think we find attractive merely moves us instinctively to successful reproductive outcomes, whose value is finally biological rather than individual. But if the driver of sexual selection or of genetically determined cooperation is aesthetic taste or costly signaling, the freeplay they allow may come to function, as they will in Eliot, to allow the ethical reading of conscious choice that she looks for.

With this account of the way an aesthetic perspective allows an escape from the inevitabilities of natural selection's causal mechanism, both in Darwin's times and still, we may outline the reasons for Eliot's slow development of an aesthetic perspective as one that enabled moral choice rather than expelled it. We know, of course, what wasn't enough in art for Eliot. In the seventeenth chapter to *Adam Bede*, in which the narrative pauses a little and over which critics pause endlessly, she values the realism to which she declares herself aligned for the moral sympathy to which it leads and which she finds most necessary. The question, though, is less what extra-aesthetic value she thinks art needs to make it valuable than why she thinks realism will lead to that value. Within the chapter itself, having instanced her taste for Dutch painting, she imagines an idealist friend reacting, "What clumsy, ugly people!" (195; ch.17), and one wonders why she doesn't think this response might be more widespread. Certainly John Ruskin, whose realism she praised, did not return the favor and criticized *The Mill on the Floss* for its unidealized portraiture (377).

Although sympathy always has a primary moral value in Eliot, one should note that by *Middlemarch* it is an epistemological achievement made in the face of our natural tendency to see ourselves as that which gives the world meaning and purpose. There is no notion that simple exposure to reality will incite it or the narrator would hardly need so strenuously to invoke our sympathetic understanding of egoism. But, more pertinently for the shift in her thinking about art, her evaluation of community feeling and of the courtship and sexual love with which it is connected start to change. Eliot starts to see reproduction and its motivation, love, first without and later with reference to Darwin, as reducing human beings to natural ends and obstructing our freedom to fashion ends for ourselves. And that change will lead to a much more positive, if still ambiguous, stance toward a formalist concept of intrinsic aesthetic value.

Written in explicit awareness of Darwin, *Middlemarch*, although it offers an ending in happy marriage, regularly construes that marriage as a failure to achieve a higher end, as a capitulation to something like a Darwinian, biological urge. And although it is not ready to oppose an aesthetic definition of self-chosen ends to what it seems to describe as a fall into marriage, that form of figuration is already there in the novel's mode of giving Dorothea a significance that its explicit analysis of human awareness won't bear. Both the awareness of Darwin and the attempt to articulate an alternative to the ends of natural selection begins with the novel's "Prelude" and its opposition of the pre-figured Dorothea with other women:

> the limits of variation [in the abilities of women] are really much wider than any one would imagine from the sameness of women's coiffure and the favorite love-stories in prose and verse. Here and there a cygnet is reared uneasily among the ducklings in the brown pond, and never finds the living stream in fellowship with its own oary-footed kind. Here and there is born a Saint Theresa, foundress of nothing, whose loving heartbeats and sobs after an unattained goodness tremble off and are dispersed among hindrances, instead of centring in some long-recognized dead. (3; Prelude)

Gillian Beer has already noted the Darwinian resonance of the word "variation" here (149), and given that the metaphor, via Hans Christian Anderson, immediately pushes forward to a distinction between species, the resonance seems quite explicit. But a distinction between two species is more absolute than one of variety. The cygnet will not just feel out of place among the ducks. It will not reproduce there. And since the different woman will have no living stream of fellowship, she as well would be denied reproduction. But the paragraph also denies that reproduction is what either we or she should want. Part of the variation is that she wants something different than that which is promised in love-stories. Further, although a cygnet could find other cygnets and thus biological fellowship, no such outcome will satisfy desires of the variety St. Theresa exemplifies.

The narrator reinforces the implication that marriage and reproduction are a descent into the biologically driven immediately in the first chapter: "Certainly such elements [being enamoured of intensity and greatness and likely to seek martyrdom] in the character of a marriageable girl tended to interfere with her lot, and hinder it from being decided according to custom, by good looks, vanity, and merely canine affection" (6; ch. 1). This opening section is, of course, decidedly ironic about Dorothea's intellectual ambitions and their results in directing her toward a marriage with Casaubon. No marriage led to by merely canine affection is more disastrous than is hers and Casaubon's. And some marriages, in the novel, grounded in canine affection are genuinely happy for the participants. But the novel never really holds up marriage as a desirable end for Dorothea. After Casaubon's death, Mrs. Cadwallader looks to find a suitable match for Dorothea as a way to bring her back into the control of the Middlemarch community: "But I see clearly a husband is the best thing to keep her in order" (333; ch. 54). And, of course, the "Finale," in response to those who questioned her marriage to Will as a successful end for her, does not argue that it is an unmitigatedly happy end for her but merely that "if the determining acts of her life were not ideally beautiful," the reason for that was that her community, "an imperfect social state," offered her no better outcome. *Middlemarch* is generally a novel about the failure of ambitions for enduring, even transcendent achievement. Because those ambitions are not merely Dorothea's but Lydgate's, Casaubon's, even Bulstrode's, the novel aligns its skepticism about them both with ironic realism about ideals and with the moral criticism of the egoistic delusions those ambitions entail. It sees the biological and psychological forces of what will come to be called sexual selection as leading to ends that are fallings from higher possibilities, that are connected with canine affection.

Sexual selection, as a concept, of course, does not yet operate in *Middlemarch*, which appeared in print only barely after the publication of *The Descent of Man*. And if Darwin's thinking about natural selection does figure there as part of the forces driving marriage and reproduction, Eliot hardly needed Darwin to arrive at her depiction of marriage as one of the ways her society kept women in order. She did not yet have the role aesthetics played to trouble sexual selection as a biological explanation to move her toward rethinking art's possibilities. And, for the most part, *Middlemarch* is as dismissive of the artistic perspective as Eliot was of Pater. Her remark about an impoverished cottage as perceivable as beautiful when seen apart from "the depressions of agricultural interest" (246; ch. 39), is fairly tangential to her ironic treatment of the landlord, Mr. Brooke, and seems more a random barb at an aesthetic so disinterested as to be unaware of human suffering. And the narrator is equally ironic about Will's tendency toward an aestheticism that would lead him to unproductive "self-culture" (286; ch. 46) were it not for his love of Dorothea.

Sexual selection is a quite conscious theme in *Daniel Deronda* precisely in the novel's resistance to it. As Beer has argued, the novel is explicitly concerned with how human beings may affect their future and, in the light of *The Descent of Man*, the role sexual selection may play in shaping the species and thus its future. But, as Beer notes, many characters seem to resist reproduction and thus, ostensibly, sexual selection. Gwendolen's and Daniel's marriages are without offspring and Mordecai's spiritual heritage, whatever its racial and cultural make-up is precisely not Darwinian (181–85). But childless couplings do not defeat sexual selection. They contribute to it: the selection occurs only if not all organisms have equal numbers of offspring. Eliot may contest Herbert Spencer's antifeminist argument that women must confine themselves to their role as mothers for the future benefit of the species (see Paxton's discussion of Rosamond's miscarriage in *Middlemarch* [177] and her argument about Spencer and *Daniel Deronda* [198–232]). But she cannot contest Darwin's claim to describe a mechanism that works regardless of choice merely by depicting a choice that still functions in terms of the mechanism described. Rather than contest sexual selection, however, the novel creates the structure of sexual selection and the passing on of blood heritage at every turn and then defeats that structure's implications precisely with the aesthetic concepts that drive both Darwin's selection—the taste of peahens for beauty without regard to fitness—and the contemporary re-explanation of it based on costly signaling, a concept that as William Flesch's argument has shown us, was all too ready to be employed as an explanation for the evolution of art because it was already aesthetic. And this conceptual role for an epistemological and analytic aesthetics that stands apart from ends and frees us from them plays an explicit role in how Deronda comes to hold deeply the ends he discovers for himself.

Critics regularly separate the Deronda section of the novel from the Gwendolen section, or at least treat them in relative isolation, considering the Gwendolen section as in the vein of Eliot's realism. And, indeed, the Gwendolen section maintains Eliot's normal resistance to idealized ends, though only by refusing what would be the natural connection between the two plots. The outcome the plot regularly predicts, one all characters in the novel are aware of, the one the opening sentence—a question not only the author but Deronda asks about Gwendolen's beauty—sets up, is, of course, Gwendolen's marriage with Deronda. Indeed, Deronda himself, retrospectively, outlines that plot as having been a likely one: "Anyone who knows him cannot wonder at his inward confession, that if all this had happened little more than a year ago, he would hardly have asked himself whether he loved her: the impetuous determining impulse which would have moved him would have been to save her from sorrow, to shelter her life forever more from the dangers of loneliness, and carry out to the last the rescue he had begun in that monitory redemption of the necklace" (655; ch. 65). One should note that, posed this way, retrospectively, this proposed ending carries its wish-fulfillment element from Gwendolen's perspective on its face. Having made the instructive bad marital choice, she would be rescued by the right one that had been there all along. One might consider, in the light of this moment, how convenient Casuabon's death was for the plot of *Middlemarch*, assuming one considers Dorothea's marriage a happy end rather than a form of failure. But from Deronda's perspective, what the passage stresses is that the expected outcome would not have been a choice, but an impulse, the kind of impulse that drives sexual selection and courtship plots.

This might seem overreading, did it not come at the climax of a plot that at key moments refers explicitly to sexual selection and connects it to courtship narrative in a way that rewrites Jane Austen quite devastatingly. Thus, for instance, in considering Grandcourt as a marriage prospect, the narrator first compares his title to the plumage on male birds, and then proceeds to a rewriting of the first sentence of *Pride and Prejudice*:

> Some readers of this history will doubtless regard it as incredible that people should construct matrimonial prospects on the mere report that a bachelor of good fortune and possibilities was coming within reach, and will reject the statement as a mere outflow of gall: they will aver that neither they or their first cousins have minds so unbridled; and that in fact this is not human nature. (76; ch. 9)

The irony here has more edges than one. It, of course, reproduces the irony of Austen's first sentence about expectations with regard to the desires of prosperous bachelors. But it attributes to its readers the ironic objection to the belief held by Austen's narrator, only to suggest that despite that conscious objection to the workings of natural impulse, impulse in fact works out according to satirized belief.[5] Thus, the courtship narrative seems reduced to the activity of sexual selection. Gwendolen, of course, also follows this narrative. Her impulses are less direct, connecting Grandcourt's clear lack of the usual courtship impulses with an unusual elegance. But, of course, this oddly aesthetic impulse explains how the peacock came to be burdened with his tail. And if Gwendolen must bear the burden of her own taste, she is available both for condemnation for moral failure and for hope for moral regeneration precisely because she acts in accord with an aesthetic that both founds and interrupts sexual selection, both enables its biological process and always threatens to make it more and less than suited for evolutionary ends.

The Deronda plot might seem more distanced from this drama of trying to avoid sexual selection and being caught up in it, but it recaptures the biological under the rubric of heritage in Daniel's finding his parentage and thus becoming available to act as Mordecai's spiritual heir. This plot, oddly, also is riddled with representations of art and artists whose activities confront, accord with, and finally redefine Deronda's final interpretation of the meaning of his heritage. One must begin by confronting how hard it is to figure out just what Deronda's supposed heritage is and what it means to him. Although Mordecai sees him as a spiritual heir of a nationhood based on racial unity and thus assumes he must be Jewish, one must note that even if this reading were the novel's, spiritual transmission is not biological heritage: Deronda must accept it regardless of his Jewishness, and once he has accepted it, one expects that that discovery could come in one way if it didn't come in another. One can imagine him declaring himself spiritually Jewish and that would not be that far from what he in fact does do. Further, as Amanda Anderson has argued, Deronda does not accept his heritage straightforwardly, posing his acceptance on a reflective distance that comes from his upbringing as an English gentleman and arguing both to his mother and to Kalonymos that he will not simply embody his grandfather's desires for him (whatever they are: although he receives a written inheritance from his grandfather and takes trouble to find out what it is, it seems never sufficiently important for it to be reproduced in the novel). Moreover, although Anderson praises that reflective distance as giving his nationalism an Enlightenment basis, one must also note that it puts Deronda more in the position of Theophrastus Such in "The Modern Hep! Hep! Hep!" praising nationalism on abstract rationalist terms that cannot really accord with the very exclusivity it praises in the way nationalists hold their nationalism. And the narrator also sees this opposition, at least to the extent that she opposes in Deronda a "reflective analysis" and a tendency resulting from it to "neutralize" sympathy (307; ch. 32). In effect, Deronda's birth seems predetermined by the narrative even as we can see that the identity the birth allows is also constructed. And this conflict in the meaning of his identity merely reflects the conflict between the way he holds his new-found identity and the way his identity seems to allow that holding to occur.[6]

This conflicted perspective precisely accords with an even more undigested conflict over the role of art in the novel. In addition to Klesmer, musicians and potential musicians in the novel include Daniel's mother, Daniel, Mirah, and Gwendolen (if we make the category "artist," we may add Hans Meyrick's painting for good measure). Nor is there any clear sense of how to take this list. Mirah's inability to be a professional singer seems connected with her idealized innocence. But if Gwendolen could have been an artist, she would have escaped her marital turmoil. And Daniel spurns singing as a profession because, as a career, it would take him away from what he thinks of as his birthright as an English gentleman, an outcome that the novel does not finally see as a bad one. Meanwhile Princess Halm-Eberstein's artistry allows her what Gwendolen's insufficient talent will not and yet we feel her somehow to blame for this. Perhaps the key to these conflicting evaluations is the reason one of Mirah's teachers give for her ultimate inability to be a professional singer: "She will never be an artist: she has no notion of being anybody but herself. That does very well now, but by-and-by you will see—she will have no more face and action than a singing-bird" (197; ch. 20). Mirah's inability to be other than herself might evidence an authenticity a true artist would lack. But oddly, its result would be to rob her of identity and make her singing as driven and lacking in interiority as that of a singing-bird. One notes that Princess Halm-Eberstein says of herself that she could act as well as she sang. And if Deronda wants to accept the Jewishness she hands down to him unwillingly, he does not seem to recognize that in his sympathy, in his claim to understand her, although he does not act, he shows the same ability to throw himself out of himself that she has. As she says, in his desire to comprehend her at least, he is not like his grandfather. In his desire to make an identity for himself that recognizes both his past cosmopolitanism and his future nationalism, he inherits, if that is the way to put the handing-off of flexibility, an aspect of her artistry. Of course, we already know that he has inherited the artistry—at least her singing ability—that led to her rebellion.

Let us conclude with the notion of costly signaling, that concept that, when the signaling is accurate, finally explains the workings of sexual selection and when it is inaccurate, can become fictiveness. Deronda's Jewishness, particularly to Mordecai (the subject of whose unsexual choice he is) functions in many of the ways such signals do. On the one hand, because he bears it as an English gentleman—and Mordecai wants his inheritor to "have been used to all the refinements of social life" (405; ch. 38)—it is a burden that shows his fitness for playing the role Mordecai wants for him. On the other hand, because the Jewishness is meant to be his identity, it should hardly be the signal; the social refinement, which would be no burden, would be that. And yet it is the signal because it verifies what Mordecai intuits about his identity rather than being what he first sees. And finally, it is simultaneously accurate, as it should be for selection, and at the least ambiguous, in accord with the artistry Daniel "inherits" from his mother and uses to redefine his commitment to Mordecai's dream. In its very disastrousness, Gwendolen's sexual selection of Grandcourt, expresses an aesthetic preference that makes an evolutionary explanation, although not inaccurate, insufficient to account for that selection entirely. More centrally, Deronda's ambiguously signifying consciousness, partaking both of the sympathy that, earlier in the novel, had threatened him with a debilitating moral neutrality, and an assumed as well as inherited identity that his moral stance leads him to take in his own way, even as it functions within the form of the heritage Mordecai proposes, creates the possibility of reflective distance that allows an ambiguously accepted nationalism. George Eliot may never have liked what she saw Darwin telling her, but she saw that he was telling her something about an aesthetic perspective that gave her a clearer protest to what she saw as the constraints of marriage and reproduction as a biological impulse and a mode of social control even in her early fiction, and led to a view of art as complex as her view of Deronda's nationalism and his identity.

NOTES

1   Herschel does not explicitly reference Kant or have him in mind, but he objects to "the Laputan method of composing books (pushed *à l'outrance*) as a sufficient account of Shakespeare," thus objecting to considering books as objects without the purpose that inten-

tion entails (qtd. in Levine, *Darwin and the Novelists* 92).

2   But one should keep in mind Steven Pinker's argument that art entails simply human beings taking advantage of certain pleasure-giving features of the brain to create much more pow-

erful pleasures than those for which they developed (524–25).

3 Here he follows the work of Lisa Zunshine.

4 It probably even rewards it, within limits, As T. H. Huxley says about a similar argument, if we have evolved moral practices of cooperation, we have certainly also evolved immoral practices of theft and murder, and there is as much evolutionary sanction for the one as for the other (80).

5 As is in fact the case in *Pride and Prejudice*, in which all prosperous bachelors do in fact marry and mostly according to the desires of Mrs. Bennett. On this, note Zunshine (174) quoting Hilary Schor.

6 On the way the narrative structure predetermines what we are supposed to think is an origin Deronda discovers, see Chase.

REFERENCES

Anderson, Amanda. "George Eliot and the Jewish Question." *The Yale Journal of Criticism* 10.1 (1997): 39–61.

Beer, Gillian. *Darwin's Plots: Evolutionary Narrative in Darwin, George Eliot and Nineteenth-Century Fiction.* London: Routledge, 1983.

Chase, Cynthia. "The Decomposition of the Elephants: Double-Reading *Daniel Deronda.*" *PMLA* 93.2 (1978): 215–25.

Darwin, Charles. *The Correspondence of Charles Darwin.* Vol. 8. Cambridge: Cambridge UP, 1993.

Darwin, Charles. *The Descent of Man.* New York: Prometheus, 1998.

Eliot, George. *Adam Bede.* Ed. Margaret Reynolds. London: Penguin, 2008.

Eliot, George. *Daniel Deronda.* Oxford: Oxford UP, 2009.

Eliot, George. *The George Eliot Letters.* Ed. Gordon S. Haight. 9 vols. New Haven: Yale UP, 1954–78.

Eliot, George. *Middlemarch.* 2nd ed. Ed. Bert G. Hornbeck. New York: Norton, 1999.

Flesch, William. *Comeuppance: Costly Signaling, Altruistic Punishment, and Other Biological Components of Fiction.* Cambridge: Harvard UP, 2007.

Hill, George Birbeck, ed. *Johnsonian Miscellanies.* Vol. 1. Oxford: Oxford UP, 1897.

Huxley, T. H. *Evolution and Ethics.* Ed. Michael Ruse. Princeton: Princeton UP, 2009.

Kant, Immanuel. *Critique of Judgment.* Trans Werner S. Pluhar. Indianapolis: Hackett, 1987.

Levine, George, ed. *Cambridge Companion to George Eliot.* Cambridge: Cambridge UP, 2001.

Levine, George, ed. *Darwin and the Novelists: Patterns of Science in Victorian Fiction.* Cambridge: Harvard UP, 1988.

Miller, Geoffrey. *The Mating Mind: How Sexual Choice Shaped the Evolution of Human Nature.* New York: Anchor, 2001.

Paxton, Nancy. *George Eliot and Herbert Spencer: Feminism, and the Reconstruction of Gender.* Princeton: Princeton UP, 1991.

Pinker, Steven. *How the Mind Works.* New York: Norton, 1997.

Ruskin, John. *Works.* Vol. 34. Ed. E. T. Cook and Alexander Wedderburn. London: George Allen, 1908.

Zahavi, Amotz and Avishag Zahavi. *The Handicap Principle: A Missing Piece of Darwin's Puzzle.* Oxford: Oxford UP, 1997.

Zunshine, Lisa. *Why We Read Fiction: Theory of Mind and the Novel.* Columbus: Ohio State UP, 2006.

Index

Works by George Eliot are entered by title, e.g. *Middlemarch,* "Lifted Veil, The." Works by other authors are entered with the author's name in parentheses after the title, e.g. *Emma* (Austen). References to members of George Eliot's family are entered as, for example, Evans, Isaac (brother of GE).

A Companion to George Eliot, First Edition. Edited by Amanda Anderson and Harry E. Shaw.
© 2013 John Wiley & Sons, Ltd. Published 2016 by John Wiley & Sons, Ltd.